W9-BTD-355

France

Vintage	Red Bordeaux		White Bordeaux		Alsace
	Médoc/Graves	Pom/St-Em	Sauternes & sw	Graves & dry	
2005	9–10	9–10	8–10	8–10	8–9
2004	7–8	7–9	5–7	6–7	6–8
2003	5–9	5–8	7–8	6–7	6–7
2002	6–8	5–8	7–8	7–8	7–8
2001	6–8	7–8	8–10	7–9	6–8
2000	8–10	7–9	6–8	6–8	8–10
99	5–7	5–8	6–9	7–10	6–8
98	5–8	6–9	5–8	5–9	7–9
97	5–7	4–7	7–9	4–7	7–9
96	6–8	5–7	7–9	7–10	8–10
95	7–9	6–9	6–8	5–9	6–9
94	5–8	5–8	4–6	5–8	6–9
93	4–6	5–7	2–5	5–7	6–8
92	3–5	3–5	3–5	4–8	5–7
91	3–6	2–4	2–5	6–8	3–5
90	8–10	8–10	8–10	7–8	7–9
89	6–9	7–9	8–10	6–8	7–10
88	6–8	7–9	7–10	7–9	8–10
87	5–7	5–7	2–5	7–10	7–8

France continued

Vintage	Burgundy			Rhône	
	Côte d'Or red	Côte d'Or white	Chablis	Rhône (N)	Rhône (S)
2005	7–9	7–9	7–9	7–8	6–8
2004	6–8	7–8	7–8	6–7	6–7
2003	6–7	6–7	6–7	5–7	6–8
2002	7–8	7–8	7–8	4–6	5–5
2001	6–8	7–9	6–8	7–8	7–9
2000	7–8	6–9	7–9	6–8	7–9
99	7–10	5–7	5–8	7–9	6–9
98	5–8	5–7	7–8	6–8	7–9
97	5–8	5–8	7–9	7–9	5–8
96	6–8	7–9	5–10	5–7	4–6
95	7–9	7–9	6–9	6–8	6–8
94	5–8	5–7	4–7	6–7	5–7
93	6–8	5–6	5–8	3–6	4–9
92	3–6	5–8	4–6	4–6	3–6

Beaujolais 05, 04, 02, 00 Crus will keep. **Mâcon-Villages** (white) Drink 04, 02, 01, now or can wait. **Loire** (Sweet Anjou and Touraine) best recent vintages: 02, 97, 96, 93, 90, 89, 88, 85; Bourgueil, Chinon, Saumur-Champigny: 05, 04, 02, 00, 99, 97. **Upper Loire** (Sancerre, Pouilly-Fumé): 05, 04, 02, 00, 99 **Muscadet** 05, 04: DYA.

Hugh Johnson's

Pocket Wine Book

2007

MITCHELL BEAZLEY

Acknowledgments

This store of detailed recommendations comes partly from my own notes and mainly from those of a great number of kind friends. Without the generous help and cooperation of innumerable winemakers, merchants, and critics, I could not attempt it. I particularly want to thank the following for help with research or in the areas of their special knowledge:

Geoff Adams	James Halliday	Jan and Carlos Read
Helena Baker	Darrel Joseph	Daniel Rogov
Charles Borden	Chandra Kurt	Stephen Skelton MW
Dr Ernö Péter Botos	Gareth Lawrence	Paul Strang
Gregory Bowden	James Lawther MW	Bostjan Tadel
Stephen Brook	John Livingstone-	Marguerite Thomas
Michael Cooper	Learmonth	Daniel Thomases
Rupert Dean	Nico Manessis	Monty Waldin
Michael Edwards	Richard Mayson	Larry Walker
Jacqueline Friedrich	Adam Montefiore	David Williams
David Furer	Jasper Morris MW	Simon Woods
Rosemary George MW	Shirley Nelson	
Robert Gorjak	John and Erica Platter	

The publishers wish to thank Riedel (www.riedel.com) for its kind permission to use the glass pictured on the cover, model 416/48 Vinum Cuvée Prestige.

Hugh Johnson's Pocket Wine Book 2007

Edited and designed by Mitchell Beazley, an imprint of
Octopus Publishing Group Limited, 2–4 Heron Quays, London E14 4JP.

Copyright © Octopus Publishing Group Limited, 1977–2006.

First edition published 1977
Revised editions published 1978, 1979, 1980, 1981, 1982, 1983, 1984,
1985, 1986, 1987, 1988, 1989, 1990, 1991, 1992, 1993, 1994, 1995, 1996,
1997, 1998, 1999, 2000, 2001, 2002(twice), 2003, 2004, 2005, 2006.

A CIP record for this book is available from the British Library.

ISBN 13: 978 184 533 102 3
ISBN 10: 184 533 102 8

The author and publishers will be grateful for any information that will assist them in keeping future editions up to date. Although all reasonable care has been taken in the preparation of this book, neither the publishers nor the author can accept any liability for any consequences arising from the use thereof, or from the information contained herein.

Commissioning Editor: Susanna Forbes
General Editor: Margaret Rand
Senior Editors: Maggie Rosen, Julie Sheppard
Sub-editor: David Tombesi-Walton
Proofreaders: Juanne Branquinho, Alyson Lacewing, Naomi Waters
Executive Art Editor: Nicky Collings
Design: Gaelle Lochner
Production: Gary Hayes

Printed and bound by Toppan Printing Company, China

Contents

The Plot So Far:

Hugh Johnson sums up thirty years of wine

A census in a rabbit warren, students in a telephone box.... I have
used all sorts of similes over the years for the job of squeezing the
wine world into your pocket. It has left little room for reflection, let
alone space to contemplate the grand sweep of history. But here we
are, thirty years on, with twice as many pages packed tighter than ever.
It is progress, not prolixity, this bulge in your pocket. More choices;
more wines from more places. Better wines? Real choices? What does
progress consist of when it comes to matters of taste?

One change has dominated the whole period: the shift of emphasis
from place to grape. Thirty years ago the name of a wine, with few
exceptions, was its place of origin. In most cases a certain grape was
mandatory or so traditional that it was taken for granted. Only new
wine regions had a choice, and naturally defined themselves by what
they chose to plant.

No single factor has made wine more understandable to the
layman. Within ten years grape varieties became the universal key.
Burgundy, Bordeaux, the Rhine and Rhône could only watch as they
saw their birthright, as they saw it, pillaged by countries with no
regulations or inhibitions – but with conditions for growing grapes that
looked enviably benign. In shorthand, the New World.

California started the revolution, at least as a conscious change of
policy. By 1977, and my first edition, "varietal" was a buzz word
signalling the new idea. Not entirely new; Australia had been using
grape names with cheerful inaccuracy for decades. In the late '70s
California started to export in earnest. In 1970 there were 220 wineries
in the state; by 1980, 500. (In the same year, for the first time in history,
Americans drank more wine than spirits). Australia was soon in pursuit,
at least in the British market. Wine is as thick as blood, it seems.
Washington and Oregon followed California. In the mid '80s, Britain
became conscious of New Zealand, by the '90s of Chile, and as the '90s
progressed South Africa and Argentina became respectable suppliers.
There was no precedent for the speed of their success, and in the new,
democratic world of wine, where what counted was a clean, strong
taste at a low price, no rapid response that Europe could give. Worse,
there was a shifting definition of what is meant by "fine", favouring the
riper flavours and higher alcohol that come easily in warmer regions.
French finesse began to look undernourished.

Europe, at least officially, was heading in the opposite direction to
this liberal trend. In the 1970s, '80s, and even '90s its governments
were still tightening regulations and raising costs. There were benefits
for some: huge benefits for the Mediterranean countries. They saw an
avalanche of money as Europe applied its social model, "rebalancing",
as they term it, the fortunes of its constituent parts. Did the brains of
Brussels foresee the result? Europe's warm regions became a new New
World on the doorstep of the Old.

Their grapes gave identities to new wines; safe ones to begin with.
Cabernet Sauvignon is a masterful grape, adaptable and recognizable.
Chardonnay became its white opposite number. Every new wine region
planted them – even Australia, where they were hardly known, and
which already had its excellent Shiraz, Semillon, and Riesling. Some

regions, like the Napa Valley, added to the world's roster of great original wines. Others just added to a growing lake of me-too "Cab" and "Chard". By the 1990s a reaction had set in: what other flavours are there, please? Each country or region volunteered its own - in most cases an early settler overlooked in the craze for Cabernet. California offered Zinfandel, Australia Shiraz, Argentina Malbec, Chile Carmenère, and all of them tried their luck with Merlot and Pinot Noir.

The situation is different in Europe's New World. Even here, Cabernet was the initial way to signal you were serious. It rapidly transformed the fortunes of Tuscany and the fame of Catalonia. But Italy has a thousand grape varieties of its own, each adapted to a niche in its prolifically varied landscape. Spain, Portugal, and Greece each have a full quiver of contenders. The next phase, then, was to put them on parade. It is where we are now. High streets are already bazaars of ethnic cooking: why would the consumer not want to try Nero d'Avola, Trincadeira, or Agiorgitiko?

These are the tectonic movements that have multiplied our choice tenfold, and doubled the number of pages in this book. Compared with the creation of a new wine world, the old seems hardly to have stirred. The lists of Bordeaux's classed growths and Burgundy's grands crus are no longer than they were, and these regions would deny that they have changed in any essential way. They are informed by science, of course, as we all are. The pooling of technical knowledge is as important to them as to anyone. But in a sense they hardly dare to change: they are defined by the vines and soil they inherit. Their terroir is their very being. And so far most, if not all, of the inheritors have kept faith with it, even in the face of a public looking for something different.

For taste has changed. The wines of warm countries are now the norm, rather than, as they used to be, an aberration. Where the north strains for ripe grapes, the south has them on demand. Lower acidity, less astringent tannin and higher alcohol are all popular. It is tempting to make them your goal, and American critics reward those who do.

What do you want from wine, is finally the question. A thirst-quencher? An investment vehicle? A trophy to impress? The perfect accompaniment to food that it can be, the art form developed by the French and Italians over centuries of inspired research? There is little consensus, apparently, over the answer, either among those who drink wine or those who make it. In every other industry, choice is being eroded. Globalization, they said, would be the end of variety; all wines would eventually taste the same.

As I read it, the exploration of what wine can be to different people has only just begun. Its resources of style and flavour are far greater than we realize. We are beginning to discover Greek grapes, and Sicilian, but Eastern Europe is undeveloped, and the Middle East unexplored. What do we know of the flavours of Georgia, with perhaps the oldest of all wine-grape varieties, or how they will be interpreted by populations who have yet to meet wine at all? One day China will have a wine culture, and India, and even, one distant day, perhaps Arabia. It cartwheeled all my preconceptions when recently I drank Thai wine grown on tropical islands in the Mekong delta. The taste was different, but it was wine and I enjoyed it. My guess is that in another thirty years no pocket will be big enough for this book.

Agenda 2007

How much alcohol should there be in wine? Can you have too little? And, more importantly, how much is too much? These are topical questions because alcohol levels are rising; and indeed have been rising for fifteen years or more. But what at first looked like an admirable trend towards greater ripeness now looks like an obsession with overripeness for its own sake; a misplaced belief that in wine more is always better. Wines that twenty years ago had 12 or 12.5 degrees of alcohol may now pack a punch at 14.5 or 15 degrees or even more; balance disappears, and drinkability is thought wimpish. Like human bodies packed with steroid-driven muscle, these wines do not fulfil any useful purpose; they are merely made to win competitions.

Of course, the weather helps. Wine regions across Europe have been reporting warmer summers for ten or fifteen years now; and winemakers have been seizing the advantage this gives and exaggerating it – sometimes as much as they can. But is red wine better for tasting like port? Is white wine better for tasting like peaches in brandy?

I'm overstating the case, of course – although I've recently come across wines from the 2005 vintage that taste just like those two things. Mostly what excess alcohol does is muddy the flavours and blur the aromas, so that you lose definition and focus and complexity. Such wines are initially impressive but quickly become boring. To make one of the world's most magical substances boring takes some doing, but a combination of fashion and climate can do it.

The New World has always produced wines of higher alcohol than Europe. That's not a problem in itself: if a California Cabernet is balanced at 14.5 degrees, it can be just as fascinating as a Bordeaux at 13.5%. "Balance" is the key word. Balance is what makes a wine sing, rather than shout or grunt.

It used to be the case that more alcohol meant less grape sugar remaining in the wine. Now, with warm wine regions and super-efficient yeasts, you can have lots of alcohol and residual sugar – and that, it turns out, is what a lot of people like in their wine. A recent survey of French drinkers indicated that the most popular wines (and I'm talking about wines that purport to be dry) are those with considerable sweetness. And when they were asked what they would like more of in wine, they said, "more sweetness".

This has always been the case, of course. The wine trade has always known that a lot of people like their dry wines to be remarkably sweet. It's why Piat d'Or was so successful all those years ago (rumour had it that the market research for this brand – popular in Britain but not in France, no matter what the advertisements said – was done with Liebfraumilch and red food colouring). But the problem is that those same people are snobbish about sweet wines – or they think they ought to be. And so the wine trade goes to enormous lengths to disguise the fact that many of its big New World brands are sweet and sugary. It's not going to come clean, because sweet wines like Liebfraumilch are laughed at as being the taste of a previous generation. New World brands, on the other hand, are seen as modern. The fact that all that has really changed is the alcohol degree is neither here nor there.

It's a curious thing, modernity in wine. On one hand, one might define "modern" wine as being clear, focused, and defined, with clean fruit flavours to the fore. But winemakers are turning back to terroir: what they increasingly want is minerality in their wines, and a sense of place. Even in California, where for a long time the soil was mostly regarded as just the stuff that held the vines upright, the mass replanting that was forced on growers by phylloxera in the 1990s has led to a new interest in what goes on below ground, what the structure of the soil is in each part of a vineyard, and why it matters. True, they're still wary of the term "terroir", but they're beginning to get quite close to it.

Some winemakers are also beginning to look nervously at ever-increasing alcohol degrees. They're working out how to beat the climate and make lighter wines in spite of what nature is throwing at them. So it's beginning to look as though modernity has taken another turn, and that it won't be long before words like "elegance" and "finesse" are buzz words again. For some of us, of course, they never went away.

It all happens because winemakers and grape-growers are insatiably curious. And they're delighted if their researches bring them back to some technique practised by winemakers of two or three generations back and since discarded – although probably never quite forgotten. Ideas and information are passed through generations of winemakers in a way that they are not among computer engineers or car manufacturers. There, once an idea has been surpassed, it's over for good. With wine, since people are working with the same soils and the same plants that were there 100 or 200 years ago, increasing knowledge can shed new light on an old idea. When you hear a winemaker start a sentence with, "Well, you know, the old guys used to say...", you know you're listening to modernity in the making. Everything changes, but not always for very long.

How to use this book

The top line of most entries consists of the following information:

❶   **❸**

| **Aglianico del Vulture** Bas | r dr (s/sw sp) | ★★★ | 96' **97** 98 99' 00 01' 02 (03) |

        ❷   **❹**

❶ Wine name and the region the wine comes from.

❷ Whether it is red, rosé or white (or brown/amber), dry, sweet or sparkling, or several of these (and which is most important):

r	red
p	rosé
w	white
br	brown
dr	dry*
sw	sweet
s/sw	semi-sweet
sp	sparkling

( ) brackets here denote a less important wine
*assume wine is dry when **dr** or **sw** are not indicated

❸ Its general standing as to quality: a necessarily rough-and-ready guide based on its current reputation as reflected in its prices:

★	plain, everyday quality
★★	above average
★★★	well known, highly reputed
★★★★	grand, prestigious, expensive

So much is more or less objective. Additionally there is a subjective rating:

★ etc   Stars are coloured for any wine which in my experience is usually especially good within its price range. There are good everyday wines as well as good luxury wines. This system helps you find them.

❹ Vintage information: which of the recent vintages can be recommended; of these, which are ready to drink this year, and which will probably improve with keeping. Your choice for current drinking should be one of the vintage years printed in **bold** type. Buy light-type years for further maturing.

00 etc	recommended years that may be currently available
96'etc	vintage regarded as particularly successful for the property in question
97 etc	years in **bold** should be ready for drinking (those not in bold will benefit from keeping).
98 etc	vintages in colour are those recommended as first choice for drinking in 2005. (See also Bordeaux introduction, p.80.)
(02) etc	provisional rating

The German vintages work on a different principle again: see p.136.

Other abbreviations

DYA	drink the youngest available
NV	vintage not normally shown on label; in Champagne, means a blend of several vintages for continuity
CHABLIS	properties, areas or terms cross-referred within the section

A quick-reference vintage chart appears on the front endpaper of this book.

Vintage report 2005

This, in much of Europe, was the year of the big, big smile. In Germany, winemakers were grinning broadly. Even when it started raining mid-harvest, they didn't stop smiling: they'd picked plenty of Auslesen and Beerenauslesen already, they said; a bit of rain would be fine, and then when it stopped they'd pick Kabinett and Spatlese. Sometimes when they measured the sugar in the grapes it was off the scale. And it was arriving in the cellars accompanied by near-perfect balancing acidity; a great year, they said; a very great year.

They said it, too, in Rioja, where they nearly ran out of adjectives and settled on "unprecedented"; even allowing for exaggeration, the wines do seem to be very good. Ribera del Duero, though, was less happy; and in Italy they weren't smiling much at all. A lot of the time you couldn't see them for umbrellas.

In Bordeaux the quality of the year was apparent from the relative silence of the proprietors. There was no hype this year; no insistence that the wines were very good, even great; just smiles. They didn't need to hype the vintage; the wines, they knew, would speak for themselves. And they would speak most loudly through price. The 2005 vintage, it became clear, was going to make the 2004 vintage look very inexpensive. The latter is the year to buy to drink; the 2005s are likely to become the stuff of speculation. In Burgundy and the Rhône the story was the same: wines even better than 2004. Only merchants, who would have to explain price rises to their customers, looked a bit nervous. In Champagne, however, the 2004 looks better: a lot of 2005 Pinot Noir is pretty and fresh, but lacks concentration. Fine for non-vintage, but expect the vintage wines to be from 2004.

Merchants nervous of prices should stick to selling Australian wines, because there won't be too many price rises in that department: Australia had its biggest-ever vintage in 2005. It was also uniformly very good. Philip Shaw, now of Cumulus Wines in Orange but previously of Southcorp, where he was chief winemaker for three years - and of Rosemount for 20 years before that - says it's the best vintage of his career. Stars of the year seem to be Margaret River whites, Clare and Eden Rieslings, McLaren Vale Shiraz, and Coonawarra Cabernet. Things weren't quite as even in New Zealand, though overall quality looks good: Sauvignon is riper, more tropical than usual.

The year in South Africa was almost biblical: either drought, or heavy rain, or plagues of beetles. The reds have survived best, and have come off pretty well unscathed thanks to clever viticulture. But beware of beetle recipes in local restaurants.

In contrast, both Chile and Argentina enjoyed rather routine years, with fresher-than-usual whites in Chile and better acidity than usual in Argentina.

Over in California, 2005 was a whopper: the biggest crop ever, with over one million tonnes of grapes more than in 2004. It may be difficult to visualize a million tonnes of grapes, but it means an awful lot more wine – and that in turn will mean lower prices. California growers are praying that 2006 will be less bountiful.

A closer look at 2004

In Bordeaux, 2004 will go down (and will be sold) as a year to drink. That is usually a euphemism for a vintage that is too dim to keep; not this year. In 2004, "drinking" means the opposite of "investing", which is probably what will happen with the 2005s. But before anyone starts accusing this book of giving financial advice – no, no, no. This is merely a description of what is likely to happen, not a suggestion to take part in it. The 2005 vintage seems to be so very good that it already has the status of 1990 or 2000, and will be expensive. The 2004s will be drinking-wines because they will look remarkably affordable in the light of the 2005s and the 2003s, and also because at their best they are beautiful wines, elegant and lively, without the thickset muscle of the 2003s.

In Burgundy it looks a more mixed year than the merchants are saying. The whites are seductive; the reds looked equally so in barrel, but as their early fruit drew back to reveal the underlying structure, it turned out that there was a vast difference between those reds with ripe tannins and those with hard, green tannins. As one grower said, the difference is between those where the tannin is inside the wine, and those where the wine is inside the tannin. Those that are good are very, very good; those that are not may well be very disappointing.

Liveliness is the characteristic of the vintage in France; what the French call "vif". The Rhône has it, especially in the south, where the wines are perfumed and supple – again, a delicious "drinking" vintage – the Loire has it. Balance and ripeness are good in most of Spain and Portugal; there'll almost certainly have been some declarations of single-quinta vintage port by the time this books appears. And these are, of course, the perfect ports to buy to drink, as opposed to buying to lay down for a decade or more.

The word most often used to describe 2004, in fact, is "classic". And it's true, it was often a classic year; but not classic in the sense of lean or austere. "Classic" here carries the subtext "compared to 2003, thank heavens" and it means a return to the sort of wines most European winemakers are accustomed to: wines with length and acidity; usually not a great vintage, but often a good to very good one. And one with concentration, too. Iin Champagne it will almost certainly be a vintage year, though the quantity of vintage that can be made will be limited by the slightly mixed quality of the Pinot Noir, and the need to replenish stocks of reserve wines after the very small 2003 vintage.

In Champagne, the hottest years have traditionally been the best, because acidity has been a constant unspoken presence; they didn't have to worry about it because, like taxation, it was always there. Now, though, there are beginning to be murmurings about the need for acidity in summers that are beginning to get gently warmer – even if they don't reach the extremes of 2003. Global warming and how to deal with it are starting to be at the forefront of growers' minds in what have always been thought of as cool regions.

However, 2004 might prove a bargain vintage for drinkers. In Bordeaux and Burgundy it is likely to be overshadowed by the greater glamour of the 2005s; in Germany the same might happen, and in Rioja it almost certainly will. This is good news: overshadowed vintages are ones to pursue, quietly, at dead of night when nobody can see. Fill your cellar while the rest of the world is running mad after fashion. The wines will offer a great deal of smug enjoyment in a few years' time.

In the United States, for buyers of California wine, the reverse will be true. The small 2003 and 2004 vintages made prices harden; once a flood of 2005s is released prices will drop again, and Two-Buck Chuck will come into its own once more. It mopped up the wine lake of 2001 and 2002; it will do so again. Buyers of better wine may also prefer to wait: 2005 offered perfect growing conditions, so if good producers couldn't make great wine they were doing something very wrong. The best 2004s are from cooler, later-ripening sites that were able to counteract the short, warm summer.

If California has another glut on the way, Australia is still living with the same one it's had for years. 2004 gave Australia a very big crop indeed, and even though new plantings are being reduced, especially of reds, and even though exports keep going up, drinkers just aren't keeping pace. Even grapes from cooler vineyards are in oversupply.

Grape varieties

I n the past two decades a radical change has come about in all
except the most long-established wine countries: the names of a
handful of grape varieties have become the ready reference to wine.
In senior wine countries, above all France and Italy (between them
producing nearly half the world's wine), more complex traditions
prevail. All wine of old prestige is known by its origin, more or less
narrowly defined, not just the particular fruit-juice that fermented.

For the present the two notions are in rivalry. Eventually the
primacy of place over fruit will become obvious, at least for wines
of quality. But for now, for most people, grape tastes are the easy
reference-point – despite the fact that they are often confused by
the added taste of oak. If grape flavours were really all that
mattered this would be a very short book.

But of course they do matter, and a knowledge of them both
guides you to flavours you enjoy and helps comparisons between
regions. Hence the originally Californian term "varietal wine" –
meaning, in principle, from one grape variety.

At least seven varieties – Cabernet Sauvignon, Pinot Noir,
Riesling, Sauvignon Blanc, Chardonnay, Gewurztraminer, and
Muscat – have tastes and smells distinct and memorable enough
to form international categories of wine. To these you can add
Merlot, Malbec, Syrah, Semillon, Chenin Blanc, Pinots Blanc and
Gris, Sylvaner, Viognier, Nebbiolo, Sangiovese, Tempranillo...
The following are the best and/or most popular wine grapes.

Grapes for red wine

Agiorgitiko (St George) Versatile Greek (Nemea) variety with juicy damson
fruit and velvety tannins. Sufficient structure for serious ageing.

Baga Bairrada (Portugal) grape. Dark and tannic. Has great potential, but
hard to grow.

Barbera Widely grown in Italy, at its best in Piedmont, giving dark, fruity, often
sharp wine. Fashionable in California and Australia; promising in Argentina.

Blaufränkisch Mostly Austrian; can be light and juicy but at best (in
Burgenland) a considerable red. LEMBERGER in Germany, KEKFRANKOS in Hungary.

Brunello Alias for SANGIOVESE, splendid at Montalcino.

Cabernet Franc, alias Bouchet (Cab Fr) The lesser of two sorts of Cabernet
grown in Bordeaux but dominant (as "Bouchet") in St-Emilion. The Cabernet
of the Loire, making Chinon, Saumur, Champigny, and rosé. Used for blending
with CABERNET SAUVIGNON, etc., or increasingly, alone, in California, Australia.

Cabernet Sauvignon (Cab Sauv) Grape of great character: spicy, herby, tannic,
with characteristic blackcurrant aroma. The first grape of the Médoc; also
makes most of the best California, South American, East European reds.
Vies with Shiraz in Australia. Its wine almost always needs ageing; usually
benefits from blending with *e.g.* MERLOT, CABERNET FRANC, SYRAH, TEMPRANILLO,
SANGIOVESE etc.. Makes aromatic rosé.

Cannonau GRENACHE in its Sardinian manifestation: can be very fine, potent.

Carignan In decline in France. Needs low yields, old vines; best in Corbières. Otherwise dull but harmless. Common in North Africa, Spain, and California.

Carmènere An old Bordeaux variety now virtually extinct in France. Widely used in Chile where until recently it was often mistaken for MERLOT.

Cinsault/Cinsaut Usually bulk-producing grape of Southern France; in South Africa crossed with PINOT NOIR to make PINOTAGE. Pale wine, but quality potential.

Dolcetto Source of soft seductive dry red in Piedmont. Now high fashion.

Gamay The Beaujolais grape: light, very fragrant wines, at their best young. Makes even lighter wine in the Loire Valley, in central France, and in Switzerland and Savoie. Known as "Napa Gamay" in California.

Grenache, alias Garnacha, Cannonau Useful grape for strong and fruity but pale wine: good rosé and *vin doux naturel* – especially in the South of France, Spain, and California – but also the mainstay of beefy Priorato. Old-vine versions are prized in South Australia. Usually blended with other varieties (*e.g.* in Châteauneuf-du-Pape).

Grignolino Makes one of the good everyday table wines of Piedmont.

Kadarka, alias Gamza Makes healthy, sound, agreeable reds in East Europe.

Kékfrankos Hungarian BLAUFRÄNKISCH; similar lightish reds.

Lambrusco Productive grape of the lower Po Valley, giving quintessentially Italian, cheerful, sweet, and fizzy red.

Lemberger See BLAUFRÄNKISCH. Württemberg's red.

Malbec, alias Côt Minor in Bordeaux, major in Cahors (alias Auxerrois) and especially in Argentina. Dark, dense, tannic wine capable of real quality.

Merlot Adaptable grape making the great fragrant and plummy wines of Pomerol and (with CABERNET FRANC) St-Emilion, an important element in Médoc reds, soft and strong (and à la mode) in California, Washington, Chile, Australia. Lighter but often good in North Italy, Italian Switzerland, Slovenia, Argentina, South Africa, New Zealand etc.. Grassy when not fully ripe.

Montepulciano A good central-eastern Italian grape, and a Tuscan town.

Morellino Alias for SANGIOVESE in Scansano, southern Tuscany.

Mourvèdre, alias Mataro Excellent dark aromatic tannic grape used mainly for blending in Provence (but solo in Bandol) and the Midi. Enjoying new interest in, for example, South Australia and California.

Nebbiolo, alias Spanna and Chiavennasca One of Italy's best red grapes; makes Barolo, Barbaresco, Gattinara, and Valtellina. Intense, nobly fruity, perfumed wine but very tannic: improves for years.

Periquita Ubiquitous in Portugal for firm-flavoured reds. Often blended with CABERNET SAUVIGNON and also known as Castelão.

Petit Verdot Excellent but awkward Médoc grape, now increasingly planted in Cabernet areas worldwide for extra fragrance.

Pinot Noir (Pinot N) The glory of Burgundy's Côte d'Or, with scent, flavour, and texture that are unmatched anywhere. Makes light wines rarely of much distinction in Germany, Switzerland, Austria, and Hungary. But now also splendid results in California's Sonoma, Carneros, and Central Coast, as well as Oregon, Ontario, Yarra Valley, Adelaide Hills, Tasmania, and New Zealand's South Island.

Pinotage Singular South African grape (PINOT NOIR x CINSAUT). Can be very fruity and can age interestingly, but often jammy.

Primitivo Southern Italian grape making big, rustic wines, now fashionable because genetically identical to ZINFANDEL.

Refosco In northeast Italy possibly a synonym for Mondeuse of Savoie. Produces deep, flavoursome and age-worthy wines, especially when grown in warmer climates.

Sagrantino Italian grape found in Umbria for powerful cherry-flavoured wines.

Sangiovese (or Sangioveto) Main red grape of Chianti and much of central Italy. Aliases include BRUNELLO and MORELLINO. Interesting in Australia.

Saperavi Makes good, sharp, very long-lived wine in Georgia, Ukraine etc. Blends very well with CAB SAUV (*e.g.* in Moldova).

Spätburgunder German for PINOT N. Quality is variable, seldom wildly exciting.

St-Laurent Dark, smooth and full-flavoured Austrian speciality. Also in the Pfalz.

Syrah, alias Shiraz The great Rhône red grape: tannic, purple, peppery wine which matures superbly. Very important as Shiraz in Australia, and under either name in California, Washington State, South Africa, Chile, and elsewhere.

Tannat Raspberry-perfumed, highly tannic force behind Madiran, Tursan, and other firm reds from Southwest France. Also rosé. Now the star of Uruguay.

Tempranillo Aromatic fine Rioja grape, called Ull de Llebre in Catalonia, Cencibel in La Mancha, Tinto Fino in Ribera del Duero, Tinta Roriz in Douro, Aragonez in southern Portugal. Now Australia, too. Very fashionable; elegant in cool climates, beefy in warm. Early ripening.

Touriga Nacional Top port grape grown in the Douro Valley. Also makes full-bodied reds in south Portugal.

Zinfandel (Zin) Fruity adaptable grape of California (though identical to PRIMITIVO) with blackberry-like, and sometimes metallic, flavour. Can be structured and gloriously lush, but also makes "blush" white wine.

Grapes for white wine

Albariño The Spanish name for North Portugal's Alvarinho, making excellent fresh and fragrant wine in Galicia. Both fashionable and expensive in Spain.

Aligoté Burgundy's second-rank white grape. Crisp (often sharp) wine, needs drinking in 1–3 years. Perfect for mixing with cassis (blackcurrant liqueur) to make "Kir". Widely planted in East Europe, especially Russia.

Arinto White central Portuguese grape for crisp, fragrant dry whites.

Arneis Aromatic, high-priced grape, DOC in Roero, Piedmont.

Blanc Fumé Occasional (New World) alias of SAUVIGNON BLANC, referring to its smoky smell, particularly from the Loire (Sancerre and Pouilly). In California used for oak-aged Sauvignon and reversed to "Fumé Blanc". (The smoke is oak.)

Bourboulenc This and the rare Rolle make some of the Midi's best wines.

Bual Makes top-quality sweet madeira wines, not quite so rich as malmsey.

Chardonnay (Chard) The white grape of burgundy, Champagne, and the New World, partly because it is one of the easiest to grow and vinify. All regions are trying it, mostly aged (or, better, fermented) in oak to reproduce the flavours of burgundy. Australia and California make classics (but also much dross). Italy, Spain, New Zealand, South Africa, New York State, Argentina, Chile, Hungary and the Midi are all coming on strong. Called Morillon in Austria.

Chasselas Prolific early-ripening grape with little aroma, mainly grown for eating. AKA Fendant in Switzerland (where it is supreme), Gutedel in Germany.

Chenin Blanc (Chenin Bl) Great white grape of the middle Loire (Vouvray, Layon, etc). Wine can be dry or sweet (or very sweet), but with plenty of acidity. Bulk wine in California, but increasingly serious in South Africa. See also STEEN.

Clairette A low-acid grape, part of many southern French blends.

Colombard Slightly fruity, nicely sharp grape, makes everyday wine in South Africa, California, and Southwest France.

Fendant See CHASSELAS.

Fiano High quality grape giving peachy, spicy wine in Campania.

Folle Blanche High acid/little flavour make this ideal for brandy. Called Gros Plant in Brittany, Picpoul in Armagnac. Also respectable in California.

Furmint A grape of great character: the trademark of Hungary both as the principal grape in Tokáj and as vivid, vigorous table wine with an appley flavour. Called Sipon in Slovenia. Some grown in Austria.

Garganega The best grape in the Soave blend. Top wines, especially sweet ones, age well.

Gewurztraminer, alias Traminer (Gewurz) One of the most pungent grapes, distinctively spicy with aromas like rose petals and grapefruit. Wines are often rich and soft, even when fully dry. Best in Alsace; but also good in Germany (Gewürztraminer), East Europe, Australia, California, Pacific Northwest, and New Zealand.

Grauburgunder See PINOT GRIS.

Grechetto or Greco Ancient grape of central and south Italy noted for the vitality and stylishness of its wine.

Grüner Veltliner Austria's favourite. Around Vienna and in the Wachau and Weinviertel (also in Moravia) it can be delicious: light but dry, peppery and lively. Excellent young, but the best age five years or so.

Hárslevelü Other main grape of Tokáj (with FURMINT). Adds softness and body.

Kéknyelü Low-yielding, flavourful grape giving one of Hungary's best whites. Has the potential for fieriness and spice. To be watched.

Kerner The most successful of recent German varieties, mostly RIESLING x SILVANER, but in this case Riesling x (red) Trollinger. Early-ripening, flowery (but often too blatant) wine with good acidity. Popular in Pfalz, Rheinhessen, etc.

Laski Rizling Grown in northern Italy and Eastern Europe. Much inferior to Rhine RIESLING, with lower acidity, best in sweet wines. Alias Welschriesling, Riesling Italico, Olaszrizling (no longer legally labelled simply "Riesling").

Loureiro The best and most fragrant Vinho Verde variety in Portugal.

Macabeo The workhorse white grape of north Spain, widespread in Rioja (alias Viura) and in Catalan cava country. Good quality potential.

Malvasia A family of grapes rather than a single variety, found all over Italy and Iberia. May be red, white, or pink. Usually plump, soft wine. Malvoisie in France is unrelated.

Marsanne Principal white grape (with ROUSSANNE) of the northern Rhône (*e.g.* in Hermitage, St-Joseph, St-Péray). Also good in Australia, California, and (as Ermitage Blanc) the Valais. Soft full wines that age very well.

Moschofilero Good, aromatic pink Greek grape. Makes white or rosé wine.

Müller-Thurgau (Müller-T) Dominant in Germany's Rheinhessen and Pfalz and too common on the Mosel. It was thought to be a cross between RIESLING and Chasselas de Courtellier, but recent studies suggests otherwise. Soft aromatic wines for drinking young. Makes good sweet wines but usually dull, often coarse, dry ones. Should have no place in top vineyards.

Muscadelle Adds aroma to white Bordeaux, especially Sauternes. In Victoria as Tokay it is used (with MUSCAT, to which it is unrelated) for Rutherglen Muscat.

Muscadet, alias Melon de Bourgogne Makes light, refreshing, very dry wines with a seaside tang round Nantes in Brittany.

Muscat (Many varieties; the best is Muscat Blanc à Petits Grains.) Widely grown, easily recognized, pungent grapes, mostly made into perfumed sweet wines, often fortified (as in France's *vins doux naturels*). Superb in Australia. The third element in Tokáj Aszú. Rarely (*e.g.* Alsace) made dry.

Palomino, alias Listán Makes all the best sherry but poor table wine.

Pedro Ximénez, alias PX Makes very strong wine in Montilla and Málaga. Used in blending sweet sherries. Also grown in Argentina, the Canaries, Australia, California, and South Africa.

Petit (and Gros) Manseng The secret weapon of the French Basque country: vital for Jurançon; increasingly blended elsewhere in the Southwest.

Pinot Blanc (Pinot Bl) A cousin of PINOT NOIR, similar to but milder than CHARDONNAY: light, fresh, fruity, not aromatic, to drink young. Good for Italian spumante. Grown in Alsace, northern Italy, south Germany, and East Europe. Weissburgunder in Germany. See also MUSCADET.

Pinot Gris (Pinot Gr) At best makes rather heavy, even "thick", full-bodied whites with a certain spicy style. In Germany can be alias Ruländer (sweet) or GRAUBURGUNDER (dry); Pinot Grigio in Italy. Also found in Hungary, Slovenia, Canada, Oregon, New Zealand...

Pinot Noir (Pinot N) Superlative black grape (See p.12) used in Champagne and elsewhere (*e.g.* California, Australia) for making white, sparkling, or very pale pink "vin gris".

> ### Riesling (Ries)
> Riesling is making its re-entrance on the world-stage through, as it were, the back door. All serious commentators agree that Riesling stands level with Chardonnay as the world's best white wine grape, though in diametrically opposite style. Chardonnay gives full-bodied but aromatically discreet wines, while Riesling offers a range from steely to voluptuous, always positively perfumed, and with more ageing potential than Chardonnay. Germany makes the greatest Riesling in all styles. Yet its popularity is being revived in, of all places, South Australia, where this cool-climate grape does its best to ape Chardonnay. Holding the middle ground, with forceful but still steely wines, is Austria. While lovers of light and fragrant, often piercingly refreshing Rieslings have the Mosel as their exclusive playground. Also grown in Alsace (but nowhere else in France), Pacific Northwest, Ontario, California, New Zealand, and South Africa.

Roussanne Rhône grape of great finesse, now popping up in California and Australia. Can age well.

Sauvignon Blanc (Sauv Bl) Makes very distinctive aromatic grassy wines, pungent in New Zealand, often mineral in Sancerre, riper in Australia; also good in Rueda, Austria, north Italy, Chile's Casablanca Valley, and South Africa. Blended with SEMILLON in Bordeaux. Can be austere or buxom. May be called BLANC FUMÉ.

Savagnin The grape of *vin jaune* of Savoie: related to TRAMINER?

Scheurebe Spicy-flavoured German RIES x SILVANER (possibly), very successful in Pfalz, especially for Auslese. Can be weedy: must be very ripe to be good.

Semillon (Sem) Contributes the lusciousness to Sauternes and increasingly important for Graves and other dry white Bordeaux. Grassy if not fully ripe, but can make soft dry wine of great ageing potential. Superb in Australia: old Hunter Valley Sem, though light, can be great wine. Promising in New Zealand.

Sercial Makes the driest madeira (where myth used to identify it with RIESLING).

Seyval Blanc (Seyval Bl) French-made hybrid of French and American vines. Very hardy and attractively fruity. Popular and reasonably successful in eastern States and England but dogmatically banned by EU from "quality" wines.

Steen South African alias for CHENIN BLANC, not used for better examples.

Silvaner, alias Sylvaner Germany's former workhorse grape. Rarely fine except in Franken – where it is savoury and ages admirably – and in Rheinhessen and Pfalz, where it is enjoying a renaissance. Good in the Italian Tyrol; now declining in popularity in Alsace. Very good (and powerful) as Johannisberg in the Valais, Switzerland.

Tocai Friulano North Italian grape with a flavour best described as "subtle". No relation to TOKAY, but could be Sauvignonasse (see SAUVIGNON BLANC).

Tokay See PINOT GRIS. Also supposedly Hungarian grape in Australia and a table grape in California. The wine Tokay (Tokáj) is FURMINT, HARSLEVELU and MUSCAT.

Torrontes Strongly aromatic, MUSCAT-like Argentine speciality, usually dry.

Trebbiano Important but mediocre grape of central Italy (Orvieto, Soave etc.). Also grown in southern France as Ugni Blanc, and Cognac as St-Emilion. Mostly thin, bland wine; needs blending (and more careful growing).

Ugni Blanc (Ugni Bl) See TREBBIANO.

Verdejo The grape of Rueda in Castile, potentially fine and long-lived.

Verdelho Madeira grape making excellent medium-sweet wine; in Australia, fresh soft dry wine of great character.

Verdicchio Potentially good dry wine in central-eastern Italy.

Vermentino Italian, sprightly with satisfying texture and ageing capacity.

Vernaccia Name given to many unrelated grapes in Italy. Vernaccia di San Gimignano is crisp, lively; Vernaccia di Oristano is sherry-like.

Viognier Ultra-fashionable Rhône grape, finest in Condrieu, less fine but still aromatic in the Midi. Good examples from California and Australia.

Viura See MACABEO.

Welschriesling See LASKI RIZLING.

Wine & food

The dilemma is most acute in restaurants. Four people have chosen
different dishes. The host calculates. A bottle of white and then one of red
is conventional, regardless of the food. The formula works up to a point.
But it can be refined – or replaced with something more original,
something to really bring out the flavours of both food and wine.

Remarkably little ink has been spilt on this byway of knowledge,
but thirty years of experimentation and the ideas of many friends have
gone into making this list. It is perhaps most useful for menu-planning
at home. But used with the rest of the book, it may ease menu-stress
in restaurants, too. At the very least, it will broaden your mind.

Before the meal – apéritifs

The conventional apéritif wines are either sparkling (epitomized by
Champagne) or fortified (epitomized by sherry in Britain, port in France,
vermouth in Italy, etc.). A glass of white or rosé (or in France red) table
wine before eating is presently in vogue. It calls for something light and
stimulating, fairly dry but not acidic, with a degree of character; Chenin
Blanc or Riesling rather than Chardonnay.

Warning: Avoid peanuts; they destroy wine flavours. Olives are also too
piquant for many wines; they need sherry or a Martini. Eat almonds,
pistachios or walnuts, plain crisps or cheese straws instead.

Food A–Z

Abalone Dry or medium white: Sauv Bl, Côte de Beaune Blanc, Pinot Gr,
or Grüner Veltliner. Chinese style: try vintage Champagne.

Aïoli A thirst-quencher is needed for its garlic heat. Rhône, sparkling
dry white; Provence rosé, Verdicchio.

Anchovies A robust white – or fino sherry.

Antipasti Dry white: Italian (Arneis, Soave, Pinot Grigio, prosecco,
Vermentino); light red (Dolcetto, Franciacorta, young Chianti); fino sherry.

Apples, Cox's Orange Pippins Vintage port (55 60 63 66 70 75 82).

Artichoke vinaigrette An incisive dry white: New Zealand Sauv Bl; Côtes
de Gascogne or a modern Greek; young red: Bordeaux, Côtes du Rhône.
With hollandaise Full-bodied slightly crisp dry white: Pouilly-Fuissé, Pfalz
Spätlese, or a Carneros or Yarra Valley Chard.

Asparagus A difficult flavour for wine, being slightly bitter. Sauv Bl
echoes the flavour, but needs to be ripe, as in Chile. Sem beats Chard,
esp Australian, but Chard works well with melted butter or hollandaise.
Alsace Pinot Gr, even dry Muscat is gd, or Jurançon Sec.

Aubergine purée (Melitzanosalata) Crisp New World Sauv Bl *e.g.* from
South Africa or New Zealand; or modern Greek or Sicilian dry white.
Or try Bardolino red or Chiaretto. Baked aubergine dishes can need
sturdier reds: Shiraz, Zin.

Avocado with seafood Dry or slightly sharp white: Rheingau or Pfalz
Kabinett, Grüner Veltliner, Wachau Ries, Sancerre, Pinot Gr; Sonoma or
Australian Chard or Sauv Bl, or a dry rosé. Or Chablis Premier Cru.

Avocado with vinaigrette Manzanilla sherry.

Barbecues The local wine would be Australian. Or south Italian, Tempranillo, Zin or Argentine Malbec. Bandol for a real treat.

Beef, boiled Red: Bordeaux (Bourg or Fronsac), Roussillon, Gevrey-Chambertin, or Côte-Rôtie. Medium-ranking white burgundy is gd, *e.g.,* Auxey-Duresses. Or top-notch beer. Mustard softens tannic reds, and horseradish kills everything – but can be worth the sacrifice.
roast Ideal partner for fine red wine of any kind, esp Cab Sauv.

Beef stew Sturdy red: Pomerol or St-Emilion, Hermitage, Cornas, Barbera, Shiraz, Napa Cab Sauv, Ribera del Duero or Douro red.

Beef Stroganoff Dramatic red: Barolo, Valpolicella Amarone, Cahors, Hermitage, late-harvest Zin – even Moldovan Negru de Purkar.

Beurre blanc, fish with A top-notch Muscadet-sur-lie, a Sauv Bl/ Sem blend, Chablis Premier Cru, Vouvray or a Rheingau Riesling.

Bisques Dry white with plenty of body: Pinot Gr, Chard, Gruner Veltliner. Fino or dry amontillado sherry, or montilla. West Australian Sem.

Boudin noir (blood sausage) Local Sauv Bl or Chenin Bl – esp in the Loire. Or Beaujolais Cru, esp Morgon.
blanc Loire Chenin Bl, esp when served with apples: dry Vouvray, Saumur or Savennières. Mature red Côtes de Beaune, if without apple.

Bouillabaisse Savoury dry white, Marsanne from the Midi or Rhône, Corsican or Spanish rosé, or Cassis, Verdicchio, South African Sauv Bl.

Brandade Chablis, Sancerre Rouge or New Zealand Pinot Noir.

Bread-and-butter pudding Fine 10-yr-old Barsac, Tokáj Azsú or Australian botrytized Sem.

Brill Very delicate: hence a top fish for fine old Puligny and the like.

Cajun food Works well with Fleurie, Brouilly or Sauv Bl. With gumbo: amontillado or Mexican beer.

Carpaccio, beef Seems to work well with the flavour of most wines. Top Tuscan is appropriate, but fine Chards are gd. So are vintage and pink Champagnes.

Cassoulet Red from southwest France (Gaillac, Minervois, Corbières, St-Chinian or Fitou) or Shiraz. But best of all is Beaujolais Cru or young Tempranillo.

Cauliflower cheese Crisp aromatic white: Sancerre, Ries Spätlese, Muscat, English Seyval Bl, or Schönburger.

Caviar Iced vodka. If you prefer Champagne, it should be full-bodied (*e.g.* Bollinger, Krug).

Ceviche Try Australian Ries or Verdelho; South African or New Zealand Sauv Bl.

Charcuterie Young Beaujolais-Villages, Loire reds such as Saumur, Swiss or Oregon Pinot N. Young Argentine or Italian reds. Sauv Bl can work well too.

Chicken/turkey/guinea fowl, roast Virtually any wine, including very best bottles of dry to medium white and finest old reds (esp burgundy). The meat of fowl can be adapted with sauces to match almost any fine wine (*e.g. coq au vin* with red or white burgundy). Try sparkling Shiraz with strong, sweet, or spicy stuffings and trimmings.

Chicken Kiev Alsace or Pfalz Ries, Hungarian Furmint, young Pinot N.

Cheesecake Sweet white: Vouvray or Anjou or fizz, refreshing but nothing special.

Cheese fondue Dry white: Valais Fendant or any other Swiss Chasselas, Roussette de Savoie, Grüner Veltliner, Alsace Ries, or Pinot Gr. Or a Beaujolais Cru. For Wine & cheese, see p.27.

Chilli con carne Young red: Beaujolais, Zin, or Argentine Malbec.

Chinese Food
Canton or Peking style Dry to medium-dry white – Mosel Ries Kabinett or Spätlese trocken – can be gd throughout a Chinese banquet. Light Monbazillac, too. Gewurz is often suggested but rarely works (but brilliant with ginger), yet Chasselas and Pinot Gr are attractive alternatives. Dry or off-dry sparkling cuts the oil and matches sweetness. Eschew sweet-and-sour dishes but try St-Emilion ★★, New World Pinot N, or Châteauneuf-du-Pape with duck. I often serve both white and red wines concurrently during Chinese meals.
Szechuan style Verdicchio, Alsace Pinot Blanc or very cold beer.

Chocolate Generally only powerful flavours can compete. California Orange Muscat, Bual, Tokáj Aszú, Australian Liqueur Muscat, 10-yr-old tawny port; Asti for light, fluffy mousses. Experiment with rich, ripe reds: Syrah, Zin, even sparkling Shiraz. Médoc can match bitter black chocolate. Banyuls for a weightier partnership. Or a tot of good rum.

Chowders Big-scale white, not necessarily bone dry: Pinot Gr, Rhine Spätlese, Albariño, Australian Sem, buttery Chard. Or fino sherry.

Choucroute garni Alsace Pinot Blanc, Pinot Gris, Ries. Or beer.

Christmas pudding, mince pies Tawny port, cream sherry, or liquid Christmas pudding itself, Pedro Ximénez sherry. Asti or Banyuls.

Cold meats Generally better with full-flavoured white than red. Mosel Spätlese or Hochheimer and Côte Chalonnaise are v.gd, as is Beaujolais. Leftover cold beef with leftover Champagne is bliss.

Cod If roast, a good neutral background for fine dry whites: Chablis, Meursault, Corton-Charlemagne, cru classé Graves, Grüner Veltliner, German (medium) Kabinett or dry Spätlesen or a gd light red, *e.g.* Beaune.

Coffee desserts Sweet Muscat inc Australia liqueur or Tokáj Aszú.

Confit d'oie/de canard Young tannic red Bordeaux Cru Bourgeois, California Cab Sauv and Merlot, and Priorato all cut the richness. Choose Alsace Pinot Gr or Gewurz to match it.

Consommé Medium-dry amontillado sherry or sercial madeira.

Coq au vin Red burgundy. In an ideal world, one bottle of Chambertin in the dish, two on the table.

Crab Crab and Ries are part of the Creator's plan.
cioppino Sauv Bl; but West Coast friends insist on Zin. Also California

sparkling wine – or any other full-bodied sparkler.

cold, with salad Alsace, Austrian or Rhine Ries; dry Australian Ries or Condrieu. Show off your favourite white.

softshell Top Chard or top-quality German Ries Spätlese.

with black bean sauce A big Barossa Shiraz/Syrah.

Creams, custards, fools, syllabubs See also Chocolate, Coffee, Ginger, and Rum. Sauternes, Loupiac, Ste-Croix-du-Mont, or Monbazillac.

Crème brûlée Sauternes or Rhine Beerenauslese, best Madeira or Tokáj. (With concealed fruit, a more modest sweet wine.)

Crêpes Suzette Sweet Champagne, Orange Muscat or Asti.

Crostini Morellino di Scansano, Montepulciano d'Abruzzo, Valpolicella, or a dry Italian white such as Verdicchio or Orvieto.

Crudités Light red or rosé: Côtes du Rhône, Minervois, Chianti, Pinot N; or fino sherry. For whites: Alsace Sylvaner or Pinot Blanc.

Dim-Sum Classically, China tea. For fun: Pinot Grigio or Ries; light red (Bardolino or Loire). NV Champagne or gd New World fizz.

Duck or goose Rather rich white: Pfalz Spätlese or off-dry Alsace Grand Cru. Or mature gamey red: Morey-St-Denis, Côte-Rôtie, Bordeaux, or burgundy. With oranges or peaches, the Sauternais propose drinking Sauternes, others Monbazillac or Ries Auslese.

Peking See Chinese food.

wild duck Big-scale red such as Hermitage, Bandol, California or South African Cab Sauv, or Barossa Shiraz – Grange if you can find it.

with olives Top-notch Chianti or other Tuscans.

Eel, jellied NV Champagne or a nice cup of (Ceylon) tea.

smoked Strong/sharp wine: fino sherry or Bourgogne Aligoté. Schnapps.

Eggs See also Soufflés. Difficult: eggs clash with most wines and can actually spoil gd ones. But local wine with local egg dishes is a safe bet. So ★ ·★★ of whatever is going. Try Pinot Bl or not too oaky Chard. As a last resort I can bring myself to drink Champagne with scrambled eggs.

Quail's eggs Blanc de Blancs Champagne.

Seagull's (or gull's) eggs Mature white burgundy or vintage Champagne.

Oeufs en meurette Burgundian genius: eggs in red wine calls for wine of the same.

Escargots Rhône reds (Gigondas, Vacqueyras), St-Véran or Aligoté. In the Midi, v.gd Petits-Gris go with local white, rosé or red. In Alsace, Pinot Bl or Muscat.

Fennel-based dishes Sauv Bl, or young, fresh red like Beaujolais.

Fish and chips, fritto misto (or tempura) Chablis, white Bordeaux, Sauv Bl, Pinot Bl, Gavi, fino, montilla, Koshu, tea; or NV Champagne and Cava.

Fish baked in a salt crust Full-bodied white or rosé; Meursault, Rioja, Albariño, Sicily, Côtes de Lubéron or Minervois.

Fish pie (with creamy sauce) Albariño, Soave Classico, Pinot Gr d'Alsace.

Fish terrine Pfalz Ries Spätlese Trocken, Grüner Veltliner, Chablis Premier Cru, Clare Valley Ries, Sonoma Chard; or manzanilla.

Foie gras White. In Bordeaux they drink Sauternes. Others prefer a late-harvest Pinot Gr or Ries (inc New World), Vouvray, Montlouis, Jurançon Moelleux or Gewurz. Tokáj Aszú 5 puttonyos is a Lucullan choice. Old dry amontillado can be sublime. If the foie gras is served hot, mature vintage Champagne. But never Chard or Sauv Bl.

Frankfurters German Ries, Beaujolais or light Pinot N. Or Budweiser (Budvar) beer.

Fruit
fresh Sweet Coteaux du Layon or light sweet Muscat.
poached Sweet Muscatel: try Muscat de Beaumes- de-Venise, Moscato di Pantelleria or Spanish dessert Tarragona.
dried fruit (and compotes) Banyuls, Rivesaltes or Maury.
flans and tarts Sauternes, Monbazillac; sweet Vouvray or Anjou.
salads A fine sweet sherry or any Muscat-based wine.

Game birds, young, plain-roasted The best red you can afford.
older birds in casseroles Red (Gevrey-Chambertin, Pommard, Santenay or Grand Cru St-Emilion, Napa Valley Cab Sauv or Rhône).
well-hung game Vega Sicilia, great red Rhône, Lebanon's Chateau Musar.
cold game Mature vintage Champagne.

Game pie, hot Red: Oregon Pinot N.
cold Gd quality white burgundy, cru Beaujolais or Champagne.

Gazpacho A glass of fino before and after. Or Sauv Bl.

Ginger desserts Sweet Muscats, New World botrytized Ries and Sem.

Goat's cheese (warm) Sancerre, Pouilly-Fumé or New World Sauv Bl. Chilled Chinon, Saumur-Champigny or Provence rosé. Australian sparkling Shiraz or strong east Mediterranean reds: *e.g.* Greek or Turkish.

Goulash Flavoursome young red such as Hungarian Zin, Uruguayan Tannat, Morellino di Scansano or a young Australian Shiraz.

Gravadlax Akvavit or iced sake. Grand Cru Chablis; California, Washington or Margaret River Chard; Mosel Spätlese (not Trocken).

Guacamole California Chard, Sauv Blanc, dry Muscat or NV Champagne. Or Mexican beer.

Haddock Rich dry whites: Meursault, California or New Zealand Chard, Marsanne or Albariño.
smoked, mousse or brandade A wonderful dish for showing off any stylish full-bodied white, inc Grand Cru Chablis or Chard from Sonoma or New Zealand.

Haggis Fruity red, eg young claret, Châteauneuf-du-Pape or New World Cab Sauv. Or of course malt whisky.

Hake Sauv Bl or any fresh fruity white: Pacherenc, Tursan, white Navarra.

Halibut As for turbot.

Ham, raw or cured Alsace Grand Cru Pinot Gr, crisp Italian white or sweetish German white (Rhine Spätlese). Soft Pinot Noir or lightish Cab Sauv. With Spanish *pata negra* or *jamon*, try fino sherry or tawny port.

Hamburger Young red: Beaujolais or Australian Cab Sauv, Chianti or Zin.

Hare Calls for flavourful red: not-too-old burgundy or Bordeaux, Rhône (*e.g.* Gigondas), Bandol, Barbaresco, Ribero del Duero or Rioja Reserva. Australia's Grange would be an experience.

Herrings, raw or pickled Dutch gin (young, not aged) or Scandinavian akvavit, and cold beer. If wine is essential, try Muscadet 2003.
fried/grilled Need a white with some acidity to cut their richness. Rully, Chablis, Bourgogne Aligoté, Greek white or dry Sauv Bl. Or try cider.

Houmous Pungent, spicy dry white, *e.g.* Furmint or modern Greek white.

Ice-creams and sorbets Fortified wine (Australian liqueur Muscat, Banyuls, PX sherry); sweet Asti or sparkling Moscato. Amaretto liqueur with vanilla; rum with chocolate.

Indian food Medium-sweet white, very cold: Orvieto Abboccato, South African Chenin Bl, Alsace Pinot Bl, Indian sparkling, Mateus Rosé, cava and NV Champagne. Or emphasize the heat with a tannic Barolo or Barbaresco, or deep-flavoured reds such as Châteauneuf-du-Pape, Cornas, Australian Grenache or Mourvèdre, or Valpolicella Amarone.

Kedgeree Full white, still or sparkling: Mâcon-Villages, South African Chard. At breakfast: Champagne.

Kidneys Red: St-Emilion or Fronsac: Nuits-St-Georges, Cornas, Barbaresco, Rioja, Spanish or Australian Cab Sauv or top Alentejo.

Kippers A gd cup of tea, preferably Ceylon (milk, no sugar). Scotch? Dry oloroso sherry is surprisingly gd.

Lamb, roast One of the traditional and best partners for v.gd red Bordeaux – or its Cab Sauv equivalents from the New World, esp Napa and Coonawarra. In Spain, the partner of the finest old Rioja and Ribera del Duero Reservas. New Zealand Pinot N for spicy lamb dishes.
cutlets or chops As for roast lamb, but a little less grand.

Lamproie à la Bordelaise 5-yr-old St-Emilion or Fronsac. Or Douro reds with Portuguese lampreys.

Lemon desserts For dishes like **Tarte au Citron**, sweet Ries from Germany or Austria, or Tokáj Aszú; the sharper the lemon, the sweeter the wine.

Lentil dishes Sturdy reds such as southern French, or Zin or Shiraz.

Liver Choose a young red: Beaujolais-Villages, St-Joseph, Cab Sauv, Merlot, Zin or Portuguese.
Calf's Red Rioja crianza, Salice Salentino Riserva or Fleurie.

Lobster, richly sauced Vintage Champagne, fine white burgundy, cru classé Graves, California Chard or Australian Ries, Pfalz Spätlese.
salad NV Champagne, Alsace Ries, Chablis Premier Cru, Condrieu, Mosel Spätlese, Penedès Chard or Cava.

Mackerel Hard or sharp white: Sauv Bl from Touraine, Gaillac, Vinho Verde, white Rioja or English white. Guinness is gd.
smoked An oily wine-destroyer. Manzanilla sherry, proper dry Vinho Verde or Schnapps, peppered or bison-grass vodka. Or lager.

Mediterranean vegetable dishes Vigorous young red: Chianti, New Zealand Cab Sauv or Merlot; young red Bordeaux, Gigondas or Coteaux du Languedoc. Or characterful white.

Meringues Recioto di Soave, Asti or Champagne doux.

Mezze A selection of hot and cold vegetable dishes. Sparkling is a gd all-purpose choice, as is rosé from the Languedoc or Provence. Fino sherry is in its element.

Mille-feuille desserts Delicate sweet sparkling white such as Moscato d'Asti or demi-sec Champagne.

Monkfish Often roasted, which needs fuller rather than leaner wines. Try Australian/New Zealand Chard, Oregon Pinot N or Chilean Merlot.

Moussaka Red or rosé: Naoussa from Greece, Sangiovese, Corbières, Côtes de Provence, Ajaccio or New Zealand Pinot N.

Mullet, red A chameleon, adaptable to gd white or red, esp Pinot N.

Mullet, grey Verdicchio, Rully or unoaked Chard.

Mussels Muscadet-sur-lie, Chablis Premier Cru or a lightly oaked Chard.

Nuts Finest oloroso sherry, madeira, vintage or tawny port (nature's match for **walnuts**), Vin Santo or Setúbal Moscatel.

Orange desserts Experiment with old Sauternes, Tokáj Aszú, or California Orange Muscat.

Osso buco Low tannin, supple red, such as Dolcetto d'Alba or Pinot N. Or dry Italian whites such as Soave and Lugana.

Oxtail Match with a rather rich French red such as St-Emilion, Pomerol, Pommard, Nuits-St-Georges, Barolo, Châteauneuf-du-Pape. Or Rioja Reserva or Ribera del Duero. Or California or Coonawarra Cab Sauv.

Oysters, raw NV Champagne, Chablis Premier Cru, Muscadet, white Graves, Sauv Bl or Guinness.
cooked Puligny-Montrachet or gd New World Chard. Champagne is gd with either.

Paella Young Spanish wines: red, dry white or rosé from Penedès, Somontano, Navarra or Rioja.

Panettone Jurançon moelleux, late-harvest Ries, Barsac, Vin Santo or Tokáj Aszú.

Pasta Red or white according to the sauce or trimmings:
cream sauce Orvieto, Frascati or Alto Adige Chard.
meat sauce Montepulciano d'Abruzzo, Salice Salentino or Merlot.
pesto (basil) sauce Barbera, Ligurian Vermentino, New Zealand Sauv Bl, Hungarian Hárslevelü or Furmint.
seafood sauce (e.g. vongole) Verdicchio, Soave, top white Rioja, Cirò, or Sauv Bl.
tomato sauce Barbera, south Italian red, Zin, or South Australian Grenache.

Pastrami Alsace Ries, young Sangiovese, or Cab Fr.

Pâté
chicken liver Calls for pungent white (Alsace Pinot Gr or Marsanne), a smooth red like a light Pomerol or Volnay, or even amontillado sherry.
duck pâté Châteauneuf-du-Pape, Cornas, Chianti Classico, or Pomerol.
fish pâté Muscadet, Mâcon-Villages, or Australian Chard (unoaked).
Pâté de campagne A dry white ★★: Gd vin de pays, Graves, Pfalz Ries.

Pears in red wine A pause before the port. Or try Rivesaltes, Banyuls or Ries Beerenauslese.

Pecan pie Orange Muscat or Australian liqueur Muscat.

Peperonata Dry Australian Ries, Western Australia Sem or New Zealand Sauv Bl. Red drinkers can try Tempranillo or Grenache.

Perch, sandre Exquisite freshwater fish for finest wines: top white burgundy, Alsace Ries Grand Cru or noble Mosels. Or try top Swiss Fendant or Johannisberg.

Pigeon Lively reds: Savigny, Chambolle-Musigny; Crozes-Hermitage, Chianti Classico, or California Pinot N. Or try Franken Silvaner Spätlese. **squab** Fine white or red burgundy, Alsace Ries Grand Cru or mature claret.

Pipérade Rosé, or dry South Australian Ries.

Pimentos, roasted Sauv Bl, or light reds.

Pizza Any ★★ dry Italian red. Or Rioja, Australian Shiraz, southern French red or Douro red.

Pork, roast A gd rich neutral background to a fairly light red or rich white. It deserves ★★ treatment – Médoc is fine. Portugal's suckling pig is eaten with Bairrada Garrafeira. Chinese is gd with Pinot N.

Pot au feu, bollito misto, cocido Rustic red wines from the region of origin; Sangiovese di Romagna, Chusclan, Lirac, Rasteau, Portuguese Alentejo or Yecla and Jumilla from Spain.

Pumpkin/Squash dishes Full-bodied fruity dry or off-dry white: Viognier or Marsanne, demi-sec Vouvray, Gavi or South African Chenin Bl.

Prawns, shrimps or langoustines Fine dry white: burgundy, Graves, New Zealand Chard, Pfalz Ries – even fine mature Champagne. ("Cocktail sauce" kills wine, and in time, people.)

Quail Alsace Ries Grand Cru, Rioja Reserva, mature claret or Pinot N.

Quiches Dry full-bodied white: Alsace, Graves, Sauv Bl, dry Rheingau; or young red (Tempranillo, Periquita), according to ingredients.

Rabbit Lively medium-bodied young Italian red or Aglianico del Vulture; Chiroubles, Chinon, Saumur-Champigny, or New Zealand Pinot Noir.

Raspberries (no cream, little sugar) Excellent with fine reds which themselves taste of raspberries: young Juliénas, Regnié, even Pomerol.

Risotto, with seafood Pinot Gr from Friuli, Gavi, youngish Sem, Dolcetto or Barbera d'Alba. **with fungi porcini** Finest mature Barolo or Barbaresco.

Rum desserts (baba, mousses, ice-cream) Muscat – from Asti to Australian liqueur, according to weight of dish.

Salads As a first course, esp with blue cheese dressing, any dry and appetizing white wine. **salade niçoise** Very dry, ★★, not too light or flowery white or rosé: Provençal, Rhône, or Corsican; Fernão Pires, Sauv Bl. **NB** Vinegar in salad dressings destroys the flavour of wine. If you want salad at a meal with fine wine, dress the salad with wine or a little lemon juice instead of vinegar.

Salmon, seared or grilled Fine white burgundy: Puligny- or Chassagne-Montrachet, Meursault, Corton-Charlemagne, Chablis Grand Cru; Grüner Veltliner, Condrieu, California, Idaho or New Zealand Chard, Rheingau Kabinett/Spätlese, Australian Ries. Young Pinot N can be gd. Salmon fishcakes call for similar, but less grand, wines.
smoked A dry but pungent white: fino sherry, Alsace Pinot Gr, Chablis Grand Cru, Pouilly-Fumé, Pfalz Ries Spätlese or vintage Champagne. Also vodka, schnapps or akvavit.
carpaccio Puligny-Montrachet, Condrieu, California Chard or New Zealand Sauv Bl.

Sand-dabs This sublime fish can handle your fullest Chard (not oaky).

Sardines, fresh grilled Very dry white: Vinho Verde, Soave, Muscadet, or modern Greek.

Sashimi If you are prepared to forego the wasabi, sparkling wines will match. Or Washington or Tasmanian Chard, Chablis Grand Cru, Rheingau Ries and English Seyval Bl. Otherwise, iced sake, fino sherry or beer. Trials have matched 5-putt Tokáj with fat tuna, sea urchin and anago (eel).

Satay Australia's McLaren Vale Shiraz. Gewurz from Alsace or New Zealand.

Sauerkraut (German) Lager or Pils. But a Ries Auslese can be amazing.

Scallops An inherently slightly sweet dish, best with finest whites.
in cream sauces German Spätlese, Montrachet, top Australian Chard, or dry Vouvray.
grilled or seared Hermitage Blanc, Grüner Veltliner, Entre-Deux-Mers, vintage Champagne, or Pinot N.
with Asian seasoning New Zealand, South African Sauv Bl, Verdelho, Australian Ries, or Gewurz.

Sea bass Weissburgunder from Baden or Pfalz. V.gd for any fine or delicate white: Clare Valley dry Ries, Chablis or Châteauneuf-du-Pape.

Shark's fin soup Add a teaspoon of Cognac. Sip amontillado.

Shellfish Dry white with plain boiled shellfish, richer wines with richer sauces. With *plateaux de fruits de mer*: Muscadet, Chablis, unoaked Chard or dry Ries.

Skate with brown butter White with some pungency (*e.g.* Pinot Gr d'Alsace), or a clean straightforward wine like Muscadet or Verdicchio.

Snapper Sauv Bl if cooked with Oriental flavours; white Rhône with Mediterranean flavours.

Sole, plaice, etc.: plain, grilled or fried Perfect with fine wines: white burgundy, or its equivalent.
with sauce Depending on the ingredients: sharp dry wine for tomato sauce, fairly rich for sole *véronique* with its sweet grapes, etc.

Soufflés As show dishes these deserve ★★★ wines.
fish Dry white: ★★★ Burgundy, Bordeaux, Alsace, Chard, etc.
cheese Red burgundy or mature Cab Sauv.
spinach (tougher on wine) Light Chard (Mâcon-Villages, St-Véran), or Valpolicella. Champagne can also be gd with many kinds of soufflé.
sweet soufflés Sauternes or Vouvray moelleux. Or a sweet (or rich) Champagne.

Steak au poivre A fairly young Rhône red or Cab Sauv.

Steak tartare Vodka or light young red: Beaujolais, Bergerac or Valpolicella.

Korean Yuk Whe (The world's best steak tartare.) Sake.

filet, tournedos, T-bone, fiorentina (bistecca) Any top red (but not old wines with Béarnaise sauce: top Californian Chard is better). My choice: Château Haut-Brion.

Steak and kidney pie or pudding Red Rioja Reserva, Douro red, or mature Cabernet.

Stews and casseroles Red burgundy comes into its own; otherwise lusty full-flavoured red, such as Toro, Corbières, Barbera, Shiraz, or Zin.

Strawberries and cream Sauternes or similar sweet Bordeaux, Vouvray Moelleux or Jurançon Vendange Tardive.

Strawberries, wild (no cream) Serve with red Bordeaux (most exquisitely Margaux) poured over.

Summer pudding Fairly young Sauternes of a gd vintage (95 96 97 98).

Sushi Hot wasabi is usually hidden in every piece. German QbA trocken wines, simple Chablis, or NV brut Champ. Or, of course, sake or beer.

Sweetbreads A grand dish, so grand wine, but not too dry: Rhine Ries or Franken Silvaner Spätlese, top Alsace Pinot Gr or Condrieu, depending on the sauce.

Swordfish Full-bodied dry white of the country. Nothing grand.

Tagines These vary enormously, but fruity young reds are a gd bet: Beaujolais, Tempranillo, Sangiovese, Merlot and Shiraz.

Tapas Perfect with fino sherry, which can cope with the wide range of flavours in both hot and cold dishes.

Tapenade Manzanilla or fino sherry, or any sharpish dry white or rosé.

Taramasalata A rustic southern white with personality. Fino sherry works well. Try white Rioja or a Marsanne. The bland supermarket version goes well with any delicate white or Champagne.

Thai food Ginger and lemongrass call for pungent Sauv Bl (Loire, South Africa, Australia, New Zealand) or Ries (German Spätlese or Australian). **coconut milk** Hunter Valley or other ripe, oaked Chards; Alsace Pinot Bl for refreshment; Gewurz or Verdelho. And of course sparkling.

Tiramisú This Italian dessert works best with Vin Santo, but also with young tawny port, Muscat de Beaumes-de-Venise or Sauternes and Australian Liqueur Muscats.

Tongue Gd for any red or white of abundant character, esp Italian. Also Beaujolais, Loire reds, New Zealand reds and full dry rosés.

Trifle Should be sufficiently vibrant with its internal sherry.

Tripe Red (*e.g.* Corbières, Roussillon) or rather sweet white (*e.g.* German Spätlese). Better: Western Australian Sem/Chard, or cut with pungent dry white such as Pouilly-Fumé or fresh red such as Saumur-Champigny.

Trout Delicate white wine, *e.g.* Mosel (Saar or Ruwer), Alsace Pinot Bl.

smoked Sancerre, California or South African Sauv Bl. Rully or
Bourgogne Aligoté, Chablis or Champagne. But Mosel Spätlese is best.

Tuna, grilled or seared White, red, or rosé of fairly fruity character; a
top St-Véran, white Hermitage, or Côtes du Rhône would be fine.
Pinot N or a light Merlot are the best reds to try.
carpaccio Viognier, California Chard or New Zealand Sauv Bl.

Turbot Serve with your best rich dry white: Meursault or Chassagne-
Montrachet, mature Chablis or its California, Australian or New Zealand
equivalent. Condrieu. Mature Rheingau, Mosel or Nahe Spätlese or
Auslese (not trocken).

Veal, roast A good neutral background dish for any fine old red which
may have faded with age (*e.g.* a Rioja Reserva), a German or Austrian
Ries, or Vouvray, or Alsace Pinot Gr.

Venison Big-scale reds inc Mourvèdre – solo as in Bandol, or in blends
– Rhône, Bordeaux or California Cab of a mature vintage; or rather rich
whites (Pfalz Spätlese or Hunter Semillon).

Vitello tonnato Full-bodied whites esp Chard; or light reds (*e.g.* young
Cabernet or Valpolicella) served cool.

Whitebait Crisp dry whites: Chablis, Verdicchio, Greek, Touraine Sauv
Bl, or fino sherry.

Zabaglione Light-gold marsala, Australian botrytized Sem or Asti.

Wine & cheese

The notion that wine and cheese were married in heaven is not born out
by experience. Fine red wines are slaughtered by strong cheeses: only
sharp or sweet white wines survive. Principles to remember, despite
exceptions, are first: the harder the cheese the more tannin the wine can
have. And second: the creamier the cheese is the more acidity is needed
in the wine. The main exception constitutes a third principle: wines and
cheeses of a region usually sympathise. Cheese is classified by its
texture and the nature of its rind, so its appearance is a guide to the
type of wine to match it. Individual cheeses mentioned below are only
examples taken from the hundreds sold in good cheese shops.

Fresh, no rind – cream cheese, crème fraîche, Mozzarella
Light crisp white – Simple Bordeaux Blanc, Bergerac, English unoaked
whites; or rosé – Anjou, Rhône; or very light, very young, very fresh red
such as Bordeaux, Bardolino or Beaujolais.

**Hard cheeses, waxed or oiled, often showing marks from cheesecloth –
Gruyère family, Manchego and other Spanish cheeses, Parmesan, Cantal,
Comté, old Gouda, Cheddar and most "traditional" English cheeses**
Particularly hard to generalize here; Gouda, Gruyère, some Spanish,
and a few English cheeses complement fine claret or Cab Sauv and
great Shiraz/Syrah wines. But strong cheeses need less refined wines,
and preferably local ones. Sugary, granular old Dutch red Mimolette or
Beaufort are gd for finest mature Bordeaux. Also for Tokáj Aszú.

Blue cheeses Roquefort can be wonderful with Sauternes, but don't extend the idea to other blues. It is the sweetness of Sauternes, esp aged, which complements the saltiness. Stilton and port, preferably tawny, is a classic. Intensely flavoured old oloroso, amontillado, madeira, marsala, and other fortified wines go with most blues. The acidity of Tokáj Aszú also works well.

Natural rind (goat's or sheep's cheese) with bluish-grey mould (the rind is wrinkled when mature), sometimes dusted with ash – St-Marcellin Sancerre, Valençay, light fresh Sauv Bl, Jurançon, Savoie, Soave, Italian Chard or English whites.

Bloomy rind soft cheeses, pure white rind if pasteurized, or dotted with red: Brie, Camembert, Chaource, Bougon (goat's milk 'Camembert') Full dry white burgundy or Rhône if the cheese is white and immature; powerful, fruity St-Emilion, young Australian (or Rhône) Shiraz/ Syrah or Grenache if it's mature.

Washed-rind pungent soft cheeses, with rather sticky orange-red rind – Langres, mature Epoisses, Maroilles, Carré de l'Est, Milleens, Munster Local reds, esp for Burgundy cheeses; vigorous Languedoc, Cahors, Côtes du Frontonnais, Corsican, southern Italian, Sicilian or Bairrada. Also powerful whites, esp Alsace Gewurz and Muscat.

Semi-soft cheeses, grey-pink thickish rind – Livarot, Pont l'Evêque, Reblochon, Tomme de Savoie, St-Nectaire Powerful white Bordeaux, Chard, Alsace Pinot Gr, dryish Ries, southern Italian and Sicilian whites, aged white Rioja or dry oloroso sherry. But the strongest of these cheeses kill most wines.

Food & finest wine

With very special bottles, the wine sometimes guides the choice of food rather than the usual way around. The following suggestions are based largely on the gastronomic conventions of the wine regions producing these treasures, plus much diligent research. They should help bring out the best in your best wines.

Red wines

Red Bordeaux and other Cabernet Sauvignon-based wines (very old, light and delicate: e.g. pre-60) Leg or rack of young lamb, roast with a hint of herbs (but not garlic); entrecôte; roast partridge or grouse, sweetbreads; or cheese soufflé after the meat has been served.

Fully mature great vintages (e.g. Bordeaux 61 66 75) Shoulder or saddle of lamb, roast with a touch of garlic, roast ribs, or grilled rump of beef.

Mature but still vigorous (e.g. 85 86 89) Shoulder or saddle of lamb (inc kidneys) with rich sauce. Fillet of beef *marchand de vin* (with wine and bone-marrow). Avoid Beef Wellington: pastry dulls the palate.

Merlot-based Bordeaux (Pomerol, St-Emilion) Beef as above (fillet is richest) or venison.

Côte d'Or red burgundy (Consider the weight and texture, which grow lighter/more velvety with age. Also the character of the wine: Nuits is earthy, Musigny flowery, great Romanées can be exotic, Pommard renowned for its four-squareness, etc.). Roast chicken, or better, capon, is a safe standard with red burgundy; guinea-fowl for slightly stronger wines, then partridge, grouse, or woodcock for those progressively more rich and pungent. Hare and venison (*chevreuil*) are alternatives.
great old burgundy The classic Burgundian formula is cheese: Epoisses (unfermented). A fabulous cheese but a terrible waste of fine old wines.
vigorous younger burgundy Duck or goose roasted to minimize fat.

Great Syrahs: Hermitage, Côte-Rôtie, Grange; or Vega Sicilia
Beef, venison, well-hung game; bone-marrow on toast; English cheese (esp best farm Cheddar) but also hard goat's milk and ewe's milk cheeses such as Berkswell and Ticklemore.

Rioja Gran Reserva, Pesquera... Richly flavoured roasts: wild boar, mutton, saddle of hare, or whole suckling pig.

Barolo, Barbaresco Risotto with white truffles; pasta with game sauce (*e.g. pappardelle alla lepre*); porcini mushrooms; Parmesan.

White wines

Top Chablis, white burgundy, other top Chards
White fish simply grilled or *meunière*. Dover sole, turbot, halibut are best; brill, drenched in butter, can be excellent.

Supreme white burgundy (Le Montrachet, Corton-Charlemagne) or equivalent Graves Roast veal, organic chicken stuffed with truffles or herbs under the skin, or sweetbreads; richly sauced white fish or scallops as above. Or lobster or wild salmon.

Condrieu, Château-Grillet or Hermitage Blanc Very light pasta scented with herbs and tiny peas or broad beans.

Grand Cru Alsace
Ries Truite au bleu, smoked salmon or choucroute garni.
Pinot Gris Roast or grilled veal.
Gewurztraminer Cheese soufflé (Münster cheese).
Vendange Tardive Foie gras or Tarte Tatin.

Sauternes Simple crisp buttery biscuits (*e.g.* Langue-de-Chat), white peaches, nectarines, strawberries (without cream). Not tropical fruit. Pan-seared foie-gras. Experiment with blue cheeses.

Supreme Vouvray moelleux, etc. Buttery biscuits, apples, or apple tart.

Beerenauslese/Trockenbeerenauslese Biscuits, peaches, greengages. Desserts made from rhubarb, gooseberries, quince, or apples.

Tokáj Aszú (4–6 putts) Foie gras is thoroughly recommended. Fruit desserts, cream desserts, even chocolate can be wonderful.

Great vintage port or madeira Walnuts or pecans. A Cox's Orange Pippin and a digestive biscuit is a classic English accompaniment.

Old vintage Champagne (not Blanc de Blancs) As an apéritif, or with cold partridge, grouse or woodcock.

A selection for 2007

Alongside recommendations in the main entries, this list represents a small compilation of choice bottles as an easy-reference guide. While some of the wines are much easier to find than others, all show a level of quality and individuality in their category which makes them worth seeking out.

Exploring Riesling
2005 Grosset Polish Hill, Australia
2002 Steingarten, Eden Valley, Australia
Kupljen Renski Rizling, as mature as possible, Slovenia
2005 Pegasus Bay, New Zealand
2004 Framingham Classic, New Zealand
2003 Forrest Estate Dry, New Zealand
2003 Steiner Hund Reserve, Nikolaihof, Austria
2005 Schloss Gobelsburg, Austria
2004 Brauneberger Juffer Sonnenuhr Auslese, Schloss Lieser, Mosel-Saar-Ruwer, Germany
1995 Absberg Trockenbeerenauslese, Maximin Grunhaus, Mosel-Saar-Ruwer, Germany
2004 von der Fels, Keller, Rheinhessen, Germany

Quirky Southern Hemisphere
2002 Pirramimma Petit Verdot, Australia
2004 Clonakilla Shiraz Viognier, Australia
1998 McWilliam's Elizabeth Semillon Cellar Release, Australia
2001 Clover Hill sparkling, Tasmania
2005 Steenberg Vineyards Semillon, Constantia, South Africa
2004 Kanu Kia Ora Noble Late Harvest, Stellenbosch, South Africa
2004 Boukenhoutskloof Semillon, Franschhoek, South Africa
2002 Craggy Range Le Sol Syrah, New Zealand
2002 Fromm Fromm Vineyard Pinot Noir, New Zealand
2003 Casa Silva Gran Reserva Lolol Shiraz, Chile

Discovering sherry
Barbadillo Obispo Gascon Palo Cortado
Domecq La Ina Fino
Emilio Hildago Privilegio 1860 Palo Cortado
González-Byass Noe PX
Gutiérrez Colosía Viejissimo Palo Cortado
Harvey's Palo Cortado
Herederos de Argüeso Viejo Amontillado
Hidalgo-La Gitana Manzanilla
Lustau Puerto Fino
Osborne Fino Quinta
Rey Fernando de Castilla Antique PX
Tradición Oloroso
Valdespino Tio Diego Amontillado
Williams & Humbert 15 year sweet Oloroso

Organic and Biodynamic

2003 The McNab, Fetzer Bonterra Vineyards, Mendocino County, California

2004 Château Moulin-du-Cadet, St Emilion Grand Cru Classé, Bordeaux

2004 Coyam, Viñedos Organicos Emiliana, Chile

2003 Domaine Leflaive Bourgogne Blanc, Burgundy

2004 Grasberg Blanc, Domaine Marcel Deiss, Alsace

2004 Le Soula Blanc, Domaine du Soula, VdP des Côtes Catalanes, Roussillon

2004 Clos du Bourg Sec, Domaine Huet, Vouvray

2004 The Ladybird Red, Laibach Estate, Stellenbosch, South Africa

2004 Zind, Domaine Zind-Humbrecht, Alsace

2001 Temple Bruer Reserve Cabernet Sauvignon Petit Verdot, Australia

2001 Hidden Valley Cabernet Sauvignon, Stellenbosch, South Africa

2003 The Observatory Syrah/Carignan, Paarl, South Africa

France

More heavily shaded areas
are the wine-growing regions

The following abbreviations
are used in the text:

Al   Alsace
Beauj   Beaujolais
Burg   Burgundy
B'x   Bordeaux
Champ   Champagne
Lo   Loire
Prov   Provence
Pyr   Pyrenees
N/S Rh   North/South Rhône
SW   Southwest

AC   *appellation contrôlée*
ch/x   château, châteax
dom/s   domaine, domaines

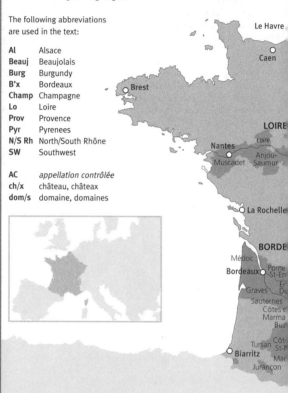

Oh, dear, poor old France. French wines seem to be turning into
something of an easy target, abused as hopelessly *démodé* by every
bien-pensant drinker of discounted, branded New World Merlot. And if it's
not old-fashioned, it's overpriced (compared to those branded New World
Merlots). And if it's not overpriced, it is, in some mysterious way, elitist.

France does have its problems. Its wines are hedged about by
bureaucracy and it has more than its share of failing growers. Its wines can't
be as cheap as those of, say, Chile, because land and labour are expensive,
and economies of scale more difficult. But there are plus points: the same
bureaucracy that prevents growers in Bordeaux from growing Syrah has
kept alive marvellous grapes like Petit Manseng and Viognier during years
when, had fashion had its way, they would have been ripped out to make

way for Chardonnay. Now Viognier is insinuating itself into so many countries and regions that it's beginning to look like the Next Small Thing: blends of Shiraz and Viognier are currently flavour-of-the-month in Australia.

If France didn't exist, the wine world would certainly have to invent it. Where else would it get so many ideas from? Where else would it get so many benchmark wine styles from? And who else could show it quite so effectively both the best, most outward-looking attitudes and the worst, most inward-looking ones?

Poor old France. It is changing, but patchily. The trouble is, the rest of the world isn't waiting for it.

France entries also cross-refer to Châteaux of Bordeaux section.

Recent vintages of the French classics

Red Bordeaux

Médoc/red Graves For some wines bottle-age is optional: for these it is indispensable. Minor châteaux from light vintages need only two or three years, but even modest wines of great years can improve for 15 or so, and the great châteaux of these years can profit from double that time.

2005 Perfect weather conditions throughout the year. Dry season and harvest. Rich, balanced, long-ageing wines from an outstanding vintage.

2004 Dry, sunny Sept and early Oct but rain during the Cabernet harvest. Mixed bag. Abundant vintage, which needed curbing. Good if selective.

2003 Hottest summer on record. Cabernet Sauvignon can be tremendous. A typical but rich, powerful wines at best, unbalanced at worst. Yields right down.

2002 Saved by a dry, sunny Sept. The later-ripening Cabernet Sauvignon benefited most. Yields down. Some good wines if selective. Keep.

2001 A cool Sept and rain at vintage meant Cabernet Sauvignon had difficulty in ripening fully. Some fine fresh wines to drink now–2012.

2000 Late flowering and a somewhat damp start to the summer looked worrying but the final product is outstanding – superb wines throughout. Keep.

1999 Vintage rain again diluted ripe juice, so-so wines to drink now–2015.

1998 Rain at vintage *again*. But Aug heat ripened (even roasted) grapes. Good, but the Right Bank is clearly the winner this year. Drink now–2015.

1997 Uneven flowering and summer rain were a double challenge. Top wines still of interest, but the rest have faded.

1996 Cool summer, fine harvest. Good to excellent. Drink now–2020.

1995 Heat-wave and drought; saved by rain. Good to excellent. Now–2020+.

1994 Hopes of a supreme year; then heavy vintage rain. The best good, but be careful. Drink now–2010.

1993 Ripe grapes but a wet vintage. Attractive drinking now–2008.

1992 Rain at flowering, in Aug and at vintage. A huge crop; light wines. Avoid.

1991 Frost in April halved crop and rain interrupted vintage. The northern Médoc did best. Drink up.

1990 A paradox: a drought year with a threat of over-production. Self-discipline was essential. Its results are magnificent. To 2020+.

1989 Early spring, splendid summer. Top wines classics of the ripe, dark kind: elegance, length. Some better than 1990. Small châteaux uneven. To 2020.

1988 Generally very good; tannic, balanced, beginning to open. Keep top wines. To 2010.

1987 Much more enjoyable than seemed likely. Drink up.

1986 Another splendid, huge, heat-wave harvest. A long-term prospect to 2020.

1985 Very good vintage, in a heat-wave. Very fine wines now–2010.

Older fine vintages: 75 70 66 62 61 59 55 53 49 48 47 45 29 28.

St-Emilion/Pomerol

2005 Same conditions as the Médoc. An overall success.

2004 Merlot often better than 2003 (Pomerol). Good Cabernet Franc. Variable.

2003 Merlot suffered in the heat, but exceptional Cabernet Franc. Very mixed. Some over-extraction again.

2002 Problems with rot and ripeness; some over-extraction. Modest to good.

2001 Less rain than Médoc during vintage. Some powerful Merlot, but variable.

2000 Similar conditions to Médoc. Less kind to Merlot but a very good vintage.

1999 Careful, lucky growers made good wines but rain was again a problem.

1998 Earlier-ripening Merlot largely escaped the rain. Some excellent wines.

FRANCE

1997 Merlot suffered in the rain. Only a handful of wines still of interest.
1996 Cool, fine summer. Vintage rain. Less consistent than Médoc. Now–2015.
1995 Perhaps even better than Médoc/Graves. Now–2012.
1994 Good, especially Pomerol. Now–2015.
1993 Pomerol better than Médoc; good despite terrible vintage weather.
1992 Very dilute Avoid.
1991 A sad story. Many wines not released.
1990 Another chance to make great wine or a lot of wine. Now–2020.
1989 Large, ripe, early harvest; an overall triumph. To 2020.
1988 Generally excellent. But some châteaux over-produced. Drink soon.
1987 Some very adequate wines (especially in Pomerol). Drink up.
1986 A prolific vintage; but top St-Emilions have a long life ahead.
1985 One of the great years, with a long future. To 2010+.
Older fine vintages: 71 70 67 66 64 61 59 53 52 49 47 45.

Red burgundy

Côte d'Or Côte de Beaune reds generally mature sooner than bigger wines of Côte de Nuits. Earliest drinking dates are for lighter commune wines – e.g. Volnay, Beaune; latest for biggest wines of, e.g., Chambertin, Romanée. But even the best burgundies are more attractive young than equivalent red Bordeaux.
2005 Expected to be outstanding – slightly below average in volume, though.
2004 Good except where hail has caused significant damage.
2003 Reds coped with the heat better than the whites. Muscular, rich wines. Best wines outstanding, others short and hot.
2002 Avoided the rains of southern France. A very exciting, stylish vintage to drink and keep.
2001 Just needed a touch more sun for excellence.
2000 Difficult. Fragile grapes in Côte de Beaune. Much better in Côte de Nuits.
1999 Big ripe vintage; good colour, bags of fruit, silky tannins. Wines to keep.
1998 Ripe fruit but dry tannins. Those in balance need keeping.
1997 Again the gods smiled. Very ripe grapes, with low acidity. Lovely wines mostly ready now.
1996 Fine summer and vintage. Top wines must be kept. 2008–2020.
1995 Small, excellent crop, despite rain. Grapes were very ripe. Start drinking.
1994 Compromised by vintage rain. Generally lean, but exceptions in Côte de Nuits. Drink up.
1993 An excellent vintage: concentrated. Now–2010. Drink up Côte de Beaune.
1992 Ripe, plump, pleasing. No great concentration. Drink up.
1991 Very small harvest; some wines very tannic. Côte de Nuits best. Drink soon.
1990 Great vintage: perfect weather compromised only by touches of drought and some over-production. Long life ahead but start to enjoy. To 2020.
1989 Year of great charm, not necessarily for long maturing. Drink up all but best.
1988 Very good, but tannic. Now–2015 (but only the best).
Older fine vintages: 85 78 71 69 66 64 62 61 59 (all mature).

White burgundy

Côte de Beaune Well-made wines of good vintages with plenty of acidity as well as fruit will improve and gain depth and richness for some years – up to ten. Lesser wines from lighter vintages are ready for drinking after two or three.
2005 Small but outstanding crop of dense, concentrated wines.
2004 Really promising for aromatic, balanced wines for medium-term ageing.
2003 Opulent wines to drink young. Not many keepers from this hot vintage.
2002 Ripe healthy grapes; medium-sized crop of great promise. Stylish wines.
2001 Generally good results despite lower sugar levels. Drink soon.

2000 A big crop of ripe, healthy grapes. Exciting wines.
1999 Another generous vintage of good, fresh, well-balanced wines.
1998 Difficult year for white. Chassagne was successful. Drink up.
1997 Overall an excellent vintage: forward and charming. Drink soon.
1996 Not developing as well as hoped. Over-acidic.
1995 A potentially great vintage, diluted in places. Now–2010.
1994 Patchy. Top growers: very fine potent wines but not for keeping. Drink up.
1993 Poor reputation, but best wines have turned out really well. Drink soon.
1992 Ripe, aromatic, and charming. Mostly ready. Drink up.

The white wines of the Mâconnais (Pouilly-Fuissé, St-Véran, Mâcon-Villages)
follow a similar pattern, but do not last as long. They are more appreciated
for their freshness than their richness.

Chablis *Grand cru* Chablis of vintages with both strength and acidity can age
superbly for up to ten years; *premiers crus* proportionately less.
2005 Small but outstanding crop of dense, concentrated wines.
2004 Difficult vintage, with mildew a problem, but larger than 2003.
2003 Small crop of ripe wines, but acidity is low and balance in question.
2002 Excellent; may be the equal of 2000.
2001 Too much rain. Relatively weak. Drink up.
2000 Fine weather for harvesting ripe grapes – excellent.
1999 Another ripe vintage, some of it compromised by rain. Drink soon.
1998 Cool weather and some hail. Wines fair to good: not for long keeping.
1997 Another fine vintage; *grands crus* excellent now.
1996 Ideal harvest but hail on top vineyards. Classic keeping Chablis. Now–2010.
1995 Very good to very, very good. Drink now.
1994 Downpours on a ripe vintage. Easy wines; drink up.
1993 Fair to good quality; nothing great. Drink up.
1992 Ripe and charming wines. *Grands crus* splendid. Drink up.
1991 Generally better than Côte d'Or. Useful wines. Drink now.
1990 *Grands crus* magnificent; others lack intensity and acidity. Drink now.

Beaujolais 05: brilliant, concentrated wines. **04**: light, some weak, some
pretty. **03**: too much heat on the grapes, but some excellent. **02**: too much
rain for top quality. **01**: very good if picked before the rain. **00**: excellent. **99**:
splendid, rich, and deep. **98**: very good, if patchy; best *crus* will keep. **97**:
very good. **95**: excellent; older wines should be finished.

Southwest France
2005 Generally a dry year, but without the excessive heat of 2003. Some
  areas affected by hail (southern Bergerac and parts of Jurançon)
  otherwise there is general optimism. Quantities up.
2004 A cool wet Aug dampened hopes of a great year. Those who controlled
  yields and picked before more rain in Oct, have made good wines. Very
  good in Jurançon, which escaped autumn rain.
2003 Little or no rain between March and Sept combined with the fiercest heat
  in France, resulted in small yields, high alcohol, low acidity. Hail in Gaillac
  ruined the vintage. Very good in Jurançon.
2002 Indian summer saved late-picking vineyards (Madiran, Cahors, Jurançon).
  Otherwise disappointing.
2001 Hot summer and perfect vintage conditions. Perhaps too much sugar/alcohol.
2000 Better than forecast despite heavy rain in Sept. Better reds should keep.
1999 Patchy weather spoiled the vintage for some, but far from disastrous.
1998 Outstanding everywhere.

The Midi

2005 A beautifully balanced year, with sunshine and rain at the right times throughout the region.

2004 Marked by Aug storms and a fine Sept. Wines are elegantly balanced, with lower alcohol than 03 or 01.

2003 The year of the heat-wave, in sharp contrast to 02, often resulting in a greatly reduced crop, but also many fine wines from skilled winemakers.

2002 Not an easy year with heavy rain in early Sept causing problems. Varies widely from AC to AC, and grower to grower.

2001 Quantity lower than average. Quality generally very good with a hot summer making for ripe, concentrated wines.

2000 A warm summer throughout, giving ripe fruity wines in Roussillon and Provence, and healthy grapes and balanced wines in Languedoc.

1999 Bad weather failed to ruin vintage in Roussillon; patchy in Languedoc (good in La Clape, not in Pic St-Loup). Good results in Provence.

1998 Drought in Roussillon meant small crop of concentrated wines. Wonderful vintage in Languedoc made ripe, fruity wines with great potential. Well-balanced fruity wines in Provence.

Northern Rhône

2005 Promising depth in reds after dry year, some late rain helped. Very promising Hermitage. Whites appear gd for mid-term drinking.

2004 Stop-start: drought was followed by Aug rain and fine Sept. Mid-weight, mid-term year; best reds are from top sites. Excellent whites.

2003 A muscled, half-sized crop. Intense sun gave cooked "southern" flavours, high degrees, low acidity. Best (not all) reds show genuine richness.

2002 Try before you buy. Best growers abandoned half their crop. Decent red St-Josephs, light Hermitage, Côte-Rôtie. Pretty good whites, esp Condrieu.

2001 Very good, lively year if picked before Sept rain. Fresh fruit, good acidity, can age well. Top year at Côte-Rôtie. Often very good whites.

2000 Decent density, quite warm and rich. Some stewed flavours. Hermitage good in parts, Cornas did well, Côte-Rôtie variable. Good Condrieu, sumptuous. Reds simpler than 99/01.

1999 Very successful. Full, ripe fruit. Delicious, likely to live long. More balance than the 98s. Harmony a key word. Ace Côte-Rôties. Sound whites.

1998 Big, robust vintage. More overt tannins than 99, but have fused well, with rich oily textures. Tasty open flavours. Good Marsanne-based whites.

1997 Good to very good. Fat, fleshy wines, fast evolutions. Lower acidity means rich, smooth flavours. Drinking well now.

1996 Mineral, leathery, grainy textures with age. Acidity still evident. Can be complex – track progress for right moment. Drink top wines 2006–08.

1995 Lots of full, ample flavour. Drink up Crozes, enjoy mature St-Josephs now. Top names should be tried now, with tannins softening.

1994 Good in general, very good in Côte-Rôtie. Well-framed wines with sound core. More mineral than the 95s. Top wines showing well now.

Southern Rhône

2005 Good, but beware high alcohol levels, with very heady crop esp Grenache. Punchy wines with greater balance than the 03s. Best sites to the fore again. Whites are big, best drunk young.

2004 Uneven ripening until stable Sept retrieved the situation. If picked too early the Côtes du Rhônes have sharp flavours. Sound, direct wines from Châteauneuf, will suit European palates. Gigondas not always rounded. Be patient; let the wines settle. Good fresh whites.

2003 A classic, chunky, potent, and warm year from the best, eg Châteauneuf – better than Gigondas, Vacqueyras. Two-speed ripening, so not all balanced. Go for the best names, best areas.

2002 Nature's payback. Floods around Châteauneuf. Simply-fruited reds (drink early) and acceptable whites. No super-*cuvées* this year. Gigondas did best.

2001 Excellent classic vintage, where grape, not oak, tannins prevail. Complex reds, lots of life ahead, be patient for top areas. Cracking Châteauneufs.

2000 Tasty wines, led by fruit; juicy and fat. Not a very long-lived year. Go for leading names. Gigondas may edge Châteauneuf in quality. Best reds starting to sing now.

1999 Very good overall. Ripe, open fruit with correct structure in the best wines. Châteauneuf reds have moved up a gear with age, very fine fruit on show.

1998 Very good. Warm wines, at a funky, cooked-fruit, mineral stage now.

1997 Fruit can be cooked. Best to drink by 2007, unless top name and low yields.

1996 Uneven. Tannins are brusque. The best will age for 10+ years.

1995 Deeply flavoured wines, hitting their stride now. Best will live to 2014–19.

1994 Good extract with noticeable tannins, now at secondary mineral stage.

Champagne

2005 Almost as big a harvest as 2004 but much less even in quality: some great Chardonnays, selectively good Pinot Noirs – but indifferent Pinot Meuniers.

2004 Mixed summer, sunny Sept weather. Huge crop, healthy wines of "vintage" quality especially Chardonnays.

2003 Torrid, difficult year. Tiny harvest, esp from hail-struck Chardonnay. Wines lack acidity – most will be for NV blends.

2002 Ideal harvest yielded rich, complex wines, especially Pinots. Potentially great.

2000 Fine harvest sun produced structured wines showing complexity as they age. Vintage year.

1999 Warm summer with breaks of refreshing rain. Ripe, expressive wines, ready soon. Exceptional Bollinger Grande Année Rosé.

1998 Well-constituted, classic wines. Vintage wines now on the market. Outstanding Pol Roger Blanc de Chardonnay.

1997 Brilliant Sept weather saved vintage. Ripe, low-acid wines for easy early drinking. Drink up.

1996 Champagnes of monumental structure, high in alcohol and acidity, real keepers. Drink 2007–16. Magnificent Jacquesson Grand Cru Avize.

Older fine vintages: 95 90 89 88 85 82

The Loire

2005 Excellent across the board. Buy without fear. Everything that could go right during a growing season did go right. Only "problem": the weather was so dry there was very little botrytis. The sweet wines are more likely to be the product of shrivelled grapes than noble rot, and extravagantly rich *cuvées* will be rare.

2004 Huge crop; success for those who reduced yields. In general better for reds than whites. There were little or no sweet wines in Vouvray/Montlouis. Anjou's whites are fewer and less sweet than usual.

2003 An atypical vintage. Some areas hit by spring frost. Wines are big and supple, though not flaccid. For early drinking. Good year for sweet wines.

2002 Best since 97. Vivid fruit and vibrant acidity in the dry whites. Some fine sweet Chenins. Where yields were kept low, the reds are juicy and deeply coloured. (Beware a whiff of rot in many of the Gamay-based wines.)

2001 Warm, wet winter left soils gorged with water. Best wines are from those who harvested late. But Muscadet perfect. Taste before buying.

2000 Muscadet, Sancerre, Touraine: satisfactory to good. Cabernet Franc deeply coloured but not rich. Drink now. Vouvray: good for sec, demi-sec.

1999 Looked to rival the great 89 until the rains came. Cabernet Franc marked by musky "animal" aromas. Vouvray: good for secs and demi-secs.

Alsace

2005 A large crop of healthy grapes harvested after an Indian summer. Ripe and well-balanced wines. Some good sweet wines, too.

2004 Despite it being a difficult year, growers who picked early and kept yields low produced classic wines.

2003 Earliest harvest since 1893. Small crop of variable wines. Best are ripe, but with low acidity (hence acidification allowed for the first time ever).

2002 Better than most of France. Late-picked wines are good to very good.

2001 Unsettled weather in Sept. Well-balanced wines, good but not great.

2000 Superb – probably best since 90. Very good for Vendanges Tardives and Sélections des Grains Nobles.

1999 Growers who kept yields down made good, well-balanced wines.

1998 The fourth fine vintage in a row. Good wines despite heat-wave.

1997 Almost perfect growing season ending with dry, sunny conditions produced concentrated dry wines and outstanding sweet ones.

Abel-Lepitre Middle-rank CHAMPAGNE house. V.gd BRUT Millésimé (**96**).

Abymes Savoie w ★ DYA Hilly area nr Chambéry; light, mild Vin de Savoie AC from Jacquère grape has alpine charm. SAVOIE has many such *crus* for local pleasure.

AC See APPELLATION CONTRÔLÉE.

Agenais SW France r p (w) ★ DYA VIN DE PAYS of Lot-et-Garonne, mostly from co-ops at Goulens, Donzac, Monflanquin, Mézin. Also from Marmandais co-ops.

Ajaccio Corsica r p w ★→★★ 00 01 02 03 04 05 The capital of CORSICA. AC for some original Sciacarello reds and Vermentino whites. Top grower: Peraldi (try his Vermentino). Also CLOS Capitoro, Jean Courrèges (Dom de Pratavone).

Aligoté Second-rank burgundy white grape and wine. Should be pleasantly tart and fruity with local character when young. BOUZERON is the one commune to have an all-Aligoté appellation. The shining example is de Villaine's, but try others from gd growers. Try PERNAND-VERGELESSES.

Alliet, Philippe Lo r ★★★ 89 90 95 96 97 02 03 04 05 Top-notch producer of long-lived, barrel-aged Chinons: esp Coteau du Noire CUVÉE. Now making a small amount of white.

Aloxe-Corton Burg r w ★★→★★★ 90' 95 96' 97 98 99' 01 02' 03 05' Village at N end of CÔTE DE BEAUNE famous for two GRANDS CRUS: CORTON (red), CORTON-CHARLEMAGNE (white). Village wines are lighter but to try.

Understanding Alsace grapes

Riesling Greatest grape of Alsace, normally crisp and dry and less flowery than in Germany. Good ageing potential. Ideal with grilled fish (in the region with pork dishes).

Gewurztraminer You either love it or you hate it. Flowery, spicy, sometimes tropical, it goes very well with Asian food, smoked salmon, and cheeses such as Munster.

Pinot Gris Alsace produces exceptionally fine examples, often quite full-bodied, slightly off-dry, and with good underlying acidity. Another good choice with oriental food and the superlative choice with foie gras.

Muscat A lovely crisp, dry style of Muscat with delightful grapey character. This is the apéritif of choice in the region. Also v.gd with fresh asparagus.

Pinot Blanc Alsace's alternative to CHARD: extremely versatile.

Alsace Al w (r sp sw) ★★→★★★★ **98 99 00 01 02 04** Region inc E foothills of Vosges mountains, esp Strasbourg-Mulhouse. Wines: aromatic, fruity, full-strength, mostly dry and expressive of variety, but too often sweet. See VENDANGE TARDIVE, SÉLECTION DES GRAINS NOBLES. Much sold by variety (Pinot Bl, Ries, GEWURZ). Matures well (except Pinot Bl, MUSCAT) 5–10 yrs; GRAND CRU even longer. Gd-quality and value CRÉMANT. Pinot N is v gd but can be hard to find.

Alsace Grand Cru W ★★★→★★★★ **89' 90 93 95 96 97 98 99 00 01 02 04** AC restricted to 51 (KAEFFERKOPF added in 2006) of the best-named v'yds (approx 1,600 ha, 800 in production) and four noble grapes (Ries, Pinot Gr, GEWURZ, MUSCAT) mainly dry, some sweet. Not without controversy but generally v.gd, expressive of terroir.

Ampeau, Robert Burg ★★★ Exceptional grower and specialist in MEURSAULT and VOLNAY; also POMMARD. Perhaps unique in releasing only long-matured bottles.

André, Pierre Burg ★ NÉGOCIANT at CH Corton-André, ALOXE-CORTON; 38 ha of v'yds in CORTON (Gd Corton-Charlemagne, Corton Blanc), SAVIGNY, GEVREY-CHAMBERTIN, etc. Also owns REINE PEDAUQUE.

d'Angerville, Marquis Burg ★★★★ Top grower with immaculate 14-ha estate all in VOLNAY. Top wines: Champans, and intense, potent CLOS des Ducs. 2003 sadly saw the passing of Jacques d'Angerville after over 50 yrs in charge.

Anjou Lo p r w (sw dr sp) ★→★★★★ Both region and Loire AC. Many styles: juicy red inc surprisingly potent AC Anjou Gamay; improving dry white. Gd ANJOU-VILLAGES; strong, usually dry, SAVENNIÈRES; luscious COTEAUX DU LAYON Chenin Bl.

Anjou-Coteaux de la Loire Lo w s/sw SW ★★→★★★ **02 03** 04 05 Tiny AC for whites made from Chenin Bl. The sweet not as rich as COTEAUX DU LAYON. Esp Musset-Roullier, CH de Putille, Doms du Fresche, de Putille.

Anjou-Villages Lo r ★→★★★ 02 **03** 04 05 Superior central ANJOU AC for reds (mainly Cab Fr, some Cab Sauv). Juicy, tannic young; gd value, esp Dom de Brize, CHX de Coulaine, Philippe Delesvaux, Dom les Grandes Vignes, Ogereau, CH PIERRE-BISE. New sub-AC to watch: Anjou-Villages-Brissac, esp Bablut, Montigilet, RICHOU, Rochelles.

Appellation Contrôlée (AC or AOC) Government control of origin and production (*not* quality) of all the best French wines.

Apremont Savoie w ★★ DYA One of the best villages of SAVOIE for pale, delicate whites, mainly from Jacquère grapes, but recently inc CHARD.

Arbin Savoie r ★★ Deep-coloured lively red from MONDEUSE grapes, rather like a gd Loire Cab Sauv. Ideal après-ski. Drink at 1–2 yrs.

Arbois Jura r p w (sp) ★★→★★★ Various gd and original light but tasty wines; speciality is VIN JAUNE. On the whole, DYA except excellent VIN JAUNE.

l'Ardèche, Coteaux de r p (w) ★→★★ Hilly area W of Rhône, buzzing along well. New DOMAINES; fresh oaked reds; Viognier (*e.g.* Mas de Libian) and Marsanne. Best from pure Syrah, Gamay, Cab Sauv (Serret). Powerful, almost burgundian CHARD Ardèche by Louis LATOUR; Grand Ardèche is very oaked. Also Doms du Colombier, Favette, Flacher, Mazel, Vigier.

Ariège SW r ★ **02 04** 05 New VIN DE PAYS from 1998 plantings of Cab Sauv, Merlot, Côt, and Tannat under leadership of Dom de RIBONNET. Also Dom des Coteaux d'Engravies. Will keep.

l'Arlot, Domaine de ★★★ Outstanding producer of excellent NUITS-ST-GEORGES, esp CLOS de l'Arlot, red and white. Owned by AXA Insurance.

Armagnac SW The alternative brandy; more tasty, rustic, and peppery than COGNAC. Table wines: CÔTES DE GASCOGNE, GERS, TERROIRS LANDAIS.

Armand, Comte Burg ★★★ Excellent POMMARD wines, esp CLOS des Epéneaux. Especially brilliant since 1999.

Aube Southern extension of CHAMPAGNE. Now known as Côte des Bar.

Aujoux, J-M Beauj Substantial grower/merchant of BEAUJOLAIS. Swiss-owned.

Auxey-Duresses Burg r w ★★→★★★ 90' 95 96 98 99' 02' 03 05' Second-rank (but very pretty) CÔTE DE BEAUNE village: affinities with VOLNAY, MEURSAULT. Best estates: Diconne, HOSPICES DE BEAUNE (Cuvée Boillot), LEROY, M Prunier. Drink whites in 3–4 yrs. Top white: LEROY's Les Boutonniers.

Avize Champ One of the top Côte des Blancs villages. All CHARD.

Aÿ Champ One of the best Pinot N-growing villages of CHAMPAGNE.

Ayala Once-famous AŸ-based CHAMPAGNE house, now owned by BOLLINGER. Longer ageing on lees and more Pinot in blends are raising quality. Brut **98**; BLANC DE BLANCS **98**; Perle d'Ayala **98**.

Bandol Prov r p (w) ★★★ 88' 89' 90' 91 92 93 94 95' **96** 97 98' 99' 00' 01 02 03 04 Little coastal region nr Toulon producing PROVENCE's best wines; splendid, vigorous, long-lasting reds mainly from Mourvèdre. Stars include Dom TEMPIER, Pibarnon, Pradeaux, Mas de la Rouvière, La Suffrène, Lafran Veyrolles. Rosés from young vines.

Banyuls Pyr br sw ★★→★★★ One of best VINS DOUX NATURELS, chiefly from Grenache (Banyuls GRAND CRU: over 75% Grenache, aged for 2 yrs+): a distant relation of port. Best are RANCIOS, with long ageing, from Doms la Rectorie, du Mas Blanc (★★★), Vial Magnères, at 10–15 yrs old. Cheap NVs end up in bars.

Barrique The BORDEAUX (and COGNAC) term for an oak barrel holding 225 litres (300 bottles). Barrique-ageing to flavour almost any wine with oak was craze in late 1980s, with some sad results. Current oak prices should urge discretion.

Barsac B'x w sw ★★→★★★★ 83' 86' 88' 89' 90' 95 96 97' 98 99' 01' 02 03' (05) Neighbour of SAUTERNES with similar superb golden wines from lower-lying limestone soil; generally less powerful with more finesse. Richly repays long ageing. Top CH'X: CLIMENS, COUTET, DOISY-DAËNE, DOISY-VÉDRINES.

Barthod, Ghislaine Burg ★★★→★★★★ Impressive range of archetypal CHAMBOLLE-MUSIGNY. Marvellous poise and lightness with depth.

Barton & Guestier BORDEAUX shipper since 18th C. Produces a wide range.

Bâtard-Montrachet Burg w ★★★★ 89' 90' 92 93 95 96 97' 99' 00 02' 03 04' 05' Neighbour of MONTRACHET (22 ha). Should be long-lived: intense flavours, rich texture. Bienvenues-B-M is an adjacent 3.6-ha GRAND CRU; very rare. Criots-Bâtard-Montrachet (1.6 ha) is even rarer. Seek out: BOUCHARD PÈRE & FILS, BOILLOT, CARILLON, DROUHIN, GAGNARD, Louis LATOUR, LEFLAIVE, MOREY, Pernot, RAMONET, SAUZET.

Baudry, Domaine Bernard Lo r p w ★★→★★★ 89 90 95 **96** 97 02 **03** 04 05 Impeccable CHINONS in a range of styles from Chenin Bl-based whites to several excellent red CUVÉES. Les Grezeaux, CLOS Guillot, Les Croix Boissées.

Baumard, Domaine des Lo ★★→★★★★ **95 96 97 99** 02 03 04 05 Leading grower of ANJOU wine, esp SAVENNIÈRES (Clos St Yves, Clos du Papillon), COTEAUX DU LAYON (CLOS Ste-Catherine), and QUARTS DE CHAUME. Baumard makes one of the best CRÉMANTS DE LOIRE and a tasty VIN DE TABLE from VERDELHO. Get it while it lasts. New convert to screwcaps.

Béarn SW Fr r p w ★→★★ w p DYA r **02 04 05** Pyrenean AC centred on co-op at Bellocq. Also ★★ Dom de Guilhémas.

Beaujolais r (p w) ★ DYA Simple AC of the very big BEAUJOLAIS region: light short-lived fruity r from Gamay. Beaujolais Supérieur is little different.

Beaujolais de l'année The BEAUJOLAIS of the latest vintage, until the next.

Beaujolais Primeur, or Nouveau Same as above, made in a hurry (often only 4–5 days' fermenting) for release at midnight on the third Wednesday in November. Ideally soft, pungent, fruity, and tempting; too often crude, sharp, too alcoholic. BEAUJOLAIS-VILLAGES should be a better bet.

Beaujolais-Villages r ★★ **99 00 01** Wines from better (N) half of BEAUJOLAIS; should be much tastier than plain BEAUJOLAIS. The ten (easily) best villages are the *crus*: FLEURIE, ST-AMOUR, JULIÉNAS, CHÉNAS, MOULIN-À-VENT, CHIROUBLES, MORGON, REGNIÉ, CÔTE DE BROUILLY, BROUILLY. Of the 30 others the best lie around Beaujeu. *Crus* cannot be released EN PRIMEUR before 15 December. Best kept until spring (or considerably longer).

Beaumes-de-Venise S Rh br r (p w) ★★→★★★ 01' **03** 04 05 for reds. DYA for MUSCAT. Widely regarded as France's best dessert MUSCAT, from S CÔTES DU RHÔNE; can be highly flavoured, subtle, lingering (*e.g.* CH St Sauveur, Doms Coyeux, Durban, JABOULET, Pigeade, VIDAL-FLEURY). Increasingly important for midweight, sometimes tannic reds (CH Redortier, Dom Cassan, du Fenouillet, Durban, Les Goubert, co-op) with own AC since 05. W and p are still CÔTES DU RHONE.

Beaumont des Crayères Champ Bijou Côte d'Epernay co-op making excellent Pinot Meunier-based Grande Réserve NV and very fine Fleur de Prestige (**97 98**). Exceptional Chard-led Cuvée Nostalgie (**97**). Great value.

Beaune Burg r (w) ★★★ **90' 95 98 99' 01** 02' 03 04 05' Historic wine capital of Burgundy. Wines: classic burgundy – but no GRAND CRU. Négociants' CLOS wines (usually PREMIER CRU) often best – *e.g.* DROUHIN'S superb CLOS des Mouches (esp w), JADOT'S CLOS des Ursules. Beaune du Château is a BOUCHARD PÈRE & FILS brand. Best v'yds: Bressandes, Fèves, Grèves, Marconnets, Teurons.

Becker, Caves J ★→★★ Proud old family firm at Zellenberg, ALSACE, now making even finer wines. Classic Ries Hagenschlauf and GRAND CRU Froehn MUSCAT.

Bellet Prov p r w ★★★ The local wine of Nice; fashionable, expensive, original; esp w from Rolle. Ageing potential. A few small producers, esp CH de Bellet.

Bergerac Dordogne r w p dr sw ★→★★★ (r) **00 01' 02** 05 Effectively, but not politically, an eastward extension of BORDEAUX with no clear break in style/quality. Top properties inc ★★★ La Tour des Gendres, CLOS de la Colline, CLOS des Verdots. CH Masburel. Dom l'Ancienne Cure. Otherwise ★★ Les Hauts de Caillevel, Les Marnières, CHX Belingard-Chayne, Grinou, de la Jaubertie, les Eyssards, Jonc Blanc, de la Mallevieille, Les Miaudoux, le Paradis, Pion, le Raz, Thénac. See also MONBAZILLAC, ROSETTE, SAUSSIGNAC, PECHARMANT, MONTRAVEL.

Besserat de Bellefon Champ Grande Tradition NV; Cuvée des Moines Brut and Rosé NV; Grande Cuvée NV; BRUT and Rosé (**99 00**). CHAMPAGNE house in Epernay, known for lightish wines, not to keep. Owned by MARNE ET CHAMPAGNE.

Beyer, Léon ★★→★★★★ ALSACE specialist: v. fine, intense, dry wines often needing 10 yrs+ bottle age. Superb Ries. Comtes d'Eguisheim, but no mention on label of PFERSIGBERG: Beyer does not recognize GRAND CRU system. V.gd GEWURZ.

Bichot, Maison Albert Burg One of BEAUNE's largest growers/merchants. V'yds (13-ha Dom du CLOS Frantin ★★: excellent): CHAMBERTIN, RICHEBOURG, CLOS DE VOUGEOT; Dom Long-Depaquit (★★) in CHABLIS; also many other brands.

Billecart-Salmon Frey investment in this exceptional family CHAMPAGNE house brought a supply of grapes from 80 ha of top vineyards. NV; Rosé NV; Nicolas François Billecart (**90 96' 98**); BLANC DE BLANCS (**97' 98**); Elisabeth Salmon Rosé (**99'**). Exquisite long-lived wines, vintage CUVÉES wholly fermented in wood from 2000. New single-v'yd St-Hilaire BLANC DE NOIRS (**96' 98**).

Bize, Simon Burg ★★★ Admirable r burgundy grower; 14 ha at SAVIGNY-LÈS-BEAUNE. Usually model wines in racy, elegant SAVIGNY style; some surprisingly gd w.

Blagny Burg r w ★★→★★★★ (w) **95 96' 97 99' 00' 01** 02' **03'** 04 05' Hamlet between MEURSAULT and PULIGNY-MONTRACHET: whites have affinities with both (and sold under both ACS), reds with VOLNAY (sold as AC Blagny). Gd ones need age; esp AMPEAU, JOBARD, LATOUR, LEFLAIVE, Matrot, G Thomas.

Blanc de Blancs Any white wine made from white grapes only, esp CHAMPAGNE. Not an indication of quality, but should be of style.

Blanc de Noirs White (or slightly pink or "blush") wine from red grapes.

Blanck, Paul et Fils ★★→★★★ Grower at Kientzheim, ALSACE, producing huge range of wines. Finest from 6 ha GRAND CRU FURSTENTUM (Ries, GEWURZ, Pinot Gr) and GRAND CRU SCHLOSSBERG (Ries). Also gd Pinot Bl.

Blanquette de Limoux Midi w sp ★★ Gd-value fizz from nr Carcassonne; claims older history than Champagne. Dry and tasty, with CHARD, Chenin Bl, and improving basic Mauzac, esp in more recent AC CRÉMANT de LIMOUX.

Blaye B'x r w ★→★★ 00' 01 03 04 (05) As of 2000, designation for top, concentrated reds (lower yields, longer ageing, etc.) from PREMIÈRES CÔTES DE BLAYE. Also declining AC for simple dry whites.

Boillot, J-M ★★★ POMMARD-based dom: though best known for very fine, oaky whites from PULIGNY-MONTRACHET, Bâtard, and remarkable MONTAGNY.

Boisset, Jean-Claude Burg Far and away the biggest Burgundy merchant based in NUITS-ST-GEORGES. Owner of Bouchard-Aîné, Lionel Bruck, F Chauvenet, Delaunay, Jaffelin, Morin Père et Fils, de Marcilly, Pierre Ponnelle, Thomas-Bassot, Vienot, CELLIER DES SAMSONS (BEAUJOLAIS), Moreau (CHABLIS), and a share in MOMMESSIN. Now involved in projects in Canada, California, Chile, Uruguay, and the Languedoc. Used to be fairly dire, but Boisset label now resurrected. From 1999 own v'yds separated as Dom de la VOUGERAIE (★★★). Potentially v.gd.

Boizel Quality Epernay family CHAMPAGNE house; brilliant, aged BLANC DE BLANCS NV and prestige Joyau de France (**96** 98). Also Grand Vintage Brut (**96** 98) and Cuvée Sous Bois. Part of Boizel Chanoine.

Bollinger NV Special Cuvée; Grande Année (**96 97' 99**); Rosé (**96 99'**). Great individualistic CHAMPAGNE house, esp good in "lesser" vintages (*viz.* 97). Luxury wines: RD (**88 90 95**), VIEILLES VIGNES Françaises (**96** 98 **96** 99) from ungrafted Pinot N vines, La Côte aux Enfants, AŸ (**97 99**). See also LANGLOIS-CHÂTEAU.

Bonneau du Martray, Domaine Burg ★★★★ (w) ★★ (r) Biggest grower (8.9 ha) of CORTON-CHARLEMAGNE. Highest quality. Also red GRAND CRU CORTON all on a high since 90. Cellars at PERNAND-VERGELESSES. Whites can outlive reds.

Bonnes-Mares Burg r ★★★→★★★★ 78' 85' 88' 89 90' 91 93 95 96' 97 98 99' 00 01 02' 03 04 05' GRAND CRU (15 ha) between CHAMBOLLE-MUSIGNY and MOREY-ST-DENIS. Sturdy long-lived wines, less fragrant than MUSIGNY; to rival CHAMBERTIN. Best: DUJAC, GROFFIER, JADOT, ROUMIER, Dom des Varoilles, de VOGÜÉ, VOUGERAIE.

Bonnezeaux Lo w sw ★★★→★★★★ 76 78 88 89 90 95 96 97 02 03 04 05 Velvety, structured, complex sweet Chenin Bl, potentially best of COTEAUX DU LAYON. Esp: Angeli/Ferme de la Sansonniere, CH DE FESLES, Dom du Petit Val (Goizil), CH la Fresnaye. Ages well, but very tempting young.

Bordeaux B'x r w (p) ★→★★ 00' 01 03 (05') Huge, catch-all AC for generic Bordeaux. Mixed quality, but can be great value when good.

Bordeaux Supérieur B'x r ★→★★ 00' 01 03 04 (05') Superior denomination to above. Higher minimum alcohol, lower yield, and longer ageing. 75% of production bottled at the property, the reverse of AC Bordeaux.

Borie-Manoux Admirable BORDEAUX shipper, chx-owner, owned by Castéja family. CHX CH Batailley, BEAU-SITE, Dom de L'ÉGLISE, HAUT-BAGES-MONPELOU, TROTTEVIEILLE.

Bouchard Père & Fils Important burgundy shipper (established in 1731) and grower; excellent v'yds (94 ha), mainly CÔTE DE BEAUNE; cellars at CH de Beaune.

Bouches-du-Rhône Prov r p w ★ VINS DE PAYS from Marseille environs. Warming reds from southern varieties, plus Cab Sauv, Syrah, and Merlot.

Bourgeois, Henri Lo ★★→★★★★ 02 **03** 04 05 Leading SANCERRE grower/merchant in Chavignol; also owns Laporte. Also POUILLY-FUMÉ, MENETOU-SALON, Giennois. Top wines: CLOS Henri, MD de Bourgeois, La Bourgeoise (r w), Sancerre Jadis, D'Antan Sancerrois, Le Chêne St-Etienne (r w). Also owns New Zealand v'yd.

Bourgogne Burg r w (p) ★★ 02' 03' 04 05' Catch-all AC, with higher standards than basic BORDEAUX. Light, often gd flavour, best at 2–4 yrs. Top growers make bargain beauties from fringes of CÔTE D'OR villages; do not despise.

FRANCE

BEAUJOLAIS *crus* (except REGNIÉ) may be labelled Bourgogne, though Gamay.

Bourgogne Grand Ordinaire r (w) ★ DYA Lowest Burgundy AC, also allowing Gamay. Rare. White may inc ALIGOTÉ, Pinot Bl, Melon de Bourgogne.

Bourgogne Passe-Tout-Grains r (p) ★ Age 1–2 yrs, junior burgundy: min 33% Pinot N, the balance Gamay, mixed in vat. Not as heady as BEAUJOLAIS.

> **Bourgogne** is the generic word for the cheaper end of Burgundy. As well as some indifferent mass-produced wines, it also covers out-lying areas which have their own subdivisions within the AC Bourgogne. **Coulanges-la-Vineuse, Epineuil,** and **Vézélay** (Yonne départment) **Chatillonais, Hautes Côtes de Beaune** and **Hautes Côtes de Nuits** (Côte d'Or) **Côte Chalonnaise** and **Couchois** (Saône et Loire). The best tip is to buy **Bourgogne Rouge** or **Blanc** from good growers in the famous villages of the Côte d'Or – they will be delicious, simple wines with more style than négociant bottlings.

Bourgueil Lo r (p) ★★→★★★(★) 95 96 97 02 03 04 05 Brawny, fruity TOURAINE (mainly Cab Fr). Deep-flavoured; ages like BORDEAUX in top yrs. ST-NICOLAS-DE-BOURGUEIL often lighter. Gd: Yannick Amirault, Audebert, Billet, Jacky Blot, Breton, Caslot/Dom de la Chevalerie, Cognard, Delaunay, Druet, Gambier/Dom des Ouches, Lamé-Delisle-Boucard, Mailloches, Nau.

Bouvet-Ladubay Lo ★→★★★ Major sparkling SAUMUR house, controlled by TAITTINGER. Wines inc vintage BRUT Saphir, oak-fermented deluxe Trésor (w p), CRÉMANT Excellence, Instinct. Also still wines (Les Nonpareils); gd sweet Grand Vin de Dessert. CUVÉES: Brut Zero, Trésor Rouge.

Bouzeron Burg w ★ CÔTE CHALONNAISE AC specifically for ALIGOTÉ. Age 1–2 yrs. Top grower: de Villaine. Also see BOUCHARD PÈRE & FILS.

Bouzy Rouge Champ r ★★★ 90 95 96 97 99 02 Still red of famous Pinot N village. Like very light burgundy, but can last well in sunny vintages.

Brocard, J-M Burg ★★ CHABLIS grower to note for fine value, crisp, and typical wines, inc Montmains, Montée de Tonnerre. Expanding into new terroir.

Brouilly Beauj r ★★ 03' 04 05' Biggest of the ten *crus* of BEAUJOLAIS: fruity, round, refreshing wine, can age 3–4 yrs. CH DE LA CHAIZE is largest estate. Top growers: Michaud, Dom de Combillaty, Dom des Grandes Vignes.

Brumont, Alain SW ★★★ Best known – but no longer unchallenged as clear leader – in MADIRAN. Specialist in highly extracted and oaked 100% Tannat wines – *e.g.* Le Tyre. Revived the Co-op at Castelnau-Rivière-Basse. Flagship wines: Dom Bouscassé, and gd-value Torus brand.

Brut Term for the dry classic wines of CHAMPAGNE.

Brut Ultra/Zéro Term for bone-dry wines in CHAMPAGNE.

Bugey Savoie r p w sp ★→★★ DYA VDQS for light sparkling, still, or half-sparkling wines from Roussette (or Altesse) and CHARD (gd). Best from Montagnieu; also Rosé de Cerdon, mainly Gamay.

Buisse, Paul ★→★★★ Reliable Montrichard merchant. Range of, esp TOURAINE, wines.

Burguet, Alain Burg ★★→★★★★ Superb GEVREY-CHAMBERTIN; esp Mes Favorites village wine.

Buxy Burg w Village in AC MONTAGNY with gd co-op for CHARD and Pinot N.

Buzet SW France r (w p) ★★ 99 00 01' 03 04 (05) Region SE of BORDEAUX; similar wines, sometimes a bit pruney. Dynamic co-op; some single properties (*e.g.* Châteaux de Gueyze, Mazelières). Local character from (independent) ★★★ Dom de Pech, ★★ CHX du Frandat, de Salles, Sauvagnères, Tournelles.

Cabardès Midi r (p w) ★→★★ 98 99 00 01 02 03 04 05 Where Bordeaux and the Midi meet, with blends of Cabernet, Merlot, Syrah, and Grenache. Best is Dom De Cabrol; also CHX Pennautier and Ventenac.

Cabernet d'Anjou Lo p s/sw ★ DYA Delicate, grapey, traditionally sw rosé. Ageworthy; some venerable bottles survive. Bablut, Dom les Grandes Vignes, CH PIERRE-BISE.

Cabrières Midi p (r) ★★ DYA COTEAUX DU LANGUEDOC. Sound village co-op.

Cahors SW France r ★→★★★★ 88 89 90' 95 98 00 01' (02) (05) Fast-reviving v'yd Auxerrois (Malbec). Ranges from tannic to atypical quick-drinking. Top producers: ★★★ CLOS DE GAMOT (inc CLOS St Jean), D'Un Jour, CHX du Cèdre, Lamartine, and Dom Cosse-Maisonneuve. ★★ CLOS Coutale, CHX du Cayrou, La Coustarelle, La Caminade, Les Croisille, Garinet, Gaudou, Les Hauts d'Aglan, La Reyne, Les Ifs, Latuc, Les Rigalets. Doms de la Bérangeraie, de Cause, Paillas, Pineraie, Savarines, Eugénie. CH Lagrézette owned by MD of Cartier, priced accordingly.

Cairanne S Rh r p w ★★ 95' 98' 99' 00' 01' 03 04' 05 One of best CÔTES DU RHÔNE-VILLAGES: solid, robust, classy fullness, esp Doms D & D, Alary, Ameillaud, Brusset, Castel Mireio, Hautes Cances, l'Oratoire St-Martin, Rabasse-Charavin, Richaud. Some improving whites; best whites with food.

Canard-Duchêne CHAMPAGNE house owned by Alain THIÉNOT. Increased presence in US as well as EU. Kind prices for lively Pinot N-tasting wines. V.gd Charles VII Grande CUVÉE in BRUT, Rosé and now BLANC DE NOIRS. Also Vintage Brut (**99 00**).

Canon-Fronsac B'x r ★★ →★★★ 95 96 98 00' 01 03 (05) Full tannic reds of improved quality from W of POMEROL. Try CHX Barrabaque, CANON-DE-BREM, Cassagne Haut-Canon, Gaby, Lamarche Canon Candelaire, Pavillon, La Fleur Caillou, Grand-Renouil, Mazeris, Moulin-Pey-Labrie, Vraye-Canon-Boyer.

Cap Corse Corsica w br ★★ →★★★ CORSICA'S wild N cape. Rich MUSCAT from CLOS Nicrosi (Rogliano); rare, soft Vermentino w. *Vaut le détour*, if not *le voyage*.

Caramany Pyr r (w) ★ 96 97 98 99 00 01 02 03 04 Notionally superior AC for single-village CÔTES DU ROUSSILLON-VILLAGES.

Carillon, Louis Burg ★★★ PULIGNY-MONTRACHET dom consistently in top league. Esp PREMIER CRU Referts, Perrières, and tiny amount of GRAND CRU Bienvenues-Bâtard.

Cassis Prov w (r p) ★★ DYA Seaside village E of Marseille with reputation for dry whites with a certain character, goes with bouillabaisse (*e.g.* Dom de la Ferme Blanche, CLOS Ste Magdeleine, CLOS d'Albizzi). Do not confuse with cassis: blackcurrant liqueur from Dijon.

Cave Cellar, or any wine establishment.

Cave coopérative Wine-growers' co-op winery; over half of all French production. Usually well run, well equipped, and wines reasonable value for money.

Cellier des Samsons ★ BEAUJOLAIS/MACONNAIS co-op at Quincié which has 2,000 grower-members. Wines widely distributed; now owned by BOISSET.

Cépage Variety of vine, *e.g.* CHARD, Merlot.

Cérons B'x w dr sw ★★ 96 97' 98 99' 01' 02 03' (05) Tiny neighbour of SAUTERNES with gd sw, less intense wines, *e.g.* CHX de Cérons, Chantegrive, Grand Enclos.

Chablis Burg w ★★ →★★★ 95 96' 97 99 00' 02' 03 04 05' Unique, flavoursome, dry, minerally wine of N Burgundy, CHARD; a total of 4,047 ha for all levels. PETIT CHABLIS from a gd house can be a gd substitute.

Chablis Grand Cru Burg w ★★★ →★★★★ 89 90' 92 93 95' 96' 97 98 99 00' 02' 03 04 05' In maturity a match for great w burgundy: often dumb in youth, at best with age combines mineral cut with hint of SAUTERNES. V'yds: Blanchots, Bougros, CLOS, Grenouilles, Preuses, Valmur, Vaudésir. See also MOUTONNE.

Chablis Premier Cru Burg w ★★★ 90' 95' 96' 97 98 99 00' 02' 03 04 05' Technically second-rank but at best excellent; more typical of CHABLIS than its GRANDS CRUS. Can outclass more expensive MEURSAULT and other CÔTE DE BEAUNE. Best v'yds inc Côte de Léchet, Fourchaume, Mont de Milieu, Montée de Tonnerre, Montmains, Vaillons. See "Chablis" box (overleaf) for producers.

> ### Chablis
> There is no better expression of the all-conquering CHARDONNAY than the
> full but tense, limpid but stony wines it makes on the heavy limestone
> soils of Chablis. Chablis terroir divides into three quality levels (four
> including Petit Chablis) with great consistency. Best makers use little or
> no new oak to mask the precise definition of variety and terroir: Barat,
> Bessin*, Billaud-Simon*, Bouchard Père & Fils, Boudin*, J-M Brocard,
> J Collet*, D Dampt, R & V Dauvissat*, J Dauvissat, B, D et E, and J Defaix,
> Droin, Drouhin*, Duplessis, Durup, Fèvre*, Geoffroy, J-P Grossot*,
> Laroche, Long-Depaquit, Dom des Malandes, L Michel, Picq*, Pupillon,
> Raveneau*, G Robin*, Servin, Tribut, Vocoret. Simple unqualified
> "Chablis" may be thin; best is PREMIER CRU or GRAND CRU. The co-op La
> Chablisienne has high standards (esp Grenouille*) and many different
> labels (it makes one in every three bottles). (* = outstanding)

Chai Building for storing and maturing wine, esp in BORDEAUX.

Chambertin Burg r ★★★★ 78' 85' 88 89 90' 91 93 95 96' 97 98 99' 00 01 02' 03 04
05' A 13-ha GRAND CRU; some of the meatiest, most enduring, best red burgundy.
20 growers inc Bertagna, BOUCHARD, CHARLOPIN, Damoy, DROUHIN, LEROY, MORTET,
PONSOT, Rossignol-Trapet, ROUSSEAU, Trapet.

Chambertin-Clos de Bèze Burg r ★★★★ 78' 85' 88 89 90' 91 93 95 96' 97 98 99' 00
01 02' 03 04 05' Neighbour of CHAMBERTIN (15 ha). Similarly splendid wines. May
legally be sold as CHAMBERTIN. 15 growers, inc Bruno CLAIR, Damoy, DROUHIN,
Drouhin-Laroze, FAIVELEY, GROFFIER, JADOT, ROUSSEAU.

Chambolle-Musigny Burg r ★★★ ·★★★★ 88 89 90' 91 93 95' 96' 97 98 99' 00 01 02'
03 04 05' CÔTE DE NUITS village (170 ha): fabulously fragrant, complex, but never
heavy wine. Best v'yds: Les Amoureuses, part of BONNES-MARES, Les Charmes,
MUSIGNY. Growers to note: BARTHOD, DROUHIN, FAIVELEY, GROFFIER, HUDELOT-NOËLLAT, JADOT,
MUGNERET, MUGNIER, RION, ROUMIER, Serveau, de VOGÜÉ.

Champagne Sparkling wines of Pinots N and Meunier and/or CHARD, and its region
(over 30,000 ha, 145 km/90 miles E of Paris); made by MÉTHODE TRADITIONELLE.
Bubbles from elsewhere, however gd, cannot be Champagne.

Champy Père & Cie Burg ★★·★★★ Oldest négociant, in BEAUNE, rejuvenated by
Meurgey family (also brokers DIVA). Range of very well-chosen wines.

Chandon de Briailles, Domaine Burg ★★★ Small estate at SAVIGNY. V.gd CORTON and
wonderful PERNAND-VERGELESSES, esp PREMIER CRU Ile de Vergelesses.

Chanson Père & Fils Burg ★·★★★ Old grower-négociant at BEAUNE (45 ha), now
owned by BOLLINGER. Esp BEAUNE CLOS des Fèves, PERNAND-VERGELESSES, SAVIGNY, CORTON.
Fine quality now.

Chapelle-Chambertin Burg r ★★★ 89' 90' 91 93 95 96' 97 98 99' 00 01 02' 03 04
05' A 5.2-ha neighbour of CHAMBERTIN. Wine more "nervous", not so meaty. Top
producers: Damoy, JADOT, Rossignol-Trapet, Trapet.

Chapoutier N Rh ★★·★★★★ Long-established grower and trader of full Rhônes;
Biodynamic. Note special CUVÉES CHÂTEAUNEUF Barbe Rac (r), HERMITAGE: L'Ermite, Le
Pavillon (r), L'Ermite, Cuvée d'Orée (w), Le Méal (w). Also CROZES red Les Varonniers,
St-Joseph w Les Granits. Sound Meysonniers Crozes. New holdings in BANYULS,
COLLIOURE, COTEAUX DU TRICASTIN, COTEAUX D'AIX-EN-PROVENCE promising. Also Australian
joint ventures, esp Jasper Hill.

Chardonnay As well as a white wine grape, also the name of a MÂCON-VILLAGES
commune. Hence Mâcon-Chardonnay.

Charlopin, Philippe Burg ★★★ Modern-style GEVREY-CHAMBERTIN estate.

Charmes-Chambertin Burg r ★★★ 88 89' 90' 91 93 95 96' 97 98 99' 00 01 02' 03 04
05' CHAMBERTIN neighbour, inc AC MAZOYÈRES-CHAMBERTIN. Supple, rounder wines; esp
Bachelet, DUGAT, DROUHIN, DUJAC, LEROY, Perrot-Minot, ROTY, ROUMIER, ROUSSEAU, VOUGERAIE.

Chassagne-Montrachet Burg w r ★★★→★★★★ r (★★) 90' 95 96' 97 98 99' 01 02' 03 04 05'; w 92 95 96 97 98 99' 00' 01 02' 04 05' CÔTE DE BEAUNE village (304 ha). Sterling, hefty red; excellent rich, dry white rarely with quite the finesse of PULIGNY next door, but often costs less. Best v'yds inc part of MONTRACHET, BÂTARD-MONTRACHET, Boudriottes (r w), Caillerets, CRIOTS-B-M, Morgeot (r w), Ruchottes, Clos St-Jean (r). Growers inc Amiot, Blain-Gagnard, COLIN-DELEGER, DROUHIN, Fontaine-Gagnard, J N GAGNARD, Gagnard-Delagrange, Jouard, Lamy-Pillot, CH de la Maltroye, MOREY, Morey-Coffinet, Niellon, Pillot, RAMONET.

Château d'Arlay ★→★★★ Major JURA estate; 65 ha in skilful hands. Wines inc v.gd VIN JAUNE, VIN DE PAILLE, Pinot N, and MACVIN.

Château de Beaucastel S Rh r w ★★★★ 78' 79 81' 83 85 86' 88 89' 90' 94' 95' 96' 97 98' 99' 00' 01' 03' 04' 05 One of biggest, best-run CHÂTEAUNEUF estates. Deep-hued, complex wines; unusual varietal mix inc one-third Mourvèdre. Small amount of wonderful Roussanne: keep 5–14 yrs. Top-notch CÔTES DU RHÔNE red (lives 8+ yrs) and white Coudoulet de Beaucastel. V.gd organic Perrin Nature CÔTES DU RHÔNE, VACQUEYRAS. (See also Tablas Creek, California.)

Château du Cèdre SW r ★★★ 98' 00 01' 02 03 (04) (05) Fashionable excellent CAHORS estate. Also delicious white VIN DE PAYS from Viognier.

Château de la Chaize Beauj r ★★★ Best-known BROUILLY estate.

Château de Fesles Lo r w sw p ★★→★★★ 95 96 97 02 03 04 05 Historic estate in Bonnezeaux; entire range of ANJOU wines. Inc COTEAUX DE LAYON la Roulerie.

Champagne growers to watch in 2007

Edmond Barnaut Bouzy. Complex, fine Champagnes mainly from Pinot N culminate in first-rate Sélection Ultra Brut.

Claude Cazals Most improved estate in Le Mesnil/Oger now run by daughter Delphine. Cuvée Vive Extra Brut perfect apéritif and magnificent single-site Clos Cazals (96 ★★★★).

Richard Cheurlin One of best grower/winemakers of the Aube. Rich but balanced Carte d'Or and vintage-dated Cuvée Jeanne (95 96).

Pierre Cheval-Gatinois Aÿ. Impeccable producer of mono-*cru* Champagnes and excellent still Aÿ Coteaux Champenois (97' 99).

Michel Genet Fine Chouilly domaine run by younger generation (Vincent & Antoine). Fresh yet supple and mature expressions of GRAND CRU CHARD. First-rate Prestige de la Cave (98 99 00).

Pierre Gimonnet Leading Côte des Blancs grower at Cuis. Superb bone-dry Cuvée Oenophile (96 99 00) is ideal with oysters.

Henri Giraud Thoughtful grower/merchant with enviably sited plots in Aÿ making exceptional Pinot-led Champagne. Excellent Prestige Cuvée fermented in Argonne oak (93 95 96).

Larmandier-Bernier Vertus; top-flight BLANC DE BLANCS grower-maker, especially Terre de Vertus non dosé (2003) and Cramant GRAND CRU VIEILLES VIGNES (2000 ★★★★).

Jean Milan Oger grower. Top range of Chard. Champagnes, very dry – ripeness, minerality, and expression of terroir in perfect balance. Sumptuous Symphorine 2000.

Serge Mathieu Avirey-Lingey. Outstanding eco-friendly Aube domaine. BLANC DE NOIRS.

José Michel Doyen of Côte d'Epernay making fresh yet mature Carte Blanche NV. Also excellent BLANC DE BLANCS (95' ★★★★ 00) and vintage (97' ★★★).

Alain Robert Great Le Mesnil grower/winemaker with magnificent older CUVÉES: Mesnil Tête de Cuvée (86').

Château Fortia S Rh r (w) ★★ 78' 81' 88 90 95' 96' 97 98' 99 00' 01' 03' 04' (05) Traditional 30-ha CHÂTEAUNEUF property. Owner's father, Baron Le Roy, launched the AC system in 1920s. Better form recently, inc special Le Baron and whites.

Château Fuissé Burg w ★★→★★★ Now being challenged as the top estate in POUILLY-FUISSÉ. Numerous CUVÉES, made to mature more rapidly than before.

Château de Meursault Burg r w ★★★ 61-ha estate owned by PATRIARCHE; gd v'yds and wines in BEAUNE, MEURSAULT, POMMARD, VOLNAY. Cellars open to public.

Château de Mont-Redon S Rh r w ★★ 78 85 88 89 90' 94' 95' 97' 98' 99' 00 01' 03' 04' (05) Gd 100-ha CHÂTEAUNEUF estate. Fine, complex red, needs 6+ yrs; aromatic white. Also gd red (mainly Grenache), white wines from Cantegril v'yd (LIRAC).

Château de Montaigne Dordogne w (sw) ★★ Home of great philosopher Michel

> **Château**
> Means an estate, big or small, good or indifferent, particularly in Bordeaux (see Châteaux of Bordeaux). Elsewhere in France, château tends to mean, literally, castle or great house, as in most of these entries. In Burgundy, "domaine" is the usual term.

de M, now making sweet CÔTES DE MONTRAVEL; part-owns CH PALMER (MARGAUX).

Château La Nerthe S Rh r w ★★★ 78' 81' 88 89' 90' 94 95' 96' 97 98' 99' 00 01' 03' 04' 05 Very high-quality 90-ha CHÂTEAUNEUF estate. Solid, refined modern-style wines, esp special CUVÉES Cadettes (r) and oaked Beauvenir (w). Takes 5 yrs to show. Also run Prieuré Montézargues Tavel, Dom de la Renjarde CÔTES DU RHÔNE, CH Signac Chusclan – all good.

Château Pierre-Bise Lo r w ★★→★★★★ 88 89 90 95 96 97 99 02 03 04 05 Top-notch producer of ANJOU range, esp COTEAUX DE LAYON, inc QUARTS DE CHAUME, vinifed and bottled by terroir. Also SAVENNIÈRES and ANJOU-VILLAGES under both CLOS de Coulaine and Pierre-Bise labels.

Château Rayas S Rh r (w) ★★★ 78' 79 81' 85 86 88' 89 90' 93 94' 95' 96' 98' 99 00 01 03 04 Famous old-style estate in CHÂTEAUNEUF. Soft, subtle Grenache ages superbly. Traditional white Rayas can be v.gd. Gd-value second label: Pignan. V.gd CH Fonsalette, CÔTES DU RHÔNE. All benefit from decanting.

Château Simone Prov r p w ★★→★★★ Famous old property synonymous with AC PALETTE, nr Aix-en-Provence. Red is warm and spicy; the white is herbal and rewards bottle-ageing. Fine rosé.

Château de Villeneuve Lo r w ★★→★★★ 89 90 93 94 95 96 97 02 03 04 05 First-rate SAUMUR estate. Exciting Saumur Blanc (esp Les Cormiers) and SAUMUR-CHAMPIGNY (esp VIEILLES VIGNES, Grand Clos).

Château-Chalon Jura w ★★★ Not a CHÂTEAU but AC and village. Unique dry, yellow, sherry-like wine (Savagnin grape). Develops *flor* (see Spain) while ageing in barrels for min 6 yrs. Ready to drink when bottled (62-cl clavelin bottle), but ages almost forever. A curiosity.

Château-Grillet N Rh w ★★ 91' 93' 95' 98' 00' 01' 04 A 3.6-ha terraced granite v'yd of Viognier; one of France's smallest ACS. Overpriced, but clear signs of revival. Mainly cask-reared. Drink 6 yrs+. Decant first.

Châteaumeillant Lo r p ★→★★ DYA A tiny VDQS area nr SANCERRE. Gamay and Pinot N for light reds and rosés.

Châteauneuf-du-Pape S Rh r (w) ★★★ 78' 80 81' 83 85 86 88 89' 90' 94 95' 96 98' 99' 00' 01' 03' 04' 05 3,318 ha nr Avignon with core of 30 or so doms for very fine wines (quality variable over remaining 90). Mix of up to 13 varieties led by Grenache, Syrah, Mourvèdre. Best are dark, strong, exceptionally long-lived. Whites fruity and zesty or rather heavy: many now DYA. Top growers inc: CHX DE BEAUCASTEL, FORTIA, Gardine, MONT-REDON, LA NERTHE,

RAYAS; Doms de Beaurenard, Bosquet des Papes, Les Cailloux, Font-de-Michelle, Grand Veneur, Marcoux, Millière, Pegaü, VIEUX TÉLÉGRAPHE, Vieille Julienne, Villeneuve, Henri Bonneau, CLOS du Mont-Olivet, CLOS DES PAPES, CLOS St-Jean, P Usseglio (Pusseglio), Jean Versino, Vieux Donjon.

Châtillon-en-Diois Rh r p w ★ DYA Small AC E of Rhône in pre-Alps. Adequate largely Gamay reds; white (some ALIGOTÉ) mostly made into CLAIRETTE DE DIE.

Chave, Gérard and Jean-Louis N Rh ★★★★ Wonderful HERMITAGE family dom. Nine hillside sites: 10 ha r; 4.8 ha w. Fleshy, gourmand, very long-lived wines (inc gd ST-JOSEPH), also occasional VIN DE PAILLE. Fruity new J-L Chave brand ST-JOSEPH.

Chavignol Picturesque SANCERRE village with famous v'yd, Les Monts Damnés. Chalky soil gives vivid wines that age 4–5 yrs (or longer); esp from BOURGEOIS and Cotat. (Produces highly regarded goats' cheese of same name.)

Chénas Beauj r ★★★ 02 03 04 05' Smallest BEAUJOLAIS *cru* and one of the weightiest; neighbour to MOULIN-À-VENT and JULIÉNAS. Growers inc Benon, Champagnon, Charvet, CH Chèvres, DUBOEUF, Lapierre, Robin, Trichard, co-op.

Chevalier-Montrachet Burg w ★★★★ 89' 90 92 95 96 97 98 99' 00' 01 02' 04 05' Neighbour of MONTRACHET (6.8 ha) making similarly luxurious wine, perhaps less powerful. Inc 1-ha Les Demoiselles. Growers inc: LATOUR, JADOT, BOUCHARD PÈRE & FILS, COLIN-DELEGER, LEFLAIVE, Niellon, PRIEUR, CH de Puligny.

Cheverny Lo r p w ★→★★ 02 04 05 Loire AC nr Chambord. Dry, crisp white from Sauv Bl and Chard. Also Gamay, Pinot N, or Cab Sauv; light but tasty. Cour-Cheverny uses local Romorantin grape. Sparkling use CRÉMANT DE LOIRE and TOURAINE ACS. Esp Cazin; CLOS Tue-Boeuf; Huards; OISLY & THÉSÉE; Dom de la Desoucherie.

Chevillon, R ★★★ 13-ha estate at NUITS-ST-GEORGES; soft and juicy wines.

Chidaine, Francois Lo dr sw w sp ★★ Serious young Montlouis producer who recently took over the v'yds of CLOS Baudoin (formerly Prince Poniatowski) in VOUVRAY. Biodynamic principles followed in both DOMAINES.

Chignin Savoie w ★ DYA Light, soft white from Jacquère grapes for alpine summers. Chignin-Bergeron (with Roussanne grapes) is best and liveliest.

Chinon Lo r (p w) ★★→★★★★ 89 90 93 95 96 97 02 03 04 05 Juicy, variably rich TOURAINE Cab Fr. Drink cool, young; treat v.gd yrs like BORDEAUX. An increasing amount of crisp, dry Chenin Bl. Top growers inc Bernard BAUDRY, ALLIET, COULY-DUTHEIL (CLOS de l'Echo and Olive), CH de la Bonneliere, Dom du Noire.

Chiroubles Beauj r ★★★ 03 04 05' Gd but tiny BEAUJOLAIS *cru* next to FLEURIE; fresh fruity silky wine for early drinking (1–3 yrs). Growers inc: Bouillard, Cheysson, DUBOEUF, Fourneau, Passot, Raousset, co-op.

Chorey-lès-Beaune Burg r (w) ★★ 96' 98 99' 01 02' 03 04 05' Minor AC N of BEAUNE. Three fine growers: Arnoux, Germain (CH de Chorey), TOLLOT-BEAUT.

Chusclan S Rh r p w ★→★★ 01' 03 (04) 05 CÔTES DU RHÔNE-VILLAGES with able co-op. Soft reds, sound rosés. Labels inc CUVÉE de Marcoule, Seigneurie de Gicon. Also CH Signac (can age) and special CUVÉES from André Roux. Drink most young.

Clair, Bruno Burg ★★→★★★ Leading MARSANNAY estate. V.gd wines from there and GEVREY-CHAMBERTIN (esp CLOS DE BÈZE), FIXIN, MOREY-ST-DENIS, SAVIGNY.

Clairet Very light red wine, almost rosé. BORDEAUX Clairet is an AC.

Clairette Traditional white grape of the MIDI. Its low-acid wine was a vermouth base. Revival by Terrasses de Landoc is full and zesty.

Clairette de Bellegarde Midi w ★ DYA Tiny AC nr Nîmes: fresh, neutral white.

Clairette de Die Rh w dr s/sw sp ★★ NV Popular dry or (better) semi-sweet Tradition MUSCAT-flavoured sp wine from pre-Alps in E Rhône; or straight dry CLAIRETTE, can age 3–4 yrs. Worth trying. Achard-Vincent, A Poulet, J-C Raspail.

Clairette du Languedoc Midi w ★ DYA Nr Montpellier. Full-bodied white AC, some barrel-ageing and improving late-harvest wines. CHX La Condamine Bertran, St-André, and Cave d'Adissan are looking gd.

Clape, Auguste and Pierre N Rh ★★★ Supreme 5+ ha Syrah v'yd at Cornas, many old vines. Traditional reds, need 6+ yrs. Epitome of unspoilt, hands-off winemaking, always good in lesser vintages. Gd CÔTES DU RHÔNE also.

Clape, La Midi r p w ★★→★★★ *Cru* of note in AC COTEAUX DU LANGUEDOC. Warming reds from sun-soaked hills between Narbonne and the Med. Tangy herbal whites age well. Gd: Châteaux Rouquette-sur-Mer, Mire l'Etang, Pech-Céléyran, Pech-Redon, CH de l'Hospitalet, La Négly.

Claret Traditional English term for all red BORDEAUX.

Climat Burgundian word for individually named v'yd, *e.g.* BEAUNE Grèves.

Clos A term carrying some prestige, reserved for distinct (walled) v'yds, often in one ownership (esp Burgundy and ALSACE).

Clos, Les CHABLIS's grandest *cru.*

Clos de Bèze See CHAMBERTIN-CLOS DE BÈZE.

Clos de Gamot SW France ★★★ 82 83' 85 89 90' 95 96 98 00 01 (02) (03) (04) (05) One of the most famous CAHORS estates. Ultra-traditional, long-lived benchmark wines. Top CUVÉE CLOS St Jean is outstanding.

Clos des Lambrays Burg r ★★★ 90' 93 95 97 99' 00 02' 03 04 05' GRAND CRU v'yd (6 ha) at MOREY-ST-DENIS. Great potential here, beginning to be realized.

Clos des Mouches Burg r w ★★★ Splendid PREMIER CRU BEAUNE v'yd, largely owned by DROUHIN. White and red wines, spicy and memorable – and consistent.

Clos des Papes S Rh r w ★★★ 90' 95' 98' 99' 00 01' 03' 04' 05 Gd 32-ha (18 plots) CHÂTEAUNEUF estate Avril-family-owned for centuries. Usually long-lived, stylish red (mainly Grenache, Mourvèdre) and white (5–15 yrs).

Clos de la Roche Burg r ★★★ 78' 85' 88 89' 90' 91 93' 95 96' 97 98 99' 00 01 02' 03 04 05' MOREY-ST-DENIS GRAND CRU (15 ha). Powerful and complex, like CHAMBERTIN. Amiot, BOUCHARD PÈRE & FILS, DUJAC, LEROY, H Lignier, PONSOT, ROUSSEAU.

Clos du Roi Burg r ★★★ Part of GRAND CRU CORTON. Also a BEAUNE PREMIER CRU.

Clos Rougeard Lo r (sw) ★★★ 88 89 90 95 96 97 02 03 04 05 The Foucault brothers have a cult following of the intense SAUMUR-CHAMPIGNY aged in new (or nearly new) BORDEAUX barrels. Also tiny amount of luscious COTEAUX DE SAUMUR.

Clos St-Denis Burg r ★★★ 78' 85' 88 89' 90 91 93' 95 96' 97 98 99' 00 01 02' 03 04 05' GRAND CRU at MOREY-ST-DENIS (6.4 ha). Splendid sturdy wine growing silky with age. Growers inc: Bertagna, DUJAC, and PONSOT.

Clos Ste-Hune Al w ★★★★ Greatest Ries in ALSACE. V. fine, initially austere; needs 5–10+ yrs ageing. Comes from GRAND CRU ROSACKER, not mentioned on label.

Clos St-Jacques Burg r ★★★ 78' 85' 88 89' 90' 91 93 95' 96' 97 98 99' 00 01 02' 03 04 GEVREY-CHAMBERTIN PREMIER CRU (6.8 ha). Excellent, powerful, velvety long-ager, often better than some GRANDS CRUS, esp ESMONIN, JADOT, CLAIR, Fourrier, ROUSSEAU.

Clos de Tart Burg r ★★★★ 85' 88' 89' 90' 93 95 96' 97 98 99' 00 01 02' 03 04 GRAND CRU at MOREY-ST-DENIS, owned by MOMMESSIN. At best wonderfully fragrant.

Clos de Vougeot Burg r ★★★ 78' 85' 88 89' 90' 91 93' 95 96' 97 98 99'00 01 02' 03' 04 04' A 50-ha CÔTE DE NUITS GRAND CRU with many owners. Occasionally sublime. Maturity depends on grower's philosophy, technique, and position. Top growers inc CH de la Tour, DROUHIN, ENGEL, FAIVELEY, GRIVOT, GROS, HUDELOT-NOËLLAT, JADOT, LEROY, Chantal Lescure, MÉO-CAMUZÉT, MUGNERET, VOUGERAIE.

Coche-Dury Burg ★★★★ 8.4-ha MEURSAULT DOMAINE (plus 0.5 ha of CORTON-CHARLEMAGNE) with the highest reputation for oak-perfumed wines. Even MEURSAULT-Villages is great (with age). Also v.gd ALIGOTÉ and reds.

Cognac Town and region of the Charentes, W France, and its brandy.

Colin-Deléger Burg ★★★ Leading CHASSAGNE-MONTRACHET estate. Superb, rare PULIGNY-MONTRACHET Les Caillerets. From 2004 split between sons Bruno and Philippe.

Collines Rhodaniennes N Rh r w ★ Popular, lively Rhône VIN DE PAYS. Also young vine CÔTE-RÔTIE. Mainly red, mainly Syrah, also Merlot, Gamay. Some Viognier, CHARD.

Collioure Pyr r ★★ **97 98 99 00 01 02** 03 04 05 Full-bodied, dry red from BANYULS area. Tiny production. Top growers inc Le CLOS des Paulilles, Doms du Mas Blanc, de la Rectorie, La Tour Vieille, Vial-Magnères. Also rosé and new white AC retrospectively from 02 vintage, based on Grenache Bl.

Comté Tolosan SW r p w ★0DYA VIN DE PAYS. Covers multitude of sins and whole of the SW. Mostly co-op wines. Pioneering ★★ DOM DE RIBONNET (Christian Gerber, S of Toulouse) for range of varietal wines, some long keepers.

Condrieu N Rh w ★★★ **01' 02 03 04'** 05 Soft fragrant w of great character (and price) from Viognier. Can be outstanding, but rapid growth of v'yd (now 117 ha; 75 growers) has made quality more variable, and increased use of young oak is a doubtful move. Best: Y Cuilleron, DELAS, Dumazet, Gangloff, GUIGAL, JABOULET, F Merlin, A Perret, Niéro, C Pichon, Vernay (esp long-lived Coteau de Vernon), Verzier. Dubious move to VENDANGE TARDIVE style by some growers.

Confuron, J-J Burg r ★★★ Tiny NUITS-ST-GEORGES. Modern-style, full of fruit.

Corbières Midi r (p w) ★★→★★★ **98 99 00 01 02 03** 04 05 Vigorous bargain reds from warm, stony hillsides N of Pyrenees. AC, with new CRU Boutenac. Production dominated by co-ops but best estates are CHX Aiguilloux, la Baronne, Lastours, des Ollieux, Les Palais, de la Voulte Gasparet, Doms de Fontsainte, du Vieux Parc, de Villemajou, Villerouge le Château, Cabriac. Co-ops: Embrès-et-Castelmaure, Camplong, Tuchan.

Cornas N Rh r ★★→★★★ **78' 83' 85' 88' 89' 90' 91' 94' 95' 96 97' 98'** 99' 00' 01 02 03' 04' 05 Sturdy, mineral-edged very dark Syrah from 105-ha steep granite v'yds S of HERMITAGE. Needs to age 5–15 yrs but always keeps its rustic character. Top: Allemand, Colombo (but beware new oak), CLAPE, Courbis, DELAS, Dumien-Serrette, J Lionnet, JABOULET (esp St-Pierre CUVÉE), R Michel (esp Geynale), Tardieu-Laurent (modern, expensive), Voge.

Corsica (Vin de Corse) Characterful wines of all colours. ACS are: AJACCIO and PATRIMONIO, and better CRUS Cap Corse and Calvi. VIN DE PAYS: ILE DE BEAUTÉ.

Corton Burg r (w) GRAND CRU ★★★ **88 89' 90' 91 93 95' 96' 97 98** 00 01 02' 03' 04 05' The only GRAND CRU red of the CÔTE DE BEAUNE. 81 ha in ALOXE-CORTON inc CLOS DU ROI, Les Bressandes. Rich and powerful, should age well. Rare white Corton from HOSPICES DE BEAUNE and CHANDON DE BRIAILLES.

Corton-Charlemagne Burg w ★★★★ **89' 90' 92' 95 96 97 98** 99' 00' 01 02' 03 04 05' White section (one-third) of CORTON. Rich, spicy, lingering, the GRAND CRU Chablis of the Côte d'Or; ages like a red. Top growers inc BONNEAU DU MARTRAY, COCHE-DURY, FAIVELEY, HOSPICES DE BEAUNE, JADOT, Javillier, LATOUR, ROULOT, VOUGERAIE.

Costières de Nîmes S Rh r p w ★→★★ **99 00 01 03 04** 05 Mainly warm r with easy appeal; best will age. Also some stylish w. Look for CHX de Campuget, Grande Cassagne, Mas Neuf, Mourgues-du-Grès, Roubaud, de la Tuilerie, Mas des Bressades, Tardieu-Laurent, Dom du Vieux Relais. Best reds are substantial: 6–8 yrs. Some stylish whites (inc Roussanne) worth a look.

> **Côte(s)** Means hillside; generally a superior vineyard to those on the plain. Many ACS are prefixed by "Côtes" or "Coteaux", meaning the same. In St-Emilion, distinguishes valley slopes from higher plateaux.

Côte de Beaune Burg r w ★★→★★★★ Used geographically: the S half of the CÔTE D'OR. Applies as an AC only to parts of BEAUNE itself.

Côte de Beaune-Villages Burg r ★★ **99' 02' 03 04** 05' Regional APPELLATION for lesser wines of classic area. Cannot be labelled "Côte de Beaune" without either "-Villages" or village name added.

Côte de Brouilly Beauj r ★★ **03' 04 05'** Fruity rich BEAUJOLAIS CRU, one of the best.

Côte Chalonnaise Burg r w sp ★★ V'yd area between BEAUNE and MÂCON. See also BOUZERON, GIVRY, MERCUREY, MONTAGNY, RULLY. Alias "Région de Mercurey".

FRANCE

Côte de Nuits Burg r (w) ★★→★★★★ N half of CÔTE D'OR. Mostly red wine.

Côte de Nuits-Villages Burg r (w) ★★ 99' 02' **03 04** 05' A junior AC for extreme N and S ends of CÔTE DE NUITS; well worth investigating for bargains.

Côte d'Or *Département* name applied to the central and principal Burgundy v'yd slopes: CÔTE DE BEAUNE and CÔTE DE NUITS. Not used on labels.

Côte Roannaise Central France r p ★→★★ **03** 04 05 AC W of Lyon. Silky, focused Gamay. Doms, Lapandéry, du Pavillon, des Millets, Serol.

Côte-Rôtie N Rh r ★★★→★★★★ 78' 83' 85' 88' 89' 90' 91' 94' 95' 97 98' 99' **00** 01' 03' 04 05 Finest Rhône red, from S of Vienne, mainly Syrah, touch of Viognier. Rich, complex softness and finesse with age (esp 5–10+ yrs). Top growers inc: Barge, Bernard, Bonnefond, Burgaud, CHAPOUTIER, Clusel-Roch, DELAS, Gaillard, J-M Gérin, GUIGAL, Jasmin, Levet, Ogier, ROSTAING, VIDAL-FLEURY.

Coteaux d'Aix-en-Provence Prov r p w ★→★★★ From hills N of Aix. Good properties inc: CHX Calissanne, Vignelaure, Dom des Béates (CHAPOUTIER-owned), Dom du CH Bas. See also COTEAUX DES BAUX-EN-PROVENCE.

Coteaux d'Ancenis Lo r p w (sw) ★ DYA VDQS E Of Nantes. Light Gamay red and rosé, sharpish dry Chenin Bl. Semi-sweet from Malvoisie, esp Guindon.

Coteaux de l'Aubance Lo w sw ★★→★★★★ 89 90 **95 96 97** 02 03 04 05 Similar to COTEAUX DU LAYON, but nervier sweet wines from Chenin Bl. A few SÉLECTIONS DES GRAINS NOBLES. Esp Bablut, Haute-Perche, Montgilet, RICHOU, Rochelles.

Coteaux des Baronnies S Rh r p w ★ DYA Rhône VIN DE PAYS nr Nyons. Syrah, Cab Sauv, Merlot, CHARD, plus traditional grapes. Fresh textures, from good altitudes. Doms du Rieu-Frais and Rosière worth noting.

Coteaux des Baux-en-Provence Prov r p ★→★★★ 98 99 00 **01 03** 04 05 From hills to N and S of Alpilles. Once part of COTEAUX D'AIX, now AC for red and rosé. TRÉVALLON is best of all, but VIN DE PAYS: Syrah and Cab Sauv, but no Grenache in v'yd so not AC.

Côteaux de Chalosse SW France r p w ★ DYA. Gd country wines from co-op at Mugron (Landes).

Coteaux Champenois Champ r w (p) ★★★ DYA (whites) AC for non-sparkling CHAMPAGNE. Vintages follow those for CHAMPAGNE. Not worth inflated prices.

Coteaux du Giennois Lo r p w ★ DYA Small area N of POUILLY promoted to AC in 1998. Light r: blend of Gamay and Pinot N; Sauv Bl à la SANCERRE. Best: Paulat.

Coteaux de Glanes SW France r ★★ DYA Lively VIN DE PAYS from nr Bretenoux (Lot). Co-op only producer. Mostly drunk in local restaurants. Excellent value.

Coteaux du Languedoc Midi r p w ★★→★★★ 97 98 99 00 **01 02** 03 04 05 Large area between Narbonne and Nimes, numerous sub-divisions, and more recently Grès de Montpellier and Terrasses du Larzac. Pézenas in the pipeline. Numerous fine estates, with quality improving dizzily.

Coteaux du Layon Lo w s/sw sw ★★→★★★★ 75 76 88 **89 90 95 96 97** 02 03 04 05 Heart of ANJOU: sweet Chenin Bl; admirable acidity, ages almost forever. New SÉLECTION DES GRAINS NOBLES; cf ALSACE. Seven villages can add name to AC. Top ACS: BONNEZEAUX, QUARTS DE CHAUME, Ctx du Layon-Chaume. Growers inc Badouin, BAUMARD, Cady, Delesvaux, des Forges, Dom de Juchepie, Ogereau, Papin (CH PIERRE-BISE), Jo Pithon, du Breuil Yves Guegniard, CH la Fresnaye.

Coteaux du Loir Lo r p w d sw ★→★★★ **02 03** 04 05 The Loir is a northern tributary of the Loire. Small region N of Tours, inc JASNIÈRES. Sometimes fine Chenin Bl, Gamay, Pineau d'Aunis, Cab Sauv. Top growers: Chaussard/le Briseau, de Rycke, Fresneau, Gigou, Nicolas/Dom de Belliviere, Robinot.

Coteaux de la Loire See ANJOU-COTEAUX DE LA LOIRE.

Coteaux du Lyonnais Beauj r p (w) ★ DYA Junior BEAUJOLAIS. Best EN PRIMEUR.

Coteaux de Peyriac Midi r p ★ DYA Much-used VIN DE PAYS name in Aude.

Coteaux de Pierrevert S Rh r p w ★ Easy-drinking co-op red, rosé, fresh white from nr Manosque. Dom la Blaque, CH Régusse CH Rousset. AC since 1998.

Coteaux du Quercy SW France r ★→★★ 00 **01' 02 03** 04 **(05)** S of CAHORS VDQS, queuing for AC. Private growers work with v.gd co-op nr Monpezat inc ★★ de Merchien, ★ Doms de la Combarade, la Garde, d'Aries, de Guyot, de Lafage.

Coteaux de Saumur Lo w sw ★★→★★★ 89 90 97 93 04 05 Rare potentially fine semi-sw Chenin Bl. VOUVRAY-like sweet (MOELLEUX) best. Esp CLOS ROUGEARD, CH Tour Grise, Retiveau-Retif, Regis Neau.

Coteaux et Terrasses de Montauban SW France r p ★→★★ DYA Dominated by co-op at LAVILLEDIEU-DU-TEMPLE. Better: ★★ Dom de Montels and ★ Doms de Biarnès.

Coteaux du Tricastin S Rh r p w ★★ **01' 03** 04 05 Fringe mid-Rhône AC of increasing quality. Best inc Doms de Bonetto-Fabrol, Grangeneuve (esp VIEILLES VIGNES), de Montine, St-Luc, and CH La Décelle (inc white CÔTES DU RHÔNE).

Coteaux Varois-en-Provence Prov r p w ★→★★ 99 00 01 02 03 04 05 Substantial AC zone, originally Coteaux Varois *tout court*, betw COTEAUX D'AIX and CÔTES DE PROVENCE. Warming red from Routas, la Calisse, Doms les Alysses, du Deffends.

Coteaux du Vendômois Lo r p w ★→★★ DYA Fringe Loire VDQS W of Vendôme; also AC. The most characteristic wines are *vins gris* from Pinot d'Aunis, which also gives peppery notes to red blends. Whites based on Chenin Bl. Producers inc Dom du Four à Chaux, Cave du Vendôme-Villiers, Patrice Colin.

Côtes d'Auvergne Central Fr r p (w) ★→★★ DYA Small VDQS. Mainly Gamay. Best: Cave St-Verny and Dom de Peyra (sells its wines as VIN DE PAYS).

Côtes de Bourg B'x r w ★→★★ 99 00' 01 02 03 04 (05) AC for earthy red and dry white from E of the Gironde. Consistent quality. CHX inc Brûlesécaille, Bujan, Falfas, Fougas, Garreau, Guerry, Haut-Guiraud, Haut-Maco, Haut Mondésir, Macay, Mercier, Nodoz, Roc de Cambes, Rousset, Sociondo, Tour de Guiet.

Côtes du Brulhois SW France r p (w) ★→★★ **03 04** 05 Nr Agen. Mostly centred on Donzac co-op.

Côtes de Castillon B'x r ★→★★ 98 99 00' 01 02 03 04 (05) Flourishing region E of ST-EMILION; similar wines. Ageing potential. Best chx inc de l'A, d'Aiguilhe, Cap de Faugères, La Clarière-Laithwaite, CLOS l'Eglise, Clos Les Lunelles, CLOS Puy Arnaud, de Laussac, Pitray, Veyry, Vieux Château Champs de Mars.

Côtes de Duras Dordogne r w p ★→★★ **01' 02 03** 04 **05** BORDEAUX satellite. Top inc Doms des Allegrets, du Grand Mayne, de Laulan, Mouthes-les-Bihan, Petit Malromé and CHX Condom-Perceval and Lafon. Gd co-op (Berticot).

Côtes de Francs B'x r w ★★ 98 00' 01 03 04 (05) Fringe BORDEAUX from E of ST-EMILION. Mainly red but some white: tasty and attractive. Reds can age a little. Best chx inc Charmes-Godard, Laclaverie, Marsau, Pelan, PUYGUERAUD, La Prade.

Côtes de Gascogne SW w (r p) ★ DYA VIN DE PAYS branch of ARMAGNAC. Very popular, led by Plaimont co-op and Grassa family (CH de Tariquet). Best known for fresh fruity Colombard-based white. Best: Doms de Joy, Papolle, Bergerayre, Maubet, Sancet, CH Monluc. Also from MADIRAN growers.

Côtes du Jura r p w (sp) ★ DYA Many light tints/tastes. ARBOIS more substantial.

Côtes du Lubéron S Rh r p w ★→★★ **01' 03 04'** 05 Greatly improved country wines from S Rhône, can often reflect modern techniques. A proliferation of new producers inc actors and media-magnates. Star is CH de la Canorgue. Others inc: CH Val-Joanis, Dom de la Citadelle, and co-op Cellier de Marrenon.

Côtes de la Malepère Midi r ★ DYA Aspiring AC on boundary between Midi and SW, nr Limoux, using grape varieties from both. Watch for fresh eager reds.

Côtes du Marmandais Dordogne r p w ★→★★★ **01' 02** 03 **04 05** Ever more serious AC. Excellent Elian da Ros (CLOS Bacqueys). V.gd: Dom des Geais, CH de Beaulieu (best are weighty, need ageing). Gd: La Verrerie.

Côtes de Montravel Dordogne w dr sw ★★ dr DYA sw **97' 98** 00 **01' 03'** 04 05 Part of BERGERAC; traditionally med-sweet, now less common. MONTRAVEL SEC is dry, HAUT-MONTRAVEL is sweet.

Côtes de Provence Prov r p w ★→★★★ r 00 01 02 03 04 05 (p w DYA) Revolutionized by new attitudes and investment. Leaders: Castel Roubine, Commanderie de Peyrassol, Doms Bernarde, de la Courtade, Dom Ott with CH de Selle and Clos Mireille, des Planes, Rabiéga, Richeaume, CH Ste-Rosaline. See COTEAUX D'AIX, BANDOL.

Côtes du Rhône S Rh r p w ★ 00' 01' 03 04' (05) Basic Rhône AC, mainly Grenache, also Syrah. Best drunk young, even as PRIMEUR. Wide quality variations: some heavy over-production. Look for estate bottlings or big Rhône merchants.

> **Top Côtes du Rhône producers:** CHX Courac, La Courançonne, l'Estagnol, Fonsalette, Grand Moulas, Hugues, Montfaucon, St-Estève, Trignon (inc Viognier); Clos Simian; Co-ops Chantecotes (Ste-Cécile-les-Vignes), Villedieu (esp white); Doms La Bouvade, Charvin, Combebelle, Coudoulet de Beaucastel (r w), Cros de la Mûre, Espigouette, Fond-Croze, Gourget, Gramenon, Janasse, Jaume, Perrin, Réméjeanne, St-Georges, Soumade, Vieille Julienne, Vieux Chêne, Guigal, Jaboulet.

Côtes du Rhône-Villages S Rh r p w ★→★★ 95' 98' 99' 00' 01' 03 04' 05 Wine from 18 best S Rhône villages across 3,055 ha. Substantial, mainly reliable, sometimes delicious. Red base is Grenache; but Syrah and Mourvèdre now used. Growing white quality, often with Viognier, Roussanne. See BEAUMES-DE-VENISE, CAIRANNE, CHUSCLAN, LAUDUN, RASTEAU, SABLET, SÉGURET, ST-GERVAIS. New villages from 2005: Massif d'Uchaux, Plan de Dieu, Puymeras, Plateau de Signargues. Sub-category with non-specified village name. Gd-value, e.g. CH Fontségune, Signac, Doms Cabotte, Deforge, Grand Moulas, Grand Veneur, Mas Libian, Montbayon, Rabasse-Charavin, Renjarde, Romarins, Ste-Anne, St Siffrein, Saladin, Valériane, Vieux Chêne, Cave Estézargues.

Côtes du Roussillon Pyr r p w ★→★★★ 98 99 00 01 02 03 04 05 E Pyrenees AC. Hefty Carignan red at its best, can pack a punch (e.g. Gauby). Some whites.

Côtes du Roussillon-Villages Pyr r ★★ 98 99 00 01 02 03 04 05 Region's best reds, 28 villages. Best labels: Co-op Baixas, Cazes Frères, Doms des Chênes, la Cazenove, Gauby (also characterful white VIN DE PAYS), CH de Jau, Co-op Lesquerde, Dom Piquemal, Co-op Les Vignerons Catalans, Dom Seguela.

Côtes du Roussillon des Aspres Newish AC (red only). First wines 03 vintage, based on Grenache Noir, Carignan, Syrah, and Mourvèdre.

Côtes de St-Mont SW France r w p ★ (r) 03 04 05 (w) Highly successful Gers VDQS still seeking AC status, imitating MADIRAN, PACHERENC. Co-op Plaimont all-powerful. Sweet CUVÉE Saint-Albert (★★★) is outstanding.

Côtes du Tarn SW France r p w ★ DYA VIN DE PAYS overlaps GAILLAC; same growers esp co-ops, CH de Vigné-Lourac, Doms de Labarthe, d'Escausses Sarrebale.

Côtes de Thongue Midi r w ★ DYA Improving VIN DE PAYS from HERAULT. Dynamic area with some gd wines, esp Doms Arjolle, les Chemins de Bassac, Coussergues, Croix Belle, Magellan, Montmarin, Monplézy.

Côtes de Toul E France (Lorraine) p r w ★ DYA Very light wines; mainly VIN GRIS.

Côtes du Ventoux S Rh r p (w) ★★ 01' 03 04' 05 Booming AC (over 6,000 ha) betw Rhône and PROVENCE for tasty red (café-style to much deeper flavours), easy rosé, and gd white. Cool flavours from altitude for some. Best: La Vieille Ferme (r) owned by BEAUCASTEL's J-P Perrin; Co-op Bédoin, Goult, St-Didier, Dom Anges, Brusset, Cascavel, Fondrèche, Martinelle, Font-Sane, Murmurium, Verrière, CHX La Croix des Pins, Pesquié, Pigeade, Valcombe, JABOULET.

Côtes du Vivarais S Rh r p w ★ 03 04 (05) DYA over 1,000 ha across several Ardèche villages W of Montélimar; promoted to AC in 1999. Improving simple CUVÉES, strong Syrah role; substantial oak-aged reds.

Coulée de Serrant Lo w dr sw ★★★★ 92 93 95' 96 97 98 99 00 01 02 03 04

A 6.4-ha Chenin Bl v'yd at SAVENNIÈRES. Ferociously biodynamic. Intense strong fruity/sharp wine, gd apéritif and with fish. Decant the day before drinking.

Couly-Dutheil Lo r p w ★★→★★★ 90 93 95 96 97 98 99 00 01 02 03 04 Major CHINON grower/merchant; range of reliable wines. CLOS d'Olive and l'Echo are top wines. New CUVÉE, Crescendo (oak-aged).

Courcel, Dom ★★★ Leading POMMARD estate – top PREMIER CRU Rugiens.

Crémant In CHAMPAGNE meant "creaming" (half-sparkling). Since 1975, an AC for quality classic-method sparkling from ALSACE, Loire, BOURGOGNE, and most recently LIMOUX – often a bargain. Term no longer used in CHAMPAGNE.

Crémant de Loire Lo w sp ★★→★★★ NV High-quality sp, esp SAUMUR and TOURAINE. Producers inc BAUMARD, Berger, Delhumeau, LANGLOIS-CHATEAU, Nerleux, Passavant.

Crépy Savoie w ★★ DYA Light, soft, Swiss-style white from S shore of Lake Geneva. *Crépitant* has been coined for its faint fizz.

Crozes-Hermitage N Rh r (w) HH 90' 95' 97' 98' 99' 00' 01' 03' 05 Nr Hermitage: larger v'yds (1,355 ha). Syrah: some fruity, early-drinking (2+ yrs), some cask-aged (4–6 yrs). Gd: Batellerie, Belle, Y Chave, Ch Curson, Darnaud, Doms du Colombier, des Entrefaux (oak), du Pavillon-Mercurol, de Thalabert of Jaboulet, Chapoutier. Drink white early (esp gd 04).

Cuve close Short-cut method of making sparkling wine in a tank. Sparkle dies away in glass much quicker than with MÉTHODE TRADITIONELLE wine.

Cuvée Wine contained in a *cuve*, or vat. A word of many uses, inc synonym for "blend" and first-press wines (as in CHAMPAGNE); in Burgundy interchangeable with *cru*. Often just refers to a "lot" of wine.

Dagueneau, Didier Lo ★★★ 00 01 02 Top POUILLY-FUMÉ producer. Pouilly's *enfant terrible* has created new benchmarks for the AC and Sauv Bl. Top CUVÉE: barrel-fermented Silex. Has also started a vineyard in JURANÇON.

Daumas Gassac See MAS DE DAUMAS GASSAC.

De Castellane Brut NV; BLANC DE BLANCS; Brut (95 96 98 99); Prestige Florens de Castellane (90 95 96). Traditional Epernay CHAMPAGNE house linked with LAURENT-PERRIER. Best for vintage wines; esp CUVÉE Commodore Brut (95 96).

Degré alcoolique Degrees of alcohol, *i.e.* per cent by volume.

Deiss, Domaine Marcel ★★→★★★ Grower at Bergheim, ALSACE. GRANDS CRUS SCHOENENBOURG CHAMPAGNE house at Le Mesnil, owned by LAURENT-PERRIER.

Delas Frères N Rh ★→★★★ Old, worthy firm of Rhône specialists with v'yds at CONDRIEU, CÔTE-RÔTIE, HERMITAGE. Top wines: CONDRIEU, CÔTE-RÔTIE Landonne, Hermitage M de Tourette (r w), Bessards. Owned by ROEDERER. Quality high.

Delbeck Small fine CHAMPAGNE house revitalized by partners Martin/ Giraudière. Find excellent Pinot N-led vintages (90 95' 96) GRAND CRU Aÿ and Cramant.

Delorme, André ★★ Leading CÔTE CHALONNAISE merchants and growers. Specialists in v.gd CRÉMANT DE BOURGOGNE and excellent RULLY, etc.

Demi-sec Half-dry: in practice more like half-sweet (*e.g.* of CHAMPAGNE).

Deutz Brut Classic NV; Rosé NV; Brut (96' 98); BLANC DE BLANCS (96' 98). One of top small CHAMPAGNE houses, ROEDERER-owned. Superb CUVÉE William Deutz (95 96').

Dom Pérignon Cuvée 90' 95 96 98; Rosé 96 98 Luxury CUVÉE of MOËT & CHANDON, named after the legendary cellarmaster who first blended CHAMPAGNE. Astonishingly consistent quality and creamy character, esp with 10–15 yrs bottle-age. Wine library of late-disgorged limited-release vintages back to 62.

Domaine (Dom) Property, particularly in Burgundy and rural France. See under name, *e.g.* TEMPIER, DOMAINE.

Dopff & Irion ★→★★★ 17th-C ALSACE firm at Riquewihr now part of PFAFFENHEIM. Famed MUSCAT les Amandiers, GEWURZ Les Sorcières. Also gd CRÉMANT D'ALSACE.

Dopff au Moulin ★★ Ancient top-class family wine house at Riquewihr, ALSACE. Best: GEWURZ GRANDS CRUS Brand, Sporen; Ries SCHOENENBOURG; Sylvaner de Riquewihr. Pioneers of ALSACE sp wine; gd CUVÉES: Bartholdi and Julien.

Dourthe, Vins & Vignobles BORDEAUX merchant with wide range and quality emphasis: gd CRUS BOURGEOIS, inc BELGRAVE, LE BOSCQ, TRONQUOY-LALANDE. Beau-Mayne and Dourthe No 1 are well made. Essence v. concentrated, modern.

Doux Sweet.

DRC See ROMANÉE-CONTI, DOMAINE DE LA.

Drappier, André Leading AUBE CHAMPAGNE house. Family-run. Vinous NV, BRUT Zéro, Rosé Saignée, Signature BLANC DE BLANCS (**95'** 99 00), Millésime d'Exception (**99 00**), Sumptuous prestige CUVÉE Grande Sendrée (**96 98 99** 00).

Drouhin, J & Cie Burg ★★★→★★★★★ Deservedly prestigious grower (61 ha). Cellars in BEAUNE; v'yds in Beaune, CHABLIS, CLOS DE VOUGEOT, MUSIGNY, etc., and Oregon, USA. Best inc (esp) (w) BEAUNE-CLOS DES MOUCHES, CHABLIS LES CLOS, CORTON-CHARLEMAGNE, PULIGNY-MONTRACHET, Les Folatières (r) GRIOTTE-CHAMBERTIN, MUSIGNY, GRANDS-ECHÉZEAUX.

Duboeuf, Georges ★★→★★★ Top-class merchant at Romanèche-Thorin. Region's leader in every sense; huge range of admirable wines. Also MOULIN-À-VENT atypically aged in new oak, white MÂCONNAIS, etc.

Duclot BORDEAUX négociant; top-growth specialist. Linked with J-P MOUEIX.

Ducournau, Patrick Exclusive MADIRAN grower also known as inventor of MICROBULLAGE and now sadly trading in oak chips.

Dugat Burg ★★★ Cousins Claude and Bernard both make excellent, deep coloured wines in GEVREY-CHAMBERTIN under their respective labels.

Dujac, Domaine ★★★ Burg grower (Jacques Seysses) at MOREY-ST-DENIS with v'yds in that village and BONNES-MARES, ECHÉZEAUX, GEVREY-CHAMBERTIN, etc. Splendidly vivid and long-lived wines. Other top v'yds VOSNE-ROMANÉE, Malconsorts, CHAMBERTIN CLOS DE BEZE purchased in 2005. Now also négociant for village wines as Dujac Fils & Père. Also venture with other grapes in COTEAUX VAROIS.

Dulong BORDEAUX merchant making unorthodox Rebelle blends. Also VINS DE PAYS.

Durup, Jean Burg ★★→★★★ One of the biggest CHABLIS growers with 152 ha, inc Dom de l'Eglantière and admirable CH de Maligny.

Duval-Leroy Fleur de Champagne Brut NV; Extra Brut; Brut 98 **99** 00; BLANC DE BLANCS **95' 96 99 98 99** 00; Rosé de Saignée NV; Prestige Cuvée des Rois **96' 98 99**. Rising Côte des Blanc house; fine quality, gd value. Many labels.

Echézeaux Burg r ★★★ 78' 88 89' 90' 91 93 95 96' **97** 98 99' **00** 01 02' 03 04 05' GRAND CRU (30 ha) between VOSNE-ROMANÉE and CLOS DE VOUGEOT. Can be superlative, fragrant, without great weight.

Ecu, Dom de l' Lo dr w r ★★★ 85 86 87 88 89 90 **93** 95 96 97 02 **03** 04 05 Producer of Biodynamic MUSCADET and Gros Plant. Also Cab Fr and sp.

Edelzwicker ALSACE w ★ DYA Modest blended light white. Popularity has waned.

d'Eguisheim, Cave Vinicole ★★ V.gd ALSACE co-op often offering excellent value: fine GRAND CRUS Hatschbourg, HENGST, Ollwiller, Spiegel. Owns Willm. Top label: WOLFBERGER. Best: Grande Réserve, Sigillé, Armorié. Gd CRÉMANT and Pinot N.

Engel, R ★★★ Top grower of CLOS DE VOUGEOT, ECHÉZEAUX, GRANDS-ECHÉZEAUX, and VOSNE-ROMANÉE. Tragic early death of Philippe Engel in 2005.

En primeur See PRIMEUR.

Entraygues SW France r p w DYA ★ Fragrant VDQS. Try Chenin Bl-based Dom Méjannassère.

Entre-Deux-Mers B'x w ★→★★ DYA Much-improved dry w BORDEAUX from between Rivers Garonne and Dordogne (aka E-2-M). Esp CHX BONNET, Fontenille, Marjosse, Nardique-la-Gravière, Sainte-Marie, Tour de Mirambeau, Toutigeac.

Esmonin, Sylvie Burg ★★★ Very classy GEVREY-CHAMBERTIN, esp CLOS ST-JACQUES.

L'Etoile Jura w dr sp (sw) ★★ Sub-region of the JURA known for stylish whites, inc VIN JAUNE, similar to CHÂTEAU-CHALON; gd sp.

Faiveley, J Burg ★★→★★★★★ Family-owned growers and merchants at NUITS-ST-GEORGES. V'yds (109 ha) in CHAMBERTIN-CLOS DE BEZE, CHAMBOLLE-MUSIGNY, CORTON, MERCUREY, NUITS. Consistent high quality rather than charm.

Faller, Théo/Domaine Weinbach ★★→★★★★ Top ALSACE grower (Kaysersberg). To age up to 10 yrs. Esp GRANDS CRUS SCHLOSSBERG (Ries), FURSTENTUM (GEWURZ).

Faugères Midi r (p w) ★★ 98 99 00 **01 02 03** 04 05 Isolated COTEAUX DU LANGUEDOC village with exceptional terroir based on schist. Reds and pinks gained AC status 1982; white in 2004, from Marsanne, Roussanne, Rolle.

Fessy, Sylvain Beauj ★★ Dynamic BEAUJOLAIS merchant with wide range.

Fèvre, William Burg ★★★ CHABLIS grower with biggest GRAND CRU holding Dom de la Maladière (18 ha). Outstanding since bought by HENRIOT in 1998.

Fiefs Vendéens Lo r p w ★ DYA VDQS for light wines from the Vendée, just S of MUSCADET on the Atlantic coast. Wines from CHARD, Chenin Bl, Colombard, Grolleau, Melon (whites), Cab Sauv, Pinot N, Negrette, and Gamay for reds and rosés. Esp: Coirier, Michon/Dom St-Nicolas, CH Marie du Fou.

Filliatreau, Domaine Lo r ★★→★★★ **02 03** 04 05 Filliatreau's r range from supple, juicy Jeunes Vignes to nuanced VIEILLES VIGNES and La Grande Vignolle.

Fitou Midi r ★★ 98 99 00 **01 02** 03 04 05 Powerful r, from hills S of Narbonne, Ages well. Best from co-ops at Cascastel, Paziols, Tuchan. Experiments with Mourvèdre. Gd estates inc CH Nouvelles, Dom Lérys, Rolland.

Fixin Burg r ★★★ 90' 95 **96' 97 98 99'** 01 02' **03** 04 05' Worthy and under-valued N neighbour of GEVREY-CHAMBERTIN. Often splendid reds. Best v'yds: CLOS du Chapitre, Les Hervelets, CLOS Napoléon. Growers inc Bertheau, R Bouvier, CLAIR, FAIVELEY, Gelin, Gelin-Molin, Guyard.

Fleurie Beauj r ★★★ **03 04 05'** The epitome of a BEAUJOLAIS *cru*: fruity, scented, silky, racy wines. Esp from Chapelle des Bois, Chignard, Depardon, Després, DUBOEUF, CH de Fleurie, Métras, the co-op.

Floc de Gascogne SW France r p w ARMAGNAC'S answer to PINEAU DES CHARENTES. Apéritif from unfermented grape juice blended with ARMAGNAC.

Frais Fresh or cool. **Frappé** Ice-cold. **Froid** Cold.

Fronsac B'x r ★→★★★ 95 96 98 00' **01 03** (05) Hilly area W of ST-EMILION; increasingly fine, often tannic red. CHX inc de Carles, DALEM, LA DAUPHINE, Fontenil, La Grave, Mayne-Vieil, Moulin-Haut-Laroque, LA RIVIÈRE, La Rousselle, Tour du Moulin, Les Trois Croix, La Vieille Cure, Villars. See also CANON-FRONSAC.

Frontignan Midi golden sw ★★ NV Small AC for sweet fortified MUSCAT. Experiments with late-harvest unfortified wines. Quality steadily improving.

Fronton SW France r p ★★ **02 03 04 05'** Called the "BEAUJOLAIS of Toulouse". DYA but Cab Sauv red needs longer. Gd growers inc Doms de Caze, Joliet, du Roc; CHX Baudare, Bellevue-la-Forêt, Boujac, Cahuzac, Cransac, Plaisance.

Furstentum ALSACE GRAND CRU at Kientzheim and Sigolsheim renowned for superb ripening ability. See FALLER DOM WEINBACH and Paul BLANCK.

Gagnard, Jean-Noel Burg ★★★ Jean Noel's daughter, Caroline l'Estimé, has pushed this DOMAINE to the top of the Gagnard clan. Beautifully expressive GRAND CRU, PREMIER CRU, and village wines in CHASSAGNE-MONTRACHET. Also cousins Gagnard-Delagrange, Blain-Gagnard, Fontaine-Gagnard.

A guide to good Gaillac

All-rounders Mas Pignou, Mas d'Aurel, Doms de Barreau, Labarthe, and d'Escausses, CH de Mayragues, co-op at Técou (esp. "Passion" range).

Reds (★★) Doms de Cailloutis, Canto Perlic, Larroque, Pialentou, Salvy, and La Chanade.

Local varieties PLAGEOLES, Doms de Ramaye, Causse-Marines (all ★★★).

Sweet whites Doms de Causse-Marines, Rotier, Long Pech, Mas de Bicary.

Dry whites Dom de Causse-Marines, CHX d'Arlus, Vigné-Lourac (★★→★★★★).

Sparkling Doms La Tronque, Peyre Combe, de Vayssette.

Vins de pays Dom Borie-Vieille (Muscadelle), Dom Sarrabelle (CHARD)

Perlé Dom de Salmes.

Gaillac SW France r p w dr sw sp ★→★★★ Mostly DYA except oaked reds **02** 03 **04** (05). Also sweet whites **01 02** 03 **04** 05.

Garage *Vins de garage* are (usually) B'x made on such a very small scale. Rigorous winemaking but a bottle costs much the same as a full service.

Gard, Vin de Pays du Languedoc ★ The Gard *département* by the mouth of the Rhône is an important source of sound VIN DE PAYS production, inc Coteaux Flaviens, Pont du Gard, SABLES DU GOLFE DU LION, Salavès, Uzège, Vaunage.

Gers r w p ★ DYA Indistinguishable from nearby CÔTES DE GASCOGNE.

Gevrey-Chambertin Burg r ★★★ **88** 90' **93 95** 96' **97 98** 99' **00** 01 02' 03 04 05' Village containing the great CHAMBERTIN, its GRAND CRU cousins and many other noble v'yds (*e.g.* PREMIERS CRUS Cazetiers, Combe aux Moines, Combottes, CLOS ST-JACQUES, CLOS des Varoilles). Growers inc Bachelet, L Boillot, BURGUET, Damoy, DROUHIN, DUGAT, ESMONIN, FAIVELEY, Harmand-Geoffroy, Geantet-Pansiot, JADOT, Leclerc, LEROY, MORTET, ROTY, ROUSSEAU, SERAFIN, Trapet, Varoilles.

Gewurztraminer Speciality grape of ALSACE: one of four allowed for specified GRAND CRU wines. The most aromatic of ALSACE grapes: at best like rose petals to smell, grapefruit and/or lychees to taste. Now returning to more traditional, drier style.

Gigondas S Rh r p ★★→★★★ 78' 89' **90' 95' 96 97 98' 99' 00' 01' 02** 03' 04' 05 Worthy neighbour to CHÂTEAUNEUF. Strong, full-bodied, sometimes peppery, largely Grenache. Try: CH de Montmirail, Saint-Cosme, CLOS du Joncuas, P Amadieu, Dom Bouïssière, Font-Sane, Goubert, Gour de Chaulé, Grapillon d'Or, les Pallières, Piaugier, Raspail-Ay, St-Gayan, Tourelles, des Travers.

Ginestet Long-established BORDEAUX négociant now owned by Bernard Taillan.

Girardin, Vincent Burg r w ★★→★★★ Quality grower in SANTENAY, now dynamic merchant, specializing in CÔTE DE BEAUNE ACS. Modern, oak and fruit style.

Givry Burg r w ★★ 99' **02' 03 04** 05' Underrated CÔTE CHALONNAISE village: light, tasty, typical burgundy from, *e.g.*, DELORME, L LATOUR, Sarazin, BARON THENARD.

Gorges et Côtes de Millau SW France r p w ★ DYA Locally popular country wines: red best. Gd co-op at Aguessac. Some private growers for the brave.

Gosset Very old small CHAMPAGNE house at AŸ. Excellent full-bodied wine (esp Grand Millésime (**96** 98 99). Gosset Celebris (**95 96** 98) is prestige CUVÉE. Celebris Rosé (**96 97** 99), launched 1995 by Cointreau family of COGNAC Frapin.

Gouges, Henri ★★★ Reinvigorated estate for rich, complex NUITS-ST-GEORGES, with great ageing potential.

Goût Taste. *Goût anglais*: as the English like it – dry for CHAMPAGNE, or well aged.

Grand Cru One of top Burgundy v'yds with its own AC. In ALSACE one of the 50 top v'yds covered by ALSACE GRAND CRU AC, but more vague elsewhere. In ST-EMILION the third rank of CHX, inc about 200 properties.

Grande Champagne The AC of the best area of COGNAC. Nothing fizzy about it.

Grande Rue, La Burg r ★★★ 90' **95** 96' **97** 98 99' **00** 01 02' 03 04 05' VOSNE-ROMANÉE GRAND CRU, neighbour to ROMANÉE-CONTI.

Grands-Echézeaux Burg r ★★★★ 78' **85' 88' 89'** 90' **91'** 93 95 96' **97** 98 99' **00** 01 02' 03 04 05' Superlative 8.9-ha GRAND CRU next to CLOS DE VOUGEOT. Wines not weighty but aromatic. *Viz:* DROUHIN, ENGEL, DRC, GROS.

Gratien, Alfred and **Gratien & Meyer** ★★→★★★ Brut NV; Brut **95 96'** 98; Prestige Cuvée Paradis Brut and Rosé (**96' 98** 99 00). Excellent smaller family-run CHAMPAGNE house. Fine, very dry, long-lasting wine fermented in barrels. Gratien & Meyer is counterpart at SAUMUR. (V.gd Cuvée Flamme.)

Graves B'x r w ★★→★★★★ **00 01 04** (05) Region S of BORDEAUX city with excellent soft earthy r; dry w reasserting star status. PESSAC-LÉOGNAN is inner zone. Top chx inc ARCHAMBEAU, CHANTEGRIVE, CLOS FLORIDENE, Vieux-CH-Gaubert, Villa Bel Air.

Graves de Vayres B'x r w ★ DYA Small AC within ENTRE-DEUX-MERS zone. No special character.

Griotte-Chambertin Burg r ★★★★ 85' **88' 89' 90' 91** 93 95 96' **97** 98 99' 00 01 02' 03 04 05' A 5.6-ha GRAND CRU adjoining CHAMBERTIN. Similar wine, but less masculine, more "tender". Growers inc DUGAT, DROUHIN, PONSOT.

Grivot, Jean Burg ★★★→★★★★ CÔTE DE NUITS dom in five ACS. Top quality since 93.

Groffier, Robert Burg ★★★ Pure, elegant GEVREY-CHAMBERTIN, CHAMBOLLE-MUSIGNY, esp Les Amoureuses.

Gros, Domaines Burg ★★★→★★★★ Excellent family of *vignerons* in VOSNE-ROMANÉE comprising (at least) Doms Jean, Michel, Anne, Anne-François Gros, and Gros Frère & Sœur. Wines range from HAUTES CÔTES DE NUITS to RICHEBOURG.

Gros Plant du Pays Nantais Lo w ★ DYA Junior VDQS cousin of MUSCADET; sharper, lighter; from the COGNAC grape, aka Folle Blanche, Ugni Blanc, etc.

Guffens-Heynen Burg ★★★ Belgian POUILLY-FUISSÉ grower. Tiny quantity, top quality. Heady Gamay. Also CÔTE D'OR wines (bought-in grapes) as VERGET.

Guigal, Ets E N Rh Celebrated grower: 22-ha CÔTE-RÔTIE, HERMITAGE, ST-JOSEPH. Merchant: CONDRIEU, CÔTE-RÔTIE, HERMITAGE, S RHÔNE. Owns VIDAL-FLEURY. By ageing single-v'yd CÔTE-RÔTIE (La Mouline, La Landonne, La Turque) for 42 months in new oak, Guigal breaks local tradition to please (esp) American palates; all his red have big shoulders. Standard wines: gd value, reliable, esp r, w CÔTES DU RHÔNE. Also full oaky CONDRIEU La Doriane, occasional sweet Luminescence.

Guy Saget Lo ★★ Family firm with v'yds in the POUILLY-FUMÉ and Pouilly-sur-Loire appellations (Dom Saget), buying up estates throughout the Loire. négociant line accounts for half the firm's annual production of 5 million bottles.

Haut-Médoc B'x r ★★→★★★ 88' 89' 90' 95 96 98 00 01' 02 03 04 (05) Big AC in S of MÉDOC peninsula. Source of gd-value, minerally, digestible wines. Some variation in soils and wines; sand and gravel in S, so finer; heavier clay and gravel further N, so sturdier. Includes five classed growths (*e.g.* LA LAGUNE).

Haut-Montravel Dordogne w sw ★★ 95' 97 98' 00 01' 02 03' (05) Rare MONTRAVEL sweet white; rather like MONBAZILLAC. Look for CHX Moulin Caresse, Puy-Servain-Terrement, Roque-Peyre; also Doms de Libarde and de Gouyat.

Haut-Poitou Lo w r ★→★★ DYA VDQS S of ANJOU. V.gd whites from CAVE linked with DUBOEUF. Reds: Gamay, Cab Sauv. Drink young, when at its fruitiest.

Hautes-Côtes de Beaune Burg ★★ r 99' **02' 03'** 05' w **02' 03 04** 05' AC for 12 villages in hills behind the CÔTE DE BEAUNE. Best: Cornu, Devevey, Jacob, Mazilly.

Hautes-Côtes de Nuits Burg ★★ r 99' **02' 03'** 05' w **02' 03 04** 05' As above, for CÔTE DE NUITS. Best: Duband, Cornu, Jayer-Gilles, GROS. Also large BEAUNE co-op.

Heidsieck, Charles Brut Réserve NV; Brut 96' 98 99; Rosé **96** 99 Major Reims CHAMPAGNE house, now controlled by Rémy Martin. Blanc des Millénaires (90' **95**). Fine quality recently, esp innovative Mis en Cave range of NV CUVÉES showing year of bottling. NV: real bargain. See also PIPER-HEIDSIECK.

Heidsieck, Monopole Brut NV Blue Top; Red Top; Gold Top (**99** 00). Once illustrious CHAMPAGNE house; owned by VRANKEN. Red Top virtually BLANC DE NOIRS.

Hengst Wintzenheim ALSACE GRAND CRU. Excels with top-notch GEWURZ from Albert MANN; also Pinot-Auxerrois, Chasselas and Pinot N, with no GRAND CRU status.

Henriot Brut Souverain NV; BLANC DE BLANCS de CHARD NV; Brut **90 95' 96** 98; Brut Rosé **98** 99; Luxury CUVÉE: Cuvée des Enchanteleurs **88' 89 90**. Old family CHAMPAGNE house; regained independence in 1994. Very fine, fresh, creamy style. Joseph H also owns BOUCHARD PÈRE & FILS (since 1995) and FÈVRE.

Hérault Midi Biggest v'yd *département*: 106,432 ha. Some excellent AC COTEAUX DU LANGUEDOC Important source of VIN DE PAYS de l'Hérault encompassing full quality spectrum, from pioneering to basic. Also VIN DE TABLE.

Hermitage N Rh r w ★★★→★★★★ 61' 66 **78' 82** 83' **85' 88 89' 90' 91' 94 95' 96 97' 98'** 99' 00 01' 03' 04 05' Dark, powerful, profound. Truest example of Syrah from 131 ha on E bank of Rhône. Needs long ageing. Heady and golden w (Marsanne, some Roussanne); top wines mature for up to 25 yrs. Best:

Belle, CHAPOUTIER, CHAVE, Colombier, DELAS, Desmeure, Faurie, GUIGAL, Habrard (w), JABOULET, Sorrel, Tardieu-Laurent. TAIN co-op gd (esp Gambert de Loche).

Hospices de Beaune Burg Historic hospital and charitable institution in BEAUNE, with excellent v'yds (known by CUVÉE names) in BEAUNE, CORTON, MEURSAULT, POMMARD, VOLNAY. Wines are auctioned on the third Sunday of each November.

Hudelot-Noëllat, Alain ★★★ Under-appreciated VOUGEOT estate producing some excellent wines, in a light but fine style.

Huet Lo ★★→★★★★ 47 59 64 69 71 76 **88 89 90** 95 96 **97** 02 03 04 05 Leading estate in VOUVRAY, run on biodynamic principles. Anthony Hwang, who owns Kiralyudvar in Tokaj, has bought the majority share. Wines for long ageing. Single-v'yd wines best: Le Haut Lieu, Le Mont, CLOS du Bourg.

Hugel et Fils ★★→★★★★ Founded Riquewihr, ALSACE, in 1639. Best-known ALSACE house, making superb late-harvest wines. Three quality levels: Classic, Tradition, Jubilee. Strongly opposed to GRAND CRU system.

Ile de Beauté Name for VINS DE PAYS from CORSICA. Mostly red; usually varietal.

Impériale BORDEAUX bottle holding eight normal bottles (6 litres).

Irancy ("Bourgogne Irancy") Burg r (p) ★★ 99' 02' 03' 05' Gd light red made nr CHABLIS from Pinot N and the local César. The best vintages mature well.

Irouléguy SW France r p (w) ★★→★★★★ 01' **02 03 04** (05) Local wines of Basque country with a rustic twang. Dark dense Tannat/Cab Sauv reds to keep 5 yrs. Gd from Doms Abotia, Ameztia, Arretxea, Brana, Etchegaraya, Ilarria, Mouguy; co-op. Rivals MADIRAN. Excellent co-op, esp white Xuri d'Ansa.

Jaboulet Aîné, Paul N Rh Old family firm at TAIN, sold to Swiss investor late 05. Formerly leading grower of HERMITAGE (esp La Chapelle ★★★), CORNAS St-Pierre, CROZES Thalabert (gd value), Roure; merchant of other Rhône wines esp CÔTES DU RHÔNE Parallèle 45, CÔTES DU VENTOUX. Drink whites young. Quality may now rise (prices, too).

Jacquart Brut NV; Brut Rosé NV (Carte Blanche and Cuvée Spéciale); Brut 95 96 **98** Co-op-based CHAMPAGNE marque; in quantity the sixth-largest. Fair quality. Luxury brands: Cuvée Nominée Blanc **98 99** 00 and Rosé **99** 00. V.gd Mosaïque BLANC DE BLANCS **98** 99 and Rosé **99**.

Jacquesson Excellent small Dizy CHAMPAGNE house. Top Avize GRAND CRU 96'; exquisite Grand Vin Signature: white (**88**' **95**' **96**) and rosé (**96**). Corne Bautray, Dizy **00**, and excellent NV CUVÉES 728, 729, and 730.

Jadot, Louis Burg ★★→★★★★ Good-quality merchant house with v'yds (63 ha) in BEAUNE, CORTON, Magenta, CH des Jacques (MOULIN À VENT), etc. Sound across the range now.

Jardin de la France Lo w r p DYA One of France's four regional VINS DE PAYS. Covers Loire Valley: mostly single grape (esp CHARD, Gamay, Sauv Bl).

Jasnières Lo w dr (sw) ★★★ 97 02 03 04 05 Rare and almost immortal dry VOUVRAY-like wine (Chenin Bl) of N TOURAINE. Esp Aubert la Chapelle, Chaussard/Le Briseau, Gigou, Nicolas/Dom de Belliviere, Robinot.

Jayer, Henri Near-legendary Burgundy figure. See ROUGET.

Jobard, François Burg ★★★ Small MEURSAULT DOMAINE; classic, slow-evolving wines. Look out also for nephew Remi Jobard's more modern-style wines.

Joseph Perrier Cuvée Royale Brut NV; Cuvée Royale BLANC DE BLANCS NV; Cuvée Royale Rosé NV; Brut 96' **98**. Excellent smaller CHAMPAGNE house at Chalons with gd v'yds in Marne Valley. Supple fruity style; v.gd prestige Cuvée Joséphine 95 96'. Part-owned since 1998 by Alain THIÉNOT.

Josmeyer ★★→★★★★ Family house at Wintzenheim, ALSACE. V.gd long-ageing wines, esp GEWURZ, Pinot Bl. Fine Ries from GRAND CRU HENGST. Wide range.

Juliénas Beauj r ★★★ 01 03' 05' Leading cru of BEAUJOLAIS: vigorous fruity wine to keep 2–3 yrs. Growers inc CHX du Bois de la Salle, des Capitans, de Juliénas, des Vignes; Doms Bottière, R Monnet, Michel Tête, co-op.

FRANCE

Jura See CÔTES DU JURA.

Jurançon w sw dr ★→★★★ SW **95 97 98 00 01 02** (03) (04') dr **98 01 02 03 04'** (05) Racy, long-lived speciality of Pau in Pyrenean foothills. Growers: Doms du Barrère, Bellegarde, Bordenave, Capdevielle, Castéra, de Souch, du Cinquau, Cauhapé, Joly, Lapeyre, Larredya, Nigri, de Rousse, Uroulat, Bellevue, Cabarrouy, Vignau-la-Juscles. Also Les Jardins de Babylone, Didier Daguenau's tiny new v'yd. Co-op's Grain Sauvage, BRUT d'Ocean, Peyre d'Or.

Kaefferkopf ALSACE w dr (sw) ★★★ Proposed in 2006 as the 51st GRAND CRU of ALSACE; one of only two permitted to make blends as well as varietal wines. Located at Ammerschwihr.

Kientzler, André ★★→★★★ A top ALSACE Ries specialist in GRAND CRU Geisburg, esp VENDANGE TARDIVE and SELECTIONS DES GRAINS NOBLE. Equally gd from GRAND CRUS Kirchberg de Ribeauvillé for GEWURZ. Osterberg for occasional *vins de glaces* (Eisweins). Also v.gd Auxerrois, Chasselas.

Kreydenweiss Marc ★★→★★★ Fine ALSACE grower: 12 ha at Andlau, esp for Pinot Gr (v.gd GRAND CRU Moenchberg), Pinot Bl, and Ries. Top wine: GRAND CRU Kastelberg (ages 20 yrs); also fine Auxerrois Kritt Klevner and gd VENDANGE TARDIVE. One of first in ALSACE to use new oak. Gd Ries/Pinot Gr blend CLOS du Val d'Eléon. Great believer in terroir and biodynamic viticulture.

Kriter Popular sparkler processed in Burgundy by PATRIARCHE. See the fountain on the Autoroute du Soleil.

Krug Grande Cuvée; Vintage **85 88' 90** 95; Rosé; CLOS du Mesnil (BLANC DE BLANCS) **81' 85 88 89 90 92** 95; Krug Collection **62 64 66 69 71 73 76 79 81** Small, supremely prestigious CHAMPAGNE house. Rich, nutty, elegant wines, oak fermented: long ageing, superlative quality. Owned by MOËT-Hennessy.

Kuentz-Bas ★→★★ Famous ALSACE grower/merchant at Husseren-les Châteaux, esp for Pinot Gr, GEWURZ. Gd VENDANGES TARDIVES. Owned by Caves B Adam.

Labouré-Roi Burg ★★→★★★ Reliable, dynamic merchant at NUITS. Mostly white, but now also owns top red new-generation merchant Nicolas POTEL.

Ladoix-Serrigny Burg r (w) ★★ 96' 98 99' 01 02' 03 04 05' Northernmost village of CÔTE DE BEAUNE below hills of CORTON. Watch for bargains.

Ladoucette, de ★★→★★★ 02 03 04 05 Leading producer of POUILLY-FUMÉ, based at CH de Nozet. Luxury brand Baron de L can be wonderful. Also SANCERRE Comte Lafond, La Poussie, Marc Brédif.

Lafarge, Michel ★★★★ 10-ha CÔTE DE BEAUNE estate with excellent VOLNAYS, in particular Clos des Chênes and now Caillerets.

Lafon, Domaine des Comtes Burg ★★★★ Top estate in MEURSAULT, LE MONTRACHET, VOLNAY. Glorious intense white; extraordinary dark red. Also in the Maconnais.

Laguiche, Marquis de Burg ★★★★ Largest owner of LE MONTRACHET. Superb DROUHIN-made wines.

Lalande de Pomerol B'x r ★★→★★★ 90' 94 95 96 98 99 00' 01' 03 04 (05) Northerly neighbour of POMEROL. Wines similar, but less mellow. New investors and younger generation: improving quality. Top chx: des Annereaux, Bertineau-St-Vincent, La Croix-St-André, Les Cruzelles, La Fleur de Boüard, Garraud, Grand Ormeau, Les Hauts Conseillants, Jean de Gué, Perron (La Fleur), La Sergue, TOURNEFEUILLE.

Lamartine, Château SW France r ★★★ 98 00 01 02 One of top new CAHORS estates. Powerful reds which also achieve some elegance and finesse.

Landron (Domaines) Lo dr w (also Dom de la Louvetrie) Excellent organic producer of MUSCADET DE SÈVRE et MAINE with several CUVÉES, bottled by terroir, inc Fief du Breil and Amphibolite Nature.

Langlois-Château Lo ★→★★★ One of top SAUMUR sparkling houses (esp CREMANT). Controlled by BOLLINGER. Also range of still wines, esp exceptional SAUMUR Bl VIEILLES VIGNES.

Lanson Père & Fils Black Label NV; Rosé NV; Brut **96 98** 99 00 Important improving CHAMPAGNE house; owned since 06 by Boizel Chanoine group. Long-lived luxury brand: Noble CUVÉE BLANC DE BLANCS (**96 98**). Black Label improved by longer ageing.

Laroche ★★→★★★ Important grower and dynamic CHABLIS merchant, inc Doms La Jouchère and Laroche. Top wines: Blanchots (Réserve de l'Obédiencerie ★★★) and CLOS VIEILLES VIGNES. Ambitious MIDI range, Dom La Chevalière.

Latour, Louis Burg ★★→★★★ Famous merchant and grower with v'yds (49 ha) in BEAUNE, CORTON, etc. V.gd white: CHEVALIER-MONTRACHET Les Demoiselles, CORTON-CHARLEMAGNE, MONTRACHET, gd-value MONTAGNY and ARDECHE CHARD etc. Reds still underperforming. CH de Corton Grancey. Also Pinot N Valmoissine from the Var.

Latour de France r (w) ★→★★ 98 99 00 01 02 03 04 05 Supposedly superior village in AC CÔTES DE ROUSSILLON-VILLAGES. Independent growers overtaking co-op. Esp Clos de l'Oum, Clos des Fées.

Latricières-Chambertin Burg r ★★★ 89' 90' 93 95 96' **97 98** 99' **00** 01 02' 03 04 05' GRAND CRU neighbour of CHAMBERTIN (6.8 ha). Similar wine but lighter and "prettier", e.g. from FAIVELEY, LEROY, Trapet.

Laudun S Rh w r p ★ **00 01 03 04** 05 Village of CÔTES DU RHÔNE-VILLAGES (W bank). Soft reds. Attractive wines from Serre de Bernon co-op, inc fresh whites. Dom Pelaquié best, esp CH Courac, Dom Duseigneur, Prieuré St-Pierre.

Laurent-Perrier Brut NV; Rosé NV; Brut **95 96 98** 99. Dynamic family-owned CHAMPAGNE house at Tours-sur-Marne. V.gd minerally NV; excellent luxury brands: Grand Siècle La CUVÉE Lumière du Millésime (**90 96**), CGS Alexandra Brut Rosé (**96'** 99). Also Ultra Brut. Owns SALON, Delamotte, DE CASTELLANE.

Lavilledieu-du-Temple SW France r p w ★ DYA Fruity wines mostly from co-op nr Montauban, also experimenting with regional varieties. Also Dom de Rouch.

Leflaive, Domaine Burg ★★★★ Among the best white burgundy growers, at PULIGNY-MONTRACHET. Best v'yds: Bienvenues-, CHEVALIER-MONTRACHET, Folatières, Pucelles, and (since 1991) Le Montrachet. Also Macon from 2004. Ever-finer wines on biodynamic principles.

Leflaive, Olivier Burg ★★→★★★ High-quality négociant at PULIGNY-MONTRACHET, cousin of the above. Reliable wines, mostly white, but drink them young.

Leroy, Domaine Burg ★★★★ DOMAINE built around purchase of Noëllat in VOSNE-ROMANÉE in 1988 and Leroy family holdings (known as d'Auvenay). Extraordinary quality (and prices) from tiny biodynamic yields.

Leroy, Maison Burg ★★★★ The ultimate négociant-eleveur at AUXEY-DURESSES with sky-high standards and the finest stocks of expensive old wine in Burgundy.

Limoux Pyr r w ★★ AC for sparkling BLANQUETTE DE LIMOUX or better CRÉMANT de Limoux, also méthode ancestrale. Oak-aged CHARD for white Limoux AC. Red AC since 2003 based on Merlot, plus Syrah, Grenache, Cabernets, Carignan. Pinot N in CRÉMANT or for VIN DE PAYS. Growers: Doms de Fourn, des Martinolles, Rives Blanques. Gd co-op: Sieur d'Arques.

Liquoreux Term for a very sweet wine: e.g. SAUTERNES, top VOUVRAY, JURANCON, etc.

Lirac S Rh r p w ★★ 98' 99' 00' 01' 03 **04** 05 Next to TAVEL. Approachable gd-value red (often can age 5+ yrs) often soft, but firmer with increased use of Mourvèdre. Red overtaking rosé, esp Doms Cantegril, Devoy-Martine, Joncier, Lafond Roc-Epine, Maby (Fermade), André Méjan, de la Mordorée, Rocalière, R Sabon, F Zobel, Clos de Sixte, CH d'Aquéria, de Bouchassy, St-Roch, Ségriès. Gd whites.

Listel Midi r p w ★→★★ DYA Vast (over 1,600 ha) estate on SABLES DU GOLFE DU LION. Owned by VRANKEN. Best known for rosé Gris de Gris. Light vins des sables, inc sp. Also Dom du Bosquet-Canet; Dom de Villeroy; fruity, low-alcohol PÉTILLANT, CH de Malijay; also Abbaye de Ste-Hilaire; CH La Gordonne in Provence.

Listrac-Médoc B'x r ★★→★★★ 95 96 98 00' 01 03 04 (05) Neighbour of MOULIS in the southern MÉDOC. Grown-up clarets with tannic grip. Now rounded out with more Merlot. Best chx: CLARKE, FONRÉAUD, FOURCAS-DUPRÉ, FOURCAS-HOSTEN, Mayne-Lalande. Also gd co-op.

Livinière, La See MINERVOIS-LA LIVINIÈRE.

Long-Depaquit Burg ★★★ V.gd CHABLIS DOMAINE (esp MOUTONNE), owned by BICHOT.

Lorentz, Gustave ★★ ALSACE grower and merchant at Bergheim. Esp GEWURZ, Ries from GRAND CRUS Altenberg de Bergheim, Kanzlerberg. Also owns Jerome Lorentz. Equally gd for top estate and volume wines.

Loron & Fils ★→★★☉Big-scale grower and merchant at Pontanevaux; specialist in BEAUJOLAIS and sound VINS DE TABLE.

Loupiac B'x w sw ★★ 96 97' 98 99' **01 02 03'** (05) Across River Garonne from SAUTERNES. Lighter and fresher in style. Top chx: CLOS-Jean, LOUPIAC-GAUDIET, Mémoires, Noble, RICAUD, Les Roques.

Lugny See MÂCON-LUGNY.

Lussac-St-Emilion B'x r ★★ 95 98 00' 01 03 (05) Lighter and more rustic than neighbouring ST-EMILION. Co-op the main producer. Top chx: Barbe Blanche, Bel Air, Bellevue, de la Grenière, de Lussac, Mayne-Blanc, DU LYONNAT.

Macération carbonique Traditional fermentation technique: whole bunches of unbroken grapes in a closed vat. Fermentation induced inside each grape eventually bursts it, giving vivid, fruity, mild wine, not for ageing. Esp in BEAUJOLAIS; now much used in the MIDI and elsewhere, even CHÂTEAUNEUF.

Mâcon Burg r w (p) DYA Sound, usually unremarkable reds (Gamay best), tasty dry (CHARD) whites. Also MÂCON Superieur (similar).

Mâcon-Lugny Burg (r) w sp ★★ **02' 03 04 05'** Village next to VIRE with huge and v.gd co-op (4 million bottles). Les Genevrières is sold by LOUIS LATOUR.

Mâcon-Villages Burg w ★★→★★★ **02' 03 04 05'** Increasingly well-made (when not over-produced). Named after villages, *e.g.* Mâcon-Lugny, -Prissé, -Uchizy. Best co-op: Prissé, Lugny. Best: Vincent (Fuissé), THEVENET, Bonhomme, Guillemot-Michel, Lafon, Merlin (La Roche Vineuse). See VIRÉ-CLESSÉ.

The Mâconnais

This hilly zone just north of BEAUJOLAIS has outcrops of limestone where CHARD gives full, if not often fine, wines. The village of CHARD here may (or may not) be the home of the variety. Granite soils give light Gamay reds. The top Mâconnais AC is POUILLY-FUISSÉ, followed by POUILLY-VINZELLES, ST-VÉRAN, VIRÉ-CLESSÉ, then MÂCON-VILLAGES with a village name. Most wines are less than extraordinary but things are looking up.

Macvin Jura w sw ★★ AC for "traditional" MARC and grape-juice apéritif.

Madiran SW France r ★★→★★★ 95' 98 00' 01 02 03 **04** (05) Dark, vigorous, characterful Gascon red, mainly from Tannat. Needs age. Try Montus, Barbazan, Bouscassé, Berthoumieu, Chapelle Lenclos, Labranche-Laffont, Laffont, Laplace, Laffitte-Teston, Capmartin, Barréjat, du Crampilh, CLOS Fardet. Gd co-ops Crouseilles, Plaimont, Castelnau-Rivière-Basse. White AC PACHERENC DU VIC BILH.

Magnum A double bottle (1.5 litres).

Mähler-Besse First-class Dutch négociant in BORDEAUX. Has share in CH PALMER.

Mailly-Champagne Top champagne co-op. Luxury wine: Cuvée des Echansons.

Maire, Henri ★→★★★ The biggest grower/merchant of JURA wines, with half of the entire AC. Some top wines, many cheerfully commercial. Fun to visit.

Mann, Albert ★→★★★★ Top growers of ALSACE at Wettolsheim using low yields to produce rich, elegant wines. V.gd Pinot Bl Auxerrois and Pinot N, and gd range of GRAND CRU wines from SCHLOSSBERG, HENGST, FURSTENTUM and Steingrubler.

Maranges Burg r (w) ★★ 99' 01 02' 03' 04 05' CÔTE DE BEAUNE AC beyond SANTENAY (243 ha): one-third PREMIER CRU. Best from Contat-Grange, DROUHIN, GIRARDIN.

Marc Grape skins after pressing; also the strong-smelling brandy made from them (the equivalent of Italian grappa; see Italy chapter).

Marcillac SW France r p ★→★★ DYA (But prestige CUVÉES will keep.) AC from 1990. Violet-hued with grassy red-fruit character. Gd co-op at Valady. Try J-L Matha, Doms du Cros, Costes, , Mioula.

Margaux B'x r ★★→★★★★ 88' 89 90' 95 96 98 99 00' 01 02 03 04 (05) Largest communal AC in the southern MÉDOC, grouping vineyards from five villages, inc Margaux itself and Cantenac. Known for its elegant, fragrant style. Top chx inc MARGAUX, RAUZAN-SÉGLA, PALMER, etc.

Marionnet, Henry Lo ★→★★★ 02 03 04 05 Leading TOURAINE property specializing in Gamay and Sauv Bl. Top CUVÉE Le M de Marionnet. Other CUVÉES: Provignage (from Romorantin grape) and Vinifera (Chenin and Cot from ungrafted vines).

Marne & Champagne Recent but huge-scale CHAMPAGNE house, and many smaller brands, inc BESSERAT DE BELLEFON. Alfred Rothschild brand v.gd CHARD-based wines. Sold Lanson brand in 2006 to Boizel Chanoine group.

Marque déposée Trademark.

Marsannay Burg p r (w) ★★ 99' 01 02' 03 04 05' (rosé DYA) Village with fine, light red and delicate Pinot N rosé. Inc villages of Chenôve, Couchey. Growers: CHARLOPIN, CLAIR, JADOT, MÉO-CAMUZET, ROTY, Trapet.

Mas de Daumas Gassac Midi r w p ★★★ 90 91 92 93 94 95' 96' 97 98' 99 00' 01' 02 03' 04 Pioneering estate that set an example of excellence in the Midi, with Cabernet-based reds produced on apparently unique soil. Quality now rivalled by others. Wines inc new super-CUVÉE Emile Peynaud, rosé Frisant, rich, fragrant white blend to drink at 2–3 yrs. Also quick-drinking red, Les Terrasses de Guilhem, from nearby co-op and traditional Languedoc varietals (Clairette, Cinsault, Aramon, etc.) from old vines under Terrasses de Landoc label. VIN DE PAYS status. Intriguing sweet wine: Vin de Laurence (Sem, MUSCATS, Sercial).

Maury Pyr r sw ★★ NV Red VIN DOUX NATUREL of Grenache from ROUSSILLON. From Grenache grown on an island of schist amid limestone and clay. Much recent improvement, esp at Mas Amiel. Also good table wines.

Mazis- (or Mazy) Chambertin Burg r ★★★ 88' 89' 90' 91 93 95 96' 97 98 99' 00 01 02' 03 04 05' GRAND CRU neighbour of CHAMBERTIN (12 ha); can be equally potent. Best from FAIVELEY, HOSPICES DE BEAUNE, LEROY, Maume, ROTY.

Mazoyères-Chambertin See CHARMES-CHAMBERTIN.

Médoc B'x r ★★ 90' 95 96 98 00' 02 03 04 (05) AC for reds in the flatter, northern part of the MÉDOC peninsula. Good if you're selective. Earthy, with Merlot adding flesh. Top chx inc GREYSAC, LOUDENNE, LES ORMES-SORBET, POTENSAC, Rollan-de-By (HAUT-CONDISSAS), LA TOUR-DE-BY.

Meffre, Gabriel ★★ Biggest S Rhône estate, based at GIGONDAS. Owns Dom Longue Toque. Variable quality, recent progress. Also bottles and sells for small CHÂTEAUNEUF doms. Decent N Rhône Laurus (new oak) range.

Mellot, Alphonse Lo ★★→★★★ 00 01 02 03 04 Leading SANCERRE grower. La Moussière is the entry-level red and white; special CUVÉES: wood-aged CUVÉE Edmond, Génération XIX (red and white), Les Demoiselles and En Grands Champs (red). Also v'yds in Charitois (VdP), both CHARD and Pinot N.

Menetou-Salon Lo r p w ★★ DYA Highly attractive similar wines from W of SANCERRE: Sauv Bl white full of charm, Pinot N light to medium-bodied red. Top growers: Clement, Henry Pellé, Jean-Max Roger, Bourgeois.

Méo-Camuzet ★★★★ Very fine DOMAINE in CLOS DE VOUGEOT, NUITS-ST-GEORGES, RICHEBOURG, VOSNE-ROMANÉE. JAYER-inspired. Esp VOSNE-ROMANÉE Cros Parantoux. Now also some less expensive négociant CUVÉES.

Mercier & Cie, Champagne Brut NV; Brut Rosé NV; Demi-Sec Brut One of biggest CHAMPAGNE houses at Epernay. Controlled by MOËT & CHANDON. Fair commercial quality, sold mainly in France. Gd powerful Pinot N-led CUVÉE Eugene Mercier.

Mercurey Burg r ★★→★★★ 96' 98 99' 01 02' 03 04 05' Leading red wine village of CÔTE CHALONNAISE. Gd middle-rank burgundy, inc improving whites. Try CH de Chamirey, FAIVELEY, M Juillot, Lorenzon, Raquillet, Dom de Suremain.

Mercurey, Région de The alternative name for the CÔTE CHALONNAISE.

Mérode, Domaine Prince de ★★★ Once more a top DOMAINE for CORTON and POMMARD.

Mesnil-sur-Oger, Le Champ ★★★★ One of the top Côte des Blancs villages. Structured CHARD for very long ageing.

Métaireau, Louis Lo w ★★→★★★ 89 90 95 96 02 03 04 05 A key figure in the MUSCADET quality revolution. His daughter now runs the estate. Expensive well-finished wines: Number One, CUVÉES Grand Mouton and MLM.

Méthode champenoise Traditional laborious method of putting bubbles into CHAMPAGNE by refermenting wine in its bottle. Must use terms "classic method" or "méthode traditionnelle" outside region. Not mentioned on labels.

Méthode traditionnelle See entry above.

Meursault Burg w (r) ★★★→★★★★ 89' 90 92 95 97 99' 00' 01 02' 04 05' CÔTE DE BEAUNE village with some of world's greatest whites: savoury, dry, nutty, mellow. Best v'yds: Charmes, Genevrières, Perrières. Also gd: Goutte d'Or, Meursault-Blagny, Poruzots, Narvaux, Tesson, Tillets. Producers inc: AMPEAU, J-M BOILLOT, M Bouzereau, Boyer-Martenot, CH de MEURSAULT, COCHE-DURY, Ente, Fichet, Grivault, P Javillier, JOBARD, LAFON, LATOUR, O LEFLAIVE, LEROY, Manuel, Matrot, Mikulski, P MOREY, G ROULOT. See also BLAGNY.

Meursault-Blagny See BLAGNY.

Michel, Louis ★★★ CHABLIS DOMAINE with model unoaked, very long-lived wines, inc superb LES CLOS, v.gd Montmains, Montée de Tonnerre.

Microbullage Technique invented by Patrick DUCOURNAU: oxygen is injected into ageing wine to avoid racking, stimulate aeration, and accelerate maturity.

Midi Broad term covering Languedoc, Roussillon, and even Provence. A melting-pot; quality improves with every vintage. ACS can be intriguing blends; VINS DE PAYS, especially d'OC, are often varietals. Brilliant promise.

Minervois Midi r (p w) br sw ★→★★★ 98 99 00 01 02 03 04 05 Hilly AC region; gd, lively wines, esp CH Bonhomme, Coupe-Roses, la Grave, Villerembert-Julien, Oupia, La Tour Boisée, CLOS Centeilles Ste Eulalie, Faiteau; co-ops LA LIVINIÈRE, de Peyriac, Pouzols. Sw Minervois Noble being developed. See ST-JEAN DE MINERVOIS.

Minervois-La Livinière, La Midi r (p w) ★→★★ Quality village (see last entry) the only sub-appellation or *cru* in Minervois. Best growers: Abbaye de Tholomies, Borie de Maurel, Combe Blanche, CH de Gourgazaud, CLOS Centeilles, Laville-Bertrou, Doms Maris, Ste-Eulalie, Co-op La Livinière, Vipur.

Mis en bouteille au château/domaine Bottled at the CHÂTEAU, property or estate. NB *dans nos caves* (in our cellars) or *dans la région de production* (in the area of production) are often used but mean little.

Mittnacht Freres, Domaine ★★ Rising ALSACE star with v'yds in Riquewihr and Hunawihr. Lovely Pinot Bl, fine Ries (GRAND CRU ROSACKER), excellent Pinot Gr.

Moelleux "With marrow": creamy-sweet. Sweet wines of VOUVRAY, COTEAUX DU LAYON.

Moët & Chandon Brut NV; Rosé 99 00; Brut Imperial 99 00. Largest CHAMPAGNE merchant/grower with cellars in Epernay; branches in Argentina, Australia, Brazil, California, Germany, Spain. Consistent quality, esp vintages. Prestige CUVÉE: DOM PERIGNON. Impressive multi-vintage Esprit du Siècle, GRANDS CRUS Aÿ Chouilly, and Sillery bottlings. Coteaux Champenois Saran: still wine.

Moillard Burg ★★→★★★ Big family firm in NUITS-ST-GEORGES, making full range, inc dark and very tasty wines.

Mommessin, J ★→★★**O**Major BEAUJOLAIS merchant now owned by BOISSET. Owner of CLOS DE TART. White wines less successful than reds.

Monbazillac Dordogne w sw ★★→★★★★ 95' 97 98' 00 01' 02 03' (04) (05) Golden SAUTERNES-style wine from BERGERAC. At best can equal Sauternes, as at Tirecul-la-Gravière. Top producers: L'Ancienne Cure, CHX de Belingard-Chayne, Bellevue, Le Fagé, Les Hauts de Caillavel, Poulvère, Theulet, Dom de la Haute-Brie et du Caillou, and La Grande Maison. Also Co-op de Monbazillac.

Mondeuse Savoie r ★★ DYA SAVOIE red grape. Potentially gd, deep-coloured, vigorous wine. Possibly same as NE Italy's Refosco. Don't miss a chance, *e.g.* G Berlioz.

Monopole A v'yd that is under single ownership.

Montagne-St-Emilion B'x r ★★ 95 96 98 00' 01 03 (05) Largest and possibly best satellite of ST-EMILION. Similar style of wine. Top chx: Calon, Faizeau, Maison Blanche, Montaiguillon, Roudier, Teyssier, VIEUX-CH-ST-ANDRE.

Montagny Burg ★★ 02' 03 04 05' CÔTE CHALONNAISE village. Between MÂCON and MEURSAULT, both geographically and gastronomically. Top producers: Aladame, J-M BOILLOT, Cave de Buxy, Michel, CH de la Saule.

Monthelie Burg r (w) ★★→★★★ 95 96' 97 98 99' 01 02' 03 04 Little-known VOLNAY neighbour, sometimes almost equal. Excellent fragrant red, esp BOUCHARD PÈRE & FILS, COCHE-DURY, LAFON, DROUHIN, Garaudet, CH de Monthelie (Suremain).

Montille, Hubert de Burg ★★★ VOLNAY and POMMARD DOMAINE to note. Important new v'yds from 2005. Etienne de Montille is now also responsible for CH de Puligny.

Montlouis Lo w dr sw (sp) ★★→★★★ 88 89 90 93 95 96 97 02 03 04 05 Neighbour of VOUVRAY. Makes similar sweet or long-lived dry wines; also sp. Top growers inc Alex-Mathur, Berger, Chidaine, Cossais, Damien Delecheneau/la Grange Tiphaine, Deletang, Moyer, Frantz Saumon, Taille aux Loups.

Montrachet Burg w ★★★★ 1904 35 47 49 59 64 66 71 73 78 79 82 85' 86 88 89' 90 92' 93 95 96' 97 98 99 00' 01 02' 03 04 05' (Both t's in the name are silent.) 7.6-ha GRAND CRU v'yd in both PULIGNY- and CHASSAGNE-MONTRACHET. Potentially the greatest white burgundy: strong, perfumed, intense, dry yet luscious. Top wines from LAFON, LAGUICHE (DROUHIN), LEFLAIVE, RAMONET, ROMANÉE-CONTI. But THENARD disappointing.

Montravel Dordogne ★★ p dr w DYA r 01 02 04 (05) Now AC, similar to BERGERAC. Gd examples from Doms de Krevel, Gouyat, De Bloy, Jonc Blanc, Masmontet, Masburel, Laulerie, Moulin-Caresse. Separate ACS for semi-sweet CÔTES DE MONTRAVEL and sweet HAUT-MONTRAVEL.

Morey, Domaines Burg ★★★ Various family members in CHASSAGNE-MONTRACHET, esp Bernard, inc BÂTARD-MONTRACHET. Also Pierre M in MEURSAULT.

Morey-St-Denis Burg r ★★★ 88 89' 90' 93 95 96' 97 98 99' 00 01 02' 03 04 05' Small village with four GRANDS CRUS between GEVREY-CHAMBERTIN and CHAMBOLLE-MUSIGNY. Glorious wine often overlooked. Inc Amiot, DUJAC, H Lignier, Moillard-Grivot, Perrot-Minot, PONSOT, ROUMIER, ROUSSEAU, Serveau.

Morgon Beauj r ★★★ 95 96 98 99' 00 01 03 05' The firmest *cru* of BEAUJOLAIS, needing time to develop its rich savoury flavour. Try Aucoeur, CH de Bellevue, Desvignes, J Foillard, Lapierre, CH de Pizay. DUBOEUF excellent.

Mortet, Denis ★★★ Splendid perfectionist GEVREY DOMAINE. Super wines since 93, in a range of village Gevreys and excellent PREMIER CRU Lavaux St-Jacques. Ultra-concentrated style.

Moueix, J-P et Cie B'x Legendary proprietor and merchant of ST-EMILION and

POMEROL. CHX inc: LA FLEUR-PÉTRUS, MAGDELAINE, and PÉTRUS. Also in California: see Dominus. Alain Moueix, who owns CH FONROQUE in St-Emilion, is cousin to Christian Moueix, who runs J-P Moueix.

Moulin-à-Vent Beauj r ★★★ 93 95 96' 98 99 00 01 03 04 05' The biggest and potentially best wine of BEAUJOLAIS. Can be powerful, meaty, and long-lived; can even taste like fine Rhône or burgundy. Many gd growers, esp CH du Moulin-à-Vent, CH des Jacques, Dom des Hospices, Janodet, JADOT, Merlin.

Moulis B'x r ★★→★★★ 95 96 98 00' 02 03 04 (05) Inland AC in the southern MÉDOC next to LISTRAC, with several leading CRUS BOURGEOIS: CHASSE-SPLEEN, MAUCAILLOU, POUJEAUX (THEIL). Gd hunting ground.

Mousseux Sparkling.

Mouton Cadet Popular brand of blended (r w) BORDEAUX. Not a quality leader.

Moutonne ★★★ CHABLIS GRAND CRU *honoris causa* (between VAUDESIR and Preuses), owned by BICHOT.

Mugneret/Mugneret-Gibourg Burg ★★★ Superb reds from top CÔTE DE NUITS sites.

Mugnier, J-F Burg ★★★→★★★★ NUITS-ST-GEORGES CH de Chambolle estate with first-class delicate CHAMBOLLE-MUSIGNY Les Amoureuses and MUSIGNY. Also BONNES-MARES. From 2004 has reclaimed family's CLOS de la Maréchale.

Mumm, G H & Cie Cordon Rouge NV; Mumm de Cramant NV; Cordon Rouge 95 96' 98; Rosé NV Major CHAMPAGNE grower and merchant. NV much improved by new winemaker; new top GRAND CRU CUVÉE. Also in California, Chile, Argentina, South Africa (Cape Mumm).

Muré, Clos St-Landelin ★★→★★★★❶One of ALSACE's great names with 16 ha of GRAND CRU Vorbourg. Unusually ripe Pinot N, full-bodied Ries and GEWURZ, and fine MUSCAT. Also v.gd CRÉMANT.

Muscadet Lo w ★→★★★ DYA (but see below) Popular, gd-value, often delicious very dry wine from nr Nantes. Should never be sharp, but should have a faint iodine tang. Perfect with fish and seafood. Best are from zonal ACS: MUSCADET-COTEAUX DE LA LOIRE, MUSCADET CÔTES DE GRAND LIEU, MUSCADET DE SEVRE-ET-MAINE. Choose a SUR LIE.

Muscadet Côtes de Grand Lieu ★→★★ 02 03 04 Recent (1995) zonal AC for MUSCADET named after the Lac de Grand Lieu in the middle of the zone. Best are SUR LIE from, *e.g.*, Bâtard, Luc Choblet, Malidain.

Muscadet-Coteaux de la Loire Lo w ★→★★ 02 03 04 Small MUSCADET zone E of Nantes (best SUR LIE). Esp Guindon, Luneau-Papin, Les Vignerons de la Noëlle.

Muscadet de Sèvre-et-Maine ★→★★★ 90 93 95 96 97 98 99 00 01 02 03 04 Wine from delimited central (best) part of area. Top growers: Guy Bossard (ECU), Chasseloir, Coing, Bruno Cormerai, Dom de la Haute Fevrie, Michel Delhomeau, Douillard, Landron, Luneau-Papin, METAIREAU. 01 can be perfection.

Muscat Distinctively perfumed and usually sweet wine, often fortified as VIN DOUX NATUREL. Made dry and not fortified in ALSACE, where it is the main apéritif wine. Also a white white grape.

Muscat de Beaumes-de-Venise See BEAUMES-DE-VENISE.

Muscat de Frontignan See FRONTIGNAN.

Muscat de Lunel Midi golden sw ★★ NV Ditto. Small AC based on MUSCAT, usually fortified, luscious, and sweet. Some experimental late-harvest wines. Look for Dom CLOS Bellevue, Grès St Paul.

Muscat de Mireval Midi sw ★★ NV Tiny Muscat-based AC nr Montpellier. Dom La Capelle.

Muscat de Rivesaltes Midi golden sw ★★ NV Sweet MUSCAT AC wine nr Perpignan. Quality variable; best from Cazes Frères, CH de Jau.

Musigny Burg r (w) ★★★★ 85' 88' 89' 90' 91 93 95 96' 97 98 99' 00 01 02' 03 04 05' GRAND CRU in CHAMBOLLE-MUSIGNY (10 ha). Can be the most beautiful, if not

FRANCE

the most powerful, of all red burgundies. Best growers: DROUHIN, JADOT, LEROY, MUGNIER, PRIEUR, ROUMIER, DE VOGÜÉ, VOUGERAIE.

Napoléon Brand name of family-owned Prieur CHAMPAGNE house at Vertus. Excellent Carte d'Or NV and first-rate vintages, esp **95 96**.

Nature "Natural" or "unprocessed" – esp of still CHAMPAGNE.

Négociant-éleveur Merchant who "brings up" (*i.e.* matures) the wine.

Nuits-St-Georges Burg r ★★→★★★★ 90' 91 93 95 96' 97 98 99' 00 01 02' 03 04 05' Important wine town: wines of all qualities, typically sturdy, tannic, need time. Often shortened to "Nuits". Best v'yds: Les Cailles, CLOS de la Maréchale, CLOS des Corvées, Les Pruliers, Les St-Georges, Vaucrains. Many merchants and growers: L'ARLOT, Ambroise, J Chauvenet, R CHEVILLON, CONFURON, FAIVELEY, GOUGES, GRIVOT, Lechéneaut, LEROY, Machard de Gramont, Michelot, RION,

d'Oc (Vin de Pays d'Oc) Midi r p w ★→★★ Regional VIN DE PAYS for Languedoc and ROUSSILLON. Esp single-grape wines and VINS DE PAYS PRIMEURS. Tremendous technical advances recently. Main producers: VAL D'ORBIEU, SKALLI, Jeanjean, merchants and village co-ops, plus numerous small individual growers.

Oisly & Thesée, Vignerons de ★★ 02 03 04 05 Go-ahead co-op in E TOURAINE (Loire), with gd Sauv Bl (esp CUVÉE Excellence), Cab Sauv, Gamay, Côt, and CHARD. Blends labelled Baronnie d'Aignan and gd DOMAINE wines some organic.

Orléans Lo r p w ★ DYA Small VDQS for CHARD-based whites, and reds and roses from Pinot Meunier and Pinot N. Formerly Vin de l'Orléanais.

Orléans-Clery Lo r ★ Small VDQS for Cab Fr-based reds. Formerly Vin de l'Orléanais.

Pacherenc du Vic-Bilh SW Fr w dr sw ★★ The white wine of MADIRAN. Dry (DYA) and (better) sweet (age up to 5 yrs for oaked versions). For growers see MADIRAN.

Paillard, Bruno Brut Première Cuvée NV; Rosé Première CUVÉE; Chard Réserve Privée, Brut 96' 98. New Vintage BLANC DE BLANCS 96' 98. Superb Nec Plus Ultra Prestige CUVÉE (95 96). Young top-flight CHAMPAGNE house. Also owns CH de Sarrin in Provence.

Palette Prov r p w ★★ Tiny AC nr Aix-en-Provence. Full reds, fragrant rosés, and intriguing whites from CH SIMONE, the only notable producer.

Pasquier-Desvignes ★→★★★ Very old firm of BEAUJOLAIS merchants nr BROUILLY.

Patriarche Burg ★→★★★ One of the bigger burgundy merchants. Cellars in BEAUNE; also owns CH DE MEURSAULT (61 ha), sparkling KRITER, etc.

Patrimonio Corsica r w p ★★→★★★ 98 99 00 01 02 03 04 05 Wide range from dramatic chalk hills in N CORSICA. Some of the island's best. Characterful reds from Nielluccio, whites from Vermentino. Top growers: Gentile, Leccia, Arena.

Pauillac B'x r ★★★→★★★★ 82' 83 85' 86' 88' 89' 90' 93 94 95' 96' 98 99 00' 01 02 03' 04' (05) Communal AC in the MÉDOC with three first-growths (LAFITE, LATOUR, MOUTON). Famous for its powerful, long-lived wines Many other fine CHX.

Pécharmant Dordogne r ★★→★★★ 98' 00' 01 02 (04) (05) Inner AC for top BERGERAC red, for ageing. Best: La Métairie, Dom du Haut-Pécharmant, CHX Champarel, d'Elle, Terre Vieille, de Tilleraie, de Tiregand. Also (from Bergerac co-op) Doms Brisseau-Belloc, du Vieux Sapin, CH le Charmeil.

Pelure d'oignon "Onion skin" – tawny tint of certain rosés.

Perlant or **Perlé** Very slightly sparkling.

Pernand-Vergelesses Burg r (w) ★★→★★★ 96' 97 98 99' 01 02' 03' 04 Village next to ALOXE-CORTON containing part of the great CORTON-CHARLEMAGNE and CORTON v'yds. One other top v'yd: Ile des Vergelesses. Growers: CHANDON DE BRIAILLES, CHANSON, Delarche, Dubreuil-Fontaine, JADOT, LATOUR, Rapet, Rollin.

Perrier-Jouët Brut NV; Blason de France NV; Blason de France Rosé NV;

Brut **98** Excellent CHAMPAGNE house at Epernay, the first to make dry CHAMPAGNE, and once the smartest name of all; now best for vintage wines. Luxury brand: Belle Epoque **96 98** (Rosé **99**) in a painted bottle.

Pessac-Léognan B'x r w ★★★→★★★★ **90' 95 96 98** 00' 01 02 04 (05) AC for the best part of N GRAVES, inc area of most of the GRANDS CRUS, HAUT-BRION, PAPE-CLÉMENT etc. Minerally reds and also B'x's finest dry whites.

Pétillant Vinous, slightly sparkling wine from VOUVRAY and MONTLOUIS.

Petit Chablis Burg w ★ DYA Wine from fourth-rank CHABLIS v'yds. Not much character but can be pleasantly fresh. Best: co-op La Chablisienne.

Pfaffenheim ★★ Respectable ALSACE co-op. Strongly individual wines, inc gd Sylvaner and v.gd Pinots (N, Gr, Bl). GRANDS CRUS: Goldert, Steinert, and Hatschbourg. Hartenberger CRÉMANT d'Alsace is v.gd. Also owns DOPFF & IRION.

Pfersigberg Eguisheim ALSACE GRAND CRU with two parcels; very aromatic wines. GEWURZ does very well. Ries, esp Paul Ginglinger, Bruno SORG, and Léon BEYER Comtes d'Eguisheim. Top grower: KUENTZ-BAS.

Philipponnat NV; Rosé NV; Réserve Spéciale **98** 99; CLOS des Goisses **95 96'** 98 Small CHAMPAGNE house known for well-structured wines and now owned by BOIZEL Chanoine group. Remarkable single-v'yd CLOS des Goisses and charming rosé. Also Le Reflet BRUT NV.

Piat Père & Fils ★❶Big-scale merchant of BEAUJOLAIS and MÂCON. Owned by Diageo.

Pic St-Loup Midi ★→★★ r (p) **96 97 98 99 00** 01 02 03 04 Notable COTEAUX DU LANGUEDOC *cru*, anticipating own AC, from vineyards around mountain N of Montpellier. Growers: CHX de Cazeneuve, CLOS Marie, de Lancyre, Lascaux, Mas Bruguière, Dom de l'Hortus.

Picpoul de Pinet Midi w ★→★★ Improving AC exclusively from the old variety Picpoul. Best growers: CH St Martin de la Garrigue, Félines-Jourdan, Co-op Pomérols.

Pineau des Charentes Strong, sweet apéritif: white grape juice and COGNAC.

Piper-Heidsieck CHAMPAGNE-makers of old repute at Reims. Much improved Brut NV and fruit-driven Brut Rosé Sauvage; Brut **96 98** 99. Excellent new CUVÉE Sublime DEMI-SEC, rich yet balanced.

Plageoles, Robert Arch-priest of GAILLAC and defender of the lost grape varieties of the Tarn. Amazingly eccentric wines include a VIN JAUNE left to oxidize like sherry, an ultra-sweet dessert wine from Ondenc grapes left to dry in the sun. Outstanding range of wines from Mauzac, inc sparkler.

Pol Roger Brut White Foil now renamed Brut Réserve NV; Brut **90' 96' 98**; Rosé **96 98**; Blanc de CHARD **98'**. Supreme family-owned CHAMPAGNE house at Epernay, now with vines in AVIZE joining 85 ha of family vineyards. Esp gd floral-silky NV White Foil, Rosé, and CHARD. Sumptuous CUVÉE: Sir Winston Churchill (**95 96**).

Pomerol B'x r ★★★→★★★★ 85 86 88 89' 90' 94 95 96 98' 00' 01 04 (05) Next village to ST-EMILION but no limestone; only clay, gravel, and sand. Famed for its Merlot-dominated full, rich, unctuous style. Top chx inc CERTAN-DE-MAY, L'EVANGILE, LAFLEUR, LA FLEUR-PETRUS, LATOUR-À-POMEROL, PÉTRUS, LE PIN, TROTANOY, VIEUX-CH-CERTAN.

Pommard Burg r ★★★ 88' 89' 90' **95** 96' 97 98 99' 01 02' 03 04 05' The biggest CÔTE D'OR village. Few superlative wines, but many potent and tannic ones to age 10+ yrs. Best v'yds: Epenots, HOSPICES DE BEAUNE CUVÉES, Rugiens. Growers inc COMTE ARMAND, Billard-Gonnet, J-M BOILLOT, DOM DE COURCEL, Gaunoux, LEROY, Machard de Gramont, DE MONTILLE, CH de Pommard, Pothier-Rieussel.

Pommery Brut NV; Rosé NV; Brut **99** 00 Historic CHAMPAGNE house; brand now owned by VRANKEN. Outstanding CUVÉE Louise (**95 96 98**) and Rosé (**96 99**).

Ponsot ★★★★ Controversial MOREY-ST-DENIS estate. Idiosyncratic high-quality GRANDS CRUS, inc CHAMBERTIN, CHAPELLE-CHAMBERTIN, CLOS DE LA ROCHE, CLOS ST-DENIS.

Portes de la Mediterranée New regional VIN DE PAYS from S Rhône/PROVENCE. Easy reds and interesting whites, inc Viognier.

Potel, Nicolas Burg ★★→★★★ Potel founded a small négociant after his father's Dom de la POUSSE D'OR was sold. Impressive reds, esp BOURGOGNE Rouge, VOLNAY, NUITS-ST-GEORGES. Now owned by LABOURÉ-ROI.

Pouilly-Fuissé Burg w ★★→★★★ 95 97 99' 00' 02' 03 04 05' The best white of the MÂCON region, potent and dense. At its best (e.g. CH Fuissé VIEILLES VIGNES) outstanding, but usually over-priced compared with CHABLIS. Top growers: Bret Bros, Ferret, Luquet, Merlin, CH des Rontets, Saumaize, Valette, VERGET, Vincent.

Pouilly-Fumé Lo w ★★→★★★★ 02 03 04 05 Full, mineral white from upper Loire, nr SANCERRE. Must be Sauv Bl. Best CUVÉES can improve 5–6 yrs. Top growers inc Cailbourdin, Chatelain, Didier DAGUENEAU, Serge Dagueneau & Filles, CH de Favray, Edmond and André Figeat, LADOUCETTE, Masson-Blondelet, CH de Tracy, Masson-Blondelet, CAVE de Pouilly-sur-Loire, Redde.

Pouilly-Loché Burg w ★★ 99 00' 02' 03 04 05' POUILLY-FUISSÉ's neighbour. Similar, cheaper; scarce. Can be sold as POUILLY-VINZELLES.

Pouilly-Vinzelles Burg w ★★ 99 00' 02' 03 04 05' Superior neighbour to POUILLY-LOCHE, best QUARTS v'yd. Best producers Bret Bros, Valette.

Pouilly-sur-Loire Lo w ★ DYA Neutral wine from the same v'yds as POUILLY-FUMÉ but different grapes (Chasselas). Rarely seen today, ever-diminishing. Best from Serge Dagueneau & Filles.

Pousse d'Or, Domaine de la Burg ★★★ 13-ha estate in POMMARD, SANTENAY, and esp VOLNAY, where its MONOPOLES Bousse d'Or and CLOS des 60 Ouvrées are powerful, tannic, and were justly famous under Gérard Potel (manager 1964–96). Signs of gd wines under new ownership.

Premier Cru (1er Cru) First-growth in BORDEAUX; second rank of v'yds (after GRAND CRU) in Burgundy.

Premières Côtes de Blaye B'x r w ★→★★ 99 00' 01 03 04 (05) Mainly red AC E of the Gironde. Varied but improved quality. Top reds labelled BLAYE as of 2000. CHX inc Bel Air la Royère, Bertinerie, Gigault, Haut-Grelot, Haut-Sociando, Jonqueyres, Loumède, Mondésir-Gazin, Montfollet, Roland la Garde, Segonzac, des Tourtes.

Premières Côtes de Bordeaux B'x r w (p) dr sw ★→★★ 98 00' 01 03 (05) Long, narrow, hilly zone running down the right bank of the River Garonne opposite the GRAVES. Medium-bodied, fresh reds. Quality varied. CHX inc Carignan, Carsin, Chelivette, Grand-Mouëys, Lamothe de Haux, Lezongars, Mont-Pérat, Plaisance, Puy Bardens, Reynon, Suau.

Prieur, Domaine Jacques Burg ★★★ 16-ha estate all in top Burgundy sites, inc GRAND CRUS from MONTRACHET to CHAMBERTIN. Now 50% owned by ANTONIN RODET. Quality could still improve.

Primeur "Early" wine for refreshment and uplift; esp from BEAUJOLAIS; VINS DE PAYS too. Wine sold en primeur is still in barrel for delivery when bottled.

Prissé See MÂCON-VILLAGES.

Propriétaire-récoltant Owner-manager.

Provence See CÔTES DE PROVENCE, CASSIS, BANDOL, PALETTE, COTEAUX DES BAUX-EN-PROVENCE, BOUCHES-DU-RHÔNE, COTEAUX D'AIX-EN-PROVENCE, COTEAUX VAROIS-EN-PROVENCE, PORTES DE LA MEDITERRANÉE.

Puisseguin St-Emilion B'x r ★★ 95 96 98 00' 01 03 (05) Satellite neighbour of ST-EMILION; Wines firm and solid in style. CHX inc Bel Air, Branda, Durand-Laplagne, Fongaban, Laurets, Soleil. Also Roc de Puisseguin from co-op.

Puligny-Montrachet Burg w (r) ★★★→★★★★ 89' 92' 95 97 99' 00 01 02' 04 05' Smaller neighbour of CHASSAGNE-MONTRACHET: potentially even finer, more vital and complex wine (apparent finesse can be result of over-production). V'yds:

BÂTARD-MONTRACHET, Bienvenues-BÂTARD-MONTRACHET, Caillerets, CHEVALIER-MONTRACHET, Clavoillon, Les Combettes, MONTRACHET, Pucelles. Producers: AMPEAU, J-M BOILLOT, BOUCHARD PÈRE & FILS, L CARILLON, Chavy, DROUHIN, JADOT, LATOUR, Dom LEFLAIVE, O LEFLAIVE, Pernot, SAUZET.

Pyrénées-Atlantiques SW France DYA VIN DE PAYS for wines not qualifying for local ACS MADIRAN, PACHERENC DU VIC BILH, or JURANÇON.

Quarts de Chaume Lo w SW ★★★→★★★★ 88 89 90 95 96 97 02 03 04 05 Famous COTEAUX DU LAYON plot. Chenin Bl grown for immensely long-lived intense, rich, golden wine. Esp from BAUMARD, Claude Papin (CH PIERRE-BISE). V.gd Clos St-Jean.

Quatourze Midi r w (p) ★ 98 99 00 01 02 03 04 05 Minor *cru* of COTEAUX DE LANGUEDOC. Reputation maintained almost single-handedly by Dom Notre Dame du Quatourze (virtually sole producer).

Quincy Lo w ★→★★ DYA Small area: very dry SANCERRE-style Sauv Bl. Worth trying. Growers: Dom Mardon, Silice de Quincy, Tatin-Wilk.

Ramonet, Domaine Burg ★★→★★★★★ Leading (legendary) estate in CHASSAGNE-MONTRACHET with 17 ha, inc some MONTRACHET. V.gd Clos St-Jean.

Rancio The most characteristic style of VIN DOUX NATUREL, such as BANYULS, MAURY, wood-aged and exposed to oxygen and heat. The same flavour is a fault in table wine.

Rangen High-class ALSACE GRAND CRU in Thann, Vieux Thann. Owes reputation to ZIND-HUMBRECHT. Other main grower: SCHOFFIT. Esp: Pinot Gr, GEWURZ, Ries.

Rasteau S Rh r br sw (p w dr) ★★ 98' 99' 00' 01' 03 04' 05 Village for sound, robust reds, esp Beaurenard, caves des Vignerons, CH du Trignon, Doms Didier Charavin, Rabasse-Charavin, Girasols, Gourt de Mautens, Soumade, St-Gayan, Perrin (gd w, too). Grenache dessert wine is (declining) speciality.

Ratafia de Champagne Sweet apéritif made in CHAMPAGNE of 67% grape juice and 33% brandy. Not unlike PINEAU DES CHARENTES.

Récolte Crop or vintage.

Regnié Beauj r ★★ 01 03 05' *Cru* village between MORGON and BROUILLY. About 730 ha. Try DUBOEUF, Aucoeur, or Rampon.

Reine Pédauque, La Burg ★ Long-established grower-merchant at ALOXE-CORTON. V'yds in ALOXE-CORTON, SAVIGNY, etc., and CÔTES DU RHÔNE. Owned by Pierre ANDRÉ. Quality not impressive.

Remoissenet Père & Fils Burg ★★ Merchant (esp for whites and THENARD wines) with a tiny BEAUNE estate (2 ha). Give red time.

Reuilly Lo w (r p) ★★ Neighbour of QUINCY. Similar white. Also rosé (Pinots N, Gr), red (Pinot N). Esp Claude Lafond, Dom de Reuilly.

Ribonnet, Domaine de SW France ★★ Christian Gerber makes pioneering range of varietals (r p w) without benefit of AC in Haute Garonne and ARIÈGE.

Riceys, Rosé des Champ p ★★★ DYA Minute AC in AUBE for a notable Pinot N rosé. Principal producers: A Bonnet, Jacques Defrance.

Richeaume, Domaine Côte de Prov r ★★ Gd Cab Sauv/Syrah. Organic; a model.

Richebourg Burg r ★★★★ 78' 85' 88' 89' 90' 91 93' 95 96' 97 98 99' 00 01 02' 03 05' VOSNE-ROMANÉE GRAND CRU. Powerful, perfumed, expensive wine, among Burgundy's best. Growers: DRC, GRIVOT, J Gros, A Gros, T Liger-Belair, LEROY, MÉO-CAMUZET.

Richou, Dom Lo ★→★★ 95 96 02 03 04 05 Reliable ANJOU estate for wide range of wines, esp ANJOU-VILLAGES BRISSAC, COTEAUX DE L'AUBANCE, and Anj Bl Chauvigne and Rogeries.

Rimage Modern trend for a vintage VIN DOUX NATUREL. For early drinking.

Rion, Domaines Burg ★★★ Patrice Rion for exceptional CHAMBOLLE-MUSIGNY Cras and Charmes and NUITS-ST-GEORGES CLOS des Argillières. Daniel Rion & Fils for VOSNE-ROMANÉE (Les Chaumes, Les Beaumonts), Nuits PREMIER CRU Les Vignes Rondes and ECHÉZEAUX.

Rivesaltes Midi r w br dr sw ★★ NV Fortified wine made near Perpignan. A tradition very much alive, if struggling these days. Top producers worth seeking out: Doms Cazes, Sarda-Malet, Vaquer, des Schistes, CH de Jau. See MUSCAT DE RIVESALTES.

Roche-aux-Moines, La Lo w sw ★★→★★★ 88 89 90 93 95 96 97 99 02 03 04 05 A 24-ha v'yd in SAVENNIÈRES, ANJOU. Intense strong fruity/sharp wine; needs long ageing or drinking fresh.

Rodet, Antonin Burg ★★→★★★ Quality merchant with 134-ha estate, esp in MERCUREY (CH de Chamirey) and Dom de l'Aigle, nr Limoux. See also PRIEUR.

Roederer, Louis Brut Premier NV; Rich NV; Brut 90 93 95 96' 97 99; BLANC DE BLANCS 95 96' 97 99; Brut Rosé 96 97' 99. Top-drawer family-owned CHAMPAGNE-grower and merchant at Reims. Vanilla-rich NV with plenty of flavour. Sumptuous Cristal (may be greatest of all prestige CUVÉES) and Cristal Rosé (90' 95 96' 97). Also owns DEUTZ, DELAS, CH de PEZ. See also California.

Rolland, Michel Ubiquitous and fashionable consultant winemaker and Merlot specialist working in B'x and worldwide, favouring super-ripe flavours.

Rolly Gassmann ★★ Distinguished ALSACE grower at Rorschwihr, esp for Auxerrois and MUSCAT from *lieu-dit* Moenchreben. House style is usually off-dry. Made "Eiswein" in 2005.

Romanée, La Burg r ★★★★ 96' 97 98 99' 00 01 02' 03 04 05' GRAND CRU in VOSNE-ROMANÉE (0.8 ha). MONOPOLE of Liger-Belair, sold by BOUCHARD PÈRE & FILS. Liger-Belair making wine for themselves from 2002.

Romanée-Conti Burg r ★★★★ 66' 76 78' 80 82 83 85' 88' 89' 90' 93' 95 96' 97 98 99' 00 01 02' 03 04 05' A 1.7-ha MONOPOLE GRAND CRU in VOSNE-ROMANÉE; 450 cases per annum. The most celebrated and expensive red wine in the world, with reserves of flavour beyond imagination.

Romanée-Conti, Domaine de la (DRC) ★★★★ Grandest estate in Burgundy. Inc the whole of ROMANÉE-CONTI and La TÂCHE, major parts of ECHÉZEAUX, GRANDS ECHÉZEAUX, RICHEBOURG, ROMANÉE-ST-VIVANT, and a tiny part of MONTRACHET. Crown-jewel prices (if you can buy them at all). Keep top vintages for decades.

Romanée-St-Vivant Burg r ★★★★ 85' 88' 89' 90' 91 93' 95 96' 97 98 99' 00 01 02' 03 04 GRAND CRU in VOSNE-ROMANÉE (9.3 ha). Similar to ROMANÉE-CONTI but lighter and less sumptuous. Cathiard, DRC, DROUHIN, HUDELOT-NÖELLAT, LEROY.

Rosacker ALSACE GRAND CRU of 26 ha at Hunwihr. Produces best Ries in Alsace (see CLOS STE HUNE, SIPP-MACK, and MITTNACHT).

Rosé d'Anjou Lo p ★ DYA Pale, slightly sweet rosé. CABERNET D'ANJOU is better.

Rosé de Loire Lo p ★→★★ DYA Wide-ranging AC for dry rosé (ANJOU is sweet).

Rosette Dordogne w s/sw ★★ DYA Pocket-sized AC for charming apéritif wines, *e.g.* CLOS Romain, CH Puypezat-Rosette, Dom de la Cardinolle.

Rostaing, René ★★★ N Rh Growing CÔTE-RÔTIE estate with prime plots, three wines notably La Blonde (soft, elegant, 5% Viognier) and La Landonne (15–20 yrs). Accomplished style; some new oak. Also elegant CONDRIEU and Languedoc.

Roty, Joseph Burg ★★★ Small grower of classic GEVREY-CHAMBERTIN, esp CHARMES-CHAMBERTIN and MAZIS-CHAMBERTIN. Long-lived wines.

Rouget, Emmanuel Burg ★★★★ Inheritor of the legendary estate of Henri JAYER in ECHÉZEAUX, NUITS-ST-GEORGES, and VOSNE-ROMANÉE. Top wine: VOSNE-ROMANÉE-Cros Parantoux.

Roulot, Domaine G Burg ★★★ Range of seven distinctive MEURSAULTS (two PREMIERS CRUS). Look out for Tessons Clos de Mon Plaisir.

Roumier, Georges Burg ★★★★ Christophe R makes exceptional long-lived wines in BONNES-MARES, CHAMBOLLE-MUSIGNY-Amoureuses, MUSIGNY etc. High standards.

Rousseau, Domaine A Burg ★★★★ Grower famous for CHAMBERTIN etc., of highest quality. Wines are intense (not deep-coloured), long-lived, mostly GRAND CRU.

Roussette de Savoie w ★★ DYA The tastiest fresh white from S of Lake Geneva.

Roussillon Midi Top region for VINS DOUX NATURELS (*e.g.* MAURY, RIVESALTES, BANYULS). Lighter MUSCATS and younger vintage wines are taking over from darker, heavier wines. See CÔTES DU ROUSSILLON (and Villages), COLLIOURE, for table wines and VIN-DE-PAYS Côtes Catalanes.

Ruchottes-Chambertin Burg r ★★★★ 88' 89' 90' 91 93' 95 96' 97 98 99' 00 01 02' 03 04 05' GRAND CRU neighbour of CHAMBERTIN. Similar splendid lasting wine of great finesse. Top growers: LEROY, MUGNERET, ROUMIER, ROUSSEAU.

Ruinart "R" de Ruinart Brut NV; Ruinart Rosé NV; "R" de Ruinart Brut (**96 98**). Oldest CHAMPAGNE house, owned by MOËT-Hennessy. Elegant wines, esp luxury brands: Dom Ruinart (**90' 95 96'**), Dom Ruinart Rosé (**90' 96**). Minerally BLANC DE BLANCS NV.

Rully Burg r w (sp) ★★ (r) **99' 02' 03 04** 05' (w) **02' 03 04** 05' CÔTE CHALONNAISE village. Still white and red are light but tasty. Gd value, esp white. Growers inc DELORME, FAIVELEY, Dom de la Folie, Jacquesson, A RODET.

Sables du Golfe du Lion Midi p r w ★ DYA VIN DE PAYS from Mediterranean sand-dunes: esp Gris de Gris from Carignan, Grenache, Cinsault. LISTEL almost sole producer.

Sablet S Rh r w (p) ★★ **99' 00' 01 03 04' 05** Admirable, improving CÔTES DU RHÔNE village, esp Dom de Boissan, Cabasse, Espiers, Les Goubert, Piaugier, Dom de Verquière. Nicely full whites, too.

St-Amour Beauj r ★★ **03 05'** Northernmost *cru* of BEAUJOLAIS: light, fruity, irresistible (esp on 14 Feb). Growers to try: Janin, Patissier, Revillon.

St-Aubin Burg w r ★★★ (w) **99' 00 02' 03' 04** 05' (r) **99' 02' 03** 04 05' Understated neighbour of CHASSAGNE-MONTRACHET. Several PREMIERS CRUS: light, firm, quite stylish wines; fair prices. Also sold as CÔTE DE BEAUNE-VILLAGES. Top growers: JADOT, H&O Lamy, Lamy-Pillot, H Prudhon, RAMONET, Thomas.

St-Bris Burg w ★ DYA Newly promoted appellation for Sauv Bl. Nr CHABLIS.

St-Chinian Midi r ★→★★ 98 99 00 01 02 03 04 05 Hilly area of growing reputation in COTEAUX DU LANGUEDOC. AC since 1982 for red, and for white since 2005, plus new *crus* Berlou and Roquebrun. Tasty southern reds, esp co-ops Berlou, Roquebrun; CH de Viranel, Dom Canet Valette, Madura, Rimbaud.

St-Emilion B'x r ★★→★★★★ 85' 86' 88 89' 90' 94 95 96 98' 00' 01 03 04 (05) Large, Merlot-dominated district on B'x's Right Bank. ST-EMILION GRAND CRU AC the top designation. Warm, full, rounded style; some long-lived. Applying for permission to plant Petit Verdot: global warming strikes again. Best chx inc: AUSONE, CANON, CHEVAL BLANC, FIGEAC, MAGDELAINE. Gd co-op. See Bordeaux chapter.

St-Estèphe B'x r ★★→★★★★ 82' 83 85' 86' 88' 89' 90' 93 94 95' 96' 98 99 00' 01 02 03 04 (05) Most northerly communal AC in the MÉDOC. Solid, structured wines. Top chx: COS D'ESTOURNEL, MONTROSE, CALON-SEGUR, etc., and a plethora of CRUS BOURGEOIS.

St-Gall Brut NV; Extra Brut NV; Brut BLANC DE BLANCS NV; Brut Rosé NV; Brut BLANC DE BLANCS 98 99; Cuvée Orpale BLANC DE BLANCS 90 95 96 Brand name used by Union-Champagne: top CHAMPAGNE growers' co-op at AVIZE. Cuvée Orpale exceptional wine at fair price.

St-Georges-St-Emilion B'x r ★★ 95 96 98 00' 01 03 (05) Tiny ST-EMILION satellite. Usually good quality. Best chx: Calon, Macquin-St-G, Tour du Pas-St-Georges, Vieux Montaiguillon.

St-Gervais S Rh r (w, p) **01'** 03 **04 05** ★ W bank Rhône village. Sound co-op, excellent, long-lived Dom Ste-Anne red (marked Mourvèdre flavours); white inc Viognier.

St-Jean de Minervois Min w sw ★★ Fine sweet MUSCAT. Much recent progress, esp Dom de Barroubio, Michel Sigé, village co-op.

St-Joseph N Rh r w ★★ **90' 95' 98' 99' 00' 01' 02** 03' (05) AC stretching length of N Rhône (65 km/40 miles). Delicious, fruit-packed wines around Tournon;

elsewhere in the appellation quality variable. Often more structure than CROZES-HERMITAGE, esp from CHAPOUTIER (Les Granits), B Gripa, GUIGAL's Grippat; also Chave, Chêne, Chèze, Courbis, Coursodon, Cuilleron, DELAS, B Faurie, P Faury, Gaillard, Gonon, JABOULET, Marsanne, Monier, Paret, A Perret Trollat, F Villard. Gd aromatic white (mainly Marsanne, drink with food).

St-Julien B'x r ★★★→★★★★ 82' 83 85' 86' 88' 89' 90' 93 94 95' 96' 98 99 00' 01 02 03 04 (05) Mid-MÉDOC communal AC with 11 classified (1855) estates, inc three LÉOVILLES, BEYCHEVELLE, DUCRU-BEAUCAILLOU, GRUAUD-LAROSE, etc. The epitome of harmonious, fragrant, and savoury red wine.

St-Nicolas-de-Bourgueil Lo r p ★→★★ 89 90 95 96 97 02 03 04 05 Next to BOURGUEIL: similar range of Cab Fr – from lively and fruity, to chunky and tannic; the best verge on elegance. Try: Amirault, Cognard, Mabileau, Taluau.

St-Péray N Rh w sp ★★ 99' 01' 03' 04' 05 White Rhône (mainly Marsanne). Some sp – a curiosity worth trying. Still w can age, good style. Top names: S Chaboud, CHAPOUTIER, CLAPE, Colombo, B Gripa, J-L Thiers, TAIN co-op, du Tunnel, Voge. JABOULET planting here.

St-Pourçain-sur-Sioule Central Fr r p w ★→★★ DYA Pleasant country wine of the Allier. Light red and rosé from Gamay and/or Pinot N, white from Tressalier and/or CHARD (increasingly popular), or Sauv Bl. Recent vintages improved. Growers inc: Ray, Dom de Bellevue, Pétillat, and gd co-op.

St-Romain Burg w r ★★ (w) 99 00' 02' 03 04 05' Overlooked village just behind CÔTE DE BEAUNE. Value, esp for firm fresh whites. Reds have a clean cut. Top growers: De Chassorney, FÈVRE, Jean Germain, Gras, LEROY.

St-Véran Burg w ★★ 99 00' 02' 03 04 05' Next door AC to POUILLY-FUISSÉ. Best nearly as gd; others on unsuitable soil. Try DUBOEUF, Doms Cordier, Corsin, des Deux Roches, des Valanges, CH FUISSÉ.

Ste-Croix-du-Mont B'x w sw ★★ 96 97' 98 99' 01' 02 03' (05) Sweet white AC facing SAUTERNES across the River Garonne. Well worth trying, esp CHX Loubens, du Mont, Pavillon, la Rame.

Salon 82 83 85 88' 90 95 The original BLANC DE BLANCS CHAMPAGNE, from Le Mesnil in the Côte des Blancs. Awesome reputation for long lived wines – less consistent recently. Tiny quantities. Bought in 1988 by LAURENT-PERRIER.

Sancerre Lo w (r p) ★★→★★★ 96 97 02 03 04 05 The world's model for fragrant Sauv Bl, almost indistinguishable from POUILLY-FUMÉ, its neighbour across the Loire. Top wines can age 5 yrs+. Also improving, often delectable Pinot N (best drunk at 2–5 yrs) and rosé (do not over-chill). Occasional v.gd VENDANGES TARDIVES. Top growers inc: BOURGEOIS, Cotat Frères, Lucien Crochet, André Dezat, Jolivet, ALPHONSE MELLOT, Vincent Pinard, Roger, Vacheron.

Santenay Burg r (w) ★★★ 95 96' 98 99' 01' 02' 03 04 05' Sturdy reds from village S of CHASSAGNE-MONTRACHET. Best v'yds: La Comme, Les Gravières, CLOS de Tavannes. Top growers: GIRARDIN, Lequin-Roussot, Muzard, POUSSE D'OR.

Saumur Lo r w p sp ★→★★★ 02 03 04 05 Fresh, fruity, mineral whites plus a few more serious, user-friendly reds, v.gd CRÉMANT and Saumur MOUSSEUX (producers inc: BOUVET-LADUBAY, Cave des Vignerons de Saumur, GRATIEN & MEYER, LANGLOIS-CHATEAU, Dom St Just, CH Yvonne), pale rosés CH DE VILLENEUVE, Dom FILLIATREAU, CH de Targé, Retiveau-Retif, CH Tour Grise.

Saumur-Champigny Lo r ★★ →★★★ 95 96 97 02 03 04 05 Flourishing nine-commune AC for fresh Cab Fr ageing remarkably in sunny yrs. Look for CHX DE VILLENEUVE, Yvonne; Doms FILLIATREAU, Legrand, Nerleux, Roches Neuves, St Just, Val Brun; CLOS ROUGEARD. CH de Targé, Alliance Loire (Cave des Vignerons de Saumur-St-Cyr-en-Bourg).

Saussignac Dordogne w sw ★★→★★★ 98' 00 01' 02 03 (04) (05) MONBAZILLAC-style ageworthy wines. New ultra-sweet style obligatory from 2004 onwards. Dom de Richard, CHX Le Chabrier, Court-les-Muts, La Maurigne, Les Miaudoux,

Le Payral, Le Tap, Tou mentine, and Clos d'Yvigne. Former semi-sweet style now sold as Côtes de Bergerac Moëlleux.

Sauternes B'x w SW ★★→★★★★ 83' 86' 88' 89' 90' 95 96 97' 98 99' 01' 02 03' (05) District of five villages (inc BARSAC) that make France's best sweet wine, strong (14%+ alcohol), luscious and golden, demanding to be aged 10 yrs. Top CHX are d'YQUEM, GUIRAUD, LAFAURIE-PEYRAGUEY, RIEUSSEC, SUDUIRAUT, etc. Dry wines cannot be sold as Sauternes.

Sauvignon de St-Bris Burg w ★★ DYA Recent AC, cousin of SANCERRE, from nr CHABLIS. To try. Dom Saint Prix from Dom Bersan is gd. Goisot best.

Sauzet, Etienne Burg ★★★ Top-quality white burgundy estate and merchant at PULIGNY-MONTRACHET. Clearly defined, well-bred wines, better drunk young.

Savennières Lo w dr SW ★★★→★★★★ 75 76 78 85 86 **88 89** 90 93 95 96 97 99 02 **03** 04 05 Small ANJOU district for pungent, long-lived whites. Baumard, CH de Coulaine, Closel, CH d'Epiré, Eric Morgat, Dom Laureau du Clos Frémur, Tijou, Vincent Ogereau, Dom Jo Pithon, CH PIERRE-BISE. Top sites: COULÉE DE SERRANT, ROCHE-AUX-MOINES, CLOS du Papillon.

Savigny-lès-Beaune Burg r (w) ★★★ 90' 95 96' 98 99' 01 02' 03 04 05' Important village next to BEAUNE; similar mid-weight wines, often deliciously lively, fruity. Top v'yds: Dominode, Guettes, Lavières, Marconnets, Vergelesses; growers: BIZE, Camus, CHANDON DE BRIAILLES, CLAIR, Ecard, Girard, LEROY, Pavelot, TOLLOT-BEAUT.

Savoie E France r w sp ★★ DYA Alpine area with light, dry wines like some Swiss or minor Loires. APREMONT, CRÉPY, and SEYSSEL are best-known whites; ROUSSETTE is more interesting. Also gd MONDEUSE red.

Schlossberg Very successful ALSACE GRAND CRU for Ries in two parts: Kientzheim and small section at Kaysersberg. Best: FALLER/DOM WEINBACH, and Paul BLANCK.

Schlumberger, Domaines ★→★★★ Vast and top-quality ALSACE domaine at Guebwiller owning approx 1% of all ALSACE v'yds. Holdings in GRANDS CRUS Kitterlé, Kessler, Saering and Spiegel. Range includes rare Ries, signature CUVÉE Ernest, and, latest addition, Pinot Gr Grand Cru Kessler.

Saumur Blanc

The popularity of SAUMUR-CHAMPIGNY forced Saumur Bl into the background – until recently. Below are ten producers who take the wine seriously:

Cave de Vignerons de Saumur ★
Château de Targé ★★
Château la Tour Grise Organic, two CUVÉES: Les Amandiers and Les Fontenelles. ★★
Château de Villeneuve Two CUVÉES: classic and Les Cormiers, barrel-fermented. ★★★
Château Yvonne Barrel-fermented and rather Burgundian. ★★★
Clos Rougeard Barrel-fermented Breze. ★★★
Domaine de Nerleux ★
Domaine de St Just Barrel-aged Coulée de St Cyr. ★★★
Domaine du Collier Barrel-fermented La Ripaille. ★★
Domaine Filliatreau CUVÉE Imago. ★★

Schlumberger, Robert de Lo SAUMUR sp; by Austrian method. Fruity, delicate.

Schoenenbourg Very rich successful Riquewihr GRAND CRU (ALSACE): Pinot Gr, Ries, very fine VENDANGE TARDIVE and SÉLECTION DES GRAINS NOBLES. Esp from MARCEL DEISS and DOPFF AU MOULIN. Also v.gd MUSCAT.

Schoffit, Domaine ★★→★★★ Colmar ALSACE house with GRAND CRU RANGEN Pinot Gr, GEWURZ of top quality. Chasselas is unusual everyday delight.

Schröder & Schÿler Old BORDEAUX merchant, owner of CH KIRWAN.

Sciacarello Found only on CORSICA for red and rosé, *e.g.* AJACCIO, Sartène.

Sec Literally means dry, though CHAMPAGNE so called is medium-sweet (and better at breakfast, teatime, and weddings than BRUT).

Séguret S Rh r w ★★ **00 01'** 03 **04** (05) Gd S Rhône village nr GIGONDAS. Peppery quite full reds; rounded, clean whites. Esp CH La Courançonne, Dom de Cabasse, J David, Le Camassot, Garancière, Mourchon, Pourra.

Sélection des Grains Nobles Term coined by HUGEL for ALSACE equivalent to German Beerenauslese, and since 1984 subject to very strict regulations (see box, p.142). *Grains nobles* are individual grapes with "noble rot".

Serafin Burg ★★★ Christian S has gained a cult following for his intense GEVREY CHAMBERTIN VIEILLES VIGNES and CHARMES-CHAMBERTIN GRAND CRU.

Sèvre-et-Maine See MUSCADET DE SEVRE-ET-MAINE.

Seyssel Savoie w sp ★★ NV Delicate white, pleasant sp. *e.g.* Corbonod.

Sichel & Co One of BORDEAUX'S most respected merchant houses. Peter A Sichel died in 1998; his five sons continue with the family's interests in CHX D'ANGLUDET and PALMER, in CORBIÈRES, and as Bordeaux merchants (Sirius a top brand).

Sipp, Jean & Louis ★★ ALSACE growers in Ribeauvillé (Louis is also a négociant). Both make v.gd Ries GRAND CRU Kirchberg. Jean's is youthful elegance; Louis's is firmer when mature. V.gd GEWURZ from Louis, esp GRAND CRU Osterberg.

Sipp-Mack ★★→★★★ Ries specialist at Hunawihr (since 1698). Outstanding Ries from GRANDS CRUS ROSACKER and Osterberg (v.gd Pinot Gr from the latter).

Sorg, Bruno ★★→★★★ First-class small ALSACE grower at Eguisheim for GRAND CRUS Florimont (Ries) and PFERSIGBERG (MUSCAT). Also v.gd Auxerrois.

Sur Lie "On the lees." MUSCADET is often bottled straight from the vat, for maximum zest and character.

Tâche, La Burg r ★★★★ **78' 85' 88' 89' 90'** 93' 95 96' **97** 98 99' 00 01 02' 03 04 05' A 6-ha (1,500-case) GRAND CRU of VOSNE-ROMANÉE and one of best v'yds on earth: big perfumed, luxurious wine. See ROMANÉE-CONTI.

Tain, Cave Coopérative de 390 members in N Rhône ACS; owns one-quarter of HERMITAGE. Red Hermitage improved since 91 esp Gambert de Loche; modern-style CROZES. Sound whites. Gd value.

Taittinger Brut NV; Rosé NV; Brut **96 99**; Collection Brut **90 95 96**. Once fashionable Reims CHAMPAGNE grower and merchant sold to Crédit Agricole group 06. Wines have distinctive silky, flowery touch, though not always consistent. Excellent luxury brand: Comtes de Champagne BLANC DE BLANCS (**96'**), Comtes de Champagne Rosé (**96 99**), also v.gd rich Pinot Prestige Rosé NV. New CUVÉES Nocturne and Prélude. (See also California: Domaine Carneros)

Tastevin, Confrérie des Chevaliers du Burgundy's cheerful promotion society. Wine with the Tastevinage label has been approved and is a fair standard. A *tastevin* is the traditional shallow silver wine-tasting cup of Burgundy.

Tavel Rh p ★★ DYA France's most famous, though not best, rosé: strong, very full, and dry – needs food. Best growers: CH d'Aquéria, Dom Corne-Loup, GUIGAL, Maby, Dom de la Mordorée, Prieuré de Montézargues, Lafond, CH de Trinquevedel.

Tempier, Domaine r w p ★★★★ The top grower of BANDOL.

Terroirs Landais Gascony r p w ★ VIN DE PAYS, an extension in the *département* of Landes of the CÔTES DE GASCOGNE, a name that many growers prefer to use. Dom de Laballe is most-known example.

Thénard, Domaine Burg The major grower of the GIVRY appellation, but best known for his substantial portion (1.6 ha) of LE MONTRACHET. Should be better.

Thevenet, Jean Burg ★★★ Dom de la Bongran at Clessé stands out for rich, concentrated (even sweet!) white MÂCON. Expensive.

Thézac-Perricard SW Fr r p ★ **02 03 04** (05') VIN DE PAYS W of CAHORS. Same grapes but lighter style. Made by co-op at Thézac. Also independent Dom de Lancement.

Thiénot, Alain Broker-turned-merchant; dynamic force for gd in CHAMPAGNE. Grande CUVÉE **95 96'**. Brut NV, Rosé NV Brut **96 99**. Vintage Stanislas BLANC DE BLANCS (**99**) and new Vigne aux Gamins BLANC DE BLANCS **99**. Also owns Marie Stuart and CANARD-DUCHÊNE in Champ, CH Ricaud in LOUPIAC.

Thorin, J Beauj ★ Grower and major merchant of BEAUJOLAIS.

Thouarsais, Vin de Lo w r p ★ DYA Light Chenin Bl (with 20% CHARD permitted), Gamay, and Cab Sauv from tiny VDQS S of SAUMUR. Esp Gigon.

Tokay d'Alsace Old name for Pinot Gr in ALSACE in imitation of Hungarian Tokay.

Tollot-Beaut ★★★ Stylish, consistent burgundy grower with 20 ha in CÔTE DE BEAUNE, inc v'yds at Beaune Grèves, CORTON, SAVIGNY (Les Champs Chevrey), and at its CHOREY-LES-BEAUNE base.

Touraine Lo r p w dr sw sp ★→★★★ **02 03 04** 05 Big region; huge range, inc Chenin Bl (VOUVRAY), red CHINON, BOURGUEIL. Large AC with light Cab Fr, Gamay, gutsy Côt, blends; grassy Sauv Bl and MOUSSEUX; often bargains. Producers: Francois Plouzeau/Dom de la Garreliere, CLOS Roche Blanche; CH de Petit Thouars, MARIONNET, Oisly-Thesée, Jacky Marteau, Puzelat/Clos de Tue-Boeuf, Dom des Corbillieres, Dom de la Presle.

Touraine-Amboise Lo r w p ★→★★ Touraine sub-appellation. François Ier is engaging local blend (Gamay/Côt/Cab Fr). Dutertre, Xavier Frissant Damien Delecheneau/la Grange Tiphaine.

Touraine-Azay-le-Rideau Lo ★→★★ Chenin Bl-based dry, off-dry white and Grolleau-dominated rosé. Producers: James Paget and Pibaleau Père & Fils.

Touraine-Mesland Lo r w p ★→★★ Best represented by its user-friendly red blends (Gamay/Côt/Cab Fr). CH Gaillard, CLOS de la Briderie.

Touraine-Noble Joué Loire p ★→★★ DYA Ancient but recently revived rosé from three Pinots (N, Gr, Meunier) just S of Tours. Esp from ROUSSEAU and Sard. Granted AOC status (Touraine-Noble Joué) in 2000. 2005 best.

Trévallon, Domaine de Provence r w ★★★ **88' 89' 90' 91 92 93 94 95' 96 97 98** 99 00 01' 03' 04 A less-than-humble VIN DE PAYS near Les Baux, fully deserving its huge reputation. Intense Cab Sauv/Syrah to age. Tiny amount of white from Marsanne and Roussanne.

Trimbach, F E ★★★→★★★★ Growers of the greatest Ries in ALSACE (CLOS STE-HUNE) and probably the second-greatest (CUVÉE Frédéric-Emile). House style is dry but elegant with great ageing potential. Also v.gd Pinot Gr and GEWURZ. Based in Ribeauvillé; founded 1626.

Turckheim, Cave Vinicole de ★★ Important ALSACE CO-op with large range of not-always-exciting wines. V'yd area: 320 ha, inc numerous GRANDS CRUS.

Tursan SW France r p w ★★→★★★ (Most DYA) VDQS aspiring to AC. Easy-drinking holiday-style wines. Mostly from co-op at Geaune, but CH de Bachen (★★★) belongs to master-chef Michel Guérard. Super-ripe, oak-aged Sauv Bl is excellent. Also ★★ Dom de Perchade-Pourrouchet keeps better than most.

Vacqueyras S Rh r (w, p) ★★ **89' 90' 95' 96' 97 98' 99' 00' 01'** 03 04' 05 Full, peppery, Grenache-based neighbour to GIGONDAS: finer structure, often cheaper. Try JABOULET, Amouriers, Arnoux Vieux Clocher, CHX de Montmirail, des Tours; CLOS des Cazaux, Doms Archimbaud-Vache, Charbonnière, Couroulu, Font de Papier, Fourmone, Garrigue, Grapillon d'Or, Monardière, Montirius, Montvac, Pascal Frères, Sang des Cailloux.

Val d'Orbieu, Vignerons du Association of some 200 top growers and co-ops in CORBIÈRES, COTEAUX DU LANGUEDOC, MINERVOIS, ROUSSILLON, etc., marketing a sound range of selected MIDI AC and VIN DE PAYS wines. CUVÉE Mythique is flagship.

Valençay Lo r p w ★ DYA VDQS in E TOURAINE; light, easy-drinking sometimes

Vallée du Paradis Midi r w p ★ VIN DE PAYS of local red varieties in CORBIÈRES.

Valréas S Rh r (p w) ★★ 98' 99 00' 01 03 04 05 CÔTES DU RHÔNE village with big co-op. Gd mid-weight red (softer, finer than CAIRANNE, RASTEAU) and improving white. Esp Emmanuel Bouchard, Dom des Grands Devers, CH la Décelle.

Varichon & Clerc Principal makers and shippers of SAVOIE sparkling wines.

Vaudésir Burg w ★★★★ 89' 90 92 93 95 96' 97 98 99 00' 02' 03 04 05' Arguably the best of seven CHABLIS GRANDS CRUS (but then so are the others).

VDQS *vins délimités de qualité supérieure.*

Vendange Harvest. **Vendange Tardive** Late harvest. ALSACE equivalent to German Auslese (see Quality box, p.142), but usually higher alcohol.

Verget Burg ★★→★★★ The négociant business of J-M GUFFENS-HEYNEN with mixed range from MÂCON to MONTRACHET. Intense wines, often models, bought-in grapes. New Lubéron venture: Verget du Sud. Follow closely.

Veuve Clicquot Yellow Label NV; White Label DEMI-SEC NV; Vintage Réserve **90 95 96' 98 99** 00; Rosé Reserve **90' 95 96**. Historic CHAMPAGNE house of highest standing, now owned by LVMH. Full-bodied, almost rich: one of CHAMPAGNE'S surest things. Cellars at Reims. Luxury brands: La Grande Dame (**90' 95 96**), Rich Réserve (**96 98 99**), La Grande Dame Rosé (**96' 98 99**).

Veuve Devaux Premium CHAMPAGNE of powerful Union Auboise co-op in Bar-sur-Seine. V.gd aged Grande Réserve NV, Oeil de Perdrix Rosé, Prestige Cuvée D.

Vidal-Fleury, J N Rh ★→★★ Long-established GUIGAL-owned shipper of top Rhône wines and grower of CÔTE-RÔTIE, esp elegant La Chatillonne (high 12% Viognier). Steady quality.

Vieille Ferme, La S Rh r w ★★ V.gd brand of CÔTES DU VENTOUX (r) and CÔTES DU LUBERON (w) made by the Perrins, owners of CH DE BEAUCASTEL. Reliable price-quality.

Vieilles Vignes Old vines – therefore, the best wine. Used by many, esp by BOLLINGER, De VOGÜÉ, and CH FUISSÉ.

Vieux Télégraphe, Domaine du S Rh r w ★★★ 78' 81' 83 85 88 89' 90 94' 95' 96' 97 98' 99' 00 01' 03' 04' 05 A leader in vigorous, modern red CHÂTEAUNEUF, and tasty white (fuller style since 90s), which age well in lesser yrs. New gd-value second wine: Vieux Mas des Papes. Second DOMAINE: de la Roquette, fruited reds, fresh whites. Owns GIGONDAS Dom es Pallières with US importer Kermit Lynch.

Vigne or vignoble Vineyard, vineyards. **Vigneron** Vine-grower.

Vin de l'année This year's wine. See BEAUJOLAIS, BEAUJOLAIS-VILLAGES.

Vin de garde Wine that will improve with keeping. The serious stuff.

Vin de Paille Wine from grapes dried on straw mats, consequently very sweet, like Italian *passito* (see p.124). Esp in the JURA. See also CHAVE.

Vin de Pays (VDP) Most dynamic category in France (with over 140 regions). The zonal VDPs are best – *e.g.* Côtes de Gascogne, Côtes de Thongue, among others. Enormous variety and sometimes unexpected quality.

Vin de Table Category of standard everyday table wine, not subject to particular regulations about grapes and origin. Can be the source of occasional delights if a talented winemaker uses this category to avoid bureaucratic hassle.

Vin Doux Naturel (VDN) Sweet wine fortified with wine alcohol, so the sweetness is natural, not the strength. The speciality of ROUSSILLON, based on Grenache or MUSCAT. A staple in French bars, but the top wines can be remarkable.

Vin Gris "Grey" wine is very pale pink, made of red grapes pressed before fermentation begins – unlike rosé, which ferments briefly before pressing.

Oeil de Perdrix means much the same; so does "blush".

Vin Jaune Jura w ★★★ Speciality of ARBOIS: odd yellow wine like fino sherry. Normally ready when bottled (after at least 6 yrs). Best is CH-CHALON.

Vin Nouveau See BEAUJOLAIS NOUVEAU.

Vin Paillé de Corrèze SW Fr Revival of old-style VIN DE PAILLE made from Cab Fr, Cab Sauv, Chard, Sauv Bl. 25 growers and small co-op.

Vinsobres S Rh r (p w) ★ 00 01' 03 04 (05) Contradictory name of gd village given full AC status 05. Best are substantial, rounded, fruity reds, often Syrah-influenced. Look for: Doms les Aussellons, Bicarelle, Charme-Arnaud, Coriançon, Deurre, Jaume, Puy de Maupas, CH Rouanne.

Viré-Clessé Burg w ★★ 99 00' 01 02' 03 04 05' New AC based around two of the best white villages of MÂCON. Extrovert, exotic style, esp A Bonhomme, Bret Bros, CLOS du Chapitre, JADOT, Château de Viré, Merlin, and co-op.

Visan S Rh r p w ★ 01 03 04 (05) Rhône village for gd medium-weight reds. Of note: Dom des Grands Devers and Roche-Audran.

Vogüé, Comte Georges de ★★★★ First-class 12-ha BONNES-MARES and MUSIGNY DOMAINE at CHAMBOLLE-MUSIGNY. At best, esp since 90, the ultimate examples. Avoid most of the 80s.

Volnay Burg r ★★★→★★★★ 04 85' 88' 89' 90' 91 93 95 96' 97 98 99' 02' 03 04 05' Village between POMMARD and MEURSAULT: often the best reds of the CÔTE DE BEAUNE; structured and silky. Best v'yds: Caillerets, Champans, CLOS des Chênes, Santenots, Taillepieds, etc. Best growers: D'ANGERVILLE, J M BOILLOT, HOSPICES DE BEAUNE, LAFARGE, LAFON, DE MONTILLE, POUSSE D'OR.

Volnay-Santenots Burg r ★★★ Excellent red wine from MEURSAULT is sold under this name. Indistinguishable from other PREMIER CRU VOLNAY. Best growers: AMPEAU, HOSPICES DE BEAUNE, LAFON, LEROY.

Vosne-Romanée Burg r ★★★→★★★★ 85' 88' 89' 90' 91 93 95 96' 97 98 99' 00 01 02' 03 04 05' Village with Burgundy's grandest *crus* (ROMANÉE-CONTI, LA TÂCHE etc.). There are (or should be) no common wines in Vosne. Many gd growers inc: Arnoux, Cathiard, DRC, ENGEL, GRIVOT, GROS, JAYER, LATOUR, LEROY, Liger-Belair, MÉO-CAMUZET, Mongeard-Mugneret, Mugneret, RION.

Vougeot Burg r w ★★★ 90' 91 93 95 96' 97 98 99' 00 01 02' 03 04 05' Village and PREMIER CRU wines. See CLOS DE VOUGEOT. Exceptional CLOS Blanc de Vougeot, white since 12th C. Bertagna and VOUGERAIE best.

Vougeraie, Dom de la Burg r ★★→★★★★ DOMAINE uniting all BOISSET's v'yd holdings. Gd-value BOURGOGNE rouge up to fine MUSIGNY GRAND CRU.

Vouvray Lo w dr sw sp ★★→★★★★ For sw Vouvray: 47 49 59 64 69 71 76 88 89 90 95 96 97 03 05. For dr Vouvray: 89 90 96 97 02 03 04 05. Large AC E of Tours: increasingly gd and reliable. DEMI-SEC is classic style, but in gd yrs MOELLEUX can be intensely sweet, almost immortal. Gd, dry sp: look out for PÉTILLANT. Best producers: Allias, CLOS Baudoin, Champalou, (Dom de la Fontanerie/)Dhoye-Deruet, Foreau, Fouquet, CH Gaudrelle, Dom de la Haute Borne, HUET, Lemaire & Renard, Pinon, Vigneau-Chevreau, Vincent Careme.

Vranken, Champagne Ever more powerful CHAMPAGNE group created in 1976 by Belgian marketing man. CHARD-led wines of gd quality. Leading brand: Demoiselle. Owns HEIDSIECK MONOPOLE, POMMERY, and Bricout.

Wolfberger ★★ Principal label of Eguisheim co-op. Exceptional quality for such a large-scale producer. Very important for CRÉMANT.

"Y" (pronounced "ygrec") B'x 79' 80' 85 86 88 94 96 00 02 Intense dry wine produced occasionally at CH D'YQUEM. Most interesting with age.

Zind-Humbrecht, Domaine ★★★★ Outstanding ALSACE estate in Thann, Turckheim, Wintzenheim. First-rate, single-v'yd wines (esp CLOS St-Urbain), and very fine from GRANDS CRUS from RANGEN, Goldert, Brand, and HENGST. Very rich, ultra-concentrated style, sometimes at the expense of elegance.

Châteaux of Bordeaux

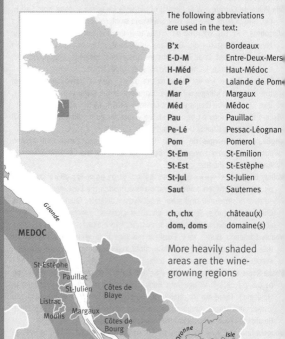

The following abbreviations
are used in the text:

B'x	Bordeaux
E-D-M	Entre-Deux-Mers
H-Méd	Haut-Médoc
L de P	Lalande de Pom
Mar	Margaux
Méd	Médoc
Pau	Pauillac
Pe-Lé	Pessac-Léognan
Pom	Pomerol
St-Em	St-Emilion
St-Est	St-Estèphe
St-Jul	St-Julien
Saut	Sauternes
ch, chx	château(x)
dom, doms	domaine(s)

More heavily shaded
areas are the wine-
growing regions

How can a wine region have so many marvellous and famous wines that people queue up to buy, and yet be destitute? How can it be a world-leader in some places, and so behind the times in others?

By being extremely large and diverse, that's how. Bordeaux covers both extremes, from the very best wines to wines that shouldn't be made at all. The classed growths and their equivalents, the top *crus bourgeois* and their equivalents, work with incredible attention to detail: at this level of quality it can take years of apparently minute adjustments in vineyard work to produce a tiny increment in ripeness or balance; but to these proprietors, it's worth it. This part of Bordeaux is flourishing, and deservedly so. But at the other end Bordeaux is not doing well at all. Many small producers of mediocre wine live on the edge of bankruptcy, and the largest chateau owner in the region is said to be the Crédit Agricole. There is just no market for poor Bordeaux any more.

Enter the merchant houses. Négociants like Sichel, Dourthe, Mau, and many others are making increasingly impressive branded blends – and in so doing are rescuing many a small proprietor who wants to make better wine but needs a lot of help to do so. These are the new everyday Bordeaux wines. Château Completely Unknown and Château Back-of-Beyond may offer occasional delights; but Sichel's Sirius and Dourthe No. 1 are well-made and contemporary. If you feel it's time you explored Bordeaux, they're a very good place to start.

d'Agassac H-Méd r ʜʜ **98 99 00' 02 03** 04 (05) "Sleeping Beauty" 14th-C moated fort. 42 ha very nr BORDEAUX suburbs. Improved quality since 1997.

Andron-Blanquet St-Est r ʜʜ **95 96 98 00'** 03 04 (05). 16-ha CRU BOURGEOIS; sister CH to COS-LABORY. Toughish wines show more charm lately.

Angélus St-Em r ʜʜʜʜ 89' 90' 92' 93 94 95 **96 97** 98' **99** 00' **01** 02 03' 04 (05) Leading 23-ha classed growth on ST-EMILION CÔTES. Precursor of the modern style; dark, rich, and sumptuous. Promoted to PREMIER GRAND CRU CLASSÉ status in 1996 (see St-Emilion classification box, p.101).

d'Angludet Cantenac-Mar r ʜʜʜ 88' 89' 90 94 95 **96' 98' 00** 02 03 04 (05) A 32-ha CRU BOURGEOIS SUPÉRIEUR owned and run by négociant Sichel; classed-growth quality. Lively long-living MARGAUX of great style popular in UK. Gd value.

Archambeau Graves r w dr (sw) ʜʜ (r) **95 96 98 00 02** 04 (05) (w) 00 01 02 04 (05) Up-to-date 27-ha property at Illats. V.gd fruity dry white; fragrant barrel-aged reds (two-thirds of v'yd).

d'Arche Saut w sw ʜʜ 89' 90 95 96 **97' 98 99 00 01' 02** 03' (05) Much improved 27-ha classed growth. Top vintages are rich and opulent. Also bed-and-breakfast in 17th-C *chartreuse*.

d'Armailhac Pau r ʜʜʜ 88' 89 90' 93 94 95' **96' 98 99** 00 01 02 03 04 (05) Formerly CH MOUTON BARONNE PHILIPPE. Substantial Fifth Growth under Rothschild ownership. 51 ha: top-quality Pauillac with more finesse than sister CLERC MILON but less power and volume. MOUTON ROTHSCHILD the big brother of CLERC MILON.

d'Arrosée St-Em r ʜʜʜ 89' 90' 94' 95 96 **98' 00 01** 02 03 04 (05) A 9.7-ha CÔTES estate with new owner and investment from 2002. Structured wines with plenty of Cab Fr and Cab Sauv (60%).

Ausone St-Em r ʜʜʜʜ 82' 83' 85 86' 88 89' 90 93 94 95 96' 97 98' **99** 00' 01' 02 03' 04 (05) Illustrious First Growth with 6.8 ha (about 2,500 cases); best

Vintages shown in light type should be opened now only out of curiosity to gauge their future. Vintages in **bold** are deemed (usually by their makers) ready for drinking. Remember, though: the French tend to enjoy the vigour of young wines, and many 88s, 89s, and 90s have at least 10 more years of development in front of them. Vintages marked ' are regarded as particularly successful for the property in question. Vintages in colour are the first choice for 2007.

position on the CÔTES with famous rock-hewn cellars. On superb form sinc 1996. Long-lived wines with added volume, texture and finesse. Second wine La Chapelle d'Ausone also excellent.

Bahans-Haut-Brion Pe-Lé r ★★★ 89' 90 93 94 95 96' 98 99 00 01 02 03 04 (05 The second wine of CH HAUT-BRION. Serious, Cab sauv-dominated. Ageing potential of 20 years.

Balestard-la-Tonnelle St-Em r ★★ 89 90' 94 95 96 98' 00' 01 03 04 (05) Histori 12-ha classed growth on limestone plateau. Fresh, firm, occasionally austere

Barde-Haut St-Em r ★★ 98 99 00 01 02 03 04 (05) The 17-ha sister property of CLC L'EGLISE and HAUT-BERGEY. Rich, modern, and opulent in style.

Bastor-Lamontagne Saut w sw ★★ 89' 90' 95 96' 97' 98 99 01' 02 03' (05) Larg (56 ha) Preignac sister to BEAUREGARD. Consistent quality; excellent, rich wines Second label: Les Remparts de Bastor. Fruity Caprice (from 2004) for earl drinking. Also CH St-Robert at Pujols: red and white GRAVES.

Batailley Pau r ★★★ 89' 90' 93 94 95 96 98 00 02 03 04 (05) Fifth Growth propert (55 ha) bordering PAUILLAC and ST-JULIEN. Fine, firm, strong-flavoured. Gd-valu PAUILLAC. Even better since 2000. Home of the Castéja family of BORIE-MANOUX.

Beaumont Cussac, H-Méd r ★★ 89' 90' 94 95 96 98 00' 02 04 (05) Over 80 h CRU BOURGEOIS SUPÉRIEUR (see "Médoc" box, p.96); easily enjoyable wines. Secon label: Ch Moulin d'Arvigny. 40,000 cases. In the same hands as BEYCHEVELLE.

Beauregard Pom r ★★★ 89' 90' 94' 95' 96' 98' 00' 01' 02 03 04 (05) A 17-ha v'yc fine 17th-C CH nr LA CONSEILLANTE. Top-rank rich wines. Advice from consultar Michel ROLLAND. Second label: Benjamin de Beauregard.

Beau-Séjour-Bécot St-Em r ★★★ 89' 90' 94 95' 96 98' 99 00' 01 02 03 04 (05 Other half of BEAUSEJOUR-DUFFAU; 18 ha. Controversially demoted in class in 198 but properly re-promoted to PREMIER GRAND CRU CLASSÉ in 1996. The Bécots als own GRAND-PONTET and LA GOMERIE.

Beauséjour-Duffau St-Em r ★★★ 89' 90' 93' 94 95 96 98 99 00 01 02 03 04 (05 Part of the old BEAU-SÉJOUR-BÉCOT Premier Grand Cru estate on W slope of th CÔTES. 6.8 ha in old family hands; only 2,000+ cases of firm-structured concentrated, even hedonistic wine.

Beau-Site St-Est r ★★ 89' 90 94 95 96 98 00 03 04 (05) CRU BOURGEOIS in sam hands as BATAILLEY etc. Usually solid and firm, if unexceptional.

Belair St-Em r ★★★ 88' 89' 90' 94 95' 96 98 99 00' 01 02 03 04 (05) Neighbour c AUSONE Biodynamically run since 1994. Fine, fragrant, elegant style; deceptivel long-lived. Second wine: CH Haut Roc Blanquant.

Bel-Air Marquis d'Aligre Soussans-Mar r ★★ 85 86 88 89 90 95' 96' 98' 0c Traditionally run MARGAUX with 13 ha of old vines giving only 3,500 cases. Fine structured wines that need bottle-age.

Belgrave St-Laurent, H-Méd r ★★ 90' 94 95 96' 98' 00' 02' 03 04' (05) 60 ha Fift Growth well managed by CVBG-Dourthe (see LA GARDE, REYSSON). Considerabl progress and investment since 1998. Second label: Diane de Belgrave.

Bel-Orme-Tronquoy-de-Lalande St-Seurin-de-Cadourne, H-Méd r ★★ 89 90 94 9 96 98' 00 02 03 04 (05) A 24-ha CRU BOURGEOIS N of ST-ESTÈPHE (see "Médoc" bo> p.96). Once known for tannic wines; more tempting since 1997.

Berliquet St-Em r ★★ 89' 90 94 95 96 97 98' 99 00' 01 03 04 (05) A 9.3-ha GRANE CRU CLASSÉ well located on the CÔTES. Moved into top gear from 1997 onwards

Bernadotte H-Méd-r ★★ 98 99 00' 01 02 03 04 (05) 30-ha estate owned an managed by PICHON-LALANDE since 1997. Fine, structured wines.

Bertineau St-Vincent L de P r ★★ 98 99 00' 01 03 04 (05) Top oenologist Miche ROLLAND owns this 4-ha estate. Consistent quality. (See also LE BON PASTEUR.)

Beychevelle St-Jul r ★★★ 89' 90' 93 94' 95 96 98 99 00 01 02 03 04 (05) Fourt Growth (90 ha) with historic mansion. Greater consistency since 1995. Wines c elegance rather than power. Second wine: Amiral de Beychevelle.

Biston-Brillette Moulis r ★★ 95 98 **00 01 02 03** 04 (05) Attractive, fruit-bound, good-value MOULIS. 24 ha in production.

Bonalgue Pom r ★★ 89 90 94 95 96 **98' 99 00 01** 03 04 (05), Dark, rich, meaty POMEROL. As good value as it gets. Michel ROLLAND consults.

Bonnet E-D-M r w ★★ (r) 98' **00 01 03 04** (05) (w) DYA Owned by André Lurton. Big producer (270 ha!) of some of the best ENTRE-DEUX-MERS and red BORDEAUX. New CUVÉE Prestige, Divinus from 2000.

Le Bon Pasteur Pom r ★★★ 89' 90' 93' 94' 95 **96' 98' 99 00 01** 02 03 04 (05) Excellent property on ST-EMILION border, owned by Michel ROLLAND. Concentrated, even creamy wines virtually guaranteed. (See also BERTINEAU ST-VINCENT.)

Le Boscq St-Est r ★★ 89' 90 95' **96' 98 00** 01 03 04 (05) Leading CRU BOURGEOIS SUPÉRIEUR, owned by CVBG-Dourthe, giving excellent value in tasty ST-ESTÈPHE.

Bourgneuf-Vayron Pom r ★★ 89' 90 94 95' 96' **98' 99 00** 01' 03 04 (05) Rich, warm, firm-edged POMEROL from this 9-ha estate on sandy-gravel soils.

Bouscaut Pe-Lé r w ★★ (r) 89 90 94 95 **98 00** 01 02 04 (05) (w) 96 98 00 01 **02 03 04** (05) Steadily improving classed growth owned by daughter of BRANE-CANTENAC's Lucien Lurton. Hitting its stride since 2000.

Boyd-Cantenac Mar r ★★★ 90 94' 95 **96' 98'** 02 03 04 (05) An 18-ha Third Growth in better form since 2000. Now has depth and purity of fruit. Second wine: Jacques Boyd. See also POUGET.

Branaire-Ducru St-Jul r ★★★ 89' 90' 93' 94 95 **96 98 99** 00 01 02 03 04 (05) Fourth Growth ST-JULIEN of 51 ha. Has set the bar of quality and consistency high. Dense, linear, cassis style. Second label: Duluc.

Brane-Cantenac Cantenac-Mar r ★★★ 89' 95 **96 98 99** 00' **01** 02 03 04 (05) Big (85-ha) Second Growth. Dense, fragrant MARGAUX. Second label: Baron de Brane.

Brillette Moulis r ★★ 95 96 98 99 **00 02** 03 04 (05) A 40-ha CRU BOURGEOIS SUPÉRIEUR. Reliable and attractive. Second label: Berthault Brillette.

Cabanne, La Pom r ★★ 95 96 **98' 00** 04 (05) Well-regarded 10-ha property. More rustic POMEROL in style. Second wine: Dom de Compostelle

Cadet-Piola St-Em r ★★ 94' **95 98 00** 01 03 04 (05) Distinguished small property (7 ha) on ST-EMILION's limestone plateau. Fresh, firm, long-lived wines.

Caillou Saut w sw ★★ 88' 89' 90' 95 96 **97 98 99** 01' 02 03' (05) Well-run second-rank 13-ha BARSAC v'yd for firm fruity wine. Private CUVÉE (**95 97' 99'**) is a top selection.

Calon-Ségur St-Est r ★★★ 3 89' 90' 94 95 **96' 98 99** 00' 01 02 03 04 (05) Big (60-ha) Third Growth with great historic reputation. Greater consistency since 1995. Second label: Marquis de Ségur.

Cambon La Pelouse H-Méd r ★★ **96' 98' 99 00 01** 02 03 04 (05) Big, accessible CRU BOURGEOIS SUPÉRIEUR. A sure bet for rich typical MÉDOC.

Camensac St-Laurent, H-Méd r ★★ 89 90 95 96' **98 00** 01 03 (05) 75-ha Fifth Growth. Quite lively if not exactly classic wines. New owner has CHASSE-SPLEEN connection; expect change. Second label: La Closerie de Camensac.

Canon St-Em r ★★★ 88 89' **96 98' 99** 00 01 02 03 04 (05) Famous first-classed growth with 22 walled-in hectares on plateau W of the town bought in 1996 by (Chanel) owners of RAUZAN-SÉGLA. Investment and restructuring of the v'yd now beginning to pay. Elegant, long-lived wines. Second label: Clos Canon.

Canon-de-Brem Canon-Fronsac r ★★ 94 95 96 **98 99 00 01** 03 04 (05) One of the top FRONSAC v'yds for vigorous wine. Formerly a MOUEIX property now under new ownership (DE LA DAUPHINE). Massive recent investment. To watch.

Canon La Gaffelière St-Em r ★★★ 89' 90' 94' 95 **96 97 98' 99** 00' **01'** 02 03 04 (05) Leading 19-ha GRAND CRU CLASSÉ on the lower slopes of the CÔTES. Same ownership as CLOS DE L'ORATOIRE and LA MONDOTTE. Stéphane Derenoncourt consults. Produces stylish, upfront, impressive wines.

Cantegril Graves r ★★ 98 99 00 **02 04** (05) Gd earthy red from CH DOISY-DAENE.

Cantemerle Macau, H-Méd r ★★★ **89'** 90 95 96' 98 **00 01** 02 03 Large 90-ha property in S MÉDOC (only 20 ha in 1980). Now merits its Fifth Growth status. Sandy-gravel soils so finer style. Second label: Les Allées de Cantemerle.

Cantenac-Brown Cantenac-Mar r ★★→★★★ 90' 94 95 96 **98 99** 00 01 02 03 04 (05) 42-ha Third Growth sold in 2006 to private investor Simon Halabi; had been owned since late 80s by AXA Millésimes Insurance. Generally powerful, robust but more elegance since 2000. Second label: Brio du Château Cantenac Brown.

Capbern-Gasqueton St-Est r ★★ 95 **96** 98 00 02 03 04 (05) Gd 34-ha CRU BOURGEOIS (see "Médoc" box, p.96); same owner as CALON-SEGUR.

Cap de Mourlin St-Em r ★★ 95 96 **98'** 99 **00 01** 03 (05) Well-known 15-ha property of the Capdemourlin family, also owners of CH BALESTARD and CH Roudier, MONTAGNE-ST-EMILION. A rich tasty ST-EMILION.

Carbonnieux Pe-Lé r w ★★★ 90' 95 **96** 98 99 00 02 04 (05) Large (90-ha), historic estate at LÉOGNAN for sterling r and w. The whites, 65% Sauv Bl (*e.g.* 96 97 98 **99** 00 01 **02 03 04** (05)), can age up to 10 yrs. Chx Le Pape and Le Sartre are also in the family. Second label: La Tour-Léognan.

de Carles Fronsac r ★★ **94 95** 96 98 99 **00 01** 02 03 04 (05) Ancient CH (named after Charlemagne). Steadily well-made, quite juicy FRONSACS. Haut Carles is the top selection.

les Carmes-Haut-Brion Pe-Lé r ★★★ 89 90' 94 95 96 98 99 00 01 02 03 04 (05) Small (4-ha) neighbour of HAUT-BRION with classed-growth standards. Old vintages show its potential.

Caronne-Ste-Gemme St-Laurent, H-Méd r ★★→★★★ 95 96' **98** 99 **00 01** 02 03 04 (05) CRU BOURGEOIS SUPÉRIEUR (40 ha). Steady, stylish quality repays patience.

Carsin Premières Côtes r w ★★ (r) **98'** 99 00 01 **02 03** (05) (w) 00 **01 02 04** (05) Ambitious enterprise: Finnish-owned, Australian-designed winery. Very attractive (esp CUVÉE Prestige and white Etiquette Grise).

Carteau Côtes-Daugay St-Em r ★★ 95 96' 98' **99 00 01 02 03** 04 (05) Consistent gd-value, 13-ha GRAND CRU; full-flavoured wines maturing fairly early.

Certan-de-May Pom r ★★★ 90' **94 95** 96 98 00' 01' 04 (05) Tiny property (1,800 cases) on the POMEROL plateau opposite Vieux-Ch-Certan with full-bodied, rich tannic wine.

Chambert-Marbuzet St-Est r ★★→★★★ 94 95 96 **98 99** 00 01 02 04 (05) HAUT-MARBUZET's tiny (8-ha) sister CH. V.gd mainly Cab Sauv, aged in new oak.

Chantegrive Graves r w ★★→★★★ 95 96 **98'** 99' **00 01 02** 03 04 (05) An 87-ha estate, half w, half r; modern GRAVES of very gd quality. Reds now more consistent. CUVÉE Caroline is top w selection (**96 97 98'** 99 00 01 **02 04** (05)).

Chasse-Spleen Moulis r ★★★ 90' **94** 95 96 **98 99** 00 01 02 03 04 (05) A 80-ha CRU BOURGEOIS EXCEPTIONNEL at classed-growth level (see Médoc box, p.96). Consistently gd, often outstanding (*e.g.* **90'**), long-maturing wine. Second label: Ermitage de C-S. One of the surest things in B'x. See also LA GURGUE, GRESSIER-GRAND-POUJEAUX, and HAUT-BAGES-LIBÉRAL.

Chauvin St-Em r ★★ 94 95 96 **98'** 99 00 01 03 04 (05) Steady performer, increasingly serious stuff. New v'yds purhased in 1998.

Cheval Blanc St-Em r ★★★★ **85'** 86 88 89 90' 93 94 95 96' **97 98'** 99 00' 01' 02 03 04 (05) 40-ha premier GRAND CRU CLASS (A) OF ST-EMILION. High percentage of Cabernet Franc (60%). Rich, fragrant, vigorous wines with some of the voluptuousness of neighbouring POMEROL. Delicious young; lasts a generation. For many, *the* first choice in B'x. Second wine: Le Petit Cheval.

Chevalier, Domaine de Pe-Lé r w ★★★ 83 89 90' 95 **96' 98' 99'** 00' 01' 02 03 04 (05) Superb estate of 38 ha at LÉOGNAN. Red is stern at first, softly earthy with age. Impressive since 1998. Complex white matures slowly and develops rich flavours (89 90' **93 94** 95 **96'** 97 **98'** 99 00 01 **02 03 04** (05)). Second wine: Esprit de Chevalier. Also look out for Dom de la Solitude, PESSAC-LÉOGNAN.

Cissac Cissac-Méd r ★★ **90** 94' **95 96' 98 00** 02 03 04 (05) Pillar of the bourgeoisie. 50-ha CRU BOURGEOIS SUPÉRIEUR (see "Médoc" box, p.96). Steady record for tasty, long-lived wine. Second wine: Les Reflets du Ch Cissac.

Citran Avensan, H-Méd r ★★ **90' 94 95 96 98 99 00 02** 03 04 (05) CRU BOURGEOIS SUPÉRIEUR of 90 ha, back in Villars-Merlaut family since 1996. Now round, ripe, supple; accessible early. Second label: Moulins de Citran. This is one to watch.

Clarke Listrac r (p w) ★★ **89' 90' 95 96' 98' 99 00 01 02** 03 04 (05) Large (54-ha) CRU BOURGEOIS SUPÉRIEUR purchased by the late Baron Edmond de Rothschild in 1973. Now benefiting from massive investment. Merlot-based red. Also a dry white Le Merle Blanc du Ch Clarke. CH Malmaison in MOULIS same connection.

Clerc Milon Pau r ★★★ **89' 90' 94 95 96' 98' 99** 00 01 02 03 04 (05) Once-forgotten Fifth Growth owned by de Rothschilds. Now 30 ha and a top performer; weightier than ARMAILHAC.

Climens Saut w sw ★★★★ 76 78 83' 85' 86' 88 89 90' 95 96 97' 98 99 01' 02 03' 04 (05) A 30-ha BARSAC classed growth making some of the world's most stylish wine (but not the sweetest) for a gd 10 yrs' maturing. (Occasional) second label: Les Cyprès. Owned by Berenice Lurton.

Clinet Pom r ★★★★ **89' 90' 93' 94 95 96 97' 98' 99 00** 01 02 03 04 (05) A 9-ha property in central POMEROL making intense, sumptuous wines from old vines. Michel Labord consults. New winery 2004. Second label: Fleur de Clinet.

Clos de l'Oratoire St-Em r ★★ **94 95 96 98 99 00'** 01' 03 04 (05) Serious performer on the NE slopes of ST-EMILION. Same stable as CANON-LA-GAFFELIÈRE and LA MONDOTTE, but lighter than both.

Clos des Jacobins St-Em r ★★ **89' 90' 94 95 96 98 00 01** 02 03 Well-known and well-run little (8.5-ha) classed growth. New ownership from 2004; new creamy style. To watch. Same family owns CH La Commanderie.

Clos du Marquis St-Jul r ★★ →★★★ **90 94 95 96 97 98 99 00 01** 02 03 04 (05) The second wine of LÉOVILLE-LAS-CASES, cut from the same cloth and regularly a match for many highly classed growths.

Clos Floridène Graves r w ★★ (r) **98' 99 00 01 02 03** 04 (05) (w) **96' 98 99 00 01' 02 03 04'** (05) A sure thing from one of B'x's most famous white-winemakers, Denis Dubourdieu. Oak-fermented Sauv Bl/Sem to keep 5+ yrs; fruity red. See also CH REYNON.

Clos Fourtet St-Em r ★★★ **89 90 94 95 96 97 98 99** 00 01 02 03 04 (05) Well-placed 20-ha First Growth on the plateau, cellars almost in town. Back on form after a middling patch. Second label: Dom de Martialis.

Clos Haut-Peyraguey Saut w sw ★★ **86' 88' 89 90' 95' 96 97' 98 99 00 01' 02** 03' 04 (05) Tiny production (12 ha) of excellent medium-rich wine. Haut-Bommes is the second label.

Clos l'Eglise Pom r ★★★ **90' 94 95 96 98 99 00'** 01 02 03 04 (05) A 6-ha v'yd on one of the best sites in POMEROL. Fine wine with more depth since 1998. Michel ROLLAND consults. Same family owns HAUT-BERGEY.

Clos René Pom r ★★ **89 90 94 95 96 98' 00' 01** 04 (05) A 12-ha CH on sand and gravel soils NW of POMEROL. Quality guaranteed. Alias CH Moulinet-Lasserre.

La Clotte St-Em r ★★ **89 90' 94 95' 96' 98' 99 00' 01 02** 03 04 (05) Tiny CÔTES GRAND CRU CLASSÉ: pungent, supple wine. Drink at owners' ST-EMILION restaurant, Logis de la Cadène. Second label: Clos Bergat Bosson.

Colombier-Monpelou Pau r ★★ **94 95 96 98 99 00'** 02 03 04 (05) Reliable small CRU BOURGEOIS SUPÉRIEUR; fair standard.

La Conseillante Pom r ★★★★ **85 86 88 89 90' 94 95' 96' 98' 99 00'** 01' 02 03 04 (05) Historic 12-ha property on plateau between PÉTRUS and CHEVAL BLANC. Some of the noblest and most fragrant POMEROL; drinks well young or old.

Corbin St-Em r ★★ **95 96 98 99 00' 01** 02 04 (05) Underperforming 12-ha GRAND CRU CLASSÉ. Steady improvement since 1999. Round and supple with soft, red fruit.

Corbin-Michotte St-Em r ★★ **90** 94' 95 96 **98' 99** 00 01 02 04 (05) Well-run, modernized, 7.6-ha property; generous, POMEROL-like wine. In same hands as CHX Calon and Cantelauze.

Cordeillan-Bages Pau r ★★ A mere 1,000 cases of rather lean PAUILLAC. Better known as a (Michelin-starred) luxury health-spa for wine writers.

Cos d'Estournel St-Est r ★★★★ **88' 89' 90'** 94 95 96' 97 **98'** 00 **01** 02 03 04 (05) A 67-ha Second Growth with eccentric chinoiserie CHAI. Most refined ST-ESTÈPHE and regularly one of the best wines of the MÉDOC. Second label: Les Pagodes de Cos. Managed by Jean-Guillaume Prats.

Cos-Labory St-Est r ★★ **88 89** 90' 94 95 96' **98' 99** 00 02 03 04 (05) Little-known Fifth Growth neighbour of COS-D'ESTOURNEL with 15 ha. Efforts since 85 have raised it to classed growth form (esp since 90). ANDRON-BLANQUET is sister CH.

Côte(s) In St-Emilion, Côtes distinguishes better valley slopes from plateau.

Coufran St-Seurin-de-Cadourne, H-Méd r ★★ **94** 95 96 98 99 00 **01** 02 03 04 (05) CRU BOURGEOIS SUPÉRIEUR Coufran and VERDIGNAN, in the extreme N of the HAUT-MÉDOC, are co-owned. Coufran is mainly Merlot for supple wine. 76 ha. SOUDARS is another, smaller sister.

Couhins-Lurton Pe-Lé w r ★★→★★★ (w) **98' 99** 00 01 **02 03 04** (05) (r) **02** 04 (05) Fine, minerally, long-lived classed-growth white produced from Sauv Bl. Now a little red from 2002. Same family as LA LOUVIÈRE.

La Couspaude St Em r ★★★ 95 96 98 99 **00' 01** 02 03 04 (05) Another to watch closely. Modern methods and full-flavoured wine.

Coutet Saut w sw ★★★ **83' 85** 86' 88' 89' 90' 95 96 97' **98' 99** 01' **02** 03' 04 (05) Traditional rival to CLIMENS; 37 ha in BARSAC. Usually slightly less rich; at its best equally fine. CUVÉE Madame is a very rich selection in the best vintages.

Couvent des Jacobins St-Em r ★★ **89 90** 95 96 **98' 99** 00' **01** 03 04 (05) Well-known 10.5-ha v'yd on E edge of St-Emilion. Splendid cellars. Lighter, easy style. Second label: Ch Beau-Mayne.

Le Crock St-Est r ★★ **89 90'** 95 96 98 99 **00' 01** 02 03 04 (05) Outstanding CRU BOURGEOIS SUPÉRIEUR of 30 ha in the same family as LÉOVILLE-POYFERRÉ. Among the best CRUS BOURGEOIS of the commune.

La Croix Pom r ★★ **88 89** 90 94 95 96 98 99 00 01 04 (05) Well-reputed 10-ha property. Appealing plummy POMEROL. Also La Croix-St-Georges, La Croix-Toulifaut, Castelot, Chambrun, and HAUT-SARPE (ST-EMILION).

La Croix-de-Gay Pom r ★★★ **89 90** 94' 95 96 98 99 00' 01' 02 03 04 (05) 12 ha in the best part of the commune. Recently on fine form. Has underground cellars (rare in POMEROL). LA FLEUR-DE-GAY is the best selection.

La Croix du Casse Pom r ★★ **89 90** 94 95 96 98 99 00' 01' 04 (05) A 9-ha property on sandy-gravel soils in the south of POMEROL. Usually rich and fine in style.

Croizet-Bages Pau r ★★ **88 89** 90' 95 96' **98** 00' 01 02 03 04 (05) A 26-ha Fifth Growth. Same owners as RAUZAN-GASSIES. A new regime in the cellar is producing richer, more serious wines, but could be better.

Croque-Michotte St-Em r ★★ **88 89'** 90' 94 95 96 98 00 01 03 04 (05) A 14-ha GRAND CRU on the POMEROL border. Gd steady wines but not grand enough to be *classé*.

Cru Bourgeois, Cru Bourgeois Supérieur, Cru Bourgeois Exceptionnel See Médoc classification box, p.96.

de Cruzeau Pe-Lé s r w ★★ (r) 95 96 **98 00 01 02** 04 (05) (w) **00** 01 02 03 **04** (05) Large 97-ha (two-thirds red) PESSAC-LÉOGNAN v'yd developed by André Lurton of LA LOUVIÈRE. Gd-value wines. Oak-fermented, Sauv Bl-dominated white.

Dalem Fronsac r ★★ **94** 95 96' **98' 99** 00 **01** 02 03 04 (05) Leading full-blooded FRONSAC. 15 ha; 85% Merlot.

Dassault St-Em r ★★ **89** 90 94 95 96 **98' 99** 00 01 02 03 04 (05) Consistent, solid, modern, oak-lined 23-ha GRAND CRU CLASSÉ (see "St-Emilion" box, p.101).

de la Dauphine Fronsac r ★★ **95** 96 **98' 99** 00 **01** 03 04 (05) Old star rejuvenated by J-P MOUEIX and sold to owners of CANON-DE-BREM in 00. New winery and cellars in 2002 – to watch.

Dauzac Labarde-Mar r ★★ ·★★★ 89' 90' 94 95 96 98' 99 00' 01 02 03 04 (05) A 49-ha Fifth Growth nr the river S of MARGAUX; underachiever for many yrs but evolution since the 1990s. Owned by an insurance company; managed by André Lurton of LA LOUVIÈRE. Second wine: La Bastide Dauzac.

Desmirail Mar r ★★ ·★★★ 90 94 95 96 98 00' 01 02 03 04 (05) Third Growth (30 ha) owned by Denis Lurton, brother of Henri of BRANE CANTENAC. Fine, delicate MARGAUX style.

Doisy-Daëne Barsac w (r) sw dr ★★★ 88' 89' 90' 95 96 97' 98' 99 01' 02 03 04 (05) Forward-looking, even experimental, 15-ha estate producing a crisp, oaky, dry w and the r CH CANTEGRIL, but above all renowned for its notably fine (and long-lived) sweet BARSAC. L'Extravagant (90 96 97 01 02 03 04) is a super-CUVÉE.

Doisy-Dubroca Barsac w sw ★★ 86 88' 89 90' 95 96 97' 99 01 03' 04 (05) Tiny (3.4-ha) BARSAC classed growth allied to CH CLIMENS.

Doisy-Védrines Saut w sw ★★ 86 88' 89 90' 95 96 97' 98 99 01' 04 (05) A 20-ha classed growth at BARSAC, nr CLIMENS and COUTET. Delicious, sturdy, rich: for keeping. A sure thing for many yrs.

La Dominique St-Em r ★★★ 88' 89' 90' 94 95 96 98 99 00' 01 03 04 (05) An 18-ha classed growth near CHEVAL BLANC. Rich, fruity, expressive wines. Second label: St Paul de Dominique.

Ducluzeau Listrac r ★★ 94 95 96 00 01 03 04 (05) Tiny sister property of DUCRU-BEAUCAILLOU. 4 ha, unusually 90% Merlot.

Ducru-Beaucaillou St-Jul r ★★★★ 82' 83' 85' 86' 89 90 93 94 95' 96' 98 99 00' 01 02 03 04 (05) Outstanding Second Growth, excellent form; 49 ha overlooking the river. Classic cedar-scented claret suited to long ageing. See also GRAND-PUY-LACOSTE, HAUT-BATAILLEY, LALANDE-BORIE. Second wine: La Croix de Beaucaillou.

Duhart-Milon Rothschild Pau r ★★★ 88 89 90 94 95 96' 98 00' 01 02 03 04' (05) Fourth Growth neighbour of LAFITE, under same management. 71 ha. Maturing vines; increasingly fine quality and reputation. Second label: Moulin de Duhart.

Durfort-Vivens Mar r ★★★ 89' 90 94 95 96 98 99 00 01 02 03 04 (05) Relatively small (32-ha) Second Growth owned and being improved by Gonzague Lurton, brother of Henri (BRANE CANTENAC) and Denis (DESMIRAIL). Recent wines have structure (lots of Cab Sauv) and class.

de l'Eglise, Domaine Pom r ★★ 89 90 95 96 98 99 00 01 02 03 04 (05) Small property: stylish, resonant wine distributed by BORIE-MANOUX.

L'Eglise-Clinet Pom r ★★★★ 89 90' 93' 94 95 96 97 98' 99 00' 01' 02 03 04 (05) A 6-ha estate. Top-flight POMEROL with great consistency; full, concentrated, fleshy wine. A CH to follow, but expensive. Second label: La Petite Eglise.

L'Evangile Pom r ★★★★ 88' 89' 90 95 96 98' 99 00' 01 02 03 04' (05) 13 ha between PÉTRUS and CHEVAL BLANC. Deep-veined but elegant style in a POMEROL classic. Bought in 1990 by Doms (LAFITE) Rothschild. New cellar in 2004.

de Fargues Saut w sw ★★★ 83 85' 86 88 89 90 95 96 97 98 99' 01 03' 04 (05) A 15-ha v'yd by ruined CH owned by Lur-Saluces, previous owner of YQUEM. Rich, unctuous wines, but balanced – maturing earlier than YQUEM.

Faurie-de-Souchard St-Em r ★★ 89 90 94 95 96 98' 00 01 03 04 (05) Small GRAND CRU CLASSÉ on the CÔTES (see "Médoc" box, p.96). See also CADET-PIOLA.

de Ferrand St-Em r ★★ 90' 94 95 96 98 00 01 03 04 (05) Big (30-ha) plateau estate. Rich oaky wines, with plenty of tannin to age.

Ferrande Graves r (w) ★★ 00 01 02 04 (05) Major estate at Castres: over 40 ha. Easy, enjoyable red and gd white wine; at their best at 1–4 yrs.

To decipher codes, please refer to "Key to symbols" on front flap of jacket, or "How to use this book" on p.8.

Ferrière Mar r ★★→★★★ **89 90 94 95 96 98 99 00** 02 03 04 (05) In same capable hands as LA GURGUE and HAUT-BAGES-LIBÉRAL. Dark, firm, perfumed wines.

Feytit-Clinet Pom r ★★ **90' 94 95 96 98 99 00 01** 03 04 (05) Tiny 6.5-ha property. Once managed by J-P MOUEIX; back with owning Chasseuil family since 2000. Improvements since. Rich, full POMEROL with ageing potential.

Fieuzal Pe-Lé r (w) ★★★ (r) 94 95' **96' 98' 00** 01 03 04 (05) (w) **95 96' 97 98' 99** 01 **02 03** (05) A 48-ha classed-growth at LÉOGNAN. Finely made, memorable wines of both colours. Classic whites since 85 are 10-yr keepers. CH Le Bonnat is sister ch vinified at FIEUZAL.

Figeac St-Em r ★★★★ 88 89' 90' 94' **95' 96 98 99 00'** 01 02 03 04 (05) First Growth, 40-ha gravelly v'yd gives one of B'x's most stylish, rich, but elegant wines, lovely to drink relatively quickly, but lasting indefinitely. Second label: Grangeneuve.

Filhot Saut w sw dr ★★ **88 90 95 96' 97' 98 99 01' 02** 03' 04 (05) Second-rank classed growth with splendid CH, 60-ha v'yd. Lightish and rather simple (36% Sauv Bl) sweet wines for fairly early drinking.

La Fleur-de-Gay Pom r ★★★ 1,000-case super-CUVÉE of CH LA CROIX DE GAY.

La Fleur-Pétrus Pom r ★★★★ 88' **89' 90'** 94 95 96 97 98' 99 00' 01 02 03 04' (05) A 13-ha v'yd flanking PÉTRUS; same management as J-P MOUEIX. Exceedingly fine, densely plummy wines. This is POMEROL at its most stylish (and expensive).

Fombrauge St-Em r ★★ ·★★★ 88' 89 90 94 95 96 **98 99 00' 01'** 02 03 04 (05) 52 ha at St-Christophe-des-Bardes, E of ST-ÉMILION. Candidate for classification. Since 1999 rich, dark, chocolatey, full-bodied wines. Second label: Cadran de Fombrauge. Magrez-Fombrauge is its GARAGE wine.

Fonbadet Pau r ★★ **89 90'** 94 95 96' **98' 00'** 01 02 03 04 (05) CRU BOURGEOIS SUPÉRIEUR of solid reputation (see box, p.96). 20 ha. Old vines; wine needs long bottle-age. Value.

Fonplégade St-Em r ★★ 88 89 90' 95 96 98 00' 01 03 04 (05) A 19-ha GRAND CRU CLASSÉ on the CÔTES W of ST-ÉMILION. At best firm and long-lasting.

Fonréaud Listrac r ★★ **88 89 90** 94 95 96 **98 00'** 02 03 04 (05) One of the bigger (39 ha) and better CRUS BOURGEOIS of its area. Investment since 1998. 2 ha of white: Le Cygne, barrel-fermented. See LESTAGE.

Fonroque St-Em r ★★★ 88 89' 90' 94 95 96 98 01 03 04 (05) 19 ha on the plateau N of ST-ÉMILION. Biodynamic culture being introduced. Big, deep, dark wine: drink or (better) keep.

Fontenil Fronsac r ★★ **90 94 95** 96 97 98' 99' 00' 01' 02 03 04 (05) Leading FRONSAC started by Michel ROLLAND in 1986. Dense, oaky, new-style. Défi de Fontenil is its GARAGE wine.

Les Forts de Latour Pau r ★★★ 85 86 88 **89' 90'** 93 94 95' 96' 97 **98 99** 00' 01 02 03 04' (05) The (worthy) second wine of CH LATOUR; the authentic flavour in slightly lighter format. Until 1990 unique in being bottle-aged at least 3 yrs before release; now offered EN PRIMEUR.

Fourcas-Dupré Listrac r ★★ **89' 90** 94 95 96' 98' **99 00'** 01 02 03 04 (05) Top-class 46-ha CRU BOURGEOIS SUPÉRIEUR making consistent wine in tight LISTRAC style. To watch. Second label: Château Bellevue-Laffont. Complete renovation in 2000.

Fourcas-Hosten Listrac r ★★ ·★★★ **89' 90'** 94 95' **96' 98'** 00 01 02 03 04 (05) A 48-ha CRU BOURGEOIS SUPÉRIEUR, often the best of its (underestimated) commune. Firm wine with a long life.

de France Pe-Lé r w ★★ (r) 90' 95' **96' 98 99 00** 02 03 04 (05) (w) **96 97 98 99 01' 02 03 04** (05) Well-known GRAVES property (the name helps) making steady progress. Michel ROLLAND consults. Try a top vintage.

Franc-Mayne St-Em r ★★ **89' 90'** 94 95 96 **98' 99 00' 01** 03 04 (05) A 7.2-ha GRAND CRU CLASSÉ. Ambitious new owners in 1996 and again in 2004. Investment and renovation. Round but firmly constituted wines. To watch.

du Gaby Canon-Fronsac r ★★ 00' **01**' **03** 04 (05) Perhaps the finest situation in France. Serious wines from new owner.

La Gaffelière St-Em r ★★★ 86' 88' 89' 90' 94 **95 96 98' 99** 00' 01 03 04 (05) A 25-ha First Growth at the foot of the CÔTES. Elegant, not rich wines. Re-equipped and improved since 1998.

Galius St-Em r ★★ 98 00 **01 03** 04 (05) Oak-aged selection from ST-EMILION co-op, to a high standard. Formerly Haut Quercus.

La Garde Pe-Lé r w ★★ (r) 96' **98' 99** 00 **01**' 02 03 04 (05) (w) **01 02 04** (05) Substantial property of 58 ha owned by négociant CVBG-Dourthe; reliable red and improving. More Merlot planted 2000.

Le Gay Pom r ★★★ 88 89' 90' 95 96 98 **99** 00 01 03 04 (05) Fine 5.6-ha v'yd on N edge of POMEROL. Major investment, with Michel ROLLAND now consulting. Usually impressive tannic wines. Ch Montviel same stable and AC.

Gazin Pom r ★★★ 88 89' 90' 94' 95 96 **98' 99** 00' 01' 02 03 04 (05) Large (for POMEROL): 23 ha, recently shining. Second label: L'Hospitalet de Gazin.

Gilette Saut w SW ★★★ **49 53 55** 59 61 **67** 70 75 76 78 79 81 82 **83 85** Extraordinary small Preignac CH stores its sumptuous wines in concrete vats to a great age. Only about 5,000 bottles of each. CH Les Justices is its sister (**96 97 99 01 02** 03' (05)).

Giscours Labarde-Mar r ★★★ 85 88 89' 90 94 95 96' **98 99** 00' 01 02 03 04 (05) Splendid 80-ha Third Growth S of Cantenac. Excellent vigorous wine in 1970s; 1980s very wobbly; new ownership from 95 and revival since. Second label: La Sirène de Giscours. Ch La Houringue is its baby sister in AC HAUT-MÉDOC.

du Glana St-Jul r ★★ 95 96 98 **99 00 02** 03 04 (05) Big CRU BOURGEOIS SUPÉRIEUR. Undemanding; undramatic; value. Second wine: Ch Sirène.

Gloria St-Jul r ★★ ·★★★ 88 89 90 95' 96 98 **99** 00' **01 02** 03 04 (05) A 45-ha ST-JULIEN estate that didn't apply for the recent CRU BOURGEOIS classification (see box, p.96). Same ownership as ST-PIERRE. Wines of vigour, with a recent return to long-maturing style. Second label: Peymartin.

La Gomerie St-Em 1,000 cases, 100% Merlot, *garagiste*. See BEAU-SÉJOUR-BÉCOT.

Grand-Corbin-Despagne St-Em r ★★ ·★★★ 89 90' 94 95 96 98 **99** 00' **01** 03 04 (05) One of the bigger and better GRANDS CRUS on the CORBIN plateau. Determined to get reinstated as GRAND CRU CLASSÉ after being demoted in 1996. Now fashionably thick wines. Also CH Maison Blanche, MONTAGNE ST-EMILION.

Grand Cru Classé see St-Emilion classification box, p.101.

Grand-Mayne St-Em r ★★★ 88 89' 90' 94 95 96 98 **99** 00' 01' 02 03 04 (05) Leading 16-ha GRAND CRU CLASSÉ on W CÔTES. Noble old CH with wonderfully rich, tasty wines.

Grand-Pontet St-Em r ★★★ 95' 96 **98' 99** 00' **01 02** 03 04 (05) A 14-ha estate revitalized since 1985. Quality much improved. See BEAU-SÉJOUR-BÉCOT.

Grand-Puy-Ducasse Pau r ★★★ 89' 90 94 95 96' **98' 99** 00 01 02 03 04 (05) Fifth Growth enlarged to 40 ha under expert management; improvements in the 1990s, but lacks the vigour of the next entry. Second label: CH Artigues-Arnaud.

Grand-Puy-Lacoste Pau r ★★★ 82' **83 85**' 86' 88' 89' 90' 94 95' 96' 97 **98 99** 00' 02 01 03 04 (05) Leading 50-ha Fifth Growth famous for excellent full-bodied, vigorous examples of PAUILLAC. Second label: Lacoste-Borie.

La Grave à Pomerol Pom r ★★★ 88 89' 90 94 95 96 **98' 00** 01 02 04 (05) Verdant CH with small but first-class v'yd owned by Christian MOUEIX. Beautifully structured POMEROL of medium richness.

Gressier-Grand-Poujeaux Moulis r ★★ ·★★★ 88 89 90 94 95 96 98 00 01 03 04 (05) V.gd CRU BOURGEOIS SUPÉRIEUR. Fine wine with gd track record. Repays patient cellaring. Since 2003, same owners as CHASSE-SPLEEN.

Greysac Méd r ★★ 95 96 98 00' **02** 03 04 (05) Elegant 70-ha CRU BOURGEOIS SUPÉRIEUR. Same management as CANTEMERLE. Fine, consistent style.

BORDEAUX

Gruaud-Larose St-Jul r нннн 85 86' 88 89' 90' 93 95' 96' 97 98 99 00' 01 02 03' 04 (05) One of the biggest, best-loved Second Growths. 82 ha. Smooth, rich, stylish claret, yr after yr; ages 20+ yrs. Second wine: Sarget de Gruaud-Larose.

Guadet-St-Julien St-Em нн 88 89 90' 94 95 96' 98 00 01 04 (05) Small GRAND CRU CLASSÉ on the plateau. Firm, classic style. Could improve.

Guiraud Saut w (r) sw (dr) нннн 86' 88' 89' 90' 95 96' 97' 98 99 01' 02 03 04 (05) Restored classed growth of top quality. Over 100 ha. At best, excellent sweet wine of great finesse; also small amount of red and dry white.

La Gurgue Mar r нн 88 89' 90 94 95' 96' 98 00' 01 02 03 04 (05) Small, well-placed 10-ha property, for MARGAUX of the fruitier sort. Same management as HAUT-BAGES-LIBERAL. Winery renovated in 2000.

Hanteillan Cissac r нн 95 96 98 00' 02 03 04 (05) Huge 82-ha v'yd: very fair CRU BOURGEOIS SUPÉRIEUR, conscientiously made. CH Laborde is the second label.

Haut-Bages Averous Pau r нн 89' 90 94 95 96 98 99 00 02 03 04 (05) The second wine of LYNCH-BAGES. Should be tasty drinking.

Haut-Bages-Libéral Pau r нннн 94 95 96' 98 99 00 01 02 03 04 (05) Lesser-known Fifth Growth of 28 ha (next to LATOUR) in same stable as LA GURGUE. Results are excellent, full of PAUILLAC vitality.

Haut-Bages-Monpelou Pau r нн 89' 90 94 95 96 98 99 00 03 04 (05) A 15-ha CRU BOURGEOIS SUPÉRIEUR stablemate of CH BATAILLEY on former DUHART-MILON land. Gd minor PAUILLAC.

Haut-Bailly Graves r нннн 88' 89' 90' 94 95 96 97 98' 99 00' 01 02 03 04 (05) Over 28 ha at LÉOGNAN. Investment in cellars. Since 1979 some of the best savoury, round, intelligently made red GRAVES have regularly come from this CH. Second label is La Parde de Haut-Bailly.

Haut-Batailley Pau r нннн 86 88 89' 90' 95 96' 98 99 00 02 03 04 (05) Smaller part of divided Fifth Growth BATAILLEY: 20 ha. Gentler than sister CH GRAND-PUY-LACOSTE. Second wine: La Tour-d'Aspic.

Haut-Beauséjour St-Est r нн 95 98 99 00 01 03 04 (05) Another CRU BOURGEOIS performing well. Owned by CHAMPAGNE house ROEDERER.

Haut-Bergey Pessac-L r (w) нн (r) 98 99 00 01 02 03 04 (05) (w) 02 03 04 (05) A 26-ha estate now producing a denser, fruit-driven GRAVES with oak overlay. Also a little dry white. Completely renovated in the 1990s. Michel ROLLAND consults. Same ownership as BARDE-HAUT and CLOS L'EGLISE. Sister CH Branon.

Haut Bommes Saut Second label of CLOS HAUT-PEYRAGUEY.

Haut-Brion Pessac, Graves r нннн (r) 70' 71 75' 76 78' 79' 81 82 83' 85' 86' 88' 89' 90' 91 93 94 95' 96' 97 98' 99 00' 01 02 03 04 (05) The oldest great CH of B'x and the only non-MÉDOC First Growth of 1855. 44 ha. Deeply harmonious, never-aggressive wine with endless, honeyed, earthy complexity. Consistently great since 75. A little full dry white: 90 93 94 95 96 97 98 99 00' 01 02 03 04' (05). See BAHANS HAUT-BRION, LA MISSION-HAUT-BRION, LAVILLE-HAUT-BRION.

Haut Condissas Méd r нн 99 00 01 02 03 04 (05) Aspiring new *cru* at Bégadan. Old-vine selection from CH Rollan de By. CHx La Clare, La Tour Séran same ownership.

Haut-Marbuzet St-Est r нннннн 82' 85' 86' 88 89' 90' 94 95 96' 98 99 00' 01 02 03 04 (05) The best of many gd ST-ESTÈPHE CRUS BOURGEOIS. Now CRU BOURGEOIS EXCEPTIONNEL. M Dubosq has reassembled ancient Dom de Marbuzet, in total 71 ha. Also owns CHAMBERT-MARBUZET, MacCarthy, Tour de Marbuzet. Haut-Marbuzet is 60% Merlot. New oak gives distinctive, if not subtle, style of great appeal.

Haut-Pontet St-Em r нн 98 00 01 03 04 (05) Reliable 4.8-ha v'yd of the CÔTES deserving its GRAND CRU status. 2,500 cases.

NB The vintages printed in colour are the ones you should choose first for drinking in 2007.

Haut-Sarpe St-Em r ★★ **86 88 89 90' 94 95 96 98 00'** 01 03 04 (05) 21-ha GRAND CRU CLASSÉ with elegant ch and park, 70% Merlot. Same owner (Janoueix) as CH LA CROIX, POMEROL.

Hortevie St-Jul r ★★ **90 95 96 98 00** 02 03 04 (05) One of the few non-classified ST-JULIENS. This tiny v'yd and its bigger sister TERREY-GROS-CAILLOU are shining examples. Now hand-harvesting only.

Hosanna Pom r ★★★★ 00 01 02 03 04 (05) Formerly Certan-Guiraud until purchased and renamed by J-P MOUEIX. Only best 4.5 ha retained. First vintages confirm its class. Worthy stablemate of PÉTRUS and TROTANOY.

Houssant St-Est r ★★ **90 95 96 98 00'** 02 03 04 (05) Typical robust well-balanced ST-ESTÈPHE CRU BOURGEOIS; well known in Denmark. Same ownership as CRU BOURGEOIS CH Leyssac.

d'Issan Cantenac-Mar r ★★★ **88 89** 90' **95 96' 98 99 00' 01** 02 03 04' (05) Beautifully restored moated ch nr Gironde with 30-ha Third Growth v'yd. Fragrant wines; more substance since late 90s. Second label: Blason d'Issan.

Kirwan Cantenac-Mar r ★★★ **82' 85 86 88 89' 90'** 94 95 96 98 99 00' 01 02 03 04 (05) A 35-ha Third Growth; from 1997 majority owned by SCHRÖDER & SCHŸLER. Michel ROLLAND advises. Mature v'yds now giving classy wines. Second label: Les Charmes de Kirwan.

Labégorce Mar r ★★ 94 95 **96 98 99 00 01** 02 03 04 (05) Substantial 38-ha CRU BOURGEOIS SUPÉRIEUR N of MARGAUX; long-lived wines of true MARGAUX quality. Significant investment since 1989.

Labégorce-Zédé Mar r ★★→★★★ **88 89' 90' 93** 94 95 **96' 98 99** 00' 01 02 03 04 (05) CRU BOURGEOIS EXCEPTIONNEL N of MARGAUX (25 ha). Typically delicate, fragrant, classic. Second label: Dom Zédé. Also 9.3 ha of AC BORDEAUX: "Z".

Lacoste-Borie The second wine of GRAND-PUY-LACOSTE.

Lafaurie-Peyraguey Saut w sw ★★★ 78 82 83' **85** 86' **88' 89' 90' 95 96' 97 98 99 01' 02** 03 04 (05) Fine 40-ha classed growth at Bommes; owners Groupe Suez Bank. One of best buys in SAUTERNES. Second wine: La Chapelle de Lafaurie.

Lafite-Rothschild Pau r ★★★★ **82' 83 85 86' 88' 89' 90' 91** 93 94 **95** 96' 97 98' 99 00' 01' 02 03' 04' (05) First Growth of famous elusive perfume and style, but never huge weight, although more density and sleeker texture from 1996. Great vintages keep for decades. Recent vintages are well up to form. Amazing circular cellars. Joint ventures in Chile (1988), California (1989), Portugal (1992), Argentina (1999), and now the Midi and Italy. Second wine: Carruades de Lafite. 91 ha. Also owns CHX DUHART-MILON, l'EVANGILE, RIEUSSEC.

Lafleur Pom r ★★★★ 82' **83** 85' 86 **88' 89' 90'** 93 94 95 96 97 98' 99' 00' 01' 02 03 04' (05) Superb 4.8-ha property. Resounding wine of the elegant, intense, less fleshy kind for long maturing and investment. 50% Cab Fr. Second wine: Pensées de Lafleur.

Lafleur-Gazin Pom r ★★ **88' 89 90** 94 95 96 **98 00 01** 04 (05) Distinguished small J-P MOUEIX estate on the NE border of POMEROL.

Lafon-Rochet St-Est r ★★★ 85 86 88' **90'** 94 95 **96' 98 99** 00' 01 02 03 04 (05) Fourth Growth neighbour of COS D'ESTOURNEL, 45 ha. Investment, selection, and a higher percentage of Merlot have made this ST-ESTÈPHE more opulent since 98. Same owner as CH PONTET-CANET. Second label: Les Pèlerins de Lafon-Rochet.

Lagrange Pom r ★★ **85' 86 88 89' 90'** 94 95 96 **98 00 01** 04 (05) An 8-ha v'yd in the centre of POMEROL run by the ubiquitous house of J-P MOUEIX. Good value but not in the same league as HOSANNA, LA FLEUR-PÉTRUS, LATOUR-À-POMEROL, etc..

Lagrange St-Jul r ★★★ **88' 89' 90'** 94 95 96 97 98 99 00' 01 02 03 04 (05) Formerly neglected Third Growth inland from ST-JULIEN. 113 ha now in tip-top condition with wines to match. Second wine: Les Fiefs de Lagrange.

La Lagune Ludon, H-Méd r ★★★ **88' 89' 90'** 94 95 96' 98 00' 01 02 03 04 (05) 80-ha Third Growth in S MÉDOC with sandy-gravel soils. Dipped in the 1990s but on form from 2000. Fine-edged, now with added structure and depth. New CHAI 2004. Owned by Jean-Jacques Frey, also a shareholder of BILLECART-SALMON.

Lalande-Borie St-Jul r ★★ **96 98 00 01 02** 03 04 (05) A baby brother of the great DUCRU-BEAUCAILLOU created from part of the former v'yd of CH LAGRANGE. Gracious, easy-drinking wine.

de Lamarque Lamarque, H-Méd r ★★ **89 90' 94 95 96 98 99 00' 02 03** 04 (05) Splendid medieval fortress in central MÉDOC, 35-ha CRU BOURGEOIS SUPÉRIEUR; competent, mid-term wines. Second wine: Donjon de L.

Lamothe Bergeron H-Méd r ★★ **88 89 90 94 95 96' 98' 00 02 03** 04 (05) Large 67-ha CRU BOURGEOIS SUPÉRIEUR in Cussac Fort Médoc making reliable claret.

Lanessan Cussac, H-Méd r ★★ **85 86' 88' 89' 90' 94 95 96' 98 00' 02** 03 04 (05) Distinguished 44-ha CRU BOURGEOIS SUPÉRIEUR just S of ST-JULIEN. Fine rather than burly, but ages well.

Langoa-Barton St-Jul r ★★★ **88' 89' 90' 94 95 96 98 99** 00' 01 02 03 04' (05) The 20-ha Third Growth sister CH to LÉOVILLE-BARTON. Very old Barton-family estate; impeccable standards, great value. Second wine: Réserve de Léoville-Barton.

Larcis-Ducasse St-Em r ★★ **85 86 88' 89' 90' 94 95 96' 98' 00** 02 03 04 (05) Top classed-growth property of St-Laurent, eastern neighbour of ST-EMILION, on the CÔTES. 12 ha in a fine situation; wines on an upward swing since management in 2002 (PAVIE-MACQUIN and PUYGUERAUD). To watch.

Larmande St-Em r ★★★ **88' 89' 90' 94 95' 96 98' 00' 01** 03 04 (05) Substantial 24-ha property. Replanted, re-equipped, and now making rich, strikingly scented wine, silky in time. Second label: CH des Templiers.

Laroque St-Em r ★★→★★★ **82' 85 86 88** 89 90 94 95 96 98 99 00' 01 02 03 04 (05) Important 58-ha v'yd on the ST-EMILION CÔTES in St-Christophe. Promoted to GRAND CRU CLASSÉ in 1996. Well-structured wines for ageing.

Larose-Trintaudon St-Laurent, H-Méd r ★★ **96' 98 00 01 02 03** 04 (05) The biggest v'yd in the MÉDOC: 172 ha. Modern methods make reliable, fruity, and charming CRU BOURGEOIS SUPÉRIEUR wine to drink young. Second label: Larose St-Laurent. Special CUVÉE (from 1996): CRU BOURGEOIS Larose Perganson; from 33-ha parcel.

Laroze St-Em r ★★ **90' 94 95 96' 98' 99 00 01** 02 (05) Large v'yd (30 ha) on W CÔTES. Fairly light wines from sandy soils, more depth from 1998; approachable when young.

Larrivet-Haut-Brion Pe-Lé r w ★★ (r) **88 89 90 94 95 96' 98' 00** 01 02 03 04' (05) LÉOGNAN property with perfectionist standards; Michel ROLLAND consulting. Rich, modern red. Also 4,500 cases of fine, barrel-fermented white (**95 96' 98' 99 00 01 02 04'** (05)). New plantings in 1999.

Lascombes Mar r (p) ★★★ **88' 89' 90' 95 96' 98' 99 00** 01 02 03 04 (05) A 97-ha Second Growth. Wines have been wobbly, but real improvements in recent vintages. Second label: Chevalier de Lascombes.

Latour Pau r ★★★★ **61' 62 64 66' 70' 75 78' 79 81 82' 83 85 86' 88' 89' 90' 91 92 93 94' 95'** 96' 97 98 99 00' 01 02 03' 04' (05) First Growth considered the grandest statement of the MÉDOC. Profound, intense, almost immortal wines in great yrs; even weaker vintages have the characteristic note of terroir and run for many yrs. 60 ha sloping to R Gironde. Latour always needs 10 yrs to show its hand. New state-of-the-art CHAI (2003) allows more precise vinification. Second wine: LES FORTS DE LATOUR; third wine: PAUILLAC.

Latour-à-Pomerol Pom r ★★★ **85' 86 88' 89' 90' 94 95 96 98' 99 00'** 01 03 04 (05) Top growth of 7.6 ha under MOUEIX management. POMEROL of great power and perfume, yet also ravishing finesse.

Latour-Martillac Pe-Lé r w ★★ (r) A 42-ha (three-quarters red) classed-growth property in Martillac. Regular quality (red and white); good value at this level. The white can age admirably (**96 97 98' 99 00 01 02 03 04** (05)).

des Laurets St-Em r ★★ **98 00 01 03 04** (05) Major property in PUISSEGUIN-ST-

EMILION and MONTAGNE-ST-EMILION (to the E), with 72 ha of v'yd evenly split on the CÔTES (40,000 cases).

Laville-Haut-Brion Pe-Lé w ★★★★ 89' 90 92 93' 94 95' 96' 97 98 99 00' 01 02 03 04' (05) Tiny production of very best white GRAVES for long, succulent maturing, made at La Mission-haut-brion. Mainly Sem. 89, 95, 96 and 04 are off the dial.

Léoville-Barton St-Jul r ★★★★ 85' 86' 88' 89' 90' 93' 94' 95' 96' 97 98 99 00' 01 02 03' 04 (05) A 45-ha portion of the great Second Growth LÉOVILLE v'yd in Anglo-Irish hands of the Barton family for over 150 yrs. Powerful, classic claret; traditional methods, very fair prices. Major investment raised already high standards to Super Second. See also LANGOA-BARTON.

Léoville-Las-Cases St-Jul r ★★★★ 82' 83' 85' 86' 88 89' 90' 91 93 94 95' 96' 97 98 99 00' 01 02 03' 04' (05) The largest LÉOVILLE; 97 ha with daunting reputation. Elegant, complex, powerful, austere wines, for immortality. Second label CLOS DU MARQUIS is also outstanding.

Léoville-Poyferré St-Jul r ★★★ 86' 88 89' 90' 95 96 98 99 00' 01 02 03' 04 (05) For yrs the least outstanding of the Léovilles; high potential rarely realized. Michel ROLLAND consults here; quality now at Second Growth level. 80 ha. Second label: Ch Moulin-Riche.

Lestage Listrac r ★★ 89' 90' 95 96 98 00 02 03 04 (05) A 42-ha CRU BOURGEOIS SUPÉRIEUR in same hands as CH FONREAUD. Firm, slightly austere claret. Second wine: La Dame du Coeur de Château Lestage.

Lilian Ladouys St-Est r ★★ 95 96 98 00 01 02 03 04 (05) Created in the 1980s: a tiny 9-ha CRU BOURGEOIS SUPÉRIEUR now making consistently good ST-ESTÈPHE.

Liot Barsac w sw ★★ 85 86 88 89' 90' 95 96 97' 98 99 01' 02 03 (05) Consistent, fairly light, golden wines from 20 ha. Good to drink early, but they last.

Liversan St-Sauveur, H-Méd r ★★ 89' 90' 94 95 96 98 00 02 03 04 (05) A 47-ha CRU BOURGEOIS SUPÉRIEUR inland from PAUILLAC. Same owner – Jean-Michel Lapalu – as PATACHE D'AUX. Quality oriented. Second wine: Les Charmes de Liversan.

Loudenne St-Yzans, Méd r w ★★ 89' 90 94 95 96' 98 00 02 03 04 (05) Beautiful riverside CH. Michel ROLLAND consults, so wines are getting bigger, blacker, denser. Well-made CRU BOURGEOIS SUPÉRIEUR r and Sauv Bl w from 63 ha. The new oak-scented white is best at 2–4 yrs, but will last (98 99' 00 01 02 04 (05)).

Loupiac-Gaudiet Loupiac w sw ★★ 89 90 95 96 97 98 99 01 02 03' (05) A reliable source of gd-value "almost-SAUTERNES", just across R Garonne.

La Louvière Pe-Lé r w ★★★ (r) 89' 90' 94' 95 96' 98' 99 00' 01 02 03 04 (05) (w) 96' 97' 98' 99 00 01 02 03 04' (05) A 55-ha LÉOGNAN estate with classical mansion restored by André Lurton. Excellent white and red of classed-growth standard. See also BONNET, DE CRUZEAU, COUHINS-LURTON, and DE ROCHEMORIN.

de Lussac St-Em r ★★ 98 99 00 03 04 (05) One of the best estates in LUSSAC-ST-EMILION. New owners and technical methods since 2000.

Lynch-Bages Pau r (w) ★★★★ 83' 85' 86' 88' 89' 90' 91 94 95' 96' 98 99 00' 01 02 03 04' (05) Always popular, now a regular star. 90 ha. Rich, robust wine: deliciously dense, brambly; aspiring to greatness. See also HAUT-BAGES-AVEROUS. From 1990, v.gd intense oaky white – Blanc de Lynch-Bages. Same owners (Cazes family) as LES ORMES-DE-PEZ and Villa Bel-Air.

Lynch-Moussas Pau r ★★ 89 90' 94 95' 96' 98 00' 01 02 03 04 (05) Fifth Growth restored by the director of Ch Batailley. On the up since 2000.

du Lyonnat Lussac-St-Em r ★★ 98 00' 01 03 04 (05) A 49-ha estate; well-distributed, reliable wine.

Macquin-St-Georges St-Em r ★★ 89 90' 95 96 98 99 00 01 03 04 (05) Steady producer of delicious, not weighty, satellite ST-EMILION at ST-GEORGES.

Magdelaine St-Em r ★★★ 82' 83' 85 86 88 89' 90' 94 95 96 98' 99 00 01 03 04

(05) Leading CÔTES First Growth: 11 ha owned by J-P MOUEIX. Top-notch, Merlot-led wine; recently powerful and fine.

Malartic-Lagravière Pe-Lé r (w) ★★★ (r) **89 90' 94** 95 96 **98 99 00'** 01 02 03 04 (05) (w) **96 97 98 99 00 01' 02 03 04'** (05) LÉOGNAN classed growth of 47 ha (majority red). Rich, modern red wine since late 1990s and a little long-ageing Sauv Bl white. Belgian owner (since 96) has revolutionized the property. Michel ROLLAND and Denis Dubourdieu now consulting.

Malescasse Lamarque, H-Méd r ★★ **89 90 94 95'** 96 98 00 01 02 03 04 (05) Renovated CRU BOURGEOIS SUPÉRIEUR with 40 well-situated hectares. Second label: La Closerie de Malescasse. Supple wines, accessible early.

Malescot-St-Exupéry Mar r ★★★ **89 90'** 94 95 96 **98 99 00'** 01 02 03 04 (05) Third Growth of 24 ha returned to fine form in the 1990s. Now ripe, fragrant, and finely structured. Michel ROLLAND consults.

de Malle Saut w r sw dr ★★★ (w sw) **83 85 86' 88 89' 90' 94** 95 96' **97' 98 99 01' 02** 03 (05) Beautiful Preignac CH of 50 ha. V.fine, medium-bodied SAUTERNES; also M de Malle dry white and GRAVES CH du Cardaillan.

Marbuzet St-Est r ★★ **89 90 94** 95' **96' 98 99** 00' 01 02 03 04 (05) Second label of COS-D'ESTOURNEL until 94. Same owners. Now a separate CRU BOURGEOIS of 7 ha

Margaux, Château Mar r (w) ★★★★ **82' 83' 85' 86' 88' 89' 90'** 91 93 94 95' **96' 97' 98' 99** 00' 01' 02 03' 04' (05) First Growth (85 ha); the most seductive and fabulously perfumed of all in its frequent top vintages. PAVILLON ROUGE **(95 96' 98 99 00'** 01 02 03 04' (05)) is second wine. Pavillon Blanc is best white (Sauv Bl) of MÉDOC, but expensive: keep 5+ yrs **(95 96 98 99 00' 01' 02 03 04'** (05)).

Marojallia Mar r ★★★ **00' 01** 02 03 04 (05) Micro-CHÂTEAU with 2 ha, looking for big prices for big, beefy, un-MARGAUX-like wines. Second wine: Clos Margalaine.

Marquis-d'Alesme-Becker Mar r ★★ **89 90** 95 98 00 01 04 (05) 17-ha Third Growth. Family ties with MALESCOT-ST-EXUPÉRY. An underperforming CRU CLASSÉ, once highly regarded. Potential here for classic MARGAUX.

Marquis-de-Terme Mar r ★★→★★★ **89' 90'** 95 **96 98 99** 00' 01 02 03 04 (05) Renovated Fourth Growth of 40 ha. Wobbled in the 1990s but looks better since 2000. Solid rather than elegant MARGAUX.

Martinens Mar r ★★ **95 96 98 99 00** 02 03 04 (05) Worthy 30-ha CRU BOURGEOIS in Cantenac.

Maucaillou Moulis r ★★ **89' 90' 94'** 95 96 98' **00' 01 02 03** 04 (05) An 80-ha CRU BOURGEOIS SUPÉRIEUR with gd standards. Cap de Haut-Maucaillou is second wine.

Mazeyres Pom r ★★ **95 96' 98'** 99 00 01 04 (05) Consistent, if not exciting lesser POMEROL. 20 ha. Better since 1996. Alain Moueix, cousin of Christian of J-P MOUEIX, manages here. See FONROQUE.

Médoc: Bourgeois confusion

In 2003, the Crus Bourgeois of the Médoc were reclassified, and many were thrown out: 247 out of 490 candidates made the grade and were classified as plain CB, CB Exceptionnel, or CB Supérieur. Cue a court case; or many court cases. The 70-odd châteaux that are suing over their non-classification may, in the meantime, continue to use the classification, but are not members of the new Association de Crus Bourgeois. In theory their cases are being reviewed by an independent body, but in practice it all seems to have gone rather quiet.

Meyney St-Est r ★★→★★★ **89' 90' 94** 95 **96 98 00** 01 02 03 04 (05) Big (50-ha) riverside property in a superb situation CRU BOURGEOIS SUPÉRIEUR; one of best in ST-ESTÈPHE. Rich, robust, well-structured wines. Second label: Prieur de Meyney.

La Mission-Haut-Brion Pe-Lé r ★★★★ **78' 82' 83** 85' **86 88 89' 90'** 93' 94' 95 96' 97 98' 99 00' 01 02 03 04' (05) Neighbour and long-time rival to HAUT-BRION;

since 1983 in same hands. Consistently grand-scale, full-blooded, long-maturing wine; even bigger than Haut-Brion and sometimes more impressive. 20 ha. Second label: La Chapelle de la Mission. White: LAVILLE-HAUT-BRION.

Monbousquet St-Em r (w) ★★★ 95 96 97 98 99 00' 01 02 03 04 (05) A familiar old property on gravel revolutionized by new owner. Now super-rich, concentrated, and voluptuous wines. Rare white (AC BORDEAUX) from 1998. New owners also acquired PAVIE and PAVIE-DECESSE in 1998.

Monbrison Arsac-Mar r ★★→★★★ 86 88' 89' 90 95 96' 98 99 00 01 02 4 (05) MARGAUX's most modish CRU BOURGEOIS SUPÉRIEUR. Elegant style. 13 ha.

La Mondotte St-Em r ★★★→★★★★ 96' 97 98' 99 00' 01 02 03 04 (05) Intense *garagiste* wines from micro-property owned by Comte Stephen von Neipperg (CANON-LA GAFFELIÈRE, CLOS DE L'ORATOIRE).

Montrose St-Est r ★★★→★★★★ 86' 88 89' 90' 91 93 94 95 96' 97 98 99 00' 01 02 03 04' (05) Real mid-Médoc Second Growth famed for deep-coloured, forceful, old-style claret. Vintages 79–85 (except 82) were lighter; but recent Montrose is almost ST-ESTÈPHE's answer to LATOUR. Second wine: La Dame de Montrose.

Moulin-à-Vent Moulis r ★★ 89 90' 94 95 96' 98 00' 02 03 04 (05) A 25-ha CRU BOURGEOIS SUPÉRIEUR; usually regular quality. Lively, forceful wine.

Moulin de la Rose St-Jul r ★★ 95 96 98 00' 01' 02 03 04 (05) Tiny 4-ha CRU BOURGEOIS SUPÉRIEUR; high standards.

Moulin du Cadet St-Em r p ★★ 89' 90' 94 95 96 98 00 01 03 (05) Little 5-ha GRAND CRU CLASSÉ v'yd on the limestone plateau, now managed by Alain Moueix (see also MAZEYRES). Fragrant, medium-bodied wines.

Moulinet Pom r ★★ 89' 90 95 96 98 00 01 04 (05) One of POMEROL's bigger CHX; 18 ha on lightish soil.

Moulin Pey-Labrie Canon-Fronsac r ★★ 89 90 94 95 96 98' 99 00' 01 02 03 04 (05) Leading property in FRONSAC. Stylish wines with elegance and structure.

Moulin-St-Georges St-Em r ★★ 95 96 98 99 00' 01 02 03 04 (05) Stylish and rich wine. Same ownership as AUSONE.

Mouton Baronne Philippe See D'ARMAILHAC. Lightish wines but recent improvements. Denis Durantou of l'EGLISE-CLINET consults. To watch.

Mouton Rothschild Pau r (w) ★★★★ 70' 75' 76 78 81 82' 83' 85' 86' 88' 89' 90' 91 93' 94 95' 96 97 98' 99 00' 01' 02 03 04' (05) Officially a First Growth since 73, though in reality far longer. 71 ha (87% Cab Sauv) can make majestic, rich wine, often MÉDOC's most opulent (also, from 91, white Aile d'Argent). Artists' labels and the world's greatest museum of art relating to wine. Second wine: Le Petit Mouton from 97. See also Opus One (California) and Almaviva (Chile).

Nairac Saut w sw ★★ 85 86' 88 89 90' 95' 96 97' 98 99 01' 02 03' 04 (05) Perfectionist BARSAC classed growth. Rich, intense, botrytized wines from 16-ha. Should age.

Nenin Pom r ★★★ 89 90 94' 95 96 97 98 99 00' 01 02 03 04 (05) LÉOVILLE-LAS-CASES ownership since 97. Massive investment. New cellars. 4 ha of former Certan-Giraud acquired in 99. Now a total of 34 ha. On an upward swing. Gd-value second wine: Fugue de Nenin.

Olivier Graves r w ★★★ (r) 95 96 98 00 01 02 03 04' (05) (w) 96 97 98' 00 01 02 03 04' (05) A 55-ha classed growth, surrounding a moated castle at LÉOGNAN. A sleeper finally being turned around. Greater purity, expression, and quality from 2002 onwards.

Les Ormes-de-Pez St-Est r ★★→★★★ 89' 90' 94 95 96 98 99 00' 01 02 03 04 (05) Outstanding 29-ha CRU BOURGEOIS EXCEPTIONNEL owned by LYNCH-BAGES. Consistently one of the most likeable ST-ESTÈPHES.

Les Ormes-Sorbet Méd r ★★ 95 96 98' 99 00' 01 02 03' 04 (05) Long-time leader in N MÉDOC. Now 21-ha CRU BOURGEOIS SUPÉRIEUR. Elegant, gently oaked wines that age. Second label: Ch de Conques.

Palmer Cantenac-Mar r ★★★★ **75' 76 78' 79' 81 82 83' 85 86' 88' 89 90 93 94 95 96' 98' 99** 00 01' 02 03 04' (05) The star of Cantenac: a Third Growth par with the Super Seconds. Wine of power, flesh, delicacy, and much Merlot. 52 ha with Dutch, British (the SICHEL family), and French owners. Second wine: Alter Ego de Palmer (a steal for early drinking).

Pape-Clément Pe-Lé r (w) ★★★→★★★★ **88' 89' 90' 94 95 96 97 98' 99 00'** 01' 02 03 04 (05) Ancient PESSAC v'yd; record of seductive, scented, not ponderous reds. Early 80s not so gd; dramatic improvement (and more white) since 85. Ambitious new-wave direction and more concentration from 2000. Watch very closely. Also CH Poumey at Gradignan.

de Parenchère r (w) ★★ **98 99 00 01 02 03 04** (05) Steady supply of useful AC Ste-Foy BORDEAUX and AC BORDEAUX SUPÉRIEUR from handsome ch with 65 ha. CUVÉE Raphael best.

Patache d'Aux Bégadan, Méd r ★★ **95 96 98 99 00 02** 03 04 (05) A 43-ha CRU BOURGEOIS SUPÉRIEUR of the N MÉDOC. Fragrant, largely Cab Sauv wine with the earthy quality of its area. See also LIVERSAN.

Pavie St-Em r ★★★ **88' 89' 90' 94 95 96 98' 99** 00' 01 02 03 04 (05) Splendidly sited First Growth; 37 ha mid-slope on the CÔTES. Great track record. Bought by owners of MONBOUSQUET, along with adjacent PAVIE-DECESSE and La Clusière. This is new-wave ST-EMILION: thick, intense, sweet, mid-Atlantic, and the subject of heated debate.

Pavie-Decesse St-Em r ★★ **89 90 95 96 98' 99** 00' 01' 02 03 04 (05) Small 3.6-ha estate. Brother to the above and on form since 1998.

Pavie-Macquin St-Em r ★★★ **89' 90' 94 95 96' 97 98' 99** 00' 01 02 03 04 (05) One of the leading GRANDS CRUS CLASSES. A 15-ha v'yd on the limestone plateau E of ST-EMILION. Astute management and winemaking by Nicolas Thienpont of PUYGUERAUD and consultant Stéphane Derenoncourt. Powerful, structured wines that need time in bottle.

Pedesclaux Pau r ★★ **95' 96 98' 99 00** 02 03 04 (05) A 20-ha Fifth Growth on the level of CRU BOURGEOIS. Most goes to Belgium. Second wine: Ch Haut-Padarnac.

Petit-Village Pom r ★★★ **90' 94 95 96 98' 99 00'** 01 03 04 (05) Top property revived. 11 ha; same owner (AXA Insurance) as PICHON-LONGUEVILLE since 1989. Powerful plummy wine. Second wine: Le Jardin de Petit-Village.

Pétrus Pom r ★★★★ **70' 71' 73 75' 76 78 79' 81 82' 83 84 85' 86 88' 89' 90 93 94 95' 96** 97 98' 99 00' 01 02 03 04' (05) The (unofficial) First Growth of POMEROL: Merlot solo *in excelsis*. 11 ha of gravelly clay giving 5,000 cases of massively rich and concentrated wine, on allocation to the world's millionaires. Each vintage adds lustre.

Peyrabon St-Sauveur, H-Méd r ★★ **98 99 00' 01 02 03** 04 (05) Serious 53-ha CRU BOURGEOIS owned by B'x négociant. Also La Fleur-Peyrabon in PAUILLAC.

de Pez St-Est r ★★→★★★ **88 89 90' 94 95' 96' 97 98' 99** 00 01 02 03 04 (05) Outstanding CRU BOURGEOIS EXCEPTIONNEL of 24 ha. As reliable as any of the village's classed growths, if not quite so fine. Bought in 95 by ROEDERER.

Phélan-Ségur St-Est r ★★ →★★★ **88' 89' 90' 94 95 96' 98 99** 00' 01 02 03 04 (05) Big and important CRU BOURGEOIS EXCEPTIONNEL (89 ha); rivals the last as one of ST-ESTÈPHE's best. From 1986 has built up a strong reputation.

Pibran Pau r ★★ **88 89' 90' 94 95 96 98 99 00'** 01 03 04 (05) Small CRU BOURGEOIS SUPÉRIEUR allied to PICHON-LONGUEVILLE. Classy wine with PAUILLAC drive.

Pichon-Longueville (formerly **Baron de Pichon-Longueville**) Pau r ★★★★ **82' 83 85 86' 88' 89' 90' 93 94' 95 96 97 98 99** 00' 01 02 03 04 (05) Second Growth (70 ha) with revitalized powerful PAUILLAC wine on a par with the following entry. Second label: Les Tourelles de Longueville.

Pichon-Longueville Comtesse de Lalande (**Pichon Lalande**) Pau r ★★★★ **75' 76 78' 79' 81 82' 83 85' 86' 88' 89' 90' 94 95 96 97 98 99** 00 01 02 03 04 (05) Supersecond-growth neighbour to LATOUR (75 ha). Always among the very top performers; a long-lived, Merlot-marked wine of fabulous breed, even in lesser yrs. Second wine: Réserve de la Comtesse. Rivalry across the road (previous entry) worth watching. Other property: CH BERNADOTTE.

Le Pin Pom r ★★★★ 82 83 85 86 88 89 90' 94 95 96 97 98' 99 00 01 02 04' (05) The original of the BORDEAUX cult mini-*crus*. A mere 500 cases of Merlot, with same family behind it as VIEUX-CHÂTEAU-CERTAN (a much better buy). Almost as rich as its drinkers, but prices well beyond PÉTRUS are ridiculous.

de Pitray Castillon r ★★ 95 96' 98' 00' 03 04 (05) Large (31-ha) v'yd on CÔTES DE CASTILLON E of ST-EMILION. Flavoursome wines, once the best-known of the AC.

Plince Pom r ★★ 88 89' 90 94 95 96 98' 99 00' 01 04 (05) Reliable 8-ha property nr Libourne. Lightish wine from sandy soil.

La Pointe Pom r ★★→★★★ 89' 90' 94 95 96 98' 99 00' 01 04 (05) Prominent 25-ha estate; wines recently plumper and more pleasing. LA SERRE is in the same hands.

Pontac-Monplaisir Pe-Lé r (w) ★★ 95 96 98 99 00 02 04 (05) 16-ha property nearly lost to B'x urbanization. Offers useful w and fragrant r of surprising quality.

Pontet-Canet Pau r ★★★ 86' 88 89' 90 94' 95 96' 97 98 99 00' 01 02' 03 04' (05) An 81-ha neighbour to MOUTON-ROTHSCHILD. Dragged its feet for many yrs. Old hard tannins were a turn-off. Since mid-90s very fine results. Very PAUILLAC in style. Second wine: Les Hauts de Pontet-Canet.

Potensac Méd r ★★ 89' 90' 94 95 96 98 99 00' 01 02 03 04' (05) Biggest and best-known CRU BOURGEOIS of N MÉDOC. Now a CRU BOURGEOIS EXCEPTIONNEL. Run and part-owned by Delon family. Class shows, in the form of rich, silky, balanced wines.

Pouget Mar r ★★ 88 89 90 94 95 96 98' 00' 02 03 04 (05) An 11-ha Fourth Growth attached to BOYD-CANTENAC. Similar wines. New CHAI in 2000.

Poujeaux (Theil) Moulis r ★★★ 89' 90' 94' 95' 96' 98 99 00' 01 02 03 04 (05) Family-run CRU BOURGEOIS EXCEPTIONNEL of 52 ha, with CHASSE-SPLEEN and Maucaillou the high-point of Moulis. 20,000-odd cases of characterful tannic and concentrated wine for a long life, yr after yr. Second label: La Salle de Poujeaux. Also CH Arnauld.

Premier Grand Cru Classé See St-Emilion classification box, p.101.

Prieuré-Lichine Cantenac-Mar r ★★★ 89' 90' 94' 95 96 98' 99 00' 01 02 03 04 (05) A 70-ha Fourth Growth brought to the fore by the late Alexis Lichine. New owners 1999; now advised by Stéphane Derenoncourt (see CANON LA GAFFELIÈRE, PAVIE-MACQUIN). Fragrant MARGAUX currently on good form. Second wine: CH de Clairefont. A gd Bordeaux Bl, too.

Puygueraud Côtes de Francs r ★★★ 95' 96 98 99 00' 01' 02 03 04 (05) Leading CH of this tiny AC. Wood-aged wines of surprising class. CHX Laclaverie and Les Charmes-Godard follow the same lines. Special CUVÉE George from 2000 with Malbec in blend. Same winemaker as PAVIE-MACQUIN (ST-EMILION).

Rabaud-Promis Saut w sw ★★→★★★ 88' 89' 90 95 96 97' 98 99 01' 02 03' (05) A 30-ha classed growth at Bommes. Nr top rank since 86. Rich stuff.

Rahoul Graves r w ★★ (r) 95 96 98' 00' 01 02 04 (05) This 30-ha v'yd at Portets is still a sleeper despite long record of gd red (60%) and v.gd white (94 95 96 97 98 99 00 01 02 04' (05)).

Ramage-la-Bâtisse H-Méd r ★★ 95 96' 98 99 00' 02 03 04 (05) Consistent and widely distributed CRU BOURGEOIS SUPÉRIEUR; 65 ha at St-Sauveur, N of PAUILLAC. CH Tourteran is second wine.

Rauzan-Gassies Mar r ★★ 90' 95 96' 98 99 00 01' 02 03' 04 (05) The 30-ha Second Growth neighbour of RAUZAN-SÉGLA that has long lagged behind it. Is something stirring? Vintages since 2000 show improvement.

Rauzan-Ségla Mar r ★★★★ 85 86' 88' 89' 90' 94' 95 96 97 98 99 00' 01 02 03 04' (05) A Second Growth (51 ha) famous for its fragrance; a great MÉDOC name back at the top. New owners since 94 (Chanel; see CANON) have rebuilt the CH and CHAIS. Second wine: Ségla. Should be the top Second Growth of all.

Raymond-Lafon Saut w sw ★★★ 83' 85 86' 88 89' 90' 95 96' 97 98 99' 01' 02 03' 04 (05) Serious little SAUTERNES estate (18 ha) acquired by YQUEM ex-manager and now run by his children. Splendid wines for ageing. Classed-growth quality.

Rayne Vigneau Saut w sw ★★★ 86' 88' 89 90' 95 96 97 98 99 01' 02 03 (05) Large 80-ha classed growth at Bommes. Good but less power and intensity than the top growths. Sweet wine and dry Rayne SEC.

Respide Médeville Graves r w ★★ (r) 99 00' 01 02 03 04 (05) (w) 95' 96' 99 00 01 02 04' (05) One of the better unclassified properties for both red and white. Drink the reds at 4–6 yrs; longer for the better vintages.

Reynon Premières Côtes r w ★★ 40 ha for fragrant white from old Sauv Bl vines (VIEILLES VIGNES) 00 01' 02 03 04' (05); also serious red (96 98 99 00 01 02 03 04' (05)). Second wine (red): CH Reynon-Peyrat. From 1996 v.gd CH Reynon Cadillac liquoreux, too. See also CLOS FLORIDÈNE.

Reysson Vertheuil, H-Méd r ★★ 95 96 00 02 03 04 (05) Recently replanted 49-ha CRU BOURGEOIS SUPÉRIEUR; managed by négociant CVBG-Dourthe (see BELGRAVE, LA GARDE). Rich, modern style.

Ricaud Loupiac w sw (r dr) ★★ 95 96 97 99 01' 02 03' (05) Substantial grower of SAUTERNES-like ageworthy wine just across the river.

Rieussec Saut w sw ★★★★ 82 83' 85 86' 88' 89' 90' 95 96' 97' 98 99 01' 02 03 04 (05) Worthy neighbour of YQUEM with 90 ha in Fargues, bought in 1984 by the (LAFITE) Rothschilds. Vinified in oak since 96. Fabulously opulent wine. Also producing a dry "R". Second wine: Carmes de Rieussec.

Ripeau St-Em r ★★ 95 98 00' 01 04 (05) Lesser 16-ha GRAND CRU CLASSÉ on sandy soils near CHEVAL BLANC. Lower yields and some improvement from 2000.

de la Rivière Fronsac r ★★ 89 90 94 95 96' 98' 99 00' 01 02 03 04 (05) The biggest and most impressive FRONSAC property, with a Wagnerian castle and cellars. Formerly big, tannic wines seem to have become more refined. New winery in 1999. Michel ROLLAND consults. Special CUVÉE: Aria.

de Rochemorin Pe-Lé r w ★★→★★★ (r) 95 96 98' 99 00' 01 02 03 04 (05) (w) 00 01 02 03 04 (05) An important restoration at Martillac by the Lurtons of LA LOUVIÈRE: 105 ha (three-quarters red) of maturing vines. New state-of-the-art winery in 2004. Fairly consistent quality and widely distributed.

Rol Valentin St-Em r ★★★ 95 96 97 98 99 00 01 02 03 04 (05) New (1994) 4.6-ha estate going for modestly massive style (and price). Owned by former footballer. 1,200 cases. Stéphane Derenoncourt consults (see CANON LA GAFFELIÈRE, PAVE-MACQUIN).

Rouget Pom r ★★ 89' 90 95 96 98' 99 00' 01' 03 04 (05) Attractive old estate on the N edge of POMEROL. 17 ha. New owners in 1992 and plenty of investment since (new cellars). Now excellent; rich, unctuous wines.

Royal St-Emilion Brand name of important, dynamic growers' co-op. See GALIUS.

St-André-Corbin St-Em r ★★ 96 98' 99 00 01 03 04 (05) A 22-ha estate in MONTAGNE and ST-GEORGES-ST-EMILION. Above-average wines.

St-Emilion: the classification system

St-Emilion has its own classification system, revised every 10 years, the last in 1996. A new classification was due to be announced in September 2006, after this book went to press. At the top are two **Premiers Grands Crus Classés "A"**: **Châteaux Ausone** and **Cheval Blanc**. Then come 11 **Premiers Grands Crus Classés "B"**. Fifty-five châteaux were elected as **Grands Crus Classés**. To be considered for classification, the châteaux must have obtained the AC St-Emilion Grand Cru certificate, which is renewable every year.

St-Georges St-Georges-St-Em r ★★ **88' 89' 90' 94 95' 96 98' 00' 01 03** 04 (05) Noble 18th-C CH overlooking the ST-EMILION plateau from the hill to the N. 51 ha (25% of St-Georges AC). Gd wine sold direct to the public.

St-Pierre St-Jul r ★★★ **82' 85 89 90' 94 95' 96' 98 99 00' 01'** 02 03 04 (05) Fourth Growth (17 ha). Stylish and consistent classic ST-JULIEN. See GLORIA.

de Sales Pom r ★★ **89' 90'** 94 95 96 98' 00' 01' 04 (05) Biggest v'yd of POMEROL (47 ha) on sandy-gravel soils, attached to grandest CH. Never poetry, lighter weight: try top vintages. Second label: CH Chantalouette.

Sansonnet St-Em r ★★ **99 00' 01** 02 03 04 (05) A small 6.8-ha estate ambitiously run in the new ST-EMILION style (rich, fat) since 1999.

Saransot-Dupré Listrac r (w) ★★ **86 88 89 90 95 96 98' 99 00' 01** 02 03 04 (05) Small 12-ha property performing tremendously well since 1986. Lots of Merlot. Also one of LISTRAC's little band of whites.

Sénéjac H-Méd r (w) ★★ **82' 85 86' 88 89' 90' 94 95 96 98 99** 00 01 02 03 A 37-ha CRU BOURGEOIS SUPÉRIEUR in S MÉDOC recently (1999) bought by the same family as TALBOT. Tannic reds to age and unusual all-Sem white, also to age Special CUVÉE: Karolus.

La Serre St-Em r ★★ **89 90 94 95 96 98' 99** 00' 01 02 03 04 (05) Small (6.5-ha) GRAND CRU CLASSÉ, same owner as LA POINTE. Pleasant stylish wines; more flesh and purity of fruit since 2000.

Sigalas-Rabaud Saut w SW ★★★ **83 85 86 88 89' 90' 95' 96' 97' 98 99 01' 02** 03' 04 (05) The smaller part of the former RABAUD estate: 14 ha in Bommes; same winemaking team as LAFAURIE-PEYRAGUEY. Very fragrant and lovely. Top-ranking now. Second wine: Le Cadet de Sigalas Rabaud.

Siran Labarde-Mar r ★★–★★★ **86 88 89' 90' 95 96 98 99** 00' 01 02 03 04 (05) A 40-ha property of passionate owner who resents lack of CLASSÉ rank. Given CRU BOURGEOIS EXCEPTIONNEL status in 2003. To follow for full-flavoured wines to age. Property is continually striving. Michel ROLLAND consults.

Smith-Haut-Lafitte Pe-Lé r (w p) ★★★ (r) **89' 90' 94 95 96 98 99 00'** 01 02 03 04' (05) (w) **95 96 97 98 99'** 00 01 02 03 04 (05) Classed growth at Martillac: 56 ha (11 ha make oak-fermented white). Ambitious owners (since 1990) continue to spend hugely to spectacular effect, inc a luxurious wine therapy (external!) clinic. Second label: Les Hauts de Smith. Also look out for their CH Cantelys, PESSAC-LÉOGNAN.

Sociando-Mallet H-Méd r ★★★ **88' 89' 90' 94 95 96' 97 98' 99** 00' 01' 02 03 04 (05) Splendid, widely followed estate at St-Seurin. Classed-growth quality; 75 ha. Conservative big-boned wines to lay down for yrs. Second wine: Demoiselles de Sociando.

Soudars H-Méd r ★★ **90 94 95 96' 98 99 00' 01** 03 04 (05) Sister to COUFRAN and VERDIGNAN; recent CRU BOURGEOIS SUPÉRIEUR doing pretty well.

Soutard St-Em r ★★★ **88' 89' 90' 94 95 96 98' 99** 00' 01 02 03 04 (05) Potentially excellent 19-ha classed growth on the limestone plateau; 70% Merlot. Potent wines can be long-lived; but also exciting when young to French palates. Forward-thinking viticultural practices. Second label: CLOS de la Tonnelle.

Suduiraut Saut w SW ★★★★ **79' 81 82' 83 85 86 88' 89' 90' 95 96 97' 98 99' 01'** 02 03' 04 (05) One of the best classed-growth SAUTERNES: 90 ha with renovated CH and gardens by Le Nôtre. New owner (AXA Insurance in 1992) has achieved greater consistency and luscious quality. See PICHON-LONGUEVILLE. Second wine: Castelnau de Suduiraut.

du Tailhas Pom r ★★ **89 90 94 95 96' 98' 99** 00 01 04 (05) 10-ha property, nr FIGEAC. POMEROL of the lighter kind.

Taillefer Pom r ★★ **89 90 94 95' 96 98' 00' 01** 02 03 04 (05) An 11-ha v'yd on the edge of POMEROL. Astutely managed by Catherine Moueix. Less power than top estates but gently harmonious.

Talbot St-Jul r (w) ★★★ **86' 88' 89' 90 94 95 96' 98' 99** 00' 02 03 04 (05) Important 102-ha Fourth Growth, for many yrs younger sister to GRUAUD-LAROSE. Wine similarly attractive: rich, consummately charming, reliable; gd value. V.gd second label: Connétable de Talbot. White: Caillou Blanc matures as well as a gd GRAVES, but drinks well young. SENEJAC same family ownership. Oenologist also oversees TOUR DE MONS.

Terrey-Gros-Caillou St-Jul r ★★ **89 90 94 95 96 98 99 00** 02 03 04 (05) Sister CH to HORTEVIE; 15 ha; at best, equally noteworthy and stylish.

du Tertre Arsac-Mar r ★★★ **88' 89' 90' 94 95 96' 98' 99** 00' 01 02 03 04' (05) Fifth Growth (50 ha) isolated S of MARGAUX. History of undervalued fragrant and fruity wines. Since 97, same owner as CH GISCOURS. New techniques and investment have produced a really concentrated, structured wine.

Tertre Daugay St-Em r ★★★ **88' 89' 90' 94 95 96 98 99 00'** 01 03 04 (05) Small, spectacularly sited GRAND CRU CLASSÉ. Currently being restored to gd order. Potent and stylish wines. Same owner as La GAFFELIÈRE.

Tertre-Rôteboeuf St-Em r ★★★★ **85 86 88' 89' 90' 93 94 95 96 97 98' 99 00' 01** 02 03' 04 (05) A cult star making concentrated, even dramatic, largely Merlot wine since 1983. The prices are frightening. The "roast beef" of the name gives the right idea. Also CÔTES DE BOURG property, Roc de Cambes.

Thieuley E-D-M r p w ★★ Supplier of consistent quality red and white AC B'x; fruity CLAIRET; oak-aged red and white CUVÉE Francis Courselle. Also owns CLOS Ste-Anne in PREMIÈRES CÔTES DE BORDEAUX.

La Tour-Blanche Saut w (r) sw ★★★ **83' 85 86 88' 89' 90' 95 96 97' 98 99 01'** 02 03 04 (05) Historic leader of SAUTERNES, now a government wine college. Coasted in 1970s; hit historic form again in 1988.

La Tour-Carnet St-Laurent, H-Méd r ★★ **82 85 86 89' 90 94' 95 96 98 99 00** 01 02 03 04' (05) Fourth Growth (65 ha) with medieval moated fortress, long neglected. New ownership (see FOMBRAUGE, PAPE-CLÉMENT) and investment from 2000 have produced richer wines in a more modern style. Second wine: Les Douvres de Château La Tour Carnet.

La Tour-de-By Bégadan, Méd r ★★ **89' 90' 94 95 96' 98 00 01** 02 03 04 (05) Very well-run 74-ha CRU BOURGEOIS SUPÉRIEUR in N MÉDOC with a name for the most attractive, sturdy wines of the area.

La Tour de Mons Soussans-Mar r ★★ **88 89 90' 94 95 96' 98' 99** 00 01 02 04 (05) Famous CRU BOURGEOIS SUPÉRIEUR of 44 ha, in the same family for three centuries. A long, dull patch but new (1995) TALBOT influence is returning to the old fragrant, vigorous, ageworthy style.

Tour-du-Haut-Moulin Cussac, H-Méd r ★★ **86' 88' 89' 90' 94 95 96 98 00'** 02 03 04 (05) Conservative grower: intense CRU BOURGEOIS SUPÉRIEUR to mature.

Tour-du-Pas-St-Georges St-Em r ★★ **95 96 98 99 00' 01 03** 04 (05) Wine from 16 ha of ST-GEORGES-ST-EMILION made by BELAIR winemaker.

La Tour du Pin Figeac-Moueix St-Em r ★★ **88' 89' 90' 95 96 98 00' 01** 04 (05) Once part of the FIGEAC estate. Now 8-ha GRAND CRU CLASSÉ owned by Jean-Michel Moueix. Firm but unexciting wines that could improve.

La Tour Figeac St-Em r ★★ **88 89' 90' 94' 95 96' 98' 99 00' 01'** 02 04 (05) A 15-ha GRAND CRU CLASSÉ between FIGEAC and POMEROL. California-style ideas since 1994. Biodynamic methods. Keep an eye on this one.

La Tour Haut Brion Graves r ★★★ **89 90 94 95 96' 98' 99** 00' 01 02 03 04' (05) Formerly second label of LA MISSION-HAUT-BRION. Up to 1983, a plainer, very tannic wine. Now a separate 4.8-ha v'yd: wines stylish, to keep.

Tour Haut-Caussan Méd r ★★ **96 98 00' 01 02** 03 04 (05) Well-run 16-ha CRU BOURGEOIS SUPÉRIEUR at Blaignan to watch for full, firm wines.

Tournefeuille Lalande de Pom r ★★ **89 90' 94 95' 98' 99 00' 01'** 02 03 04 (05) Well-known Néac CH. 17 ha. On the up-swing since 1998 with new owners.

Tour-St-Bonnet Méd r ★★ 95 96 98 99 00' 02 03 04 (05) Consistently well-made potent N MÉDOC from St-Christoly. CRU BOURGEOIS; 40 ha.

Tronquoy-Lalande St-Est r ★★ 89 90' 94 95 96 98 99 00' 02 03 04 (05) A 16-ha CRU BOURGEOIS SUPÉRIEUR: high-coloured wines to age, but no thrills.

Troplong-Mondot St-Em r ★★★ 88' 89' 90' 94' 95 96' 97 98' 99 00' 01' 02 03 04 (05) Leading GRAND CRU CLASSÉ. Well-sited 30 ha on a high point of the limestone plateau. Wines of power and depth with increasing elegance. Michel ROLLAND consults. Second wine: Mondot.

Trotanoy Pom r ★★★★ 82' 85' 88 89' 90' 94 95 96 97 98' 99 00' 01 02 03 04' (05) Potentially the second POMEROL, after PÉTRUS, from the same stable. Only 7 ha; at best (e.g. 98) a glorious fleshy, structured, perfumed wine. Wobbled a bit in the 1980s, but back on top form since 89.

Trottevieille St-Em r ★★★ 89' 90 94 95 96 98 99 00' 01 02 03' 04 (05) First Growth of 11 ha on the limestone plateau. Dragged its feet for yrs. Same owners as BATAILLEY have raised its game since 2000.

de Valandraud St-Em r ★★★★ 93 94 95' 96 97 98 99 00' 01' 02 03 04 (05) Leader among *garagiste* micro-wines fulfilling aspirations to glory. But silly prices for the sort of thick, vanilla-scented wine California can make. V'yds expanded in 1998; better terroir now, and more balance. Second and third wines: Virginie and Axelle.

Valrose St-Est r ★★ 02 03 04 (05) A newcomer since 1999, co-owned with CLINET. Special CUVÉE: Aliénor. To watch.

Verdignan Méd r ★★ 95' 96 98 99 00' 01 02 03 04 (05) Substantial 60-ha CRU BOURGEOIS SUPÉRIEUR sister to COUFRAN and SOUDARS. More Cab than Coufran. Gd value and ageing potential.

La Vieille Cure Fronsac r ★★ 95 96 98 99 00' 01' 02 03 04 (05) A 20-ha property, US-owned, leading the commune. Accesible from 4 years.

Vieux-Château-Certan Pom r ★★★★ 82' 83' 85 86' 88' 89 90' 94 95' 96' 97 98' 99 00' 01 02 04' (05) Traditionally rated close to PÉTRUS in quality, but totally different in style; almost HAUT-BRION build with plenty of finesse. 14 ha. Same (Belgian) family owns tiny LE PIN.

Vieux Château St-André St-Em r ★★ 89' 90' 94 95 96 98 99 00' 01 03 04 (05) Small 6-ha v'yd in MONTAGNE-ST-EMILION owned by winemaker of PÉTRUS until 2002. Regular quality.

Villegeorge Avensan, H-Méd r ★★ 89 90 94 95 96' 98' 99 00' 02 03 04 (05) A 15-ha CRU BOURGEOIS SUPÉRIEUR N of MARGAUX. Fine, traditional MÉDOC style. Sister CHX Duplessis in MOULIS and La Tour de Bessan in MARGAUX.

Villemaurine St-Em r ★★ 88 89 94 95 96 98 99 00' 03 04 (05) Small 8-ha GRAND CRU CLASSÉ with splendid cellars well sited on the limestone plateau by the town. Firm wine with a high proportion of Cab Sauv.

Vray Croix de Gay Pom r ★★ 88 89 90 95 96 98' 00' 04 (05) Very small (4 ha) but ideally situated v'yd in the best part of POMEROL. Has the potential for greater things.

Yon-Figeac St-Em r ★★ 90 95 96 98 99 00' 02 03 04 (05) 24-ha GRAND CRU CLASSÉ. V'yd restructured between 1985 and 1995. Improvements from 2000. Fragrant, tannic wines.

d'Yquem Saut w sw (dr) ★★★★ 75' 76' 79 80 81' 83' 85 86' 88' 89' 90' 93 94 95' 96 97' 98 99' 00 01' 02 03' 04 (05) This is the world's most famous sweet wine estate. 101 ha; only 200 bottles per hectare of very strong, intense, luscious wine, kept 4 yrs in barrel. Most vintages improve for 15+ yrs; some live 100+ yrs in transcendent splendour. After centuries in the Lur-Saluces family, in 1998 control was surrendered to Bernard Arnault of LVMH. The new management is doing well, however. Also makes dry "Y" (YGREC).

Italy

More heavily shaded areas
are the wine-growing regions

The following abbreviations
are used in the text:

Ab	Abruzzi	Sar	Sardinia
Ap	Apulia	Si	Sicily
Bas	Basilicata	T-AA	Trentino-
Cal	Calabria		Alto Adige
Cam	Campania	Tus	Tuscany
E-R	Emilia-Romagna	Umb	Umbria
F-VG	Friuli-	VdA	Valle d'Aosta
	Venezia Giulia	Ven	Veneto
Lat	Latium		
Lig	Liguria		
Lom	Lombardy	cs	Cantine Sociale
Mar	Marches	fz	frizzante
Pie	Piedmont	pa	passito

VALLE
D'AOSTA

L Come

L Maggiore

Milan

LOMBAR

Turin O
PIEDMONT

Genoa O

Po

LIGURIA

Ligurian Sea

In the middle of the first decade of the 21st century, Italy is poised to take stock of a revolution in its wines that began 30 years ago and has changed the face of a viticulture with three millennia of history. As in all Mediterranean countries, wine had always been part of daily life, an indispensable element in a diet based on wheat, the vine, and the olive; and the grape, as much as grain, was justly considered the staff of life. The country's wines, almost bewildering in their variety, were intended for local consumption, and reflected the political and geographical reality of a peninsula broken up into myriad small, independent states and authorities.

The economic boom of the post-World War II years created a national market for wine, but in the rush to modernize and mechanize its vineyards and cellars, Italy fell prey to a philosophy of high-volume production. This threatened to dilute and standardize the country's wines, and it is a credit to Italian producers that they have defended their identity.

In trying to catch up with the rest of the world, a forced internationalization would prove as risky as the quantity-oriented approach of the 1950s and 60s. The appearance of French grapes in the vineyards, of gleaming stainless-steel equipment and small oak barrels in the cellars, provoked fears that Italy was on the same slippery slope as California and Australia.

In retrospect, it is obvious that Italy had to go through this phase in order to find its way. The new millennium has seen a proud reaffirmation of its traditions, of the striking personality that the great Italian varieties can give – but with a new elegance and focus that renders them entirely different from the often too-rustic wines of the past. The techniques of the 21st century are now being put to use to give a new expressiveness to grapes and zones that were already famous in Virgil's time. And, for the world's consumers, there has never been the choice that is now available.

Recent Vintages

Tuscany

2005 Much rain and generally irregular results, most successful in the southern part of the coast, less so in Bolgheri. Sangiovese at every quality level imaginable, from first-rate to diluted.

2004 Exceptionally promising along the coast, in Montepulciano, and in Montalcino. Less consistent in cooler parts of the region (Rufina and the higher vineyards of Chianti Classico).

2003 Considerable vine stress from searing heat and three months of drought. Success with late-ripening varieties; less so with Merlot.
2002 Cool Aug, frequent rains in Sept/Oct. Dilution and rot widespread.
2001 A scorching Aug, unusually cool in early Sept, then humid when warm weather returned. Some excellent wines, but much irregularity.
2000 Very hot, dry late summer/early autumn, one of earliest vintages in memory. Full, alcoholic wines, some impressive, some unbalanced.
1999 An excellent vintage in all major zones.
1998 Very good along the coast, irregular elsewhere.
Older fine vintages: 97 95 90

Piedmont

2005 Pleasurable Dolcetto; spotty for Barbera, with some rot from persistent rains; Nebbiolo rather uneven, though promising wines are not lacking.
2004 Very long growing season, high level of quality for all major red grapes (Dolcetto, Barbera, Nebbiolo), the first since 1999.
2003 Sweltering summer, but nonetheless very positive for Barbera, Dolcetto, and Moscato. Nebbiolo more irregular, with late pickers more successful.
2002 Cool, damp growing season and serious hail damage in Barolo.
2001 Classy and firm Nebbiolo and Barbera, other grapes less successful.
2000 Excellent Barolo, Barbaresco, Barbera. Fifth sound vintage in a row.
1999 Balanced and elegant Barbaresco and Barolo; Barbera more spotty due to irregular end-of-season weather; lovely Dolcetto.
1998 Very good whites, excellent reds. For Barolo and Barbaresco, third fine vintage in a row after difficulties in 91, 92, and 94.
Older fine vintages: 97 90 89

Amarone, Veneto

2005 A difficult harvest due to damp weather, but grape-drying technology saved Amarone and Recioto wines. Less successful for Soave and whites.
2004 A damp Nov caused some concern, but a return of drier weather helped avoid rot. Classic, less concentrated and rich than 2003.
2003 The hottest and driest vintage of the post-war period. Very concentrated and sugar-rich grapes; could be outstanding.
2002 Heavy rains throughout the ripening season. A vintage to forget.
2001 Very balanced weather in the growing season. Promising and classic.
2000 Shaping up as a vintage of powerful wines.
1999 Rain in Sept, some dilution. Less successful than in other parts of Italy.
1998 Balanced grapes; powerful wines with good freshness.

Marches & Abruzzo reds

2005 A year of heavy rainfall, saved by a dry second half of October. Wines of good ripeness and structure for those who waited to pick.
2004 Considerable Oct rains; irregular results. Better in Rosso Conero than Rosso Piceno in the Marches; best in Colline Teramane DOCG, Abruzzo.
2003 One of the most successful areas in Italy in 2003, as the Montepulciano grape stood up to the heat and drought, giving first-rate results.
2002 Cool, damp year; only fair results.
2001 Ideal weather, fine balance of power and elegance in the wines, which are fragrant with much complexity and depth.
2000 Properly hot in late Aug and early Sept, a return of the heat after a cooler interval; ripe grapes of good balance; ample and classy wines.
1999 Rain in Sept; wines of a certain style, lack the usual depth and fullness.
1998 Warm and dry in early Oct, superior results for those who waited to pick.

Campania & Basilicata

2005 Traditionally the last grapes to be picked. Aglianico had weight, complexity, and character – perhaps the finest wines of all in 2005.

2004 Slow and uncertain ripening for Aglianico, and only a warm second half of Oct enabled growers to salvage the grapes. Medium-level, and spotty.

2003 Scorching and drought-stressed growing conditions, but the altitude of the vineyards worked in Aglianico's favour. Generally a success.

2002 Heavy rains; part of the crop salvaged, but little to crow about.

2001 Hot, dry and very regular from July to the end of Oct; textbook weather. Intense, perfumed, and ageworthy wines.

2000 Hotter than 1999, a powerful impetus to the ripening of the grapes. Potent and alcoholic wines built to last.

1999 Warm and dry throughout the growing season, excellent conditions.

1998 Irregular weather, rather austere wines; doubts about future evolution.

Abbazia Sant Anastasia Sicily ★★→★★★ Producer of excellent reds. Lena family now owns second important estate, Fatascià.

Abboccato Semi-sweet.

Aglianico del Vulture Bas DOC r dr (s/sw sp) ★★★ 90' 93' 94' 95 97' 98 99' 00' 01' 03' 04' 05' Among the best wines of S Italy. Ages well to rich aromas. VECCHIO after 3 yrs, RISERVA after 5 yrs. Top: Allegretti, Alovini, Basilium, Bisceglia, Francesco Bonifacio, Cantina del Notaio, Cantina di Venosa, Consiglio, Elena Fucci, Macarico, Di Palma, PATERNOSTER, Le Querce, Torre degli Svevi, Sasso, and Viticoltori Associati del Vulture.

Alba Major wine city of PIEDMONT, on River Tanaro, SE of Turin.

Albana di Romagna E-R DOCG w dr s/sw (sp) ★★→★★★ DYA Italy's first DOCG for white wine, though it was hard to see why. Albana is the (undistinguished) grape. AMABILE is usually better than dry. ZERBINA and Giovanna Madonia's botrytis-sweet PASSITO are outstanding.

Alcamo Si DOC w ★ Soft whites and reds. Rapitalà, Ceuso are best brands.

Aleatico Red Muscat-flavoured grape for sw, aromatic, often fortified wines, chiefly in S. Aleatico di Puglia DOC (best: Candido and Santa Lucia) is better and more famous than Aleatico di Gradoli (Latium) DOC. Gd Aleatico from Falesco, Massa Vecchia in Monteregio, Cecilia and Le Sughere on ELBA; v.gd from Jacopo Banti in VAL DI CORNIA and Sapereta, Acquabona on ELBA.

Alessandria, Gianfranco ★★★ Small producer of high-level ALBA wines at Monteforte d'Alba, esp BAROLO San Giovanni, BARBERA D'ALBA Vittoria, DOLCETTO.

Alezio Ap DOC p (r) ★★ Salento DOC esp for full, flavourful reds and delicate rosés. The top growers are Giuseppe Calò with fine, barrel-aged NEGROAMARO Portulan and Michele Calò with NEGROAMARO IGT Spano.

Allegrini Ven ★★★ Top-quality Veronese producer; outstanding single-v'yd IGT wines (Palazzo della Torre, Grola, and Poja), AMARONE, and RECIOTO.

Altare, Elio Pie ★★★ Pioneering, influential small producer of v. gd, modern BAROLO. Look for BAROLO Arborina, BAROLO Brunate, LANGHE DOC Larigi (Barbera), La Villa, VDT L'Insieme and DOLCETTO D'ALBA – one of the appellation's best.

Alto Adige T-AA DOC r p w dr sw sp ★→★★★ Alto Adige or SÜDTIROL DOC inc almost 50 types of wine: different grapes of different zones (inc varietals of VALLE ISARCO/Eisacktal, TERLANO/Terlaner, Val Venosta/Vinschgau, AA STA MADDALENA, AA Bozner Leiten, AA MERANESE DI COLLINA/Meraner).

Ama, Castello di, (Fattoria di Ama) ★★★ One of the best and most consistent modern CHIANTI CLASSICO estates, nr Gaiole. La Casuccia and Bellavista are top single-v'yd wines. Gd IGTS, Chard, and MERLOT (L'Apparita).

Amabile Means semi-sweet, but usually sweeter than ABBOCCATO.

Amaro Bitter. When prominent on label, contents are not wine but "bitters".

ITALY

Amarone della Valpolicella (formerly Recioto della Valpolicella Amarone) Ven DOC r ★★★ 85' 86 88' 90' 93 94 95' 97' 98' 00' 01' 03' 04' 05' Dry version of RECIOTO DELLA VALPOLICELLA: from air-dried VALPOLICELLA grapes; concentrated, long-lived. Best: Stefano Accordini, Aldigheri, Serego Alighieri, ALLEGRINI, Begali, BERTANI, BOLLA, BOSCAINI, BRUNELLI, Buglioni, BUSSOLA, Ca' La Bianca, Campagnola, Castellani, Cesari, Corteforte, Corte Sant'Alda, CS Valpantena, CS VALPOLICELLA, DAL FORNO, Farina, Guerrieri-Rizzardi, La Costa di Romagnano, LE RAGOSE, LE SALETTE, MASI, Mazzi, Nicolis, Novaia, PASQUA, QUINTARELLI, Roccolo Grassi, Sant'Antonio, Speri, TEDESCHI, Tommasi, Trabucchi, Vaona, Venturini, Villa Monteleone, Viviani, ZENATO, Zeni. Older vintages are still holding, but beginning to show their age.

An Italian choice for 2007
Aglianico del Vulture Riserva Don Anselmo 2001 PATERNOSTER
Barolo Riserva 1999 Schiavenza
Barolo Campè 2001 La Spinetta
Brunello di Montalcino Riserva 1999 La Fuga
Cervaro della Sala 2003 ANTINORI
Dedicato a Walter 2003 Poggio al Tesoro
Gladius 2003 Adolfo Spada
Poggio ai Chiari 2003 COLLE SANTA MUSTIOLA
Radicosa 2003 Coppadoro
Romangia Bianco Dettori

Anselmi, Roberto ★★★ A leader in SOAVE with his single-v'yd Capitel Foscarino and exceptional sweet dessert RECIOTO i Capitelli, now both IGT.

Antinori, Marchesi L & P ★★→★★★★ Very influential, long-established Florentine house of highest repute (mostly justified), owned by Piero A. sharing management with his three daughters and oenologist Renzo Cotarella. Famous for CHIANTI CLASSICO (Tenute Marchese Antinori and Badia a Passignano), Umbrian (CASTELLO DELLA SALA), and PIEDMONT (PRUNOTTO) wines. Pioneer of new IGT, *e.g.* TIGNANELLO, SOLAIA (TUSCANY), Cervaro della Sala (Umbria). Marchese Piero A was the "Voice of Italy" in wine circles in 1970s and 80s. Expanding into S TUSCAN MAREMMA, MONTEPULCIANO (La Braccesca), MONTALCINO, in ASTI (for Barbera), in FRANCIACORTA for sp (Lombardy), and in APULIA ("Vigneti del Sud"). V.gd DOC BOLGHERI Guardo al Tasso. See PRUNOTTO.

Apulia Puglia. Italy's heel, producing almost a sixth of Italy's wine, most blended in N Italy/France. Region to follow in increasing quality/value. Best DOC: CASTEL DEL MONTE, MANDURIA (PRIMITIVO DI), SALICE SALENTO. Producers: Appolonio, ANTINORI, Botromagno, Candido, Cantine Paradiso, Casale Bevagna, Castel di Selva, Tenuta Cocevola, Co-op Copertino, Co-op Due Palme, Conti Zecca, Coppadoro, La Corte, Li Veli, D'Alfonso del Sordo, Fatalone, Felline, Masseria Monaci, Masseria Pepe, Michele Calò, Mille Una, Ognissole, Resta, RIVERA, Rubino, ROSA DEL GOLFO, Santa Lucia, Sinfarosa, TAURINO, Valle dell'Asso, VALLONE.

Aquileia F-VG DOC r w ★→★★ (r) 99' 00 01 03 04 A group of 12 single-varietal wines from around the town of Aquileia. Gd REFOSCO, Sauv Bl. Ca' Bolani and Denis Montanar are the ones to watch.

Argiano Top BRUNELLO estate.

Argiolas, Antonio ★★→★★★ Important SARDINIAN producer. High-level CANNONAU, NURAGUS, VERMENTINO, Bovale, and red IGTS Turriga (★★★) and Korem.

Arneis Pie DOCG w ★★ DYA Fairly gd w from nr ALBA: revival of an ancient grape; fragrant, light wine. DOC: ROERO Arneis, NW of ALBA, normally better than LANGHE Arneis. Try: Almondo, Bric Cencurio, Ca' du Russ, Cascina Chicco, Correggia, Bruno GIACOSA, Malvirà, Monchiero-Carbone, Morra, Angelo Negro, PRUNOTTO.

Assisi Umb r (w) ★→★★ DYA IGT ROSSO and BIANCO di Assisi: very attractive. Sportoletti particularly gd.

Asti Major wine centre of PIEDMONT.

Asti Spumante Pie DOCG w sw sp ★→★★ NV Charming sweet, white Muscat fizz. Unfortunately, the big Asti houses are not interested in improving production of 80 million bottles. Despite unique potential, Asti is a cheap supermarket product. A few producers care: Walter BERA, CASCINA FONDA, CONTRATTO, Dogliotti-Caudrina, Vignaioli di Santo Stefano (see also MOSCATO D'ASTI).

Avignonesi ★★★ Noble MONTEPULCIANO house; highly ambitious, with a very fine range: VINO NOBILE, Desiderio, 50:50 – a SANGIOVESE/MERLOT joint venture with CAPANNELLE, a white blend, and superlative VIN SANTO (★★★★).

Azienda agricola/agraria Estates (large and small) making wine from own grapes.

Azienda/casa vinicola Négociants making wine from bought-in and own grapes.

Azienda vitivinicola A (specialized) wine estate.

Banfi (Castello or **Villa)** ★★→★★★ Space-age MONTALCINO CANTINA of biggest US importer of Italian wine. Huge plantings at Montalcino, mostly SANGIOVESE; also Syrah, PINOT N, Cab Sauv, Chard, Sauv Bl, etc.: part of a drive for quality plus quantity. Poggio all'Oro and Poggio alle Mura are ★★★ BRUNELLOS. In PIEDMONT also gd Banfi Brut, BRACCHETTO D'ACQUI, GAVI, PINOT GRIGIO. See also North America.

Barbaresco Pie DOCG r ★★→★★★★ 89' 90' 93 95' 96' 97' 98' 99' 00 01' 03 04 05 Neighbour of BAROLO; the other great NEBBIOLO wine. Perhaps marginally less sturdy. At best, palate-cleansing, deep, subtle, fine. At 4 yrs becomes RISERVA. Producers inc Marziano Abbona, Antichi PODERI di Gallina, Bera, Piero Busso, Ca' del Baio, Cascina Bruciata, Cascina Luisin, CERETTO, CIGLIUTI, Fontanabianca, FONTANAFREDDA, Fratelli Giacosa, GAJA, Bruno GIACOSA, GRESY, La Ca' Bianca, La Contea, Cortese, Lano, MOCCAGATTA, Montaribaldi, Morassino, Fiorenzo Nada, Paitin, Giorgio Pelissero, PIO CESARE, PRODUTTORI DEL BARBARESCO, PRUNOTTO, Prunset, Ressia, Massimo Rivetti, Roagna, Albino Rocca, Bruno ROCCA, RIVETTI, Ronchi, Serragilli, Sottimano, Vano, Varaldo.

Barbatella, Cascina La ★★★ Top producer of BARBERA D'ASTI: excellent single-v'yd. VIGNA dell'Angelo and MONFERRATO Rosso Sonvico (Barbera/Cab Sauv).

Barbera d'Alba Pie DOC r ★★→★★★ 97' 98' 99 00' 01' 03' 04 Tasty, fragrant r. Best age up to 7 yrs. Many excellent wines, often from fine producers of BAROLO and BARBARESCO. Top houses: Marziano Abbona, Gianfranco ALESSANDRIA, Almondo, Baudana, Bric Cencurio, Boglietti, Boroli, Bovio, Bricco Maiolica, Cascina Chicco, Cascina Cucco, Cascina Luisin, Caviola, Clerico, Aldo CONTERNO, Giovanni Conterno, Paolo Conterno, Conterno-Fantino, Cordero di Montezemolo, Corino, Damilano, De Stefanis, Gagliaso, Germano, Ghisolfi, Elio GRASSO, Silvio Grasso, Hilberg, MANZONE, Mauro Mascarello, Massolino, Molino, Monchiero-Carbone, Montaribaldi, Paolo Monti, OBERTO, Paitin, Pelissero, Luigi Pira, Principiano, PRUNOTTO, Revello, Giuseppe Rinaldi, Giorgio Rivetti, Albino Rocca, Tenuta Rocca, Rocche Costamagna, Ruggieri Corsini, Sandrone, SCAVINO, Seghesio, Sottimano, VAJRA, Varaldo, Veglio, Vietti, Roberto VOERZIO.

Barbera d'Asti Pie DOC r ★★→★★★ 97 98' 99 00' 01' 03' 04 For real Barbera-lovers: Barbera alone, tangy and appetizing, drunk young or aged up to 7–10 yrs. Top growers: Olim Bauda, BAVA, BERA, Bersano, BERTELLI, Alfiero Boffa, BRAIDA, Brema, Ca' del Fer, Ca' del Prete, Cascina Ferro, Cascina Garrettina, Cascina Tavijn, Castino, CHIARLO, Contratto, COPPO, CS Nizza, CS Vinchio e Vaglio, Dezzani, Domanda, Il Falchetto, Ferraris, Garetto, La Giribaldina, Mauro Grasso, HASTAE, Hohler, La Barbatella, La Lune del Rospo, La Meridiana, La Morandina, L'Arbiola, L'Armangia, La Tenaglia, Malgrà, Marchesi Alfieri, Marengo, Martinetti, Oddero, Agostino Pavia, Pico Maccario, PRUNOTTO, RIVETTI, Scrimaglio, Scagliola, Tenute dei Vallarino, Terre da Vino, VIETTI.

Barbera del Monferrato Pie DOC r ★→★★ DYA Easy-drinking Barbera from

Alessandria and ASTI. Pleasant, slightly fizzy, sometimes sweetish. Delimited area is almost identical to BARBERA D'ASTI but style simpler, less ambitious.

Barco Reale Tus DOC r ★★ **97 98 99** 00 01 03 DOC for junior wine of CARMIGNANO using the same grapes.

Bardolino Ven DOC r (p) ★→★★ DYA Pale, summery, slightly bitter red from Lake Garda. Bardolino CHIARETTO: paler and lighter. Best inc Buglioni Cavalchina, Giovanna Tantini, MONTRESOR, Pantini, ZENATO, Zeni.

Barolo Pie DOCG r ★★★→★★★★ 89' 90' 93' **95' 96' 97'** 98' 99' 00 01' 03, 04 Small area S of ALBA with one of Italy's supreme reds: rich, tannic, alcoholic (min 13%), dry but wonderfully deep and fragrant (also crisp and clean) in the mouth. From NEBBIOLO grapes. Ages for up to 20–25 yrs (RISERVA after five)

The Barolo role of honour

The classic style: Anselma, Ascheri, Barale, Bergadano, Giacomo Borgogno, Brovia, Cavallotto, Aldo CONTERNO, Giovanni Conterno, Paolo Conterno, Dosio, FONTANAFREDDA, Bruno GIACOSA, Bartolo MASCARELLO, Giuseppe MASCARELLO, Massolino, Monchiero, PRUNOTTO, Renato Ratti, Francesco Rinaldi, Giuseppe Rinaldi, Schiavenza, VIETTI.

A promising new generation: Gianfranco ALESSANDRIA, ALTARE, Boglietti, Bongiovanni, Boroli, Brico Cenccurio, Bruna Grimaldi, Cabutto, Camerano, Cascina Ballarin, Cascina Luisin, M CHIARLO, CLERICO, CONTERNO-FANTINO, CORDERO DI MONTEZEMOLO, Corino, Damilano, Gagliasso, Ettore Germano, Ghisolfi, Elio GRASSO, Silvio Grasso, Paolo Manzone, Giovanni MANZONE, MOLINO, OBERTO, PARUSSO, Luigi Pira, Porro, Principiano, Revello, Giorgio Rivetti, Rocche Costamagna, ROCCHE DEI MANZONI, Giovanni Rosso, Sandrone, Saffirio, SCAVINO, Fratelli Seghesio, Tenuta Rocca, VAJRA, Veglio, Gianni Voerzio, Roberto VOERZIO, and many others.

Barolo Chinato A dessert wine made from BAROLO DOCG, alcohol, sugar, herbs spices, and Peruvian bark. Producers: Cappellano, CERETTO, Giulio Cocchi.

Basciano ★★ Producer of gd DOCG CHIANTI RUFINA and IGT wines.

Bava ★★→★★★ Producer of BARBERA D'ASTI Piano Alto and Stradivarius MONFERRATO BIANCO, BAROLO CHINATO; the Bava family controls the old firm Giulio Cocchi in Asti, where it produces gd sparkling METODO CLASSICO.

Bellavista ★★★ FRANCIACORTA estate with brisk SPUMANTE (Gran Cuvée Franciacorta is top). Also Satèn (a crémant-style sp). TERRE DI FRANCIACORTA DOC and Sebino IGT Solesine (both Cab Sauv/MERLOT blends). Owner Vittorio Moretti also expanding into TUSCAN MAREMMA, Val di Cornia, and Montereggio.

Bera, Walter ★★→★★★ Small estate nr BARBARESCO. V.gd MOSCATO D'ASTI, ASTI, BARBERA D'ASTI, and LANGHE NEBBIOLO.

Berlucchi, Guido ★★★ Italy's biggest producer of sparkling METODO CLASSICO.

Bersano Historic wine house in Nizza Monferrato, with BARBERA D'ASTI Generala, and BAROLO Badarina, most PIEDMONT DOC wines inc BARBARESCO, MOSCATO D'ASTI, ASTI SPUMANTE.

Bertani ★★→★★★ Well-known, quality wines from VERONA, esp traditional AMARONE.

Bertelli ★★★ Superb wines, esp BARBERA D'ASTI, Chard, Cab Sauv; very interesting experiments with Sauv Bl, Sem, Nebbiolo, Syrah, and Marsanne/Roussanne.

Bianco White.

Bianco di Custoza Ven DOC w (sp) ★→★★ DYA Twin of SOAVE from VERONA's other side (W). Gd Corte Sant'Arcadio, Le Tende, Le VIGNE di San Pietro, MONTRESOR.

Bibi Graetz Important reds from hills of Fiesole nr Florence, old-vine SANGIOVESE, Canaiolo, and Colorino of character and depth.

Biondi-Santi ★★★★ Original producer of BRUNELLO DI MONTALCINO, from Il Greppo estate. Absurd prices, but occasional old vintages are very fine.

Boca Pie DOC r ★★ **95 96' 97'** 98' 99' 00 01 03 04 Another NEBBIOLO from N of PIEDMONT. Look for Le Piane and Poderi ai Valloni (Vigneto Cristiana ★★★).

Boccadigabbia ★★★ Top Marches producer of IGT wines: SANGIOVESE, Cab Sauv, PINOT NOIR, Chard. Proprietor Elvidio Alessandri also owns fine Villamagna estate in ROSSO PICENO DOC.

Bolgheri Tus DOC r p w (sw) ★★→★★★★ Ultra-modish region on the coast S of Livorno. Inc seven types of wine: BIANCO, VERMENTINO, Sauv Bl, ROSSO, ROSATO, VIN SANTO, and Occhio di Pernice, plus top IGTs. Newish DOC Bolgheri Rosso: Cab Sauv/MERLOT/SANGIOVESE blend. Top producers: Ca' Marcanda, Campo alla Sughera, Campo al Mare; Casa di Terra, Ceralti, Giovanni Chiapinni; Cipriana, Cipriana; Le Macchiole, Scrio (Syrah), Messorio (MERLOT); Micheletti; Enrico Santini; ORNELLAIA, Masseto (MERLOT); SAN GUIDO; ANTINORI; Meletti-Cavallari; Michele Satta; I Castagni, Poggio al Tesoro, Serni, Tringali, VIGNA al Cavaliere (SANGIOVESE).

Bolla ★★ Famous VERONA firm for VALPOLICELLA, AMARONE, SOAVE, etc. Also RECIOTO. Top wines: Castellaro, Creso (red and white), Jago. Wines, particularly AMARONE and SOAVE selections, are once again on the upswing.

Bonarda 00 01 03 Minor and confusing red grape or grapes (name often erroneously used for Croatina) widely grown in PIEDMONT, Lombardy, Emilia-Romagna, and blended with Barbera.

Bonarda Lom DOC r ★★ **97** 98 00 01 03 Soft, fresh FRIZZANTE and still wines from OLTREPÒ PAVESE, actually made from Croatina grapes.

Borgo del Tiglio ★★★→★★★★ FRIULI estate for one of NE Italy's top MERLOTS, ROSSO della Centa; also superior COLLIO Chard, TOCAI, and BIANCO. Now expanding into Marches with impressive new offerings from Sangiovese and Montepulciano.

Boscarelli, Poderi ★★★ Small estate with v.gd VINO NOBILE DI MONTEPULCIANO and barrel-aged IGT Boscarelli.

Brachetto d'Acqui Pie DOCG r sw (sp) ★★ DYA Sweet, sparkling red with enticing Muscat scent. Can be much better than it sounds. Or dire.

Braida ★★★ The late Giacomo Bologna's estate; for top BARBERA D'ASTI (BRICCO dell'Uccellone, Bricco della Bigotta, Ai Suma).

Bramaterra Pie DOC r ★★ **96 97'** 98' 99' 00 01 03 04 Neighbour to GATTINARA. NEBBIOLO grapes predominate in a blend. Gd producer: Sella.

Breganze Ven DOC ★→★★★ (r) **97'** 98 99 00 01 Catch-all for many varieties nr Vicenza. Best: Cab Sauv, Chard. Top producers: MACULAN, Miotti, Zonta.

Bricco Term for a hilltop (and by implication v.gd) v'yd in PIEDMONT.

Brindisi Ap DOC r ★★ **94 95 97 99** 00 01 03 04 Strong NEGROAMARO, esp from Due Palme, Rubino, and forthcoming wines from ZONIN.

Brolio, Castello di ★★→★★★ After a sad period under foreign ownership, the RICASOLI family has taken this legendary 900-yr-old estate in hand again. Results are heartening. V.gd CHIANTI CLASSICO and IGT Casalferro.

Brunelli ★★→★★★ V.gd quality of AMARONE and RECIOTO.

Brunello di Montalcino Tus DOCG r ★★★→★★★★ **88' 90' 93 95'** 97' 99 00 01 With BAROLO, Italy's most celebrated red: strong, full-bodied, high-flavoured, tannic, long-lived. Four yrs' ageing; after five yrs becomes RISERVA. Quality is ever improving. MONTALCINO is 25 miles S of Siena. See overleaf for "Best buys" box.

Bussola, Tommaso ★★★ Leading producer of AMARONE and RECIOTO in VALPOLICELLA.

Ca' dei Frati ★★→★★★ The best producer of DOC LUGANA: and v.gd, dry white blend IGT Pratto, sweet Tre Filer, and red IGT Ronchedone.

Ca' del Bosco ★★★★ FRANCIACORTA estate; some of Italy's best sparklers (outstanding DOCG Annamaria Clementi ★★★★), v.gd Chard, and excellent Cab Sauv blend (MAURIZIO ZANELLA), PINOT N (Pinèro). Intriguing new Carmenère.

Cafaggio, Villa ★★★ Very reliable CHIANTI CLASSICO estate with excellent IGTS San Martino (SANGIOVESE) and Cortaccio (Cab Sauv).

ITALY

> **Best Brunello di Montalcino to buy**
> Altesino, ARGIANO, BANFI, Barbi, BIONDI-SANTI, BRUNELLI, La Campana,
> Campogiovanni, Canalicchio di Sopra, Caparzo, CASANOVA DI NERI, Casanova
> delle Cerbaie, Casato Prime Donne, CASE BASSE, CASTELGIOCONDO, Castello di
> Camigliano, Cerbaiona, Cerrino, COL D'ORCIA, Collelceto, Collemattoni,
> Collosorbo, Corte Pavone, Costanti, EREDI FULIGNI, Fanti-San Filippo,
> Ferrero, La Fiorita, La Fuga, La Gerla, Gorelli, Lambardi, LISINI, La Magia,
> Marroneto, Oliveto, Siro PACENTI, Franco Pacenti, Palazzo, Pertimali, Ciacci
> Piccolomini, PIEVE DI SANTA RESTITUTA, Podere Brizio, La Poderina, POGGIO
> ANTICO, POGGIONE, La Rasina, Salvioni-Cerbaiola, San Filippo, Scopetone, La
> Serena, Sesta, Talenti, La Torre, Uccelliera, Valdicava, Vasco Sassetti,
> Verbena, Villa Le Prata, Vitanza.

Calatrasi SI ★★→★★★ Gd producer of r and w IGT labels, esp D'Istinto range.

Caldaro (Lago di Caldaro) T-AA DOC r ★ DYA Alias Kalterersee. Light, soft, bitter-almond SCHIAVA. From a huge area. CLASSICO – smaller area – is better.

Ca' Marcanda BOLGHERI estate owned by GAJA since 1996. Focus on international varieties: Cab Sauv, MERLOT, Cab Fr, Syrah.

Cannonau di Sardegna Sar DOC r (p) dr s/sw ★★ 95 96 97 98 99 00 01 02 03 04 Cannonau (Grenache) is the basic red grape of the S. From very potent to fine and mellow. Look for: ARGIOLAS, Contini, Giuseppe Gabbas, Loi, Sedilesu.

Cantalupo, Antichi Vigneti di ★★→★★★ Top GHEMME wines, esp single-v'yd Breclemae and Carellae.

Cantina Cellar or winery. See CS.

Capannelle ★★★ V.gd producer of IGT and CHIANTI CLASSICO, plus 50:50 SANGIOVESE/MERLOT joint venture with AVIGNONESI nr Gaiole.

Capezzana, Tenuta di (or Villa) ★★★ TUSCAN estate of the Contini Bonacossi family. Gd CHIANTI Montalbano, excellent CARMIGNANO (esp Villa Capezzagna, Villa Trefiano). Also v.gd B'x-style red, Ghiaie Della Furba.

Capichera ★★★ No 1 producer of VERMENTINO DI GALLURA, esp VENDEMMIA Tardiva. Now with excellent red Mantènghja from Carignano grapes.

Caprai ★★★→★★★★ Widely copied, superb DOCG SAGRANTINO, v.gd DOC ROSSO DI MONTEFALCO. Highly rated.

Capri Cam DOC r p w ★→★★ Legendary island with widely abused name. Only interesting wines are from La Caprense.

Carema Pie DOC r ★★→★★★ 89' 90' 93 95 96' 97' 98 99' 00 01 03 04 Old NEBBIOLO speciality from N PIEDMONT. Best: Luigi Ferrando (or CS).

Carignano del Sulcis Sar DOC r p ★★→★★★ 90 91 93 94 95 96 97 98 99' 00 01 02 03 04 Ageworthy red. Best: TERRE BRUNE and Rocca Rubia from CS di SANTADI.

Carmignano Tus DOCG r ★★★ 90' 93 94 95 97' 98 99' 00 01' 03 04 Region W of Florence. CHIANTI grapes plus up to 15% Cab Sauv make distinctive, reliable, excellent r. Best inc: Ambra, CAPEZZANA, Farnete, PIAGGIA, La Poggiarelle, Pratesi.

Carpenè-Malvolti Leading producer of classic PROSECCO and other sp wines at Conegliano, Veneto. Seen everywhere in Venice.

Carso F-VG DOC r w ★★→★★★ (r) 99' 00 01 02 03 04 DOC nr Trieste inc gd MALVASIA. Terrano del Carso is a REFOSCO red. Top growers: EDI KANTE, Zidanich.

Cartizze Famous, frequently too expensive, and too sweet DOC PROSECCO of top sub-zone of Valdobbiadene.

Casanova di Neri ★★★ BRUNELLO DI MONTALCINO, Pietradonice (SANGIOVESE/Cab Sauv) and v.gd ROSSO DI MONTALCINO from Neri family.

Cascina Fonda ★★★ Brothers Marco and Massimo Barbero have risen to the top in MOSCATO D'ASTI DOC. VENDEMMIA Tardiva and METODO CLASSICO ASTI SPUMANTE.

Case Basse ★★★★ Pace-setter at MONTALCINO with sublime BRUNELLO and single-v'yd BRUNELLO Intistieti.

Castel del Monte Ap DOC r p w ★★→★★★ (r) **93' 94 95 96** 97' 98 99 00 01 Dry, fresh, well-balanced wines. Rosé best known. Gd Pietrabianca and excellent Bocca di Lupo from Vigneti del Sud (ANTINORI). V.gd Il Falcone, Puer Apuliae, and Cappellaccio from RIVERA. Interesting new red from Tenuta Cocevola.

Castelgiocondo ★★★ FRESCOBALDI estate in MONTALCINO: v.gd BRUNELLO and IGT MERLOT Lamaïone.

Castellare ★★→★★★ Small but admired CHIANTI CLASSICO producer. First-rate SANGIOVESE IGT I Sodi di San Niccoló and sprightly GOVERNO di Castellare: old-style CHIANTI updated. Also Poggio ai Merli (MERLOT) and Coniale (Cab Sauv).

Castell' in Villa ★★★ V.gd CHIANTI CLASSICO estate.

Castello Castle. (See under name – *e.g.* SALA, CASTELLO DELLA.)

Castello di Albola See ZONIN.

Castelluccio ★★→★★★ Pioneering producer of quality SANGIOVESE of Romagna: IGT RONCO dei Ciliegi and RONCO dei Ciliegi. New wine: Massicone.

Caudrina-Dogliotti Romano ★★★ Top MOSCATO D'ASTI: La Galeisa and Caudrina.

Cavalleri ★★→★★★ V.gd reliable FRANCIACORTA producer, esp sparkling.

Cavicchioli E-R ★→★★ Large producer of LAMBRUSCO and other sparkling wines. Lambrusco di Sorbara VIGNA del Cristo is best. Also TERRE DI FRANCIACORTA.

Ca' Viola PIEDMONT home base of influential consultant Bepe Caviola. Classy DOLCETTO and Barbera-based wines.

Ca' Vit (Cantina Viticoltori) Group of co-ops nr Trento. Top wines: Brune di Monte (r w) and sp Graal.

Cecchi Tus ★→★★ Bottler, producer; La Gavina, Spargolo, CHIANTI CLASSICO RISERVA.

Cerasuolo Ab DOC p ★ The ROSATO version of MONTEPULCIANO D'ABRUZZO.

Cerasuolo di Vittoria Si DOCG p ★★ 99 **00 01** Garnet, full-bodied, aromatic (Frappato and NERO D'AVOLA grapes); try Planeta Valle dell'Acate, and COS.

Ceretto ★★★ V.gd grower of BARBARESCO (BRICCO Asili), BAROLO (BRICCO Rocche, Brunate, Prapò), LANGHE Rosso Monsordo, and ARNEIS. Also v.gd METODO CLASSICO SPUMANTE La Bernardina.

Chianti Tus DOCG r ★→★★★ **95' 97' 99'** 00 01 03 04 Chianti Annata DYA. Lively local wine of Florence and Siena. At best fresh, fruity, tangy. Of the sub-districts, RUFINA (★★→★★★) and COLLI Fiorentini (★→★★★) can make CLASSICO-style RISERVAS. Montalbano, COLLI Senesi, Aretini, Pisani: lighter wines. New sub-district since 1997 is Chianti Montespertoli; wines similar to Colli Fiorentini.

Chianti Classico Tus DOCG r ★★→★★★★ **97' 99'** 00 01 03 04 (single-v'yd and RISERVA) **88' 90' 93 95 97'** 99 01 03 04 Senior CHIANTI from central area. Old, pale style now rarer; top estates opt for richer, firmer wines. Some are among Italy's best wines, but too much Cab Sauv can spoil style. CONSORZIO members use the badge of a black rooster, but many top firms do not belong.

Who makes really good Chianti Classico?

AMA, ANTINORI, Bibbiano, Bossi, BROLIO, Cacchiano, CAFAGGIO, Capaccia, CAPANNELLE, Carobbio, Casa Emma, Casafrassi, Casale dello Sparviero, Casaloste, Castello di San Sano, Castel Ruggero, CASTELLARE, Castell'in Villa, Collelungo, Colombaio di Cencio, Coltibuono, Le Corti, Mannucci Droandi, FELSINA-BERARDENGA, Le Filigare, FONTERUTOLI, FONTODI, ISOLE E OLENA, Ispoli, LA MASSA, Lornano, Lucignano, LE CINCIOLE, MONSANTO, NITTARDI, PALAZZINO, PANERETTA, Panzanello, Petroio-Lenzi, Poggerino, Poggiolino, Poggio Amorelli, Poggio al Sole, Poggio Bonelli, Querceto, QUERCIABELLA, RAMPOLLA, RIECINE, Rocca di Montegrossi, Rocca di Castagnoli, RUFFINO, SAN FELICE, SAN GIUSTO A RENTENNANO, Savignola Paolina, Solatione, Selvole, Vecchie Terre di Montefili, VERRAZZANO, Villa Mangiacane, Viticcio, VOLPAIA.

Chiaretto Rosé (the word means "claret") produced esp around Lake Garda. See BARDOLINO, RIVIERA DEL GARDA BRESCIANO.

Chiarlo, Michele ★★ →★★★ Gd PIEDMONT producer (BAROLOS Cerequio and Cannubi, BARBERA D'ASTI, LANGHE, and MONFERRATO Rosso). Also BARBARESCO.

Chionetti ★★ →★★★ Makes top DOLCETTO di Dogliani (look for Briccolero).

Cigliuti, Renato ★★★ Small, high-quality estate for BARBARESCO and BARBERA D'ALBA.

Cinqueterre Lig DOC w dr sw ★★ Fragrant, fruity white from precipitous coast n La Spezia. PASSITO is known as SCIACCHETRÀ (★★→★★★). Gd from Co-op Agricola di Cinqueterre and Forlini Cappellini.

Cirò Cal DOC r (p w) ★ →★★★ 95 96 97 98 99 00 01 03 04 Strong r from Gaglioppo grapes; light, fruity w (DYA). Best: Caparra, Ippolito, LIBRANDI (Duca San Felice ★★★), San Francesco (Donna Madda, RONCO dei Quattroventi), Siciliani.

Classico Term for wines from a restricted area within the limits of a DOC. By implication, and often in practice, the best of the district. When applied to sparkling wines, it denotes the classic method (as for Champagne).

Clerico, Domenico ★★★ Constantly evolving PIEDMONT wines; the aim is for international flavour. Esp gd for BAROLO.

Col d'Orcia ★★★ Top MONTALCINO estate. Best wine: BRUNELLO.

Colle Santa Mustiola High-level SANGIOVESE from small estate just outside of VINO NOBILE DI MONTEPULCIANO zone.

Colli Hills. Occurs in many wine names.

Colli Berici Ven DOC r p w ★★ 97 99 00 01 03 04 Hills S of Vicenza. Best wine is Cab Sauv. Top producer: Villa Dal Ferro.

Colli Bolognesi E-R DOC r w ★★ SW of Bologna, eight wines, five varieties. TERRE ROSSE, the pioneer, now joined by Bonzara (★★→★★★), Santarosa, Vallona.

Colli del Trasimeno Um DOC r w ★ →★★★ (r) 97 98 99' 00 01 03 04 Lively white wines from near Perugia, but now more important reds as well. Best: Duca della Corgna, La Fiorita, Pieve del Vescovo, Poggio Bertaio.

Colli Euganei Ven DOC r w dr s/sw (sp) ★ →★★★ DYA DOC SW of Padua for seven wines. Adequate red; white and sparkling are pleasant. Best producers: Ca' Lustra, La Montecchia, Speaia, VIGNALTA.

Colline Novaresi Pie DOC r w ★→★★ DYA New DOC for old region in Novara province. Seven different wines: BIANCO, ROSSO, NEBBIOLO, BONARDA, Vespolina, Croatina, and Barbera. Inc declassified BOCA, FARA, GHEMME, and SIZZANO.

Collio F-VG DOC r w ★★→★★★★ (r) 97 99' 00 01 02 03 Makes 19 wines, 17 named after their grapes. V.gd whites from: Attems, BORGO DEL TIGLIO, Il Carpino, La Castellada, CASTELLO di Spessa, Damijan, Marco FELLUGA, Fiegl, GRAVNER, Renato Keber, LIVON, Aldo Polencic, Primosic, Princic, RONCO dei Tassi, RUSSIZ SUPERIORE SCHIOPETTO, Tercic, Terpin, Toros, Venica & Venica, VILLA RUSSIZ, Zuani.

Colli Orientali del Friuli F-VG DOC r w dr sw ★★ →★★★★ (r) 95 97 99' 00 01 03 04 Hills E of Udine. A group of 20 wines (18 named after their grapes). Both w and r can be v.gd. Best: Bastianich, Rosa Bosco, Castello di Buttrio, Centa Sant'Anna, Dorigo, Dri, LE DUE TERRE, Livio FELLUGA, Meroi, Miani, Moschioni, Perusini, Rocca Bernarda, Ronchi di Cialla, Ronchi di Manzano, Ronco delle Betulle, RONCO del GNEMIZ, SCHIOPETTO, Scubla, Specogna, Torre di Rosazzo, La Viarte, VIGNA Traverso, LE VIGNE di ZAMÒ, Vinai dell'Abate, Volpe Pasini.

Colli Piacentini E-R DOC r p w ★→★★ DYA DOC inc traditional GUTTURNIO and Monterosso Val d'Arda among 11 types grown S of Piacenza. Gd fizzy MALVASIA. Most wines FRIZZANTE. New French and local reds: Montesissa, Mossi, Romagnoli, Solenghi, La Stoppa, Torre Fornello, La Tosa.

Colterenzio CS (or **Schreckbichl**) T-AA ★★ →★★★ Pioneering quality leader among ALTO ADIGE co-ops. Look for: Cornell line of selections; Lafoa Cab Sauv and Sauv Bl; Cornelius red and white blends.

Consorzio In Italy there are two types of association recognized by wine law. One is dedicated to the observance of DOC regulations (*e.g.* Consorzio Tutela del CHIANTI CLASSICO). The second promotes the wines of their members (*e.g.* Consorzio del Marchio Storico of CHIANTI CLASSICO, previously Gallo Nero).

Conterno, Aldo ★★★★ Legendary grower of BAROLO, etc., at Monforte d'Alba. V.gd Chard Printanier and Bussiadoro, gd BARBERA D'ALBA Conca Tre Pile. Best BAROLOS: Gran Bussia, Cicala, and Colonello. Langhe Nebbiolo Favot and Langhe Rosso Quartetto both v.gd.

Conterno, Giacomo ★★★★ Iconic grower of BAROLO, etc., at Monforte d'Alba. Monfortino BAROLO: long-aged, rare, outstanding. Epitomizes grand tradition.

Conterno-Fantino ★★★ Two young families for v.gd BAROLO etc. at Monforte d'Alba.

Contini, Attilio ★ →★★★ Famous SARDINIAN producer of VERNACCIA DI ORISTANO; best is vintage blend Antico Gregori. Also gd Cannonau.

Contrada Castelletta Pioneering MONTEPULCIANO/Syrah blend from v'yd of director of Saladini Pilastri in ROSSO PICENO DOC, juicy and rich.

Contratto ★★ At Canelli (owned by GRAPPA-producing family Bocchino); produces v.gd BARBERA D'ASTI, BAROLO, SPUMANTE, ASTI (De Miranda), MOSCATO D'ASTI.

Copertino Ap DOC r (p) ★★ **97** 99 00 01 04 Savoury, ageworthy, strong red of NEGROAMARO from the heel of Italy. Look for the CS's RISERVA and Masseria Monaci, esp new barrel-aged Le Braci.

Coppo ★★ →★★★ Ambitious producers of BARBERA D'ASTI (Pomorosso), Chard.

Cordero di Montezemolo-Monfalletto ★★ →★★★ Historic maker of gd BAROLO, now with fine BARBERA D'ALBA and Chard.

Corini New house in remote area of Umbria. Produces intriguing, innovative blend of SANGIOVESE/MONTEPULCIANO/MERLOT.

Cortese di Gavi See GAVI. (Cortese is the grape.)

Corzano & Paterno, Fattoria di ★★★ Dynamic CHIANTI COLLI Fiorentini estate. V.gd RISERVA, red IGT Corzano, and outstanding VIN SANTO.

CS, Cantina Sociale Cooperative winery.

Dal Forno, Romano ★★★★ Very high-quality VALPOLICELLA, AMARONE, and RECIOTO from perfectionist grower who bottles only the best.

Del Cerro, Fattoria ★★★ Estate with v.gd DOCG VINO NOBILE DI MONTEPULCIANO (esp RISERVA and Antica Chiusina), red IGTS Manero (SANGIOVESE), and Poggio Golo (MERLOT). Controlled by insurance company SAI. Also owns excellent La Poderina (BRUNELLO DI MONTALCINO) and Colpetrone (MONTEFALCO SAGRANTINO).

Di Majo Norante ★★ →★★★ Lone star of Molise, S of Abruzzo, with v.gd Biferno ROSSO, Molise MONTEPULCIANO, Ramitello Don Luigi, and AGLIANICO Contado, white blend Falanghina-Greco and Moscato Passito Apianae.

DOC, Denominazione di Origine Controllata Means much the same as *appellation d'origine contrôlée* (see France).

DOCG, Denominazione di Origine Controllata e Garantita Like DOC but with an official "guarantee" of origin shown by an officially numbered neck label on the bottle indicating limited production.

Italy's DOCG wines: the complete list (guaranteed)

Albana di Romagna, Asti and Moscato d'Asti, Barbaresco, Bardolino Superiore, Barolo, Brachetto d'Acqui, Brunello di Montalcino, Carmignano, Cerasuolo di Vittoria, Chianti, Chianti Classico, Colline Teramane, Fiano d'Avellino, Franciacorta, Gattinara, Gavi, Ghemme, Greco di Tufo, Montefalco Sagrantino, Recioto di Soave, Roero, Rosso Conero, Soave Superiore, Sforzato, Taurasi, Torgiano Rosso Riserva, Valtellina Superiore, Vermentino di Gallura, Vernaccia di San Gimignano, Vernaccia di Serrapetrona, and Vino Nobile di Montepulciano.

Dogliotti Romano See CAUDRINA.

Dolce Sweet.

Dolceacqua See ROSSESE DI DOLCEACQUA.

Dolcetto ★→★★★ PIEDMONT's earliest-ripening red grape, for very attractive everyday wines: dry, youthful, fruity, fresh, with deep purple colour. Gives its name to several DOCs: d'Acqui; d'Asti; di Diano d'Alba (also Diano DOC), esp Alari, Bricco Maiolica, Cascina Flino, and FONTANAFREDDA; di Dogliani (esp from M & E Abbona, Francesco Boschis, CHIONETTI, Gillardi, Pecchenino, Poderi Luigi Einaudi, San Fereolo, San Romano); delle Langhe Monregalesi (look for Barone Ricatti); and di Ovada (best from La Gioia, La Guardia, Villa Sparina). Dolcetto d'Alba: ALESSANDRIA, ALTARE, Azelia, Baudana, Boglietti, Brovia, Cabutto, CA' VIOLA, Cavallotto, CLERICO, Aldo CONTERNO, CONTERNO-FANTINO, Corino, De Stefanis, Gastaldi, Germano, Bruno GIACOSA, GRESY, MANZONE, Giuseppe MASCARELLO, Massolino, Mauro Molino, Mossio, Fiorenzo Nada, OBERTO, Pelissero, Luigi Pira, Gianmatteo Pira, PRUNOTTO, Rocche Costamanga, SANDRONE, SCAVINO, Schiavenza, Fratelli Seghesio, Sottimano, VAJRA, Roberto VOERZIO.

Donnafugata Si w r ★★→★★★ Zesty Sicilian whites (best from Chiaranda and VIGNA di Gabri). Solid, improving reds, esp Mille e Una Notte and Tancredi, fine Moscato Passito di Pantelleria Ben Rye. Wines in DOC Contessa Entellina.

Duca di Salaparuta Si ★★ Vini Corvo. Popular SICILIAN wines. Sound, dry reds; pleasant, soft whites. Duca Enrico (★★→★★★) was one of SICILY's pioneeering ambitious reds. Valguarnera is premium oak-aged white.

Duca Enrico See DUCA DI SALAPARUTA.

Elba Tus r w (sp) ★→★★ DYA The island's white is very drinkable with fish. Napoleon in exile here loved the sweet red ALEATICO. Promising new wines from Sapereta, both reds and dessert. Try Acquabona, Acquacalda, Cecilia.

Enoteca Wine library; also wine shop or restaurant with extensive wine list. There are many, the impressive original being the Enoteca Italiana of Siena.

Eredi Fuligni ★★★ V.gd producer of BRUNELLO and ROSSO DI MONTALCINO.

Est! Est!! Est!!! Lat DOC w dr s/sw ★ DYA Unextraordinary white from Montefiascone, N of Rome. Trades on its oddball name. See FALESCO.

Etna Si DOC r p w ★★ (r) **95 97** 98 **99 00** 01 04 Wine from volcanic slopes. New investment in zone from Andrea Franchetti (Trinoro) and broker Marc De Grazia. Gd producers: Benanti, Cambria, Bonaccorsi.

Falchini ★★★ Producer of gd DOCG VERNACCIA DI SAN GIMIGNANO (esp CASTEL Selva and VIGNA a Solatio). Some of the area's best reds, *e.g.* IGT Campora (★★★).

Falerno del Massico ★★→★★★ Cam DOC r w ★★ (r) **90 93 94 95 97' 98 99** 00' 01 03 04 As in Falernum (or Falernian), the best-known wine of ancient times. Times change. Elegant red from AGLIANICO, fruity white from Falanghina. V.gd producer: VILLA MATILDE. Other producers: Amore Perrotta, Trabucco.

Falesco ★★→★★★ Latium estate, v.gd MERLOT Montiano and Cab Sauv Marciliano (both ★★★). Gd red IGT Vitiano and DOC EST! EST!! EST!!!

Fara Pie DOC r ★★ **90 95' 96' 97 98** 99 00' 01 03 04 Gd NEBBIOLO from Novara, N PIEDMONT. Fragrant; worth ageing; esp Dessilani's Caramino and Lochera.

Farnetella, Castello di ★★→★★★ Estate nr MONTEPULCIANO where Giuseppe Mazzocolin of FELSINA makes gd Sauv Bl and CHIANTI COLLI Senesi. Also v.gd PINOT N Nero di Nubi and red blend Poggio Granoni.

Faro Si DOC r ★★ **97 98 99 00** 01 04 Interesting full-bodied red from Messina.

Fattoria Central Italian term for an agricultural property, normally wine-producing, of a certain size. (See under name – *e.g.* MONTELLORI, FATTORIA DI.)

Fazi-Battaglia ★★ Well-known producer of VERDICCHIO, best selections: Le Moie, Massaccio, San Sisto. Owns Fassati (producer of VINO NOBILE DI MONTEPULCIANO).

Felluga, Livio ★★★ Substantial estate, consistently fine COLLI ORIENTALI DEL FRIULI wines, esp PINOT GRIGIO, Sauv Bl, TOCAI, PICOLIT, and MERLOT/REFOSCO blend.

Felluga, Marco ★★→★★★ The brother of Livio owns a négociant house bearing his name plus RUSSIZ SUPERIORE in COLLIO DOC, Castello di Buttrio in COLLI ORIENTALI DOC. Marco's daughter Patrizia is now owner of Zuani estate in COLLIO.

Felsina-Berardenga ★★★ CHIANTI CLASSICO estate; famous RISERVA VIGNA Rancia, IGT Fontalloro. Regular CHIANTI CLASSICO and RISERVA, less fashionable and less expensive, are more traditional. Also gd IGT Chard and Cab Sauv.

Ferrari T-AA ★★→★★★ Cellars making dry sp nr Trento. Giulio Ferrari RISERVA is best. Steadily improving quality. New reds from TUSCANY and Umbria as well.

Feudi di San Gregorio ★★★→★★★★ Top Campania producer, with DOCG TAURASI, DOC FIANO, Flangina, Greco di Tufo. Red IGT Serpico and Patrimo (MERLOT), white IGT Campanaro. Now active in Basilicata and APULIA as well.

Fiano di Avellino Cam DOCG w ★★→★★★ (DYA) Considered the best white of Campania. Can be intense, slightly honeyed, memorable. Best producers: Caggiano, Caputo, COLLI di Lapio, Benito Ferrara, FEUDI DI SAN GREGORIO, Grotta del Sole, MASTROBERARDINO, Villa Raiano, San Paolo, Vesevo.

Florio The major volume producer of MARSALA, controlled by Illva-Saronno.

Folonari Ambrogio Folonari and son Giovanni have split off from RUFFINO to create their own house. Will continue to make Cabreo (a Chard and a SANGIOVESE/Cab Sauv), wines of NOZZOLE (inc Cab Sauv Pareto), BRUNELLO DI MONTALCINO La Fuga, VINO NOBILE DI MONTEPULCIANO Gracciano Svetoni, with new offerings from BOLGHERI, MONTECUCCO, and COLLI ORIENTALI DEL FRIULI.

Fontana Candida ★★ One of the biggest producers of FRASCATI. Single-v'yd Santa Teresa stands out. See also GRUPPO ITALIANO VINI.

Fontanafredda ★★→★★★ Producer of PIEDMONT wines on former royal estates, inc single-v'yd BAROLOS and ALBA DOCS. V.gd SPUMANTE Brut (esp ★★★ GATTINARA).

Fonterutoli ★★★ Historic CHIANTI CLASSICO estate of the Mazzei family at Castellina. Notable new selection CASTELLO di Fonterutoli (dark, oaky, fashionable CHIANTI), IGT Siepi (SANGIOVESE/MERLOT). Mazzei also own Tenuta di Belguardo in MAREMMA, gd MORELLINO DI SCANSANO and IGT wines.

Fontodi ★★★ Top Panzano CHIANTI CLASSICO estate for CHIANTI and RISERVA, esp RISERVA del Sorbo. V.gd red IGT Flaccianello, Case Via PINOT N, Case Va Syrah.

Foradori ★★★ Elizabetta F makes best TEROLDEGO. Also oak-aged TEROLDEGO Granato, white IGT Myrto. Watch out for new estate in tuscan MAREMMA.

Forte, Podere Pasquale Forte's Val d'Orcia estate, just S of MONTALCINO, puts cutting-edge technology at the service of ambitious SANGIOVESE and Cab Sauv/MERLOT/Petit Verdot wines.

Forteto della Luja ★★★ Lone star in LOAZZOLO; v.gd Barbera/PINOT N Le Grive.

Fossi, Enrico ★★★ High-level small estate in Signa, W of Florence, very fine SANGIOVESE, Cab Sauv, Syrah, Malbec, Gamay, and Chard.

Franciacorta Lom DOCG w (p) sp ★★→★★★★ Small sparkling wine centre growing in quality and renown. Wines exclusively bottle-fermented. Top producers: Barone Pizzini, BELLAVISTA, CA' DEL BOSCO, Castellino, CAVALLERI, Gatti, UBERTI, VILLA; also v.gd: Contadi Gastaldi, Cornaleto, Il Mosnel, La Montina, Majolini, Monte Rossa, Monzio Compagnoni, Ricci Curbastri, Ronco Calino, Vezzoli. For white and red, see TERRE DI FRANCIACORTA.

Frascati Lat DOC w dr s/sw sw (sp) ★→★★ DYA Best-known wine of Roman hills: should be soft, limpid, golden, tasting of whole grapes. Most is disappointingly neutral today: look for Conte Zandotti, Villa Simone, or Santa Teresa from FONTANA CANDIDA. Sweet is known as Cannellino.

Freisa Pie r dr s/sw sw (sp) ★★ DYA Usually very dry (except nr Turin), often FRIZZANTE red, said to taste of raspberries and roses. With enough acidity it can be highly appetizing, esp with salami. Gd wines from Brezza, CIGLIUTI, Clerico, Aldo CONTERNO, COPPO, Franco Martinetti, PARUSSO, Pecchenino, Pelissero, Sebaste, Trinchero, VAJRA, Vigneti Massa, and VOERZIO.

ITALY

Frescobaldi ★★ ⋯★★★★ Ancient noble family, leading CHIANTI RUFINA pioneer at NIPOZZANO, E of Florence. Also POMINO (w) and Mormoreto (r). See MONTESODI. Owner of CASTELGIOCONDO (★★★). Now outright owners of jt venture with Mondavi nr MONTALCINO, LUCE, Lucente, and ORNELLAIA. New v'yds in COLLIO DOC and MAREMMA. Important development of v'yds to SE of Florence nr Montespertoli.

Friuli-Venezia Giulia The NE region on the Slovenian border. Many wines; the DOCS ISONZO, COLLIO, and COLLI ORIENTALI include most of the best.

Frizzante (fz) Semi-sparkling. Used to describe wines such as LAMBRUSCO.

Gaja ★★★★ Old family firm at BARBARESCO under direction of Angelo Gaja. Top-quality – and price – wines, esp BARBARESCO (single-v'yds SORÌ Tildin, Sorì San Lorenzo, Costa Russi), BAROLO Sperss. Chard (Gaia and Rey), Cab Sauv Darmagi. Latest acquisition: Marengo-Marenda estate (BAROLO), commercial Gromis label, PIEVE DI SANTA RESTITUTA (BRUNELLO). Single-v'yd BARBARESCOS and BAROLO now labelled LANGHE doc. Important new BOLGHERI project: Ca' Marcanda.

Galardi ★★★ ⋯★★★★ Producer of Terra di Lavoro, a mind-boggling blend of AGLIANICO and Piedirosso, in N Campania nr FALERNO DEL MASSICO DOC.

Galestro Tus w ★ Very light white from eponymous shaley soil in CHIANTI country.

Gambellara Ven DOC w dr s/sw (sp) ★ DYA Neighbour of SOAVE. Dry wine similar. Sweet (RECIOTO DI GAMBELLARA), nicely fruity. Top producer: La Biancara.

Gancia Famous ASTI house also producing dry sparkling.

Garganega Principal white grape of SOAVE and GAMBELLARA.

Garofoli ★★ ⋯★★★ One of quality leaders in the Marches (nr Ancona). Notable style in VERDICCHIO Podium, Macrina, and Serra Fiorese. ROSSO CONERO Piancarda and v.gd Grosso Agontano.

Gattinara Pie DOCG r ★★★ 89' 90' 93 95 96' 97' 98 99' 00 01 03 04 Very tasty NEBBIOLO-based red, historically finest from N PIEDMONT. Best: Travaglini (RISERVA), Antoniolo (single-v'yd wines). Others: Bianchi, Nervi, Torraccia del Piantavigna.

Gavi Pie DOCG w ★ ⋯★★★ DYA At (rare) best, subtle dry white of CORTESE grapes. LA SCOLCA is best-known, gd from BANFI (esp VIGNA Regale), Castellari Bergaglio, Franco Martinetti, Villa Sparina, Toledana. Broglia, Cascina degli Ulivi, CASTELLO di Tassarolo, CHIARLO, La Giustiniana, PODERE Saulino are also fair.

Geografico ★★ Co-op with rising-quality CHIANTI CLASSICO; gd RISERVA Montegiachi. IGTS Pulleraia and Ferraiolo.

Ghemme Pie DOCG r ★★ 89 90' 93 95 96 97' 98 99' 00 01 03 04 Neighbour of GATTINARA but not as gd. Best: Antichi Vigneti di Cantalupo, Rovellotti, and Torraccia del Piantavigna.

Giacosa, Bruno ★★ ⋯★★★★Inspired loner: outstanding BARBARESCO, BAROLO, and PIEDMONT wines at Neive. Remarkable ARNEIS white and sp PINOT N.

Governo Old TUSCAN custom, enjoying mild revival. Dried grapes or must are added to young wine to induce second fermentation and give a slight prickle, sometimes instead of adding must concentrate to increase alcohol.

Gradi Degrees (of alcohol), *i.e.* per cent by volume.

Grappa Pungent and potent spirit made from grape pomace (skins, etc., after pressing), sometimes excellent. Best grappa comes from PIEDMONT (Ugo Marolo, Paolo Marolo, Distilleria Artigiana, Berta), Trentino (POJER & SANDRI, Pilzer, Giovanni Poli), Friuli (Nonino), Veneto (Carlo Gobetti, Vittorio Capovilla, Jacopo Poli), Tuscany (Nannoni), Sicily (Giovi).

Grasso, Elio ★★★ V.gd BAROLO (look for Runcot, Gavarini, Casa Maté), full, barrel-aged BARBERA D'ALBA VIGNA Martina, DOLCETTO D'ALBA, and Chard Educato.

Grave del Friuli F-VG DOC r w ★ ⋯★★ (r) 95 97 99 00 01 03 DOC covering 15 different wines, 14 named after their grapes, from central part of region. Gd REFOSCO, MERLOT, and Cab Sauv. Best producers: Borgo Magredo, Le Fredis, Di Lenardo, Le Monde, Plozner, Vicentini-Orgnani, Villa Chiopris.

Gravner, Josko ★★★ Visionary COLLIO producer, leading drive for low yields, oak ageing, and ageworthy wines. Tirelessly self-critical in his search for new concepts and methods.

Grechetto White grape; more flavour than TREBBIANO. Popular in Umbria.

Greco di Bianco Cal DOC w sw ★★ 00 01 03 04 Original, smooth, fragrant sw wine from Italy's toe; worth ageing. Best from Stelitano. See MANTONICO.

Greco di Tufo Cam DOCG w (sp) ★★–★★★ (DYA) One of the best whites from the S: fruity, slightly wild in flavour, and ageworthy. V.gd examples from Caggiano, Caputo, Benito Ferrara, FEUDI DI SAN GREGORIO, Macchialupa, MASTROBERARDINO (Nuovaserra & Vignadangelo), Vesevo, Villa Raiano.

Gresy, Marchesi di (Cisa Asinari) ★★★ Consistent producer of fine BARBARESCO. Also v.gd LANGHE Rosso, Sauv Bl, Chard, MOSCATO D'ASTI, BARBERA D'ASTI.

Grevepesa CHIANTI CLASSICO co-op – quality now rising.

Grignolino d'Asti Pie DOC r ★ DYA Lively light r of PIEDMONT. Look for: BRAIDA, Castino, Due Pini, La Luna del Rospo, Marchesi Incisa della Rocchetta.

Grignolino del Monferrato Casalese Much like GRIGNOLINO D'ASTI but firmer. Try: Accornero, BRICCO Mondalino, Colonna, Mongetto, La Scamuzza, La Tenaglia.

Gruppo Italiano Vini (GIV) Complex of co-ops and wineries, inc Bigi, Conti Serristori, FOLONARI, FONTANA CANDIDA, LAMBERTI, Macchiavelli, MELINI, Negri, SANTI, and since 1997 controls Ca' Bianca (PIEDMONT) and Vignaioli di San Floriano (FRIULI). Now moving into S with recent investments in Sicily and Basilicata.

Guerrieri-Gonzaga ★★★ Top TRENTINO estate; esp San Leonardo blend.

Gutturnio dei Colli Piacentini E-R DOC r dr ★–★★ DYA Barbera/BONARDA blend from the hills of Piacenza, often FRIZZANTE. Producers: Cardinali, Castelli del Duca, La Stoppa, La Tosa, Torre Fornello.

Haas, Franz ★★★ ALTO ADIGE producer; v.gd PINOT N, LAGREIN, and IGT r and w blends.

Hastae ★★★ New super-Barbera from ASTI from group of producers: BRAIDA, CHIARLO, COPPO, PRUNOTTO, VIETTI.

Hofstätter ★★★ ALTO ADIGE producer of top PINOT N. Look for S Urbano, LAGREIN, Cab Sauv/Petit Verdot, Gewurz.

IGT, Indicazione Geografica Tipica New category for quality wines unable to fit into DOC zones or regulations; replaces the anomaly of glamorous VDTS.

Ischia Cam DOC w (r) ★–★★ DYA Wine of island off Naples. Top producer d'Ambra: DOC red Dedicato a Mario D'Ambra, IGT red Tenuta Montecorvo, IGT white Tenuta Frassitelli, and Piellero. Also gd: Il Giardino Mediterraneo, Pietratorcia.

Isole e Olena ★★★ ·★★★★ Top CHIANTI CLASSICO estate of great beauty with fine red IGT Cepparello. V.gd VIN SANTO, Cab Sauv, Chard, and L'Eremo Syrah.

Isonzo F-VG DOC r w ★★★ (r) 95 97' 98 99 00' 01 03 DOC covering 19 wines (17 varietals) in NE. Best white and MERLOT compare to COLLIO wines. Esp from Masut da Rive, LIS NERIS, Pierpaolo Pecorari, RONCO del Gelso, Borgo San Daniele, Sant'Elena, VIE DI ROMANS, Villanova.

Jermann, Silvio ★★·★★★ Family estate with v'yds in COLLIO and ISONZO: top white VDT, inc blend Vintage Tunina, oak-aged Capo Martino, and "Were dreams, now is just wine" (yes, really). Now joined by important red Pignacoluse.

Kalterersee German (and local) name for LAGO DI CALDARO.

Kante, Edi ★★·★★★ Leading light of CARSO; fine DOC Chard, Sauv Bl, MALVASIA; gd red Terrano.

Lacryma (or Lacrima) Christi del Vesuvio Cam r p w dr (sw fz) ★–★★ DYA Famous but ordinary wines in great variety from Vesuvius (DOC Vesuvio). MASTROBERARDINO and Caputo wines suggest untapped quality, as do newer offerings from De Angelis and Grotta del Sole.

La Fiorita Lamborghini family property nr Lake Trasimeno in Umbria, with touchstone SANGIOVESE/MERLOT blend Campoleone.

Lageder, Alois ★★·★★★ Top ALTO ADIGE producer. Exciting wines inc oak-aged

Löwengang Chard and Römigberg Cab Sauv. Single-v'yd Lehenhof Sauv Bl, PINOT GR Benefizium Porer, PINOT N Krafuss, LAGREIN Lindenberg, TERLANO Tannhammer. Also owns Cason Hirschprunn for v.gd IGT blends.

Lago di Caldaro See CALDARO.

Lagrein T-AA DOC r p ★★→★★★ 95' 96 97' 98 99 00' 01 02 03 04 A grape with a bitter twist. Gd, fruity wine – at best, full, minerally, and very appealing. The rosé: Kretzer; the dark: Dunkel. Best from Colterenzio co-op, Gries, Gojer, HAAS, HOFSTÄTTER, LAGEDER, Laimburg, Josephus Mayr, Thomas Mayr, Muri Gries, NIEDERMAYR, Niedrist Estates, St-Magdalena, TERLANO co-op.

La Massa ★★★ Highly rated producer of v.gd CHIANTI CLASSICO; Giorgio Primo.

Lamberti ★★ Large producer of SOAVE, VALPOLICELLA, BARDOLINO, etc., at Lazise on the E shore of Lake Garda.

Lambrusco E-R DOC (or not) r p dr s/sw ★→★★ DYA Popular fizzy red, best known in industrial s/sw version. Best is SECCO, traditional with second fermentation in bottle (with sediment). DOCS: L Grasparossa di Castelvetro, L Salamino di Santa Croce, L di Sorbara. Best: Bellei, Caprari, Casali, CAVICCHIOLI, Graziano, Lini Oreste, Medici Ermete (esp Concerto), Rinaldo Rinaldini, Venturini Baldini. Forget your prejudices – try it.

La Morandina ★★★ Small family estate with top MOSCATO and BARBERA D'ASTI.

Langhe The hills of central PIEDMONT, home of BAROLO, BARBARESCO, etc. Has become name for recent DOC (r w ★★→★★★) for eight different wines: ROSSO, BIANCO, NEBBIOLO, DOLCETTO, FREISA, ARNEIS, Favorita, and Chard. BAROLO and BARBARESCO can now be declassified to DOC Langhe Nebbiolo.

La Scolca ★★ Famous GAVI estate for gd GAVI and SPUMANTE.

Latisana F-VG DOC r w ★→★★ (r) 99 00 01 02 DOC for 13 varietal wines from 80 km (50 miles) NE of Venice. Best wine is TOCAI Friulano.

Le Cinciole ★★★ DOCG CHIANTI CLASSICO, the best is RISERVA Petresco.

Le Due Terre Small producer in COLLI ORIENTALI DEL FRIULI for choice MERLOT, PINOT N, Sacrisassi Rosso (Refosco-Schioppettino), and white Sacrisassi Bianco.

Le Fonti ★★★ V.gd CHIANTI CLASSICO house in Poggibonsi; look for RISERVA and IGT Vito Arturo (SANGIOVESE).

Le Macchiole ★★★ Outstanding red DOC BOLGHERI Paleo, TOSCANA IGTS Macchiole Rosso (SANGIOVESE/Cab Fr), Messorio (MERLOT), and Scrio (Syrah).

Le Pupille ★★★ Top producer of MORELLINO DI SCANSANO (look for Poggio Valente), excellent IGT blend Saffredi (Cab Sauv/MERLOT/ALICANTE).

Le Ragose ★★→★★★ Family estate, one of VALPOLICELLA's best. AMARONE and RECIOTO top quality; Cab Sauv and VALPOLICELLA v.gd, too.

Le Salette ★★→★★★ Small VALPOLICELLA producer: look for v.gd AMARONE Pergole Vece and RECIOTO Le Traversagne.

Lessona Pie DOC r ★★ 94 95 96' 97' 98 99' 00 01 03 04 Soft, dry, claret-like wine from Vercelli province. NEBBIOLO, Vespolina, BONARDA grapes. Best producer: Sella, plus new estate of Paolo de Marchi of ISOLE E OLENA.

Le Vigne di Zamò ★★★ First-class FRIULI estate for PINOT BL, TOCAI, Pignolo, Cab Sauv, and MERLOT from v'yds in three areas of COLLI ORIENTALI DEL FRIULI DOC.

Librandi ★★★ Top Calabria producer. V.gd red CIRÒ (RISERVA Duca San Felice is ★★★), IGT Gravello (Cab Sauv/Gaglioppo blend), and Magno Megonio from Magliocco grape. New IGT from Efeso from Mantonico grape most impressive.

Liquoroso Means strong; usually sweet and always fortified.

Lisini ★★★→★★★★ Historic small estate for some of the finest BRUNELLO.

Lis Neris ★★★ Top ISONZO estate with bevy of high-quality wines: Chard, PINOT GR, Sauv Bl, a MERLOT-based red, an aromatic Confini white blend, and lovely VDT dessert VERDUZZO.

Livon ★★→★★★★ Substantial COLLIO producer, also some COLLI ORIENTALI wines like VERDUZZO. Expanded into the CHIANTI CLASSICO and Montefalco DOCGS.

Loazzolo Pie DOC w sw ★★★ **95 96' 97'** 98' **99' 00 01'** 03 04 DOC for MOSCATO dessert wine from botrytized, air-dried grapes: expensive and sweet. Gd from Borgo Isolabella and Forteto della Luja.

Locorotondo Ap DOC w (sp) ★ DYA Pleasantly fresh southern white.

Lugana Lom and Ven DOC w (sp) ★→★★ DYA Whites of S Lake Garda: can be fragrant, smooth, full of body and flavour. Gd from CA' DEI FRATI, ZENATO.

Luce ★★★ Ambitious joint Mondavi/FRESCOBALDI venture launched in 1998, now solely FRESCOBALDI. SANGIOVESE/MERLOT blend. Could become Italy's Opus One.

Lungarotti ★★→★★★ Leading producer of TORGIANO, with cellars, hotel, and museum nr Perugia. Gd IGT Sangiorgio (SANGIOVESE/Cab Sauv), Aurente (Chard) and Giubilante. See TORGIANO.

Macchiavelli See GRUPPO ITALIANO VINI.

Maculan Ven ★★★ Excellent Cab Sauv (Fratta, Ferrata), Chard (Ferrata), MERLOT (Marchesante), and Torcolato (esp RISERVA Acininobili).

Malvasia Widely planted grape; chameleon-like: white or red, sparkling or still, strong or mild, sweet or dry, aromatic or neutral; often IGT, sometimes DOC.

Manduria (Primitivo di) Ap DOC r s/sw ★★→★★★ **97'** 98 99 00 01 Dark red, naturally strong, sometimes sweet from nr Taranto. Gd: Casale Bevagna, Felline, Feudi di San Marzano, Masseria Pepe, Pervini, Pozzopalo, Sinfarosa.

Mantonico Cal w dr sw fz ★★ **95 97** 99 00 01 Fruity, deep-amber sweet wine from Reggio Calabria. Can age remarkably well. Ceratti's is gd. Notable new dry version from LIBRANDI. See GRECO DI BIANCO.

Manzone, Giovanni ★★★ V.gd ALBA wines of much personality from Ciabot del Preve estate nr Manforte d'Alba. Single-v'yd BAROLO, BARBERA D'ALBA, DOLCETTO.

Marchesi di Barolo ★★ Important ALBA house: BAROLO (esp Cannubi and Sarmassa), BARBARESCO, DOLCETTO D'ALBA, Barbera, FREISA D'ASTI, and GAVI.

Maremma S coastal area of TUSCANY in provinces of Livorno and Grosseto. DOCs inc BOLGHERI and VAL DI CORNIA (Livorno), MONTECUCCO, MONTEREGIO, MORELLINO DI SCANSANO, PARRINA, SOVANA (Grosseto). Now attracting much interest and new investment for high-quality potential demonstrated by wines.

Marino Lat DOC w dr s/sw (sp) ★→★★ DYA A neighbour of FRASCATI with similar wine; often a better buy. Look for Di Mauro.

Marsala Sicily's sherry-type wine (★→★★★), invented by Woodhouse Bros from Liverpool in 1773. An excellent apéritif or for dessert, but mostly used in the kitchen for desserts such as *zabaglione*. Dry ("virgin"), sometimes made by the *solera* system, must be 5 yrs old. Top producers: FLORIO, Pellegrino, Rallo, VECCHIO SAMPERI. Very special old vintages ★★★★.

Martini & Rossi Vermouth and sparkling wine house now controlled by Bacardi group. (Has a fine wine-history museum in Pessione, nr Turin.)

Marzemino Trentino, T-AA DOC r ★→★★ **00** 01 03 04 Pleasant local red. Fruity and slightly bitter. Esp from Bossi Fedrigotti, CA' VIT, Gaierhof, Letrari, Longariva, Simoncelli, E Spagnolli, De Tarczal, Vallarom.

Mascarello The name of two top producers of BAROLO, etc.: Bartolo M and Giuseppe M & Figli. Look for the latter's supreme BAROLO Monprivato.

Masi ★★→★★★ Well-known, adventurous, reliable VALPOLICELLA, AMARONE, RECIOTO, SOAVE, etc., inc fine red Campo Fiorin. Also v.gd barrel-aged red IGT Toar.

Mastroberardino ★★→★★★ Campania's historic house, with quality now v. much on the upswing. Wines inc FIANO DI AVELLINO, GRECO DI TUFO, LACRYMA CHRISTI, TAURASI (look for Radici), IGT Avalon wines from Vesuvius, IGT Historia Naturalis, new top blend of AGLIANICO and Piedirosso.

Melini ★★ Long-established producers of CHIANTI CLASSICO at Poggibonsi. Gd quality/price; look for single-v'yd CHIANTI CLASSICO Selvanella and RISERVAS La Selvanella and Masovecchio. See GRUPPO ITALIANO VINI.

Meranese di Collina T-AA DOC r ★ DYA Light red of Merano.

Merlot Red grape widely grown in N (esp) and central Italy. Merlot DOCS are abundant. Best producers: BORGO DEL TIGLIO, Livio FELLUGA (Sossò), Renato Keber, LE DUE TERRE, Miani, Radikon, VILLA RUSSIZ (De la Tour) in FRIULI-VENEZIA GIULIA; Bonzara (Rocca di Bonacciara) in E-R; BOCCADIGABBIA in the Marches; FALESCO (Montiano) in Latium; PLANETA in Sicily; FEUDI DI SAN GREGORIO (Patrimo) in Campania; and TUSCAN Super-IGTS AMA (L'Apparita), FRESCOBALDI (Laimaione), La Cappella (Cantico), Cantine Leonardo da Vinci (Artisti), Castello di Bossi (Girolamo), Macchiole (Messorio), ORNELLAIA (Masseto), Pagani De Marchi (Casa Nocera), Petrolo (Galatrona), San Giusto a Rentennano (La Ricolma), Tua Rita (Redigaffi).

Metodo classico or tradizionale Now mandatory terms to identify classic method sparkling wines. "Metodo Champenois" banned since 1994 and now illegal. (See also CLASSICO.)

Mezzacorona ★★ TRENTINO co-op with gd DOC TEROLDEGO, METODO CLASSICO sp Rotari.

Moccagatta ★★→★★★ Specialist in impressive single-v'yd BARBARESCO: Basarin, Bric Balin (★★★), and VIGNA Cole. Also BARBERA D'ALBA and LANGHE.

Molino ★★★ Talented producer of elegant ALBA wines at La Morra; look for BAROLOS Gancia and Conca, Barbera Gattere, and DOLCETTO.

Monacesca, La ★★→★★★ Fine producer of VERDICCHIO DI MATELICA. Top wine: Mirus.

Monferrato Pie DOC r p w sw ★★ Hills between River Po and Apennines. Name of new DOC; inc ROSSO, BIANCO, CHIARETTO, DOLCETTO, Casalese, FREISA, and CORTESE.

Monica di Sardegna Sar DOC r ★→★★ DYA Monica is the grape of a light, dry red.

Monsanto ★★★ Esteemed CHIANTI CLASSICO estate, esp for Il Poggio v'yd and IGTS Fabrizio Bianchi (SANGIOVESE) and Nemo (Cab Sauv).

Montalcino Small town in province of Siena (TUSCANY), famous for concentrated, expensive BRUNELLO and more approachable, better-value ROSSO DI MONTALCINO.

Montecarlo Tus DOC w r ★★ DYA (w) White, and increasingly red, wine area nr Lucca in N TUSCANY. Whites are smooth, neutral blend of TREBBIANO with range of better grapes; basic reds are CHIANTI-style. Gd producers: Buonamico (red IGTS Cercatoja Rosso and Fortino), Carmignani (v.gd red IGT For Duke), red IGTS of La Torre, Montechiari, Fattoria del Teso.

Montecucco New TUSCAN DOC between MONTALCINO and MORELLINO DI SCANSANO. Try: Basile, Ciacci Piccolomini, Fattoria di Montecucco, Pegnardi, Poggio Saccone, Villa Patrizia. Much new investment: FOLONARI, MASI, Pertimali, RIECINE, Talenti.

Montefalco Sagrantino Umb DOCG r dr (sw) ★★★→★★★★ 90 91 93 94 95' 96 97' 98 99' 00' 01 03 04 Strong interesting SECCO or sweet PASSITO red from Sagrantino grapes only. Gd from Alzatura, Antigniano, Antonelli San Marco, Benincasa, CAPRAI, Castelbuono, Colpetrone, Madonna Alta, Martinelli, Le Mura Saracene, Perticaia, Scacciadiavoli, Spoleto Ducale, Tabarrini, Terra di Trinci, Tiburzi, Tudernum.

Montellori, Fattoria di ★★→★★★ TUSCAN producer making Chianti, all-SANGIOVESE IGT Dicatum, Cab Sauv/MERLOT blend Salamartano, white IGT Sant'Amato (Sauv Bl), and METODO CLASSICO SPUMANTE.

Montepulciano An important red grape of E central Italy as well as the famous TUSCAN town (see below).

Montepulciano, Vino Nobile di See VINO NOBILE DI MONTEPULCIANO.

Montepulciano d'Abruzzo Ab DOC r p ★→★★★ 90 92 94 95 97' 98' 00' 01 03 04 One of Italy's tastiest reds, full of flavour and warmth, from Adriatic coast. Best: Barba, Barone Cornacchia, Nestore Bosco, Caldora, Cataldi-Madonna, Ciccio Zaccagnini, Feuduccio, Filomusi-Guelfi, Illuminati, Masciarelli, Monti, Montori, Nicodemi, Orlandi Contucci Ponno, Terre d'Aligi, Torre dei Beati, La Valentina, VALENTINI, Valle Reale, Valori, Villa Medoro. Farnese is the big-value brand. See also CERASUOLO.

Monteregio Emerging DOC zone nr Massa Marittima in MAREMMA, high-level

SANGIOVESE and Cab Sauv wines from Campo Bargello, MORIS FARMS, Massa Vecchia, Montebelli, La Pierotta, Suveraia, Tenuta del Fontino. New investors (inc ANTINORI, BELLAVISTA, Eric de Rothschild, ZONIN) flocking in.

Montescudaio Tus DOC r w ★★ 95 97 98 99 00 01 03 04 DOC between Pisa and Livorno; best are SANGIOVESE or SANGIOVESE/Cab Sauv blends. Try Aione, Fontemorsi, Marchesi Ginori Lisci, Merlini, Poggio Gagliardo, Sorbaiano.

Montesodi Tus r ★★★ 90 93 95 97 99 01' 03 Tip-top CHIANTI RUFINA RISERVA from FRESCOBALDI.

Montevertine Radda estate; once a leading force in the renaissance of TUSCAN wine in the '70s and '80s. IGT Le Pergole Torte a pioneering example of small-barrel-aged SANGIOVESE.

Montevetrano ★★★ Small Campania producer; superb IGT Montevetrano.

Montresor ★★ VERONA wine house: gd LUGANA, BIANCO DI CUSTOZA, VALPOLICELLA.

Morellino di Scansano Tus DOC r ★·★★★ 90' 93 94 95 97 98 99' 00 01 03 04 Local SANGIOVESE of the MAREMMA, the S TUSCAN coast. Cherry-red, should be lively and tasty young or matured. Banti, Belguardo, Casina, Col di Bacche, Compagnia del Vino, Fattoria di Magliano, Fattorie LE PUPILLE, La Carletta, Malfatti, MORIS FARMS, Mantellasi, Poggio al Lupo, Poggio Argentiera, La Selva, Cantina di Scansano, Terre di Talamo, and Villa Patrizia are producers to try.

Moris Farms ★★★ Gd producer in MONTEREGIO and MORELLINO DI SCANSANO, respectively to N and S of Grosseto; look for RISERVA and IGT Avvoltore, a rich SANGIOVESE/Cab Sauv/Syrah blend.

Moscadello di Montalcino Tus DOC w sw (sp) ★★ DYA Revived traditional wine of MONTALCINO, once better known than BRUNELLO. Sweet fizz and sweet to high-octane MOSCATO PASSITO. Best: COL D'ORCIA, La Poderina, Poggio Salvi.

Moscato Fruitily fragrant ubiquitous grape for a diverse range of wines: sparkling or still, light or full-bodied, but always sweet.

Moscato d'Asti Pie DOCG w sp sw ★★·★★★ DYA Similar to DOCG ASTI, but usually better grapes; lower in alcohol, sweeter, fruitier, often from small producers. Best DOCG MOSCATO from: L Armangia, BERA, BRAIDA, Ca'd'Gal, CASCINA FONDA, Cascina Pian d'Oro, Caudrina, Il Falchetto, FONTANAFREDDA, Forteto della Luja, di GRESY, Icardi, Isolabella, Marino, Marco Negri, La Morandina, Elio Perrone, Rivetti, Saracco, Scagliola, Vajra, Vietti, Vignaioli di Sante Stefano, Viticoltori Acquese.

Moscato Giallo Aromatic ALTO ADIGE grape made into irresistible dry white, esp LAGEDER, CS CALDARO.

Müller-Thurgau Variety of some interest in TRENTINO-ALTO ADIGE and FRIULI. Leading producers: Lavis, LAGEDER, POJER & SANDRI, Zeni.

Murana, Salvatore Si ★★★ V.gd MOSCATO and PASSITO di PANTELLERIA.

Muri Gries ★★ V.gd producer of DOC ALTO ADIGE, best is DOC LAGREIN.

Nada, Fiorenzo ★★★ Fine producer of smooth, elegant DOCG BARBARESCO.

Nebbiolo The best red grape of PIEDMONT. Also in VALTELLINA (Lombardy).

Nebbiolo d'Alba Pie DOC r dr (s/sw sp) ★★ 96 97 98 99 00 01 03 04 From ALBA (but not BAROLO, BARBARESCO). Like lighter BAROLO but more approachable. Best from Marziano Abbona, Alario, BRICCO Maiolica, Cascina Chicco, La Contea, Paolo Conterno, Correggia, Damilano, De Marie, FONTANAFREDDA, GIACOSA, Bruna Grimaldi, Hilberg, Mario Marengo, Giuseppe MASCARELLO, Gianmatteo Pira, Paitin, PRUNOTTO, Rizieri, SANDRONE, Tenuta Rocca, VAL DI PRETE. See also ROERO.

Negri See GRUPPO ITALIANO VINI.

Negroamaro Literally "black bitter"; APULIAN red grape with high quality potential. See ALEZIO, BRINDISI, COPERTINO, and SALICE SALENTINO.

Nero d'Avola SICILIAN dark-red grape (Avola is S of Siracusa) with real promise, alone or in blends.

Niedermayr ★★★ V.gd DOC ALTO ADIGE, esp LAGREIN, PINOT N. Gewurz, Sauv Bl, and IGT Euforius (LAGREIN/Cab Sauv) and Aureus (sweet white blend).

Niedrist, Ignaz ★★★ Small, gifted producer of white and red ALTO ADIGE wines (esp LAGREIN, PINOT N, PINOT BL, RIES).

Nipozzano, Castello di ★★★ FRESCOBALDI estate in RUFINA E of Florence making MONTESODI CHIANTI. The most important outside the CLASSICO zone.

Nittardi ★★→★★★ Reliable source of high-quality CHIANTI CLASSICO

Nosiola (Trentino) T-AA DOC w dr sw ★ DYA Light, fruity white from Nosiola grapes. Also gd VIN SANTO. Best from Castel Noarna, POJER & SANDRI, Giovanni Poli, Pravis, Zeni.

Nozzole ★★→★★★ Famous estate now owned by Ambrogio FOLONARI, in heart of CHIANTI CLASSICO, N of Greve. Also v.gd Cab Sauv Pareto.

Nuragus di Cagliari Sar DOC w ★★ DYA Lively Sardinian white.

Oasi degli Angeli Benchmark all-MONTEPULCIANO wines from small producer in southern Marches; lush and mouth-filling.

Oberto, Andrea ★★→★★★ Small La Morra producer: top BAROLO, BARBERA D'ALBA.

Oddero ★★→★★★ Well-known La Morra estate for excellent BAROLO (look for Mondocco di Bussia, Rocche di Castiglione, and VIGNA Rionda).

Oltrepò Pavese Lom DOC r w dr sw sp ★→★★★ 14 wines from Pavia province, most named after grapes. Sometimes v.gd PINOT N and SPUMANTE. Top growers: Anteo, Barbacarlo, Casa Re, Castello di Cigognola, CS Casteggio, Frecciarossa, Le Fracce, La Versa co-op, Monsupello, Mazzolino, Ruiz de Cardenas, Travaglino, Vercesi del Castellazzo.

Ornellaia Tus ★★★★ Lodovico ANTINORI-founded estate nr BOLGHERI on the TUSCAN coast. FRESCOBALDI bought out former jt-venture partner Mondavi. Estate has many prestigious wines: excellent BOLGHERI DOC Ornellaia, superb IGT Masseto (MERLOT), v.gd BOLGHERI DOC Le Serre Nuove and VDT Le Volte.

Orvieto Umb DOC w dr s/sw ★→★★ DYA The classic Umbrian golden white, smooth, substantial; once very dull but recently more interesting, esp when sw. Orvieto CLASSICO is better. Only finest (e.g. Barberani, Co.Vi.O, Decugnano del Barbi, La Carraia, Palazzone, Vi.C.Or) age well. But see Castello della SALA.

Pacenti, Siro ★★★ Very international-style BRUNELLO and ROSSO DI MONTALCINO.

Pagadebit di Romagna E-R DOC w dr s/sw ★ DYA Pleasant traditional "payer of debts" from around Bertinoro.

Pagani De Marchi New face N of BOLGHERI, impressive IGT varietal wines from Cab Sauv, SANGIOVESE, and in particular, MERLOT.

Palazzino, Podere Il ★★★ Small estate with admirable CHIANTI CLASSICO.

Pancrazi, Marchese ★★→★★★ Estate nr Florence: some of Italy's top PINOT N.

Paneretta, Castello della ★★→★★★ To follow for very fine CHIANTI CLASSICO, IGTS Quatrocentenario, Terrine.

Pantelleria Island off the SICILIAN coast noted for MOSCATO, particularly PASSITO. Watch for Abraxas, DONNAFUGATA, Salvatore MURANA, Nuova Agricoltura.

Parrina Tus DOC r w ★★ Grand estate nr classy resorts of Argentario. Gd white Ansonica, improving reds (SANGIOVESE/Cab Sauv and MERLOT) from MAREMMA.

Parusso ★★★ Fine BAROLO (e.g. single-v'yd Bussia VIGNA Rocche and Bussia VIGNA Munie), but other wines can be less inspired

Pasqua, Fratelli ★★ Gd producer and bottler of VERONA wines: VALPOLICELLA, AMARONE, SOAVE. Also BARDOLINO and RECIOTO.

Passito (pa) Strong, mostly sw wine from grapes dried on the vine or indoors.

Paternoster ★★★ Top AGLIANICO DEL VULTURE, esp Don Anselmo and Villa Rotondo.

Patriglione ★★★ Dense, strong red IGT (NEGROAMARO/MALVASIA Nera). See TAURINO.

Piaggia Outstanding producer of Carmignano Riserva, IGT Il Sasso.

Piave Ven DOC r w ★→★★ (r) **97 99'** 00 01 03 04 (w) DYA Flourishing DOC NW of Venice for four red and four white wines named after their grapes. Cab Sauv, MERLOT, and RABOSO reds can all age. Gd examples from Duca di Castelanza, Molon, Loredan Gasparini, Villa Sandi.

Picolit F-VG DOC w s/sw sw ★★→★★★★ 00 01 03 04 Delicate sweet wine from COLLI ORIENTALI DEL FRIULI, but with an exaggerated reputation. A little like France's Jurançon. Ages up to 6 yrs, but very overpriced. Best: DORIGO, Livio FELLUGA, Meroi, Perusini, Specogna, VILLA RUSSIZ.

Piedmont (Piemonte) With TUSCANY, the most important Italian region for top-quality wine. Turin is the capital, ASTI and ALBA the wine centres. See BARBARESCO, Barbera, BAROLO, DOLCETTO, GRIGNOLINO, MOSCATO, etc.

Piemonte Pie DOC r w p (sp) ★→★★ New all-PIEDMONT blanket-DOC inc Barbera, BONARDA, BRACHETTO, CORTESE, GRIGNOLINO, Chard, SPUMANTE, MOSCATO.

Pieropan ★★★ Outstanding SOAVE and RECIOTO: deserving of its fame, esp Soave La Rocca and Calvarino, sweet PASSITO della ROCCA.

Pieve di Santa Restituta ★★★ GAJA estate for admirable BRUNELLO DI MONTALCINO.

Pigato Lig DOC w ★★ DOC under Riviera Ligure di Ponente. Often outclasses VERMENTINO as Liguria's finest white, with rich texture and structure. Gd from Bruna, colle dei Bardellini, Durin, Feipu, Foresti, Lupi, TERRE ROSSE, Vio.

Pinocchio p w sw ★ Popular in youth, famous for its nose.

Pinot Bianco (Pinot Bl) Popular grape in NE for many DOC wines, generally bland and dry. Best from ALTO ADIGE ★★ (top growers inc Colterenzio, HOFSTÄTTER, LAGEDER, NIEDRIST, TERLANO, Termeno), COLLIO ★★→★★★ (v.gd from Renato Keber, Aldo Polencic, RUSSIZ SUPERIORE, SCHIOPETTO, VILLA RUSSIZ), and COLLI ORIENTALI ★★→★★★ (best from La Viarte, Zamò & Zamò). ISONZO ★★ (from Masut da Rive).

Pinot Grigio Tasty, low-acid white grape popular in NE. Best from DOCS ALTO ADIGE (SAN MICHELE APPIANO, CALDARO, LAGEDER, Termeno), COLLIO (Renato Keber, LIVON, Aldo Polencic, RUSSIZ SUPERIORE, SCHIOPETTO, Tercic, Terpin, Venica, VILLA RUSSIZ), COLLI ORIENTALI (Livio FELLUGA), and ISONZO (Borgo San Daniele, LIS NERIS, Masut da Rive, Pierpaolo Pecorari, Ronco del Gelso, VIE DI ROMANS).

Pinot Nero (Pinot Noir) Planted in much of NE Italy. DOC status in ALTO ADIGE (the co-ops of Caldaro, Colterenzio, and Cortaccia, HAAS, Haderburg, HOFSTÄTTER, LAGEDER, Laimburg, NIEDERMAYR, Niedrist, SAN MICHELE APPIANO CO-OP, Termeno co-op) and in OLTREPÒ PAVESE (Frecciarossa, Ruiz de Cardenas). Promising trials elsewhere, *e.g.* FRIULI (LE DUE TERRE, Masut da Riva), TUSCANY (Ama, FARNETELLA, FONTODI, Pancranzi), and on Mount Etna in SICILY. Also fine from several regions: TRENTINO (Lunelli, POJER & SANDRI), Lombardy (CA' DEL BOSCO, Ronco Calino), Umbria (ANTINORI), Marches (BOCCADIGABBIA).

Pio Cesare ★★→★★★ Long-established ALBA producer. Esp BAROLO, BARBARESCO.

Planeta ★★★ Top SICILIAN producer: Segreta Bianco blend, Segreta ROSSO; outstanding Chard, Cab Sauv, Fiano, MERLOT, NERO D'AVOLA (Santa Cecilia).

Podere Small TUSCAN farm, once part of a big estate. (See under name – *e.g.* BOSCARELLI, PODERI.)

Poggio Antico ★★★ Admirably consistent, top-level BRUNELLO DI MONTALCINO.

Poggione, Tenuta Il ★★★ Very reliable estate for BRUNELLO, ROSSO DI MONTALCINO.

Pojer & Sandri ★★→★★★ Top TRENTINO producers: red and white, inc SPUMANTE.

Poliziano ★★★→★★★★ MONTEPULCIANO estate. Federico Carletti makes superior VINO NOBILE (esp Asinone) and superb IGT Le Stanze (Cab Sauv/MERLOT).

Pomino Tus DOC w r ★★★ r **95 97** 98 99' 01 Fine red and white blends (esp Il Benefizio). Esp from FRESCOBALDI and SELVAPIANA.

Primitivo Versatile red grape of far S, identified with California's Zin. See MANDURIA.

Produttori del Barbaresco ★★→★★★ Co-op and one of DOCG's most reliable producers. Often-outstanding single-v'yd wines (Asili, Montefico, Montestefano, Rabajà).

Prosecco Shorthand in wide use for a glass of dry fizz. But see next entry.

Prosecco di Conegliano-Valdobbiadene Ven DOC w s/sw sp (dr) ★★ DYA White grape for improving fashionable light sp, normally very dry; the dry, faintly bitter; the sweet fruity. Sweetest are called Superiore di Cartizze. CARPENE MALVOLTI: best known; also Adami, Bisol, Bortolin, Canevel, Case Bianche, Le Colture, Col Salice, Col Vetoraz, Nino Franco, Gregoletto, Ruggeri, Zardetto.

Prunotto, Alfredo ★★★ ›★★★★ Very serious ALBA company with top BARBARESCO BAROLO, NEBBIOLO, BARBERA D'ALBA, DOLCETTO, etc. Since 1999 Prunotto (now controlled by ANTINORI) also produces BARBERA D'ASTI (look for Costamiole) and Monferrato Rosso Mompertone, Barbera-Syrah blend.

Puglia See APULIA.

Puiatti ★★ Reliable, important producer of COLLIO; also METODO CLASSICO SPUMANTE Puiatti also owns a FATTORIA in CHIANTI CLASSICO (Casavecchia).

Querciabella ★★ ›★★★ Prominent CHIANTI CLASSICO estate with RISERVA, IGT Camartina (SANGIOVESE/Cab Sauv), barrel-fermented white Batàr, new SANGIOVESE/MERLOT.

Quintarelli, Giuseppe ★★★★ True artisan producer of VALPOLICELLA, RECIOTO, and AMARONE. At the top in both quality and price.

Raboso del Piave (now DOC) Ven r ★★ **95 97** 99' 00 01 Powerful, sharp, interesting country red; needs age. Look for Molon.

Rampolla, Castello dei ★★★ ›★★★★ Fine estate in Panzano in CHIANTI CLASSICO notable Cab Sauv-based IGT wines Sammarco and Alceo.

Recioto della Valpolicella Ven DOC r s/sw (sp) ★★ ›★★★ **95 97 98 00** 01 03 04 Potentially excellent rich and tangy red from half-dried grapes. V.gd from Stefano Accordini, Serègo Alighieri, ALLEGRINI, Baltieri, BOLLA, BRUNELLI, BUSSOLA Campagnola, Ca' Rugate, Castellani, DAL FORNO, Aleardo Ferrari, LE RAGOSE, LE SALETTE, QUINTARELLI, Sant'Alda, Speri, TEDESCHI, Trabucchi, CS VALPOLICELLA, Villa Bellini, Villa Monteleone, Viviani, and Zeldi.

Recioto della Valpolicella Amarone See AMARONE.

Recioto di Gambellara Ven DOC w sw (sp s/sw DYA) ★ Mostly half-sparkling and industrial. Best is strong and sweet. Look for La Biancara.

Recioto di Soave Ven DOCG w s/sw (sp) ★★★ **90 91 92 93 94 95 97 98 99** 00 01 03 04 SOAVE made from selected half-dried grapes: sweet, fruity, slightly almondy; high alcohol. Outstanding from ANSELMI, Gini, PIEROPAN, Tamellini, and now often v.gd from Ca' Rugate, Pasqua, Suavia, Trabuchi.

Refosco (dal Peduncolo Rosso) r ★★ ›★★★ **95 96 97'** 99' 00 01 03 Interesting, full, dark, tannic red for ageing. Best comes from COLLI ORIENTALI DOC: v.gd from Livio FELLUGA and Miani; gd from Dorigo, Moschioni, Ronchi di Manzano, Venica, Ca' Bolani, and Denis Montanara in Aquileia DOC. Often gd value.

Regaleali See TASCA D'ALMERITA.

Ribolla Colli Orientali del Friuli and Collio, F-VG DOC w ★ ›★★ DYA Highly acidic NE white. The best comes from COLLIO. Top estates: La Castellada, Damijan Fliegl, GRAVNER, Il Carpino, Primosic, Radikon, Tercic, Terpin.

Ricasoli Famous TUSCAN family, "inventors" of CHIANTI, whose CHIANTI CLASSICO is named after its BROLIO estate and castle. Other Ricasolis own Castello di Cacchiano and Rocca di Montegrossi.

Riecine Tus r ★★★ First-class CHIANTI CLASSICO estate at Gaiole, created by its late English owner, John Dunkley. Also fine IGT La Gioia SANGIOVESE.

Riesling Used to mean Riesling Italico or Welschriesling. German (Rhine) Riesling now ascendant. Best: DOC ALTO ADIGE ★★ (esp HOFSTÄTTER, Laimburg, Ignaz NIEDRIST, Kuenhof, La Vis co-op, Unterortl); DOC OLTREPÒ PAVESE (Lom) ★★ (Brega Frecciarossa, Le Fracce); excellent from RONCO del Gelso and VIE DI ROMANS (DOC ISONZO). V.gd from Le Vigne di San Pietro (Ven), JERMANN, VAJRA (Pie).

Ripasso VALPOLICELLA re-fermented on AMARONE grape skins to make a more complex, longer-lived, fuller wine. First-class is MASI's Campo Fiorin.

Riserva Wine aged for a statutory period, usually in casks or barrels.

Riunite One of the world's largest co-op cellars, nr Reggio Emilia, producing huge quantities of LAMBRUSCO and other wines.

Rivera ★★→★★★ Reliable winemakers at Andria in APULIA. ★★★ CASTEL DEL MONTE Il Falcone RISERVA; v.gd Cappellaccio; VIGNA al Monte; Puer Apuliae.

Rivetti, Giorgio (La Spinetta) ★★★→★★★★ Fine MOSCATO d'Asti, excellent Barbera, interesting IGT Pin, series of top single-v'yd BARBARESCOS. Now owner of v'yds both in the BAROLO and the CHIANTI Colli Pisane DOCGS. First vintages of BAROLO already outstanding.

Riviera del Garda Bresciano Lom DOC w p r (sp) ★→★★ r **97 99** 00 01 Simple, sometimes charming cherry-pink CHIARETTO, neutral white from SW Garda. Esp from Ca' dei Frati, Comincioli, Costaripa, Monte Cigogna.

Rocca, Bruno ★★★ Young producer with admirable BARBARESCO (Rabajà) and other ALBA wines.

Rocche dei Manzoni ★★★ Modernist estate at Monforte d'Alba. V.gd oaky BAROLO (esp VIGNA d'la Roul, Cappella di Stefano, Pianpolvere), BRICCO Manzoni (pioneer Barbera/NEBBIOLO blend), Quatr Nas (LANGHE) .

Roero Pie DOCG r ★★ **96 97' 98' 99' 00** 01' 03 04 Evolving former "drink-me-quick" NEBBIOLO. Can be firm and delicious. Best: Almondo, Buganza, Ca' Rossa, Cascina Chicco, Correggia, Funtanin, Malvirà, Monchiero-Carbone, Morra, Pace, Pioiero, Taliano, Val de Prete.

Roero Arneis See ARNEIS.

Ronco Term for a hillside v'yd in N Italy, esp FRIULI-VENEZIA GIULIA.

Ronco del Gnemiz ★★★ Small estate, very fine COLLI ORIENTALI DEL FRIULI.

Rosato Rosé; also CHIARETTO, esp around Lake Garda.

Rosato del Salento Ap p ★★ DYA From nr BRINDISI; can be strong, but often really juicy and gd. See COPERTINO, SALICE SALENTO for producers.

Rossese di Dolceacqua Lig DOC r ★★ DYA Quite rare, fragrant, light red of the Riviera. Gd from Foresti, Giuncheo, Guglielmi, Lupi, Terre Bianche.

Rosso Red.

Rosso Conero Mar DOCG r ★★→★★★ **94 95** 97' **98 00' 01'** 03 04 Some of Italy's best MONTEPULCIANO (the grape, that is): GAROFOLI's Grosso Agontano, Moroder's RC Dorico, TERRE CORTESI MONCARO's Nerone and Vigneti del Parco, Le Terrazze's Sassi Neri and Visions of J. Also gd: Casato, FAZI-BATTAGLIA, Lanari, Leopardi Dittajuti, Malacari, Marchetti, Poggio Morelli, UMANI RONCHI.

Rosso di Montalcino Tus DOC r ★★→★★★ **99'** 00 01 03 DOC for younger wines from BRUNELLO grapes. For growers, see BRUNELLO DI MONTALCINO.

Rosso di Montefalco Umb DOC r ★★→★★★ **95 96 97' 98 99'** 00' 01' 03 04 SANGIOVESE/TREBBIANO/SAGRANTINO blend. For producers, see MONTEFALCO SAGRANTINO.

Rosso di Montepulciano Tus DOC r ★★ **99'** 00 01 03 See previous two entries for VINO NOBILE. For growers see VINO NOBILE DI MONTEPULCIANO. While ROSSO DI MONTALCINO is increasingly expensive, Rosso di Montepulciano offers value.

Rosso Piceno Mar DOC r ★★ **95 97' 98' 00' 01'** 03 04 Stylish MONTEPULCIANO/ SANGIOVESE, SUPERIORE from classic zone nr Ascoli, much improved in recent years. Best inc: Aurora, BOCCADIGABBIA, Bucci, COLLI Ripani, Damiani, De Angelis, Fonte della Luna, Forano, Laila, Le Caniette, Laurentina, Montecappone, TERRE CORTESI MONCARO, Saladini Pilastri, San Giovanni, San Savino, Velenosi Ercole, Villamagna, Villa Ragnola.

Rubesco ★★ The excellent, popular red of LUNGAROTTI; see TORGIANO.

Ruchè (also Rouchè/Rouchet) Rare old grape of French origin; fruity, fresh, rich-scented red wine (s/sw). Ruchè di Castagnole MONFERRATO is recent DOC. Look for Biletta, Bologgnone, Dezzani, Garetto, SCARPA's Rouchet Briccorosa: dry (★★★).

Ruffino ★→★★★★ Outstanding CHIANTI merchant at Pontassieve, E of Florence. Best are RISERVA Ducale and Santedame. V.gd IGT Chard Solatia, SANGIOVESE/Cab Sauv Modus. Owns Lodola Nuova in MONTEPULCIANO for VINO NOBILE DI MONTEPULCIANO, and Greppone Mazzi in MONTALCINO for BRUNELLO DI MONTEPULCIANO.

ITALY

Excellent new SANGIOVESE/Colorino blend Romitorio from Santedame estate. Recent purchase: Borgo Conventi estate in FRIULI-VENEZIA GIULIA.

Rufina ★★★ Important sub-region of CHIANTI in the hills E of Florence. Best wines from Basciano, CASTELLO del Trebbio, CASTELLO DI NIPOZZANO (FRESCOBALDI), Colognole, Frascole, SELVAPIANA, Tenuta Bossi, Travignoli.

Russiz Superiore Collio (See FELLUGA.)

Sagrantino di Montefalco See MONTEFALCO.

Sala, Castello della ★★→★★★ ANTINORI estate at ORVIETO. Campogrande is the regular white. Top wine is Cervaro della Sala, oak-aged Chard/GRECHETTO. Muffato della Sala was a pioneering example of an Italian botrytis-influenced dessert wine. PINOT N also gd.

Salice Salento Ap DOC r ★★→★★★ 93 94' 95 97' 99 00 01 03 04 Resonant but clean and quenching red from NEGROAMARO grapes. RISERVA after 2 yrs. Top makers: Apollonio, Candido, Castello Monaci, Due Palme, Resya, Tornavento, TAURINO, Valle dell'Asso.

Sandrone, Luciano ★★★ Exponent of new-style BAROLO vogue with v.gd BAROLO Cannubi Boschi, Le Vigne, DOLCETTO, BARBERA D'ALBA, and NEBBIOLO D'ALBA.

San Felice ★★ Picturesque CHIANTI resort/estate. Fine CLASSICO RISERVA Poggio rosso. Also red IGT Vigorello and BRUNELLO DI MONTALCINO Campogiovanni.

San Gimignano Famous TUSCAN city of towers and its dry white VERNACCIA. Also very fine red wines: Cesani, Cusona, FALCHINI, Fontaleoni, La Rampa di Fugnano, Le Calcinaie, Le Tre Stelle, Mormoraia, Palagetto, Palagione, PARADISO.

Sangiovese (Sangioveto) Principal red grape of central Italy. Top performance used to be only in TUSCANY – CHIANTI, VINO NOBILE, BRUNELLO DI MONTALCINO, MORELLINO DI SCANSANO, various fine IGT offerings, etc. – but now competitive bottles are made elsewhere. S di Romagna often well made and v.gd value from Berti, Calonga, Ca' Lunga, Campo del Sole, Tenuta Diavoletto, Drei Donà, La Berta, La Viola, Madonia, Pandolfa, Poderi dal Nespoli, San Patrignano, San Valentino, Terragens, Tre Monti, Trere (E-R DOC), Uva delle Mura, Zerbina, IGT Ronco dell Ginestre, Ronco dei Ciliegi from CASTELLUCCIO. V.gd MONTEFALCO ROSSO and TORGIANO (Umbria). Sometimes gd from the Marches too: Maria Pia Castelli, BOCCADIGABBIA, and Ciù Ciù.

San Giusto a Rentennano ★★★→★★★★ One of the best CHIANTI CLASSICO producers (★★★). Delicious but very rare VIN SANTO. Superb SANGIOVESE IGT Percarlo (★★★★).

San Guido, Tenuta See SASSICAIA.

San Leonardo ★★★ Top estate in TRENTINO, with outstanding San Leonardo (Cab Sauv) and gd TRENTINO DOC MERLOT.

San Michele Appiano Top ALTO ADIGE co-op. Look for Sanct Valentin (★★★) selections: CHARDONNAY, PINOT GR, Sauv Bl, Cab Sauv, PINOT N, Gewurz.

Santadi ★★★ Consistently fine wines from SARDINIAN co-op, esp DOC CARIGNANO DEL SULCIS Grotta Rossa, TERRE BRUNE, Rocca Rubia, and IGT Baie Rosse (Carignano), Vermentino Villa Solais, Villa di Chiesa (VERMENTINO/Chard).

Santa Maddalena (or St-Magdalener) T-AA DOC r ★→★★ DYA Typical SCHIAVA ALTO ADIGE red. Sometimes light with bitter aftertaste; or warm, smooth, and fruity, esp: CS St-Magdalena (Huck am Bach), Gojer, Josephus Mayr, Georg Ramoser, Hans Rottensteiner (Premstallerhof), Heinrich Rottensteiner.

Santa Margherita Large Veneto (Portogruaro) merchants: Veneto (Torressella), ALTO ADIGE (Kettmeir), TUSCANY (Lamole di Lamole and Vistarenni), and Lombardy (CA' DEL BOSCO).

Santi See GRUPPO ITALIANO VINI.

Saracco, Paolo ★★★ Small estate with top MOSCATO D'ASTI.

Sardinia (Sardegna) Major potential, at times evidenced in excellent wines, *e.g.* TERRE BRUNE from SANTADI, Turriga from ARGIOLAS, Arbeskia and Dule from

Gabbas, VERMENTINO of CAPICHERA, CANNONAU RISERVAS of Jerzu, VERMENTINO and CANNONAU selections from Dettori.

Sartarelli ★★★ One of top VERDICCHIO DEI CASTELLI DI JESI producers (Tralivio); outstanding, rare Verdicchio VENDEMMIA Tardiva (Contrada Balciana).

Sassicaia Tus r ★★★★ 85' 88' 90' 93 95' 96 97' 98 99 01 03 One of the first Cab Sauvs, Italy's best by far in 1970s and '80s. Extraordinarily influential, from the Tenuta San Guido of Incisa della Rocchetta family at BOLGHERI. Promoted from SUPER TUSCAN VDT to special sub-zone status in BOLGHERI DOC. Conservative style, real finesse.

Satta, Michele ★★★ V.gd DOC BOLGHERI, IGT red blend Piastraia and Castagni.

Savuto Cal DOC r p ★★ 95 97' 98 99 00 01 03 04 Fragrant, juicy red from the provinces of Cosenza and Catanzaro. Best producer is Odoardi.

Scarpa ★★ ·★★★ Old-fashioned house with BARBERA D'ASTI (La Bogliona), rare Rouchet (RUCHÈ), v.gd DOLCETTO, BAROLO, BARBARESCO.

Scavino, Paolo ★★★ Successful modern-style BAROLO producer. Sought-after single-v'yd wines: Rocche dell'Annunziata, Bric del Fiasc, Cannubi, and Carobric. Also oak-aged Barbera and Langhe Corale.

Schiava High-yielding red grape of TRENTINO and ALTO ADIGE, used for light reds such as LAGO DI CALDARO, SANTA MADDALENA, etc.

Schiopetto, Mario ★★★ ·★★★★ Legendary late COLLIO pioneer with 25,000-case winery. V.gd DOC Sauv Bl, PINOT BIANCO, TOCAI, IGT blend Blanc de Rosis, etc. Rich and elegant new IGT offerings with wine from COLLIO and COLLI ORIENTALI vineyards.

Sciacchetrà See CINQUETERRE.

Secco Dry.

Sella & Mosca ★★ Major SARDINIAN grower and merchant with very pleasant white Torbato and light, fruity VERMENTINO Cala Viola (DYA). Gd Alghero DOC Marchese di Villamarina (Cab Sauv), and Tanca Farrà (CANNONAU/Cab Sauv). Also interesting port-like Anghelu Ruju. A safe bet.

Selvapiana ★★★ Top CHIANTI RUFINA estate. Best wines are RISERVA Bucerchiale and IGT Fornace. Also fine red DOC POMINO.

Sforzato See VALTELLINA.

Sicily Island in full creative ferment, both with native grapes (NERO D'AVOLA, Frappato, Inzolia, Grecanico) and international varieties. To watch: Abraxas, Agareno, Benanti, Bonaccorsi, Capocroce, Ceusi, Colosi, COS, Cottanera, CS Corbera, Cusumano, De Bartoli, Di Giovanna, DONNAFUGATA, DUCA DI SALAPARUTA, Fatasci, Feudo Maccari, Feudo Montoni, Feudo Santa Teresa, Firriato, Fondo Antico, Grottarossa, Gulfi-Ramada, Morgante, MURANA, Pellegrino, Principe di Butera (ZONIN), PLANETA, Rapitalà, Rudini, Sallier de la Tour, Santa Anastasia, SIV, Spadafora, TASCA D'ALMERITA, Tenuta dell'Abate, VECCHIO SAMPERI, Zemmer.

Sizzano Pie DOC r ★★ 90 93 95 96' 97' 98 99' 00 01 03 04 Full-bodied red from Sizzano, (Novara); mostly NEBBIOLO. Ages up to 10 yrs. Esp: Bianchi, Dessilani.

Soave Ven DOC w ★→★★ DYA Famous white: fresh, smooth, limpid. Standards rising (at last). Soave CLASSICO: intense fruit/minerals. Esp PIEROPAN; also Bolla, Cantina del Castello, La Cappuccina, Dama del Rovere, Fattori & Graney, Gini, Guerrieri-Rizzardi, Inama, Portinari, Pra, Ca' Rugate, Suavia, Tamellini, TEDESCHI.

Solaia Tus r ★★★★ 85 88 90 93 94' 95 96 97' 98 99' 00 01' Very fine B'x-style VDT of Cab Sauv and a little SANGIOVESE from ANTINORI; first made in 1978. Italy's best Cab Sauv in the 1990s, and a great wine by any standards.

Sorì Term for a high S-, SE-, or SW-oriented v'yd in PIEDMONT.

Sovana New MAREMMA DOC; inland nr Pitigliano. Look for SANGIOVESE, Ciliegiolo from Tenuta Roccaccia, Pitigliano, Ripa, Sassotondo, Cab Sauv from ANTINORI.

ITALY

Spanna Local name for NEBBIOLO in a variety of N PIEDMONT zones (BOCA, BRAMATERRA, FARA, GATTINARA, GHEMME, LESSONA, SIZZANO).

Sportoletti ★★★ V.gd wines from Spello, nr ASSISI in Umbria, esp Villa Fidelia.

Spumante Sparkling, as in sweet ASTI or many gd dry wines, inc both METODO CLASSICO (best from TRENTINO, ALTO ADIGE, FRANCIACORTA, PIEDMONT, OLTREPÒ PAVESE; occasionally gd from FRIULI and Veneto) and tank-made cheapos.

Stravecchio Very old.

Südtirol The local name of German-speaking ALTO ADIGE.

Superiore Wine with more ageing than normal DOC and 0.5–1% more alcohol.

Super Tuscan Term coined for innovative wines from TUSCANY, often involving pure SANGIOVESE or international varieties, barriques, and elevated prices.

Tasca d'Almerita ★★★ Historic SICILIAN producer owned by noble family (between Palermo and Caltanissetta to the SE). Gd IGT red, white, and ROSATO Regaleali; v.gd ROSSO; impressive Chard and Cab Sauv.

Taurasi Cam DOCG r ★★★ 90' 93' 94' 95 97' 98 99 00 01' 03 04 The best Campanian red, and one of Italy's outstanding wines. Tannic when young; RISERVA after 4 yrs. V.gd from Caggiano, Caputo, FEUDI DI SAN GREGORIO, MASTROBERARDINO, Molettieri, Vesevo, and Villa Raiano.

Taurino, Cosimo ★★★ Tip-top producer of Salento-APULIA, v.gd SALICE SALENTO, VDT Notarpanoro, and IGT PATRIGLIONE ROSSO.

Tedeschi, Fratelli ★★→★★★ Well-known producer of VALPOLICELLA, AMARONE, RECIOTO. Gd Capitel San Rocco IGT.

Tenuta Farm or estate. (See under name – e.g. SAN GUIDO, TENUTA.)

Terlano T-AA w ★★→★★★ DYA Terlano DOC incorporated into ALTO ADIGE. AA Terlano DOC is applicable to eight varietal whites, esp Sauv Bl. Terlaner in German. Esp from CS Terlano, LAGEDER, NIEDERMAYR, NIEDRIST.

Teroldego Rotaliano T-AA DOC r p ★★ ★★★ 95 97 99 00 01 02 03 04 Attractive blackberry-scented red; slightly bitter aftertaste; can age very well. Esp FORADORI'S. Also gd from CA' VIT, Dorigati, Endrizzi, MEZZACORONA'S RISERVA, Zeni.

Terre Brune Sard r ★★★ Splendid earthy Carignano/Bovelladda blend from SANTADI, a flag-carrier for SARDINIA.

Terre Cortesi Moncaro Mar ★★★ Marches co-op, now making wines that compete with the best of the region: gd VERDICCHIO DEI CASTELLI DI JESI, ROSSO CONERO, and ROSSO PICENO.

Terre da Vino ★→★★★ Association of 27 PIEDMONT co-ops and private estates in most local DOCS. Best: BARBARESCO La Casa in Collina, BAROLO PODERE Parussi BARBERA D'ASTI La Luna e Il Falò.

Terre di Franciacorta Lom DOC r w ★★ 97 99 00 01 Usually pleasant reds (blends of Cab Sauv, Barbera, NEBBIOLO, MERLOT); quite fruity and balanced whites (Chard, PINOT GR). Best producers: see FRANCIACORTA.

Terre Rosse ★★ Pioneering small estate nr Bologna. Its Cab Sauv, Chard, PINOT BIANCO, RIES, even Viognier, were trail-blazing wines for the region.

Terriccio, Castello di ★★★ Estate S of Livorno: excellent IGT Lupicaia, v.gd IGT Tassinaia, both Cab Sauv/MERLOT blends. Impressive new IGT Terriccio, an unusual blend of various French grapes.

Tignanello Tus r ★★★→★★★★ 88 90 93 95 96 97' 98 99' 00 01' Pioneer and leader of international-style TUSCAN reds, made by ANTINORI. Needs bottle-age.

Tocai Mild, smooth white (no relation of Hungarian Tokaji) of NE. DOC also in Ven and Lom (★→★★), but producers use most of it in FRIULI-VENEZIA GIULIA (esp COLLIO and COLLI ORIENTALI) ★★→★★★. Best producers: Aldo Polencic, BORGO DEL TIGLIO, Borgo San Daniele, LE VIGNE DI ZAMÒ, Livio FELLUGA, Masut da Rive, Meroi, Mirani, Renato Keber, RONCO del Gelso, RONCO DEL GNEMIZ, RUSSIZ SUPERIORE, SCHIOPETTO, Venica & Venica, VILLA RUSSIZ.

Torgiano Umb DOC r w p (sp) ★★ and **Torgiano, Rosso Riserva** Umb DOCG r ★★→★★★ **90 93 94 95 97 99** 00 01 03 04 Gd r from Umbria, resembles CHIANTI CLASSICO in style. RUBESCO: standard. LUNGAROTTI'S RISERVA VIGNA Montecchi was outstanding in vintages such as 75, 79, 85; keeps for many yrs. Antignano's Torgiano offers interesting contrast to historic leader LUNGAROTTI.

Traminer Aromatico T-AA DOC w ★★→★★★ DYA (German: Gewürz) Delicate, aromatic, soft. Best from various co-ops (Caldaro, Colterenzio, Prima & Nuova, SAN MICHELE APPIANO, TERLANO, Termeno) plus Abbazia di Novacella, HAAS, HOFSTÄTTER, Kuenhof, LAGEDER, Laimberg, NIEDERMAYR.

Trebbiano Principal white grape of TUSCANY, found all over Italy. Ugni Blanc in French. Sadly, a waste of gd v'yd space, with very rare exceptions.

Trebbiano d'Abruzzo Ab DOC w ★→★★ DYA Gentle, neutral, slightly tannic white from region of Pescara. Best producer: VALENTINI (also MONTEPULCIANO D'ABRUZZO), but challenged by Masciarelli. Nicodemi, La Valentina, and Valori also v.gd.

Trentino T-AA DOC r w d sw ★→★★★ DOC for 20 wines, most named after grapes. Best: Chard, PINOT BIANCO, MARZEMINO, TEROLDEGO. Region's capital is Trento.

Triacca ★★→★★★ V.gd producer of VALTELLINA; also owns estates in TUSCANY (CHIANTI CLASSICO: La Madonnina; MONTEPULCIANO: Santavenere. All ★★).

Trinoro, Tenuta di ★★★ Isolated and exceptional TUSCAN red wine estate (B'x varieties) in DOC Val d'Orcia between MONTEPULCIANO and MONTALCINO. Early vintages of Cab Sauv/Petit Verdot TRINORO are jaw-dropping. Andrea Franchetti is now developing another project on Mount Etna in SICILY.

Tuscany (Toscana) Italy's central wine region, inc DOCS CHIANTI, MONTALCINO, MONTEPULCIANO, etc., regional IGT Toscana, and – of course – SUPER TUSCAN.

Uberti ★★→★★★ Producer of DOCG FRANCIACORTA. V.gd TERRE DI FRANCIACORTA (r w).

Umani Ronchi ★★→★★★ Leading Marches merchant and grower, esp for VERDICCHIO (Casal di Serra, Plenio), ROSSO CONERO Cumaro white IGT Le Busche, red IGT Pelago. Recent wines impressively improved.

Vajra, Giuseppe Domenico ★★★ V.gd consistent BAROLO producer, esp for Barbera, BAROLO, DOLCETTO, LANGHE, etc. Also an interesting (not fizzy) FREISA.

Valcalepio Lom DOC r w ★→★★ From nr Bergamo. Pleasant red; lightly scented fresh white. Gd from Brugherata, CASTELLO di Grumello, Monzio.

Valdadige T-AA DOC r w dr s/sw ★ Name for the simple wines of the valley of the ALTO ADIGE – in German, *Etschtaler*.

Val di Cornia Tus DOC r p w ★★→★★★ **95 97** 98 **99'** 00 01' 02 03 04 New DOC nr Livorno, competing in quality with BOLGHERI. Many v.gd wines from SANGIOVESE, Cab Sauv, MERLOT, and MONTEPULCIANO. Look for: Ambrosini, Jacopo Banti, Botrona, Brancatelli, Bulichella, Tenuta Casadei, Gualdo del Re, Il Bruscello, Incontri, Le Pianacce, Montepeloso (Gabbro, Nardo), Petra, Russo, San Giusto, San Luigi, San Michele, Suveraia, Terricciola, Tua Rita (Redigaffi), and Tenuta Vignale, Villa Monte Rico.

Valentini, Edoardo ★★★ The grand tradition – and, with Gianni Mascerelli, the best maker – of MONTEPULCIANO and TREBBIANO D'ABRUZZO.

Valgella See VALTELLINA.

Vallarono, Tenute dei New project of Gancia family, high-class BARBERA D'ASTI and LANGHE ROSSO near Canelli in ASTI SPUMANTE territory.

Valle d'Aosta (VdA) DOC r w p ★★ Regional DOC for more than 20 Alpine wines inc Premetta, Fumin, Blanc de Morgex et de La Salle, Chambave, Nus Malvoisie, Arnad Montjovet, Torrette, Donnas, and Enfer d'Arvier.

Valle Isarco Eisacktal, T-AA DOC w ★★ DYA AA Valle Isarco DOC is applicable to seven varietal wines made NE of Bolzano. Gd Gewürz, MÜLLER-T, RIES, and Silvaner. Top producers: Abbazia di Novacella, CS Eisacktaler, Kuenhof.

Valpolicella Ven DOC r ★→★★★ (Superiore) **95 97 98 00** 01 03 04 (Others) DYA Attractive r from nr VERONA. Best are concentrated, complex, and merit higher prices. Delicate nutty scent, slightly bitter taste. Beware big bottles. CLASSICO more restricted; SUPERIORE aged 1 yr. Best (★★★) DAL FORNO and QUINTARELLI. Gd from Stefano Accordini, Bertani, BOLLA, BRUNELLI, Buglioni, BUSSOLA Campagnola, Ca' Rugate, Michele Castellani, Guerrieri-Rizzardi, I Saltari, LE RAGOSE, LE SALETTE, MASI, Mazzi, CS Negrar, PASQUA, Sant'Alda, Sant' Antonio Sartori, Speri, TEDESCHI, Tommasi, Trabuchi, CS VALPOLICELLA, Vaona, Venturini Villa Monteleone, Viviani, ZENATO. Interesting IGTS developing new style: MASI's Toar and Osar, ALLEGRINI's La Grola, La Poja, Palazzo della Torre (★★★).

Valtellina Lom DOC r ★★→★★★ **90 95 96 97 98** 99' 00 01 02 03 04 DOC fo tannic wines: mainly from Chiavennasca (NEBBIOLO) in N Alpine Sondric province. V.gd SUPERIORE DOCG from Grumello, Inferno, Sassella, Valgella v'yds. Best: Caven Camuna, Conti Sertoli-Salis, Fay, Nera, Nino Negri Plozza, Rainoldi, TRIACCA. Sforzato is the most concentrated type o Valtellina; similar to AMARONE.

VDT, vino da tavola "Table wine": the humblest class of Italian wine. No specific geographical or other claim to fame, but occasionally some excellen wines that do not fit into official categories. See IGT.

Vecchio Old.

Vecchio Samperi Si ★★★ MARSALA-like VDT from outstanding estate. Best i barrel-aged 30 yrs. Owner Marco De Bartoli also makes top DOC MARSALAS.

Vendemmia Harvest or vintage.

Verdicchio dei Castelli di Jesi Mar DOC w (sp) ★★→★★★ DYA Ancient white from nr Ancona, now fruity, well-structured, gd value. Also CLASSICO. Best from Accadia, Bonci-Vallerosa, Brunori, Bucci, Casalfarneto, Cimarelli, Colonnara Coroncino, FAZI-BATTAGLIA, Fonte della Luna, GAROFOLI, Laila, Lucangeli Aymeric di Laconi, Mancinelli, Montecappone, Monte Shiavo, Santa Barbara SARTARELLI, TERRE CORTESI MONCARO, UMANI RONCHI.

Verdicchio di Matelica Mar DOC w (sp) ★★→★★★ DYA Similar to above, smalle less known, longer lasting. Esp Belisario, Bisci, San Biagio, La Monacesca Pagliano Tre.

Verduno Pie DOC r ★★ (DYA) Pale red with spicy perfume, from Pelaverga grape Gd producers: Alessandria and Castello di Verduno.

Verduzzo Colli Orientali del Friuli, F-VG DOC w dr s/sw sw ★★→★★★ Full-bodie white from native grapes. Ramandolo is highly regarded sub-zone. Top Dario Coos, Dorigo, Giovanni Dri, Meroi. Superb sw VDT from LIS NERIS.

Verduzzo del Piave Ven DOC w DYA A dull little white wine.

Vermentino Lig w ★★ DYA Best seafood white of Riviera, esp from Pietra Ligur and San Remo. DOC is Riviera Ligure di Ponente. See PIGATO. Esp gd: Colle de Bardellini, Durin, Lambruschi, La Rocca di San Niccolao, Lunae Bosoni, Lup Picedi Benettini. Also Tuscan coast: ANTINORI, San Giusto, SATTA, Tenut Vignale, Terre di Talamo.

Vermentino di Gallura Sar DOCG w ★★→★★★ DYA Soft, dry, strong white c N Sardinia. Esp from CAPICHERA, Depperu, CS di Gallura, cs del Vermentino.

Vernaccia di Oristano Sar DOC w dr (sw fz) ★→★★★ **71' 80' 85' 86' 87 88 90' 9** 93' 94' 95' 97' 98 99 00 01 Sardinian speciality, like light sherry, a touc bitter, full-bodied. SUPERIORE 15.5% alcohol, 3 yrs of age. Top: CONTINI.

Vernaccia di San Gimignano Tus DOCG w ★→★★★ DYA Formerly ordinary touris wine; recent renaissance. Newly DOCG with tougher production laws. Best Cusona, Cesani, FALCHINI, Fontaleoni, Il Paradiso, Le Calcinaie, Le Rote Mormoraia, Palagetto, Palagione, Rampa di Fugnano, TERUZZI E PUTHOD.

Verona Capital of the Veneto region (home of VALPOLICELLA, BARDOLINO, SOAVE, etc. and seat of Italy's splendid annual April wine fair Vinitaly.

Verrazzano, Castello di ★★ Gd CHIANTI CLASSICO estate nr Greve.

Vestini Campagnano Small producer N of Naples specializing in forgotte local grapes. Excellent results from Casavecchia, Pallagrello Bianco, and Pallagrello Nero.

Vicchiomaggio ★★→★★★ CHIANTI CLASSICO estate nr Greve.

Vie di Romans ★★★→★★★★ Gifted young producer Gianfranco Gallo has built up his father's ISONZO estate to top FRIULI status. Excellent ISONZO Chard, PINOT GR, Sauv Bl, MALVASIA, RIES, and white blend called Flors di Uis.

Vietti ★★★ Exemplary producer of characterful PIEDMONT wines, inc BAROLO, BARBARESCO, BARBERA D'ALBA and D'ASTI at Castiglione Falletto in BAROLO region.

Vigna or vigneto A single v'yd (but, unlike elsewhere in the world, higher quality than that for generic DOC is not required in Italy).

Vignalta ★★ Top producer in COLLI EUGANEI near Padova (Veneto); v.gd COLLI Euganei Cab Sauv RISERVA and MERLOT/Cab Sauv blend Gemola.

Vignamaggio ★★→★★★ Historic, beautiful, v.gd CHIANTI CLASSICO estate nr Greve.

Villa ★★→★★★ Top producer of DOCG FRANCIACORTA.

Villa Matilde ★★★ Top Campania producer of Falerno ROSSO (Vigna Camararato) and BIANCO (Vigna Caracci), Eleusi PASSITO.

Villa Russiz ★★★ Impressive w DOC COLLIO Goriziano: v.gd Sauv Bl and MERLOT (esp "de la Tour" selections), PINOT BIANCO, PINOT GR, TOCAI, Chard.

Vino da arrosto "Wine for roast meat" – *i.e.* gd, robust dry red.

Vino Nobile di Montepulciano Tus DOCG r ★★★ **90 93 95' 97'** 98 **99'** 00 01 03 04 Impressive SANGIOVESE with bouquet and style, but often tannic; now making its name and fortune. RISERVA after 3 yrs. Best estates inc AVIGNONESI, Bindella, BOSCARELLI, Canneto, Casanova, Contucci, Dei, I Cipressi, Il Faggeto, Fassati, Fattoria del Cerro, Gracciano della Seta, Gracciano Svetoni, Icario, La Bracesca, La Calonica, La Ciarliana, Le Berne, Le Casalte, Macchione, Nottola, Palazzo Vecchio, Paterno, POLIZIANO, Romeo, Salcheto, Tre Berte, Trerose, Valdipiatta, Vecchia Cantina (look for Briareo), Villa Sant'Anna. So far, reasonably priced.

Vino novello Italy's equivalent of France's *primeurs* (as in Beaujolais).

Vin Santo or Vinsanto, Vin(o) Santo Term for certain strong, sweet wines, esp in TUSCANY: usually PASSITO. Can be very fine both in TUSCANY and TRENTINO.

Vin Santo Toscano Tus w s/sw ★→★★★ Aromatic, rich, and smooth. Aged in very small barrels called *caratelli*. Can be as astonishing as expensive, but a gd one is very rare and top producers are always short of it. Best from AVIGNONESI, CAPEZZANA, CORZANO & PATERNO, Fattoria del Cerro, FELSINA, Frascole, ISOLE E OLENA, Rocca di Montegrossi, SAN GIUSTO A RENTENNANO, San Gervasio, SELVAPIANA, Villa Sant'Anna.

Vivaldi-Arunda ★★→★★★ Winemaker Josef Reiterer makes top ALTO ADIGE sparkling wines. Best: Extra Brut RISERVA, Cuvée Marianna.

Voerzio, Roberto ★★★→★★★★ Young BAROLO pace-setter. Top single-v'yd BAROLOS: Brunate, Cerequio, Rocche dell'Annunziata-Torriglione, Sarmassa, Serra; impressive BARBERA D'ALBA.

Volpaia, Castello di ★★→★★★ First-class CHIANTI CLASSICO estate at Radda.

VQPRD Vini di Qualità Prodotti in Regione Delimitata, on DOC labels.

Zanella, Maurizio Creator of CA' DEL BOSCO.

Zenato Ven ★★→★★★ Very reliable estate for VALPOLICELLA, SOAVE, AMARONE.

Zerbina, Fattoria ★★★ New leader in Romagna; best ALBANA DOCG to date (rich PASSITO: Scacco Matto), v.gd SANGIOVESE; barrique-aged IGT Marzieno.

Zibibbo Si ★★ Local PANTELLERIA name for Muscat of Alexandria. Gd: MURANA.

Zonin ★→★★★ One of Italy's biggest private estates, based at GAMBELLARA, with DOC and DOCG VALPOLICELLA. Also in ASTI, APULIA, CHIANTI CLASSICO, SAN GIMIGNANO, FRIULI, SICILY, and now Virginia (USA). Quality rising under winemaker Franco Giacosa.

Germany

More heavily shaded
areas are the wine-
growing regions

The following abbreviations of
regional names are used in the text:

Bad	Baden
Frank	Franken
M-M	Mittelmosel
M-S-R	Mosel-Saar-Ruwer
Na	Nahe
Pfz	Pfalz
Rhg	Rheingau
Rhh	Rheinhessen
Würt	Württemberg

It's very hard to stand in a German vineyard – in somewhere like the Saar, perhaps, where the wind whistles round your ears and chills your fingers – and not wonder about the effects of global warming. "Wonder", that is, in the sense of wondering about the difference between global warming and an ice age. The Saar, even though the locals seem inured to the climate, is not a warm spot.

Yet climate change there has been, according to those same locals. Since 1988, they say, the weather has been warmer. This applies to all the wine regions of Germany: 1988 is, by general agreement, the year when extra warmth became noticeable. The trouble is, it's very hard to regret it; at least when one tastes the wines. German wines are, quite simply, superlatively good at the moment; and whether it's because of a blip in the climate statistics, or because we all drive our cars too much and too often, German growers appear to be reaping the benefits. For example, it used to be the case (admittedly, many years ago now) that *trocken* wines were skeletal, hard, bony creatures. Drinking one used to be like cuddling a laundry drier when you'd expected a labrador. Now, however, they've put on flesh and become positively playful, while regaining their poise and balance.

Curiously, too, warmer weather begins to make sense of the convoluted German system of classifying wines, which only German speakers can perfectly remember, never mind pronounce. It used to be that we Brits, brought up on the French AOC model, thought the German system – which assumes that the riper a wine is, the better it automatically is – was daft. (The French system, which believes that one vineyard is intrinsically better than another, is at first glance opposed to this, until you reflect that the reason one vineyard is better than another is because it produces better ripening: longer, slower, and more complete. But that's another subject.) But with a return to Riesling, and a realization that the new grape crossings that became so painfully popular in the 1980s and 1990s for their early and easy ripening were a mistake, the playing field has become more level than it was. Terms like Spätlese and Auslese really mean something again – but as an indication of style, not of quality. We no longer think that sweeter is necessarily better. Some of the finest, most modern German wines, for example, are Kabinetts.

The other point is that you don't have to worry so much about the vintage when every year since 1988 has been good to very good. Yes, some years are better than others, and some are ready to drink earlier than others – but warmer weather equals greater ripeness, which equals wines that can be drunk younger. It used to be said that a Kabinett needed about five years before being broached. I don't think that's necessarily the case any more.

One reason for applauding the German system is that it recognizes that individual growers can make good wines in what are generally poor years. All the growers in this chapter are focused on quality. That means that if they don't think a Spätlese or an Auslese or a Beerenauslese tastes as it should – regardless of how ripe it is according to laboratory analysis – they will demote it. So unless you actively seek out the producers who still grow Huxelrebe or Morio Muskat in order to sell Auslesen of zero flavour – and I'm not going to tell you who they are, because if you want that sort of thing, you can find it for yourself – you can trust both the vintage and the style category. If a good grower makes an Auslese in what is considered a poor year, it's because, by good fortune or good viticulture, he's managed to make a wine worthy of the name.

So climate change (if that's what it is) and riper wines – and a new emphasis on Riesling – have shifted the whole German system back into focus. It's still ridiculously complicated, and made constantly worse by the German predilection for introducing ever more categories and classifications, but that's no reason not to taste the wines.

Recent vintages

Mosel-Saar-Ruwer

Mosels (including Saar and Ruwer wines) are so attractive young that their keeping qualities are not often enough explored, and wines older than about eight years are unusual. But well-made Riesling wines of Kabinett class gain from at least five years in bottle and often much more, Spätlese from five to twenty, and Auslese and Beerenauslese anything from ten to thirty years. As a rule, in poor years the Saar and Ruwer make sharp, lean wines, but in the best years, above all with botrytis, they can surpass the whole world for elegance and thrilling, steely "breed".

2005 Superb warm autumn weather from late Sep through to Nov brought grapes to very high ripeness levels, but with better acidity than, say, 2003. Likely to be an exceptional year.

2004 A humid summer led growers to fear the worst, but the vintage was saved by a glorious autumn. At harvest, grapes were healthy and very ripe, so this has the makings of a fine year.

2003 Hot weather brought high ripeness levels but rather low acidity. Ironically, some great sites suffered from drought, while less-esteemed cooler sites often fared better. So there will be considerable variation in quality, with the best, including some powerful dry wines, superb.

2002 It is a small miracle how the Riesling grapes survived one of the wettest harvests on record to give ripe, succulent, lively wines (mostly Kabinett and Spätlese), which will be very attractive drunk young or mature.

2001 Golden Oct resulted in the best Mosel Riesling since 1990. Saar and Ruwer less exciting but still perfect balance. Lots of Spätlesen and Auslesen.

2000 Riesling stood up to harvest rain here better than most other places. Dominated by good QbA and Kabinett. Auslesen rarer, but exciting.

1999 Excellent in Saar and Ruwer, lots of Auslesen; generally only good in the Mosel due to high yields. Best will drink well young and will age.

1998 Riesling grapes came through a rainy autumn to give astonishingly good results in the Middle Mosel; the Saar and Ruwer were less lucky, with mostly QbA. Plenty of Eiswein.

1997 A generous vintage of consistently fruity, elegant wines from the entire region. Marvellous Auslesen in the Saar and Ruwer.

1996 A very variable vintage with fine Spätlesen and Auslesen, but only from top sites. Many excellent Eisweins.

1995 Excellent vintage, mainly of Spätlesen and Auslesen of firm structure and long ageing potential. Try to resist drinking too early.

1994 Another good vintage, mostly QmP with unexceptional QbA and Kabinett, but many Auslesen, Beerenauslesen, and Trockenbeerenauslesen. Rich fruit and high acidity. Drinking well now but will keep.

1993 Small, excellent vintage: lots of Auslesen/botrytis; near perfect harmony. Ready to drink except top Auslesen.

1992 A very large crop. Mostly good QbA, but 30% QmP. To drink soon.

1991 A mixed vintage. To drink soon.

1990 Superb vintage, though small. Many QmP wines were the finest for 20 years. Try to resist drinking them all too soon.

1989 Often outstanding, with noble rot giving many Auslesen etc. Saar wines best; the Mittelmosel overproduced, causing some dilution. Except for top Auslesen, ready to drink.

1988 Excellent vintage. Much ripe QmP, esp in the Mittelmosel. Lovely now but no hurry.

Fine older vintages: 76 71 69 64 59 53 49 45 37 34 21.

Rheinhessen, Nahe, Pfalz, Rheingau

Even the best wines can be drunk with pleasure when young, but Kabinett, Spätlese, and Auslese Riesling gain enormously in character by keeping for longer. Rheingau wines tend to be longest-lived, improving for fifteen years or more, but best wines from the Nahe and Pfalz can last as long. Rheinhessen wines usually mature sooner, and dry Franken and Baden wines are generally best at three to six years. Rheingau and Nahe are the longest-living.

2005 The summer was warm, but rain kept drought at bay. A very fine autumn led to high ripeness levels, accompanied by excellent acidity and extract. But the crop was about one-third less than usual. Likely to be a superb year; some compare to 1971.

2004 After an indifferent summer, a fine autumn delivered ripe healthy grapes throughout the Rhein lands. A larger than average crop, so there could be some dilution, though not at top estates. The Nahe experienced frost, storms, and hail, which may affect some wines.

2003 Very hot weather led to rich wines in the Rheingau; many lack acidity. The Pfalz produced superb Rieslings. Red wines fared well everywhere.

2002 Few challenge the best from 01, but should prove very good for both classic-style Kabinett/Spätlese and for dry; balance very good. Excellent Pinot Noir.

2001 Though more erratic than in the Mosel, here, too, this was often an exciting vintage for both dry and classic styles; excellent balance.

2000 The further south, the more difficult was the harvest, the Pfalz catching worst of harvest rain. However, all regions have islands of excellence.

1999 Quality was average where yields were high, but for top growers an excellent vintage of rich, aromatic wines with lots of charm.

1998 Excellent: rich, balanced wines, many good Spätlesen and Auslesen with excellent ageing potential. Slow-maturing; many wines still a bit closed.

1997 Very clean, ripe grapes gave excellent QbA, Kabinett, Spätlese in dry and classic styles. Little botrytis, so Auslesen and higher are rare.

1996 An excellent vintage, particularly in the Pfalz and the Rheingau, with many fine Spätlesen that will benefit from long ageing. Great Eiswein.

1995 Rather variable, but some excellent Spätlesen and Auslesen maturing well – like the 90s. Weak in the Pfalz due to harvest rain.

1994 Good vintage, mostly QmP, with abundant fruit and firm structure. Some superb Auslesen, Beerenauslesen, and Trockenbeerenauslesen. Just about ready.

GERMANY

German vintage notation

The vintage notes after entries in the German section are given in a different form from those elsewhere, to show the style of the vintage as well as its quality. Three styles are indicated:

Bold type (*e.g.* **99**) indicates classic, super-ripe vintages with a high proportion of natural (QmP) wines, including Spätlesen and Auslesen.

Normal type (*e.g.* 98) indicates "normal" successful vintages with plenty of good wine but no great preponderance of sweeter wines.

Italic type (*e.g. 96*) indicates cool vintages with generally poor ripeness but a fair proportion of reasonably successful wines, tending to be over-acidic. Few or no QmP wines, but correspondingly more selection in the QbA category. Such wines sometimes mature more favourably than expected.

N.B. Where no mention is made, the vintage is generally not recommended, or most of its wines have passed maturity.

1993 A small vintage of very good to excellent quality. Plenty of rich Spätlesen and Auslesen, which are just beginning to reach their peak.

1992 Very large vintage; would have been great but for Oct cold and rain. A third were QmP of rich, stylish quality. Most drinking well now.

1991 A middling vintage. Some fine wines are emerging. Most drinking well.

1990 Small and exceptionally fine. Drink now, but will keep for many years.

1989 Summer storms reduced crop in Rheingau. Very good quality elsewhere, up to Auslese level. Most wines mature, but no hurry to drink.

Fine older vintages: 83 76 71 69 64 59 53 49 45 37 34 21.

Achkarren Bad w (r) ★★ Village on the KAISERSTUHL, known esp for GRAUBURGUNDER First Class v'yd: Schlossberg. Wines generally best drunk during first 5 yrs Gd wines: Dr. HEGER, Michel, and co-op.

Adelmann, Weingut Graf ★★→★★★ The Adelmann estate is based at the idyllic Schaubeck castle in WÜRTTEMBERG. The specialities are subtle red blends RIES, and the rare Muskattrollinger.

Ahr Ahr r ★→★★★ **90 93 95 96 97 98 99** 00 01 02 03 04 05 Traditional specialized red wine area, S of Bonn. Light, at best elegant, SPÄTBURGUNDER esp from Adeneuer, DEUTZERHOF, Kreuzberg, MEYER-NÄKEL, Nelles, Stodden.

Aldinger, Weingut Gerhard ★★★ LEMBERGER and SPÄTBURGUNDER are the specialities of this WÜRTTEMBERG estate near Stuttgart. Gd RIES too.

Amtliche Prüfungsnummer See PRÜFUNGSNUMMER.

APNr Abbreviation of AMTLICHE PRÜFUNGSNUMMER.

Assmannshausen Rhg r ★→★★★ **89 90 93 95 96 97** 98 **99** 00 01 02 03 04 05 RHEINGAU village known for its usually pale, light SPÄTBURGUNDERS. First Class v'yd: Höllenberg. Growers inc KESSELER, Robert König, Hotel KRONE, and the STATE DOMAIN.

Auslese Wines from selective harvest of super-ripe bunches, the best affected by noble rot (*Edelfäule*) and correspondingly unctuous in flavour. Dry Auslesen are usually too alcoholic and clumsy for me.

Ayl M-S-R (Saar) w ★★★ 83 85 88 **89 90 93** 94 **95** 96 **97** 98 **99** 00 01 02 **03 04** 05 One of the best villages of the SAAR. First Class v'yd: Kupp. Growers inc BISCHÖFLICHE WEINGÜTER, Lauer, Dr. WAGNER.

Bacchus Modern, perfumed, often kitsch grape found mostly in RHEINHESSEN and FRANKEN. Best for KABINETT wines.

Bacharach ★→★★★ **89 90 93** 94 95 96 97 **98** 99 00 **01 02** 03 **04 05** Main wine town of MITTELRHEIN. Racy, austere RIES, some very fine. First Class v'yds: Hahn, Posten, Wolfshöhle. Growers inc BASTIAN, JOST, Helmut Mades, RATZENBERGER.

Bad Dürkheim Pfz w (r) ★★→★★★ 88 **89 90 93** 94 95 **96 97 98** 99 00 01 02 **03 04** 05 Main town of MITTELHAARDT, with the world's biggest barrel and an ancient Sept wine festival, the *Würstmarkt* (sausage market). First Class v'yds: Michelsberg, Spielberg. Growers: Darting, Fitz-Ritter, Schmitt, Schäfer.

Baden Bad Huge SW area of scattered v'yds with a reputation for substantial, generally dry, but supple wines that are gd with food. Fine Pinots, SPÄTBURGUNDER, RIES, GEWÜRZ. Best areas: KAISERSTUHL, ORTENAU.

Badische Bergstrasse/Kraichgau (Bereich) Widespread district of N BADEN. WEISSBURGUNDER and GRAUBURGUNDER make best wines.

Badischer Winzerkeller Germany's (and Europe's) biggest co-op, at BREISACH; 25,000 members produce up to 600 wines each year, accounting for almost half of BADEN's wine: dependably unambitious.

Badisches Frankenland See TAUBERFRANKEN.

Bad Kreuznach Nahe w ★★→★★★ 83 85 88 **89 90** 92 **93** 94 95 96 97 98 **99** 00 **01 02 03 04 05** Spa town with fine v'yds. First Class: Brückes, Kahlenberg, Krötenpfuhl. Growers inc Anheuser, Carl Finkenauer, von PLETTENBERG.

Bassermann-Jordan ★★★ 88 **89** 90 **96** 97 **98 99** 00 **01 02 03 04 05** MITTELHAARDT estate, under new ownership since 2003, with outstanding v'yds in DEIDESHEIM, FORST, RUPPERTSBERG, etc. Winemaker Ulrich Mell has put this historic estate back on top and kept it there.

Bastian, Weingut Fritz ★★ 5.6-ha BACHARACH estate. Racy, austere RIES with MOSEL-like delicacy, best from the First Class Posten v'yd.

Barriques

In 1991, German winemakers organized the German Barrique-Forum to promote this style of wine and show that German wines could be compared with oak-aged examples from anywhere in the world. In those distant days some of the wines were truly awful, while others showed a sophisticated use of oak. Now the mastery of barriques is more complete. Misguided attempts to age RIES in barriques have been abandoned, and delicate Pinot N is less likely to be swamped in new oak when it lacks the structure to support it. There is a growing band of producers, especially in BADEN and WÜRTTEMBERG, who regularly keep fruit and oak in balance, and a discreet use of barrel-ageing can also enhance the white Pinot varieties. Small oak barrels can't mask a mediocre wine, but they can give support and structure to Germany's growing number of serious reds, including the *cuvées* that blend the country's indigenous red grape varieties into a more harmonious whole.

Becker, J B ★★→★★★ Dedicated family estate and brokerage house at WALLUF. 12 ha in ELTVILLE, Martinsthal, WALLUF. Specialist in dry RIES.

Beerenauslese, BA Luscious sweet wine from exceptionally ripe, individually selected berries, usually concentrated by noble rot. Rare, expensive.

Bensheim See HESSISCHE BERGSTRASSE.

Bercher ★★★ KAISERSTUHL estate; 22.6 ha of white and red Pinots at Burkheim. Excellent WEISSBURGUNDER, RIES, and SPÄTBURGUNDER.

Bergdolt, Weingut ★★ Just south of NEUSTADT in the PFALZ, Rainer Bergdolt has long been recognized as Germany's finest producer of WEISSBURGUNDER (Pinot Bl), especially from *Grosses Gewächs* sites.

Bernkastel M-M ★→★★★★ 71 75 **83 88 89** 90 93 94 95 96 **97** 98 **99** 00 **01 02 03 04 05** Top wine town of the MITTELMOSEL; the epitome of RIES. Great First Class v'yd: Doctor, 3.2 ha; First Class v'yds: Graben, Lay. Top growers inc KERPEN, LOOSEN, MOLITOR, PAULY-BERGWEILER, PRÜM, Studert-Prüm, THANISCH, WEGELER.

Bernkastel (Bereich) Inc all the MITTELMOSEL. Wide area of deplorably dim quality and superficial flowery character. Mostly MÜLLER-T. Avoid.

Beulwitz, Weingut von ★★→★★★ Excellent RUWER estate with wines from Kaseler Nies'chen. Highly consistent.

Beware of *Bereich*

District within an *Anbaugebiet* (region). "Bereich" on a label should be treated as a flashing red light. Do not buy. See under Bereich names – *e.g.* BERNKASTEL (BEREICH).

Biffar, Josef ★★→★★★ Important DEIDESHEIM estate. 13 ha (also WACHENHEIM) of RIES. Consistently elegant wines.

Bingen Rhh w ★→★★★ **76 83** 88 **89 90 93** 94 95 **96 97** 98 **99** 00 01 02 **03 04 05** Rhine/NAHE town. Fine v'yds inc First Class Scharlachberg.

Bingen (Bereich) District name for NW RHEINHESSEN.

Bischöfliche Weingüter M-S-R ★★ Famous M-S-R estate located at TRIER, uniting cathedral's v'yds with those of two other charities, the Bischöfliches Priesterseminar and the Bischöfliches Konvikt. Owns 106 ha of top v'yds, esp in SAAR and RUWER. Quality dependable rather than exciting.

Bocksbeutel Squat, flask-shaped bottle used in FRANKEN and N BADEN.

Bodensee (Bereich) Idyllic district of S BADEN, on Lake Constance. Dry wines are best drunk within 5 yrs. RIES-like MÜLLER-T a speciality.

Boppard ★ ··★★★ 88 90 93 95 96 97 **98** 99 00 **01 02 03 04 05** Important wine town of MITTELRHEIN where quality is rapidly improving. Best sites all in amphitheatre of vines called Bopparder Hamm. Growers: Toni Lorenz, Heinrich Müller, August Perll, WEINGART. Unbeatable value for money.

Brauneberg M-M w ★★★★ 75 83 88 89 90 93 94 **95** 96 **97 98** 99 00 **01** 02 **03 04 05** Top M-S-R village nr BERNKASTEL (304 ha): excellent full-flavoured RIES – *grand cru* if anything on the Mosel is. Great First Class v'yd: Juffer-SONNENUHR. First Class v'yd: Juffer. Growers: F HAAG, W HAAG, PAULINSHOF, RICHTER, THANISCH.

Breisach Frontier town on Rhine nr KAISERSTUHL. Seat of largest German co-op, the BADISCHER WINZERKELLER.

Breisgau (Bereich) Little-known BADEN district. Gd reds and pink WEISSHERBST.

Breuer, Weingut Georg ★★★ Family estate of 24 ha in RÜDESHEIM and 7.2 ha in RAUENTHALER, giving superb, full-bodied dry RIES recently. Pioneering winemaker Bernhard Breuer died suddenly in 04, but the estate stays in his family.

Buhl, Reichsrat von ★★★ Historic PFALZ estate, returning to historic form as of 1994. 50 ha (DEIDESHEIM, FORST, RUPPERTSBERG). Leased by Japanese firm until 2005, when bought by businessman Achim Niederberger.

Bundesweinprämierung The German State Wine Award, organized by DLG: gives great (*grosse*), silver, or bronze medallion labels.

Bürgerspital zum Heiligen Geist ★★ Ancient charitable WÜRZBURG estate. 111 ha: WÜRZBURG, RANDERSACKER, etc. Rich, dry wines, esp SILVANER, RIES; can be v.gd.

Bürklin-Wolf, Dr. ★★★··★★★★ Dynamic PFALZ family estate. 95 ha in FORST, DEIDESHEIM, RUPPERTSBERG, and WACHENHEIM, inc many First Class sites. The full-bodied dry wines from these are often spectacular.

Castell'sches Fürstlich Domänenamt ★··★★★ Historic 58-ha estate in STEIGERWALD. SILVANER, RIESLANER, and a growing reputation for red wines, too.

Chardonnay Now grown throughout Germany; with over 725 ha. A few gd wines from recent vintages. Best: JOHNER, REBHOLZ, Dr. WEHRHEIM, WITTMANN.

Christmann ★★★ 15-ha estate in Gimmeldingen (PFALZ) making rich, dry RIES and SPÄTBURGUNDER from First Class v'yds, notably Königsbacher Idig.

Christoffel, J J ★★★ Tiny domain in ERDEN, URZIG. Polished, elegant RIES. Since 2001 leased to Robert Eymael of MÖNCHHOF.

Clevner (or Klevner) Synonym in WÜRTTEMBERG for Frühburgunder red grape, a mutation of Pinot N or Italian Chiavenna (early ripening black Pinot). Confusingly also ORTENAU (BADEN) synonym for GEWÜRZ.

Clüsserath-Weiler, Weingut ★★··★★★ Classic RIES from top TRITTENHEIMER Apotheke. Widely admired for fruity HALBTROCKEN.

Crusius ★★··★★★ 15-ha family estate at TRAISEN, NAHE. Vivid RIES from Bastei and Rotenfels of TRAISEN and SCHLOSSBÖCKELHEIM. Top wines age very well. Also gd SEKT and fresh fruity SPÄTBURGUNDER dry rosé.

Dautel, Weingut Ernst ★★··★★★ Since he began vinifying his own wines in 1978, Dautel has proved himself one of WÜRTTEMBERG's, and indeed Germany's, few masters of serious red wines, esp SPÄTBURGUNDER and LEMBERGER.

Deidesheim Pfz w (r) ★★··★★★★ 71 83 88 89 90 92 93 **94** 95 **96** 97 **98** 99 00 **01 02 03 04 05** Largest top-quality village of the PFALZ (405 ha). Richly flavoured, lively wines. Also SEKT. First Class v'yds: Grainhübel, Hohenmorgen, Kalkofen, Kieselberg, Langenmorgen, Leinhöhle. Top growers: BASSERMANN-JORDAN, BIFFAR, BUHL, BÜRKLIN-WOLF, DEINHARD, WOLF.

Deinhard In 1997 the WEGELER family sold the 200-yr-old merchant house and SEKT producer Deinhard to sparkling wine giant Henkell-Söhnlein. But the splendid Deinhard estates remain in family ownership (see WEGELER).

Deinhard, Dr. ★★★ Fine 35-ha estate: some of DEIDESHEIM's best v'yds.

Deutscher Tafelwein Officially the term for very humble German wines. Now, confusingly, the flag of convenience for some costly novelties as well (*e.g.* BARRIQUE wines).

Deutsches Weinsiegel A quality seal (*i.e.* neck label) for wines that have passed a statutory tasting test. Seals are: yellow for dry, green for medium-dry, red for medium-sweet. Means little; proves nothing.

Deutzerhof, Weingut ★★→★★★ AHR estate producing concentrated, BARRIQUE-aged SPÄTBURGUNDER. Fine quality, high prices.

Diel, Schlossgut ★★★ Fashionable 16-ha NAHE estate; pioneered ageing GRAUBURGUNDER and WEISSBURGUNDER in BARRIQUES. Its traditional RIES is among the finest of NAHE wines. Makes serious SEKT and delectable AUSLESE.

DLG (Deutsche Landwirtschaftgesellschaft) The German Agricultural Society at Frankfurt. Awards national medals for quality – far too generously – at BUNDESWEINPRÄMIERUNG.

Domäne German for "domain" or "estate". Sometimes used alone to mean the "State Domain" (STAATSWEINGUT, or Staatliche Weinbaudomäne).

Dönnhoff, Weingut Hermann ★★★★ 89 90 94 95 96 97 **98** 99 00 01 02 03 04 05 16-ha leading NAHE estate with fine RIES from NIEDERHAUSEN, Oberhausen, SCHLOSSBÖCKELHEIM. Some of Germany's greatest wines. Dazzling EISWEIN.

Dornfelder Red grape making deep-coloured, usually rustic wines. An astonishing 7,700 ha are now planted throughout Germany.

Durbach Baden w (r) ★★→★★★ **90** 94 96 97 **98** 99 00 01 02 **03** 04 05 Village with 314 ha of v'yds inc a handful of First Class sites. Top growers: LAIBLE, H. Männle, Schloss Staufenberg, WOLFF METTERNICH. Choose their KLINGELBERGERS (RIES) and CLEVNERS (TRAMINER).

Edel Means "noble". *Edelfäule* means "noble rot".

Egon Müller zu Scharzhof ★★★★ 75 76 79 82 **83** 85 86 88 **89** 90 92 **93 94 95** 96 **97** 98 **99** 00 **01** 02 03 04 05 Top SAAR estate of 8 ha at WILTINGEN. Its rich and racy SCHARZHOFBERGER RIES in AUSLESEN vintages is among the world's greatest wines; best are given gold capsules. Vintages: 93 95 97 99 01 02 03 are sublime, honeyed, immortal. Le Gallais is a second estate in WILTINGER Braune Kupp; good quality, but the site is less exceptional.

Eiswein Dessert wine made from frozen grapes with the ice (*i.e.* water content) discarded, producing very concentrated wine in flavour, acidity, and sugar – of BEERENAUSLESE ripeness or more. Alcohol content can be as low as 5.5%. Very expensive. Sometimes made as late as Jan/Feb of following year. 02 looks to be the best Eiswein vintage since 98, possibly since 96 and 83.

Eitelsbach M-S-R (Ruwer) w ★★→★★★★ 75 83 85 88 89 90 93 94 95 96 **97 98** 99 00 01 02 03 04 05 RUWER village bordering TRIER, inc superb Great First Class KARTHÄUSERHOFBERG v'yd site. GROSSLAGE: Römerlay.

Elbling Grape introduced by the Romans, widely grown on upper MOSEL. Can be sharp and tasteless, but capable of real freshness and vitality in the best conditions (*e.g.* at Nittel or SCHLOSS THORN in the OBERMOSEL).

Eltville Rhg w ★★→★★★ **83** 89 90 93 94 **95** 96 **97** 98 **99** 00 01 02 **03** 04 05 Major wine town with cellars of RHEINGAU STATE DOMAIN, FISCHER, and Langwerth von SIMMERN estates. First Class v'yd: Sonnenberg.

Emrich-Schönleber ★★★ Located in NAHE village of Monzingen. Since the late

1980s winemaker Werner Schönleber has shown that his RIES can match those of any other producer in the region, esp his sumptuous EISWEIN.

Enkirch M-M w ★★→★★★ 89 90 93 94 95 96 **97** 98 99 **00** 01 02 **03** 04 05 Little-known MITTELMOSEL village, often overlooked, but with lovely light, tasty wine. The best grower is IMMICH-BATTERIEBERG.

Erbach Rhg w ★★★ 83 85 88 **89 90 92 93** 95 96 97 98 99 00 01 02 **03** 04 05 RHEINGAU area: big, perfumed, ageworthy wines, inc First Class v'yds: Hohenrain, MARCOBRUNN, Siegelsberg, Steinmorgen, Schlossberg. Major estates: SCHLOSS REINHARTSHAUSEN, SCHLOSS SCHÖNBORN. Also BECKER, Jakob Jung, KNYPHAUSEN, Langwerth von SIMMERN, etc.

Erben Word meaning "heirs", often used on old-established estate labels.

Germany's quality levels

The official range of qualities and styles in ascending order are:

1 **Deutscher Tafelwein**: sweetish light wine of no specified character. (From certain producers, can be very special.)
2 **Landwein**: dryish Tafelwein with some regional style.
3 **Qualitätswein**: dry or sweetish wine with sugar added before fermentation to increase its strength, but tested for quality and with distinct local and grape character.
4 **Kabinett**: dry or dryish natural (unsugared) wine of distinct personality and distinguishing lightness. Can occasionally be sublime.
5 **Spätlese**: stronger, often sweeter than Kabinett. Full-bodied. Today many top Spätlesen are *trocken* or completely dry.
6 **Auslese**: sweeter, sometimes stronger than Spätlese, often with honey-like flavours, intense and long. Occasionally dry and weighty.
7 **Beerenauslese**: very sweet, sometimes strong, intense. Can be superb.
8 **Eiswein**: (Beeren- or Trockenbeerenauslese) concentrated, sharpish, and very sweet. Can be very fine or too extreme, unharmonious.
9 **Trockenbeerenauslese**: intensely sweet and aromatic; alcohol slight. Extraordinary and everlasting.

Erden M-M w ★★★ 71 75 **83 88 89** 90 93 94 95 96 **97** 98 99 00 **01** 02 **03** 04 05 Village between ÜRZIG and KRÖV: noble, full-flavoured, vigorous wine (more herbal and mineral than the wines of nearby BERNKASTEL and WEHLEN but equally long-living). Great First Class v'yds: Prälat, Treppchen. Growers inc BISCHÖFLICHE WEINGÜTER, CHRISTOFFEL, LOOSEN, Meulenhof, MÖNCHHOF, Peter Nicolay.

Erstes Gewächs Literally translates as "first growth". See box on p.151.

Erzeugerabfüllung Bottled by producer. Being replaced by GUTSABFÜLLUNG, but only by estates. Co-ops will continue with *Erzeugerabfüllung*.

Escherndorf Frank w ★★→★★★ **88 90 92 93** 95 96 **97** 98 **99** 00 01 02 **03** 04 **05** Important wine town near WÜRZBURG. Similar tasty, dry wine. First Class v'yd: Lump. GROSSLAGE: Kirchberg. Growers inc Michael Fröhlich, JULIUSSPITAL, H SAUER, Rainer Sauer, Egon Schäffer.

Eser, Weingut August ★★ 8-ha RHEINGAU estate at OESTRICH. V'yds also in Hallgarten, RAUENTHAL (esp Gehrn, Rothenberg), WINKEL. Variable wines.

Feinherb Imprecisely defined term for wines with around 10–20 g of sugar per litre. Favoured by some as a more flexible alternative to HALBTROCKEN. Used on label by, among others, KERPEN, VON KESSELSTATT, MOLITOR.

Filzen M-S-R (Saar) w ★★→★★★ 88 **89 90** 94 **95** 96 **97** 98 **99** 00 **01** 02 **03** 04 **05** Small SAAR village near WILTINGEN. First Class v'yd: Pulchen. Grower to note: Piedmont.

Fischer Erben, Weingut ★★★ RHEINGAU estate at ELTVILLE, with high traditional standards. Long-lived classic wines.

Forschungsanstalt Geisenheim See HESSISCHE FORSCHUNGSANSTALT.

Forst Pfz w ★★→★★★★ 83 89 90 94 95 96 97 98 99 00 01 02 03 04 05 MITTELHAARDT village with over 200 ha of Germany's best v'yds. Ripe, richly fragrant, full-bodied but subtle wines. First Class v'yds: Jesuitengarten, Kirchenstück, Freundstück, Pechstein, Ungeheuer. Top growers inc: BASSERMANN-JORDAN, BURKLIN-WOLF, DEINHARD, MOSBACHER, Eugen Müller, H Spindler, Werlé, WOLF.

Franken Frank Franconia region of distinctive dry wines, esp SILVANER, always bottled in round-bellied flasks (BOCKSBEUTEL). The centre is WÜRZBURG. Bereich names: MAINDREIECK, STEIGERWALD. Top producers: BURGERSPITAL, CASTELL, FÜRST, JULIUSSPITAL, LÖWENSTEIN, RUCK, H SAUER, STAATLICHER HOFKELLER, WIRSCHING, etc.

Franzen, Weingut Rheinhold ★→★★★ From Europe's steepest v'yd, Bremmer Calmont, Franzen makes dependable dry RIES and EISWEIN.

Friedrich-Wilhelm Gymnasium ★★ Important charitable estate based in TRIER, with v'yds throughout M-S-R. In 2003 it was bought by the BISCHÖFLICHE WEINGÜTER, but some of its v'yds were then sold off.

Fuhrmann See PFEFFINGEN.

Fürst ★★★ Small, 17-ha estate in Bürgstadt making some of the best wines in FRANKEN, particularly Burgundian SPÄTBURGUNDER (widely considered Germany's finest) and oak-aged WEISSBURGUNDER.

Gallais Le See EGON MÜLLER ZU SCHARZHOF.

Geisenheim Rhg w ★★→★★★ 85 89 90 93 94 95 96 97 98 99 00 01 02 03 04 05 Village famous for Germany's best-known wine school and v.gd aromatic wines. First Class v'yds: Kläuserweg, Rothenberg. Top growers: JOHANNISHOF, SCHLOSS SCHÖNBORN, WEGELER, VON ZWIERLEIN.

Gemeinde A commune or parish.

Gewürztraminer (or **Traminer**) Highly aromatic grape, speciality of Alsace, also impressive in Germany, esp in PFALZ, BADEN, SACHSEN, WÜRTTEMBERG.

Gimmeldingen Pfz w ★★ 89 90 93 94 96 97 98 99 00 01 02 03 04 05 Village just S of MITTELHAARDT. At best, rich succulent wines. GROSSLAGE: Meerspinne. Growers inc CHRISTMANN, MÜLLER-CATOIR.

Graach M-M w ★★★ 75 83 88 89 90 92 93 94 95 96 97 98 99 00 01 02 03 04 05 Small village between BERNKASTEL and WEHLEN. First Class v'yds: Domprobst, Himmelreich, Josephshof. Many top growers: VON KESSELSTATT, LOOSEN, J J PRÜM, S A PRÜM, SCHAEFER, SELBACH-OSTER, WEINS-PRÜM.

Grans-Fassian ★★★ Fine MOSEL estate at Leiwen. V'yds there and in TRITTENHEIM. EISWEIN a speciality. Dependable high quality since 1995.

Grauburgunder Synonym of RULÄNDER or Pinot Gr: grape giving soft full-bodied wine. Best in BADEN and S PFALZ.

Grosser Ring Group of top (VDP) MOSEL-SAAR-RUWER estates, whose annual September auction regularly sets world-record prices.

Grosses Gewächs Translates as "great/top growth". This is the top tier in the v'yd classification launched in 2002 by the growers' association VDP, except in the RHEINGAU, which has its own ERSTES GEWÄCHS classification (see box, p.151). Wines released as *Grosses Gewächs* must meet strict quality criteria.

Grosslage A collection of individual sites with seemingly similar character.

Gunderloch ★★★→★★★★ 89 90 93 95 96 97 98 99 00 01 02 03 04 05 At this NACKENHEIM estate Fritz Hasselbach makes some of the finest RIES on the entire Rhine, inc spectacular BEERENAUSLESEN and TROCKENBEERENAUSLESEN. Also owns well-known Balbach estate in NIERSTEIN.

Remember that vintage information for German wines is given in a different form from the ready/not ready distinction applying to other countries. See the explanation at the bottom of p.137.

GERMANY

Guntrum, Louis ★★ Large (27-ha) family estate in NIERSTEIN, OPPENHEIM, etc. G●
SILVANER and GEWÜRZ as well as RIES. Moderate quality.

Gutedel German name for the ancient Chasselas grape, used in S BADEN. Fresh●
but neutral, white wines.

Gutsabfüllung Estate-bottled. Term for genuinely estate-bottled wines.

Haag, Weingut Fritz M-S-R ★★★★ 71 75 76 79 82 83 84 85 86 88 89 90 92 93 9●
95 96 97 98 99 00 01 02 03 04 05 BRAUNEBERG's top estate, run for decade●
by Wilhelm Haag, president of GROSSER RING. MOSEL RIES of crystalline purity and
racy brilliance for long ageing. Haag's son runs SCHLOSS LIESER estate.

Haag, Weingut Willi M-S-R ★★ 6-ha BRAUNEBERG estate. Full, old-style RIES●
Some fine AUSLESEN. Improving quality since 1995.

Haart, Reinhold ★★★ The best estate in PIESPORT. Refined, aromatic wine●
capable of long ageing. Also the lead producer of wines from WINTRICH.

Hain, Weingut Kurt ★★ Small but focused PIESPORT estate of steadil●
increasing quality.

Halbtrocken Medium-dry (literally "semi-dry"), with 9–18 g of unfermented
sugar per litre. Popular category, often better balanced than TROCKEN.

Hattenheim Rhg w ★★→★★★★ 83 89 90 92 93 95 96 97 98 99 0●
01 02 03 04 05 Superlative 202-ha wine town, though not all producers
achieve its full potential. The First Class v'yds are Mannberg●
Nussbrunnen, Pfaffenberg, Wisselbrunnen, and, most famously●
STEINBERG (ORTSTEIL). Estates inc KNYPHAUSEN, LANG, RESS, SCHLOSS SCHÖNBORN●
SIMMERN, STATE DOMAIN.

Henkell See DEINHARD.

Heger, Dr. ★★★ Leading estate of KAISERSTUHL in BADEN with excellent dry
WEISSBURGUNDER, GRAUBURGUNDER, and powerful oak-aged SPÄTBURGUNDER reds●
Wines from rented v'yds released under Weinhaus Joachim Heger label.

Heilbronn Würt w r ★→★★ 93 94 96 97 98 99 00 01 02 03 04 05 Wine
town with many small growers. Best wines are RIES and LEMBERGER. Top●
growers inc Amalienhof, Drautz-Able, Schäfer-Heinrich.

Hessen, Prinz von ★★→★★★ Famous 42-ha estate in JOHANNISBERG, KIEDRICH, and
WINKEL. Rapidly improving quality since the late 1990s.

Hessische Bergstrasse w ★★→★★★ 90 93 96 97 98 99 00 01 02 03 04 0●
Smallest wine region in W Germany (444 ha), N of Heidelberg. Pleasan●
RIES from STATE DOMAIN v'yds at Bensheim, Bergsträsser co-op, Simon●
Bürkle, and Stadt Bensheim.

Hessische Forschungsanstalt für Wein-Obst & Gartenbau Famous wine schoo●
and research establishment at GEISENHEIM, RHEINGAU. Gd wines inc reds. The
name on the label is Forschungsanstalt.

Heyl zu Herrnsheim ★★★ Leading NIERSTEIN estate, 70% RIES. Since fine
96 vintage owned by Ahr family. Dry RIES, SILVANER, WEISSBURGUNDER of classica●
elegance. Occasional sweet wines of equal quality.

Heymann-Löwenstein ★★★ Estate in Lower or "Terrace MOSEL" with most●
consistent dry RIES in MOSEL-SAAR-RUWER and some remarkable AUSLESEN and
TROCKENBEERENAUSLESEN. Spectacular wines in 01. A rapidly rising star.

Hochgewächs Supposedly superior level of QBA RIES, esp in MOSEL-SAAR-RUWER.

Hochheim Rhg w ★★→★★★★ 75 83 85 88 89 90 92 93 94 95 96 97 98 99 00
01 02 03 04 05 242-ha wine town 15 miles E of main RHEINGAU area, once
thought of as best on Rhine. Wines with an earthy intensity, body, and
fragrance of their own. First Class v'yds: Domdechaney, Hölle, Kirchenstück●
Königin Viktoria Berg (12-acre monopoly of Hupfeld of OESTRICH). GROSSLAGE●
Daubhaus. Growers inc Hupfeld, KÜNSTLER, W J Schaefer, SCHLOSS SCHÖNBORN●
STAATSWEINGUT, WERNER.

Hock Traditional English term for Rhine wine, derived from HOCHHEIM.

Hoensbroech, Weingut Reichsgraf zu ★★ Top KRAICHGAU estate. Dry WEISSBURGUNDER (often the best wines here), GRAUBURGUNDER, SILVANER, *e.g.* Michelfelder Himmelberg.

Hohenlohe-Oehringen, Weingut Fürst zu ★★ Noble 17-ha estate in Oehringen, WÜRTTEMBERG. Earthy, bone-dry RIES and powerful reds from SPÄTBURGUNDER, LEMBERGER, and other grapes.

Hövel, Weingut von ★★★ Very fine SAAR estate at OBERMOSEL (Hütte is 4.8-ha monopoly) and in SCHARZHOFBERG. Superbly racy wines.

Huber, Bernhard ★★★ Leading estate of Breisgau area of BADEN, with powerful oak-aged SPÄTBURGUNDER reds, MUSKATELLER, and Burgundian-style WEISSBURGUNDER, CHARD.

Ihringen Bad r w ★★→★★★ 90 92 **93** 95 **96 97** 98 **99** 00 **01** 02 **03** 04 05 One of the best villages of the KAISERSTUHL, BADEN. Proud of its SPÄTBURGUNDER red, WEISSHERBST, and GRAUBURGUNDER. Top growers: Dr. HEGER, Stigler.

Immich-Batterieberg, Weingut ★★→★★★ Grown on 4.5 ha of dynamite-blasted slate slopes, this ENKIRCH estate produces gd, sometimes excellent, RIES in varying styles.

Ingelheim Rhh r w ★★ **90 93 97** 98 **99** 00 01 02 **03** 04 05 Town opposite RHEINGAU historically known for its SPÄTBURGUNDER. Few wines today live up to reputation. Top v'yds are Horn, Pares, Sonnenberg, and Steinacker.

Iphofen Frank w ★★→★★★ 88 89 90 92 **93** 94 96 **97** 98 **99** 00 01 02 03 **04** 05 Village nr WÜRZBURG. Superb First Class v'yds: Julius-Echter-Berg, Kalb. GROSSLAGE: Burgweg. Growers: JULIUSSPITAL, RUCK, WIRSCHING.

Jahrgang Year – as in "vintage".

Johannisberg Rhg w ★★ →★★★★ 75 76 **83** 85 88 **89** 90 92 **93** 94 **95** 96 **97** 98 **99** 00 **01** 02 03 **04** 05 A classic RHEINGAU village with superlative subtle RIES. First Class v'yds: Hölle, Klaus, SCHLOSS JOHANNISBERG. GROSSLAGE: Erntebringer. Top growers: JOHANNISHOF, SCHLOSS JOHANNISBERG, HESSEN.

Johannisberg (Bereich) District name for the entire RHEINGAU. Avoid.

Johannishof ★★★ JOHANNISBERG family estate, aka HH Eser. RIES that are often the best from the great Johannisberg v'yds. Since 1996 also fine RÜDESHEIM wines.

Johner, Karl-Heinz ★★★ Small BADEN estate at Bischoffingen, in the front line for New World-style SPÄTBURGUNDER and oak-aged WEISSBURGUNDER, CHARD, GRAUER BURGUNDER.

Josephshof First Class v'yd at GRAACH, the sole property of von KESSELSTATT.

Jost, Toni ★★★ Perhaps the top estate of the MITTELRHEIN: 9 ha, mainly RIES, in BACHARACH, and also at WALLUF in the RHEINGAU.

Juliusspital ★★★ Ancient WÜRZBURG religious charity with 140 ha of top FRANKEN v'yds and many superb wines. Look for its dry SILVANERS and RIES and its top white blend called BT.

Kabinett See "Germany's quality levels" box on p.142.

Kaiserstuhl Outstanding BADEN district, with notably warm climate and volcanic soil. Villages inc ACHKARREN, Burkheim, IHRINGEN. GROSSLAGE: Vulkanfelsen.

Kallstadt Pfz w (r) ★★→★★★ 90 92 **93** 94 **95 96** 97 **98 99** 00 01 02 **03** 04 05 Village of N MITTELHAARDT. Often underrated fine, rich, dry RIES and Pinot N. First Class v'yd: Saumagen. GROSSLAGEN: Feuerberg, Kobnert. Growers inc Henninger, KOEHLER-RUPRECHT.

Kanzem M-S-R (Saar) w ★★★ **89** 90 **93** 94 **95** 96 **97** 98 **99** 00 01 02 **03** 04 05 Small neighbour of WILTINGEN. First Class v'yd: Altenberg. GROSSLAGE: SCHARZBERG. Growers inc Othegraven, J P Reinert, Reverchon.

Karlsmühle ★★★ Small estate with two Lorenzhöfer monopoly sites making classic RUWER RIES; also wines from First Class KASEL v'yds sold under Patheiger label. Consistently excellent quality.

Karthäuserhofberg ★★★★ Outstanding RUWER estate of 19 ha at Eitelsbach. Easily recognized by bottles with only a neck label. Since 1993 estate has been back on top form. Also gd TROCKEN wines.

Kasel M-S-R (Ruwer) w ★★→★★★ 83 85 88 89 90 93 94 95 96 97 98 99 00 01 02 03 04 05 Stunning flowery RIES. First Class v'yds: Kehrnagel, Nies'cher. Top growers: KARLSMÜHLE, von BEULWITZ, von KESSELSTATT.

Keller Wine cellar.

Keller, Weingut ★★★★ Deep in newly fashionable southern RHEINHESSEN, the Kellers show what can be achieved with scrupulous site selection. Superlative, crystalline RIES from Dalsheimer Hubacker, esp TBA.

Kellerei Winery (*i.e.* a big commercial bottler).

Kerner Modern aromatic grape variety, earlier ripening than RIES. Makes wines of fair quality but without the inbuilt grace and harmony of RIES. Best in SACHSEN.

Kerpen, Weingut Heribert ★★ Small gd estate in BERNKASTEL, GRAACH, WEHLEN specializing in elegant sweeter styles.

Kesseler, Weingut August Rhg ★★★ 20-ha estate making the best SPÄTBURGUNDER reds in ASSMANNSHAUSEN. Also v.gd classic-style RIES.

Kesselstatt, von ★★★ The largest private MOSEL estate, 650 yrs old. Now belongs to Reh family. Some 40 ha in GRAACH, KASEL, PIESPORT, WILTINGEN, etc producing aromatic, generously fruity MOSELS. Consistently high quality, often magnificent, wines from JOSEPHSHOF monopoly v'yd, PIESPORTER Goldtröpfchen, and SCHARZHOFBERG.

Kesten M-M w ★→★★★ 83 89 90 92 93 94 95 96 97 98 99 00 01 02 03 04 05 Neighbour of BRAUNEBERG. Best wines (from Paulinshofberg v'yd) similar. Top growers: Bastgen, Kees-Kieren, PAULINSHOF.

Kiedrich Rhg w ★★→★★★★ 83 90 93 94 95 96 97 98 99 00 01 02 03 04 05 Neighbour of RAUENTHAL; equally splendid and high-flavoured. First Class v'yds: Gräfenberg, Wasseros. Growers inc KNYPHAUSEN, Speicher-Schuth. WE now top estate.

Klingelberger ORTENAU (BADEN) term for RIES, esp at DURBACH.

Kloster Eberbach Rhg Glorious 12th-C Cistercian abbey in HATTENHEIM forest. Monks planted STEINBERG, Germany's Clos de Vougeot. Now the label of the STATE DOMAIN with a string of great v'yds in ASSMANNSHAUSEN, RÜDESHEIM, RAUENTHAL, etc. New director Dieter Greiner is proving innovative and quality-oriented.

Klüsserath M-M w ★→★★★ 90 93 94 95 96 97 98 99 00 01 02 03 04 05 Little known MOSEL village whose wine-growers have joined forces to classify its top site, Brüderschaft. Growers: Bernhard Kirsten, FRIEDRICH-WILHELM GYMNASIUM, Regnery.

Knebel, Weingut ★★★ WINNINGEN may not be among the most prestigious MOSEL wine villages, but Knebel showed how its sites could produce remarkable RIES in all styles. The founder died tragically in 2004; the estate continues.

Knipser, Weingut ★★→★★★ Brothers Werner and Volker specialize in BARRIQUE-aged SPÄTBURGUNDER and other red wines, but dry RIES and other varieties can be at the same high level. Can lack consistency.

Knyphausen, Weingut Freiherr zu Rhg ★★ Noble 22-ha estate on former Cistercian land (see KLOSTER EBERBACH) in ELTVILLE, ERBACH, HATTENHEIM, and KIEDRICH. Classic RHEINGAU wines in a full range of styles.

Koehler-Ruprecht ★★★★ 76 83 85 86 88 89 90 91 92 93 94 95 96 97 98 99 00 01 02 03 04 05 Highly rated KALLSTADT grower. Traditional winemaking, very long-lived dry RIES from K Saumagen. Outstanding SPÄTBURGUNDER and striking BARRIQUE-aged Pinot varieties under the Philippi label.

Kraichgau Small BADEN region S of Heidelberg. Top grower: HOENSBROECH.

Krone, Weingut Rhg ★★ The cosy Hotel Krone in ASSMANNSHAUSEN has its own estate, producing a wide range of SPÄTBURGUNDER in every conceivable style. Best sampled at its own restaurant.

Kröv M-M w ★→★★★ **90 93** 94 96 **97 98** 99 00 01 02 **03** 04 **05** Popular tourist resort famous for its GROSSLAGE name: Nacktarsch, or "bare bottom". Be very careful. Best grower: Martin Müllen.

Künstler, Franz Rhg ★★★★ HOCHHEIM estate expanded in 1996 by purchase and incorporation of well-known Aschrott estate. Superb dry RIES, esp from First Class Domdechaney, Hölle, and Kirchenstück; also excellent AUSLESE.

Kuntz, Sybille M-S-R ★★ Successful protagonist of untypical dry MOSEL RIES of AUSLESE strength.

Laible, Weingut Andreas ★★★ 7-ha DURBACH estate. Fine sweet and dry RIES, SCHEUREBE, GEWÜRZ (First Class Plauelrain v'yd). KLINGELBERGER can be utter joy. Consistently rewarding quality.

Landwein See "Germany's quality levels" box on p.142.

Lang, Weingut Hans Rhg ★★ Reliable RIES and other varieties from one of HATTENHEIM's most versatile growers.

Leitz, J ★★★ Fine RÜDESHEIM family estate for elegant dry and sweet RIES. Now achieving long-overdue recognition.

Leiwen M-M w ★★→★★★ **88 89 90 92 93** 94 95 96 **97 98 99** 00 **01 02** 03 04 **05** First Class v'yd: Laurentiuslay. Village between TRITTENHEIM and TRIER. GRANS-FASSIAN, Carl LOEWEN, SANKT URBANS-HOF, and Rosch demonstrate how fine these little-known v'yds can be.

Lemberger Red variety imported to Germany and Austria in the 18th C, from Hungary, where it is known as Kékfrankos. Blaufränkisch in Austria. Deep-coloured, moderately tannic wines; can be excellent. Or rosé.

Liebfrauenstift A 10.5-ha v'yd in city of Worms; origin of Liebfraumilch.

Lieser M-M w ★★ **90** 92 **93** 94 **95** 96 **97** 98 **99** 00 01 02 **03** 04 **05** Little-known neighbour of BERNKASTEL. Lighter wines. First Class v'yd: Niederberg-Helden. Top grower: SCHLOSS LIESER.

Lingenfelder, Weingut ★★ Small innovative Grosskarlbach (PFALZ) estate: gd dry and sweet SCHEUREBE, full-bodied RIES, hit-and--miss SPÄTBURGUNDER.

Loewen, Carl ★★★ Top grower of Leiwen on MOSEL making ravishing AUSLESE from town's First Class Laurentiuslay site. Also fine EISWEIN.

Loosen, Weingut Dr. M-M ★★★★ **76** 85 **88** 89 **90 92 93** 94 **95** 96 **97 98 99** 00 **01** 02 **03** 04 05 Dynamic 12-ha St-Johannishof estate in BERNKASTEL, ERDEN, GRAACH, ÜRZIG, WEHLEN. Deep, intense RIES from old vines in great First Class v'yds. Superlative quality since 1990. Also leases WOLF in the PFALZ since 1996. Joint-venture RIES in Washington State with Ch Ste Michele: Eroica (dry) first vintage 99; never seems quite as good as it should be.

Lorch Rhg w (r) ★→★★ **89 90** 92 93 **94** 95 96 97 98 99 00 **01 02** 03 **04 05** Extreme W of RHEINGAU. Some fine MITTELRHEIN-like RIES. Best grower: von Kanitz.

Löwenstein, Fürst ★★★ Top FRANKEN estate. Intense savoury SILVANER from historic Homberger Kallmuth, very dramatic slope. Also Hallgarten estate long rented by SCHLOSS VOLLRADS, independent since 1997.

Lützkendorf, Weingut ★→★★ Probably the best of the SAALE-UNSTRUT estates, particularly favoured by recent warm vintages.

Maindreieck (Bereich) District name for central FRANKEN, inc WÜRZBURG.

Marcobrunn Historic RHEINGAU v'yd; one of Germany's very best. See ERBACH.

Markgräflerland (Bereich) District S of Freiburg, BADEN. Typical GUTEDEL wine can be delicious refreshment when drunk very young, but best wines are the BURGUNDERS: WEISS-, GRAU-, and SPÄT-. Also SEKT.

GERMANY

Maximin Grünhaus M-S-R (Ruwer) w ★★★★ 71 75 76 83 85 88 89 90 92 93 94 95 96 **97** 98 99 00 01 02 **03 04 05** Supreme RUWER estate of 34 ha at Mertesdorf. Wines, dry and sweet, of firm elegance and great subtlety to mature 20 yrs plus.

Meyer-Näkel, Weingut ★★★ AHR estate; 13 ha. Fine SPÄTBURGUNDERS in Dernau and Bad Neuenahr exemplify modern oak-aged German reds.

Mittelhaardt The N central and best part of the PFALZ, inc DEIDESHEIM, FORST, RUPPERTSBERG, WACHENHEIM, largely planted with RIES.

Mittelhaardt-Deutsche Weinstrasse (Bereich) Name for N and central PFALZ.

Mittelmosel M-M The central and best part of the MOSEL, inc BERNKASTEL, PIESPORT, WEHLEN, etc. Its top sites are (or should be) entirely RIES.

Mittelrhein Northern Rhine area of domestic importance (and great beauty), inc BACHARACH and BOPPARD. Some attractive, steely RIES, often underrated.

Molitor, Markus M-M ★★★ With 20 sites throughout the MOSEL and SAAR, Molitor has in one decade become a major player based in WEHLEN. Magisterial sweet RIES, and acclaimed if earthy SPÄTBURGUNDER.

Mönchhof, Weingut M-M ★★→★★★ From an exquisite manor house in ÜRZIG, Robert Eymael makes fruity, stylish RIES from ÜRZIG and ERDEN. Also leases CHRISTOFFEL estate.

Morio-Muskat Stridently aromatic grape variety now on the decline.

Mosbacher, Weingut Pfz ★★★ Fine 14-ha estate for some of best dry and sweet RIES of FORST. Best wines are dry GROSSES GEWÄCHS. Decent Sauv Bl.

Mosel The TAFELWEIN name of the area. All quality wines from the Mosel must be labelled MOSEL-SAAR-RUWER. (Moselle is the French – and English – spelling.)

Moselland, Winzergenossenschaft Huge MOSEL-SAAR-RUWER co-op, at BERNKASTEL, inc Saar-Winzerverein at WILTINGEN. Its 3,200 members, with a collective 2,400 ha, produce 25% of M-S-R wines (inc classic-method SEKT), but little is above average.

Mosel-Saar-Ruwer M-S-R 9,533-ha QUALITÄTSWEIN region between TRIER and Koblenz; inc MITTELMOSEL, RUWER, and SAAR. See box below.

Germany's most dynamic region: Mosel-Saar-Ruwer

Nowhere else in Germany are there so many exciting new producers to be discovered as in the MOSEL-SAAR-RUWER. Perhaps this is the result of the special mentality of the Moselaner as much as the international interest in the elegant and subtly aromatic RIES that this archetypal cool-climate region produces. These are four names to watch for:

Clemens Busch Clemens and Rita Busch's organic estate in Pünderich is situated in one of the least well-known sections of the MOSEL Valley and produces unusually powerful, dry RIES as well as great AUSLESE.

Herrenberg A tiny SAAR estate owned and run by Claudia and Manfred Loch. The styles of wine vary according to vintage conditions: some years give mostly sweet wines, other years give rich dry wines of surprising power and complexity.

Daniel Vollenweider A young Swiss who bought vines in the excellent but forgotten MOSEL site of Wolfer Goldgrube in 2000 and specializes in classic-style SPÄTLESE and AUSLESE inspired by the famous names of the Middle Mosel.

Van Volxem An historic SAAR estate brought back to life by owner Roman Niewodniczanski and winemaker Gernot Kollmann. Good classic KABINETT and SPÄTLESE, but it is the vineyard-designated dry wines that stand out.

Müller-Catoir, Weingut Pfz ★★★ 83 85 88 **89 90 92 93** 94 95 **96** 97 **98 99** 00 **01** 02 **03 04 05** Outstanding NEUSTADT estate. Very aromatic powerful wines (RIES, SCHEUREBE, GEWÜRZ, RIESLANER, WEISSBURGUNDER, GRAUBURGUNDER, and MUSKATELLER). Consistent quality and gd value; dry/sweet equally impressive. Retirement of its long-term winemaker in 2001 led to a slight (but temporary) dip in quality.

Müller-Thurgau Fruity, early ripening, usually low-acid grape; most common in PFALZ, RHEINHESSEN, NAHE, BADEN, and FRANKEN; decreasingly planted in favour of RIES over the past 8 yrs. Should be banned from all top v'yds by law.

Münster Nahe w ★→★★★ 83 88 **89 90 93** 94 95 96 97 **98** 99 00 **01 02 03 04 05** Best N NAHE village; fine, delicate wines. First Class v'yds: Pittersberg, Dautenpflänzer, Kapellenberg. Top growers: Göttelmann, Kruger-Rumpf.

Muskateller Ancient aromatic white grape with crisp acidity. A rarity in the PFALZ, BADEN, and WÜRTTEMBERG, where it is mostly made dry.

Nackenheim Rhh w ★→★★★★ **89 90 93** 95 **96 97 98** 99 00 **01** 02 **03 04 05** NIERSTEIN neighbour also with top Rhine terroir; similar best wines (esp First Class Rothenberg). Top grower: GUNDERLOCH.

Nahe Na Tributary of the Rhine and high-quality wine region. Balanced, fresh, clean, but full-bodied, even minerally wines; RIES best. BEREICH: NAHETAL.

Nahetal (Bereich) BEREICH name for amalgamated BAD KREUZNACH and SCHLOSSBÖCKELHEIM districts.

Neckar The river with many of WÜRTTEMBERG's finest v'yds, mainly between Stuttgart and HEILBRONN.

Neipperg, Graf von ★★→★★★ Noble estate in Schwaigern, WÜRTTEMBERG: elegant dry RIES and TRAMINER, and gd reds, esp from LEMBERGER. MUSKATELLER up to BEERENAUSLESE quality a speciality.

Neumagen-Dhron M-M w ★★ Fine neighbour of PIESPORT. The top grower is Heinz Schmitt.

Neustadt Central town of PFALZ with a famous wine school. Top growers: MÜLLER-CATOIR, Weegmüller.

Niederhausen Nahe w ★★→★★★★ 76 83 88 **89 90 93** 94 95 **96** 97 **98** 99 00 01 02 **03 04 05** Neighbour of SCHLOSSBÖCKELHEIM. Graceful, powerful wines. First Class v'yds inc Hermannsberg, Hermannshöhle. Growers: esp CRUSIUS, DÖNNHOFF, Gutsverwaltung Niederhausen-SCHLOSSBÖCKELHEIM, Mathern.

Nierstein Rhh w ★→★★★★ 83 88 **89 90 92 93** 94 95 **96** 97 **98** 99 00 **01 02 03 04 05** Famous but treacherous village name. 526 ha. Superb First-Class v'yds: Brüdersberg, Glöck, Hipping, Oelberg, Orbel, Pettenthal. Notorious GROSSLAGEN: Auflangen, Rehbach, Spiegelberg. Ripe, aromatic, elegant wines. Beware GROSSLAGE Gutes Domtal: a supermarket deception now disappearing from shelves. Try Braun, GUNTRUM, HEYL ZU HERRNSHEIM, ST-ANTONY, SCHNEIDER, Strub.

Nierstein (Bereich) Large E RHEINHESSEN district of ordinary quality.

Nierstein Winzergenossenschaft ★→★★ The leading NIERSTEIN co-op, with above-average standards. (Formerly traded under the name Rheinfront.)

Nobling New white grape: light fresh wine in BADEN, esp MARKGRÄFLERLAND.

Norheim Nahe w ★★→★★★ **89 90 93** 94 95 **96 97 98** 99 00 01 02 **03 04 05** Neighbour of NIEDERHAUSEN. First Class v'yds: Dellchen, Kafels, Kirschheck. GROSSLAGE: Burgweg. Growers: CRUSIUS, DÖNNHOFF, Mathern.

Oberemmel M-S-R (Saar) w ★★→★★★ 83 85 **89 90 93** 94 95 96 **97** 98 **99** 00 01 02 **03 04 05** Next village to WILTINGEN. Very fine from First Class v'yd Hütte, etc. GROSSLAGE: Scharzberg. Growers: von HÖVEL, von KESSELSTATT.

Remember that vintage information for German wines is given in a different form from the ready/not ready distinction applying to other countries. See the explanation at the bottom of p.137.

Obermosel (Bereich) District name for the upper MOSEL above TRIER. Wines from the ELBLING grape, generally uninspiring unless very young.

Ockfen M-S-R (Saar) w ★★→★★★ 75 76 83 85 88 89 90 92 93 94 95 96 97 98 99 00 01 02 03 04 05 Superb fragrant, austere wines. First Class v'yd: Bockstein. GROSSLAGE: Scharzberg. Growers: Dr. FISCHER, SANKT URBANS-HOF, WAGNER, ZILLIKEN.

Oechsle Scale for sugar content of grape juice.

Oestrich Rhg w ★★→★★★ 83 88 89 90 93 94 95 96 97 98 99 00 01 02 03 04 05 Big village; variable, but some splendid RIES. First Class v'yds: Doosberg, Lenchen. Top growers: August ESER, Peter Jakob Kühn, Querbach, Spreitzer, WEGELER.

Offene weine "Wines by the glass", the way to order it in wine villages.

Oppenheim Rhh w ★→★★★ 89 90 93 94 95 96 97 98 99 00 01 02 03 04 05 Town S of NIERSTEIN; spectacular 13th-C church. First Class Herrenberg and Sackträger v'yds: top wines. Growers inc: GUNTRUM, C KOCH, Kühling-Gillot. None of these, though, is realizing the full potential of these sites.

Ortenau (Bereich) District just S of Baden-Baden. Gd KLINGELBERGER (RIES), SPÄTBURGUNDER, and RULÄNDER. Top village: DURBACH.

Ortsteil Independent part of a community allowed to use its estate v'yd name without the village name – *e.g.* SCHLOSS JOHANNISBERG, STEINBERG.

Palatinate English for PFALZ.

Paulinshof, Weingut M-M ★★ 8-ha estate, once monastic, in KESTEN and BRAUNEBERG. Stylish TROCKEN and HALBTROCKEN wines.

Pauly-Bergweiler, Dr. ★★★ Fine BERNKASTEL estate. V'yds there and in WEHLEN, etc. Peter Nicolay wines from ÜRZIG and ERDEN are usually best. EISWEIN can be sensational.

Perlwein Semi-sparkling wine.

Pfalz Pfz 23,400-ha v'yd region S of RHEINHESSEN (see MITTELHAARDT and SÜDLICHE WEINSTRASSE). Warm climate: grapes ripen fully. The classics are rich wines, with dry RIES increasingly fashionable and well made. Biggest RIES area after MOSEL-SAAR-RUWER. Formerly known as the Rheinpfalz.

Pfeffingen, Weingut ★★★ Messrs Fuhrmann and Eymael make v.gd RIES and sometimes remarkable SCHEUREBE at UNGSTEIN.

Piesport M-M w ★→★★★★ 75 83 88 89 90 92 93 94 95 96 97 98 99 00 01 02 03 04 05 Tiny village with famous vine amphitheatre: at best glorious rich aromatic RIES. Great First Class v'yds: Goldtröpfchen, Domherr. Treppchen far inferior. GROSSLAGE: Michelsberg (mainly MÜLLER-T; avoid). Esp gd are GRANS-FASSIAN, HAART, Kurt Hain, von KESSELSTATT, SANKT URBANS-HOF, Weller-Lehnert.

Plettenberg, von Na ★★ 41-ha estate at BAD KREUZNACH. Renowned property but quality is middling.

Portugieser Second-rate red wine grape now often used for WEISSHERBST.

Prädikat Special attributes or qualities. See QMP.

Prinz, Fred Rhg w ★★ Best RIES in the village of Hallgarten.

Prüfungsnummer Official identifying test-number of a quality wine, the APNR.

Prüm, J J ★★★★ 69 71 75 76 79 80 82 83 84 85 86 87 88 89 90 92 93 94 95 96 97 98 99 00 01 02 03 04 05 Superlative and legendary 19-ha MOSEL estate in BERNKASTEL, GRAACH, WEHLEN, ZELTINGEN. Delicate but long-lived wines, esp in Wehlener SONNENUHR. Plain Prüm RIES is a bargain. Some wines are hard to taste when young but reward patience.

Prüm, S A (Raimond Prüm) ★★→★★★ 83 84 85 **86 88 89 90** 92 93 94 **95** 96 **97** 98 **99** 00 **01 02 03 04 05** If WEHLEN neighbour J J PRÜM is resolutely traditional, Raimond Prüm has dipped his toe into the late 20th C. Sound, if sometimes inconsistent, wines from WEHLEN and GRAACH.

QbA, Qualitätswein bestimmter Anbaugebiete The middle quality of German wine, with sugar added before fermentation (as in French chaptalization), but controlled as to areas, grapes, etc.

QmP, Qualitätswein mit Prädikat Top category, for all wines ripe enough not to need sugaring (KABINETT to TROCKENBEERENAUSLESE). See p.142.

Randersacker Frank w ★★→★★★ 88 89 90 92 **93 94** 95 96 **97** 98 **99** 00 01 02 **03** 04 **05** Leading village for distinctive dry wine. First Class v'yds inc Marsberg, Pfülben, Sonnenstuhl. GROSSLAGE: Ewig Leben. Top growers inc BURGERSPITAL, JULIUSSPITAL, STAATLICHER HOFKELLER, Robert Schmitt, Schmitt's Kinder.

Ratzenberger, Jochen ★★ Estate making racy dry and off-dry RIES in BACHARACH; best from First Class Posten and Steeger St-Jost v'yds. Good SEKT, too.

Rauenthal Rhg w ★★★→★★★★ 83 **89 90 93** 94 95 96 **97 98 99** 00 01 02 **03 04 05** Supreme village: spicy, complex wine. First Class v'yds: Baiken, Gehrn, Nonnenberg, Rothenberg, Wülfen. GROSSLAGE: Steinmächer. Top growers: BREUER, KLOSTER EBERBACH, Langwerth von SIMMERN.

Rebholz Pfz ★★★→★★★★ Top SÜDLICHE WEINSTRASSE estate for 50 yrs. Makes some of the best dry MUSKATELLER, GEWÜRZ, CHARD (Burgundian style), and SPÄTBURGUNDER in PFALZ. Outstanding GROSSES GEWÄCHS sites and wines.

Regent New Dark-red grape enjoying some success in PFALZ and RHEINHESSEN. 1,400 ha are now planted.

Ress, Balthasar ★★ RHEINGAU estate (32 ha), cellars in HATTENHEIM. Also runs SCHLOSS REICHARTSHAUSEN. Commercially astute, with original artists' labels, but variable-quality wine.

Restsüsse Unfermented grape sugar remaining in (or in cheap wines added to) wine to give it sweetness. TROCKEN wines have very little, if any.

Rheingau Rhg Best v'yd region of Rhine, W of Wiesbaden. 3,160 ha. Classic, substantial but subtle RIES, yet on the whole recently eclipsed by brilliance

---

Erstes Gewächs

From 1 September 2000, the RHEINGAU's vineyard classification came into force and with it the designation *Erstes Gewächs* or "First Growth". It applies to wines produced according to strict rules (including maximum yield and blind-tasting test). The weakness of the scheme is that the classification takes in just over 35% of the region's vineyards, including some rather poor sites. The scheme is open for SPÄTBURGUNDER and RIES, which may be dry or sweet. With each successive vintage, the ranks of *Erstes Gewächs* are growing and usually represent the finest efforts of each participating estate.

---

elsewhere. BEREICH name for whole region: JOHANNISBERG.

Rheinhessen Rhh Vast region (26,171 ha of v'yds) between Mainz and Worms, bordered by River NAHE, mostly second-rate, but inc top RIES from NACKENHEIM, NIERSTEIN, OPPENHEIM, etc. Newly fashionable.

Rheinhessen Silvaner (RS) New uniform label for earthy dry wines from SILVANER – designed to give a modern quality image to the region.

Rheinpfalz See PFALZ.

Richter, Weingut Max Ferd ★★★ Top MITTELMOSEL estate, at Mülheim. Fine barrel-aged RIES made from First Class v'yds: BRAUNEBERG Juffer-SONNENUHR, GRAACH Domprobst, Mülheim (Helenenkloster), WEHLEN SONNENUHR. Produces superb EISWEIN from Helenenkloster almost every yr.

Rieslaner Cross between SILVANER and RIES; makes fine AUSLESEN in FRANKEN where most is grown. Also superb from MÜLLER-CATOIR.

Riesling The best German grape: fine, fragrant, fruity, long-lived. Only CHARD can compete as the world's best white grape.

Ruck, Weingut Johann ★★ Reliable and spicy SILVANER and RIESLANER from IPHOFEN in FRANKEN.

Rüdesheim Rhg w ★★→★★★★ 75 76 83 85 86 88 **89 90 92 93** 94 95 **96 97 98 99** 00 **01** 02 **03 04** 05 Rhine resort with First Class v'yds; the three best are called Rüdesheimer Berg-. Full-bodied wines, fine-flavoured, often remarkable in off years. Many of the top RHEINGAU estates own some Rüdesheim v'yds. Best growers: BREUER, JOHANNISHOF, August KESSELER, LEITZ, SCHLOSS SCHÖNBORN, STATE DOMAIN.

German regions to watch out for in 2007

Mittelrhein had a string of poor vintages to contend with, but in 2002 and 2003 it proved that it is capable of producing great classic RIES.
Rheinhessen is producing a wave of new-style, clean, harmonious dry white wines that are often excellent value for money.
Saale-Unstrut has finally shaken off the legacy of its communist past and is starting to make some surprisingly full-bodied, supple dry whites.
Sachsen too, has overcome the same problems and is making sleeker and more aromatic dry whites than Saale-Unstrut.
Württemberg is beginning to produce some serious red wines, though quality is still patchy, and there is a tendency to use too much oak.

Ruländer Pinot Gris: now more commonly known as GRAUBURGUNDER.

Ruppertsberg Pfz w ★★ →★★★ **89 90 94** 95 **96** 97 **98** 99 00 **01** 02 **03 04 0**5 Southern village of MITTELHAARDT. First Class v'yds inc Linsenbusch, Nussbein, Reiterpfad, Spiess. Growers inc: BASSERMANN-JORDAN, BIFFAR, BUHL, BÜRKLIN-WOLF, CHRISTMANN.

Ruwer 76 83 88 **89 90** 94 95 96 **97** 98 **99** 00 01 02 **03 04** 05 Tributary of MOSEL nr TRIER. Very fine, delicate but highly aromatic and well structured wines. RIES both sweet and dry. Villages inc EITELSBACH, KASEL, Mertesdorf.

Saale-Unstrut 93 94 95 *96* **97** 98 99 **00 01** 02 03 04 **05** Region of 650 ha around confluence of these two rivers at Naumburg, nr Leipzig. The terraced v'yds of WEISSBURGUNDER, SILVANER, GEWÜRZ, RIES, etc, and red PORTUGIESER have Cistercian origins. Quality leaders: Böhme, LÜTZKENDORF, Landesweingut Kloster Pforta, Pawis, Thüringer Weingut.

Saar 75 76 83 85 86 88 **89 90** 91 92 **93** 94 **95** 96 **97** 98 **99** 00 **01** 02 **03 04** 05 Hill-lined tributary of the MOSEL S of RUWER. The most brilliant, austere steely RIES of all. Villages inc Ayl, OCKFEN, Saarburg, SERRIG, WILTINGEN (SCHARZHOFBERG). GROSSLAGE: Scharzberg. Many fine estates here.

Saar-Ruwer (Bereich) District covering these two regions.

Sachsen 94 95 96 97 **98 99** 00 01 02 03 04 **05** A region of 446 ha in the Elbe Valley around Dresden and Meissen. MÜLLER-T dominant, but WEISSBURGUNDER, GRAUBURGUNDER, TRAMINER, and RIES give dry wines with real character. Best growers: SCHLOSS PROSCHWITZ, Vincenz Richter, Klaus Seifert, Schloss Wackerbarth, Klaus Zimmerling.

St-Antony, Weingut ★★★ Excellent estate. Rich, intense, dry and off-dry RIES from First Class v'yds of NIERSTEIN.

St-Ursula Well-known merchants at BINGEN.

Salm, Prinz zu Owner of SCHLOSS WALLHAUSEN in NAHE and Villa Sachsen in RHEINHESSEN. President of VDP, which implemented the vineyard classification system against some stern opposition.

Salwey, Weingut ★★★ Leading BADEN estate at Oberrotweil, esp for RIES, WEISSBURGUNDER, and RULÄNDER. SPÄTBURGUNDER can be v.gd too, and fruit schnapps are an intriguing sideline.

Samtrot Red WÜRTTEMBERG grape. Makes Germany's closest shot at Beaujolais.

Sankt Urbans-Hof ★★★ New star based in LEIWEN, PIESPORT, and OCKFEN. Limpid RIES of impeccable purity and raciness from 38 ha.

Sauer, Horst ★★★ Eschendorfer Lump is one of FRANKEN's top sites, and Sauer is the finest exponent of its SILVANER and RIES. Notable dry wines, and sensational TROCKENBEERENAUSLESEN.

Schaefer, Willi ★★★ The finest grower of GRAACH (but only ha).

Schäfer-Fröhlich, Weingut ★★★ Increasingly fine RIES, dry and nobly sweet, from this 11-ha estate in Nockenau, NAHE.

Scharzhofberg M-S-R (Saar) w ★★★★ 71 75 76 83 88 **89 90 93 94 95** 96 **97** 98 **99** 00 **01 02 03 04 05** Superlative SAAR v'yd: austerely beautiful wines, the perfection of RIES, best in AUSLESEN. Top estates: BISCHÖFLICHE WEINGÜTER, EGON MÜLLER, VON HÖVEL, VON KESSELSTATT, VAN VOLXEM.

Schaumwein Sparkling wine.

Scheurebe Aromatic grape of high quality (and RIES parentage), esp used in PFALZ. Excellent for botrytis wine (BEERENAUSLESEN, TROCKENBEERENAUSLESEN).

Schillerwein Light red or rosé QBA; speciality of WÜRTTEMBERG (only).

Schlossböckelheim Nahe w ★★→★★★★ 83 85 88 **89 90** 92 **93 94 95** 96 97 **98** 99 00 **01 02 03 04 05** Village with top NAHE v'yds, inc First Class Felsenberg, In den Felsen, Königsfels, Kupfergrube. Firm yet delicate wine. Top growers: CRUSIUS, DÖNNHOF, Gutsverwaltung NIEDERHAUSEN-SCHLOSSBÖCKELHEIM.

Schloss Johannisberg Rhg w ★★★ 76 83 89 90 93 94 95 **96** 97 98 **99** 00 **01** 02 **03 04 05** Famous RHEINGAU estate of 35 ha owned by Princess Metternich and the Oetker family. Deservedly popular tourist destination, but more importantly the original Rhine "first growth". Wines inc fine SPÄTLESE, KABINETT, TROCKEN. Since 1996 there has been a return to form, though there still seems to be an element of complacency.

Schloss Lieser ★★★ Small estate owned by Thomas Haag, from Fritz HAAG estate, making pure racy RIES from underrated v'yds of LIESER.

Schloss Neuweier ★★★ Leading producer of dry RIES in BADEN, from Mauerberg and Schlossberg v'yds.

Schloss Proschwitz ★★ A resurrected princely estate at Meissen, which leads former E Germany in quality, esp with dry WEISSBURGUNDER and GRAUBURGUNDER.

Schloss Reichartshausen Rhg 4-ha HATTENHEIM v'yd run by RESS.

Schloss Reinhartshausen ★★ Fine estate in ERBACH, HATTENHEIM, KIEDRICH, etc. Originally property of Prussian royal family, now in private hands. Model RHEINGAU RIES. The mansion beside the Rhine is now a luxury hotel. After a run of disappointing vintages, the estate is returning to form.

Schloss Saarstein, Weingut ★→★★★ 75 88 89 90 93 95 96 **97** 98 **99** 00 01 **02 03 04** 05 Steep but chilly v'yds in SERRIG need warm yrs to succeed but can deliver steely brilliant AUSLESE and EISWEIN.

Schloss Schönborn ★★★ One of the biggest RHEINGAU estates, based at HATTENHEIM. Full-flavoured wines, variable, but excellent when at their best. Also v.gd SEKT.

Schloss Sommerhausen, Weingut ★★ Ancient FRANKEN estate producing gd dry whites and a dependable range of SEKT.

Schloss Thorn Ancient OBERMOSEL estate; remarkable ELBLING, RIES, and castle.

Schloss Vollrads Rhg w ★★→★★★ **71 76 83 89** 90 93 94 95 96 97 **98 99** 00 **01** 02 **03 04 05** One of the greatest historic RHEINGAU estates, owned by a bank since the sudden death of owner Erwein Count Matuschka in 1997. Since 1998, quality, under director Rowald Hepp, is much improved.

Schloss Wallhausen ★★ The 12-ha NAHE estate of the Prinz zu SALM, one of Germany's oldest. 60% RIES. V.gd TROCKEN. Variable quality.

Schneider, Weingut Georg Albrecht ★★ An impeccably run 13-ha estate. Classic off-dry and sweet RIES in NIERSTEIN, the best from Hipping v'yd.

Schoppenwein Café (or bar) wine, *i.e.* wine by the glass.

Schwarzer Adler, Weingut ★★★ Franz Keller and son Fritz make top BADEN dry GRAU-, WEISS-, and SPÄTBURGUNDER on 48 ha at Oberbergen, KAISERSTUHL.

Schweigen Pfz w r ★★★ **93** 94 **96 97 98** 99 00 **01** 02 03 04 05 Southern PFALZ village. Best growers: Fritz Becker, esp for SPÄTBURGUNDER, Bernhart.

Sekt German (QBA) sparkling wine, best when the label specifies RIES, WEISSBURGUNDER, or SPATBURGUNDER.

Selbach-Oster ★★★ ZELTINGEN estate among MITTELMOSEL leaders. Also makes wine from purchased grapes, but estate bottlings are best.

Serrig M-S-R (Saar) w ★★→★★★ **75 88 89 90 93** 94 **95 96 97** 98 99 00 **01** 02 **03 04 05** Village giving steely wines, excellent in sunny years. First Class v'yds: Herrenberg, Schloss Saarstein, WÜRZBERG. Top growers: Schloss Saarstein, Bert Simon.

Silvaner Third-most-planted German white grape variety, generally underrated; best examples in FRANKEN: the closest thing to Chablis in Germany. Worth looking for in RHEINHESSEN and KAISERSTUHL, too.

Simmern, Langwerth von Weingut ★★ Famous ELTVILLE family estate. Top v'yds: Baiken, Mannberg, MARCOBRUNN. After disappointing quality during the 1990s back on form since 01.

Sonnenuhr Sundial. Name of several v'yds, esp First Class sites at WEHLEN and ZELTINGEN.

Spätburgunder Pinot N: the best red wine grape in Germany – esp in BADEN and WÜRTTEMBERG and increasingly PFALZ – generally improving quality, but most still underflavoured or over-oaked.

Spätlese Late harvest. One better (riper, with more alcohol, more substance and usually more sweetness) than KABINETT. Gd examples age at least 5 yrs, often longer. TROCKEN Spätlesen can be very fine with food. See box, p.142.

Spreitzer, Weingut ★★ Since 1997, brothers Andreas and Bernd Spreitzer in OESTRICH, RHEINGAU, have been making deliciously racy RIES.

Staatlicher Hofkeller ★★→★★★ The Bavarian STATE DOMAIN. 150 ha of the finest FRANKEN v'yds with spectacular cellars under the great baroque Residenz at WÜRZBURG. Quality can be a hit-and-miss affair.

Staatsweingut (or Staatliche Weinbaudomäne) The state wine estates or domains; esp KLOSTER EBERBACH. Some have been privatized in recent yrs.

State Domain See STAATSWEINGUT.

Steigerwald (Bereich) District name for E part of FRANKEN.

Steinberg Rhg w ★★★ 71 76 83 89 90 92 93 94 **95** 96 97 98 **99** 00 01 02 **03 04 05** Famous 32-ha HATTENHEIM walled v'yd, planted by Cistercian monks 700 yrs ago. Now owned by STATE DOMAIN, ELTVILLE. Some glorious wines; some in the past were sadly feeble.

Steinwein Wine from WÜRZBURG's best v'yd, Stein.

Südliche Weinstrasse (Bereich) District name for S PFALZ. Quality has improved tremendously in last 25 yrs. See ILBESHEIM, REBHOLZ, SCHWEIGEN, Dr. WEHRHEIM.

afelwein See "Germany's quality levels" box on p.142.

auberfranken (Bereich) New name for minor Badisches Frankenland BEREICH of N BADEN: FRANKEN-style wines.

esch, Weingut ★★ Since 1996 Dr. Martin Tesch has transformed a previously unremarkable estate in Langenlonsheim, NAHE, into a fine source of rich, rounded dry RIES.

hanisch, Weingut Dr. H ★★→★★★ BERNKASTEL estate, inc part of the Doctor v'yd. Confusingly two estates share the same name.

raben-Trarbach M-M w **★★ 89 90 93 95** 96 **97** 98 **99** 00 **01** 02 **03** 04 **05** Major wine town of 324 ha, 87% of it RIES. Top v'yds: Ungsberg, Würzgarten. Top growers: Louis Klein, Martin Müllen, and RICHTER.

raisen Nahe w **★★★ 76 83 85 88 89 90 93** 94 **95 96** 97 98 99 00 **01 02 03** 04 **05** Small village inc First Class Bastei and Rotenfels v'yds, capable of making RIES of concentration and class. Top grower: CRUSIUS.

raminer See GEWÜRZTRAMINER.

rier M-S-R w **★★→★★★** Great wine city of Roman origin, on MOSEL, nr RUWER, now also inc Avelsbach and EITELSBACH. Big Mosel charitable estates have cellars here among imposing Roman ruins.

rittenheim M-M w **★★ 85 89 90 93** 94 **95** 96 97 98 **99** 00 **01** 02 **03** 04 **05** Attractive S MITTELMOSEL light wines. Top v'yds were Altärchen, Apotheke, but now inc second-rate flat land; First Class v'yds are Felsenkopf, Leiterchen. GROSSLAGE: Michelsberg (avoid). Growers inc E Clüsserath, Clüsserath-Weiler, GRANS-FASSIAN, Milz.

rocken Dry. *Trocken* wines have a maximum 9 g of unfermented sugar per litre. Some are austere, others (better) have more body and alcohol. Quality has increased dramatically since the 1980s, when the majority were tart, even sour.

rockenbeerenauslese (TBA) Sweetest, most expensive category of German wine, extremely rare, with concentrated honey flavour. Made from selected shrivelled grapes affected by noble rot (botrytis). See also EDEL. *Edelbeerenauslese* would be a less confusing name.

rollinger Pale red grape variety of WÜRTTEMBERG; over-cropped but locally very popular.

ngstein Pfz w **★★→★★★ 89 90** 92 **93** 94 **95 96** 97 **98 99** 00 **01** 02 **03 04 05** MITTELHAARDT village with fine harmonious wines. First Class v'yds inc Herrenberg, Weilberg. Top growers inc: Darting, Fitz-Ritter, PFEFFINGEN, Pflüger, Karl Schäfer.

Jrzig M-M w **★★★★ 83 88 89 90** 92 **93** 94 **95** 96 **97** 98 **99** 00 **01** 02 **03 04** 05 Village on red sandstone and red slate, famous for firm, full, spicy wine unlike other MOSELs. First Class v'yd: Würzgarten. Growers inc CHRISTOFFEL, LOOSEN, MÖNCHHOF, Peter Nicolay, WEINS-PRÜM.

an Volxem, Weingut ★★→★★★ Lacklustre SAAR estate revived by brewery heir Roman Niewodniczanski since 1999. Very low yields from top sites result in ultra-ripe dry RIES.

DP, Verband Deutscher Prädikats und Qualitätsweingüter The pace-making association of premium growers. Look for its eagle insignia on wine labels. President: Prinz zu SALM.

ereinigte Hospitien ★★ "United Hospices". Ancient charity at TRIER with large holdings in PIESPORT, SERRIG, TRIER, WILTINGEN, etc. Wines recently well below their wonderful potential.

Wachenheim Pfz w **★★★→★★★★ 83 89 90 93 94** 95 **96 97 98** 99 **00 01** 02 **03 04 05** 340 ha, inc exceptional RIES. First Class v'yds: Belz, Gerümpel, Goldbächel, Rechbächel, etc. Top growers: BIFFAR, BÜRKLIN-WOLF, WOLF.

GERMANY

Wagner, Dr. ★★★ Saarburg estate. Many fine wines inc TROCKEN.

Walluf Rhg w ★★★ **89 90 92** 94 95 96 **97** 98 **99** 00 01 02 **03 04** 05 Neighbo of ELTVILLE; formerly Nieder- and Ober-Walluf. Underrated wines. First Clas v'yd: Walkenberg. Growers inc BECKER, JOST.

Walporzheim Ahrtal (Bereich) District name for the whole AHR Valley.

Wawern M-S-R (Saar) w ★★→★★★ 83 85 88 **89 90** 92 **93** 94 **95** 96 **97** 98 **99** 01 02 **03** 04 Small village, fine RIES. First Class v'yd: Herrenberg.

Wegeler ★★ Important family estates in OESTRICH, MITTELHARDT, and BERNKASTE The Wegelers owned the merchant house of DEINHARD until 1997. Estat wines remain of high quality.

Wehlen M-M w ★★★ 83 85 88 **89 90 93** 94 95 96 **97** 98 **99** 00 **01 02 04** 05 Neighbour of BERNKASTEL with equally fine, somewhat richer wine Location of great First Class v'yd: SONNENUHR. GROSSLAGE: Münzlay. The to growers are: Heribert KERPEN, LOOSEN, J J PRÜM, S A PRÜM, Studert-Prüm SELBACH-OSTER, WEGELER, and WEINS-PRÜM.

Wehrheim, Weingut Dr. ★★★ In the warm SÜDLICHE WEINSTRASSE Pinot varieti as well as RIES ripen fully. Both whites and reds highly successful here.

Weil, Weingut Robert ★★★★ 89 90 93 94 95 **96** 97 **98 99** 00 **01 02 03 04** Outstanding estate in KIEDRICH; now owned by Suntory of Japan. Super QMP, EISWEIN, TROCKENBEERENAUSLESEN, BEERENAUSLESEN; standard wines also v.g since 1992. Widely considered to be RHEINGAU's No 1 in sweet wines, both i quality and price.

Weingart, Weingut ★★→★★★ Much improved MITTELRHEIN estate, with 10 ha BOPPARD. Superb value.

Weingut Wine estate. (See under name, *e.g.* LOOSEN, WEINGUT DR.)

Weinkellerei Wine cellars or winery. See KELLER.

Weins-Prüm, Dr. ★★→★★★ Classic MITTELMOSEL estate; 4.8 ha at WEHLEN. WEHLE SONNENUHR is usually top wine. Scrupulous winemaking from owner Be Selbach.

Weinstrasse Wine road: a scenic route through v'yds. Germany has several.

Weintor, Deutsches See SCHWEIGEN.

Weissburgunder Pinot Blanc Most reliable grape for TROCKEN wines: lo acidity, high extract. Also much used for SEKT.

Weissherbst Usually a pale pink wine, QBA or above and occasionall BEERENAUSLESE, made from a single variety. Speciality of BADEN, PFALZ, an WÜRTTEMBERG.

Werner, Domdechant ★★★ Family estate on best HOCHHEIM slopes: top wine excellent; others only fair.

Wiltingen M-S-R (Saar) w ★★→★★★★ 83 88 89 90 93 94 **95** 96 **97** 98 00 01 02 **03 04** 05 The centre of the SAAR. 320 ha. Beautifully subtle austere wine. Great First Class v'yd is SCHARZHOFBERG (ORTSTEIL); and Firs Class are Braune Kupp, Hölle. Top growers: EGON MÜLLER, von KESSELSTATT VAN VOLXEM, etc.

Winkel Rhg w ★★★ 83 89 90 92 **93** 94 95 **96** 97 **98 99** 00 01 02 **03 04 0** Village famous for full, fragrant wine. First Class v'yds inc Hasensprung Jesuitengarten, SCHLOSS VOLLRADS, Schlossberg. Growers inc Prinz vo HESSEN, von Mumm, Balthasar RESS, SCHLOSS SCHÖNBORN, etc.

Winningen M-S-R w ★★ Lower MOSEL town near Koblenz: unusually full RIES fc region. Excellent dry wines. First Class v'yds: Röttgen, Uhlen. Top growers HEYMANN-LÖWENSTEIN, KNEBEL, Richard Richter.

Wintrich M-M w ★★→★★★ 88 89 90 92 **93** 94 **95** 96 **97 98 99** 00 **01 02** 03 04 Neighbour of PIESPORT; similar wines. First Class v'yd: Ohligsberg. To grower: Reinhold HAART.

Winzergenossenschaft (WG) A wine-growers' cooperative, often makin sound and reasonably priced wine. Referred to in this text as "co-op".

Vinzerverein The same as above.

Virsching, Hans ★★★ Estate in IPHOFEN and in FRANKEN. Wines from RIES and SILVANER can be firm, elegant, and dry, but quality is variable. 69 ha in First Class v'yds: Julius-Echter-Berg, Kalb, etc.

Wittmann, Weingut ★★→★★★ Philipp Wittmann since 1999 has propelled this 25-ha organic estate to the top ranks in RHEINHESSEN. Powerful, dry GROSSES GEWÄCHS RIES and magnificent TROCKENBEERENAUSLESEN.

Vöhrwag, Weingut ★★→★★★ Just outside Stuttgart, this 2-ha WÜRTTEMBERG estate produces succulent reds and often brilliant RIES, esp EISWEIN.

Wolf J L ★★★ Formerly run-down estate in WACHENHEIM leased long-term by Ernst LOOSEN of Bernkastel. From first vintage (1996) strong, dry PFALZ wines with a MOSEL-like finesse. Superb quality since 1998.

Wolff Metternich ★★ Noble DURBACH estate: some gd RIES.

Wonnegau (Bereich) District name for S RHEINHESSEN.

Württemberg Wurt **89 90 93** 94 95 96 **97** 98 99 00 **01** 02 **03** 04 05 Vast southern area, little known for wine outside Germany despite some v.gd RIES (esp NECKAR Valley) and frequently unrealized potential to make gd reds: LEMBERGER, SAMTROT, TROLLINGER.

Würzburg Frank ★★→★★★★ **76 83 85 88 89 90** 92 **93 94** 96 **97** 98 99 **00 01** 02 03 **04** 05 Great baroque city on the Main, centre of FRANKEN wine: fine, full-bodied, dry. First Class v'yds: Abtsleite, Innere Leiste, Stein. See MAINDREIECK. Growers: BÜRGERSPITAL, JULIUSSPITAL, STAATLICHER HOFKELLER.

Zell M-S-R w ★→★★★ **90 93 95** 96 **97** 98 99 00 **01** 02 **03** 04 05 Best-known lower MOSEL village, esp for awful GROSSLAGE: Schwarze Katz (Black Cat). RIES on steep slate gives aromatic wines. Top grower: Kallfelz.

Zell (Bereich) District name for whole lower MOSEL from ZELL to Koblenz.

Zeltingen M-M w ★★→★★★★ **75 83 85 88 89 90 93** 94 **95** 96 **97 98 99** 00 01 02 **03 04** 05 Top MOSEL village nr WEHLEN. Lively crisp RIES. First Class v'yd: SONNENUHR. Top growers: Markus MOLITOR, PRÜM, SELBACH-OSTER.

Zilliken, Forstmeister Geltz ★★★ Former estate of Prussian royal forester with 10 ha at Saarburg and OCKFEN, SAAR. Intensely minerally RIES, inc superb AUSLESE, EISWEIN with excellent ageing potential.

Zwierlein, Freiherr von ★★ 22-ha family estate in GEISENHEIM. 100% RIES.

Luxembourg

Luxembourg has 1,400 hectares of vineyards on limestone soils on the Moselle's left bank. High-yielding Elbling and Rivaner (Müller-Thurgau) vines dominate, but there are also significant acreages of Riesling, Gewürztraminer and (usually best) Auxerrois, Pinot Blanc, and Pinot Gris. These give light to medium-bodied (10.5–11.5% alcohol), dry, Alsace-like wines. The highly competent Vins Moselle co-op makes seventy per cent of the total, including quantities of very fair fizz. Domaine et Tradition estates association, founded in 88, promotes quality from noble varieties. The following vintages were all **good**: 89 90 92 95 97; **outstanding** 97; **average** 98; similar but **softer** 99; **poor** 2000; much **better** 2001; while 2003 and 2005 look good for Pinot Noir. Best from: Aly Duhr et Fils, M Bastian, Caves Gales, Bernard Massard (surprisingly good Cuvée de l'Ecusson classic method sparkling), Clos Mon Vieux Moulin, Ch de Schengen, Sunnen-Hoffmann.

Spain & Portugal

More heavily shaded areas
are the wine-growing regions

The following abbreviations are used in the text:

Alen	Alentejo
Bair	Bairrada
Bul	Bullas
Cos del S	Costers del Segre
El B	El Bierzo
Emp	Empordà-Costa Brava/Ampurdán
Est	Estremadura
La M	La Mancha
Mont-M	Montilla-Moriles
Nav	Navarra
Pen	Penedès
Pri	Priorato/Priorat
Rib del D	Ribera del Duero
Rib del G	Ribera del Guadiana
R Ala	Rioja Alavesa
R Alt	Rioja Alta
RB	Rioja Baja
Set	Setúbal
Som	Somontano
U-R	Utiel-Requena
res	reserva

MADEIRA (off west coast of Africa)

If anyone wants examples of the benefits of EU membership, they should look to Spain and Portugal. Twenty-five years ago Spain had, effectively, just Sherry and Rioja to boast about, plus a few individual companies like Vega Sicilia and Torres. Portugal had Port and Madeira, Vinho Verde, and the old-fashioned delights of Dão and Bairrada.

Now, with massive EU grants translated into new winery kit, the big names are, in Spain, Penedès, Priorat, Ribera del Duero, Navarra, Toro, and Jumilla; and for whites, Rías Baixas, Rueda, and Somontano. And Rioja, still (just) the most prestigious. In Portugal, it's the Douro and Alentejo; Dão, Bairrada, and Vinho Verde have been slower to reinvent themselves.

In Portugal, too, after decades of cooperative dominance, the small estates or *quintas* are making the running with highly individual wines. Most of the excitement is coming from red grapes like Touriga Nacional, Tinta Roriz, and Trincadeira (sometimes alone, but mostly in blends), with Syrah becoming ever more significant in the south. And whereas Spain has DO-fever – there are now over 60 demarcated regions – in Portugal many of the most enterprising wines are not from the traditional DOCs but from the Vinho Regional category that gives winemakers more leeway to experiment.

Navarra
Rioja
Somontano
Ampurdán-
Costa Brava
les
Campo de Borja
Costers del Segre
Conca de
Barbera
Ribera del
Duero
Calatayud
Cariñena
Alella
Rueda
Montsant
Penedès
Tarragona
Vinos de
Madrid
entrida
Utiel-
Requena
Valencia
Binissalem
La Mancha
Plà i Llevant
Almansa
Valencia
Valdepeñas
Jumilla
Alicante
alquivir
Bullas
Yecla
ntilla Moriles
ilaga

Sherry, port, and madeira have a separate chapter on p.178.

Spain

Recent vintages of the Spanish classics
Rioja

2005 A large, healthy, and plentiful harvest, with exceptionally favourable
weather. Quality rated as "exceptional" and "unprecedented".

2004 A large harvest with "magnificent" quality expectations for those who
were selective enough given the tricky weather.

2003 Biggish harvest of fair quality, but few examples yet on the market.

2002 Small harvest of doubtful quality, like a cross between 1999 and 2000.

2001 Medium-sized harvest of excellent quality; wines fulfilling their promise.

2000 Huge harvest; wines distinctly bland, with little real flavour or definition.

1999 A difficult harvest, which produced light but very graceful wines that
have mainly peaked.

1998 A huge vintage of high quality; its wines are now largely mature.

1997 Cool and wet with spring and summer frosts. Poor.

Ribera del Duero

2005 A long, bitterly cold winter, followed by sparse rainfall yet high temperatures in May, June, and the run-up to an early harvest – with one major frost in mid-Sept. Not only 30% below expectations, with musts of tremendous aromas and extract, but alcohol levels often too high. Those who picked too early have green, unbalanced wines. V.gd only for the true professionals.

2004 A better year than in most regions. Despite extremes of temperature in Sept, good quality wines and a plentiful harvest.

2003 A cold winter, mild spring, scorching summer, and Oct rains resulted in a tricky harvest. The best wines are of good colour, glycerine, and alcohol, but low in acidity.

2002 Hot weather followed by heavy rain in late summer led to a large harvest. Quality generally very good.

2001 Medium-sized harvest of excellent quality; wines fulfilling their promise.

2000 Very large harvest but ripening was uneven. Some bodegas made spectacular wines; but in general good.

1999 Almost perfect weather and bumper harvest, but rainfall around harvest time resulted in lack of acidity. Very good.

1998 Torrential rain in early autumn and record grape prices. Good.

1997 Cool and wet with spring and summer frosts. Poor.

Navarra

2005 Possibly the region's best-ever vintage, with perfect climatic conditions and virtually no rain, resulting in optimum ripeness and wines of immense colour, full flavours, and sweet, powerful tannins.

2004 Low spring and summer temperatures with much rain. Good wines for those who picked late and selectively.

2003 The hot, dry summer was followed by extended torrential rain and outbreaks of botrytis and mildew. As in 2002, only the best and most professional producers obtained decent results.

2002 Torrential Aug rains affected the quality of wines from the south of the region; others are excellent.

2001 An excellent year, with big, ripe, well-balanced wines.

2000 Very dry year of prolific yields, calling for rigorous selection. Best wines are big and fleshy, and age well. Very good.

1999 Most frost-afflicted vintage of the decade, with soaring grape prices. Wines are well-structured and long-ageing. Excellent.

1998 Spring frosts but dry, hot summer. Well-structured wines with excellent colour and elegant aromas. Very good.

1997 Dank, overcast summer. Short-lived wines. Poor.

Penedès

2005 The hardest drought of the last 50 years reduced yields by 30–40%, but thanks to cold summer nights quality was excellent for reds and whites.

2004 A cold spring and late summer rains delayed the harvest, but sunny days and cold nights in autumn resulted in a memorable year for red wines.

2003 A very dry and long summer, refreshed with rains in Aug, then cool nights and sunny days in Sept, resulted in a great vintage.

2002 A splendid Sept gave wines of good quality.

2001 April frosts reduced the yield but warm summer produced very good wines.

2000 Perfect ripening of the grapes gave well-balanced wines. Very good.

1999 Dry summer but abundant harvest. Very good.

1998 Very good whites and excellent reds.

1997 Large harvest. Good white wines and very good reds.

Abadía Retuerta Castilla y León r ★★★ 96 97 98 99 00 01 02 03 04 Non-DO, one of the two most famous non-DO wineries in Spain (the other is Mauro) – and one of the most modern. With top B'x help, is making exceptional Temp, Cab Sauv, and Merlot with prices to match. Esp Negralada (02).

Agapito Rico Jumilla r ★★★ 98 99 01 02 03 04 Young BODEGA making some of Spain's best *vinos jóvenes* (see JOVEN) in JUMILLA, esp 98 99. Carchelo wines (Syrah, Merlot, or Monastrell with Temp and Merlot). Also excellent CRIANZA.

Agramont See PRÍNCIPE DE VIANA, BODEGAS.

Albariño High-quality, aromatic w grape of GALICIA, maybe the best regarded w. See CERVERA, GERARDO MENDÉZ, GRANBAZÁN, PAZO DE BARRANTES, RÍAS BAIXAS.

Albet y Noya Pen r w p ★★→★★★ 00 01 02 03 04 Spain's most famous organic producer; huge prices. A formidable range; styles can be old-fashioned. Excellent barrel-fermented Chard and outstanding Col-lecció Syrah (00).

Alella r w (p) dr sw ★★ DYA Small, demarcated region N of Barcelona. Pleasantly fruity wines. Three producers only: Marqués de Alella, PARXET, and Roura, which occasionally makes a fantastic, though unreliable Merlot.

Alicante r (w) ★ 98 99 00 01 04 DO. Most wines still stringy and over-alcoholic. Enrique Mendoza does good delicate Moscatel de la Marina.

Alión Rib del D r ★★★→★★★★ 95 96 99 00 01 02. Since discontinuing its 3-yr-old VALBUENA in 1997, VEGA SICILIA has acquired this second BODEGA to make 100% Temp; impressive results, esp 01 02.

Allende, Finca R Ala r ★★★→★★★★ 96 97 98 99 00 01 02 03. Much-praised BODEGA and the only really new-wave one in Rioja, aiming for a balance of fruit and wood: elegant, oak-aged Temp. Aurus (96 97 98 01 02) and single-estate Calvario with wild black-fruit flavours (01 02 03). Family also in LA MANCHA.

Álvaro Palacios Pri r ★★★★ 98 99 00 01 02 03 Gifted emigré from RIOJA making some of the most expensive and fashionable red wine in Spain, inc outstanding Finca Dofi that keeps, L'Ermita (drink within 2 yrs unless you like it tarry), and Les Terrasses (one of the best standard Prioratos).

Artadi Bodegas (Cosecheros Alaveses) R Ala r (w p) ★★★→★★★★ 94 95 96 97 98 00 01 02 03 04 Up-and-coming former co-op, esp for gd, young, unoaked red Artadi, splendid Viñas de Gain, Viña El Pisón, Pagos Viejos RES.

Barbier, René Pen r w res ★★ 96 98 01 Owned by FREIXENET, known for fresh white Xarel-lo, Chard, and drinkable young reds.

Barón de Ley RB r (w) res ★★★ 95 99 00 03 04 Newish RIOJA BODEGA linked with EL COTO: gd single-estate wines, esp Finca del Monasterio (01).

Berberana, Bodegas See BODEGAS UNIDAS.

Beronia, Bodegas R Alt r w res ★★→★★★ 95 99 01 04 Modern BODEGA making reds in traditional, oaky style and fresh whites. Owned by GONZÁLEZ-BYASS.

Bierzo 96 98 99 00 01 02 03 04 DO N of Léon becoming very fashionable, with many new BODEGAS using the indigenous red Mencia. Top wines: Luna Beberide, Prada a Tope, Dominio de Tares, Bodegas Pittacum.

Bilbaínas, Bodegas R Alt r w (p) w dr sw sp res ★★→★★★ 96 98 99 00 01 03 Historic Haro BODEGA, well known for its red Viña Pomal and lighter Zaco. New owner CODORNÍU has some way to go in introducing less oaky modern-style wines. Best are RES La Vicalanda (96 99) and gd Royal Carlton CAVA.

Binissalem r w ★★ 98 99 00 01 03 04 Best-known MALLORCA DO.

Blanco White.

Bodega Spanish term for (i) a wineshop; (ii) a concern occupied in the making, blending, and/or shipping of wine; and (iii) a cellar.

Bodegas de Crianza Castilla la Vieja Rueda w dr sp ★★→★★★ Makes some of RUEDA's liveliest whites under a variety of labels using Verdejo, Viura, Sauv Bl.

NB Vintages in colour are those you should choose first for drinking in 2007.

Bodegas Unidas Umbrella organization controlling MARQUÉS DE MONISTROL, BERBERANA, and Vinícola Mediterráneo with its holiday wines. A new departure are the *haciendas* situated in the v'yds, both making wine and putting up visitors. Unidas also owns the winery of late Prince Hohenlohe in Ronda, famous for its pure Petit Verdot (oo), and is brand owner of the workman-like MARQUÉS DE GRIGÑON Riojas.

Bodegas y Bebidas Part of Pernod Ricard which owns wineries all over Spain. Mainly mid-market brands. Also controls various prestigious firms – *e.g.* AGE, Marqués del Puerto, YSIOS.

Bodegas y Viñedos del Jalón Calatayud r (w dr p) ★★ **03 05** Leading brands are the very drinkable Castillo Maluenda and Viña Alarba.

Bretón, Bodegas R Alt r res ★★★ **94 95 96 98 99** Respected Loriñon range and little-seen, expensive, concentrated Dominio de Conté (**96**) and Alba de Bretón (**98**). Current wines are disappointingly astringent.

Briones Small Riojan hill-top town nr Haro, which, apart from the BODEGAS of FINCA ALLENDE and MIGUEL MERINO, boasts one of the finest and most comprehensive wine museums in the world, El Museo de la Cultura de Vino. Do not miss.

Calatayud ★→★★ **00 01 02 03 04 05** Aragón DO (one of four): esp Garnacha. See also BODEGAS Y VIÑEDOS DEL JALÓN.

Campo Viejo See JUAN ALCORTA, BODEGA.

Canary Islands (Islas Canarias) r w p ★→★★ Until recently there were few quality wines aside from dessert Malvasías (BODEGAS El Grifo and BODEGAS Mozaga on Lanzarote). But nine DOS have been created; modernized BODEGAS, esp on TENERIFE, are making better, lighter wines. Worth investigating.

Can Rafols dels Caus Pen r p w ★★★ **98 00 01 02** 03 04 Young, small PENEDÈS BODEGA: own-estate, fruity Cab Sauv, pleasant Gran Caus Chard/Xarel-lo/ Chenin Bl. Best whites: El Rocallis, Pairal; best reds: Ad Fines **01** , Lubis.

Casa Castillo Jumilla r (w p) ★★→★★★ **00 01 02 03** 04 Some of the best wines from JUMILLA, but Parker-esque: for immediate, brambly oak impact.

Castaño, Bodegas Yecla r res (w dr) ★★ **01 02 03** 04 Trailblazer in remote YECLA making sound and pleasant blends of Monastrell with Cab Sauv, Temp, and Merlot under the names Castaño, Colección, Hécula, and Pozuelo.

Castellblanch Pen w sp ★★ PENEDÈS CAVA firm, owned by FREIXENET. Look for Brut Zero and Gran Castellblanch GRAN RESERVAS.

Castell del Remei Cos del S r w p ★★→★★★ **96 99 01 02 03** Historic v'yds/winery revived, re-equipped, and replanted since 1983. Best wines: Gotim Bru red blend, new designer-style Oda Merlot, and Top 1780 (**99 00 01**).

Castilla-la Mancha, Vino de la Tierra In 1999 some 600,000 ha of this vast region were granted VINO DE LA TIERRA status by the EU. Since then dozens of large firms have moved into the area to make wines.

Castillo de Monjardín Nav r w ★★→★★★ **98** 01 02 03 **04** Newish winery making fragrant, oaky Chard (03) and v.gd reds and rosé, esp blends of Merlot.

Castillo de Perelada, Caves Emp r w p res sp ★★→★★★ **98** 01 02 03 04 Large range of both still wines and CAVA, inc Chard, Sauv Bl, Cab Sauv (esp superb Gran Claustro **01**), Finca Garbet (**01**), sp Gran Claustro Extra Brut.

Castillo de Ygay R Alt r w ★★★★ (r) **25 52 64 68 75 78 82 85 87 89 94 95** 98 Legendary wines (see "Old vintages" box p.166) from the MARQUÉS DE MURRIETA.

Cataluña 00 01 03 04 DO covering the whole Catalan area. Wines may be registered as from an existing DO or from the new global DO, but not both.

Cava Any classic-method Spanish sp, and the DO covering the areas up and down Spain where it is made, though Rueda and Galicia are not included.

Cavas Conde de Caralt Pen r w sp res ★★→★★★ CAVA wines from outpost of FREIXENET, esp gd, vigorous Brut NV; also pleasant still wines.

Celler de Capçanes Montsant, Pri r ★★→★★★ 01 02 03 Large ex-co-op in MONTSANT with some of the best new-wave wine from the Tarragona area. Typical is the **99**: meaty, concentrated, and somewhat tannic.

Cervera, Lagar de Rías Baixas w ★★★ DYA Maker of one of best ALBARIÑOS: flowery and intensely fruity with subdued bubbles and a long finish.

Chacolí País Vasco w (r) ★★ DYA Fragrant though sometimes alarmingly sharp, pétillant wine from the Basque coast; two DOS for some 450 ha. 9–11% alcohol. Best producers: Txomin Etxaniz (Guetaria), Aretxondo (Vizcaya).

Chivite, Bodegas Julián Nav r w (p) dr sw res ★★★★ 95 96 98 99 00 01 02 03 04 The biggest and best NAVARRA BODEGA. Now some of Spain's top reds, deep-flavoured, very long-lived; flowery, well-balanced white, esp Chivite Colección 125 (01), v.gd rosé (04), and superb Vendimia Tardía Moscatel (03), the best from Spain. See GRAN FEUDO.

Cigales, Bodega Cooperativa de Cigales r w d ★★ Its luscious red Torondos (sold in the UK as La Serrana Temp) is outstanding value for money.

Clos Mogador Pri r ★★★→★★★★ 99 00 01 02 03 René Barbier (no connection with FREIXENET) produces first-rate Clos Mogador PRIORATO.

Codorníu Pen w sp ★★→★★★ One of the two largest firms in SAN SADURNÍ DE NOYA making gd CAVA: very high-tech, 10 million bottles ageing in cellars. Mature Non Plus Ultra, fresh Anna de Codorníu or premium Jaume de Codorníu RES. Also owns RAÍMAT, BILBAINAS, Bach, and part-owns Scala Dei (Pri).

Compañía Vinícola del Norte de España (CVNE) R Alt r w dr (p) ★★→★★ 98 99 00 02 03 04 Famous RIOJA BODEGA. Young wines less gd than formerly, though some older Viña Real and Imperial RES are spectacular. See also CONTINO.

Conca de Barberà w (r p) 98 99 00 00 02 03 04 Catalan DO region growing Parellada grapes for making CAVA. But its best wines are the superb MILMANDA Chard and red Grans Muralles, both from TORRES.

Con Class Rueda w dr ★★ →★★★ DYA Brand name for exciting Verdejo/Viura and Sauv Bl from the Sanz family.

Condado de Haza Rib del D r ★★★ 96 99 00 01 02 04 Pure, oak-aged Tinto Fino (Temp). Similar to PESQUERA but more consistent and better value. Avoid the pricey and disappointing 95 and 96 Alenza.

Conde de Valdemar See MARTÍNEZ-BUJANDA.

Consejo Regulador Organization for the control, promotion, and defence of a DO.

Contino R Ala r res ★★★ 96 99 00 01 02 03 Very fine single-v'yd red made by a subsidiary of COMPAÑÍA VINICOLA DEL NORTE DE ESPANA. Look for 100% Graciano (01) and premium Viña del Olivo (01).

Vintage tips

Most large Spanish wineries make a range of red, white, and rosé. The vintages at the top of an entry refer to the best of a bodega's red *crianzas* and *reservas*, and are only a rough guide, since the vintages and degree of maturity may well vary from one wine to another. When individual wines are named in the text, preferred vintages are given in brackets.

Cosecha Crop or vintage.

Cosecheros Alaveses See ARTADI BODEGAS.

Costers del Segre Cos del S r w p sp ★★→★★★ 95 96 97 98 99 00 01 02 03 04 Small, demarcated area around city of Lleida (Lérida), famous for v'yds of RAÍMAT, CASTELL DEL REMEI, and Cellers de Cantonella.

Costers del Siurana Pri r (sw) ★★★→★★★★ 96 97 98 99 01 03 A star of PRIORATO. Carlos Pastrana makes the prestigious Clos de l'Obac, Misere, and Usatges from Garnacha/Cab Sauv, sometimes plus Syrah, Merlot, Temp, and Cariñena.

Criado y embotellado por... "Grown and bottled by..."

SPAIN

Crianza Literally "nursing"; the ageing of wine. New or unaged wine is *sin crianza* or JOVEN. Reds labelled *crianza* must be at least 2 yrs old (with 1 yr in oak, in some areas 6 months), and must not be released before the third year.

Dinastía Vivanco R Alt r ★★ Major new BODEGA at BRIONES.

DO, Denominación de Origen Official wine region.

DOCa, Denominación de Origen Calificada Classification for wines of the highest quality; so far only RIOJA (since 1991) and PRIORATO (DOQ – the Catalan equivalent – since 2002) benefit.

Domecq R Ala r (w) res ★★→★★★ 96 00 01 02 03 RIOJA outpost of sherry firm. Excellent Marqués de Arienzo RES, fragrant, and medium-bodied.

Don Darias/Don Hugo Alto Ebro r w ★ Huge-selling, modestly priced wines, very like RIOJA, from undemarcated BODEGAS Vitorianas. Sound red and white.

Dulce Sweet.

El Coto, Bodegas R Ala r (w) res ★★★ 98 99 00 01 04 BODEGA best known for light, soft, red El Coto and Coto de Imaz RES.

Empordà-Costa Brava/Ampurdán Emp r w p ★→★★ 98 99 00 01 03 04 Demarcated region abutting Pyrenees in NE. Mainly co-op-made rosés and reds, though some boutique wineries emerging. DO wants "Costa Brava" removed from its name now that good boutique producers are emerging.

Enate Som DO r w p res ★★★ 01 02 03 04 Gd wines from SOMONTANO in the N: light, clean, fruity, inc barrel-fermented Chard (02; one of best in Spain) and Cab Sauv blends (the CRIANZA is full and juicy). Wonderful 03 Merlot.

Espumoso Sparkling (but see CAVA).

Faustino, Bodegas R Ala r w (p) res ★★→★★★ 96 01 04 Long-established BODEGA, formerly F Martínez, with gd reds. GRAN RES is Faustino I. Top is Faustino de Autor (96). Faustino V is reliable. Also middle-of-the-road Rioja from Campillo and new Norman Foster-designed winery in RIBERA DEL DUERO.

A Spanish choice for 2007

Toro Albalá, Don PX Gran Reserva 1971 Montilla-Moriles
Bodegas La Tapada, Guitián (Sobre Lías) 2004 VALDEORRAS
Torres, Fransola 2004 PENEDÈS
Jaume Codorníu Brut CAVA
Artadi, Viña El Pisón 2002 RIOJA
Bodegas Aragonesas, Coto de Hayas Garnacha 2003 Campo de Borja
Bodegas Mauro 2, Viña San Román 2002 TORO
César Príncipe, Tempranillo 2002 CIGALES
Marqués de Murrieta, Castillo Ygay 1999 RIOJA

Fillaboa, Granxa Rías Baixas w ★★★ DYA. Makers of unusually pineappley ALBARIÑO

Finca Farm. (See under name – *e.g.* ALLENDE, FINCA.)

Freixenet, Cavas Pen w sp ★★→★★★ Huge CAVA firm, rivalling CODORNÍU in size. Gd sp, notably bargain Cordón Negro in black bottles, Brut Barroco, RES Real and Premium Cuvée DS. Also owns Gloria Ferrer in California, Champagne Henri Abelé (Reims), and a sparkling-wine plant in Mexico. Also tentacles in PRIORATO, RIBERA DEL DUERO, RÍAS BAIXAS.

Galicia Rainy NW Spain: esp for fresh, aromatic but pricey w. Reds, based on Mencia grape, are astringent and best drunk locally and chilled, or avoided. Occasionally interesting w from lesser DOS: Ribeiro, VALDEORRAS, Monterrei.

Generoso Apéritif or dessert wine rich in alcohol.

Gerardo Méndez Rías Baixas ★★→★★★ Tiny family estate making modern exuberant new-style ALBARIÑO inc minute production from old vines (200 yrs with touch of botrytis. Name on label is Albariño do Ferreiro.

Gramona Pen r w dr sw res ★★→★★★ Established and sizeable family firm make gd Chard, Sauv Bl, Gewurz, Merlot. Also excellent CAVA: clean, not esp exciting.

Granbazán w dr ★★★ DYA Agro de Bazán produces a classic, fragrant ALBARIÑO with mouth-cleansing acidity and loopy labels.

Gran Feudo Nav w Res ★★→★★★ 96 98 00 03 04 Brand name of fragrant white, refreshing rosé (04); soft, plummy red; the best-known wines from CHIVITE.

Gran Reserva See RESERVA.

Gran Vas Pressurized tanks (French *cuves closes*) for making cheap sparkling wines; also used to describe this type of wine.

Guelbenzu, Bodegas r (w) res ★★→★★★ Non-DO estate in Navarra making concentrated, full-bodied reds: Vierlas, Azul, Evo new Graciano (05) and splendid Lautus (01). Family now has two estates in same valley – Ribera del Quieles is the appellation on the label. Also now in Chile.

Guitán Godello Valdeorras w ★★★→★★★★ 03 04 Made by BODEGAS La Tapada, these splendidly fruity, fragrant, complex 100% Godello wines, rated among the top whites in Spain, typify renaissance of native grapes in GALICIA. The lees-aged *sobre lías* type has the edge; barrel-aged is less exciting.

Haro Wine centre of the RIOJA ALTA, a small but stylish old town.

Iljalba, Viña R Alt r w dr p ★ →★★★ 95 98 00 01 A newish BODEGA with a reputation for organically made younger wines and a rare 100% Graciano.

Joven (vino) Young, unoaked wine. Also see CRIANZA.

Juan Alcorta, Bodega R Alt r (w) res ★ →★★★ 97 98 00 01 02 100% Temp Alcorta; big, fruity red RES, esp Marqués de Villamagna. See BODEGAS Y BEBIDAS.

Jumilla r (w p) ★→★★★ 96 98 99 00 03 04 DO in mountains N of Murcia. Its traditionally over-strong wines are being lightened by earlier picking and better winemaking. The Monastrell grape can yield dark and fragrant wines to rival those of RIBERA DEL DUERO. They can be fantastic while young and brambly, but don't last in bottle: drink within 2 years. See AGAPITO RICO and CASA CASTILLO.

Juvé y Camps Pen w sp ★★★ 00 01 02 Family firm. Top-quality CAVA from free-run juice only, esp RES de la Familia and Gran Juvé y Camps.

Kripta Brut GRAN RES CAVA made by Agusti Torello and probably the best in Spain.

LAN, Bodegas R Alt r (p w) res ★★→★★★ 98 99 01 02 03 Huge, modern BODEGA. Recently reorganized; making improved Lan, Lanciano, new-style Ediciones Limitados, and premium Culmen de Lan (01'). Mid-level wines gd, boutique end screamingly expensive and extremely woody.

Lanzarote Canary Island with very fair, dry Malvasía, *e.g.* El Grifo. Seldom seen elsewhere due to prohibitive shipping costs and buoyant local market.

León, Jean Pen r w res ★★★ 96 97 99 02 03 Small firm; TORRES-owned since 1995. Current styles somewhat dilute compared to blockbusting intensities of yore. Gd oaky Chard and outstanding Merlot.

López de Heredia R Alt r w (p) dr sw res ★★→★★★ 54 57 61 64 68 70 73 78 81 87 93 94 97 99 (See "Old vintages" box on p.166). Old-established family BODEGA in HARO with cellars cut into the rock and a wealth of oak vats. Very long-lasting and traditional wines; best are the really old RES. Vintage differences used to be v. marked; since c.1981 vintages have been more homogeneous.

Los Llanos Valdepeñas, La M r (p w) res ★★ One of growing number of VALDEPEÑAS BODEGAS to age wine in oak. RES, GRAN RES; premium Pata Negra GRAN RES: 100% Cencibel (Temp). Clean, fruity, v.gd white Armonioso. Reds made their name as good, cheaper Rioja look-alikes, but Rioja has moved on, and Pata Negra is now looking slightly old fashioned.

Málaga Once-famous DO that has now all but vanished because producers had to bottle within city limits where premises became too expensive. TELMO RODRIGUEZ has a joint venture here, making clear, subtle, sweet white Molino Real Moscatel, mostly sold in the US.

SPAIN

Mallorca Interesting things are happening on the island at last, inc fresh Chard (better unoaked), Merlot, Syrah, Cab Sauv. Also traditional varieties and blends: Manto Negro and Callet are local red grapes, rugged and prone to oxidize. Ánima Negra, Franja Roja (biggest name), Heredad de Ribas (fantastic top cuvée), Miguel Oliver, Pere Seda, Son Bordils (highly priced minerally red), and Jaume Mesquida are leaders.

Mancha, La La M r w ★→★★ 92 93 94 96 97 98 99 00 01 02 03 04 Vast demarcated region N and NE of VALDEPEÑAS. Mainly white wines and mostly still v. ordinary. If picked in July and drunk before Christmas, can have good lime fruit; the reds lack the liveliness of the best VALDEPEÑAS but are improving. Interesting moves with Syrah. See also CASTILLA-LA MANCHA, VINO DE LA TIERRA.

Marqués de Cáceres, Bodegas R Alt r p w res ★★★ 96 98 01 02 04 Gd red RIOJAS made by modern French methods inc premium Gaudium (98) and MC (02); surprisingly light, fragrant, white (DYA), barrel-fermented Antea, and semi-sweet Satinela.

Old vintages
Extended lists of old vintages, still occasionally available at a price, are given for wines such as VEGA SICILIA, LÓPEZ DE HEREDIA, and CASTILLO DE YGAY from Murrieta. At their best, these wines are memorable and of great complexity, but a great deal depends on their provenance and cellarage, and they must be acquired from entirely reliable sources. Faking of old vintages, especially of VEGA SICILIA, is rife.

Marqués de Griñón Dominio de Valdepusa r w ★★★ 00 01 02 Enterprising nobleman initiated very fine Cab Sauv, delicious Syrah (01 02), and Petit Verdot at his Dominio de Valdepusa nr Toledo, S of Madrid. Not formerly known for good wine, but now PAGO denominated. Fruity wines to drink fairly young, esp new blend Summa. See also BODEGAS UNIDAS. The Griñón name also appears on a cheap Rioja from Berberana – a leftover from a distribution deal.

Marqués de Monistrol, Bodegas Pen p r sp dr sw res ★★→★★★ 01 03 04 Old BODEGA now owned by BODEGAS UNIDAS. Good, reliable CAVAS. Adequate, fresh blends of Cab Sauv, Merlot, and Temp.

Marqués de Murrieta R Alt r p w res ★★★→★★★★ 25 42 50 52 54 60 64 68 70 75 78 87 89 94 95 97 99 00 01 (See "Old vintages" box). Historic old BODEGA at Ygay nr Logroño, growing all its own grapes and meticulously modernized by the late Conde de Creixel. Famous for its magnificent red CASTILLO DE YGAY and old-style, oaky whites; successful newer introduction is the premium red Dalmau (01), a blend of Temp, Cab Sauv, Graciano. See also PAZO DE BARRANTES.

Marqués de Riscal R Ala & Rueda r (p) w dr ★★★→★★★★ 91 92 94 95 96 97 99 00 01 (see "Old vintages" box) Best-known BODEGA in R Ala, now greeting the 21st century with a hotel and restaurant designed by Frank Gehry of Bilbao fame. Gd, fairly light reds and a splendid Barón de Chirel RES (99, 01) made with 50% Cab Sauv. Fragrant whites from RUEDA include an oak-aged 100% Verdejo Limousin.

Marqués de Vargas, Bodegas R Ala ★★★ 96 00 01 00 04 Relative newcomer making a RES and a Privada (01) both with good concentration and balance. Not as new wave as is sometimes thought.

Martínez-Bujanda, Familia R Ala r p w res ★★★ 94 95 99 01 02 This Riojan family, based in Oyón, has been making wines since 1890. It now controls Bodegas Valdemar, making and shipping the wines formerly sold as Martínez Bujanda, including the fine Valdemar RES; Finca Valpiedra, makers of the premium single-v'yd Temp of that name; and the new Finca Antigua, producing worthwhile reds in La MANCHA.

Mascaró, Antonio Pen r p w sp ★★→★★★ Top brandy maker, gd CAVA; fresh, lemony, dry white Viña Franca and Ánima Cab Sauv. Gd CAVA hardly exists beyond Barcelona.

Mas Martinet Pri r ★★★→★★★★ 95 96 98 00 01 03 Maker of Clos Martinet and a pioneer of the exclusive boutique PRIORATOS.

Mauro, Bodegas r 94 95 96 98 99 00 02 03 Young BODEGA in Tudela del Duero; v.gd, round, fruity TINTO del País (Temp) red, superb Tereus (01) and VENDIMIA Seleccionada (01). Not DO, since some of the fruit is from outside RIBERA DEL DUERO. Now making excellent TORO San Román (02). The same winemaker, Mariano García, formerly of VEGA SICILIA, also makes headlining RIBERA DEL DUERO Aalto (01).

Milmanda Premium barrel-fermented Chard from TORRES, one of three best Chards in Spain.

Montecillo, Bodegas R Alt r w (p) res ★★ 96 98 00 01 RIOJA BODEGA owned by OSBORNE (see Sherry chapter, p.183). Old GRAN RES are magnificent.

Montsant r ★→★★★ 02 03 04 Tiny new DO (since 2001) in an enclave of PRIORATO, sharing much in common with its wines – and initially also cheaper. But the soil is different, the wines can be astringent, and prices have soared. Castell de Falset 00 probably best bet, from co-op. Capçanes is most famous, but is blander than of old.

Muga, Bodegas R Alt r (w sp) res ★★★→★★★★ 95 96 98 00 01 03 Small family firm in HARO, known for some of RIOJA's best strictly traditional reds, all made and aged in oak vats. Wines are light but highly aromatic, with long, complex finish. Best is Prado Enea (a masterpiece, but fades quickly once it peaks) and the extraordinarily concentrated, new-wave Torre Muga (98 00 01). The barrel-fermented white is almost burgundian.

Navajas, Bodegas R Alt r w res ★★→★★★★ 01 02 03 04 Family firm making young fruity reds and gd traditional oaky CRIANZAS and RES. Also excellent oak-aged white Viura (03).

Navarra Nav r p (w) ★★→★★★ 94 95 96 98 99 00 01 02 03 04 Demarcated region. Stylish Temp and Cab Sauv reds, rivalling RIOJAS in quality and trouncing many in value, although the DO has gradually been allowing larger yields, and wines at the mid-level are less concentrated than they were. See CHIVITE, GUELBENZU, OCHOA, PRÍNCIPE DE VIANA. Inurrieta also gd.

Ochoa Nav r p w res ★★→★★★ 98 01 99 01 02 04 Small family BODEGA; excellent Moscatel (04), but better known for well-made red and rosés, inc 100% Temp and 100% Merlot (01). Wines less concentrated than they were.

Pago A v'yd or area of limited size giving rise to exceptional wines. The term now has legal status, *e.g.* DO Dominio de Valdepusa (see MARQUÉS DE GRIÑÓN).

Pago de Carraovejas Rib del D r res ★★→★★★ 99 01 02 03 Large estate; produces some of the region's most stylish, densely fruity Tinto Fino/Cab Sauv in minimal supply.

Palacio, Bodegas R Ala r p w res ★★★ 01 02 03 04 Gd old BODEGA rescued from Seagram ownership. Very sound Gloriosa, Especial, and RES Privada and Cosme Palacio (03). V.gd.

Palacio de Bornos Rueda w sp ★★★ 04 05 First-rate Sauv Bl and Verdejo wines. See BODEGAS DE CRIANZA CASTILLA LA VIEJA.

Palacio de Fefiñanes Rías Baixas w dr ★★★ DYA Oldest-established of the BODEGAS in RÍAS BAIXAS, now making excellent, light, lemony, modern-style ALBARIÑOS. Experimenting with smaller batches: a barrel-fermented version, which is successful in Spain; and a lees-aged version called III.

Parxet Alella w p sp ★★→★★★ DYA Excellent fresh, fruity, exuberant CAVA (only one produced in ALELLA): esp Brut Nature and unusual Pinot N CAVA in expensive dessert version, and delicious, pricey barrel-fermented Chard, Titiana. Elegant w ALELLA (DYA): MARQUÉS DE ALELLA. Also stylish and concentrated Tionio (**03**) from new winery in RIBERA DEL DUERO.

Paternina, Bodegas R Alt r w (p) dr sw res ★→★★ Vina Vial is quite good but avoid Banda Azul. Most consistent is Banda Dorada white (DYA).

Pazo Ribeiro r p w ★★ DYA Brand name of the huge Ribeiro co-op, whose wines are akin to Vinhos Verdes. Rasping red is local favourite, and okay if ice-cold with octopus. Pleasant, slightly fizzy Pazo whites are safer.

Pazo de Barrantes Rías Baixas w ★★★ DYA ALBARIÑO from RÍAS BAIXAS; estate owned by late Conde de Creixels of Murrieta. Firm, delicate, exotic, variable, but top quality when good.

Pazo de Señorans Rías Baixas w dr ★★★ DYA Exceptionally fragrant wines from a BODEGA considered a benchmark of the DO, with beautiful buildings and gardens.

Penedès Pen r w sp ★→★★★ 93 95 96 97 98 99 00 01 03 04 Demarcated region inc Vilafranca del Penedès and SAN SADURNÍ DE NOYA. See also TORRES. CAVA and TORRES are famous; Penedès much less so.

Pérez Pascuas Hermanos Rib del D r res ★★★ 98 99 00 01 02 03 Immaculate, tiny BODEGA. In Spain, its fruity and complex red VIÑA Pedrosa and mature Gran Selección (**99**) are rated among the best of the region. Wines can have a whiff of sheep because of the sheep manure used as fertilizer. Don't keep Pedrosa unless you're Spanish and like that kind of thing.

Pesquera Rib del D r ★★★ 95 96 00 01 02 03 Small quantities of benchmark RIBERA DEL DUERO from pioneer Alejandro Fernández. Robert Parker rated it level with finest B'x, and this has never been forgotten. Janus GRAN RES (**95**). Also CONDADO DE HAZA.

Pingus, Dominio de Rib del D r ★★★ 00 01 03 Temp-based (only 450 cases). Winemaker/owner: Peter Sisseck. Spain's answer to *garage* wines of B'x. Absurdly expensive and hardly ever seen, but also makes more reasonably priced Flor de Pingus.

Piqueras, Bodegas Almansa r (w dr p) ★★→★★★ 00 01 02 03 04 Family BODEGA. Some of La MANCHA's best: Castillo de Almansa CRIANZA, Marius GRAN RES. Chewy, smoky, old-fashioned wines, but with fruit.

Pirineos, Bodega Som w p r ★★→★★★ 99 00 01 02 03 04 Former co-op and SOMONTANO pioneer. Gd Gewurz and excellent red Marboré (**01**).

Plá i Llevant de Mallorca r w dr ★→★★★ 99 00 01 03 Up-and-coming new DO in MALLORCA and home to some of its most innovative wineries – Pere Seda, Jaime Mesquida, Miquel Oliver.

Plastic stoppers Increasingly rammed into bottles of less expensive wine and sometimes impossible to remove. If necessary, claim from the supplier for replacement, broken corkscrews, sprained wrist, heart attack, etc.

Príncipe de Viana, Bodegas Nav r w p ★★ Large firm (formerly Cenalsa), blending and maturing co-op wines – as well as utilizing its own 400 ha – and shipping a range from NAVARRA, under Pleno label but also inc flowery, new-style white and fruity red Agramont. Expect another level of quality to appear soon.

Priorato/Priorat Pri br r ★★★ 93 94 95 96 98 99 00 01 03 DO enclave of TARRAGONA, traditionally known for alcoholic RANCIO and huge-bodied, almost black red. At its brambly best, one of Spain's triumphs. COSTERS DE SIURANA, MAS MARTINET, and CLOS MOGADOR rightly rank among Spain's stars. DOCA since 02 vintage. Clos Daphne imposs to find but v.gd. Clos l'Obac makes delicious sweet red Dolç, but standard red not so exciting.

Raïmat Cos del S r w p sp ★★→★★★ 94 95 96 00 **02 03 04** Clean, structured wines from DO nr Lérida, planted by CODORNÍU with Cab Sauv, Chard, other international vines. Gd 100% Chard CAVA. Value.

Raventós i Blanc Pen w sp ★★→★★★ Excellent CAVA aimed at top of market. Also fresh El Preludi white and 100% Chard.

Remelluri, La Granja R Ala w d r r res ★★★ 99 01 02 Small estate making v.gd traditional red RIOJAS all from its own mountainous 105 ha of native grapes. Top wine Colección (01).

Reserva Gd-quality wine matured for long periods. Red *reservas* must spend at least 1 yr in cask and 2 in bottle; *gran reservas*, 2 yrs in cask and 3 in bottle. Thereafter, many continue to mature for years.

Rías Baixas W ★★→★★★ DYA NW DO embracing sub-zones Val do Salnés, O Rosal, and Condado do Tea, now for some of the best (and priciest) cold-fermented Spanish whites, mainly from ALBARIÑO grapes.

Ribera del Duero Rib del D 91 94 95 96 98 99 00 01 02 03 04 Fashionable, fast-expanding DO E of Valladolid (the Duero becomes the Portuguese Douro). Excellent for Tinto Fino (Temp) reds. Many excellent wines, but high prices. See ALIÓN, PAGO DE CARRAOVEJAS, PÉREZ PASCUAS HERMANOS, PESQUERA, TORREMILANOS, VEGA SICILIA. Also non-DO MAURO. An invasion of new people has not necessarily brought exciting new wines.

Rioja r p w sp ★★→★★★★ 64 70 75 78 81 82 85 89 91 92 94 95 96 98 99 00 01 02 03 04 N upland region along River Ebro for many of Spain's best red table wines in scores of BODEGAS *de exportación*. Temp predominates. Sub-divided into the following three areas:

Rioja Alavesa N of the R Ebro, produces fine red wines, mostly light in body and colour, but particularly aromatic.

Rioja Alta S of the R Ebro and W of Logroño, grows most of the finest, best-balanced red and white wines; also some rosé.

Rioja Baja Stretching E from Logroño, makes stouter red wines, often from Garnacha and high in alcohol, and often used for blending.

> **Vinos de Alta Expresión**
>
> These select and very pricey wines found a market in Spain because of rising Spanish prosperity and the reluctance of Spaniards to buy non-Spanish wines. They are marked by dark, brooding fruit and an extremely lavish use of new oak. Some of the boutique wineries from which they originate border on exercises in vanity and the domestic market is now aproaching saturation point which may not be such a bad thing. From RIOJA: Cáceres Gaudium; MARQUÉS DE RISCAL Barón de Chirel; Remírez de Ganuza; RODA Cirsión; MUGA Torre Muga. From CONCA DE BARBERÀ: TORRES Grans Muralles. From PRIORATO: CLOS MOGADOR res; ÁLVARO PALACIO FINCA Dolfi. From RIBERA DEL DUERO: VEGA SICILIA Único. From NAVARRA: GUELBENZU Lautus. From SOMONTANO: Blecua. Expect to pay.

Rioja Alta, Bodegas La R Alt r w (p) dr (sw) res ★★★ 89 90 94 95 96 98 99 00 Excellent traditional RIOJAS made with no concessions to modernity, esp red RES VIÑA Alberdi, velvety Ardanza RES, lighter Arana RES, RES 904, and marvellous RES 890 (**89**). Still unbelievably oaky, though Arana is a bit more modern.

Riojanas, Bodegas R Alt r (w p) res ★★→★★★ 94 95 96 98 00 01 Ultra-traditional BODEGA now introducing fruity new-style wines such as Gran Albina (01) and Monte Real Crianza (**04**). Increasingly reliable.

Roda, Bodegas R Alt r ★★★★ 95 96 00 01 03 Founded in 1989 by a Catalan couple who decided that only in HARO could they make their dream wines.

Not as new wave as is often thought. Superb costly Roda I (which has the edge) and Roda II. Cirsión (03).

Rosado Rosé.

Rovellats Pen w p sp ★★→★★★ Small family firm making only gd (and expensive) CAVAS, stocked in some of Spain's best restaurants.

Rueda br w ★★→★★★ 96 97 98 99 03 04 Small, historic DO W of Valladolid. Traditional *flor*-growing, sherry-like wines up to 17% alcohol; now for fresh whites, esp MARQUÉS DE RISCAL. Badly affected by the 2005 drought, its image is also under threat from a massive influx of mercenary outsiders, seeking to exploit its success. The number of wineries has doubled and prices are rising. Barrel-fermented, bottle-aged Verdejo from Belondrade y Lurtón has a reputation as a curiosity.

Ruíz, Santiago Rías Baixas w ★★→★★★ DYA Small, prestigious company, owned by LAN: fresh, lemony ALBARIÑOS, not quite up to former standards.

Sandoval, Finca Manchuela ★★★ First vintage, 02, showed black, chargrilled fruit with lovely wild, minty character. Owned by Spanish wine writer Victor de la Serna.

San Sadurní de Noya Pen w sp ★★→★★★ Ugly town S of Barcelona, hollow with CAVA cellars. Standards can be very high, though the flavour (of Parellada and other grapes) is quite distinct from Champagne.

Seco Dry.

Segura Viudas, Cavas Pen w sp ★★→★★★ CAVA from SAN SADURNÍ (FREIXENET-owned). Buy the Brut Vintage, Galimany, or esp RES Heredad.

Solagüen, Bodega R Ala r p w dr ★→★★★ 98 99 01 03 Old-established and first-rate RIOJA co-op. Young, juicy Montebuna, gd Solagüen CRIANZAS and RES, an+d top Manuel Qintano RES (01).

Solís, Félix w dr p r ★★ 95 99 02 04 BODEGA in VALDEPEÑAS making sturdy, oak-aged reds, VIÑA Albali RES, and fresh white. RIOJA style for less money.

Somontano Som ★★→★★★ 94 95 96 98 99 00 01 02 03 04 Fashionable DO in Pyrenean foothills. Given the cool conditions, future could lie with whites and Pinot N. Reds tend not to ripen, so get over-extracted and over-oaked. Best-known BODEGAS: old French-established Lalanne BODEGA PIRINEOS, VIÑAS DEL VERO and Viñedos y Crianzas del Alto Aragón (excellent ENATE range). Also superb red Blecua (02). Monclus somewhat eccentric, sporadically good.

Telmo Rodríguez, Compañía de Vinos r w ★★→★★★ HQ in Logroño, controlled by gifted oenologist Telmo Rodríguez, formerly of REMELLURI. Excellent DO wines in TORO, RUEDA (Basa), NAVARRA (Baso), ALICANTE. His Molina Real 100% Moscatel from MÁLAGA is exceptional.

Tenerife r w ★→★★ DYA Now five DOS, mostly for political reasons; sometimes more than merely drinkable young wines. Best BODEGAS: Flores, Monje, Insulares (VIÑA Norte label). Mostly sold locally, for hefty prices.

Tinto Red.

Toro r ★★★ 94' 95 98 99 00 01 02 03 04 Increasingly fashionable DO 240 km (150 miles) NW of Madrid. VEGA SICILIA's Pintia (01/02) and MAURO'S San Román (02) show what can be done; however, wines such as this are few and far between. In the main, some very clumsy, alcoholic Temp holds sway, from a flat plateau that is either v. hot or v. cold, which can make subtlety difficult.

Torremilanos Rib del D r (p) res ★→★★★ 01 02 03 Label of BODEGAS Peñalba López, old-established family firm with extensive v'yds and a hotel for visitors nr Aranda de Duero. Quite old-fashioned wines.

Torres, Miguel Pen r w p dr s/sw res ★★→★★★★ 95 96 97 98 99 00 02 03 World-famous family firm making a huge range, all gd and some outstanding Beyond the PENEDÈS it now has vineyards in CONCA DE BARBERA, PRIORATO, RIBERA

DEL DUERO, JUMILLA, and Lérida, as well as foreign outposts in the US, Chile, and China. White wines include Viña Sol (04/05), Gran Viña Sol Parellada (04/05), Waltraud Ries (04/05), premium Fransola Sauv Blanc (04/05), and barrel-fermented Chard (03/04) Milmanda. Reds are Sangre de Toro, Gran Sangre de Toro (01/02), Gran Coronas, award-winning Mas la Plana Cab Sauv RESERVAS (96 99 00 03), soft Atrium Merlot (04), Magdala and Mas Borras Pinot N (03/04). Of the newer wines, the young Nerola, with DO Cataluña, is an innovative blend of Mediterranean grapes; Bellaterra is made from fruit grown in PRIORATO; the superb Grans Muralles (01) contains some of the reintroduced native Garot, and finally there is a magnificent and vastly expensive Res Viña Real (00). See also Jean LÉON.

Utiel-Requena U-R r p (w) ★→★★ 96 98 00 01 02 03 04 Region W of VALENCIA, and a satellite of it. Can be interesting, but is finding it hard to establish its own reputation. Sturdy reds, often made of Bobal, popular for blending; also light, fragrant rosé.

Valbuena Rib del D r ★★★★ 89 90 91 92 95' 97 99 00 01 Made with the same grapes as VEGA SICILIA but sold when 5 yrs old. Best at about 10 yrs; ome prefer it to its elder brother, but see ALIÓN.

Valdeorras Galicia r w ★→★★★ 99 00 03 04 DO E of Orense. Fresh, dry wines; at best, Godellos rated among top white wines in Spain. See GUITÁN GODELLO.

Valdepeñas La M r (w) ★→★★ 95 96 98 99 00 01 02 03 04 Demarcated region nr Andalucían border. Mainly reds, high in alcohol but surprisingly soft in flavour when made from strawberryish Cencibel grape, the local Temp. Best wines (e.g. LOS LLANOS, FÉLIX SOLÍS, CASA DE LA VIÑA) now oak-matured.

Valduero, Bodegas Rib del D (w p) ★★→★★★ 90 96 98 01 Now more than 10 yrs old; growing reputation for well-made wine and v.gd-value RES though now much pricier than they used to be, and also more traditional: Rib del D's main market is inside Spain.

Valencia r w ★ 98 99 00 01 03 04 Demarcated region exporting vast quantities of clean and drinkable table wine; also refreshing whites, esp Moscatel. Small, emerging producers inc Celler del Roure, Los Frailes.

Vega Sicilia Rib del D r res ★★★★ 53 60 62 64 66 68 70 73 75 76 80 81 82 83 85 86 89 90 91 94 95 (See "Old vintages" box p.166). Most prestigious and costliest of Spanish wines, matured very slowly in oak and best at 12–15 yrs. Wines are deep in colour, with aromatic cedarwood nose, intense and complex in flavour, finishing long. See also VALBUENA, ALION, Pintia in TORO, and Oremus Tokaji (Hungary).

Vendimia Vintage.

Viña Literally, a v'yd. But wines such as Tondonia (LÓPEZ DE HEREDIA) are not necessarily made only with grapes from the v'yd named.

Viñas del Vero Som w p r res ★★→★★★ 01 02 03 04 SOMONTANO estate. Gd varietal wines: Chard, Ries, Gewurz. Best red: Secastilla (03).

Vinícola de Castilla La M r p w ★★ 98 99 00 02 03 04 One of the largest La MANCHA firms. Red and white Castillo de Alhambra are palatable. Top are Cab Sauv, Cencibel (Temp), Señorío de Guadianeja GRAN RESERVAS.

Vinícola Navarra Nav r p w dr res ★★ 97 99 00 03 04 Old-established firm, now part of BODEGAS Y BEBIDAS, but still thoroughly traditional. Best wines Castillo de Javier rosé (04), Las Campañas RES (97).

Vino común/corriente Ordinary wine.

Vino de la Tierra (VdT) Table wine of superior quality made in a demarcated region without DO.

Ysios, Bodega R Ala r res ★★→★★★ 01 Best known for its wavy modern roof-line, the BODEGA, owned by BODEGAS Y BEBIDAS, makes easy-drinking wines that have shown marked improvement in recent vintages.

Portugal

Recent vintages

2005 An extraordinarily dry summer, esp in S, produced unbalanced wines.
2004 A cool, wet summer but a glorious Sept and Oct. Well-balanced reds.
2003 Hot summer produced soft, ripe, early-maturing wines, especially in the
   South. Best Bairrada for a decade.
2002 Challenging vintage with heavy rain during picking. Better in the South.
2001 Large vintage throughout. Those producers who undertook careful
   selection made very good wines.
2000 Small harvest in fine weather led to ripe-flavoured wines from all regions.

Adega A cellar or winery.
Alenquer Est r w ★★ →★★★ 05, 04, 03' **02 01** Sheltered DOC making gd reds
   just north of Lisbon. Gd estate wines from PANCAS and MONTE D'OIRO (Syrah).
Alentejo r (w) ★ →★★★ 00' 01 02 03 04' 05 Vast tract of S Portugal. Most
   vineyards concentrated around Reguengos, Borba, and Vidigueira. Portugal's
   "New World", making v.gd, ripe-flavoured reds. Estate wines from CARMO (part
   Rothschild-owned), CARTUXA, CORTES DE CIMA, Herdade de MOUCHÃO, João RAMOS,
   José de SOUSA, and ESPORÃO have potency and style. Best co-ops are at BORBA,
   REDONDO, and REGUENGOS. Now classified as a DOC in its own right with BORBA,
   REDONDO, REGUENGOS, PORTALEGRE, Evora, Granja-Amarejela, Vidigueira, and Moura
   entitled to their own sub-appellations. Also VINHO REGIONAL Alentejano.
Algarve r w ★ →★★ Wines from holiday coast are covered by DOCS Lagos, Tavira,
   Lagoa, and Portimão. Nothing special, but Cliff Richard has a v'yd nr Albufeira.
Aliança, Caves Bair r w sp res ★★ →★★★ Large BAIRRADA-based firm making gd
   reds and classic-method sp. Also interests in ALENTEJO, DÃO, and the DOURO.
Alorna, Quinta de Ribatejo r w →★★ DYA Enterprising estate with a range of
   gd varietals: CASTELÃO, TRINCADEIRA, and Cab Sauv.
Altano Douro DYA Gd new r from Symington family (Dow's port). Look out for RES.
Alvarinho White grape in extreme N of Portugal and increasingly elsewhere
   making fragrant, attractive w. Known as ALBARIÑO in neighbouring Galicia.
Ameal, Quinta do w ★★★ DYA One of best VINHOS VERDES available. 100% LOUREIRO.
Aragonez Successful red grape in ALENTEJO for varietal wines. See TINTA RORIZ.
Arinto White grape. Best from central and S Portugal, where it retains acidity
   and produces fragrant, crisp, dry, white wines.
Arruda r w ★ DOC in ESTREMADURA with large co-op.
Aveleda, Quinta da w →★★ DYA Reliable VINHO VERDE made on the Aveleda
   estate of the Guedes family. There are also gd varietal wines from LOUREIRO,
   ALVARINHO, and Trajadura. Reds: Charamba (DOURO).
Azevedo, Quinta do w ★★ DYA Superior VINHO VERDE from SOGRAPE. 100%
   LOUREIRO grapes.
Bacalhoa, Quinta da Set r res ★★★ 00 01 02 Estate nr SETÚBAL. Its fruity,
   reliable, mid-weight Cab Sauv/Merlot blend is made by BACALHOA VINHOS.
   Palaçio de Bacalhoa has more Merlot in the blend.
Bacalhoa Vinhos JP Vinhos (formerly the producer of João Pires Dry Muscat) has
   been renamed after its leading estate, Quinta de Bacalhoa. Wide range of well-
   made reds inc BACALHOA, inexpensive JP, Serra de Azeitão, TINTO DA ANFORA, Só
   (varietal Syrah), JP GARRAFEIRA. Also Cova da Ursa Chard, SETÚBAL dessert wine.
Bairrada Bair r w sp ★ →★★★ 90' 94 97' 98 99 00 01 03' 04 05' DOC in central

Portugal for solid (astringent) reds from the challenging Baga grape. Best wines: CASA DE SAIMA, LUÍS PATO, and Caves SÃO JOÃO will keep for yrs. Most white used by local sparkling-wine industry.

Barca Velha Douro r res ★★★★ 52 54 58 64 65 66' 78 81 82 85 91' 95' Portugal's most famous red, made in v. limited quantities in the high Douro by port firm of FERREIRA (now owned by SOGRAPE). Powerful, resonant wine with deep bouquet, but facing increasing competition from other Douro reds. Second wine known as Reserva Ferreirinha.

Beiras ★→★★ VINHO REGIONAL covering DÃO, BAIRRADA, and granite mountain ranges of central Portugal.

Beira Interior ★ Large, isolated DOC nr Spain's bdr. Huge potential from old v'yds.

Boavista, Quinta da Est ★★ DYA Large property nr ALENQUER with pioneering José Neiva at helm making gd-value range of red and white: Palha Canas, Quinta das Sete Encostas, Espiga, and a Chard, Casa Santos Lima.

Borba Alen r ★→★★ Small DOC; also well-managed co-op making fruity reds.

Branco White.

Brejoeira, Palácio de w ★★ DYA Best-known ALVARINHO from Portugal; facing increasingly stiff competition from VINHO VERDE estates around Moncão.

Bright Brothers ★★ DYA Australian flying winemaker based in Portugal: interests as far-flung as Argentina, Sicily, and Spain. Range of well-made wines from DOURO, RIBATEJO, ESTREMADURA, and BEIRAS. See also FIUZA BRIGHT.

Buçaco Beiras r w (p) res ★★★★ (r) 53 59 62 63 70 78 82 85 89 92 Legendary speciality of the Palace Hotel at Buçaco, N of Coimbra, not seen elsewhere. An experience worth the journey.

Bucelas Est w ★★ DYA Tiny demarcated region N of Lisbon with three main producers. Quinta da Romeira makes attractive wines from the ARINTO grape.

Cabriz, Quinta de ★★→★★★ 03 04 Large, successful venture in S DÃO. Gd, well-priced reds. Also has wine interests in Brazil.

Cadaval, Casa Ribatejo r w ★★ 00 01' 02 03 Gd varietal reds esp TRINCADEIRA. Also Pinot N, Cab Sauv, and Merlot. Stunning new r res, Marquês de Cadaval.

Campolargo r w Bair 03 04 Large, quirky estate making gd reds from local Baga, Cab Sauv, and Pinot N.

Carcavelos Est br sw ★★★ NV. Minute DOC W of Lisbon. Rare, sweet apéritif or dessert wines average 19% alcohol and resemble honeyed MADEIRA.

Carmo, Quinta do Alen r w res ★★ 99 00' 01 Beautiful, small ALENTEJO ADEGA, partly bought in 1992 by Rothschilds (Lafite). 50 ha, plus cork forests. Fresh white; red better. Second wine: Dom Martinho.

Cartuxa, Herdade de Alen ★★→★★★ r 00 01 03 04 w DYA 200-ha estate nr Evora, rather disappointing in recent vintages. Pera Manca (**94 95 97 98**) big but pricey red. Also Foral de Evora, Cerca Nova, EA.

Carvalhais, Quinta dos Dão ★★★ r 99 00 01 03 04 05 w DYA Excellent single-estate SOGRAPE wine. Gd red varietals (TOURIGA NACIONAL, Alfrochiero Preto) and white Encruzado.

Casal Branco, Quinta de Ribatejo r w ★★ Large family estate making gd red and white wines. Best red: Falcoaria (**00 01 03**).

Casal García w ★★ DYA Big-selling VINHO VERDE, made at AVELEDA.

Casal Mendes w ★ DYA The VINHO VERDE from Caves ALIANÇA.

Castelão A grape planted throughout S Portugal, particularly in TERRAS DO SADO. Nicknamed PERIQUITA. Makes firm-flavoured, raspberryish reds that take on a tar-like quality with age. Also known as João de Santarem.

Chocapalha Quinta de Est r 03 04 w DYA V. gd estate N of Lisbon. Rich-flavoured reds from TOURIGA NACIONAL, TINTA RORIZ, Alicante Bouschet, and Cab Sauv.

Chryseia Douro r ★★★→★★★★ 01' 03' Bruno Prats from B'x has come together with the Symington family to produce a dense yet elegant wine from port grapes. A star in the making. Second wine Post Scriptum (02).

Churchill Estates Douro r **02 03** Gd reds from port shipper Churchill. Single-estate red from Quinta da Gricha.

Colares r ★★ Small DOC on the sandy coast W of Lisbon. Its antique-style, dark-red wines, rigid with tannin, are from ungrafted vines. Undergoing a minor revival in fortune. One to watch.

Consumo (vinho) Ordinary (wine).

Cortes de Cima Alen r ★★★ **01 02 03 04** Estate nr Vidigueira owned by Danish family. Gd reds from ARAGONEZ (Temp), TRINCADEIRA, and PERIQUITA grapes. Chaminé: second label. Also good Syrah bottled under Incognito label.

Côtto, Quinta do Douro r w res ★★→★★★ r **99 00 01** 03 w DYA Pioneer of unfortified wines from port country; v.gd red Grande Escolha (**95 00 01** 03).

Crasto, Quinta do Douro r dr sw ★★→★★★★ **99 00 01 02 03'** Top estate for excellent oak-aged reds. Excellent varietal wines (TOURIGA NACIONAL, TINTA RORIZ) and res. Vinha do Ponte and María Theresa (**98 00' 03'**) are outstanding wines from low-yielding plots of old vines. Also Port.

Dão r w res ★★→★★★ **00' 01 02 03'** 04 Established DOC region round town of Viseu in central Portugal. It has improved, but needs to improve a lot more. SOGRAPE, ALIANÇA, and single QUINTAS making headway: solid reds of some subtlety with age; substantial, dry whites. See ROQUES, MAIAS, TERRAS ALTAS, GRÃO VASCO, DUQUE DE VISEU.

DFJ Vinhos r w ★→★★ DYA Successful partnership making well-priced wines, mainly in RIBATEJO and ESTRAMADURA. Look out for these labels: Ramada (r w), Segada (r w), Manta Preta (r), and Grand'Arte (r w).

DOC, Denominação de Origem Controlada Demarcated wine region controlled by a Regional Commission. See also IPR, VINHO REGIONAL.

Doce (vinho) Sweet (wine).

Douro r w ★★→★★★★ **95 97 00' 01** 02 **03' 04'** N river valley producing port and some of Portugal's most exciting red wines. Look for BARCA VELHA, CHRYSEIA, CRASTO, and wines from NIEPOORT (see Port chapter).

Duas Quintas Douro ★★★ r **00 01** 02 03' w DYA Gd red from port shipper Ramos Pinto. V.gd res and outstanding but expensive Reserva Especial.

Duque de Viseu Dão ★★ r **02 03 04** w DYA V.gd, inexpensive r DÃO from SOGRAPE.

Esporão, Herdade do Alen w DYA r ★★→★★★ **00 01 02 03 04** Impressive estate owned by Finagra. Wines made by Aussie David Baverstock. Main brand: Monte Velho, v.gd oaked whites and rich, ripe reds under the Esporão label, esp GARRAFEIRA. Also Vinha da Defesa, Quatro Castas. Gd varietals: ARAGONEZ, TRINCADEIRA, TOURIGA NACIONAL, Alicante Bouschet, Syrah.

Espumante Sparkling.

Esteva Douro r ★ DYA Very drinkable DOURO red from port firm FERREIRA.

Estremadura ★→★★★ VINHO REGIONAL on W coast. Large co-ops. Alta Mesa, Ramada, Portada: gd, inexpensive wines from local estates and co-ops. IPRS: Encostas d'Aire. DOCS: ALENQUER, ARRUDA, Obidos, TORRES VEDRAS.

Fernão Pires White grape making ripe-flavoured, slightly spicy whites in RIBATEJO. (Known as María Gomes in BAIRRADA.)

Ferreira Douro r ★→★★★★ Port shipper making a range of gd to v.gd red DOURO wines: Esteva, Vinha Grande, Callabriga, Quinta de Leda, Reserva Ferreirinha, and BARCA VELHA.

Fiuza Bright Ribatejo r w ★★ DYA Joint venture between Peter Bright (BRIGHT BROTHERS) and the Fiuza family. Gd inexpensive Chard, Merlot, Cab Sauv. And Portuguese varietals.

Fonseca, José María da Est r w dr sw sp res ★★→★★★ Venerable firm in Azeitão nr Lisbon. Huge range of wines inc brands Periquita, Pasmados, Quinta de Camerate, Garrafeiras, and the famous dessert SETÚBAL (Alambre). Impressive range of reds from new winery opened in 2001: Septimus, Vinya, Primum, and the Domingos Soares Franco Selecção Privado. Top of range: Optimum and Hexagon. Also with interests in DÃO (TERRAS ALTAS), ALENTEJO (José de SOUSA and d'Avillez), DOURO (Domini). Also see LANCERS.

Gaivosa, Quinta de Douro r ★★★ 00 01 03 04 Leading estate nr Régua owned by enterprising Domingos Alves de Sousa. Deep, concentrated, cask-aged reds from port grapes. Other reds inc Quinta das Caldas and Vale Raposa.

Garrafeira Label term: merchant's "private reserve", aged for minimum of 2 yrs in cask and 1 in bottle, often much longer.

Gatão w ★ DYA Standard Borges & Irmão VINHO VERDE.

Gazela w ★★ DYA Reliable VINHO VERDE made at Barcelos by SOGRAPE.

Generoso Apéritif or dessert wine rich in alcohol.

Grão Vasco Dão r w ★★ DYA One of the best and largest brands of DÃO, from SOGRAPE's high-tech ADEGA at Viseu. Fine red GARRAFEIRA; fresh, young white.

IPR Indicação de Proveniência Regulamentada. Portugal's second tier of wine regions. See also DOC.

Lagoalva, Quinta da r w ★★ 01 02 03 Important RIBATEJO property making gd reds from local grapes and Syrah. Second label: Monte da Casta.

Lancers p w sp ★ Semi-sweet (semi-sparkling) Rosé, extensively shipped to the USA by José María da FONSECA. Also Lancers ESPUMANTE Brut, a decent sparkler made by a continuous process of Russian invention.

Lavadores de Feitoria Douro r Enterprising amalgam of a number of small quality-conscious estates. Principal labels: Merug, Três Bagos.

Loureiro Best VINHO VERDE grape variety after ALVARINHO: crisp, fragrant whites.

Madeira br dr sw ★★–★★★★★ Portugal's Atlantic island making famous fortified dessert and apéritif wines. Also making unfortified red and white wines for the local market.

Maias, Quinta das Dão ★★ 00 01 w DYA New-wave QUINTA: reds to age.

Malhadinha Nova, Herdade de Alen r 03' w DYA Newcomer cutting a dash with v.gd big reds in the deep south of the Alentejo.

Mateus Rosé Bair p (w) ★ World's best-selling, medium-dry, lightly carbonated rosé, from SOGRAPE. Now made at Anadia in BAIRRADA.

Messias r w ★–★★★★ Large BAIRRADA-based firm; interests in DOURO (inc port). Old-school reds best.

Minho River between N Portugal and Spain – lends its name to a VINHO REGIONAL.

Monte d'Oiro, Quinta do Est r ★★★–★★★★★ 01 03 Outstanding Rhône-style reds from Syrah with a touch of Viognier. Gd second wine: Vinha da Nora.

Mouchão, Herdade de Alen r res ★★★ 99 00 01 03 The best traditional Alentejo estate making big, powerful wines. Top wine Tonel 3–4. Second wine Dom Rafael can be gd value but variable.

Mouro, Quinta do Alen r ★★★–★★★★★ 98 99 00 Fabulous old-style reds, mostly from traditional ALENTEJO grapes. Dry farmed, low yields, very concentrated.

Murganheira, Caves ★ Largest producer of ESPUMANTE. Now owns RAPOSEIRA.

Niepoort Douro r w ★★★–★★★★★ Family port shipper making even better DOURO wines. Redoma (r w p) 00 01 03; Batuta (r) 00 01' 03 Charme (r) 00 02. Reds age very well.

Palmela Terras do Sado r w ★–★★★★ Promising DOC, mostly on sandy soil but incorporating the limestone Serra da Arrabida. Reds from CASTELÃO can be long-lived. Best producers BACALHOA VINHOS and the Cooperativa de Pegões.

Pancas, Quinta das Est r w res ★★–★★★★ 00' 01 03 w DYA Go-ahead estate nr ALENQUER. Outstanding red Premium (00') and varietals from ARAGONEZ, Syrah, Cab Sauv, and CASTELÃO.

Pato, Luís Bair r sp ★★–★★★★ 95' 97 99 00 01' 03' Best-known estate of Bairrada but wines now classified as BEIRAS. Tremendous, single-v'yd reds

Vinha Pan and Vinha Barrosa, as well as João Pato and Quinta do Ribeirinho. Daughter Filipa making v.gd wines under Ensaios FP label.

Pegos Claros r **99 00 01** 03 Solid, traditionally made red from PALMELA area. Proof at last that PERIQUITA can make substantial wine.

Pellada, Quinta de See SAES.

Periquita The nickname for the CASTELÃO grape. Periquita is also a brand name for a successful red wine from José María da FONSECA (DYA). Robust, old-style red bottled under Periquita Classico label (**94 95**).

Pires, João w DYA Fragrant, off-dry, Muscat-based wine from BACALHOA VINHOS.

Planalto Douro w ★★ DYA Gd white wine from SOGRAPE.

Ponte de Lima, Cooperativa de r w ★ Maker of one of the best bone-dry red VINHOS VERDES, and first-rate dry and fruity white.

Portal, Quinta do Douro r w p ★→★★★ 00 01 03 04 Estate that once belonged to Sandeman now making increasingly gd red as well as ports.

Portalegre Alen r w ★→★★★ Small DOC with huge potential in the mountains of N ALENTEJO. Balanced reds from Monte de Penha and the go-ahead local co-op.

Quatro Ventos, Quinta dos r Douro **01 02 03** impressive red, esp res, from estate belonging to Caves ALIANÇA.

Quinta Estate (see under name, *e.g.* PORTAL, QUINTA DO).

Ramos, João Portugal Alen r w DYA Vila Santa and Marqués de Borba. Reservas (**01 03**) of the latter fetch a high price.

Raposeira Douro w sp ★★ Well-known fizz made by classic method at Lamego.

Real Companhia Velha ★★→★★★ r 00' 01' 02 03 w DYA One-time giant of the port trade; also produces increasingly gd range of DOURO wines: Evel (gd-value r and w) and more distinguished Evel Grande Escolha, Quinta dos Aciprestes, QUINTA de Cidro. Sweet Granjó from botrytis-affected Sem.

Redondo Alen r w ★ DOC in heart of ALENTEJO with well-managed co-op.

Reguengos Alen r (w) res ★→★★★ Important DOC nr Spanish border. Inc José de SOUSA and ESPORÃO estates, plus large co-op for gd reds.

Ribatejo Rib r w The second-largest wine-producing region in Portugal. Now promoted to DOC with a number of sub-regions Almeirim, CARTAXO, Coruche, Chamusca, Tomar, Santarem. Mid-weight reds, inc a number made from international grapes: Cab Sauv, Pinot N, Chard, and Sauv Bl. Also VINHO REGIONAL Ribatejano.

Roques, Quinta dos Dão r ★★→★★★ 00 01 03' 04 w DYA V.gd estate for big, solid, oaked reds. Varietal wines from TOURIGA NATIONAL, TINTA RORIZ, Tinta Cão, and Alfrocheiro Preto.

Roriz, Quinta de Douro r ★★★ 00' 02 03' One of the great QUINTAS of the DOURO, now making fine reds (and vintage port) with the Symingtons. Second wine: Prazo de Roriz.

Rosa, Quinta de la Douro r ★★→★★★ 00 01 02 03' Firm, oak-aged red from port v'yds. Res is esp worthwhile. Also red Dourosa. Amarela: lighter second wine.

Rosado Rosé.

Saes, Quinta de Dão r **00' 01** 02 03 Small mountain estate belonging to Álvaro Castro, making fine, polished reds. Pape is one of the best DÃO wines around. Quinta de Pellada is under the same ownership and also makes wines to a high standard.

Saima, Casa de Bair r (w DYA) ★★★ **99 00 01** 02 03' Small, traditional estate: big, long-lasting, tannic reds (esp GARRAFEIRAS **90' 91 95' 97' 01**) and some astounding whites.

Santar, Casa de Dão r ★★★ 00 01 02 03 Well-established estate now making welcome comeback. Reds much better than old-fashioned whites.

São Domingos, Comp dos Vinhos de Est See BOAVISTA.

São João, Caves Bair ★★→★★★ r **95 97 00 01** 03 w DYA Small, traditional firm for v.gd old-fashioned wines. Reds can age for decades. BAIRRADA: Frei João. DÃO: Porta dos Cavaleiros. Poço do Lobo: well-structured Cab Sauv.

Seco Dry.

Serradayres ★ DYA Everyday red enjoying something of a comeback, having been taken over by Caves Dom TEODÓSIO.

Setúbal Set br (r w) sw (dr) ★★★ Tiny demarcated region S of the River Tagus. Dessert wines made predominantly from the Moscatel (Muscat) grape. Two main producers: José Maria da FONSECA and BACALHOA VINHOS.

Sezim, Casa de w ★★ DYA Beautiful estate making v.gd VINHO VERDE.

Sogrape ★→★★★★ Largest wine concern in the country, making VINHO VERDE, DÃO, BAIRRADA, ALENTEJO, MATEUS ROSÉ, and now owners of FERREIRA, Sandeman port, and Offley port. See also BARCA VELHA.

Sousa, José de Alen r res ★★→★★★ 00 01 03 Small firm acquired by José María da FONSECA. The most sophisticated of the full-bodied wines from ALENTEJO (solid, foot-trodden GARRAFEIRAS [Mayor], although now slightly lighter in style), fermented in earthenware amphoras and aged in oak.

Teodósio, Caves Dom r w ★→★★ Large producer in the RIBATEJO now making a welcome comeback. Everyday wines under the SERRADAYRES label.

Terras Altas Dão r w res ★ DYA Brand of DÃO from José María da FONSECA.

Terras do Sado VINHO REGIONAL covering sandy plains around Sado Estuary.

Tinta Roriz Major port grape (alias Temp) making v.gd DOURO wines. Known as ARAGONEZ in ALENTEJO.

Tinto Red.

Tinto da Anfora Alen r ★★→★★★ 02 03 Reliable red from BACALHOA VINHOS. Heavyweight Grande Escolha. Lighter red Monte das Anforas.

Torres Vedras ★ Est r w DOC N of Lisbon, famous for Wellington's "lines". Major supplier of bulk wine.

Touriga Nacional Top red grape used for port and DOURO table wines; now increasingly elsewhere, esp DÃO, ALENTEJO, and ESTREMADURA.

Trás-os-Montes VINHO REGIONAL covering mountains of NE Portugal. Reds and whites from international grape varieties grown in the DOURO.

Trincadeira V.gd red grape in ALENTEJO for spicy varietal wines.

Tuella r w ★★ DYA Gd-value DOURO red from Cockburn (see Port chapter).

Vale Dona Maria, Quinta do ★★★ r 00 01 02 **03'** 04. Small, highly regarded QUINTA run by Cristiano van Zeller. Gd solid reds and value port.

Vale Meão, Quinta do Douro r ★★★★ **99 00 01'** 03 Once the source of legendary BARCA VELHA, now making great wine in its own right. Second wine: Meandro.

Vallado ★★ r **00' 01 02** 03' w DYA Family-owned DOURO estate; v.gd wines.

Ventozello, Quinta do Douro r **00 01** 03 Huge Spanish-owned property in the heart of the DOURO, making gd reds and port.

Verde Green (see VINHO VERDE).

Vidigueira Alen w r ★→★★★ DOC for traditionally made, unmatured whites and plummy reds from the hottest part of Portugal. Best producer: CORTES DE CIMA.

Vinho Regional Larger provincial wine region, with same status as French Vin de Pays. They are: ALGARVE, ALENTEJO, BEIRAS, ESTREMADURA, RIBATEJANO, MINHO, TRÁS-OS-MONTES, TERRAS DO SADO. See also DOC, IPR.

Vinho Verde w ★→★★★ r ★ DOC between River DOURO and N frontier, for "green wines" (w or r): made from grapes with high acidity and (originally) undergoing a secondary fermentation to leave them slightly sparkling. Today the fizz is usually just added carbon dioxide. Ready for drinking in spring after harvest.

Xisto Douro r 03 V.gd new red from joint venture between Quinta do CRASTO and Jean-Michel Cazes from B'x.

PORTUGAL

Sherry, Port, & Madeira

These are the three classic fortified wines of the world; and of the three, sherry is the best value. A really fine, extremely old oloroso will cost far, far less than its table-wine equivalent from Bordeaux, for example; and for the price of a halfway decent New World Chardonnay you can get a bottle of fino that will knock your socks off. But you should never buy compromise sherries, by which I mean sweetened supermarket amontillados: amontillado should be bone dry and scented with coffee and nuts, toast and dried figs. Sweetened fino (usually in the form of pale cream sherry) is the vinous equivalent of processed cheese, and a frightful fate should await the producers of such stuff.

Madeira, at its best, is equally uncompromising, but for real style and pungency you need one of at least 10 years old. Younger wines are mostly too soft to be interesting. But a bottle of really old madeira – and specialist retailers may have some of 50 or 100 years old or even more – is an incredible treat. Just the thing for a winter weekend for two when the rain is beating down outside.

Port is probably the most confusing of the three wines, with a large number of styles available. Quality is reasonably high across the board. 2001 and 2004 will be good years for single-quinta vintages; 2005 may be declared as a vintage by some houses. Both are considerably more expensive than they used to be, since the port producers have reacted to a smaller market by declaring smaller quantities of each vintage year and pricing it higher. The most attractive everyday buy is probably 10-year-old tawny – fresh, lively, and with some depth. If you want more nuts and fewer plums, try that Portuguese favourite, *colheita*.

Recent declared port vintages

2003 Hot dry summer. Powerfully ripe, concentrated wines, universally declared. Drink from 2015/2020.

2000 A very fine vintage, universally declared. Rich, well-balanced wines for the long-term. Drink from 2015.

1997 Fine, potentially long-lasting wines with tannic backbone. Most shippers declared. Drink 2012 onwards.

1994 Outstanding vintage with ripe, fleshy fruit disguising underlying structure at the outset. Universal declaration. Drink 2010–2030.

1992 Favoured by a few (especially Taylor and Fonseca) over 91. Richer, more concentrated, a better year than 91. Drink 2008–2025.

1991 Favoured by most shippers (especially Symingtons with Dow, Graham, and Warre) over 92; classic, firm but a little lean in style. Drink now–2020.

1987 Dense wines for drinking over the medium term, but only a handful of shippers declared. Drink now–2015.

1985 Universal declaration which looked good at the outset but has thrown up some disappointments in bottle. Now–2020 for the best wines.

1983 Powerful wines with sinewy tannins. Most shippers declared. Now–2020.

1982 Rather simple, early-maturing wines declared by a few shippers. Drink up.

1980 Lovely fruit-driven wines, perfect to drink now and over the next 15 years. Most shippers declared.

1977 Big, ripe wines declared by all the major shippers except Cockburn, Martinez, and Noval. Lovely now, but don't keep too long.

1975 Soft and early maturing. Drink up.

1970 Classic, tight-knit wines – the best just reaching their peak. Now–2020+.

1966 Wines combine power and elegance. The best rival 1963. Now–2020+.

1963 Classic vintage; some wines past their best, others will go on and on.

Almacenista Matured, unblended sherry aged by individuals who keep a few barrels and sell them to shippers. Often superb quality and value. See LUSTAU.

Alvaro Domecq ★★→★★★ Members of five branches of the DOMECQ sherry family purchased the SOLERAS of the Arandas – said to be the oldest bodega in JEREZ – thus re-establishing Domecq as an independent name in sherry. V.gd range of 1730 label wines. Best sherry vinegar to be found.

Alvear Largest producer of v.gd sherry-like apéritif and sweet wines in MONTILLA.

Andresen Independent port house making good COLHEITA.

Barbadillo, Antonio ★★→★★★ The largest SANLÚCAR firm with a wide range of MANZANILLAS and sherries, inc Muy Fina FINO, Solear MANZANILLA austere Principe AMONTILLADO, Obispo Garcon PALO CORTADO, Cuco dry OLOROSO, Eva Cream, and the excellent Reliquia line of AMONTILLADO, PALO CORTADO, OLOROSO seco, and PX. Also the largest producer of regional table wines with its Castillo de San Diego.

Barbeito Small, enterprising madeira firm managed by Ricardo de Freitas. Bottles delicious single-cask COLHEITAS.

Barros Almeida Large, family-owned port house with several brands (inc Feist, Feuerheerd, KOPKE): excellent 20-yr-old TAWNY and many COLHEITAS.

Barros e Sousa Tiny, family-owned madeira producer with old lodges in centre of Funchal. Extremely fine but now rare vintages, plus gd 10-yr-old wines.

Blandy The top name of the MADEIRA WINE COMPANY. Duke of Clarence Rich Madeira is the most famous wine. 10-yr-old RESERVES (VERDELHO, BUAL, MALMSEY, SERCIAL) are gd. Many glorious old vintages (*e.g.* MALMSEY 1978, SERCIAL 1962, BUAL 1954 and 1920), though mostly nowadays at auctions. New COLHEITAS from 95. 5-yr-old blend of BUAL and Malvasia called Alvada.

Borges, H M Family company; full range. V.gd 10-yr-olds and vintages: BUAL 77.

Bual (or Boal) One of the best grapes of Madeira, making a soft, smoky, sweet wine, usually lighter and not as rich as MALMSEY.

Burdon English-founded sherry bodega owned by Caballero. Puerto FINO, Don Luis AMONTILLADO, and raisiny Heavenly Cream are top lines.

Burmester Small port house now owned, along with CÁLEM, by a Galician bank. Fine, soft, sweet 20-yr-old TAWNY; also v.gd range of COLHEITAS.

Cálem Established port house sold by the family in 1998, now belonging (with BURMESTER) to a Galician bank. Velhotes is the main brand. Fine reputation for COLHEITAS (90) and v.gd vintage ports in 66' and 70'. Less gd since.

Churchill 82 85 91 94 97 00 03 Port shipper founded in 1981. V.gd traditional LBV. Quinta da Gricha is the single-QUINTA port (01). V.gd aged white port, too.

Cockburn Large multinational shipper, owned since 2005 by the US Fortune brands. No 1 in the UK market with Special Reserve. Vintage ports have been disappointing since the early 80s. Vintages: **63 67 70 75 83 91** 94 97 00. Gd single-QUINTA wines from Quinta dos Canais (01').

Colheita Vintage-dated port of a single yr, but aged at least seven winters in wood: in effect a vintage TAWNY. Bottling date shown on the label. Excellent examples: ANDRESEN, KOPKE, CÁLEM, NIEPOORT, Krohn, C da SILVA (Dalva). *Colheita* now also applies to a category of madeiras from a single yr.

Cossart Gordon Leading madeira shipper, founded 1745; with BLANDY, now one of the two top-quality labels of the MADEIRA WINE COMPANY. Wines slightly less rich than BLANDY's. Best known for the Good Company brand. Also 5-yr-old reserves, old vintages (1977 Terrantez, 1934 VERDELHO, 1908 BUAL).

Crasto, Quinta do Gd and improving single estate, esp LBV. Also makes v. modern table wines; see Portugal.

Croft One of the oldest firms, shipping VINTAGE PORT since 1678. Now part of the Fladgate Partnership alongside DELAFORCE. VINTAGE PORTS back on form since 03. Vintages: **63' 66 67 70 75 77 82 85** 91 94 00 03'. Lighter QUINTA da Roeda. Triple Crown and Distinction: most popular brands.

Sherry styles

Fino Along with MANZANILLA the lightest and finest of sherries. Completely dry, pale, delicate, but pungent. Should be drunk cool and fresh. Deteriorates rapidly once opened (always refrigerate and use half bottles if possible). *E.g.* GONZÁLEZ-BYASS Tío Pepe.

Manzanilla A pale, dry sherry with its own Denomination of Origin; often more delicate than a FINO and matured in the more maritime conditions of SANLÚCAR DE BARRAMEDA (as opposed to the other, more inland sherry towns of El Puerto de Santa Maria or JEREZ). Serving suggestions as with FINO. *E.g.* HIDALGO'S LA GITANA.

Amontillado A FINO in which the layer of FLOR has died, allowing the wine to oxidize and creating darker, more powerful characteristics. Naturally dry. *E.g.* VALDESPINO'S Tio Diego.

Oloroso Heavier, less brilliant than FINO when young, and not aged under FLOR, but matures to richness and pungency. Naturally dry, often sweetened with PEDRO XIMÉNEZ and sold as an oloroso dulce (sweet oloroso). *E.g.* DOMECQ Rio Viejo (dry), LUSTAU Old East India (sweet).

Palo Cortado A rare style somewhere between AMONTILLADO and OLOROSO. Dry, rich, complex – worth looking for. *E.g.* BARBADILLO Obispo Gascon.

Cream Sherry A blended sherry sweetened with grape must, PX, and/or Moscatel for consistent, inexpensive, medium-sweet style. Don't expect much character. *E.g.* HARVEY's Bristol Cream.

Pedro Ximénez (or PX) Grapily sweet, dark sherry from partly sun-dried PX grapes. Concentrated, unctuous, decadent, relatively inexpensive. The world's sweetest wine overall. *E.g.* REY FERNANDO DE CASTILLA's Antique.

Moscatel As with PX above, though it rarely reaches PX's level of concentration or richness. *E.g.* LUSTAU Centenary Selection Las Cruces.

Other styles Manzanilla Pasada: MANZANILLA aged longer than most, very complex and fascinating. Pale Cream: young, simple FINO sweetened with clarified grape must for dull, commercial appeal; *e.g.* CROFT.

Age-dated sherries The growers' consortium, Fedejerez, and sherry's governing body, the Consejo Regulador de Jerez, recently developed a sub-category of age-dated wines that applies only to AMONTILLADO, OLOROSO, PALO CORTADO, and PX styles. These are: 12-year-old; 15-year-old; VOS (Very Old Sherry/Vinum Optimum Signatum); VORS (Very Old Rare Sherry/Vinum Optimum Rare Signatum); and Añada (vintage). All the sherry in casks of the second and third categories must be an average of at least 20 and 30 yrs old, respectively, while sherry in casks of the final category must be of a specific vintage.

Croft Jerez Founded only in 1970 and recently bought by GONZÁLEZ-BYASS. One o' the most successful sherry firms. Best known for the sweet Croft Original Pale Cream and drier Croft Particular. Also Delicado FINO and first-rate PALO CORTADO.

Crusted Style of port favoured by the British houses, usually blended from several vintages. Bottled young and then aged so it throws a deposit, o "crust". Needs decanting like a VINTAGE PORT.

Delaforce Port shipper, part of the Fladgate Partnership. As sister-house CROFT VINTAGE PORTS are getting better. **63 66 70' 75 82 85** 92' 94 00 03 Single-QUINTA wines from Quinta da Corte. V.fine 20-yr-old TAWNY: Curious and Ancient.

Delgado, Zuleta ★★→★★★★ Old SANLÚCAR firm, best known for marvellous La Goya manzanilla pasada.

Dios Baco ★→★★★ New family-owned and run JEREZ bodega with good potential.

Domecq ★★→★★★★ Giant sherry bodega in JEREZ owned by the international conglomerate Beam Brands but still overseen by the supremely knowledgeable Beltran Domecq. Its La Ina FINO is excellent. Recently: a range of wonderful very old SOLERA sherries. Also in Rioja and Mexico.

Douro River that rises in Spain as the Duero and flows through port country, lending its name to the region and to a DOC for unfortified wines. The region divides in 3, with the best ports coming from Cima Corgo and Douro Superior.

Dow Brand name of port house Silva & Cosens. Celebrated its bicentenary in 1998. Belongs to Symington family alongside GRAHAM, WARRE, SMITH WOODHOUSE, GOULD CAMPBELL, QUARLES HARRIS, Quinta do VESÚVIO, and Quinta de RORIZ, but deliberately drier style than other shippers in group. V.gd range of ports, inc single-QUINTA Bomfim and Quinta da Senhora da Ribeira. **63 66 70 72 75 77 80 83 85** 91 94 97 00' 03. New v'yd: Quinta da Senhora da Ribeira 98 99 01.

Duff Gordon Sherry shipper best-known for El Cid AMONTILLADO. Gd FINO Feria; Niña Medium OLOROSO. OSBORNE-owned; name also second label for Osborne's ports.

Emilio Hildago ★★ →★★★★ Small JEREZ bodega making exquisite Privilegio 1860 PALO CORTADO and v.gd Santa Ana PX. FINO Panesa is gd value.

Ferreira Leading Portuguese-owned shipper belonging (along with OFFLEY and SANDEMAN) to Sogrape. Bestselling brand in Portugal. Fine 10- and 20-yr-old TAWNIES, Quinta do Porto and Duque de Bragança. Early-maturing vintages: **63 66 70 75 77 78 80 82 85 87** 91 94 95 97 00 03.

Flor Spanish word for "flower": refers to the layer of saccharomyces yeast that grows atop FINO/MANZANILLA sherry in barrel, keeping oxidation at bay and changing the wine's flavour, making it aromatic and pungent. When the *flor* dies, the wines are aged further without it, becoming AMONTILLADO.

Fonseca Guimaraens British-owned port shipper with a stellar reputation; belongs to the Fladgate Partnership. Delicious Bin 27 reserve RUBY is main brand. Robust, deeply coloured vintage wine, among very best. Vintages: Fonseca **63' 66' 70 75 77' 80 83 85'** 92 94' 97 00' 03'. Fonseca Guimaraens is the second label. Occasional single-QUINTA wine from Quinta do Panascal.

Forrester See OFFLEY.

Frasqueira The official name for madeira from a single year, bottled after at least 20 yrs in wood. Mostly referred to as "vintage".

Garvey ★→★★★ Famous old sherry shipper in JEREZ now owned by José María Ruiz Mateos. The finest wines are San Patricio FINO, Tio Guillermo AMONTILLADO, and Ochavico OLOROSO. Also the age-dated 1780 line.

González-Byass ★→★★★★ Large family bodega with the most famous and one of the best FINOS: Tío Pepe. Other brands inc La Concha AMONTILLADO, Elegante FINO, El Rocío MANZANILLA, 1847 sweet OLOROSO. Age-dated line inc del Duque AMONTILLADO, Matúsalem OLOROSO, Apóstoles PALO CORTADO and the ultra-rich Noe PX. Along with WILLIAMS & HUMBERT the only bodega offering old, vintage wines

Gould Campbell Port shipper belonging to the Symington family. Gd-value VINTAGE PORTS **70 77 80 83 85 91** 94 97 00.

Gracia Hermanos Mont-M Firm within the same group as PÉREZ BARQUERO and Compañia Vinícola del Sur making gd-quality MONTILLAS. Its labels inc María del Valle FINO, Montearruit AMONTILLADO, OLOROSO CREAM, and Dulce Viejo PX.

Graham One of the greatest names in port, belonging to the Symington family with v.gd range, esp Six Grapes RESERVE RUBY, LBV, excellent TAWNIES and some of the richest, sweetest VINTAGE PORTS **63 66 70 75 77 80 83' 85'** 91 94 97 00' 03' Owns Quinta dos Malvedos producing v.gd single-QUINTA vintage.

Gran Cruz The single biggest port brand, belonging to French drinks group Matiniquaise. Mostly light, inexpensive TAWNIES.

Guita, La ★→★★★ Esp fine pasada made by Pérez Marín in SANLÚCAR with huge presence in Spain. Also owns Gil Luque label for other sherries.

Gutiérrez Colosía ★★★ Family-owned and run former ALMACENISTA on the Guadalete river in El Puerto with a very consistent range. Underpriced old PALO CORTADO.

Hartley & Gibson See VALDESPINO.

Harvey's ★→★★★ Important sherry pillar, owned by Beam Brands, along with Domecq and brandy company Terry. World-famous shipper of Bristol Cream (medium-sweet) and Club AMONTILLADO.

Henriques, Justino The largest madeira shipper belonging, along with GRAN CRUZ ports, to Martiniquaise. Gd 10-yr-old and vintage – *e.g.* 1934 VERDELHO.

Henriques & Henriques Independent madeira shipper with wide range of well-structured, rich wines. Outstanding 15-yr-olds; extra-dry apéritif Monte Seco; very fine reserves and vintage, inc SERCIAL 1944, VERDELHO 1934, Terrantez, Malvasia, BUAL 1954. The joke says: "There are only two names in madeira..."

Herederos de Argüeso ★★→★★★ MANZANILLA specialist in SANLÚCAR with v.gd San Leon and Las Medallas bottlings; and the desirable VOS AMONTILLADO Viejo.

Hidalgo, La Gitana ★★★→★★★★ Old family sherry firm in SANLÚCAR overseen by the indefatigable Javier Hidalgo. Flagship is the excellent pale MANZANILLA La Gitana; also fine OLOROSO, lovely PALO CORTADOS, and mostly organically grown, single-v'yd Pastrana manzanilla pasada and AMONTILLADO.

Jerez de la Frontera Centre of sherry industry, between Cádiz and Seville. "Sherry" is a corruption of the name, pronounced "hereth". In French, Xérès.

Jordões, Casal dos One of few certified organic port producers – decent LBV.

Kopke The oldest port house, founded in 1638. Now belongs to BARROS ALMEIDA. Mostly early-maturing, fair-quality vintage wines, but some excellent (**70 74 75 77 78 79 80 82 83 85 87 89 91** 94 97 00 03), and excellent COLHEITAS.

Krohn Small port shipper; excellent COLHEITAS, some dating back to 1800s.

LBV (Late Bottled Vintage) Port from a single year kept in wood for twice as long as VINTAGE PORT (about 5 yrs); produced in much larger volumes, so lighter and ready to drink when bottled. Don't expect miracles. Usually no need to decant, though some LBVs are bottled unfiltered; these can age for 10 yrs or more (WARRE, SMITH WOODHOUSE, NIEPOORT, CHURCHILL, FERREIRA, NOVAL).

Leacock One of the oldest madeira shippers, now a label of the MADEIRA WINE COMPANY. Main brand is St John, popular in Scandinavia. Older vintages include 1950 SERCIAL, 1934 BUAL, and SOLERA 1860.

Lustau ★★→★★★★ Based in JEREZ and owned by the Caballero group. Wide variety of wines. Best known as a pioneer shipper of excellent ALMACENISTA and "landed age" wines; AMONTILLADOS and OLOROSOS aged in elegant bottles before shipping. First to commercialize a vintage sherry with its 1989 sweet OLOROSO.

Madeira Wine Company Formed in 1913 by two firms as the Madeira Wine Association, subsequently to inc all the British madeira firms (26 in total) amalgamated to survive hard times. Remarkably, three generations later, the wines, though cellared together, preserve their house styles. BLANDY and COSSART GORDON are top labels. Now controlled by the Symington group (see DOW), which runs it in partnership with the BLANDY family.

Malmsey The sweetest and richest form of madeira; dark amber, rich, and honeyed, yet with madeira's unique sharp tang. Word is English corruption of "Malvasia" (or the Greek "Monemvasia").

Martinez Gassiot Port firm, subsidiary of COCKBURN, known esp for excellent rich, and pungent Directors 20-yr-old TAWNY. Gd-value vintages: **63 67 70 75 82 85 87 91** 94 97 00 03. V.gd single-QUINTA wines from Quinta da Eira Velha.

Medina, José Originally a SANLÚCAR bodega, now a major exporter, esp to the Low Countries. Owns Bodegas Internacionales and WILLIAMS & HUMBERT, also Pérez Megia and Luis Paez: probably the biggest sherry grower and shipper.

Miles Madeira shipper, now part of the MADEIRA WINE COMPANY. Basic wines only.

Montecristo Mont-M Brand of big-selling MONTILLAS by Compañía Vinícola del Sur.

Montilla-Moriles Mont-M DO nr Córdoba. Not sherry, but close. Its soft FINO and AMONTILLADO, and luscious PX contain 14–17.5% natural alcohol and remain unfortified. At best, singularly toothsome apéritifs. PX sourced from Montilla but aged and bottled in sherry country so it may be called PX sherry.

Niepoort Small family-run port house with Dutch origins. Long record of fine vintages (63 66 70' **75 77 78 80 82 83** 87 91 92 94 97 00' 03). Second vintage label: Secundum. Exceptional TAWNIES and COLHEITAS.

Noval, Quinta do Historic port house now French (AXA) owned. Intensely fruity, structured, and elegant VINTAGE PORT; a few ungrafted vines at the QUINTA make small quantity of Nacional – extraordinarily dark, full, velvety, slow-maturing. Also v.gd 20-yr-old TAWNY. Vintages now back on form: **63 66 67 70 75 78 82 85** 87 91 94' 95 97' 00' 03'. Second vintage label: Silval. Also v.gd LBV.

Offley Brand name belonging to port shipper Forrester (now owned by SOGRAPE). Duke of Oporto is main brand and a big seller in Portugal. Baron de Forrester is gd TAWNY. Owns Quinta da Boa Vista. Gd but early-maturing vintages: **63 66 67 70 72 75 77 80 82 83 85** 87 89 94 95 97 00' 03.

Port and madeira selection for 2007

White port CHURCHILL.

Reserve Fonseca Bin 27, GRAHAM's Six Grapes, TAYLOR's First Estate, WARRE's Warrior.

Late Bottled Vintage Fonseca LBV 2000, GRAHAM's LBV 2000, Jose Maria da Fonseca & Van Zeller LBV 2000, TAYLOR's LBV 2000.

Tawny DELAFORCE Curious and Ancient, GRAHAM's The Tawny, GRAHAM's 20-Year-Old, NIEPOORT 20-Year-Old.

Single-quinta ports COCKBURN Quinta dos Canais 01, DOW's Quinta Senhora da Ribeira 01, Quinta do VESÚVIO 00, DOW's Quinta do Bomfim 96, Fonseca Quinta do Panascal 91 and 98, FONSECA GUIMARAENS 95, GRAHAM Malvedos 95 and 96, TAYLOR Quinta de Vargellas 92, 95, 98.

Vintage ports Fonseca 63, TAYLOR 63, Fonseca 66, GRAHAM 70, TAYLOR 70, SMITH WOODHOUSE 77, GRAHAM 80, GRAHAM 83, GRAHAM 85, TAYLOR 92, Quinta do NOVAL 94, Fonseca 94.

Madeiras BLANDY's Alvada, BARBEITO's Single Cask COLHEITAS and 20-yr-old MALMSEY, HENRIQUES & HENRIQUES 10-yr-old and 15-yr-old BUAL.

Osborne ★→★★★★ Huge Spanish firm producing sherry, a wide range of Spanish wines, and quality port. Has taken over Bobadilla sherries and brandies. Its instantly recognizable bull logo dots the Spanish countryside. Declared gd VINTAGE PORTS in 95 97 00'.

Paternina, Federico ★★→★★★★ Marcos Eguizabel from Rioja acquired the sherry firm Diez-Merito, retaining three VORS wines for his Paternina label, the excellent and unique FINO Imperial, OLOROSO, Victoria Regina, and PX Vieja SOLERA.

Pedro Romero ★→★★★ Recently expanded SANLÚCAR family operation in a rambling array of bodegas. Very wide range; frustratingly inconsistent.

Pereira d'Oliveira Vinhos Family-owned madeira company since 1850. Gd basic range; also fine old vintages back to 1850 labelled as Reserve.

Pérez Barquero Mont-M Another firm, like GRACIA HERMANOS, once part of Rumasa. Its excellent MONTILLAS inc Gran Barquero FINO, AMONTILLADO, and OLOROSO.

Pilar Plá/El Maestro Sierra ★→★★★★ Owned by JEREZ's grandest dame Pilar Plá. Wines inconsistent, but some great value at medium ages esp AMONTILLADO.

Poças Portuguese family port firm; TAWNIES and COLHEITAS. Gd LBV and v.gd recent vintages (97 00' 03). Single-QUINTA wines from Quinta Sta Barbera.

Puerto de Santa María The second city and former port of sherry, with important bodegas such as OSBORNE and former ALMACENISTA Gutierrez Colosia.

PX Pedro Ximénez grape, partly sun-dried, either bottled alone as top-class sweet wine, or used for sweetening other sherries.

Quarles Harris One of the oldest port houses, since 1680, now owned by the Symington family (see DOW). Mellow, well-balanced vintages, often v.gd value: **63 66 70 75 77 80 83 85** 91 94 97 00' 03.

Quinta Portuguese for "estate" traditionally denotes VINTAGE PORTS from shipper's single v'yds; declared in gd but not exceptional years. Several *quintas* make wines from top vintages in their own right, esp VESÚVIO, la ROSA, Passadouro.

Rainwater A fairly light, medium-dry blend of madeira – traditional in US.

Ramos Pinto Dynamic port house owned by Champagne house Louis Roederer. Outstanding single-QUINTA TAWNIES. Vintages tend to be rich, sweet but generally early maturing.

Régua Main town in Douro Valley, centre for port producers and growers.

Reserve/Reserva Premium-quality ports, mostly Reserve RUBY but some Reserve TAWNY, bottled without a vintage date or indication of age but better than the basic style, *e.g.* COCKBURN's Special Reserve, Fonseca Bin 27, TAYLOR's First Estate, WARRE's Warrior, GRAHAM's The Tawny.

Rey Fernando de Castilla ★★ →★★★★ JEREZ veteran Norwegian Jan Pettersen has made a small sherry revolution with his excellent wines, which, although he chooses not to label them Age-Dated, could easily be so. Top Antique line of AMONTILLADO, OLOROSO, and PX; FINOS less so.

Roriz, Quinta de Historic estate now controlled by the Symington family (see DOW). V.gd single-QUINTA DOURO wines and ports: 99 00' 01 02 03'.

Rosa, Quinta de la V.gd single-QUINTA port from the Bergqvist family at Pinhão. Recent return to traditional methods and stone *lagares*. Look for **94 95** 00 vintages and wines from a small plot of old vines called Vale do Inferno.

Royal Oporto The main port brand within Real Companhia Velha, now focusing on unfortified Douro wines. Some gd TAWNIES and recent vintages.

Rozès Port shipper owned by Champagne house Vranken alongside São Pedro das Aguias. Very popular in France.

Ruby Youngest (and cheapest) port style: simple, sweet, red. Best are vigorous, full of flavour; others merely strong, thin, spirity. See also RESERVE.

Sanchez Romate ★★ →★★★★ Family firm in JEREZ since 1781. Best known in Spanish-speaking world, esp for brandy Cardenal Mendoza. Gd sherry: OLOROSO La Sacristía de Romate, PX Duquesa, AMONTILLADO NPU ("Non Plus Ultra").

Sandeman ★ →★★★★ Large firm, now part of Sogrape group. Founded in 1790 by Scot George Sandeman, who set up twin establishments in Oporto and JEREZ. Scrupulously made sherries inc an aged Don FINO, and Armada CREAM. Also dry and sweet Imperial Corregidor and Royal Ambrosante OLOROSOS. Port: gd aged TAWNIES, esp 20-yr-old. Vintage patchy in recent years (63 66 70 75 77 80 82 85 94 97 00). Second label: Vau Vintage, recommended for drinking young.

Sanlúcar de Barrameda Historic seaside sherry town (see MANZANILLA, box p.180).

Santa Eufemia, Quinta de Family port estate with v.gd old TAWNIES.

Sercial Madeira grape for the driest of the island's wines – supreme apéritif.

Silva, C da Port shipper owned by Ruiz Mateos of GARVEY fame. Mostly inexpensive RUBIES and TAWNIES, but gd aged TAWNIES and outstanding COLHEITAS under Dalva label.

Smith Woodhouse Port firm founded in 1784, now owned by Symingtons (see DOW). Mostly a supplier of own-label but v.gd unfiltered LBV and some very fine vintages: **63 66 70 75 77'** 80 83 85 91 94 97 00' 03. Occasional single-estate wines from Quinta da Madelena.

Solera System used in ageing sherry. Consists of topping up progressively more mature barrels with slightly younger wine of same sort, the object being to attain continuity in final wine. Most sherries are blends of several *solera* wines. Used to be applied to madeiras. Although no longer used, there are many very fine old *solera* wines in bottle.

Tawny Style of port that implies ageing in wood (hence tawny in colour), though many basic tawnies are little more than attenuated RUBIES. Look for wines with an indication of age: 10-, 20-, 30-, or 40-yr-old or RESERVE.

Taylor, Fladgate & Yeatman (Taylor's) One of the best known port shippers, highly rated for its rich, long-lived VINTAGE PORTS. Now a member of the Fladgate Partnership alongside CROFT, DELAFORCE, and FONSECA GUIMARAENS. V.gd range inc RESERVE (First Estate), LBV and aged TAWNIES. Two prime estates, Quinta de Vargellas and Quinta de Terra Feita produce single-QUINTA vintage. Vintages: 63 66 70 75 77 80 83 85 92' 94 97 00' 03.

Terry, SA ★ →★★ Sherry bodega at PUERTO DE SANTA MARÍA; part of Beam Brands.

Tío Pepe The most famous of FINO sherries (see GONZÁLEZ-BYASS).

Toro Albalá, Bodegas Mont-M Family firm located in a 1920s power station and aptly making Eléctrico FINOS, AMONTILLADOS, and a PX that is among the best in MONTILLA and Spain.

Tradición ★★★ →★★★★ Part of the new wave of sherry bodegas focusing exclusively upon small quantities of VOS PX and VORS AMONTILLADO, PALO CORTADO, and OLOROSO, from a refurbished, art-filled cellar in back streets of JEREZ.

Valdespino ★ →★★★★ Famous JEREZ bodega producing Inocente FINO from the esteemed Macharnudo v'yd. Tío Diego is terrific dry AMONTILLADO; also SOLERA 1842 OLOROSO, Don Tomás AMONTILLADO. Matador is a popular range. In the US its sherries are sold as Hartley & Gibson.

Valdivia ★★ Newest producer of sherry. VOS-and-above levels in stylish bottles.

Vale D Maria, Quinta do Estate in the Torto Valley – gd value and beautifully aged VINTAGE PORT.

Ventozelo, Quinta de Huge, beautifully situated estate recently acquired by a Spanish family. Gd single-QUINTA VINTAGE PORTS.

Verdelho Madeira grape for medium-dry wines; pungent but without the searing austerity of SERCIAL. Pleasant apéritif and gd, all-purpose madeira. Some glorious old vintage wines.

Vesúvio, Quinta do Enormous 19th-C estate in the DOURO. Owned by Symington family independently of any of their port houses. Only vintage port, esp **91 92** 94 95' 00' 01 03'.

Vila Nova de Gaia City on the S side of the River DOURO from Oporto, where the major port shippers mature their wines in "lodges".

Vintage Port The best wines from an exceptional year, declared by an individual shipper between 1 Jan and 30 Sept in the second year after the harvest – *e.g.* 2003 declared in 2005. Bottled without filtration after 2 yrs in wood, the wine matures very slowly in bottle throwing a CRUST or deposit. Vintage port always needs decanting. Gd vintage port generally needs at least 15 yrs in bottle and may last for another 50. Single-QUINTA vintage ports are ready to drink earlier.

Warre Oldest of British port shippers (since 1670); owned by the Symington family (see DOW) since 1905. Fine, elegant, long-maturing vintage wines, gd RESERVE, vintage character (Warrior), excellent unfiltered LBV; 10- and 20-yr-old Otima TAWNY. Single-QUINTA vintage from Quinta da Cavadinha. Vintages: **63 66** 70' **75 77' 80 83 85** 91 94 97 00' 03.

White port Port made with white grapes, occasionally sweet (*lagrima*) but mostly off-dry and drunk as an apéritif. Look for wines with cask age: BARROS, NIEPOORT, CHURCHILL. Younger, paler wines can be drunk long with tonic.

Williams & Humbert ★★ →★★★★ Famous first-class sherry bodega, now owned by MEDINA group. Dry Sack (medium AMONTILLADO) is bestseller; Canasta CREAM and Walnut Brown are gd in their class; SOLERA Especial is its famous old PALO CORTADO. Occasional stupendous vintage sherry may be found at auction. Also famous Gran Duque de Alba brandy.

Switzerland

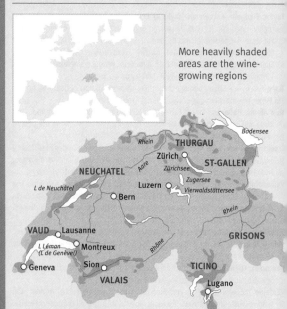

More heavily shaded
areas are the wine-
growing regions

Swiss wine has a difficult status. On the one hand, the Swiss love to drink foreign wines; on the other, foreigners know little about Swiss wine culture. Swiss wine is considered expensive – by the Swiss as well as by outsiders. This is only half true. You will not find very cheap, basic products (the high cost of living, combined with cost-intensive wine production generates a certain basic price), but high-quality wines never reach prices as high as in neighbouring France, Italy, or Germany. Top quality can be found at an average price of £12 to £15.

The invasion of New World wines provoked many wine-growers to increase their quality and focus on local specialities. More and more of the rather neutral Chasselas grape is being replaced with more attractive varieties such as Johannesberg, Sauvignon Blanc, Chardonnay, Cornalin, Syrah, or Pinot Noir. Also interesting is the increase in plantings of, for Switzerland, experimental grapes such as Malbec or Viognier. The most important vineyards are in French-speaking areas: along the south-facing slopes of the upper Rhône Valley (Valais) and Lake Geneva (Vaud, Geneva). Best Pinot Noirs come from the Grisons (Bündner Herrschaft) and best Merlots from the Ticino, the Italian-speaking zones in the south.

Recent vintages

2005 Low in quantity but high in quality.

2004 Less complex than 2003 but very promising.

2003 A style which is more elegant than full-bodied.

2002 Not the best year for everybody. Stick to the best producers.

2001 Low yields but characteristic, full-bodied wines with ageing potential.

Aargau 03 04 05 Eastern canton for fragrant Müller-THURGAU, rich BLAUBURGUNDER.

Aigle Vaud r w ★★→★★★ Well known for elegant whites and supple reds.

Amigne Traditional VALAIS white grape, esp of VÉTROZ. Full-bodied, tasty, often sweet. Best producer: André Fontannaz ★★ **03' 04** 05.

Arvine Old VALAIS white grape (also Petite Arvine): dry and sweet, elegant, long-lasting wines with a salty finish. Best in SIERRE, SION, Granges, FULLY. Producers: Benoît Dorsaz, Rouvinez, Marie-Thérèse Chappaz, Simon Maye & Fils.

Auvernier Neuchâtel r p w ★★→★★★ Old wine village on Lake NEUCHÂTEL and biggest wine-growing commune of the canton.

Basel Second-largest Swiss town and canton: divided into Basel-Stadt and Basel-Land. Best wines: Müller-THURGAU, PINOT N (104 ha).

Bern Swiss capital and canton. V'yds in W (BIELERSEE: CHASSELAS, PINOT N, white SPÉCIALITÉS) and E (Thunersee: BLAUBURGUNDER, Müller-THURGAU); 262 ha.

Bielersee r p w ★→★★ **03' 04** 05 Wine region on N shore of the Bielersee lake (dry, light CHASSELAS, PINOT N). Best producer: Domaine Grillette.

Blauburgunder German name for PINOT N; aka Clevner.

Bündner Herrschaft Grisons r p w ★★→★★★ Best German-Swiss region inc top villages: Fläsch, Jenins, Maienfeld, Malans. BLAUBURGUNDER ripens esp well due to warm Föhn wind, cask-aged v.gd. Also Chard, Müller-THURGAU, SPÉCIALITÉS. Best: Gantenbein ★★★, Davaz ★★, Fromm ★★★, Wegelin ★★ **01 02 03'** 04 05.

Chablais Vaud r w ★★→★★★ Sunny wine region on right bank of Rhône and upper end of Lake GENEVA, inc villages AIGLE, Bex, Ollon, VILLENEUVE, YVORNE. Robust, full-bodied reds and whites.

Chamoson Valais r w ★★→★★★ Largest VALAIS wine commune, esp for SYLVANER.

Chasselas (Gutedel in Germany) French cantons, white grape; neutral flavour, takes on local character: elegant (GENEVA); refined, full (VAUD); exotic, racy (VALAIS); pétillant (lakes Bienne, NEUCHÂTEL, Murtensee). Only E of BASEL. Called FENDANT in VALAIS. Accounts for almost a third of Swiss wines but increasingly replaced – a government-financed move. Best: Louis Bovard, Raymont Paccot.

Completer Native white grape, mostly used in GRISONS, making aromatic wines with high acidity. ("Complet" was a monk's final daily prayer, or "nightcap".) Related to the Valais grape Lafnetscha. Best: Adolf Boner, Malans ★★.

Cornalin ★★→★★★ **02 03'** 04 Local VALAIS speciality that has become more popular since production increased; dark, spicy, very strong red. Best: Denis Mercier, Provins, Jean-René Germanier (★★). Oldest living vine in Switzerland is a Cornalin plant in Leuk, Valais, from 1798 (www.vitisantiqua1798.ch).

Côte, La Vaud r p w ★→★★★ Largest VAUD wine area between LAUSANNE and GENEVA (N shore of lake). Whites with elegant finesse; fruity, harmonious reds. Esp from MONT-SUR-ROLLE, Vinzel, Luins, FÉCHY, MORGES, etc.

Côtes de l'Orbe Vaud r p w ★→★★ N VAUD appellation between Lake NEUCHÂTEL and Lake GENEVA esp for light, fruity reds.

Dézaley Vaud w (r) ★★→★★★ Celebrated LAVAUX v'yd on slopes above Lake GENEVA, once tended by Cistercian monks. Unusually potent CHASSELAS, develops esp after ageing. Red Dézaley is a GAMAY/PINOT N/MERLOT/Syrah rarity.

Dôle Valais r ★★→★★★ **03' 04** 05 Appellation for PINOT N, often blended with GAMAY and other reds from the VALAIS: full, supple, often v.gd. Lightly pink Dôle Blanche is pressed straight after harvest. Look for MARTIGNY, SIERRE, SION.

Epesses Vaud w (r) ★→★★★ **04 05'** LAVAUX AC: supple, full-bodied whites.

Ermitage Alias Marsanne; a VALAIS SPÉCIALITÉ. Concentrated, full-bodied dry white, sometimes with residual sugar. Best: Domaine Cornulus, Philippoz Frères.

Féchy Vaud ★→★★ Famous appellation of LA CÔTE, esp elegant whites.

Federweisser German-Swiss name for white wine from BLAUBURGUNDER.

Fendant Valais w ★→★★★ VALAIS appellation for CHASSELAS. Fuel of the ski slopes; not for wimps. Wide range of wines; best now use village names only.

Flétri/Mi-flétri Late-harvested grapes for sw/slightly sw wine (respectively).

Fribourg Smallest French-Swiss wine canton (115 ha, nr Jura). Esp for PINOT N, CHASSELAS, GAMAY, SPÉCIALITÉS from VULLY, Lake Murten, S Lake NEUCHÂTEL.

Fully Valais r w ★★→★★★ Village nr MARTIGNY: excellent ERMITAGE and GAMAY. Best producer: Marie-Thérèse Chappaz sw ★★→★★★ 01 02' 03' 04 05.

Gamay Beaujolais grape; abounds in French cantons. Mainly thin wine used in blends (SALVAGNIN, DÔLE). Gamay accounts for 14% of grapes in Switzerland.

Geneva Capital, and French-Swiss wine canton; third largest (1,425 ha). Key areas: Mandement, Entre Arve et Rhône, Entre Arve et Lac. Mostly CHASSELAS, GAMAY. Also Gamaret, Chard, PINOT N, Muscat, and gd Aligoté. Best: Jean-Michel Novelle ★★★; interesting: Jacques Tatasciere, Domaine de la Rochette ★★.

Germanier, Jean-René VÉTROZ winemaker; Cayas (100% Syrah) ★★★ 99 00' 01 02 03 04; Mitis (sweet) ★★★ 99 00 01' 02 03 04. New release: a pure Cornalin.

Gewurztraminer Grown in Switzerland as a SPÉCIALITÉ variety, esp in VALAIS. Best producer: Jean-Michel Novelle, Satigny 03' 04 05.

Glacier, Vin du (Gletscherwein) Fabled oxidized, wooded white from rare Rèze grape of Val d'Anniviers; offered by the thimbleful to visiting dignitaries.

Grand Cru Quality designation. Implication differs by canton: in VALAIS, GENEVA, and VAUD used where set requirements are fulfilled.

Grisons (Graubünden) Mountain canton, mainly in German Switzerland (BÜNDNER HERRSCHAFT, Churer Rheintal; esp BLAUBURGUNDER) and partly S of Alps (Misox, esp MERLOT). 416 ha, primarily red, also Müller-THURGAU and SPÉCIALITÉS.

Heida (Païen) Old VALAIS white grape (Jura's Savagnin) for country wine of upper Valais (VISPERTERMINEN v'yds at 1,000+ m). Gd in lower VALAIS, too. Best: Josef-Marie Chanton ★★ 00 01 02 03' 04 05. New release: a Heida from Provins.

Humagne Strong native white grape (VALAIS SPÉCIALITÉ). Humagne Rouge (unrelated, from Aosta Valley) also. Esp from CHAMOSON, LEYTRON, MARTIGNY.

Johannisberg Synonym for SYLVANER in the VALAIS.

Landwein (Vin de pays) Traditional light white and esp red BLAUBURGUNDER from E.

Lausanne Capital of VAUD. No longer with v'yds in town area, but long-time owner of classics: Abbaye de Mont, Château Rochefort (LA CÔTE); Clos des Moines, Clos des Abbayes, Domaine de Burignon (LAVAUX). Pricey.

Lavaux Vaud w (r) ★→★★★ DYA Scenic region on N shore of Lake GENEVA between Montreux and LAUSANNE. Delicate, refined whites, gd reds. Best: Calamin, Chardonne, DÉZALEY, EPESSES, Lutry, ST-SAPHORIN, VEVEY-MONTREUX, Villette.

Leytron Valais r w ★★→★★★ Commune nr SION/MARTIGNY, esp Le Grand Brûlé.

Malvoisie See PINOT GRIS.

Martigny Valais r w ★★ Lower VALAIS commune esp for HUMAGNE ROUGE and Syrah.

MDVS Mémoires des Vins Suisses – a collection of the most important Swiss wines; also older vintages, to protect the country's heritage (www.mdvs.ch).

Merlot Grown in TICINO since 1907 (after phylloxera destroyed native varieties): soft to very powerful wines. Also used with Cab Sauv. Best: Castello Luigi, Zanini.

Mont d'Or, Domaine du Valais w s/sw sw ★★→★★★ 03' 04 05 Well-sited property nr SION: rich, concentrated demi-sec and sw wines; notable SYLVANER.

Mont-sur-Rolle Vaud w (r) ★★ DYA Important appellation within LA CÔTE.

Morges Vaud r p w ★★ DYA Largest LA CÔTE/VAUD AOC: CHASSELAS, fruity reds.

Neuchâtel City and canton; 600 ha from Lake Neuchâtel to BIELERSEE. CHASSELAS: fragrant, lively (sur lie, sp). Gd OEIL DE PERDRIX, PINOT GR, Chard.

Nostrano Word meaning "ours", applied to red wine of TICINO, made from native and Italian grapes (Bondola, Freisa, Bonarda, etc).

Oeil de Perdrix Pale PINOT N rosé. DYA esp NEUCHÂTEL's; also VALAIS, VAUD.

Pinot Blanc Weissburgunder New variety producing full-bodied, elegant wines.

Pinot Gris Malvoisie Widely planted white grape for dry and residually sweet wines. Makes very fine late-harvest wines in VALAIS (called Malvoisie).

Pinot Noir Blauburgunder Top red grape (33% of v'yds). Esp BÜNDNER HERRSCHAFT, NEUCHÂTEL, THURGAU, VALAIS, ZÜRICH. Try: Gantenbein; Davaz (Fläsch); Kesseling (Ottoberg); Pircher (Eglisau); Baumann (Oberhallau) ★★★ 00 01 02 **03'** 04 05'.

Rauschling Old white ZÜRICH grape; discreet fruit and elegant acidity.

Riesling Petit Rhin Mainly in the VALAIS. Excellent botrytis wines. Try Kesseling (Ottoberg) 04' 05'.

Riesling-Sylvaner Old name for Müller-THURGAU (top white of E; a SPÉCIALITÉ in W). Typically elegant wines with nutmeg aroma and some acidity. Best producers: Hermann Schwarzenbach, Daniel Marugg ★★ **03'** 04 05'.

St-Gallen E wine canton (218 ha). Esp for BLAUBURGUNDER (full-bodied), Müller-THURGAU, SPÉCIALITÉS. Inc Rhine Valley, Oberland, upper Lake ZÜRICH.

St-Saphorin Vaud w (r) ★★→★★★ 03 04 Famous LAVAUX AC for fine, light whites. Due to hailstorm in 2005 almost no wine of this vintage will be released.

Salvagnin Vaud r ★→★★ 03 GAMAY and/or PINOT N appellation. (See also DÔLE.)

Schaffhausen German-Swiss canton and wine town on the Rhine. BLAUBURGUNDER; also Müller-THURGAU and SPÉCIALITÉS. Best: Baumann, Bad Osterfingen ★★.

Schenk Europe-wide wine giant, founded and based in Rolle (VAUD). Owns firms in France (Burg and B'x), Germany, Italy, and Spain.

Sierre Valais r w ★★→★★★ Sunny resort and famous wine town. Known for FENDANT, PINOT N, ERMITAGE, MALVOISIE. V.gd DÔLE.

Sion Valais r w ★★→★★★ Capital/wine centre of VALAIS. Esp FENDANT de Sion.

Spécialités (Spezialitäten) Wines of unusual grapes: vanishing local Gwäss, Himbertscha, Roter Eyholzer, Bondola, etc, ARVINE and AMIGNE, or modish Chenin Bl, Sauv Bl, Cab Sauv, Syrah. Of 47 VALAIS varieties, 43 are spécialités.

Süssdruck Dry rosé/bright-red wine: grapes pressed before fermentation.

Swisswine www.swisswine.ch Wine promotion body, mainly government-financed. Organizes a wine gala competition every two yrs.

Sylvaner Johannisberg, Gros Rhin White grape esp in warm VALAIS v'yds. Heady, spicy: some with marked sweetness.

Thurgau German-Swiss canton beside Bodensee Lake (265 ha). Wines from Thur Valley: Weinfelden, Seebach, Nussbaum, and Rhine. S shore of the Untersee. Typical: BLAUBURGUNDER, also gd Müller-THURGAU. SPÉCIALITÉS inc Kerner, PINOT GR, Regent. Best producer: Hans Ulrich Kesselring ★★ 02 **03'** 04' 05'.

Ticino Italian-speaking S Switzerland (with Misox), growing mainly MERLOT (gd from mountainous Sopraceneri region) and SPÉCIALITÉS. Trying Cab Sauv (oaked B'x style), Sauv Bl, Sem, Chard, Merlot white, and rosé (1,020 ha). Best producers: Luigi Zanini, Werner Stucky, Daniel Huber, Adriano Kaufmann, Christian Zündel, Guido Brivio. All ★★★ 00 **01 02 03** 04' 05.

Valais (Wallis) Rhône Valley from German-speaking upper-Valais to French lower-Valais. Largest and most varied wine canton in Switzerland (5,198 ha; source of 30% Swiss wine), now seeing a revival of quality, and ancient grapes. Near-perfect climatic conditions. Wide range: 47 grape varieties, plus many SPÉCIALITÉS. Esp white; FLÉTRI/MI-FLÉTRI wines.

Vaud (Waadt) French Switzerland's second-largest wine canton inc CHABLAIS, LA CÔTE, LAVAUX, BONVILLARS, CÔTES DE L'ORBE, VULLY. CHASSELAS stronghold.

Vétroz Valais w r ★★→★★★ Top village nr SION, esp famous for AMIGNE.

Vevey-Montreux Vaud r w ★★ Up-and-coming appellation of LAVAUX. Famous wine festival held about every 30 yrs.

Villeneuve Vaud w (r) ★★→★★★ Nr Lake GENEVA: powerful yet refined whites.

Visperterminen Valais w (r) ★→★★ Upper Valais, esp for SPÉCIALITÉS.

Vully Vaud w (r) ★→★★ Refreshing white from Lake Murten/FRIBOURG area.

Yvorne Vaud w (r) ★★ 04 05 Top CHABLAIS AC for strong, fragrant wines.

Zürich Capital of eponymous largest German-speaking canton. BLAUBURGUNDER mostly; also PINOT GR, GEWURZ, and esp Müller-THURGAU, RAUSCHLING (623 ha).

SWITZERLAND

Austria

More heavily shaded areas are the wine-growing regions

Though it produces less than one per cent of the world's wine, Austria is increasingly one of the most exciting wine countries. White grapes (which comprise two-thirds of the country's vines), especially Riesling and Grüner Veltliner from the Wachau, Kamptal, and Kremstal regions, and botrytized dessert wines from around Lake Neusiedl in Burgenland, already have stellar reputations. Some need to keep an eye on the alcohol levels, however: more is not necessarily better. Hot on their heels, red varieties such as Blaufränkisch, Zweigelt, and St Laurent are shedding excess oak and coming nicely into focus.

Recent vintages

2005 Cool, wet conditions required intensive grape selection. In Wachau, Grüner Veltliner and Riesling were fine. Despite a warm Oct, reds struggled for ripeness (disappointing for Zweigelt). Sensational botrytis conditions for Burgenland dessert wines.

2004 A cooler year. Grüner Veltliner and Riesling fared well after meticulous vineyard care, especially in Wachau. A mild Oct in Burgenland helped reds ripen nicely, while bringing plentiful botrytis for dessert wines.

2003 Very good for Grüner Veltliner and Burgenland reds, especially Blaufränkisch and Zweigelt. Little botrytis for dessert wines.

2002 Though Grüner Veltliner was hit by harvest rains, Riesling and the white Pinots did well. A difficult red wine vintage, but excellent dessert wines.

2001 Great for dry whites; very good late-harvest wines. Reds more erratic.

2000 Very good vintage in Lower Austria. Mixed in Styria due to harvest rains. In Burgenland, possibly the greatest vintage since 1945.

1999 A great vintage whose dry white wines combine concentration and elegance. The best to date for the reds.

Achs, Paul r (w) ★★→★★★ Superb GOLS estate, esp reds: Pannobile blends, Ungerberg, BLAUFRÄNKISCH and Pinot N.

Arachon TFXT r ★★★ Three growers (TEMENT, FX PICHLER, Tibor Szemes) join skills and initials to make an ultra-fashionable, ultra-polished red in Burgenland. Impeccable winemaking, but a bit short on personality.

Ausbruch PRÄDIKAT wine with sweetness levels between Beerenauslese and Trockenbeerenauslese. Traditionally produced in RUST.

Ausg'steckt ("hung out") HEURIGEN are not open all year; when they are, a green bush is hung above their doors, also to show wine is being served.

Bayer r w ★★★ Cult reds named after star signs: In Signo Leonis, In Signo Sagittarii, In Signo Tauri, plus others. Surprisingly, not just about muscle.

Blauburger Austrian red grape variety. A cross between BLAUER PORTUGIESER and BLAUFRÄNKISCH. Dark-coloured but usually produces light-bodied, simple wines.

Blauer Burgunder Pinot N. Becoming a premium winemaker's favourite, though vintages can vary markedly. Best in BURGENLAND, KAMPTAL, and the THERMENREGION (from growers P ACHS, Johanneshof, PITTNAUER, Schloss Halbturn, JURIS-STIEGELMAR, PÖCKL, UMATHUM, WIENINGER).

Blauer Portugieser Light, fruity wines to drink slightly chilled when young. Also a good blending variety. Top producers: Fischer, Lust, Bauer.

Blauer Zweigelt BLAUFRÄNKISCH/ST LAURENT cross High-yielding grape, rich in colour. Lower yields and improved methods can produce fine reds. Top producers: HEINRICH, Grassl, Markowitsch, Nittnaus, PITTNAUER, PÖCKL, Scheibhofer, UMATHUM.

Blaufränkisch Lemberger in Germany, Kékfrankos in Hungary. Austria's top-potential red grape variety, widely planted in MITTELBURGENLAND: wines with gd body and structure, peppery acidity, and a fruity, cherry taste. Often blended with Cab Sauv. Best from P ACHS, Gesellmann, HEINRICH, Iby, Igler, Krutzler, Nittnaus, TRIEBAUMER, WENINGER.

Bouvier Indigenous aromatic grape, generally producing light, low-acidity wines, esp gd for Beeren- and Trockenbeerenauslesen.

Bründlmayer, Willi r w sp ★★★→★★★★ 93 94 95 97 98 99 00 01 02 03 04 05 Leading Langenlois-KAMPTAL estate. Passionate innovator making excellent RIES, GRÜNER VELTLINER; top international styles, inc CHARD. Also Austria's best Sekt.

Burgenland Province and wine region (14,564 ha) in the E bordering Hungary. Warm climate. Ideal conditions for red wines and esp botrytis wines nr NEUSIEDLERSEE. Four areas: MITTELBURGENLAND, NEUSIEDLERSEE, NEUSIEDLERSEE-HÜGELLAND, SÜDBURGENLAND.

Buschenschank A wine tavern, often a HEURIGE country cousin.

Carnuntum r w Up-and-coming wine region SE of VIENNA now showing good reds. Best producers: Glatzer, Grassl, G Markowitsch, Pitnauer, Netzl, Weingut Marko.

Chardonnay Small amount grown; both oaked and unoaked show well. Known in STYRIA as MORILLON: strong fruit, lively acidity. Esp BRÜNDLMAYER, GROSS, LOIMER, Malat, KOLLWENTZ, POLZ, SATTLER, STIEGELMAR, TEMENT, VELICH, WIENINGER.

Deutschkreutz r (w) MITTELBURGENLAND red wine area, esp for BLAUFRÄNKISCH.

Districtus Austriae Controllatus, DAC Austria's first appellation system, introduced in 2003. Similar to France's AC and Italy's DOC. Only used so far in WEINVIERTEL, for fresh, unoaked, dry GRÜNER VELTLINER.

Donauland (Danube) w (r) Wine region, just W of VIENNA. Inc KLOSTERNEUBURG S of Danube and WAGRAM N of the river. Mainly whites, esp GRÜNER VELTLINER. Best producers inc: Ehmoser, Fritsch, Stift Klosterneuburg, Leth, Bernhard Ott, Wimmer-Czerny, R Zimmermann.

Federspiel Medium quality level of the VINEA WACHAU categories, roughly corresponding to Kabinett. Fruity, elegant, dry wines.

Feiler-Artinger Burgenland r w SW ★★★→★★★★ 93 94 95 96 97 98 99 00 01 02 03 04 05 Outstanding RUST estate with top AUSBRUCH dessert wines. Also gd dry whites and exciting red blends. Beautiful baroque house, too.

Freie Weingärtner Wachau w (r) ★★★ 94 95 96 97 98 99 00 01 02 03 04 05 Important growers' co-op in DURNSTEIN. Might now be improving after management problems. V.gd GRÜNER VELTLINER and RIES. Domaine Wachau range.

Fritsch, Weinberghof r w ★★ Depth and diversity at this Wagram estate in Donauland. V.gd GRÜNER VELTLINER, CHARD, Pinot N (Blauer Burgunder) and red blend Foggathal.

Gemischter Satz A blend of grapes (mostly white) grown, harvested, and vinified together. Traditional wine, still served in HEURIGEN.

Gobelsburg, Schloss ★★★ Renowned 35-ha KAMPTAL estate revitalized by Michael Moosbrugger. Excellent dry RIES and GRÜNER VELTLINER of discreet opulence.

Gols r w dr sw Wine commune on N shore of NEUSIEDLERSEE in BURGENLAND. Top producers: P ACHS, Beck, GSELLMANN & HANS, HEINRICH, A&H Nittnaus, PITTNAUER, Preisinger, Renner, JURIS-STIEGELMAR.

Graf Hardegg r w ★★→★★★ Top WEINVIERTEL estate steered by daring Peter Veyder-Malberg, who introduced Austria's first Viognier and port-style Forticus. V.gd Syrah, Pinot N and RIES.

Grüner Veltliner Austria's flagship white grape covering 37% of v'yds. Remarkably diverse: from lively spiced fruitiness in youth, to concentrated elegance with age. Best: BRÜNDLMAYER, HIRTZBERGER, Högl, M Huber, KNOLL, Laurenz V, LOIMER, MANTLER, NEUMAYER, NIGL, NIKOLAIHOF, OTT, PFAFFL, FX PICHLER, PRAGER, Schmelz, Sommer.

Gsellmann & Hans r w sw ★★→★★★ Formerly Gsellmann & Gsellmann, in GOLS.

G'spritzer Popular, refreshing summer drink, usually of white wine mixed with soda or mineral water. Esp in HEURIGEN.

Gumpoldskirchen w r dr sw Famous HEURIGE village S of VIENNA, centre of THERMENREGION. Distinctive, tasty, often sweet wines from ZIERFANDLER and ROTGIPFLER grapes. Best producers: Biegler, Spaetrot, Zierer.

Heinrich, Gernot r w dr sw ★★→★★★ 94 96 97 98 99 00 01 02 03 04 05 Top GOLS estate with Pannobile and (esp) red Gabarinza labels. Now focusing on balance rather than on power, and doing it v. well.

Heurige Wine of the most recent harvest, called "new wine" for one year. Heurigen are wine taverns in which growers-cum-patrons serve their own wine with simple local food – a Viennese institution.

Hirtzberger, Franz w ★★★★ 95 96 97 98 99 00 01 02 03 04 05 Leading producer with 91 ha at SPITZ AN DER DONAU. Fine dry RIES and GRÜNER VELTLINER.

Horitschon MITTELBURGENLAND region for reds: ARACHON TFXT, Anton Iby, WENINGER.

Huber, Markus (r) w ★★→★★★ Superb shooting-star TRAISENTAL producer with varying styles of GRÜNER VELTLINER. Also gd Sauv Bl and CHARD.

Illmitz w (r) dr sw SEEWINKEL region famous for Beeren- and Trockenbeeren-auslesen. Best from Angerhof, KRACHER, Martin Haider, Helmut Lang, OPITZ.

Jamek, Josef w ★★★ 97 98 99 00 01 02 03 04 05 Well-known pioneering WACHAU estate with restaurant. Not typical Wachau style: often some residual sugar.

Jurtschitsch/Sonnhof w (r) dr (sw) ★★→★★★ 97 98 99 00 01 02 03 04 05 Top KAMPTAL estate run by three brothers: v.gd whites (RIES, GRÜNER VELTLINER, CHARD).

Kamptal r w Wine region, along River Kamp N of WACHAU. Top v'yds: Langenlois, Strass, Zöbing. Best growers: Angerer, BRÜNDLMAYER, Dolle, Ehn, SCHLOSS GOBELSBURG, Hiedler, Hirsch, JURTSCHITSCH, LOIMER, Sax, Topf.

Kattus ★→★★ Producer of traditional Sekt in VIENNA.

Klosterneuburg r w Main wine town of DONAULAND. Rich in tradition, with a famous Benedictine monastery and a wine college founded in 1860. Best producers: Stift Klosterneuburg, Zimmermann.

KMW Abbreviation for Klosterneuburger Mostwaage ("must level"), the unit used in Austria to measure the sugar content in grape juice.

Knoll, Emmerich w ★★★★ 97 98 99 00 01 02 03 04 05 Traditional, highly regarded estate in Loiben, WACHAU. Showpiece GRÜNER VELTLINER and RIES.

Kollwentz-Römerhof w r dr (sw) ★★→★★★ **93 94 95 96 97 98 99** 00 01 02 03 04 05 Innovative producer nr EISENSTADT: Sauv Bl, CHARD, Eiswein, v.gd reds.

Kracher, Alois w (r) dr (sw) ★★★★ **91 93 94 95 96 97 98 99** 00 01 02 03 04 05 First-class ILLMITZ producer specializing in botryized PRÄDIKATS (dessert); some barrique-aged (Nouvelle Vague), others in steel (Zwischen den Seen); gd reds since 1997. Now right back on top form.

Kremstal r (w) Wine region esp for GRÜNER VELTLINER and RIES. Top growers: Malat, NIGL, SALOMON, S MOSER, WEINGUT STADT KREMS.

Loimer, Fred (r) w ★★→★★★ Highly innovative Kamptal producer with ultra-modern 31-ha estate, 50% GRÜNER VELTLINER; also RIES, CHARD, Pinot Gr, Pinot N. Great steel and oak versions.

Mittelburgenland r (w) dr (sw) Wine region on Hungarian border protected by three hill ranges. Makes large quantities of red (esp BLAUFRÄNKISCH). Producers: GSELLMANN, J HEINRICH, Iby, Igler, P Kerschbaum, WENINGER.

Morillon Name given in STYRIA to CHARD.

Moser, Lenz ★★ Large producer nr KREMS. LM III invented Hochkultur high-vine training system. Also inc wines from Schlossweingut Malteser Ritterorden (wine estate of Knights of Malta) and Klosterkeller Siegendorf (BURGENLAND). Perfectly all right, but could be a lot better.

Moser, Sepp ★★★ **95 97 98 99** 00 01 02 03 04 05 Founded with original LENZ MOSER v'yds. RIES, GRÜNER VELTLINER, CHARD, and Sauv Bl are elegant, dry, and highly aromatic. Also gd reds from Apetlon (Hedwighof) in NEUSIEDLERSEE region.

Müller-Thurgau See RIESLING-SYLVANER.

Muskateller Rare, aromatic grape for dry whites. Best from STYRIA and WACHAU. Top growers: Gross, HIRTZBERGER, Lackner-Tinnacher, FX PICHLER, POLZ, SATTLER.

Muskat-Ottonel Grape for fragrant, often dry whites, interesting PRÄDIKATS.

Neuburger Indigenous white grape with nutty flavour; mainly in the WACHAU (elegant, flowery), THERMENREGION (mellow and amber-bodied), and N BURGENLAND (strong, full). Best from Beck, FREIE WEINGÄRTNER, HIRTZBERGER.

Neumayer ★★★ **96 97 98 99** 00 01 02 03 04 05 Top TRAISENTAL estate making powerful, pithy, dry GRÜNER VELTLINER and RIES that take on the best of the WACHAU.

Neusiedlersee (Lake Neusiedl) Very shallow BURGENLAND lake on Hungarian border. Warm temperatures and autumn mists encourage botrytis. Gives name to wine territories of NEUSIEDLERSEE and NEUSIEDLERSEE-HÜGELLAND.

Neusiedlersee r w dr sw Wine region N and E of Lake Neusiedl. Best growers: ACHS, Beck, HEINRICH, JURIS-STIEGELMAN, KRACHER, Nittnaus, OPITZ, PÖCKL, UMATHUM, VELICH.

Neusiedlersee-Hügelland r w dr sw Wine region W of NEUSIEDLERSEE based around Oggau, RUST, and Mörbisch on the lake shores, and EISENSTADT in the Leitha Mts foothills. Best producers: FEILER-ARTINGER, KOLLWENTZ, Prieler, Schandl, SCHRÖCK, Sommer, ERNST TRIEBAUMER, WENZEL.

Niederösterreich (Lower Austria) With 58% of Austria's v'yds: CARNUNTUM, DONAULAND, KAMPTAL, KREMSTAL, THERMENREGION, TRAISENTAL, WACHAU, WEINVIERTEL.

Nigl ★★★ w **94 95 96 97 98 99** 00 01 02 03 04 05 The best in KREMSTAL, making sophisticated dry ageworthy RIES and GRÜNER VELTLINER from Senftenberg v'yd.

Nikolaihof w ★★★★ **92 94 95 97 98 99** 00 01 02 03 04 Built on Roman foundations, this Biodynamic WACHAU estate produces focused RIES from the Steiner Hund site. Impeccable winemaking across the range.

Opitz, Willi ★★★ A tiny, impressively promoted ILLMITZ estate specializing in late-harvest wines, including Schilfmandl and Opitz One, from grapes dried on reeds from Lake Neusiedl. Dry wines are less exciting.

Ott, Bernhard w ★★→★★★ GRÜNER VELTLINER specialist from DONAULAND – some of Austria's freshest. Try signature Fass 4; also Der Ott and Rosenberg.

Pfaffl ★★★ **93 94 95 96 97 98 99** 00 01 02 03 04 05 WEINVIERTEL estate nr VIENNA, in Stetten. Known for wonderful dry GRÜNER VELTLINER (Goldjoch) and RIES (Terrassen Sonnleiten). Also runs nearby Schlossweingut Bockfliess estate.

Pichler, Franz Xavier w ★★★★ 93 94 95 96 97 98 99 00 01 02 03 04 05 Top WACHAU producer and one of Austria's best. Very intense, rich RIES and GRÜNER VELTLINER (esp Kellerberg). SMARAGDS are esp good.

Pittnauer, Gerhard r (w) ★★→★★★ Another GOLS red master, with wife Brigitte, making excellent Pinot N and ST LAURENT. Keeps getting better and better.

Pöckl, Josef & René r (sw) ★★→★★★ Father-and-son team in NEUSIEDLERSEE (Mönchhof), each making red gems, esp Admiral, Reve de Jeunesse, and Rosso e Nero. Excellent Pinot N; gd Zweigelt.

Polz, Erich & Walter w ★★★ 93 95 96 97 98 99 00 01 02 03 04 S STYRIAN (Weinstrasse) growers; esp Hochgrassnitzberg: Sauv Bl, CHARD, Grauburgunder, WEISSBURGUNDER.

Prädikat, Prädikatswein Quality graded wines from Spätlese upwards (Spätlese, Auslese, Eiswein, Strohwein, Beerenauslese, AUSBRUCH, and Trockenbeerenauslese). See Germany.

Prager, Franz w ★★★★ 92 93 94 95 96 97 98 99 00 01 02 03 04 05 Pioneer, together with JOSEF JAMEK, of top-quality WACHAU dry whites. Estate now run by Anton Bodenstein; outstanding RIES and GRÜNER VELTLINER.

Ried Single v'yd.

Riesling On its own, this always means Rhine RIESLING. WELSCHRIESLING is unrelated. Top growers: Alzinger, BRÜNDLMAYER, HIRTZBERGER, Högl, KNOLL, NIGL, NIKOLAIHOF, PFAFFL, FX PICHLER, PRAGER, SALOMON.

Riesling-Sylvaner Name used for Müller-Thurgau (about 7% of Austria's grapes). Best producers: HIRTZBERGER, JURTSCHITSCH.

Rotgipfler Fragrant, indigenous grape of THERMENREGION. With ZIERFANDLER, makes lively, interesting wine. Esp Biegler, Spaetrot, Stadlmann, Zierer.

Rust w r dr sw BURGENLAND region, famous since 17th C for dessert AUSBRUCH; now also for red and dry white. Esp from FEILER-ARTINGER, Schandl, HEIDI SCHRÖCK, ERNST TRIEBAUMER, Paul Triebaumer, WENZEL.

St Laurent Traditional red grape, v.gd potential; possibly related to Pinot N. Esp from Fischer, Johanneshof, PITTNAUER, JURIS-STIEGELMAR, R Schuster, UMATHUM.

Salomon-Undhof w ★★★ V.gd KREMS producer of RIES, WEISSBURGUNDER, Traminer. Excellent quality for more than a decade.

Sattler, Willi w ★★→★★★ 94 95 96 97 98 99 00 01 02 03 04 05 Top S STYRIA grower. Esp for Sauv Bl, MORILLON. Recent vintages are more balanced.

Schilcher Rosé wine from indigenous Blauer Wildbacher grapes (sharp, dry: high acidity). A local taste, or at least an acquired one. Speciality of W STYRIA. Try: Klug, Lukas, Reiterer, Strohmeier.

Schlumberger Largest sparkling winemaker in Austria (VIENNA); wine is bottle-fermented by unique "Méthode Schlumberger". Delicate and fruity.

Schröck w sw r ★★★→★★★★ Beautiful wines of great purity and focus from an innovative, thoughtful grower. First-class AUSBRUCH.

Seewinkel ("lake corner") Name given to the part of NEUSIEDLERSEE including Apetlon, ILLMITZ, and Podersdorf. Ideal conditions for botrytis.

Smaragd Highest-quality category of VINEA WACHAU, similar to dry Spätlese.

Spätrot-Rotgipfler Typical, two-grape blend of THERMENREGION.

Spitz an der Donau w Cool WACHAU microclimate, esp from Singerriedel v'yd. Top growers are: HIRTZBERGER, Högl, Lagler.

Steinfeder VINEA WACHAU quality category for light, fragrant, dry wines.

Stiegelmar (Juris-Stiegelmar) w r dr sw ★→★★★ 96 97 98 99 00 01 02 03 04 05 Important GOLS grower. CHARD, Sauv Bl. Reds: ST LAURENT, Pinot N.

Styria Steiermark Southernmost wine region of Austria. Some gd dry whites, esp Sauv Bl. Inc SÜDSTEIERMARK, SÜD-OSTSTEIERMARK, WESTSTEIERMARK (S, SE, W Styria).

Südburgenland r w Small S BURGENLAND wine region: gd red wines. Best producers: Krutzler, Wachter-Wiesler, Schiefer.

Süd-Oststeiermark SE Styria w (r) STYRIAN region with islands of excellent v'yds. Best producers: Neumeister, Winkler-Hermaden.

Südsteiermark S Styria w Best wine region of STYRIA; makes very popular whites (MORILLON, MUSKATELLER, WELSCHRIESLING, and Sauv Bl). Best: Gross, Jaunegg, Lackner-Tinnacher, POLZ, Potzinger Sabathi, SATTLER, Skoff, TEMENT, Wohlmuth.

Tement, Manfred w ★★★ 93 94 97 98 99 00 01 02 03 04 05 Renowned S STYRIA estate with beautifully made Steirische Klassik and gently oaked Sauv Bl and MORILLON from Zieregg site. International-style wines, and esp modern reds.

Thermenregion r w dr sw Wine/hot-springs region, S of VIENNA. Indigenous grapes (e.g. ZIERFANDLER, ROTGIPFLER) and gd reds (esp ST LAURENT) from Baden, GUMPOLDSKIRCHEN, Tattendorf, Traiskirchen areas. Producers: Alphart, Biegler, Fischer, Johanneshof, Schafler, Stadelmann, Zierer.

Traisental 700 ha just S of KREMS on Danube. Dry whites can be similar to WACHAU in style, not usually in quality. Top producers: Huber, NEUMAYER.

Triebaumer, Ernst r (w) dr sw ★★★ 93 94 95 97 98 99 00 01 02 03 04 05 RUST producer; some of Austria's best reds: BLAUFRÄNKISCH (Mariental), Cab Sauv/Merlot blend. V.gd AUSBRUCH. One of several Triebaumers – known as ET

Umathum, Josef w r dr sw ★★★ 92 94 95 97 98 99 00 01 02 03 04 05 Distinguished NEUSIEDLERSEE producer. V.gd reds inc Pinot N, ST LAURENT; gd whites.

Velich w sw NEUSIEDLERSEE ★★★ Excellent Burgundian-style Tiglat CHARD (99 00 01 02 03) with fine barrel-ageing. Some of top PRÄDIKATS in the SEEWINKEL.

Vienna w (r) ("Wien" in German and on labels) Wine region in suburbs. Generally simple, lively wines, served to bus-loads of tourists in HEURIGEN, but quality producers on the rise: Mayer, Schilling, WIENINGER, Zahel.

Vinea Wachau WACHAU appellation started by winemakers in 1983 with three categories of dry wine: STEINFEDER, FEDERSPIEL, and the powerful SMARAGD.

Wachau w World-renowned Danube region, home to some of Austria's best wines. Top producers: Alzinger, FREIE WEINGÄRTNER WACHAU, HIRTZBERGER, Högl, JAMEK, KNOLL, Lagler, NIKOLAIHOF, FX PICHLER, R Pichler, PRAGER, Schmelz, Tegernseerhof, Wess.

Weingut Stadt Krems Co-op now steered by former FREIE WEINGÄRTNER WACHAU guru Fritz Miesbauer, who is transforming the quality of the whites.

Weinviertel ("Wine Quarter") w (r) Largest Austrian wine region, between Danube and Czech border. First, and so far only, to adopt DAC appellation status. Mostly refreshing whites, esp from Poysdorf, Retz. Best: Bauer, J Diem, GRAF HARDEGG, Gruber, PFAFFL, Schwarzböck, Uibel, Wöber, Weinrieder, Zull.

Weissburgunder Pinot Bl. Ubiquitous: gd dry wines and PRÄDIKATS. Esp Beck, Fischer, Gross, HEINRICH, HIRTZBERGER, Lackner-Tinnacher, POLZ, TEMENT.

Welschriesling White grape, not related to RIES, grown in all wine regions: light, fragrant, young-drinking dry wines and gd PRÄDIKATS.

Weninger, Franz r (w) ★★→★★★ Top MITTELBURGENLAND (Horitschon) estate, with fine reds, esp BLAUFRÄNKISCH, Merlot. Son Franz Reinhard runs Hungarian estate.

Wenzel r w sw ★★★★ Superb AUSBRUCH and now v.gd reds, too. Michael's father Robert pioneered the Furmint revival in RUST.

Weststeiermark W Styria p Small wine region specializing in SCHILCHER. Best from Domaine Müller, Klug, Lukas, Reiterer, Strohmeier.

Wien See VIENNA.

Wieninger, Fritz w r ★★→★★★ 94 95 97 98 99 00 01 02 03 04 05 V.gd VIENNA-Stammersdorf grower with HEURIGE: CHARD, BLAUER BURGUNDER, esp gd GRÜNER VELTLINER and RIES. Wines of great balance and depth.

Winzer Krems Important KREMSTAL co-op with 1,300 growers. Esp GRÜNER VELTLINER.

Zierfandler (Spätrot) White variety almost exclusive to THERMENREGION. Often blended with ROTGIPFLER. Best: Biegler, Spaetrot, Stadelmann, Zierer.

AUSTRIA

Central & Southeast Europe

More heavily shaded areas are the wine-growing regions

To say that parts of this region are still in transition is an understatement. But new regional autonomies and new statehoods are being followed in many cases by higher aspirations in winemaking. In a few much-publicized cases this takes the form of flying winemakers pitching their tents at vintage-time, usually to make wines acceptable to Western supermarkets from predictable grape varieties, occasionally to do far better. This affects indigenous winemaking, too – often meaning fresher and fruitier wines of intriguingly different flavours.

The decade and a half since the fall of Communism has witnessed the decline of state firms and the emergence of new family- and corporate-owned wineries. These are now establishing their own winemaking styles and market positions, with either fresh and fruity or more complex, aged wines. So far, Hungary, Bulgaria, Slovenia, and the Czech Republic have taken the lead in what has become an area to follow with fascination. The potential of other ex-Communist states has still to emerge, with Romania in particular catching up. About Greece there is no doubt: the new age of wine has well and truly arrived.

In this section, references are arranged country by country, each shown on the map on this page. Included alongside regions are producers and other terms in the alphabetical listings.

Hungary

After the privatization process, the past fifteen years have been revolutionary. Winemakers have invested capital and earnings into improving cellar equipment and procedures and expanding plantings of international grapes. The initial years of experiment gave way to proven winemaking techniques and definite wine styles.This is especially true for the reds – e.g. Villány. Tokaj, the one undisputed great wine of Central European history, remains in full renaissance, and native grapes provide the backbone for the more traditional preference for fiery, hearty, full-bodied wines. The Carpathian Basin is a special "terroir" for the Hungarian wines, mainly for whites. The situation has continued to improve following accession to the EU in May 2004, when Hungary introduced new appellation-based wine laws. The transition and EU accession period has provided difficulties as well, but in the near future further developments are likely in the Hungarian wine sector.

Alföld Hungary's Great Plain: much everyday wine (mostly international varietals), some better. Incorporates three wine districts: HAJÓS-Baja, Csongrád, KUNSÁG.

Árvay & Co TOKAJ cellar established in 2000 and headed by former DISZNÓKÖ winemaker János Árvay. First wines are on the market: ASZÚ (5/6 PUTTONYOS) and cuvée Edés Élet, Hétfürtös.

Ászár-Neszmély Wine region in NW Hungary nr the Danube. International and native grapes. Hilltop is leading winery.

Aszú Botrytis-shrivelled grapes and the sweet wine made from them in TOKAJ, similar to Sauternes. The wine is graded in sweetness, from 3 PUTTONYOS up.

Aszú Eszencia Tokaj sw ★★★★ 93 96 99 Second TOKAJ quality (see ESZENCIA). 7 PUTTONYOS-plus; should be superb amber elixir, like celestial butterscotch.

Badacsony w dr sw ★★→★★★★ Wine district on the N shore of Lake BALATON, home to the native variety KÉKNYELÜ. The basalt soil can give rich, highly flavoured white wines; well-made Ries and SZÜRKEBARÁT have fine mineral flavours. The leader is SZEREMLEY's Szent Orbán winery.

Balaton Hungary's inland sea, Europe's largest freshwater lake. Many gd wines take its name. At northside Jásdi and Figula located.

Balatonboglár r w dr sw ★★→★★★★ Name of wine district and also progressive winery owned by Henkell & Söhnlein on S shore of Lake BALATON in Dél-Balaton region. Decent whites (Chard, Sem, Muscat). Also cuve close sparkling. Other promising producers: Konyári, Katona, Légli and St Donatus.

Bikavér Eger r ★ "Bull's Blood", historic red wine of EGER: at best full-bodied and well-balanced, but highly variable in export version today. Now under supervision to protect identity and improve quality (see EGER). Mostly from KÉKFRANKOS, Cab Sauv, Cab Fr, Portugieser, Merlot. Also made in SZEKSZÁRD.

Bock, József Family winemaker in VILLÁNY. Hearty reds, both varietal and blends.

Bor "Wine": vörös is red; fehér is white; asztali is table; táj is country, a section of the market that is currently growing.

Dégenfeld, Grof Large TOKAJ estate. Traditional-style wines, plus dry FURMINT.

Disznókö Important first-class TOKAJ estate, owned by French company AXA. The Sauternes-style wines of the early years have given way to a more typically Hungarian note, imparted by a Hungarian, instead of Sauternais, winemaker.

Edes Sweet wine (but not as luscious as ASZÚ).

Eger r w dr sw ★→★★★ Best-known red-wine centre of N Hungary; Baroque city of cellars full of BIKAVÉR. Fresh LEÁNYKA (perhaps its best product), OLASZRIZLING, Chard, Cab Sauv. Top producers: Vilmos Thummerer (consistent BIKAVÉR), Tibor GÁL, Tamás Pók, Ostoros Bor, Béla Vincze, György Lőrincz, and the huge Egervin.

Eszencia ★★★★ The fabulous quintessence of TOKAJ: intensely sweet and aromatic from grapes wizened by botrytis. Properly grape juice of very low, if any, alcoholic strength, reputed to have miraculous properties: raising the dead, and the like. Its sugar content can be over 850 g per litre.

Etyek-Buda Wine region nr Budapest. Source of modern-style wines, esp Chard and Sauv Bl. Leading producer: TÖRLEY, Vinarium, Etyeki Kúria, Nyakas.

Ezerjó Literally "thousand blessings". Widespread traditional variety. In MÓR, makes one of the country's top dry whites, besides Frittman Bro Ezerjó from Soltvadkert. Has great potential: fragrant, with hint of grapefruit.

François President French-founded (1882) sparkling-wine brand now owned by TÖRLEY; winery at Budafok, nr Budapest. Vintage President very drinkable.

Furmint The classic grape of TOKAJ, with great flavour, acidity, and fire, also grown for table wine at Lake BALATON and in SOMLÓ.

Gál, Tibor EGER winemaker (deceased in 2005) for barrique-aged BIKAVÉR, also oaked GIA Chard.

Gere, Attila Family winemaker in VILLÁNY with gd, forward-looking reds, esp oak-aged Cab Sauv (00) and Cuvée Phoenix (00).

Gundel TOKAJ venture at MÁD, making wines for famous Gundel's restaurant in Budapest. Also v'yds and cellar at EGER.

Hajós Pincék Charming village in S Hungary on River Danube with 1,500 cellars. Mostly traditional, family production. Some quality lighter red wines.

Hárslevelü "Linden-leaved" grape variety used at Debrö and as 2nd grape of TOKAJ (compare Sem/Sauv Bl in Sauternes). Gentle, mellow wine; peach aroma.

Helvécia (Kecskemét) Historic ALFÖLD cellars. V'yds ungrafted: phylloxera bugs cannot negotiate sandy soil. Whites and rosés modernist; reds traditional.

Hétszölö Noble first-growth 47-ha TOKAJ estate owned by Grands Millésimes de France and Japanese Suntory. Second label, from purchased grapes: Dessewffy. Fordítás is halfway to ASZÚ in style.

Hilltop Neszmély Winery in ÁSZÁR-NESZMÉLY makes international-style wines, inc Review and Woodcutters White from Cserszegi Fuszeres hybrid.

Kadarka Traditional red grape in S, but can produce ample flavour and interesting maturity. Considered by some an essential element of BIKAVÉR.

Kecskemét Major town of the ALFÖLD. Much everyday wine, some better.

Kékfrankos Hungarian for Blaufränkisch; reputedly related to Gamay. Most widely planted red variety. Gd light or full-bodied reds.

Kéknyelü "Blue stalk". High-flavoured, low-yielding white grape making the best and "stiffest" wine of Mt BADACSONY. Best is flowery and spicy stuff.

Királyudvar Promising TOKAJ winery in old royal cellars at Tarcal. Wines inc dry and late-harvest FURMINT, Cuvee Ilona (early-bottled ASZÚ) and Jégbor (Eiswein).

Kunság Largest region in ALFÖLD. Gd KADARKA esp from Kiskörös. Izsák appellation is special for its Walton-brand sparkling wine.

Leányka "Little girl". Native Hungarian white grape. Admirable, aromatic, light, dry wine. Királyleányka ("Royal") is a different variety and supposedly superior.

Mád Old commercial centre of the TOKAJI region. Growers inc Vince Gergely, GUNDEL, József Monyok, ROYAL TOKAJI, SZEPSY.

Mátra w (r) ★★ District in foothills of Mátra range in N, nr Gyöngyös. Promising, dry SZÜRKEBARÁT (Pinot Gr), Chard, MUSKOTÁLY, Sauv Bl. Foreign investment. Szőke Mátyás and Szőlőskert producers are worth a mention.

Megyer, Château TOKAJ estate bought by Jean-Louis Laborde of Ch Clinet in Pomerol. Also owns Ch PAJZOS. Megyer is the lighter wine. Quality is fair.

Mézes Mály In TARCAL. This and SZARVAS are historically the greatest v'yds of TOKAJ.

Minöségi Bor Quality wine. Hungary's *appellation contrôlée* (see France).

Mór N Hungary w ★★→★★★★ Region long-famous for fresh, dry EZERJÓ. Now also Ries and Sauv Bl. Wines now mostly exported.

Muskotály Muscat; usually Ottonel. Muscat Bl à Petits Grains is Muscat Lunel. Makes light, but long-lived, wine in TOKAJ and EGER. A little goes into the TOKAJ blend. Very occasionally makes a wonderful ASZÚ wine solo.

Olaszrizling Hungarian name for the Italian Ries or Welschriesling. Better examples can have a burned-almond aroma.

Oremus Ancient TOKAJ v'yd of founding Rakóczi family, owned by Spain's Vega Sicilia with HQ at Tolcsva. First-rate ASZÚ. Also a lesser TOKAJ grape.

Pajzos, Château B'x-owned TOKAJ estate with some fine ASZÚ. See MEGYER.

Pécs Mecsek w (r) ★→★★ Newly renamed wine district in S Hungary, based around the city of Pécs. Known for gd whites (sp, OLASZRIZLING, Pinot Bl).

Puttonyos Measure of sweetness in TOKAJ ASZÚ. A "puttony" is a 25-kg measure, traditionally a hod of grapes. The number of "putts" per barrel (136 litres) of dry base wine or must determines the final richness of the wine, from 3 putts to 6 (3 putts = 60 g of sugar per litre, 4 = 90 g, 5 = 120 g, 6 = 150 g, 7 = 180 g). See also ASZÚ ESZENCIA and ESZENCIA.

Royal Tokaji Wine Co Pioneer Anglo-Danish-Hungarian venture at MÁD. 81 ha, mainly first- or second-growth. First wine (90) a revelation: 91 and (esp) 93 led renaissance of TOKAJ. 95, 99, 00 to follow. (I am a co-founder.)

Siklós City in S Hungary; part of VILLÁNY district. Mainly small producers, known for whites: esp HÁRSLEVELÜ. Ripe, fruity Chard promising; also TRAMINI, OLASZRIZLING.

Somló N Hungary w ★★★ Isolated small district N of BALATON: whites (formerly of high repute) from FURMINT and Juhfark ("sheep's tail") in both traditional barrel-fermented and fresh, fruity styles. Top producers inc Fekete, Inhauser.

Sopron W Hungary r ★★→★★★ Historic enclave S of Neusiedlersee (see Austria). Traditionally known for lighter reds like KÉKFRANKOS and Austrian-style sweet wines, but showing promise for whites such as Sauv Bl. Top producer Weininger, promising Jandl, Lővér, Szita.

Szamorodni Literally "as it was born"; describes TOKAJ not sorted in the v'yd. Dry or (fairly) sweet, depending on proportion of ASZÚ grapes naturally present. Sold as an apéritif. In vintage TOKAJ ASZÚ yrs, the sweet style can offer some ASZÚ character at much less cost.

Száraz Dry, esp of TOKAJ SZAMORODNI.

Szarvas TOKAJ v'yd at Tarcal; a top site. Solely owned by TOKAJ TRADING HOUSE and state-run Research Institute for Vine and Wine.

Szekszárd r ★★→★★★ District in S central Hungary; some of country's top reds from KÉKFRANKOS, Cab Sauv, Cab Fr, and Merlot. Also KADARKA which needs age (3–4 yrs); can also be botrytized ("Nemes Kadar").

Szent Orbán See SZEREMLEY.

Szepsy, István Legendary name and impeccable small production of long-ageing TOKAJ ASZÚ. Same family name as the man who created the ASZÚ method in 17th-C, though not related.

Szeremley, Huba Leader in BADACSONY. Ries, SZÜRKEBARÁT, KÉKNYELÜ, ZEUSZ are modern models. Fine KÉKFRANKOS. Szent Orbán is another label.

Szürkebarát Literally "Grey Monk": Pinot Gr. Source of sw tourist wines from BALATON. But this is one of the best: wait for great dry wines.

Tarcal TOKAJ commune with two great first growths and several gd producers.

Tiffán, Ede VILLÁNY grower, who with son Zsolt produces full-bodied, oaked reds.

Tokaj w dr sw ★★→★★★★★ Tokaj is the town; Tokay or Tokaji is the wine. Appellation covers 5,967 ha. See ASZÚ, ESZENCIA, FURMINT, PUTTONYOS, SZAMORODNI. Also dry table wine of character.

Tokajbor-Bene New TOKAJ cellar at Bodrogkeresztúr. To watch.

Tokaj Trading House Formerly state-owned TOKAJ company, now reduced to 55

HUNGARY

ha inc the magnificent SZARVAS v'yd. Also called Crown Estates. Castle Island is the brand for dry wines. Quality improving; delicious late harvest.

Törley Large company (previously Hungarovin) with cellars at Budafok nr Budapest: international varietals (Chard, Cab Sauv, Merlot), also *cuve close*, transfer, and classic sp. Owned by German sekt specialist Henkell.

Tramini Gewürztraminer, esp in SIKLÓS.

Védett eredetű bor Appellation of Origin Controlled wine.

Villány S wine region with two main towns. Villány makes mostly red, often gd-quality B'x styles. Siklós makes mostly white. High-quality producers: BOCK, Csányi, GERE, Günzer, Malatinzky, Polgár, TIFFÁN, Wunderlich, Vylyan.

Zemplén Ridge Or Zemplén Hegyhát. A less concentrated TOKAJ for younger drinkers. First vintage was 02. Couldn't they just dilute to taste?

Zéta A cross of Bouvier and FURMINT used by some in ASZÚ production.

Bulgaria

Suffering from a decline in vineyard quality and management in recent years, massive changes are now afoot in Bulgaria. Foreign investment has been on the rise to meet the demand, both nationally and internationally, for better wines combined with the awareness that there are superb indigenous grape varieties to be utilized. A French-style wine law was introduced in 2000, and updated in 2004, preparing Bulgaria for EU membership accession in 2007.

Assenovgrad r ★★ Cellar near PLOVDIV; ageworthy MAVRUD and RUBIN.

Bessa Valley Bulgaria's most exciting new winery, in Pazardjik region. Started by Bordeaux specialist Count Stephan von Neipperg and Karl-Heinz Hauptmann; with Marc Dworkin as oenologist. 135 ha planted with Merlot, Syrah, Petit Verdot, Cab Sauv. Enira label.

Blueridge r w Major Domaine Boyar winery, label.

Burgas w p (r) ★→★★ Easy whites, gd young reds, nice rosé (a speciality) from this Black Sea port area. Good Cab Sauv 03.

Controliran Like France's AC. Wine law published in 2000, updated in 2004.

Damianitza r ★★→★★★ Quality-soaring winery specializing in native MELNIK grape. V. gd Uniqato Melnik **03**. Also superb ReDark Merlot **01**, Uniqato RUBIN **03**. Gd "No Man's Land" label.

DGO "Quality wines with declared geographical origin".

Dimiat Native white grape, grown in the E. Gd examples from POMORIE.

Domaine Boyar Major exporter to UK; in receivership at time of writing.

Gamza Red grape (Kadarka of Hungary) with potential, esp from Danube region. PAVLIKENI, NOVO SELO, and PLEVEN are specialists.

Golden Rhyton Top award for Bulgarian wines. Often on labels of winning wines.

Harsovo Struma Valley region, esp for MELNIK.

Haskovo r (w) ★★ Thracian Plain winery specializing in Merlot.

Karlovo Town located in the famous Valley of the Roses. Whites, esp MISKET. Recommended: Rose Valley Kabinet Reserve.

Khan Krum Gd whites, esp Chard. Now owned by Strandzha.

Korten Boutique cellar of DOMAINE BOYAR favouring traditional winemaking styles.

Mavrud Considered the best indigenous red variety, highly popular at home. Can make highly ageworthy, dark plummy wines, esp from S. Bulgaria. Excellent from Maxxima.

Melnik Important SW village and highly prized grape variety. Dense reds that can age up to 20 years. Also ripe Cab Sauv.

Misket Indigenous grape, mildly aromatic. The basis for most country whites.

Novo Selo Gd red GAMZA from the NW.

Oriachovitza r ★★ Winery now owned by France's Belvedere SA. Also Thracian Plain area for CONTROLIRAN Cab Sauv and Merlot. Gd Res Cab Sauv.

Pamid Light, soft, everyday red in SE and NW.

Pavlikeni r Specializes in Merlot, Cab Sauv, and GAMZA.

Peruschtitza r Reds-only winery nr PLOVDIV. Esp MAVRUD, Cab Sauv, RUBIN.

Pleven N cellar for PAMID, GAMZA, Cab Sauv. Also a wine research station.

Plovdiv City in S; source of gd Cab Sauv and MAVRUD. Most winemaking at ASSENOVGRAD and PERUSCHTITZA. Many Bulgarian oenologists study at the University's Food Technology Dept here.

Pomorie w (r) ★★ Black Sea winery in E. Esp Chard and MUSKAT. Black Sea Gold Chard recommended.

Preslav w ★★ Well-known cellar in Black Sea region. Best: Chard Premium Oak 03. Also gd brandy.

Riesling Rhine Ries is grown, but Italian (Welschriesling; no relation), used for medium and dry whites, dominates.

Rkatziteli Russian grape, one of the world's most widely planted. Known as Rikat in Bulgaria, grown on 12,000 ha. Widely used in NE white blends.

Rubin Bulgarian cross (Nebbiolo x Syrah); good in blends, but gaining favour in single-varietal niche wines.

Sakar SE area with some of Bulgaria's best Merlot.

Santa Sarah S winery with fine Cab Sauv, Sauv Bl.

Shumen w r ★★ New World-style reds and esp whites from Black Sea region and winery. Barrique Chard and Merlot.

Sliven, Vini r (w) ★★ Thracian Valley winery for Merlot, MISKET, and Chard. Promising barrique-aged Cab Sauv. Best: Tuida 04.

Stambolovo Merlot specialist.

Stara Zagora r Thracian Plain winery. Esp Res Cab Sauv and Merlot.

Svishtov r (w) ★★ Winery on Danube in N, renamed Stork Nest Estates by new UK-based owners.

Targovishte w ★★ Winery in E. Quality Chard (inc barrel-fermented), Sauv Bl.

Telish r Innovative winery in N with Michel Rolland as consultant. Mainly Cab Sauv and Merlot.

Todoroff Thracia region quality winery (25 ha): Cab Sauv, MAVRUD, Merlot.

Traminer Increasingly grown in NE. Fine whites with hints of spice.

Villa Lyubimets New label, vineyard in S near Greek-Turkish borders. Mainly reds. Villa Hissar is sister white label, v'yd.

Vinimpex Major exporter of Bulgarian wines, part of Belvedere group.

Yambol r w Winery in Thracian Plain, specializing in Cab Sauv and Merlot.

Slovenia

Slovenia has a population of 2 million, and the vast majority of its wine is drunk locally. In the last two decades only a handful of top producers have made their names abroad: Kogl, Movia, and Marjan Simčič, recently joined by Barbara International, Dveri-Pax, and Jakončič. The good news is that prices remain relatively low: it is almost unheard of to pay over €20 in retail or ex-cellars even for the most prestigious names, and virtually impossible to go over €40 in restaurants even for mature vintages.

As the market becomes ever more internationally competitive, the future looks good for quality producers, and increasingly bleak for overprotected traditionalists who tend to rely on low expectations and simple tastes.

Vintages do not vary greatly, and whites are generally a notch above reds.

Barbara International ★ → ★★★ Sparklers of all types and price. NV Barbara and

Miha are gd value, while No.1 Vintage is often Slovenia's best sp.

Batič ★★ Increasingly organic v'yd from VIPAVA. Top wine: Chard; others v.gd.

Bjana ★★ Top GORIŠKA BRDA sp producer. Intense, full-bodied wines. Very popular in classier Ljubljana restaurants.

Čurin ★★ Legendary pioneer of private wine-growing from early 1970s onwards. Varietal whites and PREDIKATS of very high standards.

Cviček Locally very popular traditional pink blend of POSAVSKI. Low alcohol, high acid. Decent quality from co-op Krško, premium by Frelih (Cviček od fare).

Dveri-Pax ★★★ Excellent new company based on v'yds that, until Communism, belonged to Benedictine monks. Austrian winemaker Erich Krutzler is breaking the rules of PODRAVSKI, esp with top wines E (Ries) and Admont (w blend).

Goriška Brda Slovenian part of Collio (see Italy). Many v.gd producers, among them Blažič, Četrtič, Erzetič, JAKONČIČ, Kabaj, Klinec, Klinec, MOVIA, Prinčič, SIMČIČ, ŠČUREK, Štekar, etc. Slovenia's largest co-op of the same name produces several brands: Bagueri ★★★ (esp Chard 03 and Merlot 02), Quercus ★★ (REBULA and Cab Sauv). Super-premium r and w blends A+ (★★★).

Istenič ★→★★★ Formerly BARBARA INTL. Sp of all types and price. NV Barbara and Miha are gd value, while Gourmet vintage range is often Slovenia's best sp. Excellent 2002 rosé, v. special ultra-dry 2003.

Izbor Auslese (see PREDIKAT, and box on German quality levels, p.142).

Jagodni izbor Beerenauslese (see PREDIKAT, and box on p.142).

Jakončič ★★★ Continously improving GORIŠKA BRDA producer. Top wines are r, w, and sp Carolina. Varietals lighter, but not to be missed, esp REBULA 04.

Joannes ★★ Fine winery nr Maribor. Crisp, well-defined whites, increasingly gd MODRI PINOT. Interesting experiments with glass stoppers.

Kogl ★★★★ Hilltop winery near Ormož, dating back to 16th C. Replanted 1984. Whites among Slovenia's best, either varietal (since 01 named Solo) or Duo, Trio, and Quartet blends. Reds since 00 (MODRI PINOT, Slovenia's purest Syrah). Premium blends (r & w) Magna Domenica mature in large wooden casks. Exceptional delicate PREDIKATS.

Koper PRIMORSKI coastal district, known for REFOŠK. SANTOMAS and VINAKOPER excel.

Kras PRIMORSKI district. Several gd TERAN producers. Inc Čotar, Lisjak Boris, RENČEL.

Kupljen Jože ★★★ Quality dry wine pioneer near Ormož. Pinot N labelled Modri Burgundec; in better yrs POZNA TRGATEV. New premium line: Star of Stiria. Lovely inn and enoteca Wine Bank of Slovenia at Jeruzalem with vintages going back more than 10 yrs (spectacular RENSKI RIZLING 96 in magnums, incredible value).

Laški Rizling Welschriesling. Slovenia's most planted variety, but now in decline.

Ledeno vino Icewine. Only in exceptional yrs and can be sublime.

Ljutomer ★→★★★ Traditionally top wine district with neighbouring Ormož. Co-op called Ljutomerčan will see better times: v'yds among Slovenia's best.

Malvazija Previously underrated variety in KOPER, now making a comeback. Slightly bitter yet generous flavour, which goes very well with seafood. M by VINAKOPER is incredible value, oaked Capo d'Istria (99 00 01 02 03 04) one of more intriguing Slovenian whites. Also v.gd from Pucer, Rojac.

Mlečnik ★★★ Disciple of Italy's Joško Gravner from VIPAVA. The closest anyone in Slovenia comes to organics. Best known for very long-lived Chard.

Modra frankinja Austria's Blaufränkisch. Fruity reds mostly in POSAVSKI, best as Metliška črnina by the Metlika co-op in the Bela krajina district.

Modri Pinot Pinot N. Recently planted in all regions, with improving results.

Movia ★★★★ Best-known Slovenian winery. Releases only mature vintages of its top wines: Veliko Rdeče (r) after 6 yrs and Belo (w) after 4. Varietals usually v.gd and age for at least 5 years. Varietals usually v.gd.

Ormož ★→★★★ Top wine district with Ljutomer. Co-op named Jeruzalem Ormož. Premium brand Holermuos and gd Muscat sparkler.

Podravski Traditionally most respected Slovenian region in the NE. Recent comeback with aromatic whites and increasingly fine reds, mostly MODRI PINOT.

Posavski Conservative wine region in the SE, best known for CVIČEK. Quality producers starting to emerge: look for ISTENIČ, PRUS, Šēkoranja.

Pozna trgatev Late harvest. See PREDIKAT.

Predikat Wines made of botrytis-affected grapes with high sugar content. Term is taken from the German tradition and is used mostly in the PODRAVSKI region as POZNA TRGATEV, IZBOR, JAGODNI IZBOR, SUHI JAGODNI IZBOR, LEDENO VINO.

Primorski Region in the SW from the Adriatic to GORIŠKA BRDA. The most forward-looking Slovenian wine region for both reds and whites.

Prus Newborn star from the Bela Krajina district in POSAVSKI. Best known for PREDIKATS, also v.gd reds.

Ptujska klet ★ →★★ Winery in Ptuj with a collection of vintages from 1917. Recent vintages less notable, but the 80s were fantastic (and still great value).

Radgonske gorice ★ →★★★ District nr Austrian border, and co-op home to Radgonska Penina, Slovenia's best-known sp. Vintage Zlata (golden) is drier and fuller, also ages well; NV Srebrna (silver) often off-dry. Also very popular sweet TRAMINEC and w blend Janževec by Kapela.

Rebula Traditional white variety of GORIŠKA BRDA. Can be exceptional.

Refošk Italy's Refosco. Dark, acidic red; oaked and unoaked. Best: SANTOMAS.

Renčel ★★★★ Outstanding producer of TERAN (tiny quantities); also v.gd whites.

Renski Rizling Ries. PODRAVSKI only. Best: JOANNES, ORMOŽ, KOGL, KUPLEN, Skaza Anton.

Santomas ★★★ High-quality mature REFOŠK and international-style Cab Sauv.

Ščurek ★★ →★★★ Very reliable GORIŠKA BRDA producer (Chard, REBULA, Tokaj, Sauv Bl, Cab Fr). Very particular red (02) and white blends (04) Stara brajda and classy white Dugo.

Simčič Edi ★★★ Highly reputed GORIŠKA BRDA producer. In particular look for Chard, REBULA, SIVI PINOT. All reserve bottlings very refined and harmonious.

Simčič Marjan ★★★★ Excellent GORIŠKA BRDA producer (Chard, SIVI PINOT). REBULA-based blend Teodor is outstanding. A particular gem is Sauv Bl (reserve 02). Exceptional MODRI PINOT since 02, even better in 03.

Sivi Pinot Italy's Pinot Gr. Increasingly fine, fruity, yet full-bodied wine.

Steyer ★★ Top name from RADGONSKE GORICE. Best known for TRAMINEC, recently also v.gd Chard, RENSKI RIZLING, SIVI PINOT.

Šturm ★★★★ Long-established, yet lone star of the Bela Krajina district in POSAVSKI. Outstanding r and w PREDIKATS, from unusual varieties.

Suhi jagodni izbor Trockenbeerenauslese (see p.142).

Teran 100% REFOŠK from KRAS. The most popular Slovenian wine after CVIČEK.

Traminec Gewurz, only in PODRAVSKI. Generally sweet – also as PREDIKAT.

Valdhuber ★★★ Dry wine pioneers in PODRAVSKI. Top wine is (dry) TRAMINEC.

Vinag ★ →★★ One of largest co-ops in Slovenia, with HQ and immense cellars in Maribor. Many older vintage PREDIKATS. Recently shaky.

Vinakoper ★★★ Large company with own v'yds in KOPER. Many v.gd varietals: Chard, MALVAZIJA, Muscat (dry and sw), Cab Sauv, REFOŠK. Premium brands: Capo d'Istria (varietals), Capris (blends).

Vipava ★ →★★ District in PRIMORSKI region. Many fine producers: BATIČ, Lisjak Radivoj, MLEČNIK, Sutor, Tilia. Co-op of same name with premium brand Lanthieri ★★ (formerly Vipava 1894).

Croatia

This country is divided into two totally different regions. Kontinentalna (inland) is a region of whites, where Graševina is the first choice. Primorska (coastal) is home of many native reds and whites. In 2002, it was confirmed that Zinfandel/

SLOVENIA/CROATIA

Primitivo originated from native Dalmatian grape Crljenak. Plavac Mali is the grape to bet on, while Malvazija can produce a wine of great character in Istria.

Agrolaguna ★→★★ Co-op at Poreč, ISTRIA. Gd w and r, esp Cab Sauv.

Babić Dark, long-lived, native red from Primošten (N DALMATIA). Can be of high quality. Best by VINOPLOD **02**, 03. Unique v'yd site.

Badel 1862 ★→★★★ Big négociant and co-op. Wines and wineries from all over. Usually best: IVAN DOLAC, (PZ Svirče), DINGAČ (PZ i Vinarija Dingač).

Coronica, Moreno ★★★ Top MALVAZIJA and Gran malvazija **02 03' 04'**. Good TERAN and Gran Teran **03** from ISTRIA.

Dalmacija-vino ★ Co-op at Split: range of DALMATIAN wines. V.gd Faros.

Dalmatia Dalmacija The coast of Croatia, Zadar to Dubrovnik, inc islands. Home of many native varieties. Traditionally high in alcohol. V.gd reds; whites are old-fashioned but improving.

Dingač V'yd designation on PELJEŠAC'S steep southern slopes. "Grand cru" for PLAVAC MALI. Made from partially dried grapes, producing a full-bodied robust, dry red. Best: Bura, Kiridžija, Matuško, Miličić, Skaramuča.

Enjingi, Ivan ★★★★ Producer of excellent sw botrytized and dr whites from Požega. GRAŠEVINA, Sivi Pinot, and superb w blend Venje **98' 02**.

Graševina Welschriesling. Best from SLAVONIA. Look for Adžić, ENJINGI, KRAUTHAKER, Vinarija Daruvar, Djakovačka vina, KUTJEVO. Have a try. Gives v.gd wines of different styles. From dry and light to top botrytis wines.

Grgić, Miljenko ★★★ Californian winemaker (see Grgich Hills, California) returns to Croatian roots. Cellar on PELJEˇSAC peninsula. Makes PLAVAC and POŠIP.

Grk Rare native w of Korčula. Oldest Croatian native. Try: Cebalo Branimir.

Hvar Island in mid-Dalmatia. Some excellent reds from PLAVAC MALI grapes from steep southern slopes. Interesting native w and r from plateau. Look for: ZLATAN PLAVAC, IVAN DOLAC, Carić Faros, Tomić, PZ Svirče, PLANČić.

Istria N Adriatic peninsula. V.gd Chard, MALVAZIJA, Muscat. Look for Arman, Coronica, Degrassi, KOZLOVIĆ, MATOŠEVIĆ, Pilato, Ravalico.

Istravino ★ Co-op based in Rijeka. Legendary sp Bakarska Vodica.

Ivan Dolac V'yd area on S slopes of HVAR. "Grand cru" for PLAVAC MALI.

Kontinentalna Hrvatska Inland Croatia (N). Mostly for whites (GRAŠEVINA, Ries, Chard). But gd reds (Pinot N, Merlot) emerging.

Korak ★★ Producer of gd w from PLEŠIVICA. Chard and Beli Pinot.

Kozlović ★★★ Advanced white producer from ISTRIA. Esp MALVAZIJA. Also reds.

Krauthaker, Vlado ★★★ leading producer of Croatian w from Kutjevo, esp Chard and GRAŠEVINA . Reds are ★★. Syrah 03 is great.

Kutjevo Name shared by a town in SLAVONIJA and the ★★→★★★ co-op based there. V.gd Gewurz, GRAŠEVINA, (De Gotho **03**, 04), and botrytis.

Malvazija Malvasia 03 04. Planted in ISTRIA. A pleiad of private producers is producing a range of excellent Malvasias with character and style.

Matošević, Ivica ★★→★★★ Innovative producer of w and r from ISTRIA.

Miloš, Frano ★★ Producer from PELJEŠAC. Cult brand Stagnum (PLAVAC MALI).

Pelješac Beautiful peninsula and wine region in S DALMATIA. Some v.gd PLAVAC MALI. Mostly overrated. See GRGIĆ, Mentek, MILOŠ, POSTUP, DINGAČ.

Plančić ★★ Producer of gd native r and w on HVAR. Rare r Darnekuša.

Plavac Mali The best DALMATIAN red grape: wine of body, strength, and ageability. See DINGAČ, GRGIĆ, IVAN DOLAC, MILOŠ, POSTUP, ZLATAN OTOK. Promising at island of Brač (Murvica).

Plešivica Quality sub-region nr Zagreb, known for whites and sparkling. Look for: Korak, Režek, Šember Tomac.

Pošip Best DALMATIAN white, mostly on island of Korčula.

Postup V'yd designation just NW of DINGAČ. Medium- to full-bodied red.

Primorska Entire coastal Croatia, inc ISTRIA and DALMATIA.

Prošek Almost port-like dessert wine from PRIMORSKA. Try: Hektorovich.
Slavonija Sub-region in N for w. Try: ENJINGI, Jakobovič, KRAUTHAKER, KUTJEVO.
Stolno vino Table wine. Few v.gd wines are designated as this.
Suho Dry. *Polusuho* is semi-dry; *poluslatko* is semi-sweet, sladko is sweet.
Teran Stout, highly acidic, dark red of ISTRIA made from Refosco grape.
Vinoplod ★ Co-op from Šibenik in N DALMATIA. Gd reds, esp BABIĆ.
Vrhunsko vino A fairly rigorous designation for premium wines.
Vugava Rare w of Vis (mid-DALMATIA). Linked to Viognier. Look for Lipanovič.
Zdjelarevič ★★ White wine producer from SLAVONIJA, esp Chard.
Zlahtina Native white from island of Krk. Look for Katunar, Toljanić.
Zlatan otok ★★★ HVAR-based winery of Zlatan Plenković, uncrowned king of
    PLAVAC MALI. His Zlatan Plavac **00 01 02'** 03' 04 is considered best Croatian r.

Bosnia & Herzegovina

Since the civil war ended in 1995, wine production in Bosnia & Herzegovina
has been dominated by small, independent, family operations. Several of
these joined together in 2001 to form The Association of Herzegovinian Wine
Producers and have had some success in improving sales abroad and at home.
Blatina Native red grape and wine.
Kameno Vino White wine of unique, irrigated desert v'yd in Neretva Valley.
Mostar The area around Mostar, the unofficial wine capital city of Herzegovina, has
    been the heartland of Herzegovinian wine production since World War II.
    Cellars such as Ljubuski (the oldest in the country) and Citluk are producing
    gd-quality ZILAVKA white and slightly less impressive BLATINA red.
Samotok Light, red (rosé/*ruzica*) wine from run-off juice (and no pressing).
Zilavka White grape. Potentially dry and pungent. Fruity; faint apricot flavour.

Serbia

Serbia has 82,000 hectares of vineyards producing some 2 million hectolitres of
wine each year. Since the 2004 launch of the annual In Vino international wine
show in Belgrade, the industry has gained a higher profile. Strengths include
light, fruity reds made from the Prokupac grape, but international varieties,
notably Cabernet Sauvignon and, in the Zapadna Morava region, Sauvignon
Blanc, are doing well. Producers: Aleksandrovič, Rubin, Vrsacki Vinogradi.

Montenegro

13 July State-run co-op; high-tech Italian kit, nr Podgorica. VRANAC: high quality.
Crmnica Lakeside/coastal v'yds esp for Kadarka grape (see Macedonia).
Duklja Late-harvested, semi-sweet version of VRANAC.
Krstač Montenegro's top white grape and wine; esp from CRMNICA.
Vranac Local vigorous and abundant red grape and wine. Value.

Macedonia

Macedonia comprises three main growing areas, Pcinja-Osogovo, Povardarie
(Vardar Valley), and Pelagonija-Polog, which total approx. 30, 000 v'yd
hectares. Wine law, est. in 2004, is set to EU standards. Best wineries: Bovin,
Cekorovi, Dudin, Ezimit, Fonko, Kitvin, Popova Kula, Povardarie, Skovin, Tikveš.
Kratosija Red grape also found in Montenegro; sound wines with gd potential.
Plovdina Native grape for mild red, white; esp blended with tastier PROKUPAC.
Prokupac Top red grape of Macedonia, Serbia. Makes full reds and dark rosé
    (*ruzica*) of character. PLOVDINA often added for smoothness.
Rkatsiteli Russian (white) grape often used in blends.

Smederevka Widely planted white grape, also found in Serbia and Hungary.
Teran Less stylish than the version produced in Istria.
Tikveš Macedonia's largest winery in region of same name. Founded in 1946.
  Strong in exports. Gd native SMEDEREVKA and KRATOSIJA grapes.
Vranec Local name for Montenegro's red Vranac (qv); quality improving.
Vrvno Vino Controlled origin designation for quality wines.

The Czech Republic & Slovakia

Prior to 1989 the Czech (Moravia and Bohemia) and Slovak republics had very
little exposure to outside influences. Now much has changed with a new
investment boom leading to improved technology and better overall quality.
Since 2004, however, imports, especially bulk and cheap wines, have increased
to the point where they equal domestic production.

Moravia

Vineyards situated in SE along Austrian and Slovak borders: similar grapes,
Grüner Veltliner, Müller-T, Sauv Bl, Traminer, St Laurent, Pinot N, Pinot Bl,
Blauer Portugieser, Frankovka (Lemberger), Ries, Welschriesling, Zweigelt. Look
for: Springer and Stapleton & Springer (both Bořetice), Dobrá Vinice (Nový
Šaldorf), all young and world-standard, **Znovín** in Znojmo (modern,
internationally recognized, mostly w inc single-v'yd Šobes) and Vinselekt-
Michlovský (Rakvice). Also Baloun and SSV Research Institute (V Pavlovice).
Sonberk (Pouzdřany) and Reisten (Pavlov). Moravia also has sparkling: Sekt
Domaine Petrák (Kobylí), Znovín Classic (Znojmo), Château Bzenec. Icing on
the cake is ice and straw wine, but beware of highly priced 20-cl bottles.

Bohemia

Winemaking since 9th century. Same latitude and similar wines to E Germany.
Best made in the Elbe Valley (north of Prague) most notably at Mělník (Ries,
Ruländer, Traminer, and interesting Pinot N). Vineyard renewal, esp round
Prague, including several small boutique wineries. Producers include:
Lobkowicz-Mělník (oak-aged reds, barrel-fermented Chard, *méthode
traditionnelle* Château Mělník), Na Vinici (Konárovice), and new Vinné Sklepy
Kutná Hora. Also Kosher wine production in Chrámce. Famous castle Karlštejn
near Prague and wine from eponymous Research Institute are popular with
tourists. Sparkling wine is mostly tank-fermented using grapes from Austria.
The two biggest players, Bohemia Sekt in Starý Plzenec (Henkell-Söhnlein)
and Soare Sekt (Faber), are still expanding, thanks to foreign investment.

Slovakia

Hungarian and int'l varieties, with best wines from Malokarpatská region (in
foothills of Little Carpathians) and E Slovakia neighbouring Hungary's Tokaj.
Other key districts: Malá Tŕňa, Nové Mesto, Skalica, Bratislava, Pezinok, Modra.
Leading producers: Château Belá (Mužla) with Müller-Scharzhof involvement,
Malík (Modra), Masaryk (Skalica), Matyšák (Pezinok), Mrva & Stanko (Trnava),
J J Ostrožovič (V T ňa, Tokaj), Pavelka – Sobolič (Pezinok), Vinanza (Vráble)
and Šebo – Karpatská perla (Šenkvice). For sp: J E Hubert and Pálffy Sekt.

Romania

Romania's long winemaking tradition is being revived after decades of quality
abuse due to Soviet-influenced mass-production methods and the lack of
funds and expertise. Through this renewal, grape varieties like indigenous red

Fetească Neagră, as well as Pinot Noir, from optimal regions such as Dealul Mare, are gaining international acclaim.

Alba Iulia In cool TÂRNAVE region of TRANSYLVANIA, with aromatic and off-dry white (RIES ITALIEN, FETEASCĂ, MUSKAT OTTONEL).

Aligoté Pleasantly fresh white varietal.

Băbească Neagra Traditional "black grandmother grape" of the FOCSANI area; light body and red colour.

Banat Smallest wine region, on Serbian border, with RIES ITALIEN, SAUV BL, MUSKAT OTTONEL, local Riesling de Banat; light red Cadarca, CAB SAUV, MERLOT.

Burgund Mare Varietal name linked to Burgenland (Austria), where grape is called Blaufränkisch (Kékfrankos in Hungary).

Buzau Hills Reds (CAB SAUV, MERLOT, BURGUND MARE) from continuation of DEALUL MARE.

Cabernet Sauvignon Dark, intense wines, showing well, esp at DEALUL MARE.

Carl Reh Innovative German-owned winery with 150 ha v'yd in Oprisor. V.gd reds, esp La Cetate label.

Carpathian Winery In DEALUL MARE; excellent PINOT N, SAUV BL.

Chardonnay Dry, oak-aged, sweet styles all showing well; increasingly from MURFATLAR and TRANSYLVANIA.

Cotnari Warm region in NE with v.gd botrytis conditions. Famous sw GRASA, FETEASCĂ ALBA, TĂMAIOASĂ, Francusa.

Cramele Recas British-Romanian firm with 700 ha v'yds in Banat region. PINOT N with potential. Leads in Romanian wine exports.

Crisana W region inc historical Minis area (since 15th C): esp red Cadarca; crisp, white Mustoasa. Other areas: Silvania (esp FETEASCĂ), Diosig, Valea lui Mihai.

Dealul Mare Also Dealu Mare, "The Big Hill". Important well-sited area in SE Carpathian foothills. Excellent reds, esp FETEASCĂ NEAGRĂ, CAB SAUV, MERLOT, PINOT N. Whites from TĂMAIOASĂ. French investment.

Dobrogea Sunny, dry, Black Sea region. Inc MURFATLAR.

DOC Classification for higher-quality wines.

Drăgăsani Region on River Olt S of Carpathian Mountains. Traditional (Crâmposie Selectionată) and int'l grapes (esp Sauv Bl). Gd MUSKAT OTTONEL.

Feteasca White grape with spicy, faintly Muscat aroma. Two types: **F Alba** (same as Hungary's Leányka, ageworthy and with gd potential base for sp and sw COTNARI) and **F Regala** (gd for sp).

Feteasca Neagra "Black maiden grape" with potential as showpiece r variety. Difficult to handle, but can give deep, full-bodied wines with gd character.

Focsani Important Moldavia region, inc Cotesti, Nicoresti, and Odobesti.

Grasă Romania's version of Hungarian Furmint grape, featured esp in COTNARI wines. Botrytis-prone. Grasă means "fat".

Iași Region for fresh, acidic whites (FETEASCĂ ALBA, also RIES ITALIEN, ALIGOTÉ, sp MUSKAT OTTONEL): Bucium, Copu, Tomesti. Reds: MERLOT, CAB SAUV; top BABEASCA.

Jidvei Winery in Transylvania (Târnave); among Romania's northernmost v'yds. Gd whites: FETEASCĂ, Furmint, RIES ITALIEN, and SAUV BL.

Lechinta Transylvanian wine area. Local varieties noted for bouquet.

Merlot Romania's widely planted, workhorse red grape.

Murfatlar Area with v'yds in Dobrogea region nr Black Sea; v.gd sw CHARD and late-harvest CAB SAUV. Dry and sp on the rise.

Muskat Ottonel Muscat of E Europe; a Romanian speciality, esp in cool TRANSYLVANIA and in MOLDAVIA dry wines.

Paulis Small estate cellar in town of same name. Fine, oak-aged Merlot.

Perla Semi-sw speciality of TÂRNAVE: RIES ITALIEN, FETEASCĂ, and MUSKAT OTTONEL.

Pinot Gris Full, slightly aromatic wines, widely grown in Transylvania, MURFATLAR.

Pinot Noir Grown in the S: showing much promise.

Prahova Valley Britain's Halewood Int'l venture, producing v.gd wines, esp reds. V'yds in Dealul Mare yielding fine FETEASCĂ NEAGRĂ and PINOT N.

Premiat Reliable range of higher-quality wines for export.

Prince Stirbey 20-ha estate in Dragasani, returned to Austrian-Romanian noble family (Kripp-Costinescu). German winemaker Oliver Bauer vinifies traditional grapes inc Crâmposie Selecţionată, Fetească Regală and Tămaioasă Românească.

Riesling Italien Widely planted Welschriesling, starting to show potential.

Sauvignon Blanc Very tasty, esp when blended with FETEASCĂ.

SERVE French-founded DEALUL MARE winery and v'yds. Excellent Terra Romana label, esp Cuvée Charlotte (blend of FETEASCĂ NEAGRĂ, CAB SAUV).

Tămîioasă Românească Traditional white "frankincense" grape, with exotic aroma and taste. Often makes fine botrytis wines.

Târnave (also Tîrnave) Romania's coolest region, in Transylvania, known for PERLA and FETEASCĂ REGALA. Dry aromatic wines (esp PINOT GRIS, Gewurz) and sp. See ALBA IULIA, LECHINTA TÂRNAVE.

Tohani DEALUL MARE winery with 1,200 ha v'yd. Gd SAUV BL, FETEASCĂ NEAGRĂ.

Valea Călugărească "Valley of the Monks", part of DEALUL MARE. Nice MERLOT, CAB SAUV, PINOT N, RIES ITALIEN, PINOT GR.

Vinarte Owned by Italian producer Fabio Albisetti, comprising three domains: Villa Zorilor, Castel Bolovanu, Terase Danubiane.

Vin de Masa Basic wine classification; generally for local drinking.

Vinterra Dutch/Romanian venture reviving FETEASCĂ NEAGRĂ; also good PINOT N, MERLOT.

Vrancea E region covering Panciu, Odobesti, Cotesti, and Nicoresti.

Greece

Greek wines remain relatively unknown abroad, but they have much going for them, including a mild maritime climate and, for the most part, reliable weather. Greece has twenty appellations, or OPEs, and over eighty Vins de Pays, or TOs, making some of the most interesting wines. A panoply of over 300 indigenous grape varieties offer exciting flavours. Rediscovered grapes, such as Crete's Vilana or Kozani's Velvendino are two of the latest finds. A mosaic of diverse terroir is now becoming better understood. Farming practices are changing. Denser planting is now used to temper the vigours of Greek nature. The latest water management expertise is applied with success. Despite the language barrier, unfamiliar names of grapes and places, well-made Greek wines are a revelation. These highly individual modern wines beckon to be discovered.

Recent vintages

2005 Small harvest. Uniform ripening. Outstanding reds.

2004 Cool growing season with a late and prolonged harvest. Excellent whites.

2003 Didn't suffer the extreme lack of rain and heat of other European v'yds. Generous dry whites and very good reds.

2002 Difficult, with rain and rot. Nemea a wash-out. North fared better.

2001 Textbook weather conditions. Elegant wines on the mainland and islands.

2000 Lack of spring rains and heat stress in several regions. A few reds are very good.

Aghiorghitiko Quality NEMEA red grape leading Greek wine out of anonymity.

Agioritikos Medium whites and rosés from Agios Oros (Mount Athos), Halkidiki's monastic peninsula. Brand name for TSANTALIS.

Alpha Estate ★★→★★★★ Modern estate in cooler-climate Amindeo. V.gd barrel-aged Merlot/Syrah/XINOMAVRO blend 04, pungent Sauv Bl 04, unfiltered

XINOMAVRO 04. Top wine: Alpha 1, astonishing Tannat-Montepulciano 03.

Antonopoulos ★★→★★★ PATRAS-based merchant and v'yd(s), with MANTINIA, crisp Adoli Ghis 05, unoaked, nutty Chard, and Cab Sauv-Nea Dris (**97 98 00 01**). Top wine: violet-scented Vertzami/Cab Fr 00. To watch.

Arghyros ★★→★★★ Top SANTORINI producer with delicious (expensive) Vinsanto aged 20 yrs in cask. Current vintage: **86**. New fragrant (dry) Aidani 05.

Avantis ★★ Boutique winery in Evia with (r) v'yds in Boetia. Gd (w) Ktima 05, dense Syrah 03. Top wine: elegant single-v'yd Avantis Collection Syrah 02.

Biblia Chora ★★→★★★ V'yds and villa-like winery near Kavala. Polished New World-style wines. Grapey Sauv Bl/Assyrtiko 05. Floral Byblia Rosé 05. Ovilos (w) Sem/Assyrtiko 05. Tangy r Areti cask-aged AGHIORGHITIKO.

Boutari, J & Son ★→★★ Producers and merchants in NAOUSSA. Also v'yds and wineries in GOUMENISSA, MANTINIA, on SANTORINI and CRETE. Popular MOSCHOFILERO. Top wine: single-v'yd Filiria Goumenissa 03.

Calliga ★ KOURTAKIS-owned. Gd AGHIORGHITIKO sourced for Montenero and Rubis.

Cambas, Andrew ★ Brand owned by BOUTARI. V.gd-value Chard and Cab Sauv.

Carras, Domaine ★ Estate at Sithonia, Halkidiki, with its own AC (Côtes de Meliton). Chateau Carras 01. Under new management. Underperforming.

Cava Legal term for cask-aged still white and red wines – *e.g.* Cava Amethystos Kosta Lazaridi, Cava Hatzimihali.

Cephalonia (Kephalonia) Ionian island: gd w Robola, Muscat, Mavrodaphne.

Creta-Olympias ★★ Leading Cretan producer. Inexpensive Nea Ghi range, v.gd-value spicy w Xerolithia 05, r Mirabelo 04. New Pirorago 04 Syrah/Cab Sauv/Kotsifali blend.

Crete Improving quality. Led by Alexakis, Ekonomou, Lyrarakis, Douloufakis.

Emery ★→★★ Historic RHODES producer, specializing in local varieties. Look for brands: Villaré and Grand Rosé. V.gd-value Rhodos Athiri 05. Efreni Muscat 03.

Gaia ★★★ Top-quality NEMEA-based producer and winery on SANTORINI. Fun Notios label. Leading AGHIORGHITIKO (04). Thalassitis SANTORINI 05. Top wine Gaia Estate (**97 98 99 00 01** 03). New Anatolikos 00 dessert (sun-dried) NEMEA.

Gentilini ★→★★★ Exciting whites incl v.gd Robola. New Unique Red Blend 05.

Gerovassiliou ★★★ Perfectionist miniature estate nr Salonika. Look for benchmark fruity blend Assyrtiko/MALAGOUSIA 05, smooth Syrah/Merlot blend 03 Herby, r Avaton **03** from rare indigenous varieties.

Goumenissa (AC) ★→★★ XINOMAVRO and Negoska oaked red from MACEDONIA. Esp BOUTARI, Tatsis Bros, Aidarinis, and Ligas.

Hatzimichalis, Domaine ★ Large v'yds and merchant in Atalanti. Huge range. Greek and French varieties. Top wine: r Rahes Galanou 03 Merlot – Cab Fr.

Katoghi-Strofilia ★★ V'yds and wineries in Attica, Peloponnese, and N Epirus. Mainly Greek varieties, but also Chard, Cab Sauv, and floral Traminer 05.

Katsaros ★★→★★★ Small organic winery of very high standards on Mount Olympus. Ktima r has staying power. Cab Sauv/Merlot 03, supple Chard 05.

Kir-Yanni ★★ High-quality v'yds in NAOUSSA and at Amindeo. Vibrant white Samaropetra 05; gd Syrah 05; top NAOUSSA racy Ramnista 01.

Kouros ★ Reliable, well-marketed white PATRAS and red NEMEA from KOURTAKIS.

Kourtakis, D ★★ Athenian merchant with mild RETSINA and gd dark NEMEA.

Ktima Estate, farm. Term not exclusive to wine.

Lazaridis, Domaine Kostas ★★→★★★ V'ds and wineries in Drama and Kapandriti (nr Athens). Quality Amethystos label (w r p). Top wine: unfiltered red CAVA Amethystos 02.

Lazaridis, Nico ★→★★ Spectacular post-modernist winery and v'yds in Drama. Gd Trebbiano 05. Top wine: Magiko Vouno w (05) r (03).

Lemnos (AC) Aegean island: co-op dessert wines, deliciously fortified, lemony Muscat of Alexandria. New dry Muscats by Kyathos-Honas winery.

Macedonia Quality wine region in the N, for XINOMAVRO.

Malagousia Rediscovered perfumed white grape.

Mantinia (AC) High central Peloponnese region. Fresh, grapey MOSCHOFILERO.

Matsa, Château ★★→★★★ Historic and prestigious small estate in Attica. Top wine: Ktima Assyrtiko/Sauv Bl 05. Excellent MALAGOUSIA 05.

Mavrodaphne (AC) "Black laurel", and red grape. Cask-aged port/*recioto*-like, concentrated red; fortified to 15–22°. Speciality of PATRAS, N Peloponnese.

Mercouri ★★→★★★ Peloponnese family estate. Very fine Refosco, delicious RODITIS. New CAVA (01). Classy Refosco dal Penducolo red and dry MAVRODAPHNE blend.

Moraitis ★★ Small quality producer on the island of Paros. V.gd smoky (w) Monemvasia 05, Ktima (w) Monemvasia-Assyrtiko 05, (r) tannic Moraitis Reserve 01 Monemvasia-Mandelaria blend.

Moschofilero Pink-skinned, rose-scented high-quality, high-acid grape.

Naoussa (AC) r High-quality region for XINOMAVRO. One of two Greek regions where a "cru" notion may soon develop. Excellent vintages: 00 01.

Nemea (AC) r Region in E Peloponnese producing dark, spicy AGHIORGHITIKO wines. Recent investment has moved it into higher gear. High Nemea merits its own appellation. Koutsi front-runner for *cru* status.

Oenoforos ★★ Gd Peloponnese producer with high v'yds. Leading RODITIS w Asprolithi (05). Also delicate white Lagorthi, nutty Chard, crisp Ries 05, and stylish Syrah 04.

Papaïoannou ★★ Reliable NEMEA grower. Classy red (inc Pinot N); flavourful white. Top wine: Ktima Papaïoannou Palea Klimata (old vines) **97 98** 00 01.

Patras (AC) White wine (based on RODITIS) and wine town facing the Ionian Sea. Home of MAVRODAPHNE. Rio-Patras (AC) sweet Muscat.

Pavlidis ★★ Ambitious new v'yds and winery at Kokkinogia nr Drama. Gd Assyrtiko/ Sauv Bl (04), v.gd Assyrtio 05. New Syrah 04 and Tempranilo 04.

Rapsani Interesting oaked red from Mt Ossa. Rasping until rescued by TSANTALIS.

Retsina Attica speciality white with Aleppo pine resin added. Domestic consumption now waning.

Rhodes Easternmost island. Home to creamy (dry) Athiri white grape. Top wines inc Caïr (co-op) Rodos 2400 and Emery's Villare. Also some sparkling.

Roditis White grape grown all over Greece. Many clones. Gd when yields are low.

Samos (AC) Island nr Turkey famed for sw, pale, golden Muscat. Esp (fortified) Anthemis 00, (sun-dried) Nectar. Rare old bottlings can be great.

Santorini Volcanic island N of CRETE: luscious, sweet Vinsanto (sun-dried grapes), mineral-laden, bone-dry white from fine Assyrtiko grape. Oaked examples are gd. Top producers inc GAIA, Hatzidakis, SIGALAS.

Semeli ★★ Estates nr Athens and NEMEA. Gd-value Orinos Helios (w) 05 (r) 04.

Sigalas ★★→★★★ Top SANTORINI estate producing the leading oaked SANTORINI Oia Bareli (05). Stylish, golden-robed Vinsanto (03). Also rare r Mavrotragano.

Skouras ★★ Innovative PELOPONNESE wines. Large range. First to introduce screwcaps on Chard Dum Vinum Sperum. Top: High Nemea Grande Cuvée 03.

Spiropoulos, Domaine ★★ Gd organic producer in MANTINIA. Improving oaky, red Porfyros (AGHIORGHITIKO, Cab Sauv, Merlot). Sparkling Odi Panos has potential.

Tsantalis ★→★★ Merchant and v'yds at Agios Pavlos. AC wines. Gd r Metoxi (01), Rapsani Reserve (01), and gd-value Organic Cab Sauv (03).

Tselepos ★★→★★★ Top-quality MANTINIA producer and Greece's best Gewurz (05). Other wines: fresh, oaky Chard, solid NEMEA (03), v.gd Cab Sauv/ Merlot (03), single-v'yd Avlotopi Cab Sauv (02). Top wine: single-v'yd Kokinomylos Merlot (03).

Voyatzi Ktima ★★ Small estate nr Kozani. Aromatic white 05, classy red 04, new r Velvendino varietal 04.

Xinomavro The tastiest of many indigenous Greek red grapes – though name means "acidic-black". Grown in the cooler N, it is the basis for NAOUSSA, GOUMENISSA, and Amindeo. High potential. Ageworthy vintages: 92 93 94 97 00 01.

Zitsa Mountainous N. Epirus AC. Delicate Debina white, still or sparkling.

Cyprus

Cyprus's finest product is the historic sweet Commandaria, recorded in written sources from the eighth century BC. For years, wines were basic, but now upgrading has started. Vineyards are located in the foothills of the Troodos Mountains, and until recently only two local grapes were grown; now twelve more have emerged, alongside international varietals. Significantly, Cyprus has never had phylloxera. Today the majority of the island's wine is produced by four organizations: KEO, ETKO, SODAP, and Loel, although the number of small wineries is growing. Wines from these smaller producers are often of a high quality, but they are seldom seen outside the island. Cyprus joined the EU in 2004; how this will affect the wine industry is not yet clear.

Commandaria Gd-quality brown sweet wine traditionally produced in hills N of LIMASSOL. Region limited to 14 villages; principal village: Kalo Khorio. Made from sun-dried XYNISTERI and MAVRO grapes. Best (as old as 100 yrs) is superb. A limited quantity of vintage wine is exported.

ETKO Based in LIMASSOL. 16 different wines inc Olympus, Cornaro Carignan, Cornaro Grenache, Semeli (all red), and Nefel (white). Best: Ino Cab Sauv.

KEO Large, go-ahead firm. Production moved from LIMASSOL to regional wineries. Range inc Aphrodite (XYNISTERI), sp Bellapais, Rosella (fragrant pink), Heritage (rich oaked MARATHEFTICO), Othello (solid red), Domaine d'Ahera (velvety red). COMMANDARIA St John. Standard Dry White and Dry Red v.gd value.

Kokkineli Deep-coloured, semi-sweet rosé: the name is related to cochineal.

Limassol Southern port. Historically the home of all the large wineries.

Loel One of major producers. Reds: Orpho Negro, Hermes. Whites: varietal PALOMINO and Ries, also COMMANDARIA Alasia and brandies.

Maratheftico Vines of superior quality make concentrated red wine of tannin and colour, close to Cab Sauv; the future grape of Cyprus.

Mavro The black grape of Cyprus. Can produce quality if planted at high altitude; otherwise gives sound, acceptable wines.

Opthalmo Black grape (red/rosé): lighter, sharper than MAVRO.

Palomino Soft, dry white (LOEL, SODAP). Very drinkable ice-cold.

Pitsilia Region S of Mt Olympus. Some of best white and COMMANDARIA wines.

SODAP A co-op winery and one of the four largest producers. Wines inc: (w) Arsinoë (XYNISTERI), Artemis, Danae; (r) Afames, varietal Carignan, and Grenache. New ranges made using Australian consultancy: Island Vines is modern, fresh, and made from native grapes; Mountain Vines is made from "international" varieties. Both are inexpensive.

Xynisteri Native aromatic white grape of Cyprus, making delicate, fruity wines.

Malta

Accession to the EU has seen vineyard, winemaking, and labelling practices slowly improve, though some producers still chaptalize and/or use inferior "eating" or imported grapes. But pioneering estate Meridiana (Antinori-backed) continues, since 1994, to make excellent, quintessentially Maltese Isis and Mistral Chardonnays, Melqart Cabernet Sauvignon/Merlot, Nexus Merlot, Bel Syrah and premium Celsius Cabernet Sauvignon Reserve from island vines only. Volume producers of note are Delicata, Marsovin, and Camilleri.

England & Wales

The modern UK wine industry, although only just over fifty years old, has learned to produce wines of real individuality and style. The best still wines, based on spicy, Sauvignon Blanc lookalike Bacchus, and some sparklers based on Pinots and Chardonnay are world-class. Many of the original plantings of German crosses and French-American hybrids have been removed in recent years, as a combination of warm years (2003 and 2005 being the warmest), better understanding of sites and soils, and experience with better clones and more suitable rootstocks has prompted a wave of planting, with Champagne varieties being favourite. Chardonnay, Pinot Noir, and Pinot Meunier account for almost twenty per cent of the UK's 800 hectares. Red varieties are on the increase, with Rondo, Regent, and Dornfelder heading the lists. Since 1994, the UK has had an official appellation system for still wines: the best are labelled "Quality Wine" or "Regional Wine". Plain "UK Table Wine" is best avoided, as is "British Wine" that is made from imported concentrate.

Astley Stourport-on-Severn, Worcestershire ★★ Wines continue to win awards and medals. Late Harvest 03 and 04 and Triassic 04 v.gd.

Breaky Bottom E Sussex ★★ 99 01 Sparkling wines well worth trying, esp Cuvée Rémy Alexandre 99, and Cuvée Maman 96. Also Seyval Blanc 03.

Camel Valley Cornwall ★★★ 04 V.gd quality, esp Cornish Rosé 04. Also Bacchus 04 and Atlantic Dry 04. Excellent facilities and very welcoming to visitors.

Denbies Surrey ★★ 02 03 England's largest v'yd at 106 ha. Impressive winery worth a visit. Greenfields 99 sparkling and Hillside Chardonnay 2003 both gold medal winners. Range v.gd and improving.

English Wines Group Kent ★★★ 02 03 Largest UK producer inc Chapel Down, Tenterden, and Lamberhurst brands. Wide range of excellent wines. Pinot Reserve sparkling 00 & 01, plus Pinot N (still) 02 all gold medal winners.

Nyetimber W Sussex ★★★ 95 96 Leading UK specialist sparkling-wine maker; classic Champagne varieties. Classic Cuvée 97 and 99 gold medal winners.

RidgeView E Sussex ★★★ 01 02 Specialist sparkling-wine producer; classic Champagne varieties. Bloomsbury 02 IWSC trophy winner; Grosvenor 02 v.gd.

Sharpham Devon ★★★ 02 03 Produces consistently v.gd wines. Beenleigh Red 03 and Sharpham Pinot N 03 both gold medal winners.

Stanlake Park Berkshire (formerly Valley Vineyards) ★★ Under new ownership. King's Fumé 99 v.gd. Large range of wines of above-average quality.

Three Choirs Gloucestershire ★★ 03 04 UK's second-largest producer. Wines sometimes inconsistent, but Bacchus, Pinot N, and Siegerrebe 04s all good.

Other noteworthy producers

Barnsole All wines Quality and Regional status. Canterbury Choice 02 and 03 and Red Reserve 03 gd.

Biddenden Long-standing producer. Try Dry Ortega 04 and Dornfelder 04.

Chilford Hundred Long-established producer. Wines can be inconsistent. Try Firmin Lifget 04 and sparkling.

Davenport Good range, including Limney Dry White 04 Organic from 2003.

Heart of England Oberon Red worth trying.

Meopham Brut 00, Chardonnay 02, and Pinot Gris medal winners.

Nutbourne Bacchus 01, Nutty 02, and Sussex Reserve 03 gd.

Sandhurst Dessert 01 and Pinot N 03 v.gd.

Asia, North Africa, & The Levant

Algeria Since independence, the combined effects of Islam and the EU have seen wineries dwindle from over 3,000 to fewer than 50, while legislation banning the import of alcohol propagates uncertainty. Viticultural areas and producers of note: Tlemcen (powerful reds, whites, esp rosé – Dom de Sebra), Mascara (Dom El Bordj, Sidi Brahim), Dahra (full-bodied reds, rosés – Dom de Khadra), Zaccar (Ch Romain), Médéa (Ch Tellagh), Tessala, Aïn-Bessem-Bouira.

China Now accounting for 4.5 per cent of world wine production, China is fast becoming the world's sixth-largest producer (in terms of surface under vine and wine production). Twenty-six provinces produce wine, the most suitable being Xinjiang, Tianjin, Shandong, Lioaning, Shanxi, Hebei, and Henan. Currently, there are over 400 wineries in the country and this number is rapidly expanding. Production is still dominated by three companies – Dynasty, Changyu, and Great Wall – but there is an increasing emergence of premium producers. Quality producers such as Huadong (gd Chard and Ries) in Shandong and China Grace at Dongjia Village in Shanxi (gd Merlot, Cab Sauv, B'x blend, Chard) are being joined by the improving Lou Lan at Turpan (gd Chenin Bl and Merlot) and Suntime Manas, both in Xinjiang, and by Dragon Seal and Bodega Langes in Hebei. Other producers to watch: Tsingtao in Shandong, Maotai in Hebei, Kai Xuan Winery in Shandong.

India There are 123,000 acres of vines in India, although just 1 per cent are used for wine. Production is centred around Maharashtra, with 30 wineries; this region is home to the successful Chateau Indage (producers of Omar Khayyam sparkling wine) and the expanding Sula, producing gd Chenin Bl, Sauv Bl, Zin, and Merlot. Grover Vineyards is the other well-known producer, located in Bangalore, making gd Cab Sauv, Merlot, and Shiraz under the guidance of Michel Rolland. Other producers to watch include ND Wines and Dajeeba Wines in Maharashtra and McDowell in Bangalore.

Japan Japan has a 135-yr history of winemaking and is home to 200 wineries. The country has two large wine regions: Yamanashi (nr Mount Fuji) is the oldest and most important; and Nagano. Yet these are beset with climatic problems (summer rain followed by high humidity), and this, coupled with excessive soil fertility, has led to several producers researching new regions and indigenous varieties. Other smaller regions include Yamagata prefectures (N of Tokyo) and Hokkaido, the coldest wine region in the world, which some producers feel may offer a solution to climatic and fertility issues.

Japan has no appellation system, and only 3 per cent of Japanese wines are made locally; the rest are made with imported concentrate and bulk wine. Production is dominated by Mercian, Suntory, Sapporo (Polaire), Mann, and Kyowa Hakko Kogyo (Ste Neige).

Of the indigenous grape varieties causing the greatest buzz, Koshu (discovered 1186) is the most prominent, making gd crisp, dry whites (gd producers: Mercian, Katsunuma, Grace). Other promising indigenous varieties include Shokoshi (Coco Farm, Katsunuma) and the lighter red Yama Sauvignon (Mars).

Red production is now moving towards lighter styles. The most interesting and expensive wines are from established international varieties, such as Mann's Chard from Nagano, Mercian's Kikyogahara Merlot, Asahi Yoshu's Kainoir, and Jyonohira Cab Sauv. Smaller wineries to watch include Obuse (Sangiovese/Merlot), Takeda, Alps, Marufuji, and Yamazaki.

Morocco The finest v'yds are found on the slopes of the Atlas Mountains (esp Meknes and Fez). Cinsault, Carignan, Grenache make interesting traditional reds and "Gris", but Syrah, Cab Sauv, Merlot, Sauv Bl, Chard are now making better wines. Coastal v'yds produce notable light, fruity wines. The area under vine has declined drastically but French investment (esp Castel and William Pitters) is breathing new life. Best producer Celliers de Meknes makes around 90% of the country's wine; Cépages de Meknes and Cépages de Boulaouane also figure. Best labels inc L'Excellence de Bonassia (aged Cab Sauv/Merlot), Les Trois Domaines, El Baraka, Halana, Domaine de Sahari.

Tunisia Substantial foreign investment plus recent government initiatives have seen a new wave of producers and labels emerge; best inc Dom Hannon, Dom Atlas, Dom Magon, Dom Neferis. Muscat produces the finest traditional whites. The most successful international grapes are Ugni Blanc, Carignan, Cab Sauv, Syrah, Merlot, Pinot N, Cinsault. The main viticultural areas lie in Grombalia, Kelibia-Cap Bon, Bizerte-Mateur-Tebourba, and Thibar.

Turkey State producer Tekel recently disbanded, leaving Kavaklidere (gd white Cankaya, red Yakut) and Doluca (gd Kav/V Doluca reds) to dominate. Diren, Melen, Sarafin (v.gd international varieties), and Kocabag also make gd wine. The main area of production is Thrace/Marmara (40%); other districts are C/E/SE Anatolia and the Black Sea coast. Indigenous Sultaniye and Narince produce good whites; Bogazkere and Oküzgözü make full, powerful reds. International varieties show promise. Winemakers are increasing their own v'yds in favour of independent growers to ensure better practices.

The Old Russian Empire

This region's wines are still plagued by their Soviet heritage. Cheap, imported bulk wines make life difficult for authentic regional wine producers. Large, ex-Soviet wineries dominate. Some good wines are produced by flying winemakers. Known authentic producers are listed below:

Ukraine (inc Crimea) Second-largest wine producer in the CIS. Potential for Crimea's first-class dessert and fortified wines was revealed in 1990 by the auction of old wines from the last Tsar's Massandra Collection, nr Yalta, where production continues, though Massandra is now more of a tourist attraction. Classic brut sp from Novy Svet (Crimea, served at Tsar's coronation 1896) and Artyomovskoe. Large new investments: Sun Valley. Other Crimea wineries to watch: Inkermann, Magarach. Reds: potential (*e.g.* Massandra's Alushta). Whites: Aligoté; Artyomovskoe sp.

Georgia Possibly the oldest wine region of all: antique methods such as fermentation in clay vats (*kvevris*) still exist and a huge number of indigenous grape varieties almost untried. Reluctant to modernize, but newer techniques used for exports (Mukuzani, Tsinandali). Kakheti (E) makes two-thirds of Georgia's wine, esp lively, savoury r (the grape is Saperavi) and acceptable w (Tibaani, Rkatsiteli, Gurjaani). Foreign investors: Pernod Ricard with GWS brand; US-owned Bagrationi has cheap, drinkable sp. To watch: Talisman, Suliko, Shumi. As the region's equipment, techniques, and attitudes evolve, Georgia could be an export hit.

Moldova Most important in size and potential, but poorest, with few signs of recovery. Most wineries are privatized and supply cheap wines to Russia. Wine generates a third of Moldova's income. Wine regions: Bugeac (most important), Nistrean, Codrean, Northern. Grapes inc Cab Sauv, Pinot N, Merlot, Saperavi, Ries, Chard, Pinot Gris, Aligoté, Rkatsiteli. Top wineries: Purkar, Cahul, Kazayak, Hincesti. Also gd: Cricova. New World investment at Hincesti, and by local company Vininvest, has brought modern winemaking practices. Moldova's most modern wines: Ryman's Hincesti

Chard; Abastrele (w); Legenda (r). Progress has not been smooth but is worth following. Appellations are now in force.

Russia Moscow and St Petersburg are waking up to wine – a rapidly growing, large market. But things are not helped by imported cheap, bulk wine. Krasnodar on Northern Black Sea Coast produces 60% of Russia's wine. New winery nr Anapa: Ch Le Grand Vostock with French winemaker, equipment, and French-style blends. Australian winemaker at Myskhako (Novorossiysk) making gd Aligoté, Chard, Cab Sauv. Largest producer: Fanagoria (Temruk) – Merlot and Cab Sauv. Also look at sw Kagor from Vityazevo Winery (Anapa). Abrau Durso Brut (also Prince Golitsyn): classic sp since 1896.

The Levant

Israel New World technology and internationally trained winemakers have had dramatic effects, resulting in consistent improvement. Best v'yds are in cooler, high-altitude regions of the Upper Galilee, Golan Heights, and Judean Hills.

Amphorae r w ★ 2003s herald return to quality.

Barkan r w V.gd Barkan ★ Pinotage. Segal varietals great value.

Bazelet ha Golan Golan r Elegant, rounded Cab Sauv.

Binyamina r w Traditional winery making encouraging improvements.

Carmel r w sp ★→★★ Founded in 1882 by a Rothschild. Excellent Limited Edition (02 03'), single-v'yd Kayoumi Shiraz, Zarit Cab Sauv from Upper Galilee.

Castel Judean Hills r w ★★★ Small family estate in Jerusalem mountains. Complex Grand Vin (00' 01 02 03'); outstanding Chard (02 03' 04).

Chateau Golan Golan r (w) ★ Spicy, gamey Syrah. Gd Sauv Bl.

Chillag r Israel's most prominent female winemaker.

Clos de Gat Samson r w ★→★★ Rich and buttery Chard. Well-made reds.

Dalton U. Galilee r w ★ Reserve reds: modern, oaky, concentrated.

Efrat r w Old winery starting to upgrade its wines.

Ella Valley Samson r w ★ Dark, garnet Cab Fr with leathery finish.

Flam r (w) ★★ Intense Cab Sauv (02 03); earthy, herbal Syrah Cab.

Galil Mountain Upper Galilee r w ★→★★ Pinot N with gd varietal character.

Margalit r ★★ Ripe, concentrated B'x blend Enigma (03).

Recanati r w ★ Oaky wines very much in New World style.

Saslove r w ★ Aviv reds are easy-drinking, flavourful, and fruit-forward.

Sea Horse r Idiosyncratic *garagiste* specializing in Syrah and Zin.

Tabor Lower Galilee r w Crisp, aromatic Sauv Bl. Gd value.

Tishbi r w sp Family grower. Gd wines from Gush Etzion v'ds.

Tzora r w Kibbutz winery situated in Judean foothills.

Vitkin r Promising boutique. Carignan and Petite Sirah specialist.

Yarden Golan r w sp ★★★ Multilayered Cab Sauv (00' 01 02) and rare r Katzrin (90 93 96 00'), Heights Wine dessert wines, and Blancs de Blancs sp also gd.

Yatir Judean Hills r (w) ★★ Classy Yatir Forest (01 02) rich with velvety finish.

Lebanon The Bekaa Valley is host to new, quality wineries challenging the existing order, showing there is life after Musar. Dominant influence is French.

Chateau Musar r (w) ★★★ Unique Cab Sauv with Cinsault (91 94 95 98) improves with age. Lighter Hochar r (Cinsault/Cab Sauv). Also oaky w Obaideh.

Clos St Thomas r (w) Best value Les Emirs from Cab Sauv and Grenache.

Kefraya r w ★★ Outstanding Comte de M (99 00 01) from Cab Sauv, Syrah, Mourvèdre. Also fresh rosé.

Kouroum r w Sept Cépages is an interesting blend of seven varieties.

Ksara r w ★★ Ch Ksara is fragrant, spicy B'x blend. Reserve du Covent gd value.

Massaya r w ★ New Lebanon. Syrah/Grenache blend is very promising.

Wardy r w Private Selection – Syrah/Cab Sauv an impressive wine.

North America

California

More heavily shaded areas are the wine-growing regions

The key to Californian wine is diversity. Napa is still the best-known area, with its sometimes stunning Cabernet-family wines, and for most people, Napa Cabernet remains the star turn in the state. A string of mostly good vintages going back to the late 1990s, as well as continued advances in viticulture and winemaking, have led to a surge in quality.

But Napa is not the only Californian wine county. For example, look for wines from the Central Coast, especially Chardonnay. There is a rich selection of Zinfandel and Rhône varieties from this area as well, with outstanding Syrah, Viognier, and Rhône blends coming out of Paso Robles, Monterey, and Santa Barbara County. The Lodi American Viticultural Area (AVA) in the upper San Joaquin Valley east of San Francisco Bay is also good for quality Zinfandel, Syrah, Cabernet Sauvignon, and Chardonnay, at everyday prices. Back on the North Coast, Lake County, an inland region around a large, freshwater lake just north of Napa, is gaining a reputation for solid Cabernet Sauvignon, Syrah, and outstanding Sauvignon Blanc. And there are exciting new Pinots and Chardonnays coming from the very cool Sonoma Coast AVA.

Another major story currently unfolding is the move toward organically grown grapes and biodynamic farming of vineyards. Organic and/or biodynamic wines have consistently outperformed traditional wines in several US tastings.

Overall, it's a good time to drink California.

The principal Californian vineyard areas

Central Coast

An umbrella region stretching from San Francisco Bay south almost to Los Angeles, including the following AVAs:

Arroyo Grande San Luis Obispo County. A coolish growing region with Pacific influence. Gd Pinot N, Viognier. Zin at higher and warmer elevations away from the coast.

Arroyo Seco Monterey County. Excellent Ries both dry and late harvest, citrus Chard and Cab Sauv from warmer canyons in the Santa Lucia mountains.

Carmel Valley Monterey County. Resort area with small production of dense, concentrated Cab Sauv and Merlot on hillside v'yds and some gd Sauv Bl.

Edna Valley San Luis Obispo County. Cool winds whip through a gap in the coastal range off Morro Bay. Excellent minerally Chard.

Monterey County Wide range of soils and microclimates gives wines good varietal character. See individual listings for best regions.

Paso Robles San Luis Obispo County. Large, productive area E of coastal range. Known for Zin. Promising plantings of Syrah and Rhône varieties.

Santa Lucia Highlands Monterey County. Newish AVA above the Salinas Valley, E of the Santa Lucia mountains. Excellent Syrah and Ries; outstanding Pinot N.

Santa Maria Valley Santa Barbara County. Outstanding Pinot N, gd Chard, Viognier, and Syrah.

Santa Ynez Valley Santa Barbara County. Like Santa Maria but with warmer inland regions. Rhône grapes, Pinot N, Chard in cool areas. Sauv Bl a gd bet.

North Coast

Encompasses Lake, Mendocino, Napa, Sonoma counties, all north of San Francisco. Ranges from very cool climate near San Francisco Bay and the coast to very warm interior regions. Soils vary from volcanic to sandy loam. Includes the following regions:

Alexander Valley Sonoma County. Fairly warm AVA bordering Russian River. Excellent Cab Sauv in a ripe, juicy style. Gd Sauv Bl near the river.

Anderson Valley Mendocino County. Cool valley opening to the Pacific along the Navarro River. Outstanding sparkling wine, v.gd Gewurz and Pinot N. Hillside v'yds above the fog produce terrific old-vine Zin.

Carneros Napa and Sonoma Counties. Cool and foggy region bordering San Francisco Bay. Top site for Pinot N and Chard. V.gd sparkling wine.

Dry Creek Valley Sonoma County. Relatively warm region offering distinctive Zin and Sauv Bl, with Cab Sauv a winner on rocky hillsides.

Lake County Warm to hot mountainous region centred around Clear Lake. Gd Zin, Sauv Bl nr the lake, and lush, fruity Cab Sauv on cooler hillsides.

Mendocino County Large region N of Sonoma County with a wide range of growing regions from hot interior valleys to the coast.

Mount Veeder Napa County. High altitude AVA (v'yds planted up to 730 m) best known for concentrated Cab Sauv and rich Chard.

Napa Valley Best-known wine district, N of San Francisco Bay. Napa's v'yd land has become the most expensive outside of Europe. Great diversity of soil, climate, and topography in such a small area can produce a wide range of wines, esp the red B'x varieties and Pinot N in cooler areas. Wines have achieved international acclaim, and are priced to match.

Oakville Napa County. Located in mid-Valley, the heart of Cab Sauv County.

Redwood Valley Mendocino County. Warm interior region. Gd basic Cab Sauv, excellent Zin, everyday Chard, and Sauv Bl. Also gd plantings of Syrah.

Russian River Valley Sonoma County. Very cool area, often fog-bound until noon. Maybe best Pinot N in California; Zin and Cab Sauv on hillside v'yds. Green Valley is a small super-cool AVA located within the Russian River AVA.

Rutherford Napa County. Rivals Oakville as Cab Sauv heartland. Long-lived reds from hillside v'yds; lush, dazzling Merlots and other B'x reds nr Napa River.

Sonoma Coast Sonoma County. Trendy new region borders the Pacific. Very cool climate, very poor soils. New plantings of Pinot N show great promise.

Sonoma Mountain Sonoma County. Part of the Sonoma Valley AVA. High-elevation v'yds ideal for powerful Cab Sauv.

Sonoma Valley This is Jack London's Valley of the Moon. Varied growing regions produce everything from Cab Sauv to Zin. Separated from Napa Valley by the Mayacamas mountains.

Spring Mountain Napa County. Part of the Mayacamas range. V.gd Cab Sauv with pockets of delicious Sauv Bl at lower elevations, plus good Ries.

Stags Leap Napa County. E of Napa River, distinctive Cab Sauv and Merlot.

Bay Area

Urban sprawl has wiped out most of the vineyards that once surrounded San Francisco Bay.

Contra Costa County Historic growing district E of the Bay now succumbing to homes and shopping malls. Fine Zins, red Rhônes.

Livermore E and S of San Francisco Bay, valley soils are gravel and stone. Surprisingly gd Cab Sauv; outstanding Sauv Bl and Sem.

Marin County Old (1820s) growing region being revived with new plantings of Pinot N and Chard near the coast.

Santa Clara Valley Broad valley S of the Bay, once major wine district, now called Silicon Valley. Remnant areas like Hecker Pass can surprise today.

Santa Cruz County Pierce's Disease has wiped out many historic v'yds, but a few remain, yielding gd Cab Sauv and some Pinot N from Santa Cruz Mountains.

Central Valley

About 60% of California's v'yds are in this huge region that runs N to S for several hundred miles. Now shedding its image as a low-quality producer, as Valley growers realize they must go for quality to keep up in the global market.

Clarksburg Sacramento, Solano, and Yolo counties. Just outside the state capital Sacramento, running along the Sacramento River. Viognier, Syrah, and Sauv Bl are strong.

Lodi San Joaquin and Sacramento counties. More than a decade ago this AVA began a push for quality. It has paid off in a major way. Strengths are Zin, Sauv Bl, Muscat (sweet), and fruit-forward Chard grown nr Sacramento River.

Sacramento Valley Northern half of California's agricultural centrepiece makes affordable Rhône varietals from the Dunnigan Hills AVA.

San Joaquin Valley Hot heart of the Central Valley. Source of most jug, bag-in-a-box, and fortified dessert wine from the state. Many growers now process their own grapes, making fruity, easy-drinking varietals at a bargain price.

Sierra Foothills

Grapes were first planted here during Gold Rush days. Best regions include:

Amador County Warm region famous for old Zin v'yds producing jammy, intense wines with a signature metallic backnote, as well as crisp Sauv Bl. Top Rhône reds and Italian varietals are beginning to emerge.

Fiddletown Amador County. High-elevation v'yds produce a more understated, elegant Zin than much of Amador.

Shenandoah Valley Amador County. Source of powerful Zins and increasingly well-regarded Syrah.

Recent vintages

Because of its size and wide range of microclimates, it is virtually impossible to produce a one-size-fits-all vintage report for California. California's climate is not as consistent as its "land of sunshine" reputation suggests, and although grapes ripen regularly, they are often subject to spring frosts, sometimes a wet harvest time, and (too often) drought. Wines from the Central Valley tend to be most consistent. The Central Coast region, with its much cooler maritime mesoclimate has a different pattern of vintage quality from the North Coast or Sierra Foothills. Rain is much less of a factor and arrives later, rarely before mid-December. Grapes ripen more slowly and are harvested 3–6 weeks later than inland regions such as Napa. That said, the following vintage assessment relies most heavily on evaluation of Cabernets and Zinfandels from North Coast regions. For Chardonnay, the best vintages are: 97 99 01 03.

2005 A surprisingly large crop all across the state following a long, cool growing season. Promising reports of gd-quality wines with crisp acidity and ageing potential. Could be the best vintage since 2001.

2004 Scant winter rains and a warm spring led to bud-break and bloom at least 3 wks early. Grapes developed evenly through the summer and it was looking good until a prolonged heat-wave hit the North Coast in late Aug. Grapes ripened quickly with uneven quality. At best it looks average.

2003 A difficult year all around. Spring was wet and cool, with a series of heat spikes during the summer and some harvest rains. The size of the crop is down and quality is spotty on the North Coast, better on the Central Coast. Careful grape selection could lead to an above-average vintage.

2002 Average winter rainfall and slightly delayed bud-break with some frost damage. Heavy rain in May, cool growing season but no rain until Nov. Average-sized crop with superior quality and showing well with age.

2001 Little winter rain, sporadic heat in March, severe April frost, hottest May on record, and no rain until Oct. Excellent quality.

2000 Scares included a threatened storm from the south in early Sept, but damage was minimal. Biggest harvest on record. OK quality.

1999 Very cold spring and summer created late harvest, but absence of autumn rain left crop unscathed. Intensely flavoured and coloured wines. Outstanding quality, which is looking even better with a little age.

1998 Erratic harvest stumbled into Nov. Wines are adequate to dismal.

1997 Huge crop, but strongly flavoured and showing very well at present. Favourite vintage on record for growers; well appreciated by consumers.

1996 Tiny crop, lots of structure, lacks aromatic charm. Vintage is fading fast.

1995 Tiny crop, great vitality but slow to unfold. Good Zins, great Cabs. Best vintage for cellaring since 90.

1994 Mild growing season; dry, late harvest. Superb Zins, but a bit long in the tooth now; Cabs are supple, wonderful for drinking right now.

1993 Modest, plain-faced, serviceable year in the North Coast, but spectacular in Sierra Foothills with concentrated Zins, refreshing acidity. Drink up.

1992 Oddly inconsistent. Some empty. Some flavourful and vital.

1991 Very late harvest; very large crop: 30–50% bigger than normal and twice the size of tiny 90. Wines are lean, racy, most European-style in years.

1990 Picture-perfect California vintage and small crop: wonderful development and strong collectors' value. Cabernets magnificent.

Acacia Carneros ★★★ (Chard) 00 01 02 03 04 (Pinot N) 97 99 00 01 02 03 CARNEROS pioneer in Chard and Pinot N, moving towards darker Pinot N fruit with emphasis on single-v'yd wines.

Acorn Russian River Valley ★★→★★★ Newcomer with outstanding Zin from Heritage vines. Also v.gd Sangiovese and Syrah. Will only get better.

Alban Edna Valley ★★→★★★ Pioneer Rhône-variety planter, and (with CALERA) California benchmark for Viognier. Excellent Grenache, Roussanne, Marsanne.

Alexander Valley Vineyards Sonoma ★★→★★★ (Cab Sauv) 00 01 03 Juicy approachable Cab Sauv and Zin. Chard much improved in past few years.

Altamura Vineyards Napa ★★★ (Cab) 01 02 03 Elegant and luscious Cab Sauv. Sangiovese is one of the state's best.

Amador Foothills Winery Amador ★★ Ripe and delicious Zin and bright Sauv Bl, often blended with Sem.

Andrew Murray Sta Barbara ★★★ 00 01 02 03 04 Small winery with a goal of producing only Rhône varietals. V'yds planted on slopes thus reducing yields. Gd Syrah, great Roussanne and Viognier.

Araujo Napa ★★★ 95 97 00 01 02 03 Powerful, sleek, cultish Cab Sauv made from Eisele v'yd, bottled for years by Joseph PHELPS as a single-v'yd wine.

Armida Sonoma ★★→★★★ RUSSIAN RIVER VALLEY winery with solid Merlot, gd Pinot N, and a zippy Zin made from DRY CREEK VALLEY grapes.

Arrowood Sonoma ★★→★★★ (Chard) 03 04 (Cab) 95 97 01 02 03 Supple Cab Sauv and a sound Chard. Change of ownership obscures the future.

Artesa Napa, Carneros ★★ Former Codorníu NAPA has turned away from bubbly to still-wine production, showing steady improvement, esp the reds.

Arthur Earl Sta Barbara ★★→★★★ Small producer of Rhône and southern French varietals. V.gd Mourvédre.

Atlas Peak Napa ★★ Now owned by Beam Wines – stablemates of Clos du Bois, Geyser Peak. New emphasis here on Cab Sauv. Shows promise.

Au Bon Climat Sta Barbara ★★★ (Chard) 01 02 03 04 (Pinot N) 99 01 02 03 04 Jim Clendenen listens to his private drummer: ultra-toasty Chard, flavourful Pinot N, light-hearted Pinot Bl. Vita Nova label for B'x varieties, Podere dellos Olivos for Italianates. See also QUPÉ.

Babcock Vineyards Sta Barbara ★★★ Very cool location in W SANTA YNEZ VALLEY. Gd for Pinot N and Chard; Eleven Oaks Sauv Bl is one of California's best.

Beaulieu Vineyard Napa ★★★ (Cab) 73 78 85 90 91 95 97 00 01 02 03 04 Under André Tchelistcheff in the 1940s and 1950s, Beaulieu set the style for NAPA

Cab Sauv. Now owned by Diageo Chateau & Estate Wines. Not the jewel it was, but still quite gd, esp the Georges de Latour Private Reserve Cab Sauv.

Benessere Napa ★★★ Sangiovese and Syrah worth a try. New Super Tuscan-style blend called Phenomenon is outstanding.

Benziger Family Winery Sonoma ★★★ Family began converting vines to biodynamism in the mid-1990s. Steady improvement in wines, esp Chard and a soft, delicious Merlot.

Beringer Blass (Foster's Wine Estates) Napa ★★→★★★★ (Chard) **00 01** 02 03 04 (Cab) **87 90 91 95 97** 99 01 02 03 A NAPA classic producing wines from Central and N Coast. Single-v'yd Cab Sauv Reserves are over-the-top, but marvellous. Velvety but powerful Howell Mountain Merlot. Look for Founder's Estate bargain line. Also owns CHATEAU ST JEAN, ETUDE, MERIDIAN, ST CLEMENT, STAGS' LEAP WINERY, and Taz, a ★★★★ Pinot from Santa Barbara.

Bernardus Carmel Valley ★★★ **97** 00 01 03 Strong Meritage wines from densely-planted, high-altitude v'yd above the valley floor. Brilliant Sauv Bl.

Biale Napa ★★→★★★ Small Zin specialist using mostly NAPA fruit.

> **Biodynamics**
> The biodynamic option is coming into greater play in California. Biodynamics is the farming technique that, among other things, focuses on astrological data to guide planting and harvesting. Most winemakers admit that they don't know why it works, but it does, as tastings have shown. FETZER has walked the biodynamic path for years at some of its key vineyards for the Bonterra brand. New converts include QUIVIRA, Joseph PHELPS, BENZIGER, and FROG'S LEAP.

Boeger El Dorado ★★ First El Dorado winery after Prohibition. Mostly estate wines. Attractive Merlot, Barbera, Zin, and Meritage. More understated than many in SIERRA FOOTHILLS.

Bogle Vineyards Yolo ★→★★ Major growers in the SACRAMENTO Delta, Bogle family makes attractive line of budget varietals and an excellent old-vine Zin.

Bokisch Lodi ★★→★★★ Makes wine only from Spanish varieties. V.gd Garnacha, brilliant Albariño and one of the state's best Tempranillos.

Bonny Doon Sta Cruz Mtns ★★→★★★ Original Rhône Ranger Randall Grahm has expanded operations into S France and Italy. All wines now in screwcap. Best is Cigare Volant, his homage to Châteauneuf-du-Pape. Big House Red and Big House White are gd bargain quaffs. Brilliant Pacific Rim Ries.

Bouchaine Vineyards Napa Carneros ★★→★★★ (Chard) **01 02** 03 04 (Pinot N) **01** 02 03 Winery has had some ups and downs since its founding in 1980. Now on an up-swing with classic, sleek Chard and juicy but serious Pinot N.

Bruce, David Sta Cruz Mtns ★★★ (Pinot) Powerful Chard has improved of late, but Pinot N is first rate.

Buehler Napa ★★→★★★ Cab Sauv can be inconsistent, but look for gd to outstanding estate Zin and Chard made from RUSSIAN RIVER grapes.

Buena Vista Napa, Carneros ★★→★★★ 00 **01** 02 03 After stumbling for a few years, Buena Vista is back on track with v.gd Estate Cab Sauv and gd Sauv Bl from Lake County. Chard also worth a look.

Burgess Cellars Napa ★★→★★★ (Cab) **95 97** 99 01 02 03 Emphasis on dark, weighty Cab Sauv made from hillside vines. Powerful Zin worth seeking out.

Bynum, Davis Sonoma ★★★ (Pinot N) **00 01** 02 03 04 Marvellous single-v'yd Pinot N from RUSSIAN RIVER VALLEY. Lean, minerally Chard is a treat.

Cain Cellars Napa ★★★ (Cain Five) 85 87 90 94 **95** 97 99 01 02 Stylish, supple Cain Five anchored in estate plantings of Cab Sauv and four B'x cousins on SPRING MOUNTAIN; Cain Cuvée (declassified Cain Five) can rival the big brother.

Cafaro Napa ★★★ Winemaker label for sturdy-to-solid Cab and Merlot.

Cakebread Napa ★★★→★★★★ (Chard) **00 01 02 03** 04(Cab) **87 90 91 95 97** 00 01 02 03 Powerful Cab Sauv with well-integrated if sometimes obvious oak. One of the best Sauv Bls in the state. Chard sometimes too oaky.

Calera San Benito ★★★★ (Chard) **01 02** 03 04 (Pinot) **00 01** 02 03 04 Yale and Oxford graduate Josh Jensen went in search of the holy grail of Pinot N and found it in the dry, hot hills of San Benito. Three Pinot Ns named after v'yd blocks: Reed, Seleck, and Jensen; also, intense, flowery Viognier.

Cambria Sta Barbara ★★ Part of KENDALL-JACKSON's Artisans & Estates group. Chard routinely toasty; Pinot N more enticing.

Campion Winery Napa ★★→★★★ Pinot N guru Larry Brooks (ex-SAINTSBURY) is making only Pinot N and only single-v'yd Pinot N. Very promising beginning.

Carneros Creek Napa, Carneros Founder Frances Mahoney was one of the first to explore the potential of Pinot N in Carneros and made outstanding Pinot N and Chard in the 1990s. Winery now in transition.

Cass Paso Robles ★★ New producer; Rhône varieties. Production limited but will grow. Look for Syrah and Grenache/Syrah/Mourvèdre blend Rockin One.

Caymus Napa ★★★→★★★★ (Cab) **90 91 94 97** 99 00 **01** 02 03 The Special Selection Cab Sauv is consistently one of California's best: rich, intense, slow to mature. Also a quite gd regular bottling, balanced and a little lighter.

Cedar Mountain Winery Livermore ★★ Top marks for powerful, long-lived Cab Sauv from estate v'yds. A range of delicious port-style dessert wines as well.

Ceja Vineyards Napa ★★→★★★ 99 00 **01** 02 03 Established in 1999 and already making a mark with balanced, focused Cab Sauv and delicious Chard.

Chalk Hill Sonoma ★★→★★★ Large estate that has been up and down over the years. Usually reliable Cab Sauv made for ageing and a pleasing Chard.

Chalone Monterey ★★★→★★★★ (Chard) **01 02** 03 04 (Pinot) **00 01** 02 03 04 Mountain estate on E edge of MONTEREY. Marvellous flinty Chard and rich, intense Pinot N. Also makes a gd Chenin Bl (unusual in California) and a tasty Pinot Bl. Bought by global wine and spirits company Diageo in 2005; at this point, quality remains high.

Chappellet Napa ★★★ (Cab) 90 **94** 95 **97 99** 00 **01** 02 Beautiful amphitheatrical hill v'yd, with California's first modern winery building (1968). Ageworthy Cab Sauv has new grace-notes, esp Signature label. Chenin Bl: a NAPA classic, dry and succulent. Pleasing, understated Chard; gd Cab Fr, Merlot, sweet Moelleux.

Château Montelena Napa ★★★→★★★★ (Chard) **97 00 01 02** 03 04 (Cab) 99 00 01 02 03 04 Understated ageworthy Chard, and Calistoga Estate Cab Sauv built for long-term ageing.

Château Potelle Napa ★★★ Ex-pat French couple produce quietly impressive Chard (Reserve edition toastier) and vigorous Cab Sauv from MOUNT VEEDER estate. Outrageously gd Zin from estate-owned v'yds in PASO ROBLES.

Château St Jean Sonoma ★★→★★★ Pioneered single-v'yd Chard in California under Richard Arrowood in the 1970s, still outstanding; gd Sauv Bl. Red wine now a priority. Cinq Cepage, made from the five B'x varieties, one of the best in the state. Reliable bottlings of Sonoma County Cab Sauv and Chard. Owned by BERINGER BLASS.

Château Souverain Sonoma Winery now sold to NIEBAUM-COPPOLA. Souverain brand will be made elsewhere by Foster's Estates.

Chimney Rock Napa ★★★→★★★★ (Cab) **95 97 99 00 01** 02 03 04 STAGS LEAP AVA producer of elegant, sometimes understated Cab Sauv.

Clautiere Santa Barbara ★★ Lively, palate-pleasing wines that are fun to hang with, especially the Mon Beau Rouge, a Rhône blend and a balanced, v.gd Syrah. A winery to watch.

Cline Cellars Carneros ★→★★ Originally Contra Costa (important v'yds still there), now in SONOMA/CARNEROS and still dedicated mostly to rustic-style Rhône blends and sturdy Zin.

Clos du Bois Sonoma ★★→★★★ Large-scale Sonoma producer of quaffable everyday wines, with the exception of a single-v'yd Cab Sauv (Briarcrest) and Calcaire Chard, which can be v.gd.

Clos du Val Napa ★★★★ (Cab) 85 87 91 91 94 95 97 00 01 02 03 04 Bernard Portet and his staff create consistently elegant Cab Sauvs that are among the best ageing candidates in the state. Chard is a delight and a Sem/Sauv Bl blend called Ariadne is a charmer.

Clos LaChance Santa Cruz ★★ Relative newcomers showing gd Zin and bright Chard from sourced fruit and own vineyards.

Clos Pegase Napa ★★→★★★ Post-modernist winery/museum makes a spare, wiry NAPA CARNEROS Chard and a sleek Cab Sauv from N NAPA grapes.

Cohn, B R Sonoma ★★→★★★ Mostly estate Cab Sauvs; hard-edged and awkward in the 1990s, now showing gd juicy base and ageing potential.

Constellation Huge NY firm, formerly known as Canandaigua. Owns and operates wineries in California, NY, Washington State, Chile, Australia, and New Zealand. Produces 90 million cases of wine annually, selling more wine than any other winery in the world. Once a bottom feeder, now going for the top. Bought MONDAVI at end of 2004 and also owns FRANCISCAN, ESTANCIA, Mount Veeder, SIMI, and RAVENSWOOD.

Corison Napa ★★★→★★★★ (Cab) 94 95 97 00 01 02 03 Long-time winemaker at CHAPPELLET makes supple, flavoursome Cab Sauv promising to age well.

Cosentino Napa ★★→★★★ Irrepressible winemaker-owner Mitch Cosentino always full tilt. Results sometimes odd, sometimes brilliant, never dull. Cab Sauv always worth a look; Chard can be v.gd.

Coturri & Sons, H Sonoma ★ Organic, no-sulphite but unreliable wines. Sometimes gd Zin with an attitude. Has a cult following.

Crichton Hall Vineyard Napa ★★→★★★ Outstanding estate Chard; stylish Pinot N.

Cuvaison Napa ★★★ (Chard) 01 02 03 04 (Merlot) 98 99 00 01 02 03 04 Estate CARNEROS Chard steadily fine. Cab Sauv is catching up with the Merlot.

Dalla Valle Napa ★★★★ 97 00 01 02 03 Hillside estate is that rare thing: a cult classic with a track record. Maya is a Cab Sauv-based brawny beauty – perhaps a touch too brawny in recent vintages – and Pietre Rosso, from Sangiovese, is a brilliant showcase for that variety.

Dehlinger Sonoma ★★★★ (Pinot) 99 00 01 02 03 04 Tom D focuses on ever-plummier RUSSIAN RIVER VALLEY Pinot N, and rightly. Also gd Chard, Syrah.

Delicato Vineyards San Joaquin ★★ One-time CENTRAL VALLEY jug producer has moved up-scale with purchase of MONTEREY v'yds and several new bottlings from LODI. Watch this brand for gd quality at everyday price.

DeLoach Vineyards Sonoma ★★→★★★ Fruit-rich Chard ever the mainstay of reliable RUSSIAN RIVER VALLEY winery. Gargantuan single-v'yd Zins (Papera, Pelletti) finding an audience. Now owned by Boisset (see France).

Diamond Creek Napa ★★★★ (Cab S) 87 90 94 95 97 00 01 02 03 Austere, stunning cult Cabs from hilly v'yd nr Calistoga go by names of v'yd blocks: Gravelly Meadow, Volcanic Hill, Red Block Terrace. Wines age beautifully.

Domaine Carneros Carneros ★★★ Showy US outpost of Taittinger in CARNEROS echoes austere style of its parent in Champagne (see France) but with a delicious dollop of California fruit. Vintage Blanc de Blancs v.gd. La Rêve the luxury *cuvée*. Still Pinot N and Chard also impressive.

Domaine Chandon Napa ★★→★★★ Maturing v'yds, maturing style, broadening range taking Moët & Chandon's California arm to new heights. Look esp for NV Reserve, étoile rosé. Still wines a recent and welcome addition.

Domaine de la Terre Rouge Amador County ★★★ Former retailer is a Rhône specialist with a strong stable of growers. Syrah, Mourvèdre, and Grenache are superb. Also makes a red blend and a white blend from Rhône varieties.

Dominus Napa ★★★★ 90 95 96 97 98 99 00 01 02 03 Christian Moueix of Pomerol produces red B'x blend that is slow to open but ages beautifully; packed with power inside a silk glove. Big jump in quality in the mid-1990s.

Donum Estate Sonoma, Carneros ★★★ Exceptionally gd single-v'yd Pinot N from Martini clones. A newcomer moving quickly into the top ranks.

Dry Creek Vineyard Sonoma ★★ Sauv (Fumé) Bl set standard for California for decades. Still impressive. Pleasing Chenin Bl; gd Zin.

Duckhorn Vineyards Napa ★★★→★★★★ (Merlot) 97 00 01 02 03 Known for dark, tannic, almost plummy-ripe, single-v'yd Merlots (esp Three Palms) and Cab Sauv-based blend Howell Mountain. New winery in ANDERSON VALLEY for Golden Eye Pinot N made in an uncompromising style. Has also completed a new Napa winery for Decoy blend.

Dunn Vineyards Napa ★★★★ (Cab) 85 87 89 91 94 95 97 99 00 01 02 03 Owner-winemaker Randy Dunn makes dark, iconic Cab Sauv from Howell Mountain, which ages magnificently, slightly milder from valley floor. 4,000 cult cases.

Dutton-Goldfield Western Sonoma Co ★★★ Adroitly crafted Burgundian varieties from several top sites. Owners have the v'yd smarts to reach four stars soon.

Keeping it cool

Californian winemakers are pushing the limits of cool-climate agriculture with new plantings of Pinot N and Chard on the Pacific coast north of San Francisco. Early releases show tremendous promise with intense varietal character. Dense Pacific fog and cold winds mean these v'yds, sometimes planted within a few miles of the ocean, have very low yields, so for many winemakers it is a labour of love – to push the variety to the edge.

Duxoup Sonoma ★★★ Quirky producer of excellent Rhône-style Syrah (don't look for Shiraz here) and inky, old-vine Charbono. A promising Sangiovese under the Gennaio label. Limited production but worth seeking out.

Eberle Winery San Luis Obispo ★★★ Burly ex-footballer makes Cab Sauv and Zin in his own image: plenty of knock-your-socks-off power but, behind that, gd balance and a supple concentration.

Echelon Napa. Gd-value label featuring gd CENTRAL COAST Chard.

Edna Valley Vineyard San Luis Obispo ★★ Decidedly toasty Chard. Pinot N best drunk soon after vintage. Recent Syrah impressive.

Estancia FRANCISCAN label for gd value MONTEREY Chard, Sauv, Pinot N, Cab Sauv.

Etude Napa ★★★→★★★★ (Pinot N) 00 01 02 03 04 Rich Pinot N made from Carneros fruit. Winery part of BERINGER BLASS operation.

Far Niente Napa ★★★★ (Chard) 00 01 02 03 04 (Cab) 95 97 00 01 02 03 Opulence is the goal in both Cab Sauv and Chard from luxury NAPA estate.

Farrell, Gary Sonoma ★★★→★★★★ After yrs of sharing working space at Davis BYNUM winery while making legendary RUSSIAN RIVER Pinot N, Farrell now has his own winery. Also look for Zin and Chard.

Ferrari-Carano Sonoma ★★★ Over-the-top winery draws on estate v'yds in NAPA and SONOMA to make range of above-average wines, Merlot being the best, but don't overlook Sauv Bl and toasty Chard.

Fess Parker Sta Barbara ★★★ Owned by actor who played title role in TV's *Daniel Boone*; son Eli is winemaker. Gd Chard in tropical-fruit style, impressive Pinot N and Syrah, surprisingly gd Ries. New release is Parker Station Pinot N, a luscious little wine made from young vines.

Fetzer Mendocino ★★→★★★ A leader in the organic/sustainable viticulture movement, Fetzer has produced consistently gd-value wines from least expensive range (Sundial, Valley Oaks) to brilliant Reserve wines. Fetzer also owns Bonterra Vineyards (all organic grapes) where Roussane and Marsanne are the stars. Wines from McNabb Ranch line now farmed biodynamically.

Ficklin Vineyards Madera, Central Valley Lush and delicious port-style dessert wines made from the classic Portuguese varieties.

Fiddlehead ★★★→★★★★ Winemaker Kathy Joseph commutes between home/ office nr SACRAMENTO and two wineries where she contracts space: one in ARROYO GRANDE AVA, San Luis Obispo; the other in Oregon. She has recently formed a partnership with high-production Santa Maria Pinot N with BERINGER BLASS. Her Pinot N is always the top and she also makes several bottlings of Sauv Bl, inc a minerally B'x-style.

Firestone Sta Barbara ★★ Fine Chard overshadows but does not outshine delicious Ries. Good Merlot as well.

Fisher Sonoma ★★→★★★ Hill-top SONOMA grapes for often-fine Chard; NAPA grapes dominate steady Cab Sauv.

Flora Springs Wine Co Napa ★★★ Best here are the two Meritage wines, a red blend called Trilogy (**95 97** 00 01 02 03) and a white called Soliloquy (**00 01** 02 03 04). Juicy Merlot also worth a look. Chard can be too oaky.

Foley Estates Vineyard Santa Barbara ★★→★★★ Established in 1997; making a name for itself with balanced and delicious Chard and Pinot N.

Foppiano Sonoma ★★ Long-established wine family turns out fine reds (esp Petite Sirah, Zin) under family name. Responsible for leading the mini-renaissance in "petty sir".

Forman Napa ★★★★ 97 99 00 01 02 03 Winemaker who found fame for STERLING in the 1970s now makes his own excellent Cab Sauv and Chard.

Foxen Sta Barbara ★★★ (Pinot) **00 01** 02 03 04 Tiny winery nestled between SANTA YNEZ and SANTA MARIA VALLEYS. Always bold, frequently brilliant Pinot N overshadows stylish Chard.

Franciscan Vineyard Napa ★★★ (Cab) **97** 00 01 02 03 04 Solid producer of reliable Cab Sauv and Merlot, complex yet supple Chard. Austere Cab Sauv and red Meritage from MOUNT VEEDER label. Now owned by CONSTELLATION.

Franzia San Joaquin ★ Penny-saver wines under Franzia, Corbett Canyon, NAPA Ridge, Charles Shaw ("Two-Buck Chuck"), and other labels. Largest bag-in-box producer.

Freeman Russian River Valley ★★ New producer showing great promise with cool-climate Pinot N (Akiko's Cuvée from SONOMA COAST AVA) and RUSSIAN RIVER Pinot N. Keep an eye on this exciting new estate.

Freemark Abbey Napa ★★★ (Chard) **01 02** 03 04 (Cab) **95 97** 00 01 02 03 Underrated but consistent producer of stylish Cab Sauv (esp single-v'yd Sycamore and Bosché). V.gd, deliciously true-to-variety Chard.

Fritz Dry Creek Valley ★★ Consistently good Zin from DRY CREEK and RUSSIAN RIVER AVAs, sometimes rising to ★★★. Gd Pinot N and a reliable Cab Sauv.

Frog's Leap Napa ★★★→★★★★ (Cab S) 87 **95** 97 **99** 00 01 02 03 Small winery, as charming as its name (and T-shirts) suggest. Lean, minerally Sauv Bl, toasty Chard, spicy Zin. Supple and delicious Merlot, as well as an elegant Cab Sauv. Converting to organic and biodynamic practices.

Gallo, E & J San Joaquin ★ Having mastered the world of commodity wines, this huge family firm (the world's second biggest after CONSTELLATION) is now unleashing a blizzard of regional varietals under such names as Anapauma, Marcellina, Turning Leaf, Zabaco, and more; some from Modesto, some via GALLO SONOMA, all mostly forgettable.

Gallo Sonoma Sonoma ★★→★★★ (Chard) **01 02** 03 04 (Cab) **97 99** 00 01 02 03 DRY CREEK VALLEY winery bottles several wines from SONOMA, NORTH COAST. Cab

Sauv can be v.gd, esp the single-v'yd ones. SONOMA line impressive for value.

Geyser Peak Sonoma ★★→★★★ Reliable producer of toasty Chard, powerful, sleek Cab Sauv, and juicy Shiraz top the charts. A blend of B'x reds can be v.gd. Interesting new bottlings of single-v'yd wines worth looking out for.

Gloria Ferrer Sonoma, Carneros ★★★ Built by Spain's Freixenet for sparkling wine, now producing spicy Chard and bright, silky Pinot N, all from CARNEROS fruit. Bubbly quality remains high, esp the Royal Cuvée, inspired by a visit from King Juan Carlos of Spain.

Goosecross Cellars Napa Spicy, lively Chard. Improving reds from new v'yds.

Grace Family Vineyard Napa ★★★★ 97 99 00 01 02 03 Stunning Cab Sauv. Shaped for long ageing. One of the few cult wines actually worth the price.

Green & Red Vineyards Napa Zingy pleasing Zin from Pope Valley.

Greenwood Ridge Mendocino ★★★ Winery well above the floor of ANDERSON VALLEY made its name as producer of off-dry, perfumy Ries. Reds, esp Cab Sauv and Pinot N, also v.gd.

Grgich Hills Cellars Napa ★★★→★★★★★ (Chard) 99 00 01 02 03 04 Vastly underrated NAPA producer of supple Chard (which can age); balanced elegant Cab Sauv; jammy, ripe Zin from SONOMA grapes. Gd Sauv Bl in minerally style.

Groth Vineyards Napa ★★★→★★★★★ (Cab) 87 90 91 94 95 97 99 00 01 02 03 OAKVILLE estate Cab Sauv has been consistently four-star quality for a decade, with big, wrap-around flavours made for ageing. Chard also excellent.

Gundlach-Bundschu Sonoma ★★→★★★ Pioneer name solidly revived by fifth generation. Versatile Rhinefarm estate v'yd signals memorably individual Gewurz, Merlot, Zin. Much-improved Cab Sauv recently from hillside vines.

Hagafen Napa ★★ One of the first serious California kosher producers. Esp Chard and crisp Sauv Bl.

Hahn Estate Monterey ★★ Consistently gd Cab Sauv and reasonably priced Chard from v'yds in the SANTA LUCIA HIGHLANDS and ARROYO SECO.

Handley Cellars Mendocino ★★★ Winemaker Mila Handley makes excellent ANDERSON VALLEY Chard, Gewurz, Pinot N. Also v.gd DRY CREEK VALLEY Sauv, Chard from her family's vines. She produces a small amount of intense sparkling wine which is well worth a look.

Hanna Winery Sonoma ★★★ Has been flirting with four-star status for yrs. Recent vintages of Cab Sauv and well-made Sauv Bl are excellent.

Hanzell Sonoma ★★★→★★★★★ (Chard) 96 00 01 02 03 04 (Pinot N) 00 01 02 03 Small producer of outstanding terroir-driven Chard and Pinot N from estate vines. Always gd; quality level has risen sharply in past few years.

Harlan Estate Napa ★★★★ (Cab) 94 95 97 99' 00 01 02 03 Concentrated, sleek, cult Cab Sauv from small estate commanding luxury prices.

Harrison Napa ★★→★★★★ (Cab) 95 97 99 01 02 03 04 Located nr LONG VINEYARDS and the cult Cab Sauv of Bryant family. Predictably specializing in Cab Sauv.

Hartford Court Sonoma ★★★ Part of KENDALL JACKSON'S Artisans & Estates group showing v.gd single-v'yd Pinot Ns, tight coastal-grown Chard, and wonderful old-vine RUSSIAN RIVER Zins.

Hartwell Napa ★★★ High-end image, small producer with gd Cab Sauv potential.

HDV Carneros Chard from grower Larry Hyde's v'yd in conjunction with Aubert de Villaine of Domaine Romanée-Conti (see France).

Heitz Napa ★★★→★★★★★ (Cab) 90 91 95 97 00 01 02 03 Rich, supple, deeply flavoured, minty Cab Sauv from Martha's Vineyard. Bella Oaks and newer Trailside Vineyard rival but can't match Martha. Some feel quality has slipped in recent vintages.

Heller Estate Carmel Valley, Monterey ★★★ (Cab) 97 99 00 01 02 03 Dark and powerful wines (esp the past few years as vines mature) are acquiring something of a cult status. Chenin Bl is charming.

Hess Collection, The Napa ★★★→★★★★ (Chard) **01 02** 03 04 (Cab) **95 97** 00 01 02 03 Owned by Swiss art collector Donald Hess, who has installed a v.gd museum. New Cab Sauv from v'yds in Mt Veeder AVA step up to new quality level. Chard crisp and bright. Budget Hess Select label is v.gd value.

Hobbs, Paul Sonoma ★★★ Excellent winemaker, well known for consulting with Catena in Argentina, buying top Chard grapes in CARNEROS, Cab Sauv in NAPA, and Pinot N in RUSSIAN RIVER for own label.

Hook & Ladder ★★→★★★ When the DELOACH family sold the winery, they kept some of their best RUSSIAN RIVER v'yds. V.gd Pinot N; outstanding Zin.

Hop Kiln Sonoma ★★ Best: inky Zin from RUSSIAN RIVER and burly Petite Sirah.

Husch Vineyards Mendocino ★★ Has ANDERSON VALLEY v'yd for often fine Pinot N and Ukiah v'yd for sometimes gd Sauv Bl, Cab Sauv.

Iron Horse Vineyards Sonoma ★★★→★★★★ Chard **00 01** 02 03 04 RUSSIAN RIVER family estate producing some of California's best bubbly, especially a series of late-disgorged beauties. Chard from cool Russian River Valley is outstanding, and an above-average Cab Sauv from ALEXANDER VALLEY v'yds.

Jade Mountain Napa ★★→★★★ Outstanding producer of Rhône-style wines, esp Syrah, Mourvèdre.

Jessie's Grove Lodi ★★ Old Zin vines work well for farming family's venture.

Jordan Sonoma ★★★★ (Cab) **87 90 91 94** 95 97 99 00 01 02 03 Extravagant ALEXANDER VALLEY estate models its Cab Sauv on supplest B'x. And it lasts. Minerally Chard is made in a Burgundian style.

J Sonoma ★★★ Born part of JORDAN, now on its own in RUSSIAN RIVER VALLEY. Creamy classic-method Brut the foundation. Still, Pinot N and Pinot Gr worth a look.

Judd's Hill Napa Valley ★★★ Founders of Whitehall Lane now have their own winery, making elegant Cab Sauv that should age v. well.

Kautz-Ironstone Lodi and Calaveras County ★★ Showplace destination in SIERRA FOOTHILLS attracts visitors from all over the state. Honestly priced broad range led by fine Cab Fr.

Keenan Winery, Robert Napa ★★→★★★ Winery on SPRING MOUNTAIN: supple, restrained Cab Sauv, Merlot; also Chard.

Kendall-Jackson Sonoma ★★→★★★ Staggeringly successful style aimed at widest market: esp broadly sourced off-dry toasty Chard. Even more noteworthy for the development of a diversity of wineries under the umbrella of Kendall-Jackson's Artisans & Estates (see CAMBRIA, HARTFORD COURT).

Kenwood Vineyards Sonoma ★★→★★★★ (Jack London Cab) **97** 00 01 02 03 Single-v'yd Jack London Cab Sauv, Zin (several) the high points. Sauv Bl is very reliable value. Owned by KORBEL.

Kistler Vineyards Sonoma ★★★ (Chard) **01** 02 03 04 Still chasing the Burgundian model of single-v'yd Pinot N, most from RUSSIAN RIVER, with mixed success. Chards can be very toasty, buttery and over-the-top, though they have a loyal following.

Konigsgaard Napa ★★★ Small production of Chard, Syrah, and Roussanne from former NEWTON winemaker.

Korbel Sonoma ★★ Long-established sparkling specialist emphasizes bold fruit flavours, intense fizz; Natural tops the line.

Krug, Charles Napa ★★ Historically important winery with sound wines. Cabs at head of list. CK-Mondavi is a relentlessly sweet commodity brand.

Kunde Estate Sonoma ★★★ Long-time large grower has become solid producer with an elegant, understated Chard, flavourful Sauv Bl, peachy Viognier, and silky Merlot. All estate-bottled.

La Jota Napa ★★→★★★ Huge, long-lived Cab Sauv from Howell Mountain. Owned by MARKHAM vineyards.

Lambert Bridge Dry Creek, Sonoma ★★★ Seductive Merlot, zesty Zin, and brilliant Sauv Bl in a "B'x meets New Zealand" style.

Lamborn Howell Mountain, Napa ★★★ V'yd planted on historic 19th-C site. Big juicy Zin, Cab Sauv coming along for this cult winery.

Landmark Sonoma ★★→★★★ (Chard) 01 02 03 04 Early promise of elegant Burgundian-style Chard blunted by oaky-toasty flavours for a time in the late 1990s. Recent bottlings seem to be back on track.

Lang & Reed Napa ★★★ Specialist focusing on delicious Loire-style Cab Fr.

Laurel Glen Sonoma ★★★★ (Cab) 91 94 95 97 00 01 02 03 Floral, well-etched Cab Sauv with a sense of place from steep v'yd on SONOMA MOUNTAIN.

Lava Cap El Dorado ★★ Sierra producer making a wide range of mostly estate wines. Cab Sauv is gd, but Zin is outstanding.

Lipartia Cellars Howell Mountain, Napa ★★★ Deeply concentrated Cab Sauv, which promises long cellar life.

Livingston Moffett St Helena, Napa ★★★ Noteworthy Cab Sauv from Rutherford Ranch v'yds. Syrah also v.gd.

Lockwood Monterey ★★ Large S Salinas Valley v'yd. Gd value in Chard, Sauv Bl.

Lohr, J Central Coast ★★→★★★ Large winery with extensive v'yds; v.gd PASO ROBLES Cab Sauv Seven Oaks. Recent series of Meritage-style reds best yet. Commodity line is Cypress.

Lolonis Mendocino ★★ Pre-Prohibition Mendo growers, founded winery in 1982. Gd, solid Zin, Merlot, spicy Chard.

Long Meadow Napa ★★★ Elegant, silky Cab Sauv better with each vintage. V'yd is organically farmed. Potential cult status.

Longoria Winery Sta Barbara (★★→★★★) Rick Longoria makes brilliant Pinot N from top v'yds in the area.

Long Vineyards Napa ★★★ (Chard) 00 01 02 03 04 (Cab) 87 90 91 94 95 97 99' 00 01 Small estate owned by legendary winemakers Robert and Zelma Long. Luscious Chard silky Cab Sauv, and velvety Ries at top prices.

MacRostie Sonoma, Carneros ★★★ Toasty, ripe Chard with some complexity is flagship. Also Merlot, Pinot N from single-v'yds.

Madonna Estate Napa Carneros ★★→★★★ Outstanding single-v'yd Pinot N; however, Cab Sauv and Chard seldom rise above two stars. Formerly Mont St John Cellars.

Mahoney Vineyards Napa, Carneros ★★→★★★ Founder of CARNEROS CREEK now producing under own label. V.gd Vermentino, excellent single-v'yd Pinot N.

Marcassin Sonoma Coast Cult consultant Helen Turley's own tiny label. Worth so much at auction that few ever drink it. Concentrated Chard and dense Pinot N. Chard so densely concentrated, those who do taste it never forget.

Markham Napa ★★★ (Merlot) 98 99 01 02 03 Way underrated producer of balanced, elegant Merlot and solid Cab Sauv.

Martinelli Russian River ★★★ Family growers from fog-shrouded western hills of Sonoma, famous for old-vine Jackass Hill Vineyard Zin. Sought after Pinot N and Chard made under Helen Turley's consulting eye.

Martini, Louis M Napa ★★→★★★★ Long history making ageworthy Cab Sauv, Zin, Barbera from fine v'yds (Monte Rosso, Los Vinedos, Glen Oaks, etc.) in NAPA and SONOMA. On downslide for several years. May be on the way back after purchase by GALLO in 2002 with recent bottlings of Cab Sauv showing v. well.

Matanzas Creek Sonoma (Merlot) 00 01 02 03 04 Excellent Sauv Bl has slipped of late. Merlot outstanding; also gd Chard. Owned by KENDALL-JACKSON.

Mayacamas Napa ★★★ Pioneer boutique v'yd with rich Chard and firm (but no longer steel-hard) Cab Sauv, capable of long ageing.

Meridian San Luis Obispo ★★ Gd SANTA BARBARA Chard and PASO ROBLES Cab Sauv.

Merry Edwards Russian River ★★★★ Superstar consultant has planted her own

Pinot N v'yd in RUSSIAN RIVER district and buys in grapes from other v'yds. Already one of the top Pinot N producers in California. Also top Sauv Bl.

Merryvale Napa ★★★ Best at Cab Sauv and Merlot, which have elegant balance and supple finish. Chard being revitalized, moving away from oaky-toast to a more complex Burgundian model. Sauv Bl can be v.gd.

Mettler Family Vineyards Lodi ★★ Long-time growers now producing a sleek and tangy Cab Sauv and a powerful Petite Sirah. On the way up.

Michael, Peter Sonoma ★★★→★★★★ Stunning, complex Chard from Howell Mountain in a powerful style, and a more supple ALEXANDER VALLEY bottling. Cab Sauv on the tight side.

Michel-Schlumberger Sonoma ★★→★★★ Excellent ageing potential in supple Cab Sauv usually blended with Merlot from hillside vines.

Milano Mendocino ★★ Small producer of Zin, Cab Sauv, worth seeking out.

Mondavi, Robert Napa ★★→★★★★ Brilliant innovator bought in 2004 by CONSTELLATION, has wine at all price/quality ranges. At the top are the NAPA VALLEY Reserves (bold, prices to match), NAPA VALLEY appellation series (*e.g.* CARNEROS Chard, OAKVILLE Cab Sauv, etc), NAPA VALLEY (basic production). At the low end are various Central Coast wines, inc Robert Mondavi-Woodbridge. Some feel that the second generation had lost focus and was spread too thin. CONSTELLATION vows to bring back legendary Mondavi quality. We'll see.

Monteviña Amador ★★ Ripe and fruit-forward SIERRA Zin and one of state's best Barberas. Owned by SUTTER HOME. Top of line called Terra d'Oro.

Monticello Cellars Napa ★★★ (Cab) **90 91 94 95 97** 00 01 02 03 Consistently worth seeking out. Basic line under Monticello label, reserves under Corley. Both inc Chard and Cab Sauv.

Morgan Monterey ★★★ Top-end, single-v'yd Pinot Ns and Chards from v.gd SANTA LUCIA HIGHLANDS v'yds. Esp fine unoaked Chard called Metallico. Estate Double L v'yd is now farmed organically.

Mumm Napa Valley Napa ★★★ Stylish bubbly, esp delicious Blanc de Noirs and a rich, complex DVX single-v'yd fizz, which does improve with a few years in the bottle. Now owned by Diageo.

Murphy-Goode Sonoma ★★ Large ALEXANDER VALLEY estate. Sauv Bl, Zin are tops. Merlot better than average. Tin Roof (screwcap) line offers refreshing Sauv Bl and Chard *sans* oak, in contrast to lavishly oaked Reserve line.

Nalle Sonoma ★★★ Doug Nalle makes lovely Zins from Dry Creek fruit, that are juicy and delicious when young and will also mature gracefully for years.

Napa Wine Company Napa ★★★ Largest organic grape grower in Napa sells most of the fruit and operates a custom crush facility for several small premium producers. Offers three-star Cab Sauv under own label.

Navarro Vineyards Mendocino ★★★→★★★★ From ANDERSON VALLEY, splendidly ageworthy Chard, perhaps the grandest Gewurz in state. Even more special: late-harvest Ries, Gewurz. Pinot N in two styles, homage to Burgundy from ANDERSON VALLEY grapes, plus a brisk and juicy bottling from bought-in grapes.

Newton Vineyards Napa ★★★→★★★★ (Cab) **91 94 95 97 99** 00 01 02 03 (Merlot) **90 91 95 97 99** 00 01 02 03 Mountain estate makes some of California's best Merlot. Lush Chard and a supple Cab Sauv.

Neyers Napa ★★→★★★★ Gd quality overall; great Syrah and a lovely Chard.

Niebaum-Coppola Estate Napa ★★★(★) (Rubicon) **85 91 94 95 97** 98 00 01 02 03 "Godfather" Coppola has proven he is as serious about making wine as making movies. Now owns the historic Inglenook Estate v'yd and winery (but not the brand). Flagship Rubicon ranks with the state's best B'x red blends. Edizone Pennino concentrates on delightfuly old-fashioned Zin; gd-value Diamond series always worth a look. Recently bought the Souverain winery in Sonoma for Diamond production, but not the brand.

Ojai Ventura ★★★ Former AU BON CLIMAT partner Adam Tolmach on his own since early 1990s makes wide range of excellent wines, esp Syrah.

Opus One Napa ★★★ 85 91 94 95 97 99 00 01 02 03 There have been a lot of in and out years at Opus, but the trend has been up for the last few vintages. Now jointly owned by CONSTELLATION and Baronne Philippine de Rothschild.

Orfila Vineyards San Diego ★★ Reliable S California producer of Viognier, other Rhône varieties, and a very pretty Sauv Bl.

Pahlmeyer Napa ★★★ Cultish producer of dense, tannic Cab Sauv and more supple, fruity Merlot.

Paradigm Napa ★★★ Westside OAKVILLE v'yd with an impressive Merlot and a bright, supple Cab Sauv.

Paraiso Monterey ★★→★★★ Up-and-comer owned by large grower in Salinas, making luscious Ries and Pinot Bl. More recently bright and balanced Pinot N from SANTA LUCIA HIGHLANDS fruit and a supple Syrah.

Patz & Hall Napa ★★→★★★ Reputation for CARNEROS Chard from individual v'yds established around crisp structure and opulent winemaking. Inviting Pinot N.

Peachy Canyon Paso Robles ★★→★★★ Big bold Zin is a story worth telling.

Pedroncelli Sonoma ★★ Old-hand in DRY CREEK producing agreeable Zin, Cab Sauv, and a solid Chard.

Periano Lodi ★★ Good example of the new look of Lodi wines. Outstanding Barbera, brilliant Viognier, and v.gd Chard.

Perry Creek Eldorado ★★→★★★ An extraordinary Syrah from high-elevation vines and above-average Cab Sauv.

Phelps, Joseph Napa ★★★★ (Cab Sauv) 85 87 90 91 94 95 97 99 00 01 02 03 04 Finally beginning to get well-deserved credit as one of California's best producers. V.gd Chard, Cab Sauv (esp Backus), and Cab Sauv-based Insignia. Also look for fine Rhône series under Vin du Mistral label. Expect great things from a Pinot N-only winery Phelps is building in coastal Sonoma. Beginning to farm biodynamically.

Philips, R H Yolo, Dunnigan Hills ★→★★ The only winery in the Dunnigan Hills AVA makes a wide range of wines. Excellent job with Rhône varieties under the EXP label and gd-value Toasted Head Chard. Occasional old-vine Zin sourced from v'yds in the suburbs of Los Angeles. Owned by Vincor.

Philip Togni Vineyards Napa ★★★→★★★★ (Cab Sauv) 97 99 00 01 Veteran Napa winemaker (ex-MAYACAMAS) makes outstanding Cab Sauv from small estate v'yd on Spring Mountain.

Pine Ridge Napa ★★★ Tannic and concentrated Cab Sauvs from several NAPA AVAs which are worthy of ageing. The just off-dry Chenin Bl is a treat.

Preston Dry Creek Valley, Sonoma ★★★ Lou Preston is a demanding terroirist, making outstanding DRY CREEK VALLEY icons like Zin and fruity, marvellous Barbera. His Sauv Bl is a delicious fusion of "New Zealand meets SONOMA".

Pride Mountain Spring Mountain, Napa ★★★ Top hillside location contributes bright fruit characters to fine B'x-variety offerings with ageing potential.

Provenance Napa ★★★ Lovely, elegant, and supple Cab Sauv from heart of NAPA estate; owned by CONSTELLATION. Winemaker Tom Rinaldi also makes a superb Hewitt Vineyard Cab Sauv. New ownership makes future uncertain.

Quady Winery San Joaquin ★★ Imaginative Madera Muscat dessert wines, inc celebrated orangey Essencia, rose-petal-flavoured Elysium, and Moscato d'Asti-like Electra.

Quintessa Napa ★★★(★) 99 00 01 02 Splendid new estate on Silverado Trail, linked to FRANCISCAN and CONSTELLATION. Early releases of red Meritage-style show tremendous promise. Converting to biodynamic farming.

Quivira Sonoma ★★★ Sauv Bl, Zin, and others, from DRY CREEK VALLEY estate.

Qupé Sta Barbara ★★★ Never-a-dull-moment cellar-mate of AU BON CLIMAT.

Marsanne, Pinot Bl, Syrah are all well worth trying.

Rafanelli, A Sonoma ★★★ →★★★★ 00 01 02 03 04 Extraordinary Dry Creek Zin is strong suit. It will age, but it's so delightful when young, why bother?

Rasmussen, Kent Carneros ★★★ Crisp, lingering Chard and delicious Pinot N. Ramsay is an alternative label for small production lots.

Ravenswood Sonoma ★★★ →★★★★ Zin Master Joel Peterson pioneered single-v'yd Zin. Affordable line of SONOMA and Vintners Reserve Zin and Merlot. Now owned by CONSTELLATION, but quality appears to be holding firm.

Raymond Vineyards and Cellar Napa ★★★ (Cab) 90 91 94 95 97 99 00 01 02 03 04 Underrated Cab Sauv from family v'yds. Potential for long-term ageing.

Ridge Sta Cruz Mtns ★★★★ (Cab) 85 87 91 94 95 97 00 01 02 03 Winery of highest repute among connoisseurs. Drawing from NAPA (York Creek) and its own mountain v'yd (Montebello) for lithe, harmonious Cab Sauvs, worthy of long maturing, and from SONOMA, NAPA, Sierra Foothills and PASO ROBLES for amazing single-v'yd Zin. Most of Zin has good ageing potential, but, as noted elsewhere, it tastes so good when young, why bother? Outstanding Chard from wild-yeast fermentation is often overlooked.

Rios-Lovell Livermore ★★ New producer with an outstanding Petite Sirah and better-than-average Zin.

Rochioli, J Sonoma ★★★ →★★★★ (Pinot N) 00 01 02 03 04 Long-time RUSSIAN RIVER grower sells most of fruit to GARY FARRELL and other top Pinot N producers, but makes several own-label Pinot Ns every year that are simply super. Also v.gd Zin.

Roederer Estate Mendocino ★★★★ ANDERSON VALLEY branch of Champagne house (established 1988). Supple, elegant house style. Easily one of the top three sparklers in California and hands-down the best rosé. Top-of-the-line luxury cuvée l'Ermitage superb.

Rosenblum Cellars San Francisco Bay ★★★ Makes 7–8 single-v'yd Zins in any given year sourced from all over the state, many from old vines. Quality varies, but always well above average.

Rutz Cellars Russian River Valley Sonoma ★★ →★★★ Outstanding Chard from select RUSSIAN RIVER v'yds. Super Pinot N with more guts than most. Keep an eye on Rutz.

Saddleback Cellars Napa ★★★★ (Cab) 91 95 97 99 00 01 02 03 Owner-winemaker Nils Venge is a legend in NAPA. Lush Zin and long-lived Cab Sauv.

St Amant Lodi ★★ LODI producer could soon earn third star, esp with old-vine Zin and a nifty Syrah.

St Clement Napa ★★★ (Cab) 91 95 97 00 01 02 03 Supple, long-lived Oroppas, a Cab Sauv-based blend, is the go-to wine here. Merlot and Chard also outstanding. Owned by BERINGER BLASS.

St Francis Sonoma ★★★ (Merlot) 97 99 00 01 02 03 04 (Zin) 97 99 00' 01 02 03 Deep and concentrated Cab Sauv, fruity and lively Merlot. The old-vine Zin is super.

St-Supéry Napa ★★★ Sleek and graceful Merlot; Cab Sauv can be outstanding, as is red Meritage. Sauv Bl one of best in state. Sources some grapes from warmer Pope Valley E of NAPA VALLEY. French-owned (Skalli).

Saintsbury Carneros ★★★ (Chard) 00 01 02 03 04 (Pinot) 99 00 01 02 03 04 Outstanding Pinot N, denser than most from CARNEROS. Chard full-flavoured and oak-shy. Garnet Pinot N, made from younger vines, is a light-hearted treat.

CALIFORNIA

Sanford Sta Barbara ★★★ (Pinot) **00 01** 02 03 04 Richard Sanford was one of the first to plant Pinot N in Santa Barbara. He has now left the winery, and future quality is uncertain under new owners, Teralto. Look for supple richness in the Pinot N and a bright minerality in the Sauv Bl. Pinot N pioneer in Santa Barbara. Wines can be forward and intense, but they take on a supple richness with a few years in bottle. Sauv Bl is a beauty.

Santa Cruz Mountain Vineyard Santa Cruz ★★→★★★ (Cab Sauv) 95 97 99 00 01 02 Produces wines of strong varietal character from estate grapes. Vgd Pinot N and an exceptional Cab Sauv – big and concentrated, and capable of extended ageing.

Sattui, V Napa ★★ King of direct-only sales (*i.e.* winery door or mail order). Wines made in a rustic, drink-now style. Reds are best, esp Cab Sauv, Zin.

Sausal Sonoma ★★→★★★ ALEXANDER VALLEY estate noted for its Zin and Cab Sauv. Century Vine Zin is a stunning example of old-vine Zin.

Scherrer Sonoma ★★★ Ripe, California-style Pinot N and Chard from RUSSIAN RIVER, as well as mouth-filling, old-vine Zin from ALEXANDER VALLEY.

Schramsberg Napa ★★★★ One of California's top sparkling producers and the first to make a true *methodé champenoise* in the state in commercial quantity. Historic caves. Reserve is splendid; Blanc de Noirs outstanding (2–10 yrs). Luxury *cuvée* J Schram is America's Krug. Now making a v.gd Cab Sauv from mountain estate vines.

Schug Cellars Carneros ★★★ German-born and trained owner-winemaker dabbles in other types, but CARNEROS Chard and Pinot N are his main interests and wines. Pinot N is always near the top.

Screaming Eagle Napa ★★★★ Small lots of cult Cab Sauv at luxury prices for those who like that kind of thing.

Sebastiani Sonoma ★ Former jug-wine king has tried to go upscale with single-v'yd wines with limited success.

Seghesio Sonoma ★★★ Concentrating now on superb, ageworthy Zins from own old v'yds in ALEXANDER and DRY CREEK VALLEYS, but don't overlook smaller lots of Sangiovese.

Selene Napa ★★★→★★★★ Ace winemaker Mia Klein makes rich and concentrated Merlot and brilliant Sauv Bl.

Sequoia Grove Napa ★★★ Estate Cab Sauvs are intense and long-lived, and the trend in the past few yrs is clearly towards a fourth star. Chard is a cut above and can age.

Shafer Vineyards Napa ★★★★ (Cab) 86 87 90 91 94 95 97 99 00 01 02 03 (Merlot) 95 97 99 00 01 02 03 04 Always in the top range for Merlot and Cab Sauv, esp the Hillside Select from STAGS LEAP. CARNEROS Chard (Red Shoulder Ranch) breaking out of oak shackles. Also look for Firebreak, a single-v'yd Sangiovese.

Sierra Vista El Dorado ★★→★★★ Dedicated Rhôneist in SIERRA FOOTHILLS. Style is elegant, mid-weight, and fruit driven, with emphasis on varietal typicity.

Signorello Napa ★★★ Fairly high-end Cab Sauvs and Chards, noteworthy Pinot N from RUSSIAN RIVER, v.gd Sem/Sauv Bl blend is best value. All could do with a bit less oak.

Silverado Vineyards Napa ★★★→★★★★ (Cab) 90 91 95 97 99 01 02 03 Showy hilltop STAGS LEAP district winery offering supple Cab Sauv, lean and minerally Chard, and distinctive Sangiovese.

Silver Oak Napa/Sonoma ★★★→★★★★ (Cab Napa) 85 87 91 97 00 01 02 03 (Cab Alex Valley) 87 91 95 97 00 01 02 03 Separate wineries in NAPA and ALEXANDER VALLEYS make Cab Sauv only. Owners have ridden extreme American-oaked style to pinnacle of critical acclaim among those who admire such wines. Alexander Valley a bit more supple than Napa.

Simi Sonoma ★★→★★★ Up-and-down historic winery makes a wide range of varietals. Long-lived Cab Sauv and v.gd Chard still the heart of the matter. White Meritage Sendal is super.

Sinskey Vineyards Napa ★★★ EX-ACACIA partner started winery. Chard with a gd acidic bite and luscious Pinot N are the highlights.

Smith-Madrone Napa ★★ High up on SPRING MOUNTAIN, the Smith brothers craft a superb off-dry Ries and a lean Chard.

Sonoma-Cutrer Vineyards Sonoma ★★ (Chard) 01 02 03 04 Chard specialist in oaky-toasty territory is in a down period just now. Owned by Brown-Forman.

Spencer Roloson ★★ Négociant producer of stylish Zin and Tempranillo from single v'yds. To watch.

Spottswoode Napa ★★★★ (Cab) 87 91 94 95 97 99 00 01 02 03 Outstanding Cab Sauv from estate v'yd is long lasting, balanced, and harmonious. Brilliant Sauv Bl.

Spring Mountain Napa ★★→★★★ Famed on TV as "Falcon Crest", a mountain estate now concentrating on wine. Excellent Cab Sauv and outstanding Sauv Bl from estate vines.

Stag's Leap Wine Cellars Napa ★★★★ (Cab) 78 84 87 90 91 94 95 97 99 00 01 02 03 Celebrated for silky, seductive Cab Sauvs (SLV, Fay, top-of-line Cask 23) and Merlots. Gd Chard is often overlooked. Owner Warren Winiarski is holding the line for balance and harmony against the onslaught of over-the-top, super-concentrated Napa Cab.

Stags' Leap Winery Napa ★★ Historic estate being revived by BERINGER BLASS. Important for Petite Sirah.

Staglin Napa ★★→★★★ (Cab) 91 95 97 99 00 01 02 03 Silky and elegant Cab Sauv from Rutherford Bench originally developed for BEAULIEU when André Tchelistcheff was the wine wizard there.

Steele Wines Lake ★★→★★★ Jed Steele is a genius at sourcing v'yds for a series of single-v'yd wines under main label and a second label called Shooting Star. Chard can get a little oaky, but Pinot N and some speciality wines, such as Washington State Lemberger, are outstanding.

Sterling Napa ★★→★★★ Scenic NAPA estate now owned by Diageo Chateau & Estate Wines. Gd basic Chard and understated single-v'yd Cab Sauv. Sterling has never seemed to fulfil potential, but new owners seem determined to put winery back on course.

Stony Hill Napa ★★★★ 85 90 91 95 97 99 00 01 02 03 Amazing hillside Chard for the past 50 years, made in an elegant "homage to Chablis" style. Most wine sold from mailing list. Stony Hill was Napa's first cult winery. Wines are very long-lived.

Storybook Mountain Napa ★★→★★★ Dedicated Zin specialist makes taut and tannic Estate and Reserve wines from Calistoga v'yd.

Strong Vineyard Sonoma ★★→★★★ (Cab) 00 10 02 03 04 Cab Sauv from single-v'yd bottlings often three stars; gd RUSSIAN RIVER Pinot N.

Sutter Home Napa ★→★★ Famous for white Zin and rustic Amador red Zin. Trying to move up-scale with Signature Series and M Trinchero brands.

Swan, Joseph Sonoma ★★★ (Zin) 97 99 00 01 02 03 04 Long-time RUSSIAN RIVER producer of intense Zin and classy Pinot N.

Tablas Creek Paso Robles ★★★ Joint venture between owners of Château Beaucastel and importer Robert Hass. V'yd based on cuttings from Châteauneuf v'yds. Early results promising, with odds good that some of the state's best Rhône styles lie ahead.

Talbott, R Monterey ★★★ Chard from single v'yds in MONTEREY is the name of the game, with the famed Sleepy Hollow v'yd in the Santa Lucia Highlands AVA at the heart. Approach is Burgundian; several bottlings reach three-star level.

Tanner, Lane Santa Barbara ★★★ (Pinot N) **99 00 01** 02 03 04 Owner-winemaker with often-superb single-v'yd Pinot N (Bien Nacido, Sierra Madre Plateau) reflecting terroir with a quiet, understated elegance.

The Terraces Napa ★★★ High above the Silverado trail, this is the home of outstanding Zin and Cab Sauv with supple style.

Thomas Fogarty Santa Cruz Mtns ★★→★★★ Go here for a rich, complex Chardonnay that ages fairly well. Also gd Pinot N from estate vineyards and a delightful Gewurz from Monterey grapes.

Torres Estate, Marimar Sonoma ★★★→★★★★ (Chard) **99 00 01** 02 03 04 (Pinot N) **99 00 01** 02 03 04 Edgy Chard (ages magnificently), lovely Pinot N from RUSSIAN RIVER VALLEY. New Pinot N plantings on coast should be superb. V'yds now farmed organically.

Trefethen Napa ★★★ (Chard) **97 98** 00 01 02 03 Respected family winery. Gd off-dry Ries, balanced Chard for ageing, although recent releases have not shown as well. Cab Sauv shows increasing depths and complexity with a few years in bottle.

Tres Sabores Rutherford AVA, ★★★ Newcomer making Zin and Cab Sauv from organically grown estate grapes. Wines are consistently balanced and elegant. Should age v. well.

Truchard Carneros ★★★ From the warmer N end of CARNEROS comes one of the flavoury, firmly built Merlots that give the AVA identity. Cab Sauv and Syrah even better and the tangy lemony Chard is a must-drink. New bottlings of Tempranillo outstanding.

Turley Alexander Valley ★★★ Former partner in FROG'S LEAP, now specializing in hefty, heady, single-v'yd Zin and Petite Sirah from old vines.

Ventana Monterey ★★ Showcase for owner's v'yds: watch for Chard and Sauv Bl from Musqué clone. Exciting new Syrah and Tempranillo.

Viader Estate Napa ★★★★ (Cab Sauv) **95 97** 99 01 02 03 A blend of Cab Sauv and Cab Fr from Howell Mountain hillside estate. Powerful wines, yet balanced and elegant in best yrs. Ages well. Also look for new series of small-lot bottlings, including Syrah, Tempranillo.

Vino Noceto Amador ★★ Sangiovese one of the best in California.

Volker Eisele Family Estate Napa ★★★→★★★★ 95 99 00 01 Sleek luscious blend of Cab Sauv and Cab Fr is highlight. Also look for a spicy Sauv Bl.

Wellington Sonoma ★★→★★★ Vivid old-vine Zin and sleek, powerful Cab Sauv from selected v'yds.

Wente Vineyards Livermore and Monterey ★★ Historic specialist in whites, esp LIVERMORE Sauv Bl and Sem. But LIVERMORE estate Cab Sauv is also v.gd. Monterey sweet Ries can be exceptional. A little classic sparkling.

Williams Selyem Sonoma ★★★ (Pinot) **97 99 00** 01 02 03 Intense smoky RUSSIAN RIVER Pinot N, esp Rochioli and Allen v'yds. Now reaching to SONOMA COAST, MENDOCINO for grapes. Cultish favourite.

Young, Robert Sonoma ★★★ Outstanding Chard, Cab Sauv from famed v'yd, source of CHATEAU ST JEAN Chard for many years.

York Creek Spring Mtn, Napa ★★★ Exceptional v'yd owned by Fritz Maytag, father of microbrew revolution in US. Sells to RIDGE and now has own label. Makes a variety of wines, mostly gd, always interesting.

Zaca Mesa Sta Barbara ★★→★★★★ Now turning away from Chard and Pinot N to concentrate on Rhône grapes (esp Marsanne and Syrah) and blends (Cuvée Z) grown on estate.

Zahtila Vineyards Napa ★★→★★★ Newcomer in N NAPA specializes in elegant and inviting Cab Sauv and intense Zin (one from estate v'yd nr Calistoga). Also makes DRY CREEK and RUSSIAN RIVER Zins from SONOMA COUNTY. A winery to watch.

ZD Napa ★★ Lusty Chard tattooed by American oak is ZD signature wine.

The Pacific Northwest

The wine country spans three adjoining states. Oregon has more than 9,000 hectares of vines, concentrated in the Willamette Valley, south of Portland. Washington's roughly 11,000 vineyard hectares are concentrated in the warmer, drier half of the state, east of the Cascade mountain range. Idaho's wine country lies mostly just east of Washington's, along the Snake River, with only a handful of wineries further north, in the panhandle. There are about 25 wineries in Idaho, with vineyard plantings estimated at under 500 hectares.

The grapes of Burgundy and Alsace do well in Oregon; Dijon clones of Chardonnay and Pinot Noir promise earlier ripening and potentially more complex wines. Across the Columbia River in eastern Washington, the warmer, drier climate of the Columbia Valley allows thicker-skinned varieties (Merlot, Cabernet Sauvignon, Cabernet Franc, and the hot new favourite, Syrah) to ripen well. These same varieties also grow well in Oregon and Idaho.

There are more than 700 wineries in the three states, but most produce fewer than 30,000 cases of wine annually, and many wineries make only 2,000 to 5,000 cases. The Red Mountain AVA in Washington is one of the most exciting of the newer appellations, especially for red B'x varieties. Idaho is in the process of getting its first AVA, Snake River.

Recent vintages

2005 Generally cool harvest with rains in many parts of the Northwest. Those wineries that waited to pick during dry periods are reporting excellent wines from the vintage, with firm acidity and good varietal character.

2004 Rain during flowering led to a small crop in some cases, but in general grape quality was high. Wines could range from below average to well above average, depending on the site.

2003 A potentially mixed vintage after a season of heat and water stress.

2002 Wines with full expression and elegance.

2001 Lower acidity and less concentration than previous three years.

2000 Solid vintage. High yields, concentrated, structured wines.

Oregon

Abacela Vineyards Umpqua Valley ★★★ New producer is performing well in unfashionable area of S Oregon. Temp, Dolcetto, Cab Fr, Syrah stand out.

Adelsheim Vineyard Yamhill County ★★★→★★★★ (Pinot) 00 01 02 03 04 Smoothly balanced Pinot N. New Dijon clone Chard, Ries, top Pinots Gr and Bl: clean, bracing.

Amity Willamette ★★→★★★ Pioneer in Oregon with exceptional Ries and Pinot Bl. The Pinot often rises to ★★★.

Andrew Rich (Tabula Rasa) Willamette ★★ Ex-California winemaker. Small lots of artisan wines, including Pinot N and exceptional Syrah, solid rosé.

Archery Summit Yamhill Co ★★→★★★ 97 98' 99' 00' 01 02 Owned by Napa's Pine Ridge. Pinot N is impressive if sometimes a little oaky for Oregon fruit.

Argyle Yamhill County ★★→★★★★ An outstanding sparkling wine (esp the vintage brut) and ★★★ Pinot N form a solid base for this winery, founded by Aussie superstar winemaker Brian Croser.

Beaux Frères Yamhill County ★★ 00 01 02 03 04 Pinot N has more power than most Oregon offerings, if that's what you are looking for in Pinot N. Part-owned by Robert Parker Jr.

Bethel Heights Willamette ★★★→★★★★ 00 01 02 03 04 Deftly made estate Pinot N. Also notable Chard, Pinot Bl, Pinot Gr.

Brick House Yamhill County ★★★ 98 99 01 02 03 04 Huge estate Pinot N. Dark and brooding when young with older vintages more balanced.

Cameron Yamhill County ★★ (Pinot N) **00 01** 02 03 04 Eclectic producer of powerful, unfiltered Pinot N, Chard: some great. Also v.gd Pinot Bl.

Chehalem Yamhill County ★→★★ (Chard) **00 01** 02 03 04 Outstanding Chard with ageing potential sometimes rising to ★★★. V.gd Ries, Pinot Gr.

Cooper Mountain Willamette ★★→★★★ Outstanding Pinot Gr and Pinot N on a steady upward curve. Certified biodynamic v'yds.

Domaine Drouhin Willamette ★★★→★★★★ **99 00** 01 02 03 04 Outstanding Pinot N, silky and elegant, improving with each vintage. Chard also a winner.

Domaine Serene Willamette ★★★ **98 00** 01 02 03 04 Traditional Pinot N in a rich echo of Burgundy. Bottled unfiltered. Well worth seeking out.

Elk Cove Vineyards Willamette ★★→★★★ Outstanding Ries inc a late harvest. Pinot N often near the top; some recent improvements in Chard.

Erath Vineyards Yamhill County ★★→★★★ **98 97** 01 02 03 04 Oregon pioneer, est 1968. V.gd Chard, Pinot Gr, Gewurz, Pinot Bl. Pinots and Ries age well.

Evesham Wood Nr Salem, Willamette ★★ Small family winery with fine Pinot N, Pinot Gr, and dry Gewurz. Organically farmed.

Eyrie Vineyards, The Willamette ★★★ **97 98 00** 01 02 03 04 Pioneer (1965) winery. Chards and Pinot Gr: rich yet crisp. All wines age beautifully.

Foris Vineyards Rouge Valley ★→★★ A lovely Pinot Bl and a classic red-cherry Pinot N top the list.

Henry Estate Rouge Valley ★→★★ Big but never clumsy Cab Sauv and a light, crisp Müller-T.

Ken Wright Cellars Yamhill County ★★ **99 01** 02 03 04 Floral Pinot N and a v.gd Chard from single v'yds.

King Estate S Willamette ★★★ (Pinot) **01 02** 03 04 One of Oregon's largest wineries, now converting to biodynamic viticulture. Lovely and constantly improving Pinot N, outstanding Chard, better-than-average Zin.

Lange Winery Yamhill County ★★ Pinot N has become richer, more intense as v'yds mature. V.gd Pinot Gr.

Panther Creek Willamette ★→★★ **97** 01 02 03 04 Concentrated, meaty, single-v'yd Pinot N and pleasant Melon de Bourgogne.

Oak Knoll Willamette ★★ Pinot is the big story here, with intense but balanced bottlings. Also a v.gd off-dry Ries.

Patricia Green Cellars Yamhill County ★★→★★★ Exciting, intense Pinot N from a newish winery. Small production, but worth seeking out.

Penner-Ash Yamhill County ★★★ REX HILL winemaker Lynn Penner-Ash and her husband are making great Pinot N in a bolder style than many in Oregon.

Ponzi Vineyards Willamette Valley ★★→★★★ **98 99 00 01** 02 03 04 Small pioneering winery well known for Pinot Gr, Chard, Pinot N.

Rex Hill Willamette ★★→★★★ **97 98 00** 01 02 03 04 Excellent Pinot N, Pinot Gr, and Chard from several N Willamette v'yds. Reserves rank high.

Sokol Blosser Willamette ★★→★★★ **98 99 00 01** 02 03 04 Outstanding Pinot N, Chard, and Gewurz, usually balanced and harmonious. Intriguing Müller-T.

Torii Mor Yamhill County ★★★ **98 99 00 01** 02 03 04 Several v.gd single-v'yd Pinot N bottlings and a superior Pinot Gr.

Tyee S Willamette ★★ Small producer; v.gd Pinot N, Pinot Gr, and tasty Gewurz.

Van Duzer Winery Willamette Valley ★→★★ Bright and fruity Pinot N, and delicious Pinot Gr, from one of the cooler parts of the Willamette Valley. Wines steadily improving.

Willakenzie Estate Yamhill County ★★ **98 99 00 01** 02 03 04' Outstanding, sometimes ★★★ Pinot N. V.gd Pinot Bl.

Willamette Valley Vineyards Willamette ★→★★ Large (for Oregon) winery nr Salem. Moderate- to very high-quality Chard, Ries, Pinot N. Also owns and produces v.gd Griffin Creek and Tualatin brands.

Washington & Idaho

Andrew Will Puget Sound, Washington ★★★★ **91 92 93 94 95 96 97** 00 01 02 03 04 Owner Chris Camarda sources B'x varietals from the new Red Mountain appellation, making outstanding single-v'yd reds – some of the best reds in Washington: balanced, elegant, tremendous ageing potential.

Arbor Crest Spokane, Washington ★★ The top draw here is the Chard. Cab Sauv is steadily improving. Keep an eye on this one.

Badger Mountain Columbia Valley, Washington ★★ Washington's first organic v'yd, producing impressive Cab Sauv and gd Chard.

> **Washington looks to terroir**
> There is an added dimension and complexity to many of the new wines tasted from Washington. This is a result of winemakers finding the right sites for the right vines, such as the Red Mountain AVA for Bordeaux varieties. Washington vintners are also realizing the potential for Rhône varieties, such as Syrah and Viognier, which develop great varietal intensity during the long hours of summer sunshine. Washington wines have been very good in the past, and there is no doubt that they are going to be even better in the years ahead.

Barnard Griffin Columbia Valley, Washington ★★→★★★ Small producer: well-made Merlot, Chard (esp barrel-fermented), Sem, Sauv Bl. Top Syrah.

Canoe Ridge Walla Walla, Washginton Now owned by Constellation Brands. Gd Chard and two-star Merlot, which could rise to three stars.

Cayuse Walla Walla ★★ →★★★ Striking Syrah and Viognier with loyal following.

Château Ste-Michelle Woodinville, Washington ★★→★★★★ Ubiquitous regional giant is Washington's largest winery; also owns COLUMBIA CREST, Northstar (top Merlot), Domaine Ste-Michelle, and Snoqualmie, among others. Major v'yd holdings, first-rate equipment, and skilled winemakers keep wide range of varieties in front ranks. V.gd v'yd-designated Cab Sauv, Merlot, and Chard.

Chinook Wines Yakima Valley, Washington ★★★ (Merlot) 97 98 99 00 01 02 03 04 Lovely, elegant Merlot and Cab Sauv; outstanding Cab Fr.

Columbia Crest Columbia Valley, Washington ★★→★★★ Separately run CHÂTEAU STE-MICHELLE label for delicious, well-made, top-value wines. Cab Sauv, Merlot, Syrah, and Sauv Bl best. Also v.gd reserve wines.

Columbia Winery Woodinville, Washington ★★→★★★ (Cab) **91 95 97 99** 00 01 03 04 Pioneer (1962, as Associated Vintners) and still a leader. MW David Lake makes balanced, stylish, understated single-v'yd wines. Marvellous Syrah.

DeLille Cellars Woodinville ★★★→★★★★ **96 98 99** 00 01 02 03 04 Exciting winery for v.gd red B'x blends: ageworthy Chaleur Estate, D2 (more forward, affordable). Excellent barrel-fermented white. Look for new Syrah, Doyenne.

Dunham Cellars Walla Walla, Washington ★★→★★★ **95 96 97 99** 00 01 02 03 A silky Syrah tops the list. Extracted Cab Sauv has a strong following.

Glen Fiona Walla Walla, Washington ★★→★★★ **00 01 02** 03 04 Rhône specialist with gd Syrahs and Syrah blends, esp the Syrah/Cinsault/Counoise *cuvée*.

Hedges Cellars Yakima Valley, Washington ★★★→★★★★ Outstanding B'x reds from Red Mountain AVA. Also v.gd wines from second label CMS Cellars.

Hogue Cellars, The Yakima Valley, Washington ★→★★ Large reliable producer known for excellent, gd-value wines, esp Ries, Chard, Merlot, Cab Sauv. Produces quintessential Washington Sauv Bl. Owned by Vincor of Canada.

Hyatt Vineyards Yakima Valley, Washington ★★→★★★ Stylish Merlot is among the state's best. Seek Black Muscat Icewine when conditions are right.

Indian Creek Idaho ★→★★ Top wine here is Pinot N backed by a v.gd Ries and successful Cab Sauv.

Kiona Vineyards Yakima Valley ★→★★ Solid Red Mountain producer. Easy-drinking wines; gd value and quality. Juicy Lemberger and reliable Cab Sauv.

L'Ecole No 41 Walla Walla ★★★→★★★★ (Merlot) **94 95 97 99** 00 01 02 03 04 Blockbuster but balanced reds (Merlot, Cab Sauv, and super Meritage blend) with forward, ageworthy fruit. Gd barrel-fermented Sem.

Leonetti Walla Walla ★★★→★★★★ Harmonious Cab Sauv: fine and big-boned. Bold and ageworthy Merlot. Wines are in great demand.

Long Shadows Columbia Valley ★★→★★★ Former Château Ste-Michelle CEO Allen Shoup has leading international winemakers producing Washington wine under a separate label. V.gd early releases incl Poet's Leap Ries; Pirouette, an amazing red; Chester-Kidder, a more concentrated, New Worldish red; and a bold Australian-style Syrah. Expect great things here.

Matthews Cellars Woodinville, Washington ★★→★★★ **96 97 98 99** 00 01 02 03 04 Smaller producer of mouth-filling B'x blends sourced from eastern Washington, with best called simply Red Wine.

McCrea Puget Sound ★★ Look for gd Viognier, Syrah, and Grenache sourced from top Washington vineyards from this Rhône specialist.

Nota Bene Cellars Puget Sound ★★→★★★ Amazing wines from B'x varietals sourced in Red Mountain AVA and other top Washington v'yds. Hard to find now, but well worth looking for.

Pend d'Orielle Idaho ★→★★ Complex, at times elegant, Pinot N, Merlot, Cab Fr.

Pepper Bridge Walla Walla Valley ★★→★★★ B'x-style Cab Sauv and Merlot.

Quilceda Creek Vintners Puget Sound ★★★→★★★★ **95 96 97 98 99 01 02 03 04** Expertly crafted, ripe, well-oaked Cab Sauv from Columbia Valley grapes is the speciality. Exceptional finesse and ageability.

Reininger Walla Walla, Washington ★★→★★★ **99 00** 01 02 03 04 Small, focused producer of outstanding Merlot and exceptional Syrah.

Ste Chapelle Caldwell, Idaho ★★ Pleasant, forward Chard, Ries, Cab Sauv, Merlot, and Syrah from local and E Washington v'yds. Attractive sparkling wine: gd value and improving quality.

Salishan Vineyards SW Washingon ★★ Earthy Burgundian-style Pinot N from grapes grown across the Columbia River from Portland, OR. Worth a search.

Woodward Canyon Walla Walla, Washington ★★★→★★★★ **97 98 00** 01 02 03 Ripe, intense, but elegant Cab, Chard, and blends. Merlot coming on strong.

East of the Rockies

Producers in New York (there are now 213 in nine AVAs) and other eastern states, such as Ohio (90 in five AVAs), traditionally made wine from hardy native grapes and French-American hybrids. Today, consumer tastes plus cellar and vineyard technology largely bypass these. Chardonnay, Riesling, Cabernet Sauvignon, and even Icewine, are now firmly established. Pinot Noir is emerging with some notable results, and Cabernet Franc and Merlot may be the most promising reds. Viognier, Gewurztraminer, and Pinot Gris are fulfilling early promise. Progress, from Virginia to Ohio, is accelerating as the wines gain recognition, especially with the direct interstate shipment now in most states

Allegro Pennsylvania ★★ 03 04 05 Produces a worthy Chard and a Cab Sauv-based B'x-style blend.

Anthony Road Finger Lakes, NY ★★★ 03 04 05' Fine Ries; great late-harvest Vignoles.

Barboursville Virginia ★★★★ **99 00 01 02** 03 04 05 Oldest of the state's modern-era wineries, est 1976 by Italian Zonin family. Excellent Chard, Cab Fr, Barbera, Nebbiolo, Pinot Gr. Elegant inn and restaurant.

Bedell Long Island, NY ★★★ **01** 02 03 04 05 Excellent Merlot and Cab Sauv.

Blenheim ★★★ Young estate. 03 04 05 v.gd Chard, Petit Verdot, B'x-style blend.

Breaux Virginia ★★★ **00 01** 02 03 04 05 Beautiful 35 ha v'yd 1 hr from Washington, DC. Gd Chard, Sauv Bl.

Chaddsford Pennsylvania ★★★ 02 03 04 05 Solid producer since 1982, esp for gd Pinot Gr and B'x-style red blend.

Chamard ★★ 02 03 04 05 Connecticut's best winery, owned by Tiffany chairman. Top Chard. AVA is Southeastern New England.

Chateau LaFayette Reneau Finger Lakes, NY ★★★ **01** 03 04 Stylish Chard, Ries, and Cab Sauv from established producer. Stunning lakeside setting.

Chrysalis Virginia ★★★ **03 04** 04 05 Top-notch Viognier, also v.gd Petit Manseng and native Norton.

Clinton Vineyards Hudson River, NY ★★ **04 05** Clean, gd, dry Seyval (still and sparkling). Exceptional cassis and peach wine.

Constellation See California.

Debonné Vineyards Lake Erie, Ohio ★★ 03 04 05 Largest OHIO estate winery. Chard, Ries, Pinot Gr, and some hybrids: Chambourcin and Vidal.

Finger Lakes Beautiful, cool, upstate-NY region, source of most of state's wines. Top wineries: ANTHONY ROAD, CHATEAU LAFAYETTE RENEAU, Dr. FRANK, FOX RUN, GLENORA, King Ferry, RED NEWT, Shalestone, STANDING STONE, Swedish Hill, and WIEMER.

Firelands Lake Erie, Ohio ★★ 02 03 04 OHIO estate making Chard, Cab Sauv, Gewurz, Pinot Gr, sparkling Ries, and Pinot N.

Fox Run Finger Lakes, NY ★★★ **02** 03 04 05' Some of region's best Chard, Gewurz, Ries, and Pinot N.

Frank, Dr. Konstantin (Vinifera Wine Cellars) Finger Lakes, NY ★★★★ **01 02** 03 04 05' Continues to set the pace for serious winemaking. The late Dr. F was a pioneer in growing European vines in the FINGER LAKES. Excellent Ries, Gewurz; gd Chard, Cab Sauv, and Pinot N. Also v.gd Chateau Frank sparkling.

Glenora Wine Cellars Finger Lakes, NY ★ 04 05 Gd sparkling wine, Chard, and Ries.

Hamptons, The (aka South Fork) LONG ISLAND AVA. The top winery is moneyed WÖLFFER ESTATE. Showcase Duck Walk is owned by PINDAR.

Horton Virginia ★★★ **01 02** 03 04 05 Est early 90s. Gd Viognier, Mourvèdre, Cab Fr, Norton.

Hudson River Region America's oldest wine-growing district (37 producers) and NY's first AVA. Straddles the river, 2 hrs' drive N of Manhattan.

Jefferson Virginia ★★★ **01 03 04** 05 Nr Thomas Jefferson's landmark estate Monticello, fine Pinot Gr, Viognier, Petit Verdot, B'x blend.

Keswick Virginia ★★★ 03 04 05 Young winery already establishing reputation for elegant Chardonnay, v.gd Viognier, Touriga, and Cab-based blend.

King Family Estate/Michael Shaps Wines Virginia ★★★★ **00 01 02** 03 04 05' Excellent Chard, Merlot, Cab Fr, and red blend turned out by Burgundy-trained oenologist.

Lake Erie Largest grape-growing district in the eastern US; 10,117 ha along shore of Lake Erie, inc portions of New York, Pennsylvania, and OHIO. Long-established Concord vines rapidly being replaced by vinifera plantings. Also name of a tri-state AVA: NY's sector has seven wineries, Pennsylvania's seven and OHIO's 30. OHIO's Harpersfield sets standards for quality.

Lamoreaux Landing Finger Lakes, NY ★★★ **02 03** 04 05 Promising Chard, Ries, and Cab Fr from striking Greek-revival winery.

Lenz ★★★ **01** 02 03 04 05 Classy winery of NORTH FORK AVA. Fine austere Chard in the Chablis mode, also Gewurz, Merlot, and sparkling wine.

Linden Virginia ★★★★ **99** 01 02 03 04 05 Small (5,000 cases) Virginia producer in mountains 100 km (65 miles) west of Washington, DC. Impressive Sauv Bl, Cab Fr, Petit Verdot, and B'x-style "claret".

Long Island, New York Exciting wine region E of the Rockies and a hothouse of experimentation. Currently 1,200 ha, all vinifera (35% Merlot) and three AVAs (LONG ISLAND, NORTH FORK, THE HAMPTONS). Most of its 43 wineries are on the North Fork. Best varieties: Chard, Cab Sauv, Merlot. A long growing season; almost frost-free but hurricane-prone. The youngest generation of wineries inc Ackerd Pond, Comtesse Thérèse, Diliberto (gd reds), Martha Clara, Old Fields (first wine sold 2002), Shinn (owned by proprietors of acclaimed Manhattan restaurant Home), Sherwood House (Chard and Merlot), Raphael.

Michigan In addition to fine cool-climate Ries, impressive Gewurz, Pinot N, and Cab Fr are emerging; 44 commercial wineries and four AVAs. Best inc St-Julien Wine Co, Ch Grand Traverse, Peninsula Cellars (esp dry Gewurz), Ch Chantal, Willow, and Tabor Hill. Mawby V'yds known for sp. Fenn Valley and Lemon Creek have large regional following. Up and coming: Brys, also Round Barn Winery and Distillery with gd dry Muscat, Cab Fr, and fine eau de vie.

Millbrook Hudson River, NY ★★ 02 03 04 05 Dedicated viticulture and savvy marketing has lifted spiffy whitewashed Millbrook in big old barn into NY's firmament. Burgundian Chards; Cab Fr can be delicious.

Naked Mountain Virginia 01 02 03 04 05 Est '81; known for big, buttery Chard.

Niagara Escarpment New York's newest AVA (Sept 05); currently seven wineries.

North Carolina Upcoming region, with 55 wineries. Leaders include Biltmore Estate, Childress, Iron Gate, Old North State. Look for Chard, Viognier, Cab Fr.

North Fork LONG ISLAND AVA (of three). Top wineries: Bedell, Macari, Lieb, LENZ, PALMER, PAUMANOK, PELLEGRINI, PINDAR. 2.5 hrs' drive from Manhattan.

Ohio 94 wineries, five AVAs, notably LAKE ERIE and Ohio Valley. Notable progress with Pinot Gr, Ries, Pinot N, Cab Fr, Icewine. To watch: Grand River Valley AVA.

Palmer Long Island, NY ★★★ 02 03 04 05 Superior NORTH FORK producer and byword in Darwinian metropolitan market. High profile due to perpetual-motion marketing. Tasty Chard, Sauv Bl, and Chinon-like Cab Fr.

Paumanok Long Island, NY ★★★ 01 02 03 04 05 NORTH FORK winery; impressive Ries, Chard, Merlot, Cab Sauv; outstanding Chenin Bl; savoury late-harvest Sauv Bl.

Pellegrini Long Island, NY ★★★ 00 01 02 03 04 05 An enchantingly designed winery on NORTH FORK. Opulent Merlot, stylish Chard, B'x-like Cab Sauv.

Pindar Vineyards Long Island, NY ★★★ 01 03 04 05 A 116-ha operation at NORTH FORK (Island's largest). Wide range of blends and popular varietals, inc Chard, Merlot, sparkling, v.gd B'x-style red blend, Mythology. Popular with tourists.

Rappahannock Virginia 04 05 Young family-run estate, 2000 first vintage. Nice Viognier and Chard.

Red Newt Finger Lakes, NY ★★★ 01 02 03 04 05 Turns out top Chard, Ries, Cab Fr, Merlot, and B'x-inspired red blend. Popular bistro.

Sakonnet Little Compton, Rhode Island ★★ 02 03 04 05 Largest New England winery. Very drinkable wines; delicious sp brut *cuvée*.

Standing Stone Finger Lakes, NY ★★ 01 02 03 04 05 One of the region's finest wineries with v.gd Ries, Gewurz, and B'x-type blend.

Tomasello New Jersey ★★ 02 04 05 Gd Chambourcin, sparkling Pinot N, Cab Sauv, and Merlot.

Unionville Vineyards New Jersey ★★ 02 03 04 05 Lovely Ries and gd red blend.

Valhalla Virginia ★★★ 02 03 04 05 V'yd at 600 m (2,000 ft) atop a granite mountain yields fine Alicante Bouschet, spicy Sangiovese, and gd red blend of all five B'x grapes.

Veritas Virginia ★★★ 04 05 Recently est. Gd Chard, Cab F, gutsy Petit Verdot.

Villa Appalaccia Virginia ★★★ 02 03 04 05 Italian-inspired winery in the Blue Ridge Mountains turning out limited amounts (3,000 cases total) of Primitivo, Sangiovese, Malvasia, Pinot Gr.

Virginia With 91 bonded wineries and six AVAs, Virginia is turning out some of the best wines in the E. The modern winemaking era now encompasses virtually every part of the state, with emphasis on vinifera.

Wagner Vineyards Finger Lakes, NY ★★ 03 04 05 Barrel-fermented Chard, dry and sweet Ries, and Icewine. Also has micro-brewery and restaurant.

Westport Rivers SE New England ★★ 02 03 04 05 Massachusetts house established in 1989. Gd Chard and elegant sparkling.

Whitehall Virginia ★★★★ 01 02 03 04 05 A handsome estate nr Charlottesville. Impeccable Gewurz, lush Petit Manseng, top Chard, Cab Fr, and Cab blend.

Wiemer, Hermann J Finger Lakes, NY ★★→★★★ 01 02 03 04 05 Creative, German-born winemaker. Outstanding Ries; v.gd Chard.

Wölffer Estate Long Island ★★★ 00 01 02 03 04 05 Modish Chard and Merlot from German-born winemaker. Gd wine *can* be made on the South Fork.

Wollersheim Wisconsin ★★ 05 Winery specializing in variations of Maréchal Foch. Prairie Fumé (Seyval Bl) is a commercial success.

Southeast & central states

Missouri Continues to expand, with over 50 producers in three AVAs: **Augusta**, **Hermann**, and **Ozark Highlands**. Best wines are Seyval Bl, Vidal, Vignoles (sweet and dry versions), and Chambourcin. **Stone Hill** in Hermann produces v.gd Chardonel (a frost-hardy hybrid of Seyval Blanc and Chardonnay), Norton, and gd Seyval Blanc and Vidal Blanc. **Hermannhof** is also drawing notice for Vignoles, Chardonel, and Norton. Also notable: **St James** for Vignoles, Seyval, Norton; **Mount Pleasant** in Augusta for rich "port" and Norton; **Adam Puchta** for good port-style wines and Norton, Vignoles, Vidal Blanc; **Augusta Winery** for Chambourcin, Chardonel, Icewine; **Les Bourgeois**, gd Syrah, Norton, Chardonel, Montelle, v.gd Cynthiana and Chambourcin.

Maryland Has over 15 wineries in four distinct growing regions. Best-known producer and oldest family-run winery is **Boordy Vineyards**, making v.gd Vidal Blanc, Chard, Chambourcin, and gd Cab Fr, Merlot, Ries. **Basignani** for good Cab Sauv, Ries, and Seyval. **Fiore**: gd Chambourcin, Merlot, Cab Sauv, Ries, and Vidal Blanc. **Woodhall** has good Ries, Seyval, and Cab Sauv.

Georgia There are now over a dozen wineries here. Look for: **Three Sisters** (Dahlonega), **Habersham V'yds**, and **Chateau Elan** (Braselton), which features southern splendour with v'yds, wine, and a resort.

Southwest
Texas

The fifth-largest wine-producing state in the US has seven AVAs and over 100 bonded wineries, many winning awards both nationally and internationally.

Becker Vineyards Stonewall ★★★ V.gd Cab Sauv, Chard, Ries, Merlot, Viognier.

Delaney Vineyards Nr Dallas ★★ Gd Chard and Sauv Bl.

Dry Comal Texas Hill Country Gd Cab Sauv, Merlot, Chard, Sauv Bl.

Fall Creek Texas Hill Country ★★ V.gd Chenin Bl and blends; gd Merlot.

Flat Creek Estate Texas Hill Country ★★ V.gd Sangiovese, Moscato Bianco; gd Pinot Gr, Shiraz.

Haak Vineyard & Winery Galveston County ★ V.gd Blanc du Bois and Cab Sauv.

Llano Estacado Nr Lubbock ★★★ The pioneer (since 1976) continues on award-winning track with Chard, Chenin Bl, and Zin. V.gd blends.

Lost Creek Vineyard Texas Hill Country V.gd Chard; gd Merlot and blends.

Messina Hof Wine Cellars Bryan ★★★ Most award-winning wines in the state. Excellent Ries, Chard (Private Reserve), Merlot, Cab Sauv. V.gd port-style wines.

Pheasant Ridge Nr Lubbock V.gd Chard and Chenin Bl; promising Merlot.

Pillar Bluff Texas Hill Country V. gd Cab Sauv, Chenin Bl.

Pleasant Hill Brenham Gd Cab Sauv, Blanc du Bois, blends.

Ste-Genevieve Fort Stockton ★ Largest Texas winery, linked with Domaines Cordier (France). Well-made NV wines, esp Sauv Bl. The premium label, Escondido Valley, features Chard, Cab Sauv.

Sister Creek Boerne Boutique winery with v.gd Pinot N, Chard, Muscat Canelli.

Stone House Spicewood New and promising; gd blends and port-style wines.

New Mexico, etc.

New Mexico Continues to show promise with emphasis on vinifera grapes, though some French hybrids still used (historic Mission grape is produced at Tularosa Winery). Over 30 wineries, three AVAs. **Black Mesa**: ★★ V.gd Cab Sauv, Pinot Gr, Merlot; gd blends, esp Coyote (r). **Casa Rondeña**: ★★ V.gd Cab Fr, Cab Sauv, Ries. Gruet: ★★★ Excellent sp; v.gd Chard, Pinot N. **La Chiripada**: ★★ V.gd Ries and blends; gd port-style wine. **Milagro V'yds**: v.gd Chard, Cab Sauv. **Ponderosa Valley**: ★★ V.gd Ries, gd Pinot N, Merlot, and blends, esp Summer Sage and Jemez Red. **Santa Fe V'yds**: Gd Sauv Bl, Merlot. **La Viña**: ★★ V.gd Chard, Zin; gd blends, esp Rojo Loco. St Clair, Blue Teal V'yds, Mademoiselle V'yds, D H Lescombes, and Santa Rita Cellars all under winemaker **Florent Lescombes** have a gd variety of wines. Luna Rosa, new: trying many varieties; v.gd Zin, Symphony, Merlot.

Colorado Focus is on vinifera grapes, with over 250 ha planted, now ranging from the Grand Valley on the Western Slope, over the Rocky Mountains to the Front Range. Has over 60 wineries and two AVAs. Leading producers inc **Carlson Cellars**: ★★★ V.gd Gewurz, Ries. **Canyon Wind**: Gd Chard, Cab Sauv, Merlot. **Cottonwood Cellars**: Gd Merlot, Chard. **Garfield Estates**: V.gd Sauv Bl. **Grande River**: ★★→★★★ V.gd Chard; gd Merlot, Syrah, Viognier. **Plum Creek**: ★ V.gd Ries; gd Chard, Merlot. **Terror Creek**: ★★ Small with v.gd Pinot N, Ries, Gewurz. **Trail Ridge**: Gewurz, Ries. **Two Rivers**: V.gd Cab Sauv, Chard, Merlot. **Verso Cellars**: V.gd Cab Sauv. **Balistreri**: Gd Cab Sauv, Syrah.

Arizona Progress has been made in overall quality. Success with Rhône and Mediterranean grape varieties: Sangiovese, Syrah, Petite Sirah show promise. **Callaghan Vineyards**: ★★ Excellent Temp-based Padres, v.gd Syrah, Cab Sauv, blends. **Dos Cabezas** ★ V.gd Cab Sauv, Petite Sirah, Sangiovese. **Kokopelli**: Arizona's largest winery; sound, reasonably priced wines.

Oklahoma Expanded to over 30 wineries, now emphasizing vinifera, although some wineries include native American grapes. **Greenfield Vineyard** Chandler: Gd Merlot, Sauv Bl. **Stone Bluff Cellars** Haskell: Gd Vignoles, Cynthiana, blends. **Panther Hills** Bessie: ★★ New, boutique, vinifera emphasis; v.gd Cab Sauv. **Tidal School V'yds** Drumright: The largest; good blends.

Utah Spanish Valley (Moab) V.gd Ries (esp Late Harvest) and Cab Sauv.

Nevada Pahrump Valley Nr Las Vegas produces gd Chard, Cab Sauv. **Tahoe Ridge** (N Nevada) has extensive expansion plans and v.gd Chard.

Canada

British Columbia

The biggest concentration of wineries is in the warm, dry Okanagan Valley around a vast lake, 400 km (245 miles) east of Vancouver, especially in the desert-like southernmost part of the region. There are over 100 wineries in four appellations: Okanagan Valley, Fraser Valley, Similkameen Valley, Vancouver Island. Up and coming: Fairview Cellars (Bordeaux reds), Golden Mile (Merlot, Chardonnay), Herder (Merlot, Pinot Gris), La Frenz (Semillon), Lake Breeze (Pinot Blanc, Semillon), Mt Boucherie (Semillon).

Blue Mountain 98 00 01 02 04 05 Excellent Chard and sparkling.

Burrowing Owl 00 01 02 03 04 05 Excellent Merlot, solid whites.

Calona-Sandhill Vineyards ★★★ 00 01 02 03 04 05 Large winery. Gd Pinot Bl, Cab Fr, outstanding Syrah, and Merlot.

Cedar Creek ★★★ 00 01 **02** 03 04 05 Outstanding Chard, Ries, Pinot Bl, Pinot N, B'x-style blend, and Merlot. Tapas-style restaurant.

Gehringer Bros ★★ 03 04 05 Gd Riesling, Pinot Gr, Ehrenfelser.

Inniskillin Okanagan ★★★ Excellent Chard, Viognier, Pinot Bl.

Jackson-Triggs Okanagan ★★★ 02 03 04 05 V.gd Merlot, Meritage, Shiraz, Viognier, Ries Icewine.

Mission Hill ★→★★★ 00 01 02 03 04 05 Acclaimed Chard, Pinot Bl, Syrah, Merlot, and flagship Oculus. High culinary standards on Dining Terrace.

Quails' Gate ★★ 00 01 02 03 04 05 Ries, Merlot, Late Harvest Optima, and Old Vines Foch.

Sumac Ridge ★★ 00 01 02 04 05 Gewurz, Sauv Bl, sp among region's best. Notable Meritage and Merlot. (Owned by VINCOR.)

Ontario

Includes Canada's largest viticultural area Niagara Peninsula. Around 100 wineries. Proximity of the lake and diverse soils create distinctive growing conditions. Emerging quality-driven wineries inc Fielding, Tawse, Coyote's Run, and Stratus. Icewine is the region's international flagship. In 2005, 12 new sub-appellations were approved within the larger Niagara Peninsula appellation.

Andres 00 01 **02** 03 04 05 Second-largest Canadian winery. Owns HILLEBRAND and Peller Estates.

Cave Spring Cellars ★★★ 01 **02** 03 04 05 Benchmark Ries, sophisticated Chard from old vines, gd Gamay, and sp wines.

Château des Charmes ★★★ 00 01 **02** 03 04 05 Showplace château-style winery. Fine Chard, Viognier, Cab Sauv, Icewines, sp.

Creekside 00 01 02 03 04 05 Consistently top producer of fine Pinot N, Sauv Bl, and B'x-style red blend.

Henry of Pelham ★★★ 00 01 **02** 03 04 05 Elegant Chard and Ries; Cab Sauv/Merlot, distinctive Baco Noir, Icewine.

Hillebrand Estates ★→★★★ 00 01 **02** 03 04 05 Excellent Ries, sparkling, and B'x-style red blend. Handsome restaurant.

Inniskillin ★★★★ 00 01 **02** 03 04 05 Important (VINCOR-owned) producer that spearheaded birth of modern Ontario wine industry. Skilful Burgundy-style Chard, Pinot N; also B'x-style red. V.gd Ries, Icewine (inc sp), Pinot Gr.

Jackson Triggs ★★★ 00 **01 02** 03 04 05 State-of-the-art winery, fine Ries, Chard, B'x-style reds.

Malivoire 03 04 05 Small, innovative gravity-flow winery with very good Pinot N, Chard, and Gamay. Some organic.

Pelee Island Estate 00 01 02 03 04 05 Canada's first commercial winery (1866); largest VQA producer. Chard, Cab Fr, and Icewines.

Peninsula Ridge ★★★ 00 01 **02** 03 04 05 Est 2000. Gd Chard, Sauv Bl, and Merlot; delicious Icewine.

Vincor International ★→★★ 00 01 02 03 04 05 Fourth-largest company in N America. Produces premium wines and varietals, blends. Owns JACKSON-TRIGGS, INNISKILLIN (Chard, Cab Sauv), Sumac Ridge, California's RH PHILLIPS, Washington's HOGUE CELLARS; also Goundrey (Australia) and Kim Crawford (NZ).

Vineland Estates ★★★ 00 01 02 03 04 05 Dry and semi-dry Ries; Gewurz much admired. Vidal Icewine gd. Chard, Cab Sauv, Sauv Bl, and B'x-style red.

Vintners Quality Alliance (VQA) Canada's appellation body. Its rigid standards have rapidly raised respect and awareness of Canadian wines.

Central & South America

More heavily shaded areas
are the wine-growing regions

Chile

The annual Wines of Chile Awards, first held in 2004, have shown that
smaller, quality-minded, vineyard-focused wineries are emerging with
each new vintage and have also illustrated the development of newer,
usually cooler terroirs. In San Antonio, some vineyards lie just 4 km
(2.5 miles) from the sea, and the conditions can be distinctly brisk. In the
Elqui Valley, 500 km (300 miles) north of Santiago, as in Limarí 100 km
(60 miles) further south, the altitude and coastal influences mean this is a
cool-climate region. Over 1,000 km (600 miles) south lies Bío-Bío, source of
Chile's finest Riesling, and Malleco, home of one of Chile's top Chardonnays.
The conventional heartland of Chilean wine lies between these two extremes
in the Central Valley, but even here, cooler locations are sought.

Then there is the greater diversity of grape varieties. Syrah is proving
successful in a number of locations. Pinot Noir is blossoming in the new,
cooler regions, as is Viognier, while Malbec is also becoming popular. Look out
too for Zinfandel, Alicante Bouschet, Sauvignon Gris, and other oddities.
Cabernet Sauvignon continues to impress; Carmenère is increasingly
impressive, but still gives its best performance in a blend; while Merlot, now
without the helping hand from Carmenère (the two were thought identical for
several years) is disappointing. In whites, Chardonnay seldom rises above the
competent; but Sauvignon Blanc (as opposed to the inferior Sauvignonasse;

the two are still confused in many older vineyards) can be excellent, with a more pithy, European style than some overtly New World versions.

With their top-of-the-range wines, many producers are still looking to provide maximum impact with ripeness, concentration, and levels of oak. These can be impressive, but the cheaper wines are often more satisfying to drink. With just a little more restraint, the wines will be world-beaters.

Recent vintages

Most wines are ready to drink on release, although the better reds improve for up to five years. Curiously, odd years have been best for reds in recent vintages.
2005 Mild summer, slow but steady ripening for all varieties. Very high quality.
2004 Hot summer, cool autumn, low yields. Good for Cab Sauv, others variable.
2003 Warm, low-yielding year. High-quality reds; whites may lack crispness.
2002 Good in Maipo and Aconcagua, more patchy further south due to rain.
2001 Near-perfect conditions, generally lower yields, very high quality.

Aconcagua Nth'most quality wine region. Inc CASABLANCA, Panquehue, SAN ANTONIO.
Almaviva ★★★ Expensive but classy, claret-style MAIPO red – a joint venture between CONCHA Y TORO and BARON PHILIPPE DE ROTHSCHILD.
Altaïr ★★→★★★ Ambitious joint venture between Ch Dassault (St-Emilion) and SAN PEDRO. Pascal Chatonnet of B'x is consultant; *grand vin* (mostly Cab Sauv with Carmenère) complex and earthy, 2nd wine Sideral for earlier drinking.
Anakena Cachapoal ★→★★ Solid range. Flagship wines under Ona label include punchy Syrah; Single Vineyard bottlings and Reserve Chard also gd.
Antiyal ★★→★★★ Alvaro Espinoza's own estate, making fine, complex red from Biodynamically grown Cab Sauv, Syrah, Carmenère. Second wine Kuyen.
Apaltagua ★★→★★★ Carmenère specialist drawing on old-vine fruit from Apalta (Colchagua). Grial is rich, herbal flagship wine.
Aquitania, Viña ★★→★★★ Chilean/French joint venture making v.gd Lazuli Cab Sauv (MAIPO) and Sol de Sol Chard from Malleco. Also Paul Bruno MAIPO Cab Sauv (Paul Pontallier and Bruno Prats from B'x are partners).
Arboleda, Viña ★★ Part of the ERRÁZURIZ/CALITERRA stable, sourcing fruit from several regions, and impressing with Cab Sauv, Syrah, Carmenère, Sauv Bl, Chard.
Baron Philippe de Rothschild ★→★★ B'x company making gd Mapa varietal range, better Escudo Rojo red blend. Also see ALMAVIVA.
Bío-Bío Promising southern region. Potential for gd whites and Pinot N.
Botalcura ★★→★★★ Curicó venture involving French winemaker Philippe Debrus, formerly of VALDIVIESO. Grand Reserve Cab Fr is the star.
Calina, Viña ★→★★★ Kendall-Jackson (see California) venture. Better reds (esp Selección de Las Lomas Cab Sauv) than whites; Elite Cab Sauv the pick.
Caliterra ★→★★★ Sister winery of ERRÁZURIZ. Chard and Sauv Bl improving (more CASABLANCA grapes), reds becoming less one-dimensional, esp Res.
Cánepa, José Colchagua ★★ Solid range. Lemony Sem and spicy Zin among the more unusual wines. Best inc juicy Malbec and fragrant Syrah Res.
Carmen, Viña ★★→★★★ MAIPO winery; same ownership as SANTA RITA. Ripe, fresh Special Res CASABLANCA Chard and late-harvest MAIPO Sem top whites. Reds even better; esp RAPEL Merlot, MAIPO Petite Sirah, Gold Res Cab Sauv.
Carta Vieja ★→★★★ MAULE winery owned by one family for six generations. Reds better than whites; but Antigua Selección Chard is gd.
Casablanca Cool-climate region between Santiago and coast. Little water: drip irrigation essential. Top-class Chard, Sauv Bl; promising Merlot, Pinot N.
Casablanca, Viña ★→★★★ Sister winery to SANTA CAROLINA. RAPEL and MAIPO fruit used for some reds; but better wines – Merlot, Sauv Bl, Chard, Gewurz – from Santa Isabel Estate in CASABLANCA. Look for new super-*cuvée* Neblus.

Casa Lapostolle ★★ ⇢★★★★ Money from the family of Grand Marnier and advice from Michel Rolland (see France) result in fine range. B'x-style Sauv Bl is gd, but Cuvée Alexandre reds and Carmenère-based Clos Apalta are even better.

Casa Marín ★★★ Dynamic San Antonio white specialist, v.gd Gewurz and superb Sauv Bl. First Syrah and Pinot N promising.

Casa Rivas Maipo ★★ Part of group that includes TARAPACA, VIÑA MAR, Missiones de Rengo. Best: Sappy Sauv Bl; gentle, citrus Chard Res; blackcurrant-pastille-y Cab Sauv; generously fruity Maria Pinto Syrah/Cab Sauv Res.

Casas del Bosque ★ ⇢★★★ CASABLANCA winery, also using Cab Sauv from Cachapoal for elegant range inc juicy, svelte Pinot N and peppery Syrah Res.

Casa Silva ★★ Colchagua estate. Chunky Res Merlot and top-of-the-range Quinta Generación Red and White; white is a successful blend of Chard, Sauv Gris, and Viognier. New red, Altura, is silky and complex.

Concha y Toro ★ ⇢★★★ Mammoth, quality-minded operation. Best: subtle Amelia Chard (CASABLANCA); inky Don Melchor Cab Sauv (RAPEL); and Terrunyo Winemaker Lot single-v'yd range. Marqués de Casa Concha, Trio, Explorer, Casillero del Diablo offer v.gd value. See also BARON PHILIPPE DE ROTHSCHILD, CONO SUR, FRANCISCO DE AQUIRRE, VOE; also Viña PATAGONIA (Argentina).

Cono Sur Chimbarongo, Colchagua ★★ ⇢★★★ Owned by CONCHA Y TORO. Has v.gd Pinot N (local and CASABLANCA fruit), headed by Ocio. Other top releases appear as 20 Barrels selection (look out for 2004 Chard); new innovations under Visión label (BÍO-BÍO Ries is superb). Also dense, fruity Cab Sauv, delicious Viognier, rose-petal Gewurz, impressive new Syrah. Second label Isla Negra.

Cousiño Macul ★★ ⇢★★★ Historic MAIPO producer now relocated to Buin. Long-lived Antiguas Res Cab Sauv; zesty Sauv Gris. New (as yet unnamed) Icon wine scheduled for release late 2006. Cab Sauv rosé wonderfully refreshing.

de Martino Maipo ★★ ⇢★★★ Ambitious Carmenère pioneer and one of W MAIPO's best wineries, esp for v.gd premium *cuvée*, Gran Familia Cab Sauv.

Domus Maipo ★★ ⇢★★★ Ambitious winery making gd Chard and v.gd Domus Aurea Cab Sauv; sister Cabs Stella Aurea and Peñalolen also tasty.

Echeverría ★★ Boutique Curicó (MAULE) winery. Reliable Res Cab Sauv; gd oaked and unoaked Chard; improving Sauv Bl; elegant, fragrant Carmenère.

Edwards, Luís Felipé ★★ Colchagua winery. Citrus Chard, silky Res Cab Sauv.

El Principal, Viña ★★★ Excellent Pirque (MAIPO) estate making B'x blends with guidance of Patrick Valette in St-Emilion. El Principal is top wine.

Errázuriz ★ ⇢★★★ Main winery in ACONCAGUA's Panquehue district. Complex Wild Ferment Chard; brooding La Cumbre Syrah; best Sangiovese in Chile. Award-winning VIÑEDO CHADWICK (00), Seña (00 01). Also see ARBOLEDA, CALITERRA, SEÑA.

Falernia, Viña ★★ Winery in far N Elquí Valley, v'yds lie at around 2,000 m. Alta Tierra Syrah and Chard show potential; gd Sauv Bl, Carmenère, Merlot.

Fortuna, Viña La Lontué Valley ★★ Established winery with attractive range.

Francisco de Aguirre, Viña ★ ⇢★★ Promising Cab Sauv, Cab Fr, Chard under Palo Alto label from northerly region of Limarí; recently bought by CONCHA Y TORO.

Garcés Silva Leyda ★★ ⇢★★★ Exciting newcomer with Amayna range; SAN ANTONIO Sauv Bl is among Chile's finest; Pinot N and Chard also commendable.

Gracia de Chile ★ ⇢★★ Winery with v'yds from ACONCAGUA down to BÍO-BÍO. Res Lo Mejor Cab Sauv and Syrah (both ACONCAGUA) and BÍO-BÍO Sauv Bl are best. Part of same group as PORTA, Agustinos, VERANDA.

Hacienda Araucano ★★ ⇢★★★ The Lurton brothers' Chilean enterprise. First-class selection: complex Gran Araucano Sauv Bl (CASABLANCA), refined Carmenère/Cab Sauv blend Clos de Lolol, and heady Alka Carmenère (both COLCHAGUA).

Haras de Pirque ★★ ⇢★★★ Pirque (MAIPO) estate. Smoky Sauv Bl, stylish Chard, dense Cab Sauv/Merlot. Top wine Albis (Cab Sauv/Carmenère) is solid, smoky red made in joint venture with Antinori (see Italy).

Larose, Viña de ★→★★ RAPEL venture by Médoc Ch Larose-Trintaudon under the Las Casas del Toqui and Viña Alamosa labels. Promising top-end Leyenda Chard and Prestige Cab Sauv.

Leyda, Viña ★★→★★★ Leyda pioneers, producing elegant Chard (Lot 5 Wild Yeasts is the pick), lush Pinot N (esp Lot 21 cuvée and lively rosé), tangy Garuma Sauv Bl. Decent MAIPO Cab Sauv and RAPEL Merlot.

Maipo Famous wine region close to Santiago. Chile's best Cab Sauvs often come from higher, eastern sub-regions such as Pirque and Puente Alto.

Matetic San Antonio ★★★ Decent Pinot N and Chard from this exciting winery, but fragrant, zesty Sauv Bl and spicy, berry-scented Syrah are the stars.

Maule Southernmost region in Central Valley. Claro, Loncomilla, Tutuven Valleys.

Montes ★★→★★★ Alpha Cab Sauv can be brilliant; Merlot, Syrah, Malbec also fine; Chard v.gd. B'x blend Montes Alpha M improves each year; Folly Syrah is one of the best in Chile; Purple Angel is Carmenère at its most intense.

MontGras ★★→★★★ State-of-the-art Colchagua winery with fine limited-edition wines, inc Syrah and Zin. High-class flagship Ninquen Cab Sauv.

Morande ★★ Vast range inc César, Cinsault, Bouschet, Carignan. Limited Edition used for top wines, inc a spicy Syrah/Cab Sauv and inky Malbec. Gd value.

Odfjell ★→★★★ MAIPO-based, Norwegian-owned red specialist. Top wine: Aliara Cab Sauv. Orzada range, inc entry-level Armador, also v.gd.

Pérez Cruz ★★★ MAIPO winery with Alvaro Espinoza (see ANTIYAL) in charge of winemaking. Fresh spicy Syrah, aromatic Cot, and stylish Liguai red blend.

Porta, Viña ★→★★ MAIPO winery. Range inc supple, spicy Cab Sauv. See GRACIA.

Rapel Central quality region divided into Colchagua and Cachapoal valleys. Great "Merlot" (much is actually Carmenère). Watch for sub-region Marchihue.

La Rosa, Viña ★★ Reliable, if seldom exciting, RAPEL Chard, Merlot, and Cab Sauv under La Palmeria and Cornellana labels. Don Reca reds are the stars.

San Antonio Coastal region west of Santiago benefiting from sea breezes; very promising for whites, Syrah, and Pinot N. Leyda is a sub-zone.

San Pedro ★→★★★ Massive Curicó-based producer. Gato and 35 South (35 Sur) are reliable. Involved in Viña Tabalí in Limarí. See also ALTAÏR.

Santa Carolina, Viña ★★→★★★ Historic bodega; impressive, complex wines. All MAIPO Res wines are gd, inc rich, limey Sauv Bl. Barrica Selection range, inc earthy Carmenère and supple Syrah, better still.

Santa Inés ★★ Successful small family winery in Isla de MAIPO making ripe, blackcurranty Legado de Armida Cab Sauv. Part of DE MARTINO stable.

Santa Mónica ★→★★ Rancagua (RAPEL) winery; the best label is Tierra del Sol. Ries, Sem, and Merlot under Santa Mónica label also gd.

Santa Rita ★★→★★★★★ Quality-conscious MAIPO bodega. Best: Casa Real MAIPO Cab Sauv; but Triple C (Cab Sauv/Cab Fr/Carmenère) nearly as gd.

Selentia ★★ New Chilean/Spanish venture. Res Special Cab Sauv is fine.

Seña Polished Cab Sauv/Merlot/Carmenère blend from the ERRÁZURIZ stable.

Tabali Limarí ★★ New winery partly owned by SAN PEDRO, already making refined Chard and earthy, peppery Syrah.

Tarapacá, Viña ★★ MAIPO winery improved after investment, but inconsistent.

Terramater ★→★★★ Wines from all over Central Valley, inc v.gd Altum range.

Terranoble ★→★★★ Talca winery specializing in grassy Sauv Bl and light, peppery Merlot. Range now inc v.gd spicy Carmenère Gran Res.

Torreón de Paredes ★→★★★ Attractive, crisp Chard, ageworthy Res Cab Sauv from this RAPEL bodega. Flagship Don Amedo Cab Sauv could be better.

Torres, Miguel ★★→★★★ Fresh whites and gd reds, esp sturdy Manso del Velasco single-v'yd Cab Sauv and Cariñena-based Cordillera. See also Spain.

Undurraga ★→★★ Traditional MAIPO estate known for its Pinot N. Top wines: Res Chard, refreshing, limey Gewurz, peachy Late Harvest Sem.

CENTRAL & SOUTH AMERICA

Valdivieso ★→★★★ Major producer with new Lontué winery. Single-v'yd bottlings inc fine new Chard and NV blend Caballo Loco are pick of the range. Res bottlings also gd; basic range much improved in recent vintages.

Vascos, Los ★→★★ Lafite-Rothschild venture making Cab Sauv in B'x mould. Recent vintages show more fruit. Top wines: Le Dix and Grande Réserve.

Veramonte ★★ CASABLANCA-based operation of Agustín Huneeus (formerly of California winery Franciscan); whites from CASABLANCA fruit, red from Central Valley grapes – all gd. Top wine: Primus red blend.

Veranda ★★ Joint venture between Corpora (owners of GRACIA DE CHILE) and Boisset of Burgundy using fruit from ACONCAGUA, CASABLANCA and MAIPO.

Villard ★★ Sophisticated wines made by French-born Thierry Villard. Gd MAIPO reds, esp heady Merlot, Equis Cab Sauv, and CASABLANCA whites.

Viña Mar Casablanca ★→★★ B'x-style reds are a little scrawny, but Pinot N, Sauv Bl, and Chard all show Casablanca at its best. See CASA RIVAS.

Viñedo Chadwick Maipo ★★★ Stylish Cab Sauv improving with each vintage from v'yd owned by Eduardo Chadwick, chairman of ERRÁZURIZ.

Viñedos Organicos Emiliana (VOE) ★★ →★★★ Organic arm of Santa Emiliana (part of CONCHA Y TORO), and the world's largest Biodynamic grower. Complex, heady red blend Coyam currently heads the range, but flagship wine (provisionally named Nasca) soon to appear.

Viu Manent ★→★★ Emerging Colchagua winery. Dense, fragrant Viu 1 tops range; Secreto Malbec and Viognier also v.gd; Late Harvest Sem top notch.

Von Siebenthal ★★★ Small (in Chilean terms) Swiss-owned ACONCAGUA winery. V.gd Carabantes Syrah and B'x-inspired reds, the best of which is elegant Cab Sauv/Petit Verdot/Carmenère blend Montelig.

Argentina

Progress in Argentina continues apace, and wine-lovers have to contend with emerging regions and sub-regions, a broader palette of grape varieties, and a raft of new producers. With vineyards ranging from 500 m up to nearly 1,500 m, much effort is being put into matching varieties to site. Old-vine Malbec is the trump card, but Cabernet Sauvignon is improving rapidly, while higher vineyards boast elegant Chardonnay. A number of producers are now treating other European grapes such as Barbera, Tempranillo, Sangiovese, and Bonarda with increased respect, and the results can be very good.

Other provinces are also springing to prominence. Salta in the north has some of the highest vineyards in the world and is excelling with both reds and whites, especially with Torrontés. Between Mendoza and Salta lie Catamarca, La Rioja, and San Juan, all of which are making progress, while south of Mendoza, wine quality is improving rapidly in Neuquén and Río Negro.

Expect the trend for single vineyard old-vine Malbec to proliferate, and be prepared to wrestle for them with wine-lovers all over the world.

Recent vintages

Whites and cheaper reds should generally be drunk on release. Better reds benefit from 5+ yrs from vintage.

2005 Cool but generally fine. Ripe, structured reds; balanced, aromatic whites.
2004 Hot, dry, and largely hail-free. Whites erratic, but top-class reds.
2003 Frosts and hail, but otherwise the vintage was fine and dry.
2002 A good vintage, resulting in the best wines for more than a decade.
2001 Quality is variable, but some very good reds.

Achaval Ferrer ★★★ →★★★★ MENDOZA. Super-concentrated Altamira, Bella Vista, and Mirador single-v'yd Malbecs and Quimera Malbec/Cab Sauv/Merlot blends.

Alta Vista ★★★ French-owned MENDOZA venture specializing in Malbec. Dense, spicy Alto among best wines in the country. Also fresh, zesty Torrontés. Sister winery Navarrita makes fine Winemakers Selection Malbec.

Altos las Hormigas ★★★ Italian-owned Malbec specialist, wines made by consultant Alberto Antonini (ex-Italy's Antinori). Best: Viña las Hormigas Res.

Anubis ★★ Another venture for Susana Balbo (see DOMINIO DEL PLATA), making exciting juicy reds, esp Malbec. Budini is new and tasty entry-level range.

Balbi, Bodegas ★★ Allied-Domecq-owned San Raphael producer. Juicy Malbec, Chard, and delicious Syrah (red and rosé). Red blend Barbaro also v.gd.

Bianchi, Valentin ★ San Rafael red specialist. Familia Bianchi (Cab Sauv) is excellent flagship. Gd-value Elsa's Vineyard inc meaty Barbera. Pithy Sauv Bl.

Bodega del Fin del Mundo ★★ First winery in the province of Neuquén; Malbec a speciality, top wine Special Blend is Merlot/Malbec/Cab Sauv.

Cabernet de los Andes ★★ Promising organic (and partly Biodynamic) Catamarca estate with big, fragrant, balanced reds under Vicien and Tizac labels.

Canale, Bodegas Humberto ★★ Premier Río Negro winery known for its Sauv Bl and Pinot N, but Merlot and Malbec (esp Black River label) are the stars.

Cassone, Bodega ★★ Mendoza enterprise now benefiting from Alberto Antonini's winemaking expertise. Watch out for Obra Prima Malbec.

Catena ★→★★★★ Style can be a little international, but quality is always gd. Range rises from Malambo through Argento, Alamos, Catena, Catena Alta, to flagship Nicolas Catena Zapata and a new trio of fine single-v'yd Malbecs.

Clos de los Siete ★★ Seven parcels of French-owned vines in MENDOZA, run by Michel Rolland (see France). A juicy Malbec already exists, but each site will produce its own wine (see MONTEVIEJO).

Chakana ★★ Agrelo winery to watch for joyful Malbec, Cab Sauv, Syrah.

Chandon, Bodegas ★→★★ Makers of Baron B and M Chandon sp under Moët & Chandon supervision; promising Pinot N/Chard blend. See TERRAZAS.

Cobos, Viña ★★★ Californian Paul Hobbs plus husband and wife Andrea Marchiori and Luis Barraud. Stunning Marchiori Vineyard old-vine Malbec.

Dominio del Plata ★→★★★★ Ex-CATENA husband-and-wife pair Susana Balbo and Pedro Marchevsky produce superior wines under the Crios, Susana Balbo, and BenMarco labels. See also ANUBIS.

Doña Paula ★ Luján de Cuyo estate owned by Santa Rita (see Chile). Elegant, structured Malbec; modern fleshy Cab Sauv; tangy Los Cardos Sauv Bl.

Etchart ★★→★★★ Pernod-Ricard owned, two wineries: SALTA and MENDOZA. Reds from both regions gd, topped by plummy Cafayate Cab Sauv. Torrontés also one of the best, with intriguing late-harvest Tardio.

Fabre Montmayou ★★ French-owned Luján de Cuyo (MENDOZA) bodega; fine reds and advice from Michel Rolland (see France). Also decent Chard. Infinitus is sister bodega in Rio Negro making supple Gran Res Merlot.

Familia Zuccardi ★→★★★★ Dynamic MENDOZA estate producing gd-value Santa Julia range, led by new blend Magna, better Q label (impressive Malbec, Merlot, Tempranillo), and deep yet elegant Zeta (Malbec/Tempranillo).

Finca La Anita ★★→★★★★ MENDOZA estate making high-class reds, esp Syrah and Malbec, and intriguing whites, inc Sem and Tocai Friulano.

Finca Colomé ★★→★★★ SALTA bodega owned by Donald Hess of California's Hess Collection. Pure, intense, Biodynamic Cab Sauv, Merlot, and Malbec.

Finca El Retiro ★→★★ MENDOZA bodega for gd Malbec, Bonarda, and Temp.

Finca Flichman ★★ Long-established company, now owned by Portugal's Sogrape. Gd-value Syrah. Best: Dedicato blend (mostly Cab Sauv/Syrah). Paisaje de Tupungato (B'x blend), Paisaje de Barrancas (Syrah-based) v'gd.

Finca Las Moras ★★ San Juan bodega with chunky Tannat, chewy Malbec Res, and plump, fragrant Malbec/Bonarda blend Mora Negra.

CENTRAL & SOUTH AMERICA

Finca Sophenia Tupungato bodega co-owned by Roberto Luka, ex-president of Wines of Argentina, and with advice from Michel Rolland (see France). Malbec and Cab Sauv shine; gd Altosur entry-level range; top wine Synthesis.

Kaikén ★★→★★★ Mendoza venture for Aurelio Montes (see Chile) making user-friendly range topped by Ultra Cab Sauv and Malbec.

Luigi Bosca ★★→★★★ Small MENDOZA (Maipù) bodega with three tiers of quality – Finca La Linda, Luigi Bosca Res, and High Range. Esp gd Finca Los Nobles Malbec/Verdot and Cab Sauv/Bouchet, plus impressive new Gala blends.

Lurton, Bodegas J & F ★→★★★ MENDOZA venture of Lurton brothers. Juicy, concentrated Piedra Negra Malbec and complex, earthy Chacayes (Malbec) head range; new Flor de Torrontés more serious than most.

Marguery, Familia Top-class Malbec from old vines in the Tupungato district.

Masi Tupungato ★★ →★★★ MENDOZA enterprise for the well-known Valpolicella producer (see Italy). Passo Doble is fine *ripasso*-style Malbec/Corvina/Merlot blend; Corbec is even better Amarone lookalike (Corvina/Malbec).

Mendoza Most important province for wine (over 70% of plantings). Best sub-regions: Agrelo, Tupungato, Luján de Cuyo, and Maipú.

Monteviejo ★★→★★★ One of the vineyards of CLOS DE LOS SIETE, now with top-class range of reds headed by wonderfully textured Monteviejo blend (Malbec/Merlot/Cab Sauv/Syrah); Lindaflor Malbec also v.gd.

Navarro Correas ★★ Gd if sometimes over-oaked reds, esp Col Privada Cab Sauv. Also reasonable whites, inc very oaky Chard and Deutz-inspired fizz.

Nieto Senetiner, Bodegas ★★ Luján de Cuyo-based bodega. Quality rises from tasty entry-level Santa Isabel through Reserva to top-of-range Cadus reds.

Noemia Old-vine RÍO NEGRO Malbec from Hans Vinding-Diers and Noemi Cinzano.

Norton, Bodegas ★★★ Old bodega, now Austrian-owned. Gd whites; v.gd reds, esp Malbec and excellent value Privada blend (Merlot/Cab Sauv/Malbec).

O Fournier ★→★★★ Spanish-owned Valle de Uco bodega. Best: Tempranillo/Merlot/Malbec blends Acrux and Bcrux. New Syrah bodes well.

Patagonia, Viña ★→★★ Owned by Concha y Toro of Chile, making gd-value int'l Malbec, Syrah, Cab Sauv, Merlot, Chard under Trivento and Alta Vida labels.

Peñaflor ★→★★★ Argentina's biggest wine company. Labels inc Andean Vineyards and, for finer wines, TRAPICHE.

Poesia ★★→★★★ Exciting Luján de Cuyo bodega under same ownership as Clos l'Eglise of B'x; stylish Poesia (Cab Sauv/Malbec), chunkier but still fine Clos des Andes (Malbec), and juicy Pasodoble Malbec/Syrah/Cab Sauv blend.

Pulenta ★★→★★★ Luján de Cuyo winery. Gd Sauv Bl and v.gd reds, best of which are Gran Corte (Cab Sauv/Malbec/Merlot/Petit Verdot) and Malbec.

Río Negro Promising new area in Patagonia.

Salentein, Bodegas ★★ MENDOZA bodega, impressing with Cab Sauv, Malbec, Merlot, Primus Pinot N. Finca El Portillo (a separate estate) gd for cheaper wines; also Bodegas Callia in San Juan, where Shiraz is the focus.

Salta Northerly province with some of the world's highest v'yds. Sub-region Cafayate renowned for Torrontés.

San Pedro de Yacochuya ★★★ SALTA collaboration between Michel Rolland (see France) and the ETCHART family. Ripe but fragrant Torrontés; dense, earthy Malbec; and powerful, stunning Yacochuya Malbec from oldest vines.

Santa Ana, Bodegas ★→★★ Old-established family firm at Guaymallen, MENDOZA. New La Mascota range a distinct improvement, with weighty Cab Sauv being the pick; also bright, friendly Cepas Privadas Viognier.

San Telmo ★★ Modern Seagram-owned winery making fresh, full-flavoured Chard, Chenin Bl, Merlot. Best: Malbec and Cab Sauv Cruz de Piedra-Maipú.

Tacuil, Bodegas ★★→★★★ SALTA venture for Raul Davalos, former owner of FINCA COLOMÉ. 33 de Davalos is excellent spicy Cab Sauv/Malbec blend.

Terrazas de los Andes ★★→★★★ CHANDON enterprise for still wines made from Malbec, Cab Sauv, Chard, Syrah. Three ranges: entry-level Terrazas (juicy Cab Sauv is the star), mid-price Res, and top-of-the-tree Afincado. Joint venture with Ch Cheval Blanc of B'x making superb Cheval des Andes blend.

Torino, Michel ★★ Rapidly improving organic Cafayate enterprise, esp Cab Sauv. Altimus is rather oaky flagship.

Toso, Pascual ★★ Californian Paul Hobbs heads a team making gd-value, tasty range headed by ripe but finely structured Magdalena Toso (mostly Malbec).

Trapiche ★★→★★★ Premium label of PEÑAFLOR. Labels in ascending quality order are Astica, Trapiche (pick is Oak Cask Syrah), Fond de Cave (gd Malbec Reserva), Medalla (plummy Cab Sauv), pricy red blend Iscay, and new high-class trio of single-v'yd Malbecs.

Val de Flores ★★★★ Another Michel Rolland-driven enterprise close to CLOS DE LOS SIETE for compelling yet elegant (and Biodynamic) old-vine Malbec.

Viniterra ★→★★ Clean, modern wines under Omnium, Bykos, Viniterra labels.

Weinert, Bodegas ★→★★ Potentially fine reds, esp Cavas de Weinert blend (Cab Sauv/Merlot/Malbec), are often spoiled by extended ageing in old oak.

Other Central & South American wines

Bolivia With a generally hot, humid climate, annual domestic consumption of just one bottle per capita, only 2,000 hectares of grapes (most destined for fiery *aguardiente* brandy), and only ten wineries, this is not a major wine producer. Even so, **Vinos y Viñedos La Concepción** wines show what is possible. The vineyards, 1,000 km S of La Paz, are the highest in the world.

Brazil New plantings of better grapes are transforming a big, booming industry with an increasing home market. International investment, especially in Rio Grande do Sul and Santana do Liuramento, notably from France and Italy, are significant, and point to possible exports. The sandy Frontera region and Sierra Gaucha hills (Italian-style sparkling) to watch. Continuous harvesting is possible in some equatorial vineyards. Of the wines that do leave Brazil, 95% are made by **Vinícola Aurora** (**Bento Gonçalves**), sometimes under the **Amazon** label. Look out for newcomer **Rio Sol**.

Mexico Oldest Latin American wine industry is reviving, with investment from abroad (*e.g.* Freixenet, Martell, Domecq) and California influence via UC Davis. Best in Baja California (with Valle de Guadeloupe among the best sub-zones), Querétaro, and on the Aguascalientes and Zacatecas plateaux. Lack of water is a problem countrywide. Top Baja C producers are **Casa de Piedra** (impressive Tempranillo/Cab Sauv), **L A Cetto** (Valle de Guadaloupe, the largest, esp for Cab Sauv, Nebbiolo, Petite Sirah), **Doña Lupe** (organic specialist), **Bodegas Santo Tomás** (working with California's Wente Brothers to make Duetto, using grapes from both sides of the border), **Monte Xanic** (with Napa award-winning Cab Sauv), **Bodegas San Antonio**, and **Cavas de Valmar. Marqués de Aguayo** is the oldest (1593), now only for brandy.

Peru **Viña Tacama** exports some pleasant wines, esp the Gran Vino Blanco white; also Cab Sauv and classic-method sparkling. Chincha, Moquegua, and Tacha regions are making progress, but phylloxera is a serious problem.

Uruguay Point of difference here is the rugged, tannic grape Tannat, producing a sturdy, plummy red, best blended with Merlot and Cabernet Franc. **Carrau/Castel Pujol** is among the most impressive wineries: Amat Gran Tradición 1752 and Las Violetas Reserva show Tannat at its most fragrant, while Casa Luntro is a fine collaboration with the Lurton brothers. Top wineries: Bruzzone & Sciutto, Casa Filguera, Castillo Viejo, De Lucca, Los Cerros de San Juan, Dante Irurtia, Juanicó, Pisano, Carlos Pizzorno, and Stagnari.

SOUTH AMERICA

Australia

More heavily shaded areas
are the wine-growing regions

After a 20-year run of success, Australia has hit some problems:
it's producing too many grapes and, hence, too much wine. It
is altogether curious that we should be bemoaning two years of
perfect weather that have produced well above average yields.
In the short term, this is obviously good for consumers; equally
obviously, it's bad for growers in the irrigated Riverland and
Riverina regions, where a lot of the overproduction is coming from.

Instead of blowing up buildings, burning tractors, and
flooding roads (as in France), the response has been to graft or
remove those grape varieties in oversupply (notably Cabernet
Sauvignon in irrigated areas) and to form a "heads of government"-
style committee to look at every aspect of wine in Australia – and
to analyze the competition.

The success of the (yellow tail) brand has saved growers from
even greater pain. The downside has been the surge in "Two Dollar
Road Kill" or "Little Critters" imitations, which, inevitably, are not
as good as the originals.

More insidiously, (yellow tail) et al have reinforced the image of
Australia as the maker of cheap-and-cheerful, sunshine-in-a-bottle
wines, casting a shadow over the diversity of better, characterful,
single-estate wines. It is a shadow that Australia must dispel.

Recent vintages

New South Wales (NSW)
2005 A very good to exceptional year across almost all districts, esp the Hunter, Mudgee, and Orange.
2004 Hunter Valley suffered; other regions good to very good outcomes.
2003 Continued drought broken by heavy rain in Jan/Feb; variable outcomes.
2002 Heavy Feb rain caused problems in all but two areas. Riverina outstanding.
2001 Extreme summer heat and ill-timed rain set the tone; remarkably, Hunter Valley Semillon shone.
2000 A perfect growing season for the Hunter Valley, but dire for the rest of the state; extreme heat followed by rain during the harvest.
1999 Another Hunter success; rain when needed. Other regions variable.
1998 Good to excellent everywhere; good winter rain; warm, dry summer.
1997 Heavy rain bedevilled the Hunter; Mudgee, Orange, and Canberra shone.
1996 Yields varied, but very good wine in most regions.
1995 Severe drought slashed yields and stressed fruit; good at best.

Victoria (Vic)
2005 Rain up to end of Feb was followed by a freakish three-month Indian summer giving superb fruit.
2004 Near perfect weather throughout ripened generous yields.
2003 Overall, fared better than other states, except for bushfire-ravaged Alpine Valleys.
2002 Extremely cool weather led to tiny yields, but wines of high quality.
2001 Did not escape the heat; a fair to good red vintage, whites more variable.
2000 Southern and central regions flourished in warm and dry conditions; terrific reds. Northeast poor; vintage rain.
1999 Utterly schizophrenic; Yarra disastrous (vintage rain); some other southern and central regions superb; northeast up and down.
1998 Drought and Oct frost did not spoil an outstanding year in all regions, notably for Shiraz, Cabernet Sauvignon, and Merlot.
1997 Few grapes, but very high-quality, esp Pinot Noir in the south.
1996 Extremely variable. Far southwest, Grampians, and Bendigo did well.
1995 Disappointing; hot summer, wet autumn. Grampians and Geelong good.

South Australia (SA)
2005 Clare Valley, Coonawarra, Wrattonbully, and Langhorne Creek did best in what was a large but high-quality vintage with reds to the fore.
2004 Excellent summer and autumn weather helped offset large crops (big bunches/berries); heavy crop-thinning needed.
2003 A curate's egg. The good: Limestone Coast and Clare Riesling (yet again); the bad: rain-split Shiraz.
2002 Very cool weather led to much-reduced yields in the south and to a great Riverland vintage in both yield and quality. Fine Riesling again.
2001 Far better than 2000; Clare Valley Riesling an improbable success.
2000 The culmination of a four-year drought impacted on both yield and quality, the Limestone Coast Zone faring the best.
1999 Continuing drought was perversely spoiled by ill-timed March rainfall; Limestone Coast and Clare reds the few bright spots.
1998 Very dry year. Overall quality of reds superb, esp south of Adelaide.
1997 On-again–off-again weather upset vines and vignerons alike, with the exception of Eden and Clare Valley Riesling. Yields down overall.

1996 Classic vintage, classic wines, succulent, and long-lived.
1995 Reduced yields and quality, the low yields averting disaster.

Western Australia (WA)

2005 Heavy rain in late March and April spoiled what would have been the vintage of a generation for Cabernet and Shiraz in the south; whites uniformly excellent.
2004 More of the same; mild weather, long autumn. Good flavours, some lacking intensity.
2003 An in-between year, with ill-timed rainfall nipping greatness in the bud.
2002 Best since 84 in Swan District. In the south, quality is variable.
2001 Great Southern, the best vintage since 95; good elsewhere.
2000 Margaret River excellent, variation elsewhere; the Swan Valley ordinary.
1999 An outstanding vintage for Margaret River and Swan reds (best in more than a decade) and pretty handy elsewhere, other than the Great Southern.
1998 The Swan Valley shone again; elsewhere in the state a rainy vintage.
1997 Good reds from Margaret River and Riesling from Great Southern.
1996 The Swan Valley was cooked, but the warm year was a blessing for Margaret River and Great Southern, with lovely Cabernet the pick.
1995 Very low yields balanced by quality in the south and Margaret River.

Abercorn Mudgee, NSW r ★★ Dedicated, self-taught winemaker acquired neighbouring HUNTINGTON ESTATE late 2005. Identities to be kept separate.
Adelaide Hills SA Spearheaded by PETALUMA: cool, 450m sites in Mt Lofty ranges.

Alcohol levels

Seemingly relentless increases in the level of alcohol in many Australian wines occupy central stage. For SHIRAZ, it is seen as a badge of honour in markets such as the United States; attitudes within Australia are more ambivalent. Makers in temperate-to-warm regions suggest full flavour is not reached until the potential alcohol (Baumé or Brix) reaches 14.5 degrees or above, the sting lying in the "or above", which may be 16 degrees or more. There is little ambivalence about CHARDONNAY, where alcohol over 16 degrees is seen as wholly undesirable. Open vine canopies, climate change, super-efficient yeasts, and low-temperature fermentation are all part of a complex web of causes. Development of low-efficiency yeasts (and earlier picking) are the most obvious solutions, but are not without costs of their own. Reverse osmosis is another high-tech (and expensive) response.

Alkoomi Mount Barker, WA r w ★★★ (RIES) **99 01' 02** 03 04 05' (CAB SAUV) **96' 97'** 00 01' 02 A veteran of 30 yrs making fine RIES and potent, long-lived reds.
Allandale Hunter V, NSW r w ★★ Small winery, no v'yds, buying selected local, MUDGEE, ORANGE, and Hilltops grapes. Quality can be gd, esp CHARD.
All Saints Rutherglen, Vic r w br ★★ Historic producer making creditable table wines; great fortifieds.
Alpine Valleys Vic Geographically similar to KING VALLEY and similar use of grapes.
Amberley Estate Margaret R r w ★★ Successful maker of a full range of regional styles with off-dry Chenin Bl the commercial engine. Owned by Vincor.
Andrew Pirie N Tas r w sp ★★→★★★ A phoenix arisen, with own brand an responsibility for TAMAR RIDGE.
Angove's SA r w (br) ★→★★ Large, long-established MURRAY VALLEY fami

Annie's Lane Clare V, SA r w ★★→★★★ Part of FWE; consistently good wines, flagship Copper Trail excellent, esp RIES.

Arrowfield Hunter V, NSW r w ★→★★ Has sold Upper Hunter winery and v'yds to coalminer and relocated to former Rothbury Estate in Lower Hunter. Eviscerated Rothbury brand retained by FWE.

Ashbrook Estate Margaret R, WA r w ★★★ Minimum of fuss; consistently makes 8,000 cases of exemplary SEM, CHARD, SAUV BL, VERDELHO, and CAB SAUV.

Ashton Hills Adelaide Hills, SA r w (sp) ★★★ Fine, racy, long-lived RIES and compelling PINOT N crafted by Stephen George from 23-yr-old v'yds.

Bailey's NE Vic r w br ★★ Rich SHIRAZ, and magnificent dessert Muscat (★★★★) and "Tokay". Part of FWE.

Balgownie Estate Bendigo and Yarra V, Vic r w ★★→★★★ Rejuvenated producer of v. well-balanced wines now with separate YARRA VALLEY arm.

Balnaves of Coonawarra SA r w ★★★ Grape-grower since 1975; winery since 1996. V.gd CHARD; excellent supple, medium-bodied SHIRAZ, MERLOT, CAB SAUV.

Bannockburn Geelong r w ★★★ (CHARD) **97' 98' 00 02'** 03' 04 (PINOT N) **97 99' 00 02'** 03 Intense, complex CHARD and PINOT N produced using Burgundian techniques.

Banrock Station Riverland, SA r w ★→★★ Almost 1,600-ha property on MURRAY RIVER, 243-ha v'yd, owned by HARDYS. Impressive budget wines.

Barossa Valley SA Australia's most important winery (but not v'yd) area; grapes from diverse sources make diverse wines. Local specialities: very old-vine SHIRAZ and GRENACHE.

Barwang Hilltops, NSW r w ★★ Owned by McWILLIAM'S. Stylish estate wines.

Bass Phillip Gippsland, Vic r ★★★→★★★★ (PINOT N) **96' 97' 99'** 01' 02' 03' (05) Tiny amounts of stylish, eagerly sought-after PINOT N in three quality grades; very Burgundian in style.

Bay of Fires N Tas r w sp ★★→★★★ Pipers River outpost of HARDYS empire. Produces stylish table wines and essential components for Hardy Arras super-*cuvée* sparkler.

Beechworth Vic Trendy region; Castagna and GIACONDA are best-known wineries.

Beggar's Belief Shiraz SA Blackberries, rum, and oak in a stand-a-spoon-up-in-it tincture.

Bendigo Vic Widespread small v'yds, some v.gd quality. Notable estates: BALGOWNIE, PONDALOWIE and Passing Clouds.

Beringer Blass Barossa, SA r w (sp, sw, br) ★★★ (CAB SAUV blend) **90' 91' 94** 96' 98' 00 02' 04 (05) Founded by the ebullient Wolf Blass, now swallowed up by FWE (see also Beringer Blass, California). It is well served by winemakers Chris Hatcher (chief) and Caroline Dunn (reds).

Best's Grampians, Vic r w ★★→★★★ (SHIRAZ) **92' 94'** 96 **97'** 98' 99' 00' 03 04' (05) Conservative old family winery; v.gd mid-weight reds. Thomson Family SHIRAZ from 120-yr-old vines is superb.

Big Rivers Zone NSW and Vic The continuation of South Australia's Riverland inc the MURRAY DARLING, Perricoota, and Swan Hill regions.

Bindi Macedon, Vic r w ★★★→★★★★ Ultra-fastidious, *terroir*-driven maker of outstanding, long-lived, PINOT N and CHARD.

Blue Pyrenees Pyrenees, Vic r w sp ★★ 180 ha of mature vineyards are being better utilized across a broad range of wines.

Botobolar Mudgee, NSW r w ★★ Marvellously eccentric little organic winery.

Brand's of Coonawarra Coonawarra, SA r w ★★★ **90' 91' 96' 98' 99** 01 03 (05') Owned by McWILLIAM'S. Going from strength to strength, esp with super-premium Stentiford's SHIRAZ (100-yr-old vines) and Patron's CAB SAUV.

Brangayne of Orange Orange, NSW r w ★★ Reflects potential of relatively new region. Wines of finesse inc CHARD, SAUV BL, and SHIRAZ.

region. Wines of finesse inc CHARD, SAUV BL, and SHIRAZ.

Bremerton Langhorne Creek, SA r w ★★ Regularly produces attractively priced

---

Brettanomyces

Brett (for short, but also sometimes called dekkera) can variously be described as giving wet-sticking-plaster or meaty aromas and a metallic finish to the palate. It used to be regarded as a foreign (Old World or Californian) disease, but lower sulphur levels allowed it to populate Australian wines. Brett police, armed with brettometers, are now vigilantes, savaging any wine with the presumption of guilt, not innocence. The police, coupled with higher sulphur additions, have led to a marked reduction in its occurrence.

---

red wines with silky, soft mouthfeel and stacks of flavour.

Brini Estate McLaren Vale, SA r ★★→★★★ Family grape-growers for 50 years now have pick of the crop contract-made into velvety SHIRAZ and GRENACHE.

Brokenwood Hunter V, NSW r w ★★★ (SHIRAZ) **91' 93' 94' 95' 98'** 99 00' 01 03' Exciting CAB SAUV; SHIRAZ since 1973 – Graveyard SHIRAZ outstanding. SEM and Cricket Pitch SEM/SAUV BL fuel sales.

Brookland Valley Margaret R, WA r w ★★→★★★ Superbly sited winery (with a restaurant) doing great things, esp with SAUV BL. Owned by HARDYS.

Brown Brothers King V, Vic r w dr br sp sw ★ →★★★ (Noble RIES) **98** 99' **02'** Old family firm, with new ideas. Wide range of delicate, varietal wines, many from cool mountain districts, inc CHARD and RIES. Dry white Muscat is outstanding. CAB SAUV blend is best red.

Bullers Calliope Rutherglen, Vic br ★★★★ Rated for superb Rare Liqueur Muscat and "Tokay" (Muscadelle).

Buring, Leo Barossa, SA w ★★★ **79' 84' 91' 92** 94' **95 97** 99' **02'** 03 04 Part of FWE. Happily, now exclusive RIES producer; Leonay to label, ages superbly. Has moved to screwcap.

By Farr/Farr Rising Geelong, Vic r w ★★★ Father Gary and son Nick's own, after departure from Bannockburn. CHARD and PINOT N are minor masterpieces.

Cabernet Sauvignon 28,621 ha; 284,062 tonnes. Grown in all wine regions, best in COONAWARRA. From herbaceous green pepper in coolest regions, through blackcurrant and mulberry, to dark chocolate and redcurrant in warmer areas.

Campbells of Rutherglen NE Vic r br (w) ★★ Smooth ripe reds and gd fortified wines; Merchant Prince Rare Muscat and Isabella Rare Tokay v.gd.

Canberra District NSW Both quality and quantity on the increase; altitude dependent, site selection important.

Capel Vale Geographe, WA r w ★★★ Very successful with gd whites, inc RIES. Also top-end SHIRAZ and CAB SAUV.

Cape Mentelle Margaret R, WA r w ★★★ Robust CAB SAUV gd, CHARD even better; also ZIN and very popular SAUV BL/SEM. LVMH Veuve Clicquot owner; also Cloudy Bay (see New Zealand).

Capercaillie Hunter V, NSW r w ★★→★★★ Veteran Alasdair Sutherland goes from strength to strength, supplementing local grapes with purchases from elsewhere, inc ORANGE, MCLAREN VALE, etc.

Carlei Estate Yarra V, Vic r w ★★ Mercurial winemaker Sergio Carlei sources PINOT N and CHARD from various vineyards and cool regions to make wines with abundant character.

Casella Riverina, NSW r w ★ The (yellow tail) phenomenon has swept all before it with multimillion-case sales in US. Like Fanta: soft and sweet.

of its best grapes from ORANGE, but the winemaking skills and a large investment chequebook are there.

Central Ranges Zone NSW Encompasses MUDGEE, ORANGE, and Cowra regions, expanding in high altitude, moderately cool to warm climates.

Chain of Ponds Adelaide Hills, SA r w ★★ Impeccably made, full, flavoursome wines. SEM, SAUV BL, and CHARD to the fore.

Chalkers Crossing Hilltops, NSW r w ★★→★★★ Beautifully balanced cool-climate wines made by French-trained Celine Rousseau.

Chambers' Rosewood NE Vic br (r w) ★★→★★★ Viewed with MORRIS as the greatest maker of "Tokay" and Muscat.

Chapel Hill McLaren Vale, SA r w ★★ (r) Now owned by Swiss Schmidheiny group with multinational wine interests inc Napa's Cuvaison in California.

Chardonnay 30,507 ha; 378,287 tonnes. Best known for fast-developing, buttery, peachy, sometimes syrupy wines, but cooler regions produce more elegant, tightly structured, ageworthy examples. Oak is less heavy-handed.

Charles Melton Barossa, SA r w (sp) ★★★ Tiny winery with bold, luscious reds, esp Nine Popes, an old-vine GRENACHE/SHIRAZ blend.

Cheviot Bridge Long Flat, SE Aus r w ★★ Fast-moving part of new corporate empire that bought the Long Flat brand from TYRRELL'S.

Clare Valley (Clare V), SA Small high-quality area 90 miles N of Adelaide. Best for RIES; also SHIRAZ and CAB SAUV.

Clarendon Hills McLaren Vale, SA r (w) ★★★ Monumental (and expensive) reds from small parcels of contract grapes around Adelaide.

> **Climate change**
> As the highest per-capita producer of greenhouse gases in the world – and a Kyoto "refusenik" – Australia is in the firing line of environmentalists everywhere. Moreover, eminent viticultural researcher Dr. John Gladstones has put the proverbial cat among the pigeons by suggesting greenhouse warming in Australia is unlikely to cause viticultural migration into cooler areas. "If anything, rising atmospheric carbon dioxide concentrations will compensate, and perhaps more than compensate, for any warming, to the relative advantage of present intermediate and warm areas."
> (*Viticulture and Environment*, Winetitles, Adelaide 2002; p.271).

Clonakilla Canberra District, NSW r w ★★★ Deserved leader of the SHIRAZ/Viognier brigade. RIES and other wines also v.gd.

Coldstream Hills Yarra V, Vic r w (sp) ★★★ (CHARD) 88' 92' 96' 00' 02' 03'–04 (PINOT N) 91' 92' 96' 97 00' 02' 03 04' (05') (CAB SAUV) 91' 92' 98' 00' 02 04 (05') Established in 1985 by wine critic James Halliday. Delicious PINOT N to drink young, and Reserve to age leads Australia. V.gd CHARD (esp res wines), fruity CAB SAUV, and (from 97) MERLOT. Part of FWE.

Coonawarra SA Southernmost and perhaps finest v'yds of state: home to most of Australia's best CAB SAUV; successful CHARD, RIES, and SHIRAZ. Newer arrivals inc Murdock and Reschke.

Coriole McLaren Vale r w ★★→★★★ (SHIRAZ) 90' 91' 96' 98' 99' 02' 04 (05') To watch, esp for old-vine SHIRAZ Lloyd Reserve.

Craiglee Macedon Vic r w ★★★ (SHIRAZ) 91' 92 94' 97' 98' 00' 02' 03 (05') Re-creation of famous 19th-C estate. Fragrant, peppery SHIRAZ, CHARD.

Cullen Wines Margaret R, WA r w ★★★★ (CHARD) 99' 00' 01 02' 03 04 (05) (CAB SAUV/MERLOT) 86' 87' 90' 91' 94' 95' 96' 99' 01' 02' 04' Vanya Cullen makes strongly structured CAB SAUV/MERLOT (Australia's best), substantial but subtle SEM/SAUV BL, and bold CHARD: all real characters.

AUSTRALIA

Cumulus Orange, NSW r w ★★ The reborn Reynolds Wines, with much venture capital, the production skills of Philip Shaw (ex ROSEMOUNT), and slick marketing to push its 550,000-case production.

Cuttaway Hill Southern Highlands, NSW r w Leads the region in the production of estate-grown wines, esp CHARD, SAUV BL, Pinot Gr.

Dalwhinnie Pyrenees, Vic r w ★★★ (CHARD) **99' 00'** 02' 04' (Reds) **94' 95' 98' 99'** 00' 01 02' 03 Rich CHARD and SHIRAZ. CAB SAUV best in PYRENEES.

d'Arenberg McLaren Vale, SA r w (sw br sp) ★★→★★★ Old firm with new lease of life; sumptuous SHIRAZ and GRENACHE, lots of varieties and wacky labels.

Deakin Estate Murray Darling r w ★ Part of KATNOOK group, producing 500,000 cases of very decent varietal table wines.

De Bortoli Griffith, NSW r w dr sw (br) ★→★★★ (Noble SEM) 82' **87'** 95' **96'** 97' **99' 00'** 02 03 Irrigation-area winery. Standard red and white but splendid sweet botrytized Sauternes-style Noble SEM. See also next entry.

De Bortoli Yarra V, Vic r w ★★→★★★ (CHARD) **00' 01'** 02' 04 05' (CAB SAUV) **92' 94'** 98' 00' 02' 04 YARRA VALLEY's largest producer. Main label is quite good; second label Gulf Station and third label Windy Peak v.gd value.

Delatite Upper Goldburn (r) w (sp) ★★ (RIES) **99** 00 01 02' 03 04 05 RIES, Gewurz, CAB SAUV, and SAUV BL are specialities of this cool mountainside v'yd.

Devil's Lair Margaret R, WA r w ★★★ Opulently concentrated CHARD and CAB SAUV/MERLOT. Fifth Leg is trendy second label. Part of FWE.

Diamond Valley Yarra V, Vic r w ★★→★★★ (PINOT) **99'** 00 02' 03 04 (05) Outstanding PINOT N in significant quantities; other wines gd, esp CHARD.

Domaine A S Tas r w ★★★ Swiss owners/winemakers Peter and Ruth Althaus are ultimate perfectionists; SAUV BL (Fume Blanc) and CAB SAUV are picks.

Domaine Chandon Yarra V, Vic sp (r w) ★★★ Classic sparkling wine from grapes grown in cooler wine regions, supported by owner Moët & Chandon. Well known in UK as Green Point (label also used for table wine).

Dominique Portet Yarra V, Vic r w ★★→★★★ After 25-yr career at TALTARNI, now in his own winery for the first time, going from strength to strength.

Dromana Estate Mornington Pen, Vic r w ★★→★★★ (CHARD) **00' 01** 02' 03 04 (05') Light, fragrant CAB SAUV, PINOT N, and CHARD. Now taking Italian varieties (grown elsewhere) very seriously.

Eden Valley (Eden V), SA Hilly region home to HENSCHKE and PEWSEY VALE; RIES and SHIRAZ of very high quality.

Elderton Barossa r w (sp br) ★★ Old v'yds; flashy, rich, oaked CAB SAUV and SHIRAZ.

Evans & Tate Margaret R, WA r w ★★→★★★ (CAB) **95' 96'** 99' 00 01' 02 04' Fine elegant SEM, CHARD, CAB SAUV, MERLOT from MARGARET RIVER, Redbrook. Has suffered financial blues and stock write-downs.

Evans Family Hunter V, NSW r w ★★★ (CHARD) **99'** 00' 01 02 03' 04 Excellent CHARD from small v'yd owned by family of Len Evans. Fermented in new oak. Repays cellaring. See also TOWER ESTATE.

Ferngrove Vineyards Great Southern, WA r w ★★★ Cattle farmer Murray Burton's syndicate has established more than 400 ha of vines since 1997; great RIES.

Fox Creek McLaren Vale, SA r (w) ★★ Produces 36,000 cases of flashy, full-flavoured wines, which are inveterate wine-show winners.

Freycinet Tas r w (sp) ★★★ (PINOT N) **94'** 98 00' 01' 02' 03 04 E coast winery producing voluptuous, rich PINOT N and gd CHARD.

FWE (Fosters Wine Estates) Official name of the merged Beringer Blass and Southcorp wine groups. Has 41 brands in Australia, more than any other, excluding the virtual brands (which use contract grapes, contract wineries, contract staff) that come and go like mushrooms after spring rain.

Gapsted Wines Alpine V, Vic r w ★★ Brand of large winery that crushes grapes for 50 growers.

Geelong Vic Once-famous area destroyed by phylloxera, re-established in the mid-1960s. Very cool, dry climate: firm table wines from gd-quality grapes. Names inc BANNOCKBURN, SCOTCHMANS HILL, BY FARR, Curlewis.

Gemtree Vineyards McLaren Vale, SA r (w) ★★ Top-class SHIRAZ alongside Tempranillo, B'x blends and other exotica, linked by quality.

Geoff Merrill McLaren Vale, SA r w ★★ Ebullient maker of Geoff Merrill and Mt Hurtle. A questing enthusiast; his best are excellent, others unashamedly mass-market oriented. TAHBILK owns 50%.

Geoff Weaver Adelaide Hills, SA r w ★★★ An 8-ha estate at Lenswood. Very fine SAUV BL, CHARD, RIES, and CAB SAUV/MERLOT blend. Marvellous label design.

> **Regions: Geographical Indications**
> The process of formally defining the boundaries of the Zones, Regions, and Sub-regions, known compendiously as Geographic Indications (GIs), continues. These correspond to the French ACs and AVAs in the United States. It means every aspect of the labelling of Australian wines has a legal framework that, in all respects, complies with EC laws and requirements. The guarantee of quality comes through the mandatory analysis certificate for, and the tasting (by expert panels) of, each and every wine exported from Australia.

Giaconda Beechworth, Vic r w ★★★ (CHARD) 92' 93 94' 96' 97' 98 99' 00' 02' 03 Australia's answer to Kistler (see California). CHARD is considered by many to be the best in Australia – certainly the 96 is one of the all-time greats. PINOT N is very variable; newly introduced SHIRAZ better.

Glaetzer Wines Barossa r ★★★ Hyper-rich, unfiltered, v. ripe old-vine SHIRAZ headed by iconic Amon-Ra. V.gd examples of high-octane style much admired by US critics.

Goulburn Valley (Goulburn V), Vic Very old (TAHBILK) and relatively new (MITCHELTON) wineries in temperate mid-Victoria region. Full-bodied table wines.

Goundrey Wines Great Southern WA r w ★★ Recent expansion has caused quality to become variable. Bought by Canada's Vincor International in 2003.

Grampians Vic Region previously known as Great Western. Temperate region in central W of state. High quality, esp SHIRAZ.

Granite Belt Qld High-altitude, (relatively) cool region just N of Qld/NSW border. Esp spicy SHIRAZ and rich SEM.

Granite Hills Macedon, Vic r w ★★→★★★ 30-yr-old family v'yd and winery has regained original class with fine elegant RIES and spicy SHIRAZ.

Grant Burge Barossa, SA r w (sp sw br) ★★→★★★ 200,000 cases of silky-smooth reds and whites from the best grapes of Burge's large v'yd holdings.

Great Southern WA Remote, cool area; FERNGROVE and GOUNDREY are the largest wineries. Albany, Denmark, Frankland River, Mount Barker, and Porongurup are official sub-regions.

Grenache 2,097 ha; 25,418 tonnes. Produces thin wine if overcropped, but can do much better. Growing interest in old BAROSSA and MCLAREN VALE plantings.

Grosset Clare, SA r w ★★★→★★★★ (RIES) 93' 94' 95' 97' 99' 00' 01 02' 03 04' 05' (Gaia) 90' 91 92' 94' 96' 98' 99' 01 02 03' 04' Fastidious winemaker. Foremost Australian RIES, lovely CHARD, PINOT N, and exceptional Gaia CAB SAUV/MERLOT from dry v'yd high on MOUNT HORROCKS.

Haan Wines Barossa, SA r w ★★★ Low yields and meticulous winemaking ensure top results for Viognier, MERLOT, SHIRAZ and B'x blend (Wilhelmus).

Hamelin Bay Margaret R, WA ★★ 15-yr-old estate plantings (25 ha) are paying dividends, with top-flight CHARD leading the way.

Hamilton's Ewell Vineyards Barossa, SA r (w) ★★★ Famous family name with 160-yr history renewed by Mark and Robert Hamilton, esp classic SHIRAZ.

Hanging Rock Macedon, Vic r w sp ★→★★★★ (Heathcote SHIRAZ) **91' 97' 98' 99** 00' 01' 02' 03 Eclectic: budget brands; complex sparkler and estate varietals.

Hardys r w sp (sw) ★★→★★★★ (Eileen CHARD) **98 99' 00** 01 02' 03 04' ("Vintage Port") **51' 54' 56' 58' 75 77 82** 84' 96' 98 Historic company blending wines from several areas. Best are Eileen Hardy and Thomas Hardy series and (Australia's best) "Vintage Ports". REYNELLA's restored buildings are group HQ. Part of Constellation, world's largest wine group.

Heathcote Vic Divorce from BENDIGO in 2003 led to formal recognition of this ultra-trendy, SHIRAZ-specialist region; JASPER HILL is the founding father, but there are many aspirational newcomers.

Heathcote Estate Heathcote, Vic r ★★★ SHIRAZ specialist brimming with potential for small group of owners/executive winemakers; overlaps with YABBY LAKE.

Heggies Eden V, SA r w dr (sw w) ★★ (RIES) **98** 99 00 02' 04 **05** V'yd at 500 m owned by S SMITH & SONS but separately marketed.

Henschke Barossa, SA r w ★★★★ (SHIRAZ) **58' 61' 64' 67' 68' 80' 81' 84' 86' 90' 91' 93' 96'** 98' 99' 01 02'(CAB SAUV) **80' 85 86' 88 90' 91' 92 93** 94 96' 98' 99 01 02' A 137-yr-old family business, perhaps Australia's best, known for delectable Hill of Grace (SHIRAZ), v.gd CAB SAUV and red blends, and value whites, inc RIES. Lenswood v'yds in ADELAIDE HILLS add excitement. Fervent opponent of corks for reds, too.

Hewitson SE Aus r (w) ★★★ The virtual winery of ex-PETALUMA/ex-flying winemaker Dean Hewitson, sourcing parcels of old vines and making wines (with great skill) in rented space.

Hollick Coonawarra, SA r w (sp) ★★★ (CAB SAUV/MERLOT) **91' 93 96' 98'** 99 01 02' 03 Gd CHARD and RIES. Much-followed reds, esp Ravenswood.

Houghton Swan V, WA r w ★→★★★ The most famous old winery of WA. Soft, ripe Supreme is top-selling, ageworthy white; a national classic. Also excellent CAB SAUV, VERDELHO, SHIRAZ, etc. sourced from MARGARET RIVER and GREAT SOUTHERN. See HARDYS.

Howard Park Mount Barker and Margaret R, WA r w ★★★ (RIES) **94' 96' 97' 98'** **99' 02** 04' (CAB SAUV) **86' 88' 90' 92 94' 96'** 98' 99' 01' 02 Scented RIES, CHARD; spicy CAB SAUV. Second label: MadFish Bay is excellent value.

Hunter Valley NSW Great name in NSW. Broad, soft, earthy SHIRAZ and gentle SEM that live for 30 yrs. CAB SAUV not important; CHARD is.

Huntington Estate NSW r w ★★★ (CAB SAUV) **93 94' 95' 96' 97' 99'** 01' 02' Small winery; the best in MUDGEE. Fine CAB SAUV, v.gd SHIRAZ. Underpriced.

Jasper Hill Heathcote, Vic r w ★★★→★★★★ (SHIRAZ) **85' 86' 90' 91' 92'** 96' 97' **98'** 99' 00 01' 02' 03 Emily's Paddock SHIRAZ/Cab Fr blend and Georgia's Paddock SHIRAZ from dry-land estate are intense, long-lived, and much admired.

Jim Barry Clare V, SA r w ★★→★★★ Some great v'yds provide gd RIES, McCrae Wood SHIRAZ, and convincing Grange challenger The Armagh.

Kaesler Barossa, NSW r w (w) ★★→★★★★ Old Bastard SHIRAZ (A$180) outranks Old Vine SHIRAZ (a mere A$60). Wine in the glass gd, too (in heroic style).

Katnook Estate Coonawarra, SA r w (sp sw w) ★★★ (CAB SAUV) **90' 91' 96'** 98' 99 00 02' 03 Excellent, pricey CAB SAUV and CHARD. Also RIES and SAUV BL.

Keith Tulloch Hunter, NSW r w ★★★❶Ex-Rothbury winemaker fastidiously crafting elegant yet complex SEM, SHIRAZ, etc.

Killikanoon Clare V, SA ★★→★★★ r w Strongly regional RIES and SHIRAZ have been awesome performers in shows over past few yrs.

Kingston Estate SE Aus ★→★★★ Kalaedoscopic array of varietal wines from all over the place, consistency and value providing the glue.

King Valley (King V), Vic Important alpine region. 15,000 tonnes chiefly for purchasers outside the region. Some wineries of its own.

Knappstein Wines Clare V, SA r w ★★→★★★ Reliable CAB SAUV/MERLOT and CAB SAUV. Owned by LION NATHAN.

Lake Breeze Langhorne Ck, SA r (w) ★★ Long-term grape-growers turned winemakers, producing succulently smooth SHIRAZ and CAB SAUV.

Lake's Folly Hunter V, NSW r w ★★★★ (CHARD) **97' 98 99** 00' 01 02 03' 05' (CAB SAUV) **69 81 89' 91 93' 97'** 98' 00' 02 03' Founded by Max Lake, the pioneer of HUNTER CAB SAUV. New owners since 2000. CHARD consistently better than CAB SAUV these days.

Lamont's Swan V, WA r w ★★ Winery and superb restaurant owned by Corin Lamont (daughter of legendary Jack Mann) and husband. Delicious wines.

Lark Hill Canberra District, NSW r w ★★ Most consistent CANBERRA producer, making esp attractive RIES, pleasant CHARD, and surprising PINOT N.

Leasingham Clare V, SA r w ★★→★★★ Important mid-sized quality winery bought by HARDYS in 1987. Gd RIES, SHIRAZ, and CAB SAUV/Malbec. Various labels.

Leeuwin Estate Margaret R, WA r w ★★★★ (CHARD) **85' 87' 89 90 92' 94 95' 96** 97' 98 **99'** 00 **01'** 02' 03 Leading W Australia estate, lavishly equipped. Superb, ageworthy (and expensive) Art Series CHARD, SAUV BL, RIES, and CAB SAUV also good.

Limestone Coast Zone SA Important zone inc Bordertown, COONAWARRA, Mount Benson, Mount Gambier, PADTHAWAY, Robe, and WRATTONBULLY.

Lindemans r w ★→★★ One of the oldest firms, now owned by FWE. Low-price Bin range (esp Bin 65 CHARD) now its main focus.

Lion Nathan New Zealand brewery; owns PETALUMA, STONIER, TATACHILLA, MITCHELTON, Smithbrook, ST HALLET, and KNAPPSTEIN.

Macedon and **Sunbury** Vic Adjacent regions, Macedon at higher elevation, Sunbury nr Melbourne airport. CRAIGLEE, HANGING ROCK, VIRGIN HILLS, GRANITE HILLS.

Majella Coonawarra, SA r (w) ★★★→★★★★★ Rising to the top of COONAWARRA cream. The Malleea is outstanding CAB SAUV/SHIRAZ super-premium red. SHIRAZ and CAB SAUV also v.gd.

Margan Family Winemakers Hunter V, NSW r w ★★ Highly successful winemaker inc fascinating House of Certain Views brand.

Margaret River, WA Temperate coastal area, 174 miles S of Perth, with superbly elegant wines. Australia's most vibrant tourist wine (and surfing) region.

McGuigan Simeon Hunter V, NSW ★→★★ Nominal Hunter base of Australia's fifth-largest wine group, recently adding Miranda scalp to its collection.

McLaren Vale SA Historic region on the southern outskirts of Adelaide. Big, alcoholic, flavoursome reds have great appeal to US market.

McWilliam's Hunter V and Riverina, NSW r w (sw br) ★★→★★★ (Elizabeth SEM) **84' 86' 87' 93 94' 95 96** 98 **99** 00' 01' 02 03' 04 Famous family of HUNTER VALLEY winemakers at Mount Pleasant: SHIRAZ and SEM. Also pioneer in RIVERINA: CAB SAUV and RIES. Recent show results demonstrate high standards. Elizabeth (sold at 4 yrs) and Lovedale (6 yrs) SEMS are quite superb. Hanwood v.gd value.

Merlot The darling of the new millennium; from 9,000 tonnes in 1996, to 132,586 tonnes in 2005. Grown everywhere, but shouldn't be.

Mitchell Clare V, SA r w ★★→★★★ (RIES) **90' 94' 95 00' 01'** 02' 03' 04 05' Small family winery for excellent CAB SAUV and very stylish dry RIES.

Mitchelton Goulburn V, Vic r w (sw w) ★★ Substantial winery, now part of LION NATHAN. A wide range inc v.gd wood-matured Marsanne, SHIRAZ; GOULBURN VALLEY Blackwood Park RIES is one of Australia's best-value wines.

Mitolo McLaren Vale/Barossa, SA r ★★★ One of the best "virtual wineries" (*i.e.* contract vineyards, contract wineries, contract winemaker), paying top dollar for top-quality SHIRAZ and CAB; quality oak and winemaking by Ben Glaetzer. Heroic but (virtually) irresistible wines.

Moorilla Estate Tas r w (sp) ★★★ (RIES) **94' 97' 99 00'** 01' 02' 03' 04 05' Senior winery on outskirts of Hobart on Derwent River: v.gd RIES, Gewurz, CHARD; PINOT N now in the ascendant.

Moorooduc Estate Mornington Pen, Vic r w ★★★❶Stylish and sophisticated (wild yeast, etc.) producer of top-flight CHARD and PINOT N.

Mornington Peninsula (Mornington Pen), Vic Exciting wines in new cool coastal area 25 miles S of Melbourne; 1,000 ha. Many high-quality, boutique wineries.

Morris NE Vic br (r w) ★★→★★★★ Old winery at RUTHERGLEN for some of Australia's greatest dessert Muscats and "Tokays"; also gd low-priced table wine.

Moss Wood Margaret R, WA r w ★★★★ (SEM) **94' 95' 97' 98'** 99 01 03 (CAB SAUV) **80' 85' 87 90' 91'** 94 95' 96' 98 99' 01 To many, the best MARGARET RIVER winery (11.7 ha). SEM, CAB SAUV, CHARD, all with rich fruit flavours.

Mount Horrocks Clare V, SA w r ★★★→★★★★❶Finest dry RIES and sweet Cordon Cut in separate range from GROSSET winery.

Mount Langi Ghiran Grampians, Vic r w ★★★ (SHIRAZ) **88 90' 92 93' 96'** 98' 99' 01 03 (05') Esp for superb, rich, peppery, Rhône-like SHIRAZ, one of Australia's best cool-climate versions. Now owned by YERING STATION.

Mount Mary Yarra V, Vic r w ★★★★ (PINOT N) **97' 98 99'** 00' 02' 03 (05') (CAB SAUV/Cab Fr/MERLOT) **86' 88' 90' 92' 93' 94 95' 96'** 97' 98' 99 00' 02 03 04 Perfectionist Dr. John Middleton makes tiny amounts of suave CHARD, vivid PINOT N, and (best of all) CAB SAUV blend: Australia's most B'dx-like "claret". All will age impeccably.

Mudgee NSW Small, isolated area 168 miles NW of Sydney. Big reds, surprisingly fine SEM, and full CHARD.

Murdock Coonawarra, SA r ★★★ Long-term grower now making classic CAB SAUV.

Murray Valley SA, Vic and NSW Vast irrigated v'yds. Principally making "cask" table wines. 40% of total Australian wine production.

Nepenthe Adelaide Hills, SA r w ★★→★★★ One of a few wineries in the region. State-of-the-art kit, excellent v'yds, skilled winemaking, and sophisticated wines (esp SAUV BL, CHARD, and SEM).

Ninth Island See PIPERS BROOK.

O'Leary Walker Wines Clare V, SA r w ★★★❶Two whizz-kids have mid-life crisis and leave BERINGER BLASS to do their own thing – very well.

Orange NSW Cool-climate region giving lively CHARD, CAB SAUV, MERLOT, SHIRAZ.

Orlando (Gramp's), Barossa, SA r w sp (br sw) ★★→★★★ (St Hugo Cab) **90' 96 98'** 99 01 02' 03 Great pioneering company, now owned by Pernod Ricard. Full range, from huge-selling Jacob's Creek, to excellent Jacaranda Ridge CAB SAUV from COONAWARRA. See also WYNDHAM ESTATE.

Padthaway SA Large v'yd area developed as overspill of COONAWARRA. Cool climate; good CHARD and excellent SHIRAZ (Orlando).

Paringa Estate Mornington Pen, Vic r w ★★★★ Maker of quite spectacular CHARD, PINOT N, and (late-picked) SHIRAZ, winning innumerable trophies.

Parker Estate Coonawarra, SA r ★★★ Small estate making v.gd CAB SAUV, esp Terra Rossa First Growth. Acquired by YERING STATION mid-2004.

Pemberton WA Region between MARGARET RIVER and GREAT SOUTHERN; initial enthusiasm for PINOT N replaced by MERLOT and SHIRAZ.

Penfolds Originally Adelaide, now everywhere r w (sp br) ★★→★★★★ (Grange) **52' 53' 55' 62' 63' 66' 71' 76** 78 **80 83 86' 88 90'** 91' 94' 96' 97 98' 99' 01 (02') (Bin 707) **64 76' 86' 90' 91** 94' 96' 98' 99' 01 02' Ubiquitous and excellent: in BAROSSA VALLEY, CLARE, COONAWARRA, RIVERINA, etc. Consistently

Australia's best red wine company, if you can decode its labels. Its Grange (was called Hermitage) is deservedly ★★★★. Yattarna CHARD was released in 98. Bin 707 CAB SAUV not far behind. Other bin-numbered wines (e.g. Kalimna Bin 28 SHIRAZ) can be v.gd.

Penley Estate Coonawarra, SA r w ★★★ High-profile, no-expense-spared winery. Rich, textured, fruit-and-oak CAB SAUV; SHIRAZ/CAB SAUV blend; CHARD.

Perth Hills WA Fledgling area 19 miles E of Perth with a larger number of growers on mild hillside sites. Millbrook and Western Range best.

Petaluma Adelaide Hills, SA r w sp ★★★★ (RIES) 80' 84' 86' 94' 96' 97 99' 00' 01' **02'** 03' 04 05 (CHARD) **96'** 00 02' 03 04 (CAB SAUV) 79' 84' 86' 90' **91' 95'** **98' 99** 00' 02' (04) A rocket-like 1980s success with COONAWARRA CAB SAUV, ADELAIDE HILLS CHARD, Croser CLARE VALLEY RIES, all processed at winery in ADELAIDE HILLS. Created by the fearsome intellect and energy of Brian Croser. Red wines richer from 1988 on. Fell prey to LION NATHAN 2002.

Peter Lehmann Wines Barossa, SA r w (sp br sw w) ★★ →★★★ Defender of BAROSSA faith; fought off Allied-Domecq by marriage with Swiss Hess group. Consistently well-priced wines in substantial quantities. Try Stonewell SHIRAZ and dry RIES, esp with age.

Pewsey Vale Adelaide Hills, SA w ★★★→★★★★ Glorious RIES, esp The Contours, released with screwcap, 5 yrs bottle-age and multiple trophies.

Pierro Margaret R, WA r w ★★★ (CHARD) **95' 96' 99'** 00' 01' 02' 03 Highly rated producer of expensive, tangy SEM/SAUV BL and v.gd barrel-fermented CHARD.

Pinot Noir 4,231 ha; 36,887 tonnes. Mostly used in sparkling. Exciting wines from S Victoria, TASMANIA, and ADELAIDE HILLS; plantings are increasing.

Pipers Brook Tas r w sp ★★★ (RIES) **94' 96' 98' 99'** 00' 01' 02' 03 04 (CHARD) **97** **99' 00'** 02' Cool-area pioneer; v.gd RIES, PINOT N, restrained CHARD and sp from Tamar Valley. Second label: Ninth Island. Owned by Belgian Kreglinger family, owners of Vieux-Château-Certan (see Bordeaux).

Pirramimma McLaren Vale, SA r w ★★ Low-profile, century-old family business with first-class v'yds. Makes underpriced wines, inc excellent Petit Verdot.

Plantagenet Mount Barker, WA r w (sp) ★★★ (Reds) **94' 95' 98** 99 01' 02 The region's elder statesman: wide range of varieties, esp rich CHARD, SHIRAZ, and vibrant, potent CAB SAUV.

Pondalowie Bendigo, Vic r ★★★ Flying winemakers with exciting SHIRAZ/Viognier/Tempranillo in various combinations.

Primo Estate Adelaide Plains, SA r w dr (w sw) ★★★ Joe Grilli is a miracleworker given the climate; successes inc v.gd botrytized RIES, tangy Colombard, and potent Joseph CAB SAUV/MERLOT.

Pyrenees Vic Central Vic region producing rich, minty reds.

Red Hill Estate Mornington Pen, Vic r w sp ★★→★★★ One of the larger and more important wineries; notably elegant wines.

Redman Coonawarra, SA r ★ Famous old name in COONAWARRA; red specialist: SHIRAZ, CAB SAUV, CAB SAUV/MERLOT. Wine fails to do justice to v'yd quality.

Richmond Grove Barossa r w ★→★★★ Master winemaker John Vickery produces great RIES at bargain prices; other wines are OK. Owned by ORLANDO WYNDHAM.

Riesling 4,326 ha; 41,237 tonnes. Has a special place in the BAROSSA, EDEN, and CLARE valleys. Usually made bone-dry; can be glorious with up to 20 yrs bottle-age. Screwcaps now the only accepted closure.

Riverina NSW Large-volume irrigated zone centred around Griffith. Gd-quality "cask" wines (esp white) and great sweet, botrytized SEM. Watch for reduced yields and better quality, e.g. the marvellous 02 wines.

Robert Channon Wines Granite Belt, Qld r w ★→★★ Lawyer turned *vigneron* has 6.8 ha of permanently netted, immaculately trained v'yd producing v.gd VERDELHO (plus usual others).

Rockford Barossa r w sp ★★→★★★★ Small producer. Range of individual wines, from old, low-yielding v'yds; reds best, also iconic sparkling Black SHIRAZ.

Rosemount Estate Upper Hunter, McLaren Vale, Coonwarra, SA r w (sp) ★★→★★★ Rich, Roxburgh CHARD, McLAREN VALE Balmoral SYRAH, MUDGEE Mountain Blue CAB SAUV/SHIRAZ, and COONAWARRA CAB SAUV lead the wide range. Part of FWE.

Rutherglen and **Glenrowan** Vic Two of four regions in the NE Vic Zone, justly famous for weighty reds and magnificent, fortified dessert wines.

St Hallett Barossa, SA r w ★★★ (Old Block) **86' 90' 91' 94' 96' 98'** 99 02' 04' Rejuvenated winery. 60-plus-yr-old vines give splendid Old Block SHIRAZ. Rest of range is smooth and stylish. LION NATHAN-owned.

St Sheila's SA p sw sp **36 22 38** Full-bodied fizzer. Ripper grog, too.

Saltram Barossa, SA r w ★★→★★★ Mamre Brook (SHIRAZ, CAB SAUV, CHARD) and No 1 SHIRAZ are leaders. Metala is associated Stonyfell label for Langhorne Creek CAB SAUV/SHIRAZ. An FWE brand.

Sandalford Swan V, WA r w (br) ★→★★★ Fine old winery with contrasting styles of red and white single-grape wines from SWAN and MARGARET RIVER areas. Sandalera is amazing, long-aged sweet white.

Sauvignon Blanc 4,152 ha; 38,355 tonnes. Usually not as distinctive as in New Zealand, but amazingly popular. Many styles, from bland to pungent.

> ### Screwcaps: the great closure debate
> For many wineries, it's no longer a debate: corks have lost. Most have chosen Stelvin/screwcap for all their wines, white and red, on the basis that it's the best generally available technology. Membrane-covered corks, glass stoppers, and even stainless-steel crown seals may prove viable alternatives. Natural cork will only come back if the causes of sporadic bottle oxidation can be identified and solutions to the problem found. Taint remains a secondary issue but has been largely eradicated by the cork producers – after the horse has bolted.

Scotchmans Hill Geelong, Vic r w ★★ Makes significant quantities of stylish PINOT N, gd CHARD, and spicy SHIRAZ.

Semillon 6,282 ha; 96,727 tonnes. Before the arrival of CHARD, Sem was the HUNTER VALLEY'S answer to South Australia's RIES. Traditionally made without oak and extremely long-lived. Brief affair with oak terminated.

Seppelt Barossa, Grampians, Padthaway, etc. r w sp br (sw w) ★★★ (SHIRAZ) **56' 71' 85' 86' 91' 93' 96' 97'** 98' 99' 02' 03' 04 Far-flung producer of important wines under various labels inc Great Western; also new range of Victoria-sourced table wines. Top sp is highly regarded Salinger. Another part of FWE.

Sevenhill Clare V, SA r w (br) ★★ Owned by the Jesuitical Manresa Society since 1851. Consistently gd wine; SHIRAZ and RIES can be outstanding.

Seville Estate Yarra V, Vic r w ★★★ (SHIRAZ) **85' 91' 94 97'** 00' 02' 03 04 Multiple ownership changes have not affected quality of CHARD, SHIRAZ, PINOT N.

Shadowfax Geelong, Vic r w ★★→★★★ Stylish new winery, part of Werribee Park; also hotel based on 1880s mansion. V. gd CHARD, PINOT N, SHIRAZ.

Shantell Yarra V, Vic r w ★★→★★★ Underrated producer with 30-yr-old v'yd. SEM, CHARD, PINOT N, CAB SAUV.

Shaw & Smith McLaren Vale, SA w (r) ★★★ Founded by Martin Shaw and Australia's first MW, Michael Hill Smith. Crisp SAUV BL, complex, barrel-fermented Reserve CHARD, and MERLOT.

Shelmerdine Vineyards Heathcote/Yarra V, Vic r w ★★→★★★ Well-known family with high-quality wines from estate in the YARRA VALLEY and HEATHCOTE, the

with high-quality wines from estate in the YARRA VALLEY and HEATHCOTE, the latter with unusual elegance and low alcohol levels.

Shiraz 48,508 ha; 415,421 tonnes. Hugely flexible: velvety/earthy in the HUNTER; spicy, peppery, and Rhône-like in central and S Vic; or brambly, rum-sweet, and luscious in BAROSSA and environs (*e.g.* PENFOLDS' Grange).

Sirromet Queensland Coast r w ★★ A striking (100-ha) 75,000-case winery, with a 200-seat restaurant; biggest of many such new ventures. Wines from 100-plus ha of estate v'yds in GRANITE BELT consistently gd.

South Burnett Now Queensland's second region with 14 wineries and more births (and some deaths) imminent, symptomatic of SE corner of the state.

South Coast NSW Zone inc Shoalhaven Coast and Southern Highlands.

Southcorp The former giant of the industry; now part of FWE. Owns PENFOLDS, LINDEMANS, SEPPELT, Seaview, WYNNS, ROSEMOUNT.

Southern NSW Zone inc CANBERRA, Gundagai, Hilltops, Tumbarumba.

S Smith & Sons (alias Yalumba) Barossa, SA r w sp br (sw w) ★★→★★★ Big old family firm with considerable verve. Full spectrum of high-quality wines, inc PEWSEY VALE, HEGGIES and YALUMBA. Angas Brut, a gd-value sparkling wine, and Oxford Landing varietals are now world brands.

Stanton & Killeen Rutherglen, Vic br r ★★★ Grandson Chris Killeen has a modernist palate, makes a great dry red, outstanding "Vintage Port", and Muscat.

Stefano Lubiana S Tas r w sp ★★→★★★ Beautiful v'yds on the banks of the Derwent River 20 mins from Hobart. Sp wine specialist, but also v.gd table wines inc PINOT N.

Stonehaven Padthaway, SA r w ★★ First large (A$20m) winery in PADTHAWAY region, built by HARDYS, servicing whole LIMESTONE COAST ZONE production.

Stonier Wines Mornington Pen, Vic r w ★★★ (CHARD) 00' 01' 02' 03 04 (PINOT N) 00' 02' 03 04' Consistently v.gd; Reserves outstanding. Owned by LION NATHAN.

Suckfizzle/Stella Bella/Skuttlebutt Margaret R, WA r w ★★→★★★ Avant-garde label designs and names shouldn't obscure deadly serious commitment to quality. CAB SAUV, SEM/SAUV BL, CHARD, SHIRAZ, SANGIOVESE/CAB all shine.

Summerfield Pyrenees, Vic r (w) ★★ Consistent producer of estate-grown, blockbuster SHIRAZ and CAB SAUV, esp in reserve appellation.

Swan Valley (Swan V), WA Located 20 minutes N of Perth. Birthplace of wine in the W. Hot climate makes strong, low-acid table wines; being rejuvenated for wine tourism.

Tahbilk Goulburn V, Vic r w ★★→★★★ (Marsanne) 79' 92' 95' 97' 98' 99 00' 01 03' 04 05' (SHIRAZ) 68 71 76 86' 88 91' 98 99' 00 02' Beautiful historic family estate: long-ageing reds, also RIES and Marsanne. Reserve CAB SAUV outstanding; value for money ditto. Rare 1860 Vines SHIRAZ, too.

Taltarni Grampians/Avoca, Vic r w (sp) ★★ New management and winemaking team producing more sophisticated reds, esp Cephas.

Tamar Ridge N Tas r w (sp) ★★→★★★ Public-company ownership, Dr. Richard Smart as viticulturist, Dr. Andrew Pirie as CEO/chief winemaker, and 230-plus ha of vines make this a major player – if not the major player – in TASMANIA.

Tapanappa SA r ★★ New WRATTONBULLY collaboration between Brian Croser, Bollinger, and J-M Cazes of Pauillac (see France). To watch.

Tarrawarra Yarra V, Vic r w ★★★ (CHARD) 98' 00' 02' 04' 05' (PINOT N) 00' 02' 03 04 Has moved from idiosyncratic to (much-improved) elegant, mainstream CHARD and PINOT N. Tin Cows is the second label.

Tarrington Henty, Vic r w ★★★ Cameo winery producing jewel-like CHARD (intense, no oak) and PINOT N in miniscule quantities.

Tasmania Production continues to surge, but still tiny. Great potential for sparkling, CHARD, PINOT N, and RIES in cool climate.

AUSTRALIA

Tatachilla McLaren Vale, SA r w ★★→★★★ Significant (250,000 cases) production of nice whites and v.gd reds. Acquired by LION NATHAN in 2002.

Taylors Wines Clare V, SA r w ★★→★★★ 400,000 case production of much-improved RIES, SHIRAZ, CAB SAUV. Exports under Wakefield Wines brand (trademark issues with Taylors of Oporto).

Ten Minutes by Tractor Mornington Pen, Vic r w ★★ Amusing name and sophisticated packaging links three family v'yds that are – yes, you've guessed. SAUV BL, CHARD, PINOT N are all gd.

T'Gallant Mornington Pen, Vic w (r) ★★ Improbable name and avant-garde labels for Australia's top Pinot Gris/Grigio producer. Also makes a fragrant unwooded CHARD. Quixotic acquisition by FWE.

The Islander Estate Kangaroo Island, SA r w ★★ New, full-scale development by Jacques Lurton, planned as likely retirement venture. Flagship estate wine an esoteric blend of Sangiovese, Cabernet Fr, and Malbec. Watch this space.

TK Wines Adelaide Hills, SA r w ★★★ Estate now sole occupation of Tim Knappstein, making subtle SAUV BL, powerful CHARD, and PINOT N.

Torbreck Barossa, SA ★★★ r (w) The most stylish of the cult wineries beloved of the US; focus on old-vine Rhône varieties.

Tower Estate Hunter V, NSW r w ★★★→★★★★ Newest venture of Len Evans (and financial partners), offering luxury convention facilities and portfolio of 10 wines made from grapes grown in the best parts of Australia. Impressive stuff.

Trentham Estate Murray Darling (r) w ★→★★★ 65,000 cases of family-grown and made, sensibly priced wines from "boutique" winery on R Murray; gd restaurant, too.

Turkey Flat Barossa, SA r p ★★★ Icon producer of rosé, GRENACHE, and SHIRAZ from core of 150-yr-old v'yds. Top stuff; controlled alcohol and oak.

Two Hands Barossa, SA r ★★→★★★ Savvy wine execs have created v. successful virtual winery with top SHIRAZ from PADTHAWAY, MCLAREN VALE, LANGHORNE CREEK, BAROSSA, and HEATHCOTE stuffed full of alcohol, rich fruit, oak, and the kitchen sink.

Tyrrell's Hunter V, NSW r w ★★★ (SEM) 77' 87' **93' 94' 95' 96'** 98 99' 00' 01' 03 05' (CHARD Vat 47) **79' 97' 98' 99' 00' 01** 02 05' (SHIRAZ Vats) **75' 79' 81' 87 91'** 92' **94' 96' 97 98'** 99' 00' 02 03' (05) Some of the best traditional HUNTER VALLEY wines, SHIRAZ and SEM. Pioneered CHARD with big, rich Vat 47 – still a classic. Also PINOT N.

Upper Hunter NSW Established in early 1960s; irrigated vines (mainly whites), lighter and quicker developing than Lower Hunter's.

Vasse Felix Margaret R, WA r w ★★★ (CAB SAUV) **91 95' 96' 97** 99' 00' 01' 02 03 With CULLEN, pioneer of MARGARET RIVER. Elegant CAB SAUV, notable for mid-weight balance.

Verdelho 1,603 ha, 18,627 tonnes. Old white grape made in large volumes, unoaked and slightly sweet; cash cow.

Voyager Estate Margaret R, WA r w ★★★ 30,000 cases of estate-grown, rich, powerful SEM, SAUV BL, CHARD, CAB SAUV/MERLOT.

Wendouree Clare V, SA r ★★★★ **78 79 83 86** 89' 90' 91' 92 93 94' 96' 98' 99' 01 02' (04') Treasured maker (tiny quantities) of Australia's most powerful and concentrated reds, based on SHIRAZ, CAB SAUV, Mourvèdre, and Malbec. Immensely long-lived.

Wirra Wirra McLaren Vale, SA r w (sp sw w) ★★★ (CAB SAUV) **86 90' 91' 95 96'** 98' 99 02' 03 04' High-quality wines making a big impact. Angelus is superb, top-of-the-range CAB SAUV, ditto RSW SHIRAZ.

Woodlands Margaret R, WA r (w) ★★★→★★★★ 7 ha of 30-plus-yr-old CAB SAUV among top v'yds in region, joined by younger but still v.gd plantings of other B'x reds. Still family-owned and run, but consultancy advice has lifted quality to sensational levels, esp single-barrel Réserve du Cave releases.

Wrattonbully SA Important grape-growing region in LIMESTONE COAST ZONE for 30 years; profile lifted by recent arrival of TAPANAPPA.

Wyndham Estate Hunter V, NSW r w (sp) ★→★★★ Originally HUNTER/MUDGEE, but now no wineries there, just brands: Poet's Corner, Montrose, and RICHMOND GROVE. Part of Orlando Wyndham, owned by Pernod Ricard.

Wynns Coonawarra, SA r w ★★★ (SHIRAZ) 55' 63 86' 88' 90' 91' 93 94' 96' 98' 99 00 02' 03 (CAB SAUV) 57' 60' 82' 85' 86' 90' 91' 94' 96' 97 98' 99' 00 02 SOUTHCORP-owned COONAWARRA classic. RIES, CHARD, SHIRAZ, and CAB SAUV are all v.gd, esp John Riddoch CAB SAUV, and Michael SHIRAZ.

Yabby Lake Mornington Pen, Vic r w ★★★ Joint venture between movie-distribution magnate Robert Kirby, Larry McKenna (ex-Martinborough), and Tod Dexter (ex STONIER WINES) (affiliated to HEATHCOTE estate), utterly driven by the goal of quality.

Yalumba See S SMITH & SONS.

Yarra Burn Yarra V, Vic r w sp ★★→★★★ Estate making SEM, SAUV BL, CHARD, sp PINOT N/CHARD/PINOT M, and CAB SAUV. Acquired by HARDYS in 1995. Bastard Hill CHARD and PINOT N legitimate flag-bearers.

Yarra Valley (Yarra V) Superb historic area nr Melbourne. Growing emphasis on very successful PINOT N, CHARD, SHIRAZ, MERLOT, and sparkling.

Yarra Yarra Yarra V, Vic r w ★★★ Recently increased to 7 ha, giving greater access to fine SEM/SAUV BL and CAB SAUV, each in classic B'x style.

Yarra Yering Yarra V, Vic r w ★★★→★★★★ (Dry Reds) 81' 82' 83 84 85 90' 91' 93' 94' 95 96' 97' 98 99' 00' 01 02' 03 04 (05') Best-known Lilydale boutique winery. Esp racy, powerful PINOT N; deep, herby CAB SAUV (Dry Red No 1); SHIRAZ (Dry Red No 2). Luscious, daring flavours in red and white. Also fortified "Port-Sorts" from the correct grapes.

Yeringberg Yarra V, Vic r w ★★★ (Marsanne) 91' 92 94' 95 97 98 00' 02' 03 04 (05') (CAB SAUV) 80' 81' 84 86 88' 90 91' 92 93 94' 97' 98 99 00' 02' 04 (05') Dreamlike, historic estate still in the hands of founding family. Makes small quantities of very high-quality Marsanne, Roussanne, CHARD, CAB SAUV, and PINOT N.

Yering Station/Yarrabank Yarra V, Vic r w sp ★★★ On site of Vic's first v'yd; replanted after 80-yr gap. Extraordinary joint venture: Yering Station table wines (Reserve CHARD, PINOT N, SHIRAZ, Viognier); Yarrabank (esp fine sparkling wines for Champagne Devaux).

Zema Estate Coonawarra, SA r ★★→★★★★ One of the last bastions of hand-pruning in COONAWARRA; silkily powerful, disarmingly straightforward reds.

New Zealand

More heavily shaded areas
are the wine-growing regions

Sauvignon Blancs of breathtaking intensity, and seductively scented, supple Pinot Noirs are New Zealand's two greatest offerings to the wine world. Alone in vast seas, the country has a cool, temperate climate, ideal for classic European grape varieties. In 1982, it exported 12,000 cases; in 2005, more than 5.7 million. There are now over 22,000 vineyard hectares. Sauvignon Blanc and Chardonnay are extensively planted (over half the national total), but Pinot Noir plantings now exceed Chardonnay. Merlot and Cabernet Sauvignon are well established, with sizeable pockets of Riesling, Semillon, Pinot Gris (newly fashionable), Viognier (ditto), Gewurztraminer, Cabernet Franc, Malbec, and Syrah (revealing great potential in Hawke's Bay). Intense fruit and crisp acidity are New Zealand's hallmarks. Nowhere matches Marlborough Sauvignon for pungency. Chardonnay shines throughout the country, while Riesling's stronghold is the South Island. Marlborough has also proved itself with fine fizz. Claret-style reds (increasingly Merlot-based) from Hawke's Bay and Auckland are of improving – at best outstanding – quality. Pinot Noir makes wonderful wines in Martinborough and the South Island. There are now well over 500 wineries and 3,000 wines.

Recent vintages

2005 Much lower-yielding than 2004, due to exceptionally cold, wet, early summer. Late summer and autumn variable but often good. Excellent Marlborough Sauvignon Blanc and Pinot Noir.

2004 Record crop, reflecting fast-expanding vineyard area and heavy yields. Exceptionally wet Feb, but cool, dry autumn. Variable quality, with some Sauvignon Blanc lacking depth.

2003 Frost-affected season, yielding the lightest crop yet. Unripe flavours in some wines; excellent intensity in others.

2002 Bumper crop (50% heavier than previous record). Outstanding Chardonnay and variable reds in Hawke's Bay.

2001 Very dry in the South, wet in the North. Tiny crop in Hawke's Bay and Gisborne. Marlborough Sauvignon Blanc of variable quality. Pinot Noir excellent.

Akarua Central Otago ★★ Large v'yd at Bannockburn, producing classy, exuberantly fruity Pinot N, flinty Chard, and Pinot Gr. Supple, charming, second-tier Pinot N, labelled The Gullies.

Allan Scott Marlborough ★★ Excellent Ries (from vines more than 20 years old); gd Chard, Sauv Bl; top label Prestige.

Alpha Domus Hawke's Bay ★★ Gd Chard and concentrated reds, esp savoury, Merlot-based The Navigator, and notably dark, rich, Cab Sauv-based The Aviator. Top wines labelled AD.

Amisfield Central Otago ★★ Impressive Pinot Gr, Sauv Bl, and Pinot N. Lake Hayes is lower-tier label.

Ata Rangi Martinborough ★★★ Small but highly respected winery. Outstanding Pinot N (**00 01 02** 03'). Rich, concentrated Craighall Chard. Increasingly impressive Merlot/Syrah/Cab Sauv blend Célèbre.

Auckland (r) **00' 02** 04' 05' (w) **04** 05' Largest city in NZ. Henderson, Huapai, Kumeu, Matakana, Clevedon, Waiheke Island districts – pricey, variable quality B'x reds – nearby.

Awatere Valley Marlborough Important sub-region, slightly cooler than the larger WAIRAU VALLEY, with racy, herbaceous, minerally Sauv Bl.

Babich Henderson (Auckland) ★★→★★★ Mid-size family firm, established 1916; quality, value. AUCKLAND, HAWKE'S BAY, and MARLBOROUGH v'yds. Refined, slow-maturing Irongate Chard (**00' 02'**) and Cab Sauv/Merlot (single v'yd). Ripe, dry MARLBOROUGH Sauv Bl.

Black Ridge Central Otago ★→★★ One of the world's southernmost wineries. Noted for rich, soft Pinot N; also gd Chard, Ries, and Gewurz.

Borthwick Wairarapa ★★ Small producer nr Masterton, with freshly aromatic, high-flavoured Sauv Bl, Ries, Chard. Also warm, complex Pinot N with cherry, plum, and smoky oak flavours.

Brancott Vineyards ★→★★★ Brand used by PERNOD RICARD NEW ZEALAND in US.

Brookfield Hawke's Bay ★★ One of region's top v'yds: outstanding "gold label" Cab Sauv/Merlot; rich Chard, Pinot Gr, and Gewurz.

Cable Bay Waiheke Island ★★ Sizeable newcomer, first vintage 2002. Tight, refined Waiheke Chard and spicy, savoury, Five Hills red; subtle, finely textured MARLBOROUGH Sauv Bl.

Canterbury (r) **01' 03 04** 05 (w) **01' 03 04** 05 NZ's fifth-largest wine region; v'yds nr Christchurch and Waipara. Long, dry summers favour Pinot N, Chard, Ries.

Canterbury House Waipara ★→★★ Sizeable winery, US-owned, best known for fresh, punchy Sauv Bl; crisp, spicy Pinot Gr; and honey-sweet Noble Ries.

Carrick Central Otago ★★ Emerging Bannockburn winery with flinty, flavourful whites (Pinot Gr, Sauv Bl, Chard, Ries) and rich, velvety Pinot N.

Central Otago (r) **03' 04** (w) **03' 04** Fast-expanding, cool, mountainous region in South Island. Ries and Pinot Gr promising; Pinot N perfumed and silky, with notably intense character, but best drunk young.

Chard Farm Central Otago ★★ Fresh, vibrant Ries, Pinot Gr, and gd Pinot N.

Church Road Hawke's Bay ★★→★★★ PERNOD RICARD NEW ZEALAND winery. Rich Chard and elegant Merlot/Cab Sauv. Top res wines; prestige, claret-style red, Tom.

Churton Marlborough ★★ Owned by English wine merchant turned winemaker Sam Weaver. Subtle, complex, finely textured Sauv Bl; fragrant, spicy, v. harmonious Pinot N.

Clearview Hawke's Bay ★★→★★★ Burly, flavour-packed Res Chard; dark, rich Res Cab Fr, Enigma (Merlot-based), Old Olive Block (Cab Sauv blend).

Clifford Bay Marlborough ★★ Single-v'yd producer of fresh, lively Chard, Ries, Pinot N. Scented, intense Sauv Bl is best.

Clos Henri Marlborough ★★→★★★ Established by Henri Bourgeois (see, France). First vintage 03. Subtle, flinty, minerally Sauv Bl and vibrant, supple Pinot N.

Cloudy Bay Marlborough ★★★ Owned by the vast LVMH group. Large-volume Sauv Bl, Chard, and Pinot N are v.gd. Pelorus sp impressive. Rarer Gewurz, Late-Harvest Ries, and Te Koko (oak-aged Sauv Bl) now the greatest wines. Pinot Gr is in the wings.

Collard Brothers Auckland ★★ Long-established, small family winery. Whites, esp Rothesay Vineyard Chard.

Cooper's Creek Auckland ★★ Excellent Swamp Res Chard, gd MARLBOROUGH Sauv Bl.

Corbans Auckland ★ →★★★ Established 1902, now PERNOD RICARD NEW ZEALAND brand. Best wines: Cottage Block and Private Bin. Quality from basic to outstanding.

Craggy Range Hawke's Bay ★★→★★★ Mid-sized winery with v'yds in MARTINBOROUGH and HAWKE'S BAY. Restrained Sauv Bl, stylish Chard, dense, ripe, firm Merlot and Syrah.

Daniel Le Brun Marlborough ★★ Small winery: v.gd bottle-fermented sparkler, esp Vintage (**97**) and Blanc de Blancs (**98'**). Terrace Road table wines also gd.

Delegat's Auckland ★★ Large family winery. V'yds at MARLBOROUGH. Res Chard, Merlot, and Cab Sauv/Merlot offer v.gd quality and value. OYSTER BAY brand: deep-flavoured Chard and Sauv Bl, elegant Pinot N.

Deutz Auckland ★★★ Champagne company gives name and technical aid to fine sp from MARLBOROUGH by PERNOD RICARD NEW ZEALAND. NV: lively, yeasty, flinty. Vintage Blanc de Blancs: rich and creamy.

Dog Point Marlborough ★★ Grape-grower Ivan Sutherland and winemaker James Healy (both ex-CLOUDY BAY) produce unusually complex, finely textured, oak-aged Sauv Bl (Section 94), Chard, and Pinot N.

Dry River Martinborough ★★★ Tiny winery. Penetrating, long-lived Chard, Ries, Pinot Gr (NZ's finest), Gewurz, and ripe powerful Pinot N (**99 00 01 02** 03').

Escarpment Martinborough ★★ Sturdy, rich, Alsace-like Pinot Gr and muscular, dense Pinot N from Larry McKenna, ex-MARTINBOROUGH VINEYARD. Top label: Kupe.

Esk Valley Hawke's Bay ★★ →★★★ Owned by VILLA MARIA. Some of NZ's most voluptuous Merlot-based reds (esp Res label **00' 02'**, v.gd Merlot rosé, Chenin Bl, satisfying Chards, and Sauv Bl.

Felton Road Central Otago ★★★ Star winery in warm Bannockburn area. Pinot N Block 3 and 5 and Ries outstanding; excellent Chard and regular Pinot N.

Firstland Waikato ★→★★ Previously De Redcliffe; now owned by expatriate American. Hotel du Vin attached. Gd MARLBOROUGH whites. Improving HAWKE'S BAY reds.

Forrest Marlborough ★★ Mid-size winery; fragrant, ripe Chard, Sauv Bl, Ries; flavour-crammed HAWKE'S BAY Cornerstone Vineyard Cab Sauv/Merlot/Malbec.

Foxes Island Marlborough ★★ Small producer of rich, smooth Chard, finely textured Sauv Bl, and elegant, supple Pinot N.

Framingham Marlborough ★★ Owned by PERNOD RICARD NEW ZEALAND. Aromatic whites, notably Ries (Classic is slightly sweet, intense, and zesty; Dry is even finer) and lush, slightly sweet Pinot Gr. Rich, dry Sauv Bl.

Fromm Marlborough ★★★ Swiss-founded, focusing on very powerful red wines. Sturdy, firm Pinot N, esp under Fromm Vineyard and Clayvin Vineyard labels.

Gibbston Valley Central Otago ★★ Pioneer winery with popular restaurant. Greatest strength is Pinot N, esp robust, exuberantly fruity Reserve (**01 02'**). Racy local whites (Chard, Ries, Pinot Gr).

Giesen Estate Canterbury ★ German family winery. Gd, slightly honeyed Ries, but bulk of production is now average-quality MARLBOROUGH Sauv Bl.

Gisborne (r) 04' 05 (w) 04' 05' NZ's third-largest region. Abundant sunshine and rain, with fertile soils. Key strength is Chard (typically deliciously fragrant, ripe, and soft in its youth). Gd Gewurz and Viognier; Merlot more variable.

Goldwater Waiheke Island ★★→★★★ Region's pioneer Cab Sauv/Merlot Goldie (00' 02) is still one of NZ's finest: Médoc-like finesse, concentration, and structure. Also crisp, citrus Chard and pungent Sauv Bl, both grown in MARLBOROUGH.

Gravitas Marlborough ★★ First 02 vintage yielded exceptionally rich Sauv and Chard. Subsequent wines excellent but slightly less memorable.

Greenhough Nelson ★★→★★★ One of region's top producers, with immaculate and deep-flavoured Ries, Sauv, Chard, and Pinot N. Top label: Hope Vineyard.

Grove Mill Marlborough ★★→★★★ Attractive whites, inc vibrant Chard; excellent Ries, Sauv, and slightly sweet Pinot Gr. Gd, lower-tier Sanctuary brand.

Hawke's Bay (r) 00' 02' 04 (w) 02' 04' NZ's second-largest region. Long history of winemaking in sunny climate; shingly and heavier soils. Full, rich Merlot and Cab Sauv-based reds in gd vintages; Syrah a fast-rising star; powerful Chard; rounded Sauv Bl.

Herzog Marlborough ★★★ Established by Swiss immigrants. Power-packed, pricey, but classy Merlot/Cab Sauv, Montepulciano, Pinot N, Chard, Viognier, and Pinot Gr.

Highfield Marlborough ★★ Japanese-owned with quality Ries, Chard, Sauv Bl, and Pinot N. Also piercing, flinty, yeasty Elstree sparkling.

Huia Marlborough ★★ Mouth-filling, subtle wines that age well, inc savoury, rounded Chard and perfumed, well-spiced Gewurz.

Hunter's Marlborough ★★→★★★ Top name in intense, immaculate Sauv Bl. Fine, delicate Chard. Excellent sp, Ries, Gewurz; light, elegant Pinot N.

Isabel Estate Marlborough ★★★ Family estate with limey clay soil. Outstanding Pinot N, Sauv Bl, and Chard, but lately slightly inconsistent.

Jackson Estate Marlborough ★★ Rich Sauv Bl, gd Chard, and attractive Dry Ries. Lightish Pinot N.

Kaituna Valley Canterbury ★★→★★★ Small producer with v'yds nr Christchurch and in MARLBOROUGH. Consistently powerful, multi-award-winning Pinot N.

Karikari Northland ★★ NZ's northernmost v'yd and winery, American-owned, with rich, ripe B'x-style reds, Pinotage, and Syrah.

Kemblefield Hawke's Bay ★→★★ US-owned winery. Solid reds; ripely herbal, oak-aged Sauv Bl; soft, peppery Gewurz, and fleshy, lush Chard.

Kim Crawford Hawke's Bay ★★ Founded 1996 by ex-COOPER'S CREEK winemaker; sold in 2003 to Vincor (Canada). Numerous labels, inc rich oaky GISBORNE Chard and scented, strong-flavoured MARLBOROUGH Sauv Bl.

Kumeu River Auckland ★★→★★★ Rich, refined Kumeu Chard (02' 04' 05'); single-v'yd Mate's Vineyard Chard even more opulent. Distinctive, minerally MARLBOROUGH Sauv Bl since 04. Second label: Kumeu River Village.

Lake Chalice Marlborough ★★ Small producer with bold, creamy-rich, softly textured Chard and incisive, slightly sw Ries; Sauv Bl of excellent quality. Platinum premium label.

Lawson's Dry Hills Marlborough ★★→★★★ Weighty wines with rich, intense flavours. Distinguished Sauv Bl and Gewurz; gd Pinot Gr and Ries.

Lincoln Auckland ★ Long-established family winery. Gd-value varietals of improving quality: buttery GISBORNE Chard (top label Reserve).

Lindauer See PERNOD RICARD NEW ZEALAND.

Longridge ★ Former CORBANS brand, now owned by PERNOD RICARD NEW ZEALAND. Reliable, moderately priced wines (inc citrus, lightly oaked Chard) typically from HAWKE'S BAY.

Margrain Martinborough ★★ Small winery with firm, concentrated Chard, Ries, Pinot Gr, Merlot, and Pinot N, all of which reward bottle-age.

Marlborough (r) **03 04** 05' (w) **04 05** NZ's largest region (half of all plantings). Sunny, warm days and cool nights give intense, crisp whites. Amazingly intense Sauv Bl, from sharp, green capsicum to ripe tropical fruit. Fresh, limey Ries; very promising Pinot Gr and Gewurz. High-quality sparkling. Pinot N variable; best are among NZ's finest.

Martinborough (r) **01 03'** (w) **03'** Small, high-quality area in S WAIRARAPA (foot of North Island). Warm summers, dry autumns, gravelly soils. Success with white grapes, but most renowned for sturdy, rich, long-lived Pinot N.

Martinborough Vineyard Martinborough ★★★ Distinguished small winery; one of NZ's top Pinot Noirs (**00 01 03'**). Rich, biscuity Chard and intense Ries.

Matakana Estate Auckland ★→★★ Largest producer in Matakana district. Average to gd Chard, Pinot Gr, Sem, Syrah, and Merlot/Cab Sauv blend. Volume label: Goldridge.

Matariki Hawke's Bay ★★→★★★ Stylish white and red, extensive v'yds in stony Gimblett Road. Rich, ripe Sauv Bl; robust, spicy Quintology red blend.

Matawhero Gisborne ★→★★ Formerly NZ's top Gewurz specialist, now reduced in size and reputation. Mature wines of variable quality.

Matua Valley Auckland ★★→★★★ Highly rated, large winery, owned by Beringer Blass (see California), with v'yds in four regions. Top range Ararimu inc fat, savoury Chard and dark, rich Merlot/Cab Sauv. Numerous attractive GISBORNE (esp Judd Chard), HAWKE'S BAY, and MARLBOROUGH wines (Shingle Peak). Shingle Peak Sauv Bl top value.

Mergers and acquisitions: changing hands

The majority of New Zealand's wine output is now controlled by overseas interests. The country's wine giant, PERNOD RICARD NEW ZEALAND – for decades known as MONTANA and, latterly, as Allied Domecq Wines (NZ) – is now part of the Pacific division of Pernod Ricard, the French spirits conglomerate that also owns Orlando Wyndham in Australia.

CLOUDY BAY is part of the Louis Vuitton-Moët Hennessy luxury-goods empire. Thus, both New Zealand's biggest and most internationally prestigious wineries are in French hands.

The list goes on. NOBILO, New Zealand's second-largest winery, belongs to the world's largest wine producer, Constellation. MATUA VALLEY is owned by Beringer Blass, the wine division of the Australian brewing giant Fosters; WITHER HILLS is owned by Australian-based, Japanese-controlled Lion Nathan; KIM CRAWFORD is owned by Canada-based Vincor.

Among the many other New Zealand brands wholly or partly overseas-owned are CANTERBURY HOUSE, CLOS HENRI, CRAGGY RANGE, DRY RIVER, ESCARPMENT, FELTON ROAD, FROMM, HIGHFIELD, KARIKARI, KEMBLEFIELD, NAUTILUS, SACRED HILL, TE AWA, TRINITY HILL, and WHITEHAVEN.

Mills Reef Bay of Plenty ★★→★★★ The Preston family produces impressive wines from HAWKE'S BAY grapes. Top Elspeth range inc dense, rich B'x-style reds and Syrah. Reserve range also impressive.

Millton Gisborne ★★→★★★ Region's top small winery: mostly organic. Soft, savoury Chard (single v'yd Clos de Ste Anne is superb). Rich, long-lived Chenin Bl is NZ's finest.

Mission Hawke's Bay ★→★★ NZ's oldest wine producer, established 1851, still run by Catholic Society of Mary. Solid varietals: sweetish, perfumed Ries is esp gd value. Reserve range inc gd B'x-style reds and Chard.

Montana Auckland ★→★★★ Formerly name of NZ wine giant, now a key brand of PERNOD RICARD NEW ZEALAND. Top wines labelled Estate; Reserve is second tier. Big-selling varietals include smooth, peachy, lightly oaked GISBORNE Chard and crisp, grassy MARLBOROUGH Sauv Bl.

Morton Estate Bay of Plenty ★★ Respected mid-size producer with v'yds in HAWKE'S BAY and MARLBOROUGH. Refined Black Label Chard is one of NZ's best (**02'**). White Label Chard also v.gd. Other varietals usually gd value.

Mount Riley Marlborough ★→★★ Fast-growing company with extensive v'yds and new winery. Easy-drinking Chard; punchy Sauv Bl; dark, flavoursome Merlot/Malbec. Top wines labelled Seventeen Valley. All gd value.

Mt Difficulty Central Otago ★★ Quality producer in relatively hot Bannockburn area. Best known for vibrant, flinty Ries and very refined, intense Pinot N.

Mud House Marlborough ★→★★ Punchy, vibrant Sauv Bl and solid Pinot Gr, Ries, Merlot, and Pinot N.

Muddy Water Waipara ★★ Small, high-quality producer with beautifully intense Ries, minerally Chard, and savoury, subtle Pinot N.

Nautilus Marlborough ★★ Small range of distributors Négociants (NZ), owned by S SMITH & SON of Australia. Top wines inc stylish, finely balanced Sauv Bl, savoury Pinot N, and fragrant sparkler. Lower-tier: Twin Islands.

Nelson (r) **01 02'** (w) **03 04** Small, fast-growing region W of MARLBOROUGH; climate wetter. Clay soils of Upper Moutere hills and silty Waimea Plains. Strengths in whites, esp Ries, Sauv Bl, Chard. Pinot N is best red.

Neudorf Nelson ★★★ A top, smallish winery. Strapping, creamy-rich Chard (**02' 03 04**), Superb Pinot N, Sauv Bl, Ries.

Nga Waka Martinborough ★★ Dry, steely whites of high quality. Outstanding Sauv Bl; piercingly flavoured Ries; robust, savoury Chard. Pinot N scented and supple.

Ngatarawa Hawke's Bay ★★→★★★ Mid-sized. Top Alwyn Reserve range, inc powerful Chard, Cab Sauv, Merlot. Mid-range Glazebrook also excellent.

Nobilo Auckland ★→★★ NZ's second-largest wine company, now owned by Hardy's (see Australia). MARLBOROUGH Sauv Bl is gd but sharply priced. Superior varietals labelled Icon. V.gd Drylands Sauv Bl. Cheaper wines labelled Fernleaf and Fall Harvest. See also SELAKS.

Okahu Estate Northland ★→★★ One of NZ's northernmost wineries, at Kaitaia. Hot, humid climate. Warm, ripe reds; complex, creamy Chard.

Omaka Springs Marlborough ★→★★ punchy, herbaceous Sauv Bl, solid Ries, Chard, and leafy reds.

Oyster Bay See DELEGAT'S.

Palliser Estate Martinborough ★★→★★★ One of the area's largest and best wineries. Superb tropical-fruit-flavoured Sauv Bl, excellent Chard, Ries, Pinot N. Top wines: Palliser Estate. Lower tier: Pencarrow.

Pask, C J Hawke's Bay ★★→★★★ Mid-size winery, extensive v'yds. Gd to excellent Chard. Cab Sauv and Merlot-based reds fast improving. Rich, complex Reserves.

Pegasus Bay Waipara ★★→★★★ Small but distinguished range: notably taut, cool-climate Chard; lush, complex, oaked Sauv Bl/Sem; and very rich, zingy Ries. Merlot-based reds are region's finest. Pinot N lush and silky (esp Prima Donna).

Peregrine Central Otago ★★ Crisp, cool-climate Ries, Pinot Gr, and Gewurz of variable quality, and beautifully rich, silky, gd-value Pinot N.

Pernod Ricard New Zealand Auckland ★→★★★ NZ wine giant, formerly called Allied Domecq Wines (NZ) and, before that, MONTANA. Purchased by Pernod Ricard, which also owns Orlando (see Australia) in 2005. Wineries in AUCKLAND, GISBORNE, HAWKE'S BAY, and MARLBOROUGH. Extensive co-owned v'yds for MARLBOROUGH whites, inc top-value MONTANA Sauv Bl, Ries, and Chard

(Reserve range esp gd). Strength in sp, inc DEUTZ, and stylish, fine-value Lindauer. Elegant CHURCH ROAD reds and quality Chard. Other key brands: CORBANS, LONGRIDGE, STONELEIGH, Saints. New brand Triplebank offers intense, racy AWATERE VALLEY wines.

Providence Auckland ★★★ Rare, Merlot-based red from Matakana district. Perfumed, lush, and silky; very high-priced.

Quartz Reef Central Otago ★★ Quality producer with weighty, flinty Pinot Gr; substantial rich Pinot N; yeasty, lingering, Champagne-like sparkler, Chauvet.

Rimu Grove Nelson ★★ Small, American-owned, coastal v'yd. Concentrated, minerally Chard and Pinot Gr; rich, spicy Pinot N.

Rippon Vineyard Central Otago ★→★★ Stunning v'yd. Fine-scented, very fruity Pinot N and slowly evolving whites, inc steely, appley Ries.

Rockburn Central Otago ★★ Crisp, racy Chard, Pinot Gr, Gewurz, Ries, Sauv Bl. Fragrant, supple, rich Pinot N is best.

Sacred Hill Hawke's Bay ★★→★★★ Sound Whitecliff varietals; gd, oaked Sauv Bl (Barrel Fermented and Sauvage). Gd Basket Press Merlot and barrel-fermented Chard. Distinguished Riflemans Chard and Brokenstone Merlot. Punchy, off-dry MARLBOROUGH Sauv Bl.

Saint Clair Marlborough ★★→★★★★ Fast-growing, export-led producer with substantial v'yds. Prolific award winner. Sauv Bl, fragrant Ries, easy Chard, and plummy, early-drinking Merlot. Rich Reserve Sauv Blanc, Chard, Merlot, Pinot N.

St Helena Canterbury ★ The region's oldest winery, founded nr Christchurch in 1978. Light, supple Pinot N (Reserve is bolder). Chard variable but gd in better vintages. MARLBOROUGH Sauv Bl solid.

Seifried Estate Nelson ★★ Region's biggest winery, founded by an Austrian. Known initially for well-priced Ries and Gewurz; now also producing gd-value, often excellent Sauv Bl and Chard. Best wines: Winemakers Collection.

Selaks ★→★★ Mid-size family firm bought by NOBILO in 1998. Sauv Bl, Ries, and Chard are its strengths; reds are mostly plain but improving.

Seresin Marlborough ★★→★★★★ Established by NZ film producer Michael Seresin. Stylish, immaculate Sauv, Chard, Pinots N and Gr, Ries, Noble Ries.

Sileni Hawke's Bay ★★ Major winery with extensive v'yds and classy Chard and Merlot. Top wines: EV (Exceptional Vintage), then Estate Selection, and Cellar Selection.

Southbank Hawke's Bay ★→★★ Fast-growing new producer. Creamy, rich HAWKE'S BAY Chard and penetrating MARLBOROUGH Sauv Bl are best.

Spy Valley Marlborough ★★ Fast-growing company with extensive v'yds. Sauv Bl, Chard, Ries, Gewurz, Pinot Gr, and Pinot N are all v.gd.

Staete Landt Marlborough ★★ Dutch immigrants, producing refined Chard, Sauv Bl, and Pinot Gr; and graceful, supple Pinot N.

Stonecroft Hawke's Bay ★★→★★★ Small winery. Dark, concentrated Syrah, more Rhône than Australia. V.gd red blend Ruhanui, Chard, v. rich Gewurz.

Stoneleigh Former CORBANS brand, now owned by PERNOD RICARD NEW ZEALAND. Impressive MARLBOROUGH whites and Pinot N, esp Rapaura Reserve.

Stonyridge Waiheke Island ★★★★ Boutique winery. Famous for exceptional B'x-style red, Larose (**96 99 00'** 04' 05'). Dark, perfumed, and magnificently concentrated, it matures well for a decade.

Tasman Bay Nelson ★→★★ Best known for rich, creamy-smooth Chard. Top, single-v'yd wines sold as Spencer Hill.

Te Awa Hawke's Bay ★★ US-owned large estate v'yd. Classy Chard and Boundary (Merlot-based blend); gd larger-volume Longlands labels.

Te Kairanga Martinborough ★→★★ One of district's larger wineries. Big, flinty Chard (richer Res); perfumed, supple Pinot N (complex and powerful Res).

Te Mata Hawke's Bay ★★★→★★★★ Prestigious winery. Fine, powerful Elston Chard; stylish v. B'x-like Coleraine Cab/Merlot (**95' 98' 00'** 02). Syrah and Viognier among NZ's finest. Woodthorpe range for early drinking; Rymer's Change is third tier.

Te Motu Waiheke Island ★★ Top wine of Waiheke Vineyards, owned by Dunleavy and Buffalora families. Concentrated, brambly red. Dunleavy second label.

Terra Vin Marlborough ★★ Weighty, dry, tropical-fruit-flavoured Sauv Bl and rich, firmly structured Hillside Sel.

Thornbury ★★ V'yds in HAWKE'S BAY and MARLBOROUGH. Best known for weighty, rich, tropical-fruit-flavoured MARLBOROUGH Sauv Bl.

Tohu ★→★★ Maori-owned venture with extensive v'yds. Punchy, racy Sauv Bl and moderately complex Pinot N, both from MARLBOROUGH; full-flavoured GISBORNE Chard.

Torlesse Waipara ★→★★ Small, gd-value CANTERBURY producer of fresh, flinty Ries and firm, toasty, citrus Chard. Mid-weight Pinot N.

Trinity Hill Hawke's Bay ★★→★★★★ Firm, concentrated reds since 96, and top-flight Chard. New Homage range since 02: very stylish and expensive (Chard, Syrah, Merlot-based). V. promising Tempranillo. NZ's best Viognier.

Unison Hawke's Bay ★★→★★★★ Red specialist with dark, spicy, flavour-crammed blends of Merlot, Cab Sauv, Syrah. Selection label is oak-aged the longest.

Vavasour Marlborough ★★ Based in AWATERE VALLEY. Immaculate, intense Chard and Sauv Bl; promising Pinot N and Pinot Gr. Dashwood is the second label.

Vidal Hawke's Bay ★★→★★★★ Established in 1905 by a Spaniard, now part of VILLA MARIA. Reserves (Chard, Cab Sauv/Merlot) uniformly high standard.

Villa Maria Auckland ★★→★★★★ One of NZ's three largest wine companies, inc VIDAL and ESK VALLEY. Owned by George Fistonich. Top range: Reserve (Pinot N is powerful, lush); Cellar Selection: middle-tier (less oak); third-tier Private Bin wines can be excellent and top value (esp Ries, Sauv Bl, Gewurz). Brilliant track record in competitions.

Waimea Nelson ★→★★★ Fresh, grassy Sauv Bl; rich, gently sw Classic Ries; and bold, lush Bolitho Reserve Chard. Reds variable; Pinot N best.

Waipara Hills Canterbury ★→★★ Publicly owned, sizeable producer of MARLBOROUGH and CANTERBURY wines, esp nettly, zingy MARLBOROUGH Sauv Bl. Fast-improving quality.

Waipara Springs Canterbury ★★ Small producer with lively, cool-climate Ries, Sauv Bl, and Chard; concentrated Reserve Pinot N.

Waipara West Canterbury ★★ Co-owned by London-based Kiwi wine distributor Paul Tutton. Finely scented, lively Ries; freshly acidic, herbaceous Sauv Bl; firm, citrus Chard; and increasingly ripe and substantial Pinot N.

Wairarapa NZ's sixth-largest wine region. See MARTINBOROUGH.

Wairau River Marlborough ★★ Intense Sauv Bl. Home Block is top label.

Wairau Valley MARLBOROUGH's largest district, with most of the region's vineyards and the vast majority of its wineries.

Wellington Capital city and name of region; inc WAIRARAPA, Te Horo, MARTINBOROUGH.

West Brook Auckland ★★ Underrated, richly flavoured Chard, Sauv Bl, Ries.

Whitehaven Marlborough ★★ Excellent wines: racy Ries; scented, delicate, lively Sauv Bl; flavourful, easy Chard. Gallo is part-owner.

Wither Hills Marlborough ★★→★★★★ Sold by Marris family to Lion Nathan (see Australia) in 2002. Rich, toasty Chard; fragrant, fleshy Sauv Bl; serious, concentrated, spicy Pinot N.

NEW ZEALAND

South Africa

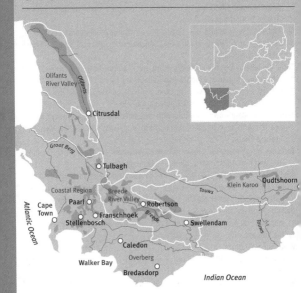

France knows the phenomenon, but the paradox has reached South Africa: consumers have responded to impressive leaps in quality by turning away from wine. Consumption has slid to 7.6 litres per head per year. South Africa is the world's ninth-largest producer, but the thirst here is for beer, so local wine depends on foreign palates. It's a recipe for vulnerability. What if the world's supermarkets dumb down even more? South Africans – and increasingly foreign investors – seem impervious to such doleful ruminations.

The government's benign neglect of the industry has been a tonic after the stultifying controls and price-fixing monopolies of the past. New punters are piling into the winelands at the rate of fifty to sixty a year: expanding vineyards, building new cellars, exploring new areas. Parallel attractions – restaurants, hotels, spas, music festivals, and wildlife parks – are proliferating. Exports have soared by 540 per cent in the past decade. Is this lift-off?

Some leading French wine luminaries seem to think so. May-Eliane de Lencquesaing of Château Pichon-Lalande, Bruno Prats (ex-Chateau Cos d'Estournel), Michel Laroche from Chablis, and Pomerol's celebrated master consultant Michel Rolland have all recently sunk serious money into the Cape. These are not quick-buck stunts straining for instant iconhood.

Perhaps as significant was a recent local augury: for the first time Cape wine producers went, en masse, to Soweto, South Africa's largest black suburb in Johannesburg. A three-day wine festival was successfully staged in the beer-drinking heartland. Can the national palate learn to like wine?

Recent vintages

2006 Dry, overly-warm winter was not best start (uneven budding later); but an uneventfully trouble-free, hot, longer summer than 2005 – by about two weeks – with average yields; the fourth sound vintage in a row.

2005 Very early, short harvest after an exceptionally dry, hot season. Small, thick-skinned berries promise concentrated reds for keeping.

2004 Drawn-out, hot year, above-average quality across most varieties. Intense reds, especially Shiraz, Pinotage.

2003 Excellent: hot, dry, generally disease-free. Concentrated, rich reds, for longer keeping. Heatwave mid-harvest denied whites some fresh, tropical flavours. Most Cape dry whites best drunk within 2–3 yrs.

2002 Wet, mildewy start, then a long heatwave in many districts; top growers made reds of good colour and fruit; generally safer to opt for the vintages before and after this one.

Alto Estate Stellenbosch r ★★ Old estate (exporting since 1920s) on rise again, sp with Cab Sauv **01'**; reputation for long life, slow maturation. Also v. popular Alto Rouge (blend Cab Sauv/Cab Fr/Shiraz) **01** 03.

Anthony de Jager Wines r ★★★ PAARL-based FAIRVIEW Estate winemaker's own label; supple, complex Shiraz/Viognier blend called Homtini Shiraz **00 03** 04.

Anwilka Stellenbosch r New joint venture: Bruno Prats and Hubert de Bouard (Ch Angelus) with South Africa's Lowell Jooste (KLEIN CONSTANTIA). 40 ha. Cab Sauv/Merlot/Shiraz. First 04 due soon.

Axe Hill r sw ★★★ Outstanding tiny specialist producer of vintage port-style at Calitzdorp. Touriga Nacional, Tinta Barocca **99 00 01 02** 03.

Backsberg r w sw ★★ Large PAARL estate. Recently added "Med-style" blend Elba – Mourvèdre, Shiraz, Malbec, Viognier 03 – to long list of labels headed by Babylonstoren B'x blend **02 03**. Also Chard, Viognier. Fine founder's cask-aged Sydney Back brandy.

Beaumont r w ★★→★★★ Walker Bay. Family-run winery, reputation for Rhône-style reds and substantial CHENIN BL: Shiraz **02** 03; dense, dark Mourvèdre **02** 03. Gd PINOTAGE **00 01 02** 03.

Bellingham r w ★→★★ Long-established, popular brand, many ranges/labels – inc Maverick range (Syrah, Viognier); also Spitz (Merlot, PINOTAGE). Popular whites (all DYA), Chard, Sauv Bl, and Chard/Sauv Bl blend Sauvenay.

Beyerskloof St'bosch r ★★→★★★ A top specialist PINOTAGE grower – Reserve **02** 03; also deep-flavoured Cab Sauv/Merlot blend **00 01** 02. Firm, bold Cape blend (PINOTAGE/Cab Sauv/Merlot) Synergy **01** 02.

Boekenhoutskloof Franschhoek r w ★★★ A Cape star, with spicy Syrah **99 00 01' 02'** 03; acclaimed Cab Sauv **99 00 01'** 02; red blend Chocolate Block **02** 03 04 supple, rich-flavoured. Consistently fine Sem. V.gd-value second label Porcupine Ridge, sp. Syrah **03** 04..

Boplaas Family Vineyards r w sw ★★ Estate in dry, hot Karoo. Earthy, deep Cape Vintage Res port-style **91 94 96 97 99' 01** 02 03, fortified Muscadels, and Cape Tawny Port NV.

Boschendal r w sp ★★ Cape's biggest single estate (250,000 cases p.a.) nr Franschhoek. Bold Res Chard, Sauv Bl. V.gd Shiraz Reserve. Also B'x blend Grand Reserve 01, Res Cab Sauv **00 01**. Popular, yeasty Cap Classique sp from Chard/Pinot N.

Bouchard-Finlayson Walker Bay r w ★★★ Leading Pinot N producer: Galpin Peak **97 99 00 01 02'** 03 and Tête de Cuvée **99 01'**. Impressive Chard sp Missionvale label, also Kaaimansgat. V.gd Sauv Bl (DYA).

Buitenverwachting r w sp ★★→★★★ Historic estate in Constantia suburbs of Cape Town. Stand-out Sauv Bl, generally DYA, Chard (Hussey's Vlei 04), B'x blend Christine **98 99 00 01'**, Cab Sauv **99 00 01'**, Merlot **99** 01.

Cabrière Estate Franschhoek ★★ Gd NV sp under Pierre Jourdan label (Brut Sauvage; Belle Rosé). Fine Pinot N in some years **00** 02.

Camberley Wines St'bosch r w ★★→★★★ Family-run red specialist: striking

Shiraz **03**; unusual but impressive, full Shiraz/Merlot blend (Philosopher's Stone) **02 03**; exceptional and massive, dark, plummy PINOTAGE **03** 04'.

Capaia Wines Philadelphia r w New name to watch. French-German collaboration: supple, fine, rich-berry Capaia B'x blend 03 04 won quick plaudits.

Cape Bay ★★ Among most successful export ranges, smooth-blended Ruby Cab and very quaffable CHENIN BL. Driven by NEWTON-JOHNSON family.

Cape Chamonix Franschhoek r w sp ★★ Consistently good Chard Res **01 02 03** and two Méthode Cap Classique Chard-based sp.

Cape Point Vineyards w ★★→★★★ Atlantic on both sides of these v'yds on the slim tip of Cape Town's Peninsula. Crisp Sauv Bl (DYA), Sauv Bl/Sem, Sem dessert.

Cederberg Wines r w ★★→★★★ Highest Cape v'yds. Fruity, crisp whites: Sauv Bl, Reserve V Generations CHENIN BL. Cab Sauv-based blend V Generations **00' 01 03'**. Exceptional, restrained Shiraz **02' 03**.

Château Libertas Blend of mainly Cab Sauv made by STELLENBOSCH FARMERS' WINERY.

Chenin Blanc Most widely planted grape; very adaptable. Sometimes v.gd; much upgrading by leading growers to improve ageability.

Cloof Darling r w ★★ Fast-rising new label; best is concentrated Crucible Shiraz **03'**, but also gd PINOTAGE and Cab Sauv-based blends.

Clos Malverne St'bosch ★★ Small estate, with reputation for PINOTAGE Res **99 00** 02, Cab Sauv/Merlot/PINOTAGE blend Auret **99 01**.

Coleraine Wines Paarl r ★★ Opulent, inky reds, garnering attention and awards: Merlot 05', Syrah **02**, Cab Sauv **02**.

Constantia Once the world's most famous sweet, Muscat-based wines (both red and white). See KLEIN CONSTANTIA.

Constantia Uitsig r w ★★→★★★ Specializing in Chard Res, Sem Res, Cab Sauv/Merlot **00 01** 03 labelled Constantia Red from premium CONSTANTIA v'yds.

Cordoba St'bosch r w ★★→★★★ Highly regarded winery/v'yds on Helderberg mountains. Usually late-developing, Cab Fr-based claret blend labelled Crescendo **98 99 00 01 02** 03; plus ripe Merlot **97 98 01' 02**.

De Krans Estate ★★→★★★ Karoo semi-desert v'yds make rich, full, impressive Vintage Reserve port-style **95 97 99 02** 03'. Also traditional fortified sw r and Muscadels.

De Toren St'bosch r ★★→★★★ Elegant B'x blend (Cab Sauv, Sauv Bl, Merlot, Petit Verdot, Malbec) Fusion V **99 00 01 02 03'**.

De Trafford Wines St'bosch r w sw ★★★ Exceptional small-scale artisan specializing in unfiltered, wild-yeast fermentation. B'x blend Elevation 393, **98 99 00 01** 03'; Cab Sauv **97 98 99 00 01 03** 04; Shiraz **98 00 01 03** 04; Merlot. Dry CHENIN BL in oak and dessert Vin de Paille (also Chenin) worth cellaring.

De Waal Wines r w ★★→★★★ From Uiterwyk, old estate SW of STELLENBOSCH. single-v'yd PINOTAGE Top of the Hill **00 01' 02** 03 among Cape's best; 50-yr-old vines. V.gd "Cape blend" Merlot/Shiraz/PINOTAGE.

De Wetshof Robertson w sw ★★ Large-scale producer, inc Chards – flagships are barrel-selected Bateleur and Finesse. Also Sauv Bl, Gewurz, Rhine Ries, Edeloes botrytis dessert. Exports own-brand Chard for supermarkets.

Delaire Winery St'bosch r w ★★ Mountain v'yds at Helshoogte Pass. Undergoing revamp since purchase by London jeweller Laurence Graff: New B'x blend from 03. Rich Chard **02 03 04**, Cab Sauv Botmaskop **98 00 02**.

Delheim St'bosch r w dr sw ★★ Family winery. Acclaimed Vera Cruz Shiraz **98' 00 01 02** 03; plummy Grand Res B'x blend **97 98 99 00 01** 03. Also Chard and Sauv Bl. Following for botrytis Steen, Edelspatz.

Diemersfontein Wines Wellington r w ★★ Growing reputation for reds, sp power-packed PINOTAGE **03** 04; Cab Sauv (03, 04) and Shiraz in Carpe Diem range.

Distell STELLENBOSCH-based conglomerate, merging Distillers and STELLENBOSCH FARMERS' WINERY, dwarfing other wholesalers. Many brands, spanning quality scales: Capenheimer, Cellar Cask, CHÂTEAU LIBERTAS, FLEUR DU CAP, Kellerprinz, MONIS, NEDERBURG, Overmeer, Tassenberg, Two Oceans, ZONNEBLOEM, etc.

Dornier Wines St'bosch r w ★★→★★★ Imposing B'x blend (with pinch of Shiraz) Donatus 02 03, worth cellaring. Slightly oaked, fruity/flinty white blend Donatus – CHENIN BL. Sauv Bl, Sem **02 03 04**.

Durbanville Hills r w ★★ Fashionably maritime-cooled v'yds owned by giant DISTELL. Best is Single-v'yd Range Caapman Cab Sauv/Merlot **99**. Also Rhinofields Range with gd Chard and Sauv Bl. DYA.

Du Toitskloof Winery r w sw Rawsonville ★→★★ Specialist in various well-priced dessert Muscats. Regular winner of local gd-value awards.

Edelkeur ★★★ Intensely sweet noble-rot white from CHENIN BL by NEDERBURG. Like all full-blown botrytis desserts, officially designated Noble Late Harvest.

Ernie Els r ★★★ South African golfing great's rich aromatic B'x blend **00** 01' **02 03** with fruit from Helderberg/STELLENBOSCH v'yds. Cape's priciest wine. Also Engelbrecht-Els Proprietor's Blend. Partnership between Ernie Els and Jean Engelbrecht (ex-Rust-en-Vrede) sourcing widely, selectively for Cab Sauv/Shiraz blend launched with promising 03. Gd third label, Guardian Peak Syrah/Mourvèdre/Grenache **01 02**.

Estate Wine Official term for wines grown and made (not necessarily bottled) exclusively on registered estates. Not a quality designation.

A choice from South Africa for 2007

Vilafonte Series C 2003, PAARL

Kaapzicht Steytler Vision 2002, STELLENBOSCH

Vergelegen V 2003, STELLENBOSCH

Rijk's Private Cellar Cab Sauv 2002, Tulbagh

De Krans Vintage Reserve 2003 Calitzdorp

Steenberg Sauv Bl Res 2005, CONSTANTIA

Vergelegen White 2004 (Sem/Sauv Bl), STELLENBOSCH

Ken Forrester FMC 2003 (CHENIN BL), STELLENBOSCH

The Foundry Syrah 2003, STELLENBOSCH

The Berrio Sauv Bl (DYA), Elim

Fairview Caldera 03, PAARL/Swartland

Fairview Jakkalsfontein Shiraz 03, PAARL/Swartland

Fairview r w dr sw ★★→★★★★ Cutting-edge winery. Eclectic wines inc many styles of individual, usually near-ready-to-drink Shiraz-based reds. Top range Red Seal, with Caldera, Solitude, Beacon Block, Jakkalsfontein (recent best: **01 03** 04); PINOTAGE Primo **00' 01**; Pegleg Carignan **01 02 03** 04; Akkerbos Chard; Oom Pagel Sem. Regular labels inc Cape's first and still v.gd Viognier. Successful with Rhône-style blends (w r p) Goats do Roam and Goat-Roti.

First Cape Vineyards Worcester/Walker Bay r w ★★ Fastest growing Cape export brand to UK, excellent price to quality: PINOTAGE Cab Sauv, Merlot, Shiraz, PINOTAGE, and blends Shiraz/PINOTAGE, Cab/Merlot, Chard/Sem. Joint venture of NEWTON-JOHNSON WINES, Brand Phoenix in Surrey, UK, and De Wet and Goudini wineries based in Worcester, Cape.

Flagstone r w ★★→★★★★ Modern Cape star, sourcing singular, quality grapes from many very individual, often far-flung v'yds. Best labels: Bowwood Cab/Merlot **02 03**, Mary Le Bow, Cab/Shiraz/Merlot 03. Regular youthful standout: The Berrio Sauv Bl (DYA). Also: The Berrio Cab Sauv **01** 04, Ruby in the Dust **02**, Longitude Shiraz/Merlot/PINOTAGE **00 02**, Writer's Block PINOTAGE 02 04.

Fleur du Cap St'bosch r w sw ★★ Giant producer DISTELL's flagship labels, inc v.gd Unfiltered Collection. Gd Cab Sauv **98 00 01** 03, Merlot **98 00 01 03**; Sauv Bl DYA, Chard **03 04**, Sem **03 04**, and Viognier 04.

Gilga Wines St'bosch r ★★→★★★ A hit with intense spicy Syrah **98 00 01 02** 03.

Glen Carlou r w ★★★ 1st-rate Cape winery, v'yds at PAARL, owned by Donald Hess (see California). Outstanding Chard and Chard Res **03 04**; B'x blend Grand Classique **99' 00 01** 02 03; full Pinot N **98 00** 01 03; spicy, powerful, elegant Syrah **02 03** 04'.

Graham Beck Winery Robertson/Franschhoek r w sp ★★→★★★ Avant-garde properties making classy MÉTHODE CAP CLASSIQUE sp inc vintage Blanc de Blancs Chard (recent plaudits for 00). Also: The Ridge Syrah **01' 02 03**; Coffeestone Cab Sauv **98 99 00** 03; Old Road PINOTAGE **98 99** 00' 01' 02; Barrel selection Cape blend Cab/PINOTAGE The William **99 00** 01 02 03.

Grangehurst St'bosch r ★★→★★★ Small, top red specialist, buying in grapes. Cape blend – PINOTAGE/Merlot – Nikela **98 99 00**. Gd PINOTAGE **97 98 00** and concentrated Cab Sauv/Merlot **97' 98 00** 01.

Groot Constantia r w ★→★★ Historic government-owned estate nr Cape Town. Legendary red and white Muscat desserts in early 19th C. 03 Grand Constance revives tradition, with same red/white Muscat grape varieties – delicious, soft, v. sweet. Also gd B'x blend Gouverneur's Reserve **97 99 00 01** 03, Shiraz **01 02 03**, Chard Res, sw Weisser (Rhine) Ries.

Groote Post Vineyards Darling r w ★★ Coastal, cool-climate benefits for Chard (oaked and unwooded) and intense Shiraz 03; also Merlot, Pinot N separately bottled, and "Old Man's Blend" featuring all together.

Hartenberg St'bosch r w ★★★ Accumulating laurels, a Cape front-ranker. New The McKenzie B'x blend 03'. Always serious Shiraz **97 00 01 02** 03', now also single-v'yd The Stork Shiraz, 03'. Fine Merlot **00 01 02** 03 04'. Lately award-winning Chard Res **03'** and sw Weisser (Rhine) Ries.

Hidden Valley St'bosch r ★★→★★★ Small, organic, Devon Valley/Helderberg v'yd. Top PINOTAGE **96 97 00 01' 04**. Classic Cab Sauv **00 01**. Shiraz 04.

Ingwe Stellenbosch r w ★★→★★★ Alain Moueix (of the Pomerol dynasty) among early 1990s French investors; elegant, minerally Merlot-based B'x blend Ingwe – **02 03**; Sauv Bl/Semillon Amehlo white. For export.

Jack & Knox Winecraft Somerset West r w ★★→★★★ Excellent dry Frostline Ries **03 05**; and subtle Green on Green Sem **03 04**.

J C le Roux St'bosch sp ★★ South Africa's largest sparkling-wine house. All MÉTHODE CAP CLASSIQUE. Top Desiderius **96 97 98** and Scintilla 98 99 (both Chard/Pinot N); also Pinot N **96 97**; Blanc de Blancs Chard, long (5–9 yrs) maturation in bottle. Well-priced NV Pongràcz.

Jean Daneel Wines Napier r w ★★★ Outstanding Signature Series CHENIN BL **02 03'** 04. Chard Brut 01 MÉTHODE CAP CLASSIQUE sp.

Joostenberg Wines Paarl r w ★★ Botrytis dessert from CHENIN BL **03 04**; also gd B'x blend **01** 03, particularly gd Shiraz/Viognier 04.

Jordan Vineyards St'bosch r w ★★★ A bright star. Dense, concentrated Chard Nine Yards Res **02' 03 04**. Cab Sauv blend Cobbler's Hill **97 98 99 00' 01** 03'; Cab Sauv **97 98 99 00 01** 03; Merlot **99 00 01 02** 03; v.gd Sauv Bl (DYA) and new 05 botrytis dessert from CHENIN BL. Husband-and-wife team.

J P Bredell St'bosch ★★→★★★ Rich Vintage Res port-style (Tinta Barocca and Souzão) **91 95 97** 98 00. A Cape benchmark.

Kaapzicht Estate St'bosch r w ★★★ Acclaimed Steytler Vision (blend PINOTAGE/Cab Sauv/Merlot) **98 00 01' 02' 03'**; Steytler PINOTAGE **98 99 00 01' 02 03'**. Well-crafted Kaapzicht Cab Sauv **97 98 99** 00 **01'** 02 03 and PINOTAGE, Shiraz.

Kanonkop St'bosch r ★★★ Retains – in an ever more crowded field – grand local status. Two formidable labels: oak-finished PINOTAGE **94 97 98 99 00 01** 02 03 and, with a fanatic following, B'x-style blend Paul Sauer **94 95 97 98' 99 00 01** 02 03, plus Cab Sauv **89 94 95 97 98 99' 00** 01.

Kanu Wines St'bosch r w sw ★★→★★★ Best known for barrel-aged CHENIN BL;

also v.gd Chard and Sauv Bl (DYA); botrytis dessert wine Kia Ora **99 01 03**.

Ken Forrester Vineyards St'bosch r w sw ★★→★★★ Helderberg producer. Outstanding Forrester-Meinert CHENIN BL, labelled FMC, from 30-yr-old+ bush vines in Icon Range, a punter's favourite. Hearty Grenache/Shiraz/PINOTAGE, called 'Gypsy', **01'** 02. Botrytis CHENIN BL named T **00 01'**.

Klein Constantia Estate r w sw ★★ →★★★ Led resurgence of historic Constantia area, now launching joint venture with Bordeaux's Bruno Prats (ANWILKA). From 1986, with Vin de Constance, recreated legendary 18th-C Cape icon dessert from Muscat de Frontignan. Only about 500 cases p.a. **93 94 95 96 97 98 99 00** 01 – last drier than norm. Bold Sauv Bl, DYA but can hang in for yrs; solid Chard. Ageworthy, just-off-dry Ries.

Kleine Zalze St'bosch r w ★★ Family Reserve Shiraz 04' tops gd reds inc Cab Sauv **01** 03 and Merlot **01 03**. Also barrel-fermented CHENIN BL and Chard.

Kloovenburg Wines Swartland r w ★★ Recently turning heads with peppery Shiraz, forward Chard.

Kumala r w sp ★→★★ Gd-value, tiered range by UK-based Western Wines, celebrated 10th anniversary in 2006. Accounts for 14% of SA's wine exports; is fourth-biggest brand in UK. Journey's End is top range: Cab Sauv **01 03** and Chard. Kumala Res range inc sound Cab Sauv, Merlot, PINOTAGE, Shiraz, Chard, Sauv Bl, and Chard Brut MÉTHODE CAP CLASSIQUE.

KWV International Paarl r w sw ★→★★★ Kooperatieve Wijnbouwers Vereniging, formerly South Africa's national wine co-op and controlling body: now partly (25.1%) black-owned. Top ranges are Laborie Estate and Cathedral Cellar: Cab Sauv **99 00 01'** 03. B'x blend Triptych **99 00 01'** 03, Shiraz, and Chard. Regular KWV labels inc traditional blend Roodeberg and a vast range of dry whites. Sherry and port-styles, fortified desserts. MÉTHODE CAP CLASSIQUE sp.

La Motte r w ★★ Lavishly appointed Rupert family (controls international luxury houses Dunhill, Cartier etc.,) estate nr Franschhoek. New to gd red stable is Pierneef Collection Shiraz/Viognier 03 B'x-style blend Millennium **99 01**; consistently friendly Shiraz **02 03**.

L'Avenir St'bosch r w ★★→★★★ Acquired by Michel Laroche of Chablis in 2005, now in a dynamic expansion phase – adding to properties in Chile. Gd Cab Sauv **00 01** 03, Chard, and Sauv Bl (DYA). Also botrytis dessert Vin de Meurveur, Cape Vintage port-style **99** 03.

Lanzerac St'bosch r w ★★ Old v'yds (and grand hotel) expensively refurbished, replanted by banking/retailing magnate Christo Wiese. Early-drinking Merlot, forward, oaky Chard.

Le Riche Wines St'bosch r ★★★ Fine Cab Sauv-based boutique wines, hand-crafted by respected Etienne le Riche. Cab Sauv Res **97' 98 00 01'**.

Long Mountain Wine ★→★★ Pernod Ricard label, buying grapes from warm-climate Breede River co-ops, exporting to 35 countries. Well-priced Cab Sauv, Ruby Cab, Cab Sauv/Merlot Res, Chard, CHENIN BL. Chard/Pinot N MCC sp recently added; upgrade to "super-premium" labels planned.

Lourensford St'bosch r w Vast project – 285 ha – new cellar, new v'yds, etc. by banker Christo Wiese (LANZERAC). Best early bottlings: delicately peachy Viognier **04**, dessert from Sem **04**, promising Cab Sauv and Sauv Bl.

L'Ormarins Private Cellar r w sw ★★ Revamp, replantings (plus name change) underway at this Rupert family property nr Franschhoek (see LA MOTTE). Best red is B'x blend Optima **98 00' 02**. Gd Cab Sauv, Merlot, Chard, Sauv Bl. Also respectable quaffers from Sangiovese and Pinot Gr in Terra del Capo range.

Lynx Wines Franschhoek r ★★ Lively newcomer; rich Shiraz **03** elegant, complex; 04 less so. Also Cab Sauv and B'x blend Xanache.

Meerlust Estate St'bosch r w ★★→★★★ Prestigious old estate, probably South Africa's best-known quality red label. After 25 years, a new winemaker. Aims to fine-tune rather than makeover; stressing elegance over impact. Flagship Rubicon B'x blend with Cab Sauv about 75% **95 97 98** 99 00 01; Merlot **97 98 99** 00; Pinot N Reserve **98 99 00**. Lately lighter, less oaky Chard. Gd-value 2nd label Meerlust Red, for years when Rubicon "declassified" – **90 02**.

Meinert Wines St'bosch r ★★→★★★ Small-scale producer/consultant Martin Meinert does two fine blends, Devon Crest (B'x) and Synchronicity (Cab Sauv/Cab Fr/Merlot/PINOTAGE) **00 01** 03. Merlot **00 01 03** from Devon Valley v'yds.

Méthode Cap Classique (MCC) South African term for classic-method sp wine.

Monis Paarl DISTELL-owned: enduring quality from oldest (1906) fortified wine producer of tawny-port-styles and Muscadels.

Morgenhof Estate St'bosch r w sw sp ★★→★★★ French-owned. Gd track record for three reds: Merlot Res **98' 00 01'** 03. B'x blend Première Sélection **98 99 00 01** 03. Cab Sauv Res **98 01** 03. V.gd whites (DYA) and ageworthy CHENIN BL, dry and botrytis; port-style LBV **95 01** and Vintage **98 00**; Brut Res MCC from Chard/Pinot N.

Morgenster Estate St'bosch r ★★★ Serious Italian investment with Pierre Lurton consulting. Cab Sauv and Cab Fr-based B'x blend is fine; supple proprietary label, **00 01** 03. Lourens River Valley B'x blend is similarly restrained 2nd label **98 99 00 02** 03.

Mulderbosch Vineyards St'bosch r w ★★★ Penetrating – usually scintillating too – Sauv Bl (DYA, but can age). Two Chards: oak-fermented and fresh, less oaky. V.gd barrel-fermented CHENIN BL Steen op Hout. Easy, B'x-style blend, Faithful Hound **00 01** 03.

Nederburg Paarl r w p dr sw s/sw sp ★→★★★ Large winery est 1937. Now headed by Romanian winemaker Razvan Macici. Improving Classic Range reds inc Edelrood blend **00 01 02** 03 and Cab Sauv **00 01 02**. Also Chard, Sauv Bl, Ries, and sp. Small quantities of Limited Vintage, Private Bins for auction, some outstanding (Private Bin 163 Cab Sauv 03'; Private Bin PINOTAGE **99 00 01**; Shiraz **00 01 03** Private Bin Sangiovese/Barbera/Nebbiolo – 03 not as mixed up as it sounds. A 1970s pioneer of botrytis wines. Stages Cape's celebrity annual wine event, the Nederburg Auction. See also EDELKEUR.

Neethlingshof St'bosch r w sw ★★ Large estate, many labels. Best in flagship Lord Neethling range is Laurentius red blend (Cab Sauv/Cab Fr and Shiraz) **98 00 01'**; also gd PINOTAGE; Shiraz; Chard and excellent Gewurz, and blush Blanc de Noirs. Champion botrytis wines from Weisser Riesling.

Neil Ellis Wines St'bosch r w ★★★ 1980s pioneer of sourcing single-v'yd grapes for site expression. Forthright wines vinified at Jonkershoek Valley. Top-flight Res V'yd Selection Cab Sauv **98 99 01** 03, Syrah **01 03**. Premium STELLENBOSCH range. Always excellent Cab Sauv, PINOTAGE, Shiraz and Sauv Bl, inc Groenkloof and Elgin (DYA), and full bold Chards from STELLENBOSCH and Elgin.

Newton-Johnson Wines r w ★★→★★★ Dedicated family winery, with v'yds at Walker Bay, sourcing grapes widely. Among few v.gd Cape Pinot N growers (**01 02 04**). Also lemony Chard, intense Sauv Bl. Delicious peppery Shiraz/Mourvèdre blend in **03 04**. See also FIRST CAPE VINEYARDS, CAPE BAY.

Nitida Cellars Durbanville r w ★★ Small v.gd range, sea-cooled v'yds; fresh, vital Sauv Bl (DYA) and Sem 03'. Also gd Cab Sauv, 03, B'x blend Calligraphy.

Omnia Wines ★→★★★ A 2.5-million-case-p.a. STELLENBOSCH operation (merger of Stellenbosch Vineyards and Vinfruco) with more than 40 labels in eight brands/ranges: Kumkani (gd Shiraz and Shiraz/Cab Sauv, gd-value PINOTAGE, Sauv Bl Lanner Hill and dry white blend VVS – Viognier/Verdelho/Sauv Bl); Credo Range; Arniston Bay Range mainly entry-level export); Inglewood Range; etc.

Overgaauw Estate St'bosch r w ★★ Old (1783) family estate. Dependable Merlot **01 02** 03 and B'x blend Tria Corda **99 01** 02 03; v.gd Cab Sauv **99 00 01** 03. Two excellent port-styles: Cape Vintage and Reserve. Estate was early to buy into Touriga Nacional grapes for port-style blend.

Paarl Town 30 miles NE of Cape Town and the wine district around it.

Paul Cluver Estate r w ★★ Gd Pinot N **01 03** from these cooler upland v'yds E of Cape Town. Also elegant Chard; intense botrytis dessert from Weisser (Rhine) Riesling; also off-dry Ries. Aromatic off-dry Gewurz.

Pinotage: South Africa's speciality

This red Pinot N/Cinsault cross was "born" in 1926. It can be delicious – with intriguing boiled-sweets and banana flavours – and has shown potential if carefully matured in oak. But coarse, estery flamboyance can dominate (and often does). Pinotage is now featuring in "Cape blends", a local term sometimes used – without official sanction yet – to differentiate these from B'x blends, where Pinotage is usually absent.

Plaisir de Merle r w ★★ Grand, DISTELL-owned cellar, v'yds nr PAARL. Approachable Merlot **01 02 03**, weightier Grand Plaisir B'x blend **01 02** . New star is single-v'yd Cab Fr (**03**).

Quoin Rock St'bosch r w ★★★ Grapes from southerly Cape Agulhas v'ds. Plush Merlot **01 03**; elegant/spicy Syrah **03**; lightly oaked white flagship Oculus. Clean-cut Chard and Sauv Bl.

Raats Family St'bosch r w ★★ Deep-scented, minerally Cab Franc **01 03** and two acclaimed, oaked and unoaked, CHENIN BL, both worth keeping a few yrs.

Raka Walker Bay r w ★★ Award-winning Shiraz **02 03** 04, from Swartland grapes; plus full five-varieties B'x blend 02, and complex, individual Sauv Bl.

Remhoogte Estate Stellenbosch r ★★→★★★ Classically styled Bonne Nouvelle 02 03 – (Cab Sauv/Merlot/PINOTAGE) joint-venture between proprietor Murray Boustred and Michel Rolland; also B'x blend Estate Wine and Cab Sauv.

Ridgeback Wines Paarl r w ★★→★★★ Standout Syrah **02 03**, Cab Fr/Merlot **03**, and Viognier.

Rijk's Private Cellar Tulbagh r w ★★★ New (small-scale) Cape star. Depth, intensity in Cab Sauv 01 **02'** and Shiraz 02; matched by Sem 02 03 and CHENIN BL.

Robertson District Inland from Cape. Mainly dessert (notably Muscat) and white wines. Determined effort now to increase red v'yds.

Robertson Winery Robertson r w sw ★→★★ Often underrated, gd value from warm-climate, co-op-scale (29,000 tons p.a.) winery. Vineyard Selection range: 2 gd Shiraz labels, Constitution Rd and Wolfkloof; Phanto Ridge PINOTAGE; King's River Chard. Ries Wide River Noble Late Harvest (01') superb.

Rudera Wines St'bosch r w ★★→★★★ Rising star. Classy Cab Sauv **00 01**, Syrah **01 02 03**; CHENIN BL, fresh, oak-fermented, and botrytis Noble Late Harvest (**03 04 05'**), but all outstanding.

Rupert & Rothschild Vignerons r w ★★★ Top v'yds, cellar at Simondium, Paarl. Joint venture between Baron Benjamin Rothschild and the Ruperts, two old French and South African wine families. Roving French guru Michel Rolland is consultant. Mellow, soft Cab Sauv/Cab Fr/Merlot 98 00 01 named Baron Edmond since 1998. Chard Baroness Nadine is a deep-flavoured classic.

Rustenberg Wines r w ★★★ Prestigious STELLENBOSCH estate, founded 300 yrs ago, making wine continuously for more than 100 yrs. Flagship is single-v'yd Peter Barlow Cab Sauv **97 98 99' 01'** 03; Rustenberg B'x blend John X Merriman **97 98 99 01'** 03. Outstanding Chard Five Soldiers **01 02 03**. Local favourite Chard Five Soldiers is single v'yd. Also top 2nd label Brampton.

Rust en Vrede Estate r ★★★ Estate E of STELLENBOSCH: frequent trophy winner known for strong, individual red blend Rust en Vrede Estate Wine, **98 99 00' 01**. Solid Cab Sauv, and Shiraz.

Sadie Family Wines Swartland r ★★★ Painstakingly – trendily/traditionally –

made (wild-yeast fermented, unfined, unfiltered) Columella (Shiraz/Mourvèdre) **00 01 02** 03 now spoken of as Cape benchmark. Complex, intriguing (citrus/apricots) white blend Palladius **01 02** (Viognier, CHENIN BL, Chard, Grenache Blanc). Star winemaker Eben Sadie.

Seidelberg Estate Paarl r w ★★ Reserve Merlot **00 01 03**, Syrah **01**, B'x blend Un Deux Trois **00** 02, Chard, promising Viognier, and CHENIN BL.

Signal Hill Cape Town r w sw ★★ French flair in lively range, widely sourced grapes, for new downtown Cape Town winery, Jean-Vincent Ridon collaborating with Zulu winemaker Khulekani Buthelezi. Malbec, Petit Verdot, Furmint (Tokaji lookalike Mathilde Aszu), Muscat and PINOTAGE all feature.

Simonsig Estate St'bosch r w sp sw ★★→★★★ Malan family winery. Extensive range inc red blend Tiara **99 00 01** 02, Merindol Syrah **01' 02** 03, Frans Malan Reserve **99 00 01** 02, Red Hill PINOTAGE **99 00 01 02** 03, v.gd Chard, and dessert-style Gewurz. First (30 yrs ago) Cape MÉTHODE CAP CLASSIQUE, Kaapse Vonkel brut from Pinot N/Chard.

Simonsvlei International r w p sw sp ★ Leading co-op cellar, just outside PAARL. Many tiers of quality, from Hercules Paragon (Merlot) to Mount Marble.

Spice Route Wine Company Malmesbury r w ★★★ Front-running Cape specialist in Rhône style; top label is Malabar **02** 03' (Syrah/PINOTAGE/Mourvèdre/Grenache/Viognier). Also rich Flagship Syrah **99 00 01 02** 03, Merlot **99 01' 03**, PINOTAGE **98 99 00 01**; full, barrel-fermented CHENIN BL and Viognier **04**.

Spier Cellars St'bosch r w ★★ Well-made ranges, best in Private Collection Cab Sauv 01 03, Merlot 99 01 03, plus PINOTAGE/Shiraz, CHENIN BL/Viognier and dessert botrytis Ries/CHENIN BL. Recently award-winning CHENIN BL. Pan-African restaurant Moyo, golf course, wildlife and conf centre, hotel.

Springfield Estate Robertson ★★→★★★ Individual wines from whole-berry and native yeast fermentation. Three v.gd, softer-style Cab Sauvs, unfiltered, unfined: Whole Berry **00 01'** 03, Méthode Ancienne (native yeast) and The Work of Time (B'x blend) **01 02**. Also crisp Sauv Bl (DYA) and rich, wild yeast Chard under Méthode Ancienne.

Stark-Condé St'bosch r ★★→★★★ Ripe, full Cab Sauv **00 02** 03 and Syrah **03**.

Steenberg Vineyards Constantia r w ★★★ Showcase Cape winery/v'yds under winemaker John Loubser. Serious, elegant Merlot **01 02 03** and red blend Catharina **99 00 01 02'** 03. Arresting Sauv Bls: flinty single-v'yd Res and fruitier Regular. Two single-v'yd Sems, oaked and unoaked. Gd sparkling Steenberg Brut 1682 NV. One of Cape's few Nebbiolos (minerally, taut).

Stellenbosch St'bosch. Oak-shaded university town, second oldest in South Africa, and demarcated wine district 30 miles E of Cape Town. Heart of the wine industry – the Napa of the Cape. Many top estates, especially for reds, tucked into mountain valleys and foothills; extensive wine routes, many restaurants.

Stellenbosch Farmers' Winery (SFW) Part of SA's biggest wine conglomerate Distell: equivalent of 14 million cases per year. Ranges inc NEDERBURG; ZONNEBLOEM. Wide selection of mid- and low-price wines.

Stellenzicht St'bosch ★★ Modern winery, mountainside v'yds. V.gd Syrah **98 99 01 02**, consistent B'x blend Stellenzicht **99 00**, PINOTAGE **99 01**, Sem Res. Golden Triangle range inc gd value Cab Sauv, Malbec, PINOTAGE, Shiraz.

The Foundry St'bosch r ★★★ Sources grapes in STELLENBOSCH and PAARL. Syrah **02 03**; also Viognier 05.

The Observatory Paarl r ★★→★★★ Expanding Rhône-style specialist with organic/Biodynamic methods. Perfumed Syrah **01 02**; juicy, frontal Carignan/Syrah **02** (Syrah/Carignan 03), and unusually elegant PINOTAGE/Syrah **04**.

The Winery (formerly Radford-Dale) r w ★★→★★★ Premium export label of young, ambitious "multinational" (Brit-, Aussie-, and French-owned, enthusiastically operated). Includes unfiltered Shiraz (04), Merlot **01 03**

and Gravity (Merlot/Cab/Shiraz) combo **03** 04. Also caramelly Chard. Other ranges: Vinum, Black Rock, New World, and Winery of Good Hope.

Thelema Mountain Vineyards St'bosch r w ★★★→★★★★ Winemaker Gyles Webb and Thelema still at the top of their game; one of v. few iconic Cape names. Cab Sauv **91 92 93 94 95 97 98 99 00 01** 03', rich Merlot Res **99 01** 03', elegant Shiraz **01' 02 03**, Chard, and Sauv Bl and Sutherland Sauv Bl from Elgin v'yd (DYA). Individual, spicy, rich Ed's Reserve Chard. Among best (off-dry) ageworthy Ries. Immaculate v'yds.

Tokara St'bosch r w ★★★ Hang-the-cost winery, v'yds under direction of Gyles Webb (THELEMA). First releases outstanding, lightly oaked Tokara White Sauv Bl 04' and fresh unoaked **05**; very elegant Cab Sauv/Merlot blend 03 and Chard **04**. Second label Zondernaam Sauv Bl (DYA). Also gd Cab Sauv and PINOTAGE.

Veenwouden r ★★→★★★★ Family-run PAARL property. Reputation for Merlot and B'x blend Veenwouden Classic.

Vergelegen St'bosch r w ★★★→★★★★ Cape's currently most celebrated (and trophy-laden) wine farm. Inspired winemaker André van Rensburg given his head by owners, mining giant Anglo-American Corp. Luxury-priced flagship is new V Cab Sauv 01' 03 – forsakes restraint for power and impact; but stablemate B'x blend Vergelegen **98 99' 00 01'** 03' offers sumptuous, lower-key alternative. Ditto Cab Sauv 98 99 00 01' 03, Merlot 99 00 01 **03**, exceptional Shiraz **01' 02** 03'. Estate White is taut, barrel-fermented Sem-led blend. Superb, lemony Chard, and racy Schaapenberg and Res Sauv Bl.

Vilafonté Paarl r ★★★ First US-South African joint venture. California's Zelma Long (ex-Simi) and Phil Freese (ex-Mondavi viticulturalist) teaming up with WARWICK ESTATE's Mike Ratcliffe. Two B'x blends (03): mainly Cab Sauv C Series and mainly Merlot M Series, both fine, supple – C more firmly structured, for longer keeping. Top international notices for maiden releases.

Villiera Wines St'bosch r w sp ★★→★★★ Big family-run v'yds and winery with excellent quality/value range. Five MÉTHODE CAP CLASSIQUE bubblies inc: Brut Natural, virtually organic Blanc de Blancs and Monro Brut Première Cuvée. Sound red B'x blend Monro **99 00 01** 02. Consistently gd Bush Vine Sauv Bl (DYA); dessert botrytis CHENIN BL (00); port-style Fired Earth.

Vredendal Cooperative r w dr sw ★ South Africa's largest co-op winery in warm Olifants River region. Improving reds, inc Shiraz Mt Maskam. Huge range, mostly white. Big exporter of various supermarket labels.

Vriesenhof Vineyards St'bosch r w ★★★ Run by Cape wine (and rugby) legend, Jan Boland Coetzee. Highly rated, inc Talana Hill (B'x blend Royale and Chard) and Paradyskloof labels. B'x blend Kallista is flagship 95 **97 98 99** 00 01' 03. Now also Pinot N **00 01 04'**; PINOTAGE-based blend Enthopio 00 01 02 03.

Warwick Estate St'bosch r w ★★→★★★ Consistently gd B'x blend Trilogy Estate Reserve **99 00' 01'** and Cape blend Three Ladies Cab Sauv/Merlot/PINOTAGE **00 01'** 02. Fine individual Cab Fr 00 01 02 03. Old Bush Vines PINOTAGE has following **00 01 02 03** 04. V.gd Chard, Sauv Bl Prof Black.

Waterford St'bosch r w ★★→★★★ Showpiece winery. Outstanding Kevin Arnold Shiraz **01 02 03**, Cab Sauv **01 02** 03'. V.gd Sauv Bl (DYA) and Chard.

Welgemeend Estate Paarl r ★★→★★★ Boutique estate: B'x-style blend Estate Reserve **98 00 01**. Ripe, fruity PINOTAGE/Shiraz **01 02**. Malbec-based blend Douelle **00 01 02**.

Wine of Origin The Cape's "AC", but without French crop-yield etc. restrictions. Certifies vintage, variety, region of origin.

Zonnebloem r w sw (Cab Sauv) ★★ STELLENBOSCH FARMERS' WINERY's top range, widely sourced. Generally gd value: B'x blend Laureat **01 02** 03, plus dependable if unremarkable PINOTAGE, Shiraz, Cab Sauv. Easy drinking, well-priced Chard, Sauv Bl and Blanc de Blanc (CHENIN BL/Sauv Bl).

About the contributors

The store of detailed recommendations comes partly from my own notes and mainly from those of a great number of kind friends. Without their generous help and cooperation, I could not attempt it. I particularly want to thank the following for their help with research or in the areas of their special knowledge.

Geoff Adams is a freelance wine writer and author of *Greek Wines: A Comprehensive Guide* (Winemaster Publishing, 2002). Adams has contributed chapters on Greece and Southeastern Europe to *Wines of the World* (Dorling Kindersley) and writes for *Harpers*, *The Wine and Spirit Weekly* and *Decanter*. He has been a judge at numerous international wine competitions.

Helena Baker was born in Prague. She translated *Hugh Johnson's Pocket Wine Book 2003* and publishes her own Czech Republic Wine Guide, in addition to the first comprehensive Czech-language book on Italian Wines, and *Coq au Vin* (a cookbook). She is a founder and member of several wine and food organizations, including the Prague Wine Society, Czech Convivium of Slow Food, and Ladies of Wine.

Charles W Borden is a Moscow-based American businessman and writer who has worked with wineries of the former Soviet Union since 1994, writing about them in the English-language press. He is wine and business editor for Moscow's *Passport* magazine.

Dr. Ernő Péter Botos is director of the Hungarian Research Institute for Vine & Wine (Kecskemét) and assistant professor at Corvinus University in Budapest. He writes for numerous academic and trade publications, specializing in the Tokaj and Villány wine regions. He is also chairman of the Hungarian Wine Appellation Board and vice-president of the Hungarian Wine Academy.

Gregory Bowden fell in love with Alsace after graduating from Oxford. A winner of the Grands Maisons d'Alsace Scholarship, Bowden is a wine merchant and author of various books, including a history of British gastronomy. He also lectures to Diploma students at the Wine & Spirit Education Trust (WSET).

Stephen Brook has been a contributing editor to *Decanter* since 1996. His numerous books, including *Liquid Gold: Dessert Wines of the World* (Beech Tree Books, 1987) and *Bordeaux: People, Power, Politics* (Mitchell Beazley, 2000), have won many major wine-writing awards. His latest book is *Bordeaux: Médoc and Graves* (Mitchell Beazley, 2006).

Michael Cooper is a leading authority on New Zealand wine. He was appointed an Officer of the New Zealand Order of Merit in 2004 for services to wine writing. An award-winning journalist and author, Cooper has written several books, including the *Wine Atlas of New Zealand* and the bestselling annual *Michael Cooper's Buyer's Guide to New Zealand Wines* (Hodder and Stoughton). He is wine editor of New Zealand's *Cuisine* magazine, and chairman of its New Zealand wine-tasting panel.

Rupert Dean has over 20 years' experience in the international wine trade. The first European to earn a Master's Degree in Wine Business from Roseworthy Wine College, University of Adelaide, Dean speaks regularly at conferences in Australia, New Zealand, Europe, and Asia, where he has both lived and worked several times. He has written extensively about wine and the Asian market.

Michael Edwards joined London wine shippers Laytons in 1968. A wine journalist and former chief inspector for the *Egon Ronay Guide*, Edwards wrote the award-winning *Champagne Companion* (Apple Press) and *Pocket Guide: Champagne & Sparkling Wine* (Mitchell Beazley).

Jacqueline Friedrich, an American who lives in France, is the award-winning author of *A Wine & Food Guide to the Loire* (Henry Holt). An erstwhile actress, recovering lawyer, and homesick New Yorker, Friedrich has a passion for food, wine and whisky, Argentine tango, and rock 'n' roll. She is currently working on a guide to French wine.

David Furer is the author of *Wine Places* (Mitchell Beazley, 2005) and has written for many publications including *Wine Report*, *Which? Wine Guide*, and *Wine Business Monthly*. An industry consultant and lecturer, Furer has taught wine classes at the University of Chicago, Oxford, Cambridge, and the Volkshochschulen in Germany. He currently promotes sherry in the UK.

Rosemary George MW is the author of ten books, including *The Wines of the South of France, from Banyuls to Bellet* (Faber & Faber, 2001) and *Treading Grapes; Walking through the Vineyards of Tuscany* (Mitchell Beazley). George was one of the first women to pass the Master of Wine exams, in 1979, and she worked in the wine trade before becoming a writer.

Robert Gorjak is based near Ljubljana, Slovenia, from where he has written about wine since 1994. Beside regular contributions to Slovenian periodicals, he contributes to the *Oxford Companion to Wine*. He has also judged several national and international wine competitions. He and his wife founded Slovenia's first wine school, where he also teaches.

James Halliday co-founded Australian wineries Brokenwood and Coldstream Hills. A winemaker and viticulturist from 1971–2000, he has been judging and chairing national and international wine shows since 1975. He is a regular contributor to *The Weekend Australian*, *Gourmet Traveller Wine*, *Decanter*, and others. Halliday has written or contributed to over fifty books and received numerous awards. He says he "tastes Australian, drinks French and German".

Darrel Joseph is based in Vienna, Austria, from where he writes about the wines and wine regions of Central and Eastern Europe. Joseph's articles have appeared in *Decanter*, *Wine Spectator*, *Harpers*, *The Wine and Spirit Weekly*, and others. He also teaches at home and abroad, and specializes in the rise of Grüner Veltliner and the renaissance of Hungary's Tokaji Aszú.

Chandra Kurt is based in Switzerland and has written several wine books including the bestselling *Weinseller*. Kurt contributes to both wine-oriented and general-interest publications, including *Cash*, *Al Dente*, and *SchweizerFamilie*. She is a wine consultant to Swiss International Airlines and several Swiss retail institutions.

Gareth Lawrence is curriculum manager of the WSET School, the training arm of the Wine and Spirit Education Trust. He has developed an interest in the wines and spirits of the Eastern Mediterranean and Near East over a number of years and has contributed to the *Oxford Companion to Wine* and *Hugh Johnson's World Wine Atlas*.

James Lawther MW joined the wine trade in 1983, selling wine at Steven Spurrier's Caves de la Madeleine in Paris and lecturing at the Académie du Vin. He passed his Master of Wine examination in 1993. Based in Bordeaux since 1996, Lawther is an independent wine writer, lecturer, and contributing editor to *Decanter*. He also leads tours in the wine regions of France.

John Livingstone-Learmonth is author of *The Wines of the Rhône* (Faber, 1992) and *The Wines of the Northern Rhône* (University of California Press, 2005). Livingstone-Learmonth has also written about the wines of the Loire, Beaujolais, and Bordeaux, for numerous publications including *Decanter*, *Wine International*, and *Harpers*, *The Wine and Spirit Weekly*.

Nico Manessis, based in Geneva, is an expert on wines of his native Greece, and his books include *The Illustrated Greek Wine Book* and *The Greek Wine Guide*. He has contributed to *Decanter*, *The International Herald Tribune*, and numerous other publications and wine books. He is the wine critic for *Athens Insider*. He is a wine show judge, and he lectures on Greek wine at various French and Swiss universities.

Richard Mayson was raised in Portugal and wrote his undergraduate dissertation on the microclimate of Douro Valley vineyards. He has written four books, including the award-winning *The Wines and Vineyards of Portugal* and *Port and the Douro* (both published by Mitchell Beazley). He writes for *Decanter* and *The World of Fine Wine*, owns a vineyard in the Alentejo, Portugal, and is working on a book about madeira wine.

Jasper Morris founded and developed UK-based wine merchants Morris & Verdin Ltd, which was sold in 2003 to Berry Bros & Rudd, for which he is now buying director. He became a Master of Wine in 1985 and lectures and writes frequently on Burgundy, where he now lives for part of the year. He contributed the articles on Burgundy to the *Oxford Companion to Wine*.

Shirley Nelson is a freelance wine writer and Southwest editor for www.wineandcuisine.org. She has judged at numerous state, national, and international wine competitions throughout the Southwestern and Western US. In the 1980s, she was assistant winemaker at Sangre de Cristo Winery in New Mexico.

John and Erica Platter launched South Africa's bestselling annual pocket wine guide, *John Platter's South African Wines*, twenty-six years ago. Both former journalists, they farmed and made wines in the Cape for twenty years before selling their interest in the guide to do more travelling. They wrote *Africa Uncorked: Travels in Extreme Wine Territory*, and John has contributed to the *Oxford Companion to Wine*, *New World of Wine* (Mitchell Beazley), and other international publications and has judged widely round the wine world. He served on the South African Wine and Spirits Board and, as a government trustee of the South African Wine Industry Trust, is tasked with the post-apartheid transformation of Cape wine.

Margaret Rand is a previous editor of *Wine* magazine, *Wine & Spirit International*, and *Whisky Magazine*. She contributes to a wide range of publications including *Decanter*; *Square Meal*; *The World of Fine Wine*, where she is a member of the regular tasting panel; and *Harpers*, *The Wine and Spirit Weekly*. She is general editor of *Hugh Johnson's Pocket Wine Book* and general editor of Mitchell Beazley's Classic Wine Library series. Her latest book, *Grapes & Wines* (with Oz Clarke; Time Warner), is now out in paperback.

Jan Read trained as a research scientist but developed an interest in the wines of

Spain while writing scripts in Hollywood. He has published many of the key books on the subject. He has contributed to the *Pocket Wine Book* since its inception.

Carlos Read, Jan's son, is a shipper of Spanish wines and has pioneered the sale in the UK of wines from regions such as Rueda, Navarra, and Calatayud.

Daniel Rogov writes *Rogov's Guide to Israeli Wines*, published annually, as well as weekly wine and restaurant columns in the newspaper *Haaretz* and the section on Israel for Tom Stevenson's *Wine Report*. Rogov also maintains a wine and food website: *Rogov's Ramblings*.

Adam Sebag Montefiore was born in London and worked in the English wine trade before he went to live in Israel. Since then he has worked for Israel's two most famous wineries, Carmel Winery and Golan Heights Winery, and has spearheaded the development of Israeli wines worldwide. He wrote the section on Israel for the new *Oxford Wine Companion* by Jancis Robinson MW. He regularly writes about wine for Israeli and international publications.

Stephen Skelton MW has been a winemaker and viticulturalist since 1975, and in 1977 he established Tenterden Vineyards in Kent, where he made wine for twenty-three vintages. He was also winemaker and general manager at Lamberhurst Vineyards from 1988 to 1991. Skelton is a consultant to the English wine industry and has written and lectured widely. His *Wines of Britain and Ireland* is the standard work on the subject. He currently runs Thameside Wines in London.

Paul Strang was described by a colleague as "the man who knows every centimetre of the Southwest". He has had a home in the Aveyron *département* of southwest France since 1961. With thirty years' experience visiting growers there, he wrote the first wine book about the area, *Wines of South-West France* (Kyle Cathie, 1994), as well as *Languedoc-Roussillon: The Wines & Winemakers* (Mitchell Beazley, 2002). His latest book, *South-West France: The Wines & Winemakers'*, will be published in 2007 by Grub Street.

Bostjan Tadel has been wine editor of the Sunday edition of Slovenia's major daily newspaper since 1999. He wrote a wine column for the country's most widely distributed free magazine, *Delniãar*, and has, since 2002, been editor-in-chief of *Polet*, a weekly lifestyle magazine supplement. He has been a marketing consultant to a number of Slovenian winemakers.

Marguerite Thomas is the travel editor at *The Wine News*. She writes a column, "Intrepid Gastronome", for the *Los Angeles Times* International Syndicate and is also a columnist at www.winereviewonline.com. She is the author of two books about wines of the Eastern United States, *Wineries of the Eastern States* and *Touring East Coast Wine Country* (both WW Norton/Countryman Press publications).

Daniel Thomases was educated at Harvard University and was the principal collaborator of Luigi Veronelli, Italy's leading wine and food critic, from 1985 to 2004. Thomases has been writer and editor for *I Vini di Veronelli*, the annual guide to Italian wine, as well as Italian correspondent for *Wine Spectator*, *International Wine Cellar*, *The Wine Advocate*, and a contributor to the *Oxford Companion to Wine*. He is a wine columnist for *24*, the monthly magazine of *Il Sole 24 Ore*, Italy's leading financial newspaper.

Monty Waldin became interested in organic and Biodynamic viticulture and vinification as a student, when he grew disillusioned with the conventionally farmed Bordeaux and Chilean vineyards. He has worked in organic and Biodynamic vineyards in Germany, the Roussillon, and California, with the Fetzer family, pioneers in this field. *Biodynamic Wines* (Mitchell Beazley, 2006) is his fifth book and the world's first to focus exclusively on Biodynamic wines.

Larry Walker writes on food, wine, travel, and environmental issues. He contributes to a number of magazines, including *Quarterly Review of Wines* and *Wines & Vines*. With his wife, Ann Walker, he has written six books: *A Season in Spain*, *The Pleasures of the Canary Islands*, *Tequila: the Book*, *Tapas*, *The Best of California*, and *To the Heart of Spain*. The Walkers are currently working on a food and travel book about France's Languedoc-Roussillon area. His most recent book, *The Wines of the Napa Valley*, was published by Mitchell Beazley in 2005. Other books on California wine include *The Wine Guide* from Williams-Sonoma and *The Wine Companion to Napa and Sonoma*.

David Williams is deputy editor of *Wine & Spirit* magazine. Previously deputy editor of *Harpers*, *The Wine and Spirit Weekly*, Williams has contributed to a variety of different publications including *Time Out*, *The World of Fine Wine*, and *The Face*.

Simon Woods has been a wine correspondent for the *Financial Times*, co-editor of the annual *Which? Wine Guide*, and co-ordinator of the International Wine Challenge, the world's largest wine competition. His book *Vine to Bottle* (Mitchell Beazley, 2001) won the prize of "Best in the World Wine Book for Professionals" at the 2001 Gourmand World Cookbook Awards. He has also written the award-winning *I Don't Know Much About Wine* (Mitchell Beazley), and contributes to many publications.

And the score is...

It seems that America and the rest of the world will never agree about the idea of scoring wines. America is seemingly besotted with the 100-point scale devised by Robert Parker, based on the strange US school system in which 50 = 0. Arguments that taste is too various, too subtle, too evanescent, too wonderful to be reduced to a pseudo-scientific set of numbers fall on deaf ears. Arguments that the accuracy implied by giving one wine a score of 87 and another 88 is a chimera don't get much further. Numbers are too useful to investors.

European critics do use numbers, but smaller, less dramatic ones. A 20-point system is popular among professionals; others use a 7-point scale, and the magazine *Decanter* a 5-star system which works well for its readers. Amateurs (the French word fits wine-lovers perfectly) will always be sceptical about claims of total precision. The pleasure principle is the one they believe in.

The Johnson System

I offer a tried and tested alternative way of registering how much *you* like a wine. The Johnson System reflects the enjoyment (or lack of it) that each wine offered at the time it was drunk with inescapable honesty. Here it is:

One sniff	the minimum score. Emphatically no thanks
One sip	one step up
Two sips	faint interest (or disbelief)
A half glass	slight hesitation
One glass	tolerance, even general approval

Individuals will vary in their scoring after this (they do with points systems, too). You should assume that you are drinking without compunction – without your host pressing you or the winemaker glowering at you. But you have time and you are thirsty.

Two glasses	means you quite like it
	(or there is nothing else to drink);
Three glasses	you find it more than acceptable;
Four	it tickles your fancy;
One bottle	means satisfaction:
A second bottle	is the real thumbs up.

The steps grow higher now:

A full dozen	means you are not going to miss out on this one... and so on.
	The logical top score in the Johnson System is, of course, the whole vineyard.